BAN

Graham Stewart is the author of the internationally acclaimed *Burying Caesar: Churchill, Chamberlain and the Battle for the Tory Party*. He was educated at St Andrews and Cambridge universities and is a senior research fellow of the Humanities Research Institute at Buckingham University. His other books include *Friendship and Betrayal, The Murdoch Years* volume of the official history of *The Times* and *Britannia: 100 Documents that Shaped a Nation*.

'Graham Stewart has done a terrific job. His book brings the decade vividly back to life and convincingly places it in perspective. Not only does he include all the major political and economic episodes of the period – the Falklands War, the miners' strike and the Big Bang – he also covers some of the more momentous moments in mass culture ... Stewart is a gifted writer. He possesses a novelist's ability to engage the reader's interest.'
Toby Young, *Mail on Sunday*

'Superb ... Throughout this carefully researched history, Stewart conjures the urban decay and collapsed industries of early-80s Britain ... Rarely has history seemed so close to us, yet so far.'
Ian Thomson, *Observer*

'Stewart properly says that it is too soon to prepare a long-term profit and loss account, but in a detailed record of political, social and cultural events he provides an entertaining and insightful summary of interesting times.'
The Times

'For those like me, for whom, the Eighties were their formative years, Stewart's book is an illuminating reminder of a decade that crackled with creative energy and social tension. Those born afterwards have a fascinating introduction in store.'
Fergus Kelly, *Daily Express*

'Sensationally good ... Stewart is clever, stylish, learned and occasionally funny. His grasp of social affairs is also as comprehensive as any of our current crop of era-historians... Absorbing'
Roger Hutchinson, *Scotsman*

'Stewart has written an accomplished, politically minded history of a decade in which Britain was painfully reborn.'
Dan Jones, *Daily Telegraph*

'Lively, incisive and valiantly thorough … Stewart is particularly good on Thatcher's strengths and weaknesses.'
John Preston, *Spectator*

'The book's greatest strengths are in its meticulous account of the economic crisis that confronted the incoming Thatcher government in 1979 and how it was resolved, and its masterly description of the reform of the city, which culminated in the Big Bang that gives the book its title.'
Andy McSmith, *Independent*

'A racy account of the 1980s, which will take its place with John Campbell's biography of Margaret Thatcher and Richard Vinen's *Thatcher's Britain* as a standard guide … It is especially good on political history'
Vernon Bogdanor, *TLS*

'[Stewart's] control of a complex narrative here is masterly, his style lively and easy to read, and there are many shrewd insights.'
Donald Trelford, *Literary Review*

'*Bang!* chronicles the intellectual and political insurgency that transformed the British economy and which continues to be relevant today.'
Rohan Silva, *Prospect*

'A definitive look back … He's covered almost everything: the politics, economics and the culture'
Peter York, *Management Today*

'*Bang!* isn't all juntas and public-sector borrowing requirements. As you would expect, pop culture muscles its way in with padded shoulders. There is a long and generally sound résumé of synth-pop and Stewart is also surprisingly insightful on The Smiths, offering a far more sensitive and nuanced portrait than many specialist rock writers have managed … Crammed with detail, anecdote and juxtapositions'
Stuart Maconie, *New Statesman*

'Margaret Thatcher bestrides a stirring tale which is superbly and fairly told by Graham Stewart.'
Northern Echo

Also by Graham Stewart

Burying Caesar: Churchill, Chamberlain and the Battle for the Tory Party
His Finest Hours: The War Speeches of Winston Churchill
The History of The Times (Volume VII): *The Murdoch Years*
Friendship and Betrayal: Ambition and the Limits of Loyalty
Britannia: 100 Documents That Shaped a Nation

BANG!

A HISTORY OF BRITAIN IN THE 1980s

GRAHAM STEWART

Atlantic Books
London

Published in Great Britain in 2013 by Atlantic Books, an imprint of Atlantic Books Ltd.

10 9 8 7 6 5 4 3 2 1

A CIP catalogue record for this book is available from the British Library.

Hardback ISBN: 9781848871458

Ebook ISBN: 9781782391371

Paperback ISBN: 9781848871465

Printed in Italy by 🐾 Grafica Veneta

Atlantic Books
An Imprint of Atlantic Books Ltd
Ormond House
26–27 Boswell Street
London
WC1N 3JZ

www.atlantic-books.co.uk

For my good friend, Jean-Marc Ciancimino

CONTENTS

Contents

ACKNOWLEDGEMENTS

Britain in the 1980s does not lend itself easily to dispassionate analysis. It was a time of primary colours, clashing ideologies and divisive personalities. Any effort now to dodge contentiousness by painting it in gentler, pastel shades can only miss its vibrant power to shock, disturb and excite. Rather than skirt around its arguments, the historian can only join them.

At the same time, I am conscious of the dangers of allowing personal experiences of the decade to cloud judgment. For this reason I have tried to let neither my own partial and perhaps hindsight-contaminated recollections (I was a Scottish teenager for almost all of the eighties) nor the possibly unreliable memories of those who shaped the period, rather than merely grew up in it, assume undue influence. Wherever possible, it is always best to garner the evidence from what is recorded during, or soon after, the events.

For their help in gathering this material I should particularly like to thank Eamon Dyas and Nick Mays at the News International Archive and Record Office and the staff at the London Library and the British Library for all their assistance. Any historian of the politics of the period is also indebted to the Margaret Thatcher Foundation, whose exemplary website provides an easily accessible treasure trove of primary material.

Among the secondary sources that have most influenced this book, I should like to single out John Campbell for his remarkable two-volume biography of Margaret Thatcher, Francis Beckett and David Henche for their history of the miner's strike, Ivor Crewe and Anthony King for their work on the SDP, Simon Reynolds on early-eighties pop, Matthew Collin on the late-eighties dance scene and David Kynaston for his magisterial study of the City of London. The responsibility for the interpretations drawn from these and other works of scholarship listed in the bibliography is, of course, entirely my own.

At Atlantic Books, I consider myself extremely fortunate to have had Toby Mundy as my commissioning editor, while James Nightingale expertly saw the book through from manuscript to printing press. As ever, my agent, Georgina Capel, has been a tireless advocate and supporter.

Finally, for their kindness, encouragement, ideas and stimulating conversation during the writing of this book I would particularly like to thank

Nicholas Boys Smith, Jane Clark, Mark Craig, Thomas Harding, Daniel Margolin, Duncan Reed, Luke Rittner, Cita and Irwin Stelzer, Paul Stephenson, Eleanor Thorp, Edward Wild and Nicole Wright. Jean-Marc Ciancimino has been a very good friend over many years and it is in recognition of this that I should like to dedicate this work.

ILLUSTRATIONS

INTRODUCTION

The paradox of the eighties is simply put. Everywhere we look around and see its profound influence and yet the decade itself – its tastes, obsessions and alarms – is beginning to seem remote to the point of becoming exotic.

The realization that Britain in the eighties did not, in fundamental respects, resemble the country of today presents an opportunity worth grasping. It suggests that we are gaining distance and critical detachment from events and personalities that divided opinion to a degree that seemed remarkable even at the time. Of course, it is the extremes and peculiarities of any age that tend to be remembered while the quiet continuities remain unexamined or taken for granted. Some Britons rioted and went on protest marches while others hung patriotic bunting and bought shares in British Telecom. Impervious to stereotype, a few may have done all four. Many more did none of these things; history may be shaped by trendsetters but is not just inhabited by them. With the help of selective, and at times repetitive, archive footage to accompany television and newspaper commentary, shoulder pads and striking miners are portrayed as emblematic of the eighties. At the same time, sales of denim jeans held up pretty well and millions of employees simply got on with their work and, every once in a while, won promotion.

Nevertheless, it would take an essayist of wearisome contrariness to argue that the period of the eighties had little that was distinctive, let alone unique, about it and should be conceded no meaning beyond that dictated by the calendar. For a start, no decade had seen Britain served continuously by the same prime minister since William Pitt the Younger in the 1790s; and unlike Pitt (whose terms of office stretched from 1783 to 1801 and 1804 to 1806), Margaret Thatcher's Downing Street tenure (1979 to 1990) almost perfectly framed the intervening decade as if it were her own. Perhaps this might not have been so significant had she possessed a more technocratic and less commanding personality. That she proved to be one of the dominant figures of modern British history is a defining characteristic of the period. While this book encompasses politics, economics, the arts and society, it has a unifying theme: the attraction or repulsion, in each of these areas, to and from the guiding spirit of the age. That Thatcher was the personification of that spirit is perhaps the least contentious aspect of what will unfold.

There is another recurring theme. It is that what happened during the eighties in the UK was not just significant for those who lived there. The country's influence was worldwide to an extent that is easily forgotten in the first decade of the twenty-first century. The Cold War and the major strategic role of British forces in defending the 'Free World' against the Soviet Union stand out with particular clarity. Thatcher was the first Western leader to identify Mikhail Gorbachev as someone with whom, to paraphrase her, business could be done. She was an important bridge between him and Ronald Reagan. The legacy from that most fruitful of détentes was of unambiguous benefit to mankind, which for the previous four decades had been forced to ponder what, at times, looked like its imminent destruction in nuclear war. Necessarily, though, the 'cold thaw' diminished Britain's strategic significance in the world.

NATO and diplomatic special relationships were only a part of Britain's significance during the eighties. The international penetration by British youth and progressive cultures was remarkable, with British acts accounting for a third of pop music sales in the United States. On 13 July 1985, it was estimated that more than one fifth of the planet's inhabitants watched the most spectacular charity appeal in history, coming to them from a stadium in north-west London. In the Live Aid audience at Wembley was Diana, Princess of Wales, an international fashion icon of the period without European, or possibly global, compare.

Political debate, though, remained at the heart of Britain's influence. If we now take it for granted that a major Western country's head of government could be a woman, it is primarily because Thatcher made it so. Thirty years on from her election, it is right to argue over Thatcher's legacy but difficult to dismiss out of hand at least the general sentiment of her official biographer, Charles Moore, that

> She is the only post-war British prime minister (her successors included) who stands for something which is recognized and admired globally. 'Ah, Mrs Thatcher – very strong woman!' taxi drivers have said to me in Melbourne, Moscow, Paris, Tokyo, New York, Delhi and Cape Town. Indeed, and still the only woman in the history of democratic government to have made a real difference to the world.[1]

Such admiration was not always felt everywhere, least of all at home. For a while, other nations looked on in horror at the signs of social, economic and political division that run through the narrative of this book. Then – for good or ill – they began to copy the policies that Thatcher's Britain had experimented with, enacted and promoted. Britain in the eighties was both an inspiration and a warning to the rest of the world to an extent that it has rarely been during the succeeding twenty years. What follows is an attempt to describe, analyse and argue over that momentous period in the nation's history.

1 JIM'LL FIX IT

Waiting at the Church

The prime minister had a farm: Upper Clayhill spread out across 138 acres of the Sussex Downs. To the west was the medieval town of Lewes, where more than seven hundred years previously the 'Father of Parliament', Simon de Montfort, and his fellow barons had defeated a royal army and taken the hapless King Henry III prisoner. To the south was Glyndebourne, home since the 1930s of the celebrated summer opera festival. Set beside a water meadow, the farmhouse at Upper Clayhill was part-Elizabethan, part-Georgian. Built in old Sussex brick, it retained many of its original oak beams and an impressive Tudor fireplace. James Callaghan had taken out a loan to buy it in 1968 shortly after a Cabinet reshuffle had switched him from the Treasury to the Home Office. He found that farming was not only a money-making venture but also a welcome distraction, and it provided him with a weekend retreat where his family could gather for Sunday lunch. Upon becoming prime minister in 1976, he gladly exchanged a pokey flat in Lambeth for 10 Downing Street, and even though he also gained the official country house at Chequers, parting with Upper Clayhill was never his intention. It did not come with the job and it could not be taken away with the job. Its rustic, homely feel contrasted with the formal town-house dimensions of Downing Street. Only the historical bric-a-brac on the walls suggested an occupant with an interest in the vigorous projection of British power in the world: the rooms were decorated with prints and paintings of Royal Navy men-o'-war, sails puffed out and cannons ready to repel the enemy.

This artistic taste might have suggested a nostalgic Tory busy fortifying his old-fashioned dwelling against the sombre realities of 1970s Britain, a nation whose relative decline was a recurring subject of discussion in the media, at home and abroad.[1] But James Callaghan was the leader of the Labour Party. He had no particular pining for lost imperial glories. What was more, as prime minister, he was as engaged as anyone in the realities of the present and more optimistic than most that years of prosperity lay ahead, especially if his government could, through a partnership with the trade unions, ensure industrial peace and maintain wage restraint as the means to bring down inflation. The 'sick man of Europe' epithet, once used of the Ottoman Empire, may have attached itself to the United Kingdom during the decade as economic dislocation followed an energy crisis and international economists like J. K. Galbraith spoke regretfully of the 'British disease', yet, unlike the other major European nations, the United Kingdom possessed an asset that seemed destined to protect her from subsequent shocks and through which a dramatically more prosperous future could be secured.

North Sea oil promised riches the like of which previous post-war prime ministers could scarcely have dreamt. 'Black gold' was the abundant substance that would fund higher public spending *and* remove the burden from the average taxpayer. In June 1977, Gavyn Davies (who would later be chairman of the BBC but was then a member of the Downing Street Policy Unit) sent Callaghan a 'medium-term assessment' which forecast that through a policy of controlled reflation and rising North Sea oil revenues, Labour might be able to reduce income tax to 15 per cent by 1982.[2] The eighties could be a decade of dynamic growth, enhanced public sector investment and Scandinavian-style social democracy.

However, if Callaghan wanted to lead this national revival he had first to win a general election. When to call polling day was what particularly preoccupied him during August 1978. With Parliament on its summer recess, Upper Clayhill Farm provided the perfect setting for calm and measured deliberation. After completing his usual early morning tour of the acres, the fields of barley, checking the welfare of the cattle and assessing the likelihood of rain,[3] his mind turned to forecasting the consequences if he called a snap general election in the autumn.

There was no need to do so until late the following year since, constitutionally, it was not until November 1979 that there had to be an election. The main argument for waiting until the full five-year term had expired was a powerful one given that the country had only recently emerged from a recession. The longer Callaghan could put off the campaign, the more time there was for a sustained economic recovery to improve the voters' sense of material well-being. But prime ministers were out of the habit of going the distance. In search of a workable parliamentary majority in 1966, Harold Wilson had called – and won – an election seventeen months into his first term of office. In 1970, he went to the polls again, nine months before it was necessary to do so. His Tory vanquisher on that occasion, Edward Heath, proceeded to gamble, unsuccessfully, on a February 1974 election, sixteen months early. Then, in October 1974, the third general election within four years was held. Between 1966 and 1974, declaring early had worked twice and failed twice.

One handicap in calling a snap election was that it could look suspicious.

Did the prime minister know something ominous was on the horizon and was trying to secure re-election before the storm hit? It was therefore helpful that the vote should be held not just after several months of improving conditions but in an atmosphere marked by continuing optimism. Both criteria appeared to be met in the summer of 1978. Furthermore, Callaghan's generally avuncular public persona – he was dubbed 'Sunny Jim' – was an obvious asset in this respect. The opinion polls suggested he was both more popular than his own Labour Party and more popular than the leader of the opposition, Margaret Thatcher, whose popularity was lower than that of her Conservative Party. Were it to be a presidential contest, the advantage was clearly with Callaghan. Nonetheless, even the reality of a parliamentary election was not necessarily bad news for Labour. Although the psephological evidence was mixed, with private polling provided to the prime minister by Bob Worcester of MORI suggesting the Tories were clinging on to the slenderest of advantages, other opinion polls showed Labour leads of up to 4 per cent. By October, that lead had grown to between 5 and 7 per cent.[4] Seven per cent represented a decent majority.

Had Callaghan enjoyed a working majority at Westminster, the argument for continuing in office well into 1979 would have been especially strong. But no such luxury was at his disposal. The general election that had ousted Edward Heath's Conservative government in February 1974 had produced no overall majority and when the incoming Labour prime minister, Harold Wilson, finally won a second election later that year, it was with a parliamentary majority of just three. Subsequent by-election defeats soon removed even that slender advantage. In April 1976, Wilson retired as prime minister and, after a Labour leadership election, Callaghan took over. From the spring of 1977 to the summer of 1978, he stayed in office thanks to the 'Lib–Lab' pact which Labour had negotiated with the Liberal Party.

The Liberals only had thirteen MPs – only two more than the Scottish Nationalists – but dealing with them suited Callaghan because it provided the cloak of political necessity to cover his preference for steering policy away from the demands of Labour's left-wingers and towards the centre ground. It also suited the Liberals, who were keen to avoid fighting an election campaign so soon after they had hurriedly replaced their leader, Jeremy Thorpe. The flamboyant Thorpe was facing charges of conspiracy to murder a talkative stable lad turned male model whom he had picked up and encountered unexpected difficulties in letting go. In Thorpe's place, the Liberals chose as their new leader David Steel, who, as the son of a Church of Scotland minister, seemed an altogether safer bet. Yet Steel was still in his late thirties and was struggling to assert himself against the condescending appellation 'the Boy David'. Other than staving off an expensive and awkwardly timed election campaign, the Liberals secured little from their Westminster assignations with Labour's chief whip. Having run its course, the Lib–Lab pact broke up in July 1978, more in ennui than acrimony. Thus, as Callaghan weighed his options over the summer, he recognized that when Parliament reconvened in November, the government would be unable to carry its business through the House of Commons unless it brokered deals with the Scottish and Welsh nationalists and satisfied the divergent aspirations of the Ulster Unionists and the Irish nationalists of the SDLP. Labour's outright victory in an October 1978 general election would be the means of escaping this wearisome prospect.

Securing a dissolution of Parliament was a prime minister's prerogative, and though Callaghan sought the opinions of his Cabinet colleagues he could divine no consensus.[5] There were also other important figures in public life whose views the prime minister thought worth soliciting – the union bosses. Almost alone among his senior Cabinet colleagues, Callaghan had been a national trade union official.* Indeed, one of his claims to the party leadership was his rapport with both the parliamentary and trade union wings of the Labour movement. The unions had good cause to regard him as their friend. In 1969, Harold Wilson's employment secretary, Barbara Castle, had proposed legislation to curb unofficial strikes in a white paper, *In Place of Strife*. Opposition to it within the Cabinet had been led by Callaghan, who forced the proposals to be dropped in favour of a face-saving, and meaningless, 'solemn and binding undertaking' by the TUC to discourage wildcat strikes.

On 1 September 1978, four days before he was due to speak at the TUC annual conference, Callaghan invited six of Britain's most senior trade unionists down to dinner at his farm. It was a beautiful summer's evening. The food was cooked by his wife, Audrey, a woman noted for her culinary expertise as well as her experience in local government (although the press tended to focus on her frumpy appearance, dubbing her the 'Yorkshire Pudding').[6] She was half of a happy and stable marriage, Callaghan having met her when she was a sixteen-year-old Baptist Sunday school teacher in Maidstone and he a junior clerk at the Inland Revenue. The courses were served by their granddaughter, Tamsin Jay, whose father, Peter Jay, had been plucked from writing about economics in *The Times* to become ambassador to the United States amid inevitable accusations of prime ministerial nepotism. In this easy, relaxed, family-oriented life at Upper Clayhill, the union

---

* He had been assistant secretary of the small, white-collar union, the Inland Revenue Staff Federation, between 1936 and 1943.

fraternity found a warm welcome. Round the dining-room table was assembled the 'Labour aristocracy' of Len Murray (general secretary of the TUC), Moss Evans (the new general secretary of the Transport and General Workers' Union), and David Basnett of the General and Municipal Workers' Union, who was also organizer of Trade Unionists for a Labour Victory, together with Lord Allen, Hugh Scanlon of the Amalgamated Union of Engineering Workers, and Geoffrey Drain of the local government workers' union, NALGO. To all but the most casual of newspaper readers or news bulletin viewers, these were some of the most well-known names in British public life. Between courses, Callaghan discussed with them whether he should call the general election, raising arguments for why delay was worth considering. He failed to convince. Of his six guests, five felt he should hesitate no longer and go for October. Only Scanlon argued for deferring the date. Callaghan listened and remained non-committal. Nonetheless, it was clear what the union leaders thought, and as they delivered their parting thanks and goodbyes they had grounds for assuming the hospitable prime minister had digested their advice.[7]

This was far more of a historic occasion than its attendees realized, for at no time over the succeeding quarter-century would a prime minister solicit in this way the opinions of the trade union high command on such prime ministerial prerogatives as when to call a general election. The eighties changed that relationship abruptly and fundamentally. But Callaghan belonged to a different world and a contrasting set of values. He was bound to the union bosses by history, by temperament and, most importantly of all, by expedient, for their connivance was essential if the government's pay restraint policies were to control inflation. Enjoying vigorous mental and physical health, Callaghan was sixty-six years old, having been born two years before the First World War began. As he had gone straight from school to the workplace, joining a union had been for him a rite of passage into adulthood and wider responsibility. He had been in Parliament since 1945, having been elected – aged only thirty-three – to a Cardiff constituency in Clement Attlee's Labour landslide and proceeding to occupy all four of the great offices of state, serving as Chancellor of the Exchequer from 1964 to 1967, Home Secretary from then until 1970, and Foreign Secretary from 1974 until 1976, when he became prime minister. Although in private he could display a sharp temper and a tendency to bully colleagues, in public Callaghan seemed at ease with himself. Without a hint of embarrassment or contrived showmanship, he had cheerfully sung 'I'm the man, the very fat man, who waters the workers' beer' at a Durham miners' gala. At least to those who did not cross him personally, it all seemed part of 'Sunny Jim's' affable nature and rootedness in the culture of working-class struggle.

He was driven precociously into public life and Labour politics by the disadvantages he experienced in childhood. He was the son of an Englishman of Irish descent called James Garoghan, who had used the assumed name Callaghan when enlisting in the Royal Navy and had seen action at the battle of Jutland on board the dreadnought HMS *Agincourt*, rising through the ranks to become a chief petty officer. In 1921, however, he had suddenly died of a heart attack when his son was nine years old, leaving a family without financial security and reduced to living in a succession of cheap rented rooms. There was no pension upon which to draw until provision was extended by the first Labour government in 1924, along with a grant that ensured the fatherless boy would manage to stay on at school until the age of seventeen. It was a socialist administration's helping hand that the young James Callaghan grasped, although the limits of state assistance in the inter-war period were soon brought home: his grades were good enough, but the lack of further grants made going on to university out of the question. He felt this social handicap for the rest of his life – perhaps one reason why he sometimes considered himself closer to union leaders than to such Oxford-educated luminaries of the Labour front bench as Hugh Gaitskell, Harold Wilson, Roy Jenkins, Tony Crosland, Denis Healey and Michael Foot. Tellingly, the first words that came from Callaghan's lips when told he had made it to 10 Downing Street were, 'Prime minister of Great Britain! And never went to university!'[8]

Unlike typical representatives of the university-educated intelligentsia drawn to the progressive cause of the Labour Party, Callaghan was not a liberal. In many respects, he was a traditionalist, revering the heritage and structure not only of the trade unions but of the armed forces and the monarchy as well. He never shared the anti-militarist, anti-American sentiments that engaged radicals of the sixties' generation. His internationalism found no conflict with a sense of patriotism. In the Second World War, he had served, albeit uneventfully, as a seaman in the Royal Navy, and his natural admiration for royalty was apparent during the outpouring of popular sentiment accompanying the Queen's silver jubilee in 1977. One of the vessels framed on his walls at Upper Clayhill Farm was King Edward VII's royal yacht, *Victoria and Albert*, upon which his father had served as a rigger. As her prime minister, Callaghan enjoyed a warm rapport with Queen Elizabeth, with whom he shared an elevated, idealistic, view of the British Commonwealth's importance. It was, though, in his attitude to the social changes of the sixties that he demonstrated how fully he did not share what became the prevailing attitudes and assumptions of the left after 1979. Reversing the tone of his predecessor as Home Secretary, Roy Jenkins, Callaghan assured the House of Commons of his determination 'to call a halt to the rising tide of permissiveness', which was 'one of the most unlikeable words that has been invented in recent years'.[9] Although he had long lost the Baptist faith, or any strong Christian faith, of his upbringing, he believed in traditional family structures. He was repulsed by pornography, vigorously opposed tolerance of even soft drugs, and struggled to conceal his distaste for homosexuality.[10] In these respects, his views were perhaps no different from those of most of his Conservative opponents – or of a broad, cross-party, swathe of the electorate.

On 5 September 1978, the delegates for the annual TUC conference gathered in a brightly lit hall in Brighton to hear Callaghan's address to them. They were joined by ranks of journalists waiting expectantly for the telltale comments that would surely give the game away that he was about to call a general election. His speech opened with an overview of problems surmounted and achievements to be built upon. Taxes were being cut, benefits and pensions were being increased and, if wage restraint was accepted, inflation, which had previously let rip, would continue on its downward path. Then he did something so wholly unexpected that it would dominate news coverage that evening. The prime minister broke into a music hall song, which he misattributed to the Edwardian entertainer, Marie Lloyd:*

There was I waiting at the church,
All at once he sent me round a note,
Here's the very note,
This is what he wrote,
'Can't get away
To marry you today,
My wife won't let me!'

The delegates responded by erupting into laughter and applause, although it was not really clear who he was leaving in the lurch – them, the media or Margaret Thatcher. Emboldened, Callaghan went on to the offensive. 'I have promised nobody that I shall be at the altar in October, nobody at all. So all I want to add this afternoon is that I certainly intend to indicate my intentions very shortly on this matter.'[11] The unions responded by offering £1 million to the election fund, and *The Times* assured its readers that 'seasoned political hands' were united in believing the Cabinet would be meeting on 7 September to agree a dissolution of Parliament for an election on 5 October.[12]

On the morning of 7 September, the members of the Cabinet were duly told by Callaghan that their fate was deferred. Rather than call a snap poll,

---

* It was actually by Vesta Victoria.

he would settle first the referendums on Welsh and Scottish devolution and ensure the economic recovery was given a few more months to work its balm upon the nation's mood. That evening, Callaghan broadcast to the nation announcing there would be no election. There was much astonishment. A momentum of expectation had developed only to be suddenly and belatedly quashed. Callaghan, however, did not like others assuming what he would do and was determined to lay out fresh proposals for the coming decade. 'We are discontented with the way of the things we observe: the football hooligans, the litter in the streets,' he jotted down. 'There is much to be done – indeed the job is never-ending. We must put forward a realistic socialist policy for [the] '80s.'[13]

Most of all, Callaghan simply did not think the opinion poll lead was big enough, or sufficiently sustained, to risk it. He was aware that a new electoral register would come into force in February 1979 which, it was estimated, would benefit Labour by about six seats. Given the existing arithmetic, that might be the difference between forming a government and going into opposition. Years later, when holidaying with his wife in Scotland, Callaghan met David Steel, who asked him why he had not called an autumn 1978 election. Callaghan explained that he had been primarily influenced by the possibility that he might win but without a working majority in the Commons. To a leader of a minority party like the Liberals, a hung parliament would be a godsend, not a catastrophe, and Steel expressed surprise that such an outcome would have been considered so unpalatable to the Labour Party.[14] In saying this, Steel perhaps underestimated the toll that the unrelenting daily political management inflicted upon the prime minister. Callaghan had seemingly reached the point where merely prolonging the agony of minority government no longer seemed a prize worth fighting for. Instead, he believed the economic prospects were favourable for 1979 and that, far from Britain being in a state of systemic decline, it had merely suffered a few turbulent years of mismanagement under Edward Heath's Conservative government, which Labour was demonstrably rectifying. Another six months or so of sustained improvement would convince the electorate to give Labour a full mandate to govern.

Floating or Sinking?

Certainly, there seemed a marked contrast between Heath's last period in office and the situation facing Callaghan in the autumn of 1978. Within a couple of years of winning power in 1970, Heath had been assailed by problems. In the midst of a world boom, financial constraints were relaxed in order to pursue a 'dash for growth'. Low interest rates and easy credit powered a spectacular, and highly speculative, property boom. In place since the end of the Second World War, the Bretton Woods system of international fixed currency exchange rates had broken down in August 1971 and various anti-volatility mechanisms had been put in place in an effort to maintain stability. However, in June 1972, the decision was taken to cut sterling free from its corset. For the first time since the 1930s, Britain had a currency whose value 'floated' against other currencies. Heath's Chancellor, Anthony Barber, announced that it was only 'a temporary measure'[15] (apart from the abortive experience of the European Exchange Rate Mechanism of 1990–2, the currency was still floating well into the second decade of the twenty-first century). At first, Heath saw this freedom from constantly having to intervene to keep sterling at a fixed rate as a carte blanche to do as he pleased, as if Britain had entered a consequence-free economic world. Although the pound initially ascended above its December 1971 fixed value of $2.60, it was soon not so much floating as sinking, the extent of Heath's extravagantly reflationary policies worrying holders of sterling into selling it. Alarmed as the pound's descent gathered momentum, and also concerned at soaring inflation, Heath changed course and tried deflationary measures and – a heresy to those who believed in the free market – a statutory incomes policy. It was 'stop–go' economics at its most primitive. Interest rates were raised to record levels and public spending cut. Indirect controls were forced upon bank lending. Then, in December 1973, with winter temperatures chilling the country, the National Union of Mineworkers chose its moment to call a 'work to rule' overtime ban in support of a 35 per cent pay increase.

It was the miners' second strike in successive years. Such had been the success of their picketing of power stations in 1972 that Heath had called a state of emergency. Businesses and houses lost electricity for several hours each day until Heath hoisted the flag of surrender. In the succeeding months, the Arab–Israeli Yom Kippur War and the embargo on Western countries enforced by the oil producers' cartel, OPEC, quadrupled the price of petrol. To the miners' leaders, it was the perfect opportunity to strike again. Facing acute energy shortages in mid-winter, the government once more fell back on emergency powers, this time forcing businesses to cut down to a 'three-day week'. With the nation's power supply switched off, Britons were reduced to groping around by candlelight. Taking malicious glee in this humbling of a once mighty power, Uganda's military dictator, Idi Amin, duly launched a 'Save Britain Fund', urging Ugandans to 'come forward and help their former colonial masters'.[16]

The sense of defeatism went to the heart of Whitehall. Feebly, the best that Heath's unofficial 'deputy prime minister' and head of the civil service, Sir William Armstrong, could offer his colleagues was to announce that the government's task was to 'oversee the orderly management of decline'. Even a fighting retreat proved beyond the administration's reach, with Sir William a personal casualty in the rout. Suffering a mental breakdown, he was at one stage found under his table muttering incoherently about 'moving the red army from here and the blue army from there', although he later recovered sufficiently to be appointed chairman of the Midland Bank.[17] More telling was the experience across the English Channel. There, the British shambles was not repeated. Other major European economies were still expanding, their ability to cope with the oil price shock only rubbing in Britain's humiliation. The extent to which Heath had lost control was the unfortunate sub-text of his February 1974 general election slogan 'Who Governs?' If the question had to be asked, then the answer was clear. Albeit by the narrowest of margins, Labour returned to power amid hopes that it could find a workable compromise with the trade unions. Seventy million working days had been lost to strikes during Heath's three and half years in Downing Street. Labour quickly bought off the miners and by 1976 relative industrial peace had broken out for the first time in the decade.

Stabilizing the economy and restoring growth were more difficult. In 1974, the economy had contracted by almost 2 per cent. Inflation continued to soar. By the summer of 1976, the annual rate had reached 26 per cent. The savings of the provident were being swiftly eroded. The assault worsened by the year's end, when the London Stock Exchange crashed. The *Financial Times* index (established at 100 in 1935) plunged towards 150. Denis Healey, the florid, bushy eye-browed Chancellor of the Exchequer, raised taxes in his April 1975 budget. The basic rate of income tax rose to 35 per cent. The upper rate was fixed at 83 per cent. These were deflationary measures intended to combat acutely rising prices, but they nonetheless helped convince many middle-class taxpayers that redistributing their diminishing income was a deliberate part of socialism in action. The *Wall Street Journal*'s leading article, entitled 'Goodbye, Great Britain', all but read the country's last rites: 'the British government is now so clearly headed towards a policy of total confiscation that anyone who has any wealth left is discounting furiously at any chance to get it out of the country.'[18] The US Secretary of State, Henry Kissinger, assured the president, Gerard Ford, that 'Britain is a tragedy – it has sunk to begging, borrowing, stealing, until North Sea oil comes in . . . That Britain has become such a scrounger is a disgrace.'[19] A few disgruntled reactionaries drew admiring parallels with Augusto Pinochet's recent right-wing coup in Chile. Some even went so far as to lay the groundwork for action.[20] The view from most boardrooms, however, was that salvation would come not from men in uniform but from officialdom in Brussels. Opinion polls, which had suggested most Britons opposed joining the European Economic Community before entry was negotiated by Heath, now indicated growing support. Articulating the view that the country's problems were so severe that only foreigners could solve them, Christopher Soames, Winston Churchill's diplomat son-in-law, asserted: 'This is no time for Britain to consider leaving a Christmas Club, let alone the Common Market.'[21] In June 1975, a national referendum on the issue (called primarily to solve the internecine debate within the Labour Party) produced a resounding verdict, with 67 per cent voting in favour of remaining within the EEC.

With the run on the pound continuing during 1976, it was indeed down to foreigners to get Britain out of its financial misery. When the British ambassador asked the usually anglophile German Chancellor, Helmut Schmidt, if German funds might be forthcoming, Schmidt responded with a lecture on Britain's economic incompetence, comparing the country's management unfavourably with that of communist East Germany. Another potential rescuer was the International Monetary Fund. An emergency loan from the IMF would come with strings attached, requiring the government to balance the budget and cut public spending, forcing Labour to choose between fighting unemployment or quelling inflation. The number of those out of work had long passed one million and, at over 6 per cent of the workforce, was well above the post-war 2 per cent level that constituted 'full employment.' For Labour, whose heritage was steeped in the depression of the 1930s, cutting unemployment benefit was especially distasteful. On the other hand, an alternative Keynesian prescription of a reflationary stimulus looked reckless at a time when inflation was at its highest level for three hundred years, double the rates of Britain's major competitors, and, it was feared, on the verge of replicating the situation in South America where currencies were becoming virtually worthless amid mounting chaos and military crackdowns.

In the Cabinet, the left-wing case against accepting an IMF bail-out, with its accompanying requirement to cut public spending, was made by the energy secretary, Tony Benn. He advocated creating a siege economy, with the normal inflows and outflows of the market being replaced by socialist planning and tariffs against imports. Even the Foreign Secretary, Tony Crosland, proposed threatening sweeping import controls on the calculation that 'as the IMF was even more passionately opposed to protectionism than it was attached to monetarism, this threat would be sufficient to persuade the IMF to lend the money without unacceptable conditions'.[22] Full-scale protectionism was a dangerous bluff, wholly inconsistent with the EEC membership that had so recently been reaffirmed. Yet such was the level of panic that even Britain's forward role in NATO seemed to be tradable: the decision was taken to warn West Germany that unless she helped bail Britain out, British forces might have to be withdrawn from the country.

The succession of events that brought these options to the Cabinet table unfolded during the autumn of 1976. The government's budget deficit had broken records. The pound had slumped to $1.57, despite interest rates hiked to 15 per cent. The markets looked at Britain's spiralling public sector borrowing requirement and concluded sterling was not a currency to hold on to. The nadir came on 27 September. Scheduled to attend an IMF conference in Manila, via Hong Kong, Healey's chauffeur-driven car got as far as Heathrow airport before its passenger panicked. So acute was the pound's free fall that he concluded he could not afford to spend seventeen hours on a flight and out of telephone contact. The television cameras captured his limousine turning round and heading back towards the Treasury. There, Healey brought forward the scenario he had already concluded was inevitable. Britain would have to appeal to the IMF for a loan. The following day, Callaghan found himself virtually shouting at the delegates at the Labour Party conference in Blackpool:

> We used to think that you could just spend your way out of recession . . . I tell you in all candour that that option no longer exists and that insofar as it ever did exist, it only worked by injecting a bigger dose of inflation into the economy . . . Higher inflation, followed by higher unemployment. That is the history of the last twenty years.[23]

The pronouncement was not to prove, as was subsequently assumed, the beginning of full-throttle monetarism – the money supply grew more quickly between 1976 and 1979 than between 1975 and 1976[24] – but it was, perhaps, the end of the more simplistic interpretation of Keynesian economics. Two days later, Healey announced Britain was going begging to the IMF for $3.9 billion, the largest loan in the fund's history. Indeed, the sum necessary to bankroll Britain was so great that the IMF had not enough money itself and needed to seek additional resources from other lenders. In return, it would instruct Her Majesty's Treasury how to run its affairs. Between 1975 and 1978, the Labour government slashed public spending in real terms by 8 per cent,[25] a far more swingeing cut than Margaret Thatcher ever achieved in the 1980s. In the space of three years, from 1973 to 1976, Britain had experienced not just galloping inflation but stagflation – rising prices and falling output – as well as massive industrial unrest, the temporary switching off of energy supplies, serious civil unrest in Northern Ireland which claimed over eight hundred lives and spread to the British mainland, a stock market collapse, a secondary banking crisis, credit controls and a begging mission to the IMF. Apart from the darkest days of the Napoleonic conflict and the two world wars when the prospect of military annihilation had loomed (and notwithstanding the one-off embarrassment of the Suez fiasco), it was surely the greatest convocation of visible humiliations visited upon the country since the civil wars of the seventeenth century. What effect this had on the national psyche was difficult to tell: 'Britain is a country that resents being poor,' concluded *The Times* on New Year's Eve 1976, 'but is not prepared to make the effort to be rich.'[26]

It was thus perhaps understandable that the popular response to the Queen's silver jubilee in 1977 was not to behead the monarch but to rejoice that in Elizabeth II there was at least the embodiment of one state institution that remained secure and fit for purpose. Yet, almost contemporaneous with the red, white and blue bunting strung across lamp posts and shopfronts in celebration of the Queen's twenty-five years on the throne, there came early signs that recovery was under way. Following the enforcement of spending cuts, wage inflation was being brought under control. Unemployment figures stopped going up. The pound was climbing towards \$1.90 and reserves, depleted during the crisis of 1976, were replenished as sterling assumed the status of a petro-currency. Indeed, the exchange rate strengthened to the extent that it became Treasury policy to prevent it from rising beyond a rate deemed uncompetitive for British exporters, for in 1977 the country's trade balance had moved into surplus for the first time since the 1960s. While going begging to the IMF was an act of national degradation, it nonetheless impressed investors, convincing them that Britain was adopting the right medicine. In consequence, less than half of the IMF loan needed to be drawn. Suddenly, it seemed that Britain might buck the trend of ex-imperial powers that had gone into long-term decline, its period in the doldrums merely a matter of a few unfortunate years rather than the drawn-out process of decades.

Healey deemed the signs of recovery sufficient to allow a mild relaxation of his tough deflationary measures. Further amelioration was dependent upon the inflation rate continuing to fall. The government had made wage restraint the centrepiece of its anti-inflationary strategy, believing the key to success lay with its own forecasting skills and the willing compliance of the trade unions not to push for pay deals above what the government decreed should be the 'norm'. More than half of all employees were members of trade unions. The leverage exerted by the state on pay policy was considerable given that almost 30 per cent of Britain's workforce was employed by the state, either in the public services or the nationalized industries. Eighty per cent of those on the public sector payroll were also members of unions. Thus an anti-inflationary policy that relied upon partnership between government and unions was founded upon three assumptions: that inflation was caused by big pay rises, that the state remained the dominant employer, and that the unions were far more likely to reach agreement with a Labour administration than risk undermining it and putting their Conservative antagonists in power.

This form of corporatist government was a relatively recent innovation. Until the late 1960s, Whitehall had not deployed meaningful industrial relations policies, believing that this was best left to collective bargaining between individual unions and employers. The Wilson and Callaghan governments, however, made incomes policy a central tool of economic management. Whereas Heath had found himself with a statutory incomes policy because the unions would not work amicably with a Tory government, Labour in power believed it could achieve similar results through its goodwill with the union high command. Each year, the government announced the 'norm' pay increases. In July 1975, a maximum £6 per week increase (with no increase at all for anyone earning above £8,500 per year) was set. A year later, the pay increase was a mere 5 per cent, up to a maximum of £4 per week. Ten per cent was permitted in 1977. Only 5 per cent was allowed in 1978. All these increases were below the rate of inflation. Almost every week, the media ran stories about the 'norm': where it had been breached, what efforts were being made to arbitrate a compromise or what a government minister proposed to say or do about it. The front steps of ACAS, the arbitration service, became almost as familiar a backdrop for news reports as College Green, outside the soot-covered Houses of Parliament.

To match the incomes policy there was a statutory prices policy. This, indeed, was the mechanism whereby supposedly voluntary pay deals were indirectly enforced by a statutory Price Code which legally prevented any company from passing on in higher prices any wage increase above the 'norm'. The Price Commission acted as an ombudsman to police 'unearned' price rises. Large firms, labelled 'Category I', had to give twenty-eight days' advance notification of price rises to the Price Commission; fourteen days were required by 'Category II' firms (which included manufacturers and public utilities), except for those in distribution, construction and professional services, which were let off with a mere compulsion to report. The Price Code laid out what sort of cost increases could be taken into account before prices were increased. The government also intervened with targeted subsidies to specific everyday items, in particular foods, in order to depress the cost of living.[27] Taken together, the incomes and prices policies provided some of the clearest contrasts between how the state intervened in daily life in the 1970s and how it left it to the free market in the thirty years thereafter.

In the short term, the incomes and prices polices produced favourable results. By February 1978, inflation had fallen below 10 per cent. The unions, however, had had enough of squeezing their members' salaries because the government told them to do so. Higher pay awards in the private sector left those in the public sector struggling in comparison. And in order to counterbalance private sector increases, the government was particularly keen to crack down further on wage increases in the sector of the economy it could more easily control. When the unions refused to cooperate any further, the result was the 'Winter of Discontent' and the downfall of James Callaghan's corporatist vision for Britain.

Crisis? What Crisis?

Four months after James Callaghan had informed his colleagues that there would be no autumn general election he was back in the Cabinet Room at 10 Downing Street marshalling their views on whether to call a national state of emergency. Within this short space of time, the government's claim to have sorted out the industrial anarchy inherited from Edward Heath's Tories in 1974 was tested to destruction. Between December 1978 and March 1979, the 'Winter of Discontent' fatally undermined claims that a cure had been found for the 'British disease' of dismal industrial productivity, strikes and poor relations between government, management and unions. The opinion polls, which had shown a clear Labour lead in October 1978, started suggesting the result of the next election would be a Conservative landslide.[28]

That the Labour government's reputation with swing voters was seriously damaged by the sudden outbreak of trade union militancy was the inescapable conclusion from data collected by Gallup and other market research companies. For Callaghan, the unions' actions were a personal betrayal. He had built his career in the Labour Party as a union man. He had risked his Cabinet position in 1969 in order to scupper legislation intended to restrict the unions' ability to flex their muscles at will. A decade on, they had offered him no reward for his support, made no attempt to meet his pleas for self-sacrifice. It seemingly counted for nought that his government had passed legislation to increase the unions' powers to enforce closed shop rules, whereby union shop stewards enjoying exclusive bargaining rights with a company could legally prevent the company from employing anyone who refused to join their union. The fractious winter of 1978/9 seemed a world away from the bucolic charm of Upper Clayhill Farm in August, when Audrey's cooking had provided a convivial dinner for the union leaders and her husband had failed to take their advice to get a move on with the election campaign.

The first sign of trouble came on the opening day of the Labour Party conference on 2 October 1978. In response to Callaghan's announcement that the pay 'norm' for the coming year would be 5 per cent, delegates (their numbers distorted in the ballot by the union block-voting system) passed a motion calling for the abolition of pay restraint by an emphatic 4 million to 1.9 million votes.

Callaghan intended to ignore the conference vote, but three days later his economics adviser, David Lipsey, tried to persuade him that it was clear the unions would not accept his 5 per cent pay norm. 'Abandoning 5 per cent,' Lipsey wrote, 'will be embarrassing. But could we win an election after a winter of discontent in which a large chunk of the Parliamentary Labour Party will be sympathizing with the malcontents?' Callaghan seemed surprisingly unperturbed.[29] Overriding his Chancellor's hesitations, he calculated that an incomes policy of just 5 per cent would be anti-inflationary. Augmented by additional emoluments and staggered payments from the previous year, 5 per cent would end up equating to an inflation rate of around 8 per cent. He was not, therefore, asking for a below-inflation wage rise.

With hindsight, Callaghan's sanguinity seems complacent, an episode of wishful thinking from a prime minister who, without seeking the full range of alternative means of combating inflation, lacked weapons beyond his personal powers of persuasion with union leaders and the threat that destabilizing a Labour government was not in their long-term interests. Callaghan's delusion was, however, built upon recent experience. While many of the images that came to seem representative of the period were of picket lines manned by union officials warming themselves next to braziers, the actual period of industrial unrest was a short one. Until that winter, Labour had not presided helpless over a strike-bound country. Although there had been a particularly vicious confrontation at the Grunwick Film Processing Laboratories in the summer of 1977, and a firemen's strike at the end of that year, most of the strikes since Labour's return to office in 1974 had been relatively small-scale affairs and did not compare with the serious unrest visited upon the Tory administration of Edward Heath.

Callaghan's ability to keep the industrial peace had been maintained through the good relations he enjoyed with Len Murray, the TUC general secretary and Jack Jones of the Transport and General Workers' Union, which was the country's biggest union, with two million members. Jones had been one of the kingmakers of the decade. A 1977 Gallup poll suggested that a majority of Britons believed him more powerful than the prime minister,[30] which, if true, would certainly have added weight to Heath's 'Who Governs?' election slogan. Born into poverty and wounded fighting fascism in the Spanish Civil War (after which, according to one well-informed testimony, he remained a paid Soviet agent until the 1980s),[31] Jones had been Callaghan's union ally in scuppering Barbara Castle's *In Place of Strife* proposals in 1969 and had done as much as anyone to make Heath's union legislation unworkable. However, in 1978 he finally retired with a triumphant send-off from 2,500 guests assembled at the Royal Festival Hall and was made a Companion of Honour by the Queen. Rather than impose a deal negotiated in Downing Street, his successor, Moss Evans, along with his union's national organizer, Ron Todd, believed in devolved union management, preferring to let the shop stewards on the ground make what they thought were appropriate claims. The ebbing of power from the union high command downwards to the activists undermined corporatist planning, since on the shop floor the primary interest was, understandably, in maximizing pay and conditions rather than conforming with the government's nationwide anti-inflationary strategy.

In October 1978, 57,000 TGWU members at Ford Motors went out on strike, demanding, with Evans's endorsement, a 30 per cent pay increase. Concluding that the lengthy disruption to productivity was more harmful than the cost of raising wages, Ford was keen to reach a deal and, after seven weeks, the strike was called off in return for a 17 per cent pay rise. It was a deal that shattered the government's 5 per cent norm. Unable and unwilling to declare war on the TGWU, Callaghan decided to punish the Ford management (among whose executives was numbered his son, Michael) by withdrawing government subsidies to the firm. This infuriated those Labour MPs who thought it outrageous that financial sanctions should be introduced against generous pay deals in blue-collar industries. With John Prescott among a group of left-wing MPs refusing to support the measure in the Commons, the vote was duly lost, and Callaghan scurried to regain his parliamentary authority by calling an immediate vote of confidence.

The episode underlined a fundamental weakness in the government's position. Not only was it unable to control those unions who were no longer willing to do its bidding, but there was a conflict of interest – financial as well as ideological – involving a large section of the Parliamentary Labour Party that was sympathetic to union demands and was directly union-sponsored. An administration with no working majority at Westminster was ill placed to take on the TGWU when so many of its MPs were sponsored by the TGWU. Without union funds, Labour could not hope properly to finance the forthcoming election campaign. The divided loyalty was personified in Derek Gladwin, who was both Labour's chief election campaign manager and the southern regional secretary of the GMWU, a union actively engaged in the coming Winter of Discontent.

The great industrial conflict followed swiftly from the TGWU's victory in the Ford dispute. Emboldened, the TGWU's militancy swiftly spread beyond the car makers to the road haulage drivers, with unofficial strikes in December developing into all-out nationwide action in the New Year in pursuit of a 20 per cent pay rise. In the midst of the season of goodwill, the spectre presented itself of shops being unable to restock because of the inactivity of the lorry drivers. Nor was everything normal for those seeking entertainment at home. An electricians' strike took both BBC 1 and BBC 2 off the air just before Christmas. What caused the government particular alarm was the prospect of renewed power cuts once the 8,500 TGWU drivers of oil tankers heralded in the New Year by going on strike in pursuit of 25 per cent. Callaghan was presented by the Cabinet Office's central contingencies unit with Operation Drumstick, a plan to cancel the Christmas leave of 9,000 soldiers, who would be redeployed to drive oil tankers which the state would requisition using emergency powers. In the event, the strike was settled before a final decision on Drumstick was taken. With some petrol supplies beginning to run low, the oil companies awarded their drivers a 13 per cent increase.[32]

On 4 January, Callaghan flew out to a world leaders' summit in Guadeloupe, where he secured international backing for British arms sales to China and a replacement for Polaris as Britain's independent nuclear deterrent. Before returning, he stopped off for a few days of talks, rest and relaxation in Barbados. The contrast with the strike-bound British midwinter was too much for critical newspapers to ignore, and one paper's photographer managed to accentuate the contrast by persuading some especially lithesome air hostesses to frolic in the pool next to the prime minister when he went for a dip. The affectionate nickname 'Sunny Jim' took on a more irritating connotation. The annoyance was compounded when he decided to call a press conference upon his arrival back at Heathrow airport on 10 January. As the microphones were thrust towards him, the prime minister made light of his sunbathing, issuing the complacent reproach: 'If you look at it from outside – and perhaps you're taking a rather parochial view at the moment – I don't think that other people in the world would share the view there is mounting chaos.' *The Sun*'s headline 'Crisis? What Crisis?' captured the spirit, if not the actual words, of Callaghan's efforts to lighten the mood.

The railways followed the road hauliers in coming out on strike. With secondary picketing blockading key ports, the nation's commercial arteries were ceasing to function. The transport minister, Bill Rodgers, was especially anxious. His mother was dying of cancer and the chemotherapy drugs she needed were stuck at Hull docks. No union member would move them. But it was not just medical supplies that were running low. Hospital care itself was crippled when the public sector union NUPE began a series of strikes. Nurses joined picket lines. Ambulance staff downed stretchers. On 22 January, the TGWU, GMWU, NUPE and COHSE banded together for a 'day of action', bringing out 1.5 million workers in a remarkable flexing of their muscles. Strikes, which had previously afflicted the private sector, like the car workers, or nationalized industries like the mines, now spread across public sector service provision. The casualties were no longer just a managerial class sitting in their boardrooms and fretting over the consequences of a few more pounds a week to their workers. Instead, the victims were increasingly the helpless and defenceless, the old, the infirm, the bereaved. Labour's environment secretary, Peter Shore, later reflected on a time of 'occupational tribal warfare' in which 'every separate group in the country had no feeling and no sense of being part of a community but was simply out to get for itself what it could'.[33] Society appeared to be breaking down.

Schools began closing when their caretakers and dinner ladies walked out, depriving the pupils of heating, eating and safe keeping. Old people's homes were affected. When refuse collectors struck, unsightly piles of rat-infested rubbish started piling up in the streets, creating not only a noxious stink but a clear public health hazard. In late January, Liverpool's gravediggers went out on strike. Funeral cortèges were blocked, mourners sent back with their coffins by GMWU members picketing cemeteries. Corpses started to be piled in a disused factory. With some of the remains over ten days old, the city council became increasingly anxious about how to dispose of them. They considered burying them at sea. One government minister's response when asked by the Lord Chancellor what could be done was simply: 'Let the dead bury the dead.'[34] Ultimately, it was easier to give the GMWU gravediggers the pay rise they wanted, though not before a potent metaphor for Britain's decay had taken hold in the popular imagination.

On 15 January, the Cabinet discussed calling a state of emergency. Troops would be brought out on to the streets. The soldiers' main tasks would be to clear the piled-high rubbish before disease started spreading across cities, to drive ambulances and lorries carrying essential medical supplies, and to grit the frozen roads. It was a desperate option to which there were many objections: there were not enough troops to do the jobs required, their presence might exacerbate tensions, and it could be seen as an attempt to politicize the armed forces by deploying them as strike-breakers. A compromise was advocated by the transport secretary, Bill Rodgers, who hoped to avoid a formal state of emergency while nonetheless selectively deploying soldiers to perform potentially life-saving activities. Troops had, after all, provided emergency cover using their own 'green goddess' fire engines during the 1977 firemen's strike. The problem now was the sheer scale of the operation. How many troops could be withdrawn from Northern Ireland or West Germany to keep Britain going? How psychologically damaging to Britain's international status would be the sight of her legions coming home to prop up civil order? After protracted deliberation, a decision on using troops was deferred. Instead, Moss Evans was warned that if his members did not start moving essential supplies, the army would be called in.

This, and the accompanying offer of up to 20 per cent pay rises, persuaded the lorry drivers to call off their strike at the end of January. Elsewhere, above-inflation increases helped bring the other strikes to a close in February and March. In the meantime, Callaghan summoned the TUC General Council to Downing Street and announced a new understanding with Len Murray: the 5 per cent norm was effectively dropped and the TUC, in return for being brought yet more closely into the government's economic counsels, would in future provide guidance to unions on good strike conduct. Murray thought the accord, announced on St Valentine's Day, would not work.

Whether its endurance would be counted in weeks or months, the accord manifested the collapse of the Labour government's efforts to control inflation by a tight incomes policy. During 1979, inflation moved back up into double digits. The problems that afflicted Britain in the desperate months before the IMF bail-out had returned. The experience of the Winter of Discontent and the return of accelerating price rises also raised an important question. If inflation could not be brought down by a wage-restraint pact with the unions, how else was it to be controlled? Might monetarism be the answer? Controlling the money supply rather than doing deals with the unions was certainly an intellectually attractive idea to those in the Conservative Party getting ready to plot an alternative course for Britain in a general election that could only now be months, perhaps weeks, away.

The Ayes to the Right

James Callaghan was in a bind. He had until November to face a general election. The longer he held out, the more chance there would be that memories of the Winter of Discontent would fade and the new accord with the unions might hold. Alternatively, the longer he postponed his fate, the more time there was for the higher pay deals to fuel soaring inflation and for the St Valentine's Day engagement to be broken off in the clear absence of heartfelt commitment. Grimly, government strategy rested upon hoping that something might turn up. Reworking an already tired metaphor, the prime minister's policy adviser, Bernard Donoughue, compared the mood to like 'being on the sinking *Titanic* without the music'.[35]

The sense of desperation was sharpened by the want of a parliamentary majority. During its life, the government had lost over thirty Commons divisions. The continually tight arithmetic had produced countless moments of drama. As early as 1976, tempers had turned violent when, through conscious deceit, the Labour whips overturned the parliamentary procedure decreed by the Speaker for a select committee and secured the nationalization of the shipping and aviation industries by one vote – by suddenly rushing a 'paired' Labour MP through the lobbies without informing his Tory 'pair', who, in a previous mutual arrangement, had agreed not to vote. Unable to contain their glee, Labour MPs burst into raucous jeering on the floor of the Commons. Amid chanting of 'The Red Flag', fisticuffs broke out behind the bar of the House as the two sides vented their fury while, to gasps of astonishment, an incensed shadow minister for industry, Michael Heseltine, seized with both hands the symbol of Commons authority, the Mace. He subsequently claimed he had been offering it to the Labour benches as a protest against their unconstitutional actions, although by the time the story had grown with the retelling (television broadcasts were still banned from the chamber) he was depicted as wielding it like an offensive weapon.[36] The consequences included the abandonment of the pairing system, ensuring that late-night sittings became torturous as the Conservatives kept pushing Labour's whips to the limits of their disciplinary powers, hoping a late vote might catch them off guard. The consequence of this style of warfare was that politicians were reluctant to stray far from the Palace of Westminster's precincts. Inevitably, this made Parliament's extensive range of in-house bars the natural assembly point. Alcohol-fuelled emotions ran high in Annie's Bar and the Strangers' Bar, the latter generally known as the 'Kremlin' on account of its hard-drinking, left-wing clientele. When the Labour whips could not run their quarry to ground there, they patrolled the gentlemen's lavatories and, where necessary, extracted their intoxicated and sometimes unwell MPs from behind locked cubicle doors.[37]

When not corralling their own supporters, Labour whips were also kept busy plying the eleven Scottish Nationalist MPs with alcohol. The withdrawal of Liberal Party support made it critical that the SNP's continuing will to vote with the government was fortified. The result was memorably described by the journalist Alan Watkins, who observed of this period that, for the Scot Nats, every night was Burns Night.[38] The political price paid for their allegiance was the devolution of powers to Scotland and, on a lesser scale, to Wales. It was a cause close to few hearts in the Cabinet, certainly not to the prime minister's, even though – or, rather, because – he was the member for Cardiff South. Nonetheless, devolution seemed necessary not just to shore up the government's position in the Westminster lobbies but also as a measure of appeasement which, it was hoped, would dissuade the Scottish and Welsh electorates from embracing the campaigns for outright independence of the SNP and Plaid Cymru.

There was a problem. The devolution legislation passed through Westminster, but it did so badly mauled by Labour backbenchers who shared the doubts best articulated within their ranks by Tam Dalyell, MP for West

Lothian. His 'West Lothian Question' asked why should Scottish MPs have a vote on English matters at Westminster but English MPs have no right to intervene in Scottish matters in a Scottish Parliament. Not only did the government have to commit itself to subjecting its devolution proposals to referendums in Scotland and Wales, an amendment by George Cunningham, a Scots Labour MP who sat for Islington, introduced a new electoral rule – that a simple majority of those voting would not be enough and endorsement by 40 per cent of the total electorate would be needed before devolution was introduced. This created a huge hurdle. The Welsh vote was effectively lost even before the campaign got under way. In Scotland, the 'yes' campaign was hampered by Labour's sliding support and, arguably, by the Scottish football team's dismal first-round exit from the 1978 World Cup in Argentina (despite a heroic victory over Holland, Ally MacLeod's much-hyped team lost to Peru and only scraped a draw with Iran, taking what comfort it could from England's failure to qualify). The two referendums were held on 1 March 1979. Welsh voters rejected devolution by a margin of four to one. The Scottish vote went narrowly in favour, by a margin of 52 per cent to 48 per cent. Representing almost 33 per cent of the total electorate, however, the 'yes' vote failed to clear the 40 per cent hurdle.

Having failed to secure devolution, the SNP no longer saw any reason to continue propping up an increasingly unpopular Labour administration. On 21 March, the party tabled a vote of no confidence in the government. Quickly seeing the chance of causing an upset, the Conservatives immediately did likewise. The Commons vote was held on 28 March. Both sides realized it would be tantalizingly close. One highly canvassed possibility was that the division would end in a tie. In that case, the Speaker would cast his vote for the government.

Throughout the day of 28 March, political horse-trading became the principal occupation of those charged with bringing out the vote. Roy Hattersley, the secretary of state for prices, spent the day wooing two Ulster Unionist MPs, who agreed to support the government in return for a special price index for Northern Ireland. Hattersley duly put the deal in writing. Unfortunately, he signed it with a green biro. Refusing to have anything to do with a document confirmed in the colour of Irish nationalism, the Ulster Unionists demanded that the whole statement be retyped, allowing the signatures to be written again in black. With even greater reluctance, Hattersley importuned Enoch Powell, the former Tory turned Ulster Unionist. The intended bribe was the construction of a gas pipeline from the mainland to Northern Ireland. This effort failed, as much as anything because of Callaghan's reluctance. Indeed, while Hattersley was trying to square the Ulster Unionists, the prime minister received Gerry Fitt, the moderate leader of the Irish nationalist SDLP, in Downing Street. Fitt did not want to bring

Callaghan down but made it clear that Ulster's nationalist community wanted Roy Mason, the Northern Ireland secretary, to be sacked. At this, Callaghan, a non-drinker, nodded to an assistant who had a bottle of gin brought in. The gesture went down badly. Fitt was not going to be intoxicated into surrender and ended up abstaining in the division.

By contrast, nothing could have been more appealing than alcoholic blandishments to Frank Maguire, the Independent Republican MP for Fermanagh and South Tyrone. A pub-owner in Lisnaskea, Maguire had once shocked Fitt by confiding that he did not condemn IRA atrocities for fear the IRA might blow up his pub. Relishing his opportunity to be put on the government's hospitality account, Maguire chose the no-confidence debate to make one of his rare flights across the Irish Sea to Westminster. Jock Stallard, a government whip who also happened to be Roman Catholic, was assigned to act as Maguire's saloon minder, shielding him from opposition solicitations as he moved seamlessly from bar to bar. Even an increasingly furious Fitt was unable to get near him. It was all in vain. During the evening, the flush-faced and increasingly disoriented Maguire gave Stallard the slip. His wife found him and took him home, ensuring that he missed the division. Such was the Labour whips' desperation that they next tried to keep the government alive by carrying a fatally ill man through the division lobby on a stretcher. Sir Alfred 'Doc' Broughton was the Labour MP for Batley and Morley, and the idea was to bring him down from Yorkshire by ambulance. He agreed to make the sacrifice, but in the event it proved impossible to get him down and he died five days later.

Leaving nothing else to chance, at 7 p.m., the government whips ordered all Labour MPs to assemble for a headcount. Meanwhile, in the Commons chamber the no-confidence debate was reaching its denouement. The rhetorical highlight came when the government's case was summed up by the Leader of the House, Michael Foot. In a sparkling performance which relied on humour to cover the seriousness of the situation, the finest Labour orator of the age chided Thatcher while reserving his sarcasm for the Liberal leader, David Steel. Thatcher, Foot declaimed, was 'leading her troops into battle, snuggling concealed behind a Scottish Nationalist shield, with the Boy David holding her hand'. He was less worried about Thatcher – 'she can look after herself' – than about Steel: 'But the leader of the Liberal party – and I say this with the utmost affection – has passed from rising hope to elder statesman without any intervening period whatsoever.' The government benches rocked with laughter. Labour knew the Liberals would vote against them. The trial of their former leader, Jeremy Thorpe, for conspiracy to murder, was due to begin in the spring and the party now wanted the election over and done with before the court case got under way.

The judgement on Callaghan's future came far sooner, with the calling of the division at 10 p.m. The BBC was transmitting live coverage, although because of the prohibition on televising parliamentary debates, viewers across the country had to make do with a sound-only broadcast adorned by a mixture of footage of Big Ben and occasional sketched images of the (empty) chamber. Rumours quickly spread, based on little more than who was last seen smiling or looking relaxed. Jimmy Hamilton, a Labour whip, was observed giving the thumbs-up. Labour thought they had won. 'I don't believe it!' stuttered Mrs Thatcher, who came to the same conclusion when her whips passed her their tally. In the excitement, they had forgotten to include their two tellers in the vote. Moments later, the truth was revealed when the tellers came into the chamber with the Conservatives standing on the right. The declaration was made. The Speaker repeated the result in his precise Welsh intonation: 'The Ayes to the right, 311. The Noes to the left, 310. So the Ayes have it.'

Tory MPs rose exultantly to their feet, cheering and waving their order papers. They had won by one vote, beating Labour and its remaining allies with the help of thirteen Liberals, eleven Scottish Nationalists and eight of the eleven Ulster Unionists. No Commons vote had forced a general election since 1924, when the first Labour administration, also a minority government, fell. More extraordinarily, it was the first time a government had been brought down on a vote of no confidence since 1841. Callaghan rose to his feet, stood at the dispatch box and announced: 'Now that the House of Commons has declared itself, we shall take our case to the country.' Several left-wing MPs, chief among them a young Welsh member called Neil Kinnock, broke into a stirring and heartfelt rendition of 'The Red Flag'.

2 HELLO MAGGIE!

Marketing Maggie

'Labour Isn't Working' proclaimed the poster, its play on words illustrated by a queue of the jobless snaking towards the entrance to an unemployment office. This proved to be a famous moment in billboard history. Twenty years later, it was voted 'poster of the century' by *Campaign*, the advertising industry's leading magazine. Its success supposedly showed that advertising companies had come of age. They were not just about marketing cold beer to men and refrigerators to women. They could sell a political party too. No less an authority than the Conservative Party chairman, Lord Thorneycroft, credited the poster with deciding the election result. And he had not even liked it when he first saw it.[1]

Encouraging the belief that the 1979 general election was won by a poster obviously suited those who made their career in the commerce of persuasion. It was surely fitting that a decade in which public relations, marketing and advertising were portrayed as thrusting 'growth industries' – at a time when 'real industries' were in decline – should have been launched in this way. The claim not only suited ad men in their efforts to drum up new business but also chimed with critics of the extravagant, eye-catching and sometimes deceitful public pseudo-art that adorned eighties Britain. To detractors, 'Labour Isn't Working' was emblematic of everything that was worst about advertising's powers of superficial appeal: the punning slogan persuaded voters to elect a Conservative government that presided over far longer dole queues than existed under Labour.

Rarely has so slight an advertising promotion been credited with such influence. In fact, the 'Labour Isn't Working' posters only appeared on twenty billboards during the summer of 1978 in anticipation of the autumn election that never happened. The image had been knocked up at the last moment and given relatively low priority in the campaign put together by Saatchi & Saatchi, the advertising firm engaged by the Tories. According to the poster's creator, Martyn Walsh, the agency's co-founder, Charles Saatchi, was sceptical of its value and it was nearly never used. But it gained fleeting notoriety because Denis Healey, the Chancellor of the Exchequer, made the tactical error of complaining about it in the chamber of the House of Commons. Not only did this raise its profile by turning it into a news story, but Healey failed to land his blow. His claim that the Tories had reached a new low by 'selling politics as if it was soap powder' concerned the specific accusation that those in the queue were not really unemployed but were paid actors. In fact, those forming the jobless queue were neither unemployed nor paid actors but volunteers from Hendon Young Conservatives, and because less than twenty of them could be mustered the long queue had been created by the photographic trick of taking multiple photos of them in different poses and then superimposing the images to make it look as if there were hundreds of people stretching to infinity.[2]

Whatever impact the poster made was short-lived, its newsworthiness quickly receding alongside the prospect of an autumn 1978 election. Although it was resurrected with an amended slogan, 'Labour *Still* Isn't Working', in the weeks leading up to the eventual polling day on 3 May 1979, the claim that it – or, for that matter, the rest of Saatchi & Saatchi's campaigning tricks – swung the election for the Conservatives seems overblown. The period of its launch in the late summer of 1978 coincided with Labour regaining an opinion poll lead which it then extended in the two months thereafter. As for the spring of 1979, far from Saatchi & Saatchi's campaign being so slick that the Tories' lead over Labour widened, the reverse was true: Conservative support crumbled during the five-week campaign, starting at around 50 per cent of the vote and sliding towards 43 per cent on the eve of the poll.[3] And research by MORI suggested that the electorate actually thought Labour's election broadcasts were the more successful.[4]

But if Britain did not get its first woman prime minister because she had the slickest ad men, it was nevertheless a paradox that the supposed 'conviction politician' kept such masters of style over substance within her intimate counsels. Surprisingly, for an instinctive puritan, she enjoyed being feted by the colourful, even louche, band of courtiers that constituted her image-making team. Their close presence was also encouraged by those among Thatcher's colleagues who deemed her a liability. She had none of Jim Callaghan's unaffected common touch with which to endear herself to the non-committed voter. Nor had she displayed any ability to win in more structured debates. Lacking instinctive wit and verbal dexterity, she had shown herself to be a leaden parliamentary performer as leader of the opposition. Callaghan regularly basted her at Prime Minister's Questions, condescendingly treating her like a schoolgirl swot who had learned some statistics but failed, due to her limitations, to see the bigger picture.[5] Her failure became more apparent beyond Westminster's confines when, in 1978, permission was finally given for parliamentary debates to be broadcast on the radio.* Such was the dissatisfaction within her own ranks about her overall performance that there was a clear likelihood that she would have faced a direct challenge to her leadership if she had lost the general election expected in the autumn of 1978. She appeared to recognize the tenuousness of her grip upon remaining leader, confessing that she did not think she would be given a second chance if she lost the election, not least because 'there's only one chance in life for women. It is the law of life.'[6] Even going into the 1979 election campaign, the polling statistics suggested the Tories' greatest vulnerability was not their policies but their leader. When, on 12 April, Gallup asked its sample 'who would make the better prime minister?' Callaghan was preferred by 39 per cent to 33 per cent. The efforts of Thatcher's public relations experts to improve her image reached extraordinary limits as the campaign intensified. At one stage she was even persuaded to stride into a field and cradle a defenceless calf for a full thirteen minutes until her husband, Denis, warned her that if she cuddled it any longer it might die on her.[7] Whether in hard or soft focus, the more the electorate saw of her, the less impressed they pronounced themselves. On the eve of the poll, Callaghan's lead over Thatcher as the preferred premier had risen further and he was trouncing her by the vast margin of 44 per cent to 25 per cent.[8]

In seeking to capitalize on his greater popularity and ease of manner, Callaghan challenged Thatcher and the Liberal leader, David Steel, to a television debate. No incumbent prime minister had agreed to go head to head on television with the leader of the opposition since the idea had first been mooted for the 1964 general election.[9] Callaghan had rejected the idea as recently as 1978. But in the spring of 1979, with Labour trailing in the opinion polls, televising the leaders' sparring would have presented an opportunity to turn the campaign into a presidential race – to Callaghan's clear advantage. David Steel was keen to attend, naturally leaping at the chance to get equal billing with the leaders of the two main parties. Thatcher, too, was up for the scrap, but was pulled up by her advisers who saw no gain in turning the election from policy, where they were ahead, to personality, where they were behind. Some Tory tacticians even thought no good could come of her debating on equal terms with a man, for, as the party chairman,

---

* The broadcasts began in April 1978, although there had previously been a trial run in 1975 – the first time the proceedings of the House of Commons were ever broadcast. Television cameras were not permitted in the Commons until 1990.

Lord Thorneycroft, put it: 'If she had won the argument, which we thought she would, a lot of people wouldn't have liked that in a woman,' because men might have thought, '"There's my wife," and it wouldn't have been a good thing.'[10]

Labour strategists were certain that the Conservatives' weakest spot was their leader. For all the downsides of a five-week campaign, they believed it would at least provide enough time for Thatcher first to sound shrill and then, with any luck, to lose her voice entirely. In the Tory camp, too, there was no shortage of those who feared she lacked the breadth of vision and appeal to win through. Thorneycroft's attempts to get Edward Heath positioned alongside her at election rallies particularly irked her,[11] the clear implication being that she could not carry the campaign without the support of the man she had replaced. While Heath – eyeing up the Foreign Office as his reward – was keen to be seen and heard in the weeks before polling day, his successor was privately certain that she wanted to rid Britain of his political legacy almost as much as that of Harold Wilson and James Callaghan.

Those given the task of marketing Thatcher encountered the problem of deciding which version of her to portray. On the one hand she was the grammar school-educated, Methodist chapel-going, provincial girl from a Lincolnshire market town, who had learned life's often hard commercial realities from her father's corner shop and won a place at Oxford through her own endeavours. As such, she was by birth, sex, upbringing, religion and region an outsider from the traditional establishment. Her personal success was evidence of her strength of character and that she was a battler against difficult odds. This, however, was only the first half of her story. As soon as opportunity presented itself, she had switched Wesleyanism for Anglicanism, turning her back on Grantham for more material rewards as the London and suburban Kent-based wife of a millionaire businessman, with a son and daughter who had been looked after by a nanny before proceeding, respectively, to Harrow and to St Paul's Girls' School. Only occasionally – usually when roused to anger or disdain – did her voice still betray a Lincolnshire lilt. Mostly, she sounded like the privileged and somewhat patronizing stockbroker-belt southerner whose tones she had quickly adopted upon becoming Mrs Denis Thatcher in 1951.

In 1974, Enoch Powell assumed she had no chance of succeeding Edward Heath because the party 'wouldn't put up with those hats and that accent'.[12] Among the image-makers' first tasks was to steer her away from her tendency to dress as if she were on her way to a garden party in the weald of Kent or to take tea with Mrs Mary Whitehouse. By 1979, the fight against millinery had been won, leaving her crowned only by a bouffant lion's mane of golden hair. Under the guidance of Gordon Reece, a former television producer seconded from EMI, work continued to be done on the pitch of her voice. Laurence Olivier was only one of a succession of experts drafted in to demonstrate how she could sound less ladylike. Vocal training made her sound progressively deeper, more measured, less shrill and no longer redolent of the Queen in her coronation year.

As director of publicity, Reece did more than lower Thatcher's voice and ditch the dated hats. He recognized the importance of the tabloid and mid-market press, building bridges with, in particular, *The Sun*. The Tories had gone into previous elections without the support of a single mass-market newspaper, a disability that was about to be remedied. Furthermore, Reece was instrumental in getting Saatchi & Saatchi hired to handle the party's advertising, and its managing director, Tim Bell, became another key member of the Thatcher posse. Reece also taught his charge how to improve her indifferent television performances, encouraging her to see an interview question as a cue to make her case to the viewers rather than, as was her instinct, to assume it was a starting gun to argue with the interviewer. It was another key member of her image team, Ronald Millar, who forced her to memorize the mantra 'Cool, calm – and elected'.[13] Millar was a successful playwright, whose West End hits included adaptations of C. P. Snow's novels and the Tudor historical drama *Robert and Elizabeth*. He quickly identified Thatcher as his modern Gloriana, injecting the Tilbury spirit into her major oratorical performances. For, while she took infinite care over the crafting of her set-piece speeches, fully involving herself in their content rather than leaving speech writers free rein to put whatever substance they liked into her mouth, it was Millar who provided her with her more memorable lines. He shared her love of aphorism, fusing an outlook from the sort of proverbs and homespun wisdom that had been familiar components of American speech since at least the days when Benjamin Franklin's *Poor Richard's Almanack* was a colonial best-seller. Indeed, Millar knew he had found his leading lady when she approached him for help with her opening broadcast as party leader in 1975. When he recited to her some apposite lines by Abraham Lincoln –

> You cannot strengthen the weak by weakening the strong.
> You cannot bring about prosperity by discouraging thrift.
> You cannot help the wage-earner by pulling down the wage-payer . . .

– Thatcher excitedly snapped open her handbag and retrieved from it a crumpled and faded cutting with exactly the same lines on it. 'It goes wherever I go,' she assured him.[14] Yet, while America's Great Emancipator had succinctly summarized her view of life, perhaps nobody did more for her public image than the Soviet Army paper *Red Star*, which responded to her anti-communist rhetoric in 1976 by dubbing her the 'Iron Lady'. Delighted by the backhanded compliment, she repeated the phrase for both domestic and foreign consumption, bolstering her claim to be not just the irritating schoolgirl of Callaghan's twice-weekly baiting but some kind of modern Boudicca. 'Sunny Jim' the prime minister might have been in the hot summer of 1976, but it was not a helpful sobriquet for the Winter of Discontent. By contrast, Thatcher hit home her advantage and demonstrated her new actress-like sense of timing: 'The Russians said I was an Iron Lady. [*pause*] They were right. [*pause*] Britain needs an Iron Lady. [*cheers*]'[15]

Labour clung to the hope that the long general election campaign would expose Thatcher's tendency to make unguarded statements at variance with what had been agreed with her shadow Cabinet. Instead, she accepted her advisers' strategy to save her energies until late in the campaign. Gordon Reece encouraged her to get her mind off politics by going to the theatre. So off she promptly took herself to see . . . *Evita*.

With Reece and Millar's help, the showbiz side of politics was turned to her advantage. At one of her rallies, Lulu, Ken Dodd and the DJ Pete Murray provided warm-up entertainment before she breezed onstage to the theme of *Hello Dolly*, re-lyricized to 'Hello Maggie!' Indeed it was not until 16 April 1979, nearly halfway through the election campaign, that Thatcher cheekily made her first major public speech, on Callaghan's home turf of Cardiff. 'I am a conviction politician,' she assured the assembled believers. 'The Old Testament prophets didn't go out into the highways saying, "Brothers I want consensus." They said, "This is my faith and my vision! This is what I passionately believe!"'[16] Not for the only time in her career, she risked being accused of displaying messianic tendencies, but the speech emphasized that she represented a galvanizing force in British life.

It was Thatcher's advantage that she embodied change merely by being a woman. Nor was she afflicted by any snobbish attitude towards modern methods of reaching out to those disengaged by traditional politics. Her team understood that the media, particularly television, needed visual material to accompany reports. Giving them the right photo-opportunity was the surest way of securing airtime. The shots of her doing the shopping were deemed particularly helpful because ordinary voters, particularly women, were assumed to relate to her at this level. What was more, it showed her as she wanted to be portrayed: the grocer's daughter who well understood how to manage a household budget as a precursor to getting the nation's finances back into the black. Callaghan doing the shopping could never have struck the same chord. All the same, as the market research suggested, it was his team's less inventive approach that won the propaganda war of 1979. The press's cameramen were tipped off in time to photograph Callaghan with his grandchildren emerging from a local church service, even though few could recall him being a noted attendee outside of election time. When, as the campaign reached its denouement, he walked out of an interview because he objected to the persistent line of questioning about the unions, his team leant on ITN to broadcast neither the interview nor his temper tantrum.[17] ITN duly obliged. Deference to Downing Street was not entirely dead.

Five Weeks that Shaped a Decade?

Despite the claims of both sides that the very future of a prosperous or fair Britain was at stake, the 1979 election never descended into a slanging match, with both Thatcher and Callaghan avoiding making personal remarks about each other. Front-bench spokesmen in danger of offering policy hostages to fortune – Tony Benn for Labour and the Conservative Sir Keith Joseph – were kept from fronting press conferences as much as possible. Indeed, the only major gaffe came from Callaghan's predecessor, Harold Wilson, who appeared to suggest his wife Mary might vote for the Conservatives because they were led by a woman.

At the campaign's outset, on 30 March, a bomb exploded under the car of Airey Neave, the shadow secretary of state for Northern Ireland, as it pulled out of the House of Commons car park. An IRA splinter group, the INLA, claimed responsibility. Neave, a Colditz escapee, had been Thatcher's campaign manager for the Tory leadership in 1975. His murder brought both cross-party condemnation and the fear that the election campaign might be marred by bombings and assassination attempts. Instead, the five weeks passed without further serious incident, although Callaghan was dogged by hecklers from a group calling itself (without evident irony) Socialist Unity, who tried to break up the Labour leader's speaking engagements by chanting 'Troops out of Northern Ireland'.

The handling of Ulster's Troubles was one of the few areas in which Labour and the Conservatives were in close agreement. Although on some other issues the difference was only a matter of degree: the Tories promised not to cut NHS spending, focusing instead on reversing their opponents' discouragement of private health provision; both parties were committed to keeping British forces in NATO, although only the Tories promised significant increases in the defence budget. Labour's preparedness to nationalize more companies was kept imprecise, with merely a pledge to keep 'using public ownership to sustain and create new jobs'. The Tories restricted their privatization crusade to those industries most recently nationalized – shipbuilding and aerospace – and the National Freight Corporation. The big industries and utilities – coal, steel, telephones, gas, etc. – would remain in state ownership. There would be no dramatic dismantling of the mixed economy. While a subsequent generation came to see 1979 as marking the end of the post-war consensus, voters at the time actually perceived the main parties to be closer than during the heyday of 'Butskellism': in 1955, 74 per cent of those polled by Gallup believed there were important differences between the main parties; in 1979, only 54 per cent did so.[18]

The ideological chasm might have been broader but for the fact that the Labour leader kept tight reins on what went into his party's manifesto, while the Conservative leader had much less input into what went into hers. Callaghan's insistence that nothing became an election pledge unless he agreed with it ensured that proposals to nationalize one or more of the big four banks or to give up the nuclear deterrent were dropped. Overcoming fellow members of a drafting committee that included Michael Foot and Tony Benn necessarily involved some brinkmanship on the prime minister's part, and it was perhaps surprising that the one issue over which he threatened to resign if it were included was a commitment to abolish the House of Lords.[19] *The Economist* duly pronounced the resulting manifesto, *The Labour Way Is the Better Way*, 'as moderate as any on which the Labour Party has campaigned during its 79 years' existence'.[20]

If Labour's manifesto was driven by its party's right wing, the content of the Tory manifesto was cast by its left wing – in the guise of its drafters from the Conservative Research Department, Adam Ridley and, particularly, the up-and-coming young voice of Heathite moderation, Chris Patten. Even Mrs Thatcher's introductory message was prepared for her by Sir Ian Gilmour, who was not remotely from her wing of the party. Mostly absent was the authentic, uncompromising voice of the leader herself. Nevertheless, even if Thatcher had been left unchecked to write the whole manifesto, it might be mistaken to imagine that it would have been as radical as the monetarist and free-market think tanks would have wished. For all her talk of being a conviction politician, she could be remarkably cautious if she felt the circumstances were not propitious. As Nigel Lawson later wrote of the Tories' preparations for government, 'little detailed work had been done' on privatization policy, because of 'Margaret's understandable fear of frightening the floating voter'.[21] It was sometimes the manifesto's omissions that showed where Thatcher's influence on policy had been greatest: her predecessor's support for Scottish devolution was ditched, and there was no flirtation with proportional representation – despite the feeling of many within her shadow Cabinet that proportional representation and European integration might be the only mechanisms available to curtail a future radically left-wing government. To Margaret Thatcher, the thought of office being dependent upon the sufferance of David Steel did not appeal.

For all the efforts of James Callaghan and Chris Patten to remove the ideology from election issues, there were five battlegrounds on which Labour and the Conservatives offered very clear choices over what would become of Britain in the eighties. These were housing and education policy, trade union power, how to control inflation, and the level of taxation.

In 1979, a third of Britain's housing stock was owned and maintained by local councils. This represented an all-time high which Labour promised to supplement by building more council flats, seeing the further extension of council estates as the answer to the nation's needs. In stark contrast, the Tories believed the future lay with home ownership and promised that local authority tenants would have the right to buy their own council houses. This was to give impetus to one of the most important shifts of the 1980s, the vast increase in home ownership, bringing with it a revolution in the nation's attitude to borrowing and personal finance.

On education policy, the two parties were also polls apart. Labour pledged to wipe out the last remaining grammar schools with the single sentence: 'Universal comprehensive education, which is central to our policy, must be completed in the 1980s.' But it was not just the few examples of selection in the state sector that the party had in its sights. 'Independent schools still represent a major obstacle to equality of opportunity. Labour's aim is to end, as soon as possible, fee-paying in such schools' and to abolish their 'remaining public subsidies and public support'. There was thus a genuine prospect that the long tradition of private education was about to end in Britain. The future for such institutions looked bleak even if the legislation to make them illegal did not get through Parliament and the courts, since without the retention of charitable status their fees would place all but the most well endowed beyond the reach of their main clientele, the middle classes, whose available resources were, in any case, feeling the squeeze from an 83 per cent top rate of income tax. Only a few of the great public schools might have survived, perhaps by relocating abroad – rather in the manner of the Jesuit academies that had once decamped across the English Channel to avoid seventeenth-century religious persecution. To those who saw private education as one of the most divisive props of the British class system, the expectation that they might soon be axed presented a thrilling opportunity to improve the life chances of the many. To their defenders, however, it seemed the state was about to destroy what was reputedly one of the world's most rigorous education systems, ending choice in the free market just as it had crushed selection in the maintained sector. Here, then, was to be a modern version of the dissolution of the monasteries – somewhat ironically given that the Henrician dissolution had created some of the public schools in the first place. For the independents as for the grammar schools, only a Conservative victory promised salvation, or at least a stay of execution.

In contrast to the ancient academies, Labour intended to leave the traditional institutions at the heart of its own movement unreformed. Despite the fact that the Winter of Discontent had pushed trade unions to the forefront of debate, unions received little mention in the Labour manifesto, except in the emphasis placed upon their central role in helping to curb inflation. So sensitive was the fragile truce brokered by the TUC that the government simply could not afford to risk it with some ill-timed criticism. The best that Callaghan could hope for was that the union leaders would keep their financial dues flowing into Labour's coffers without rocking the boat while the election campaign was in the balance. Most had the sense to toe the official line. A few remained resolutely off-message: Sid Weighell, general secretary of the National Union of Railwaymen, spoke hopefully of messing up a future Tory government's appeal for wage restraint: 'I don't see how we can talk to Mrs Thatcher . . . I will say to the lads, come on, get your snouts in the trough.'[22]

While such comments helped the Conservatives make their case that union militancy needed muzzling, the potentially disastrous consequences of attempting to do so fostered fears that a Tory victory was far from a recipe for industrial peace. So concerned were the Conservatives on this front (and still bruised from the drubbing the unions had given Heath's administration) that had the general election been called in 1978, they would have avoided firm commitments to curb union power. This was the cautious message the consensus-minded shadow employment secretary, Jim Prior, had successfully pressed upon his leader. It was only the severity of the Winter of Discontent that made such appeasement incredible. Thus the manifesto included pledges to restrict secondary picketing (where picket lines were manned by union members not actually employed by the company where there was a strike). In an attempt to make the unions more democratic, public money would be offered to encourage their use of secret ballots instead of the existing habit of open voting by a show of hands. There would also be help for those victimized by the closed shop (where no worker could be employed by a company unless they were a member of the recognized union), with measures taken to prevent its further spread where it was not overwhelmingly endorsed by the workforce. But there was no promise to end the closed shop. Here again, Thatcher was persuaded to proceed with caution, despite her instinct for action.

Prices had doubled during Labour's term in office and it was on how best to curb inflation that Labour and the Conservatives most clearly demonstrated their contrasting views over whether Britain needed a more or less interventionist state. Labour announced that it aimed to cut inflation to 5 per cent. This would be achieved not just by continuing to work with and involve the unions in setting pay policy norms, but also by giving the Price Commission greater statutory powers forcibly to cut prices where, in its judgement, they were higher than they ought to be. The Conservatives did not conceal their belief that relying on the opinions of a price-fixing committee to curb inflation was nonsense. They would scrap the Price Commission. As for wages, what pay the private sector set for its employees was its own affair – it was not for the state to determine. The Treasury should set targets for the money supply, rather than income norms, for 'to master inflation, proper monetary discipline is essential, with publicly stated targets for the rate of growth of the money supply'.[23] This was not entirely the great dividing line that many on both sides made it out to be. Albeit with mixed results, the Labour government had also been actively pursuing monetary targets since 1976, while being coy about trumpeting the fact too publicly. What was different was the centrality the Tories gave to monetary discipline. Even here, though, there was caution. The CBI still supported an incomes policy and it was not until after the Winter of Discontent that the Conservatives ceased being ambiguous about whether they would persevere with the policy in government. This was a victory for Thatcher, who saw incomes policies not only as a means whereby the unions would always have a lever on economic policy, but as a mechanism that focused national attention away from the indicator that really mattered. As she told an audience in March 1979: 'Only when we stop being obsessed with pay and start being obsessed with productivity are we going to prosper.'[24] Focusing on the money supply would prove an alternative obsession. But part of its appeal was that it came part and parcel with reducing the size of the state: public spending would be cut, as would government borrowing and taxes.

Taxation was the last of the five main battlegrounds dividing the parties, and the one on which the Conservatives believed they were on the strongest ground. While Labour skated over their fiscal intentions, its manifesto was nevertheless not embarrassed about proclaiming that 'The Labour Party's priority is to build a democratic socialist society in Britain' – which was presumably not going to be achieved by giving taxpayers a slice of their money back. Indeed, Callaghan went into the election promising a new burden on top of the already historically record-breaking level of income tax. This came in the shape of an annual wealth tax on those who had more than £150,000 squirreled away. The very idea was naturally anathema to the Tories, who announced they would cut the top rate of income tax to the European average (which was at the time around 60 per cent). They also undertook to raise the threshold at which those on low incomes paid tax. But there was a sting in the shape of a switch from taxing income to taxing spending. As Labour pointed out, increasing VAT would both be inflationary and would disproportionately affect those on lower wages, for whom the shopping bill consumed a relatively larger share of their income.

MORI's private polling, commissioned by Labour, showed that the Conservatives led on every policy issue except the National Health Service and industrial peace. On the two issues cited as the most important by respondents – taxation and law and order – the Tory lead over Labour was 30 per cent.[25] This was especially important because cutting taxes was the centrepiece of the Conservative campaign. Yet the apparent support for tax cuts was far less clear-cut when the question was balanced by eliciting respondents' views on retaining the existing level of welfare provision. Opinion surveys by Gallup suggested that those believing tax cuts should be enforced even at the expense of front-line public services slid from 34 to 30 per cent during the course of the campaign.[26]

The Tory manifesto was noticeably short of detail, especially when it came to where the state would be rolled back. As Denis Healey put it, finding Tory costings was 'like looking for a black cat in a dark coal cellar'.[27] Labour suggestions about where their opponents' spending axe would fall proved effective, and as each week of the campaign went by the Tory lead narrowed from around 11 per cent to 5 per cent. By 28 April, with five days to polling, MORI had the Tories' lead down to 3 per cent. Two days later, an NOP poll showed Labour 0.7 per cent ahead. With the Liberals gaining ground, Britain appeared to be heading back towards a hung parliament. This boded especially ill for the Tories given that Thatcher had come close to ruling out a coalition by stating that 'the experiences of the last two or three years have been utterly abhorrent. It reduced the whole standard of public life and parliamentary democracy to a series of wheels and deals.'[28]

Certainly, official statistics released during the campaign helped Labour's cause – inflation remained below 10 per cent and unemployment was edging down. The one bad set of statistics, the trade figures, was not released because of a civil servants' strike. Nonetheless, Labour's fightback was all the more remarkable considering the extent to which the Tories were outspending them on advertising and the attitude of much of the print media. Aside from the *Mirror* group of newspapers and the *Guardian*, the national press was overwhelmingly supportive of the Tories. Gaining the endorsement of *The Sun* was the biggest coup – a case of the editor (Larry Lamb) telling his proprietor (Rupert Murdoch) to switch the paper's allegiance, rather than, as is more usually assumed, the other way round.[29] On election day, *The Sun*'s front page proclaimed: 'A message to Labour supporters: VOTE TORY THIS TIME, It's the only way to stop the rot.' The paper's editorial stated: '*The Sun* is above all a RADICAL newspaper. And we believe that this time the only radical proposals being put to you are being put by Maggie Thatcher and her Tory team.' The *Daily Mirror* settled for the equally partisan: 'Back to the Tories or FORWARD WITH THE PEOPLE, Vote Labour today.' Arguably the most telling commentary on Britain's industrial problems was provided by the silence of *The Times* and the *Sunday Times*. They were off the streets at the time – and would remain so for eleven months, their owners having shut them down in a failed attempt to force union members who printed the papers to allow journalists to use computer terminals.

In the peroration of his final television broadcast, Callaghan again returned to the great white hope: 'Let me in conclusion before you vote sum up my attitude to the eighties. We have got great opportunities if we work together. North Sea oil has given us a wonderful chance. We must use its resources and revenues to modernize our own industry to create more wealth.'[30] Where the prime minister appeared to be pinning his hopes on a new way to pay for more of the same, the leader of the opposition was emphasizing that she stood for a whole new approach, telling the audience at her final rally of the campaign:

> There's a worldwide revolt against big government, excessive taxation and bureaucracy . . . an era is drawing to a close . . . At first . . . people said, 'Ooh, you've moved away from the centre!' But then opinion began to move too, as the heresies of one period became, as they always do, the orthodoxies of the next.[31]

Had she but known it, Callaghan was privately, if reluctantly, agreeing with her. To his senior policy adviser, Bernard Donoughue, he confessed: 'It then does not matter what you say or do. There is a shift in what the public wants and what it approves. I suspect there is now such a sea-change – and it is for Mrs Thatcher.'[32]

The polling day weather was clement. The first results came in at 11.34 p.m. and quickly pointed to a clear, rather than overwhelming, Conservative victory. Turnout was high, at 76.2 per cent. The swing exceeded 5 per cent. The Conservatives gained fifty-one of the seventy-four seats that changed hands, giving them a total of 339 seats. Labour's tally fell to 269. Winning 42 per cent of the vote, Thatcher triumphed with a good working majority of forty-three seats.

Compared with the last election, in October 1974, the Conservatives had failed to make up any additional ground among the middle and professional classes. Their gains had come from among the so-called C1 and C2 categories, dominated by skilled workers. Among this group they enjoyed an 11 per cent swing, giving them 40 per cent of those that voted. There was an 8.5 per cent swing towards the Tories from trade union members, ensuring that about a third of them voted Conservative. While there was equality in the ratio of men and women voting Tory, with Labour there remained a clear male predominance. The Tories made gains among young, first-time voters, where they ended up almost neck and neck with Labour.[33] Regionally, the swing to the Tories was greatest in the south and the Midlands. But one of the most dramatic regional results was in Scotland, where the SNP contracted from eleven to just four MPs, justifying Callaghan's jibe when they deserted him that they were like 'turkeys voting for Christmas'. Meanwhile, the first-past-the-post system again did its best to marginalize the Liberal Party, its 14 per cent of the vote translating into a mere eleven seats.

At 2.30 p.m., Callaghan was driven to Buckingham Palace, where he formally resigned. His job done, he departed for the calm of his farm, its familiar bric-a-brac and pictures of fighting ships. An hour later, Thatcher arrived at the palace to kiss hands with her monarch, a female first minister for a female head of state – the first instance in the history of the world.

Callaghan was gracious in defeat. For a woman to hold the office of prime minister was, he said, 'a tremendous moment in the country's history'.[34] Indeed, Margaret Thatcher was the first woman prime minister of any European or American country.[35] Her achievement was sufficiently ahead of its time that, with the exception of Norway, no electorate on either continent had followed Britain's example by the time she departed from power eleven years later.

A Woman in Power

As Margaret Thatcher acknowledged the cheers (and some boos) in Downing Street on 4 May 1979, she delivered the homily – misattributed to St Francis of Assisi – that Ronald Millar had suggested she memorize. The opening line, 'Where there is discord may we bring harmony,' was the sort of pious wish Edward Heath might have expressed. But the next two lines suggested there was now a tenant in No. 10 who was not searching for compromise solutions: 'Where there is error may we bring truth. Where there is doubt may we bring faith. And where there is despair may we bring hope.'[36]

Next to St Francis of Assisi, the other man Margaret Thatcher paid tribute to from the pavement outside 10 Downing Street was Alderman Alfred Roberts. 'I just owe almost everything to my own father,' she replied to a question as she prepared to enter her new home for the first time.[37] At such a moment, personal reflections on life and the people and events that had shaped its course were understandable. Thatcher's father had died in 1970, just before his younger daughter entered Edward Heath's Cabinet. Her mother, a less significant figure in her development, had died in 1960, the year after she was elected to Parliament. Yet, it was not just the private memory of Alfred Roberts that the new prime minister cherished. The Victorian values of his outlook and the equally sober commercial realities of his shop-keeping business were what his daughter preached as the only hope for Britain in the 1980s. As one of her most perceptive biographers, John Campbell, has put it: 'Alfred Roberts' grocery had become a British equivalent of Lincoln's log cabin.'[38]

Neither Alfred Roberts nor his wife, Beatrice, had enjoyed more than an elementary education. Beatrice was a seamstress, whose father marked time as an attendant in a railway cloakroom. While Beatrice was essentially a homemaker to her two daughters, Muriel and Margaret, it was from Alfred Roberts's example of hard work, discipline and status in the local commu-nity that Margaret drew the most inspiration. Early lessons in public speaking came through listening to him deliver sermons as a lay preacher in Grantham's Wesleyan church. Having to attend church four times every Sunday, and with the comforts of the material world strictly rationed, Thatcher later con-ceded 'there was not a lot of fun and sparkle' in her early life.[39] But there was politics. Elected to the town council as an 'Independent', her father was the sort of teetotal Nonconformist whose historic adherence to the Liberal Party gradually realigned itself to the Conservatives as the practical alternative to socialism. During the 1930s, the anti-appeasement *Daily Telegraph* was the Roberts family's newspaper, and in 1938 they gave sanctuary to an Austrian Jewish girl who had escaped the Nazis, taking it in turns with other local Rotarians to let her live with them in their Spartan flat above the corner shop. Roberts became mayor of Grantham in 1945. When, forty years later, his daughter recalled how in 1952 the Labour Party had controversially used their newly won majority on the council to remove him as an alderman after twenty-seven years' service, she started to cry.[40]

Having missed out on a secondary education, Alfred Roberts disciplined himself to spend what minimal spare time he had on self-improving study, selecting his daughter's reading matter at the same time: 'Each week my father would take two books out of the library – a "serious" book for himself (and me) and a novel for my mother. As a result, I found myself reading books which girls of my age would not generally read.'[41] Winning a place at the competitive Kesteven and Grantham Girls' School freed the eleven-year-old Margaret from the culture prevalent in mixed-sex schools before the war, where girls' interests and aspirations were often taken less seriously than those of boys. Instead, she got her chance to focus on what she was good at – the sciences – rather than what was deemed appropriate for girls. Thus armed, she won a place at Oxford. In doing so, she belonged to the last generation that made its way in the world without the financial and institu-tional support of the welfare state.* In her experience, meritocracy was not a creation of the post-war social consensus.

---

* She went up to grammar school in 1936, six years before the Beveridge Report and eight years before

She went up to Oxford during wartime, when many of her male contemporaries were absent, serving in the armed forces. Thus her Oxford was not the enchanted playground of formal balls and male-oriented pastimes like rowing and dining clubs. It was one of the few times in the university's modern history when showing off was considered bad form. This suited a serious, provincial girl like Margaret Hilda Roberts, who would never have been an adornment to the milieu of a Sebastian Flyte or Charles Ryder. Rather, rationing was in force in 1943 and social life revolved around drinking cheap coffee and toasting crumpets in the rooms of her women's college, Somerville. After a brief flirtation with cigarettes, she decided the money would be more wisely invested buying *The Times*. However, in working for her chemistry degree she did not read widely on other subjects and her dogged commitment to the Conservative Party, an adherence she brought with her fully formed from Grantham, was deemed odd and unimaginative by contemporaries at a time when Oxford's visible undergraduate intellectual life looked overwhelmingly to socialism for its answers. The Oxford Union was still all-male and it was primarily through her superb organizational skills that she became only the second female chairman of the Oxford University Conservative Association, in 1946. She was never considered a great or memorable 'character' and formed no lasting friendships while at Oxford. Academically, she was good if not outstanding, gaining a second-class degree in Natural Sciences and going on to be awarded a BSc in chemistry in 1947.

It was this qualification as a research chemist that allowed her to eschew the common 1940s destinations for women graduates of teaching or the civil service and instead to enter the male-dominated world of industry, first at a plastics company and then at the massive J. Lyons cafe-owning and cake-baking firm. There, she made ice cream fluffier by pumping more air into it. But it was not her heart's desire to become Mrs Whippy. She had campaigned for the Tories in both Oxford and Grantham during the 1945 general election and got herself on to the party's candidates list in time for the next election. This showed considerable self-confidence. After all, there was only one woman sitting in Parliament on the Conservative benches at the time. A mere fourteen had got as far as being adopted as Tory candidates in 1945. She started off contesting the no-hope constituency of Dartford, where the Labour incumbent's majority exceeded twenty thousand. Undaunted, her determination to reach out to every voter was such that she found a way of getting round the prohibition on women in Dartford's men's club by briefly enrolling there as a barmaid. Soliciting working men's votes

---

Rab Butler's education act. Kesteven and Grantham Girls' School charged nominal fees to the majority of the parents of pupils who, like the Robertses, were able to afford them.

while serving them pints of mild and bitter, and dating a wealthy divorced man named Denis Thatcher, certainly suggested that ambition was straining the leash of her Methodist upbringing. On election day in 1950, she managed to chip down the Labour majority to twelve thousand, but, according to a report circulated in Conservative Central Office, she had been so 'outstanding' that Labour canvassers were forced to stay on in Dartford rather than flood the next-door marginal of Bexley, thereby allowing another promising young Tory, Edward Heath, to enter Parliament with a majority of 133.[42]

More remarkable, however, was the fact that an unmarried, 23-year-old woman, only two years out of university, had even won the chance to fight. At the time of her birth, in 1925, women of twenty-three did not even enjoy the right to vote. With no professional experience to speak of, it was extraordinarily precocious of her to put herself forward. In the decade that followed, as she went about trying to gain selection for a winnable constituency, she discovered that Conservative associations preferred men, often with the advantage of a distinguished war record. Against the braid of military decorations and life experiences gained at the sharp end, she was hardly able to compete. And when, after her marriage to Denis Thatcher, she became a mother of twins, selection committees asked her pointedly whether she really thought she ought to be at Westminster rather than attending to her motherly duties. A decade passed between her adoption at Dartford and her selection in time for the 1959 general election. In being selected for the north London constituency of Finchley, she narrowly saw off rival prospective Tory candidates including one man who had won the Military Cross and another who had served in the Special Operations Executive. Finchley's retiring MP was so appalled that the nominees to succeed him included someone called Peter Goldman and another called Margaret Thatcher that he grumbled: 'We've got to choose between a bloody Jew and a bloody woman!'[43] The 'bloody woman' proceeded to win Finchley with an increased majority – of sixteen thousand – and to hold on to it in nine successive elections over her thirty-three years in the House of Commons. During which time she showed that, as Alfred Sherman put it: 'A woman from the provincial lower-middle class, without family connections, oratorical skills, intellectual standing or factional backing of any sort, established herself as leader of a great party which had represented hierarchy, social stratification and male dominance.'[44]

But by then she was far less of a social outsider, thanks to the other man in her life besides her father. Unusually for many men of his class and generation, Denis Thatcher combined traditional right-wing views and a successful business career with a recognition that his wife should not only be free to follow her career but that he should support and encourage her in her ambition. It was his wealth that had allowed her to forsake the consistency of

Lyons Maid ice cream, to employ a nanny for her two young children and to read for the bar, which was a profession far better suited in its hours and challenges to someone with political ambitions. Between 1954 and her 1959 victory in Finchley, she honed her advocacy and attention to detail as a barrister specializing in taxation law (an area useful to a politician but in which exceedingly few women specialized at that time). Her husband's tolerance and material support were advantages she enjoyed over many women of her generation for whom motherhood, social attitudes and financial constraints proved insurmountable hurdles. Yet, for all her staunch attachment to Denis, she rarely made due acknowledgement of the head start his support gave her over most women. Despite her considerable personal experience of patronizing, sexist attitudes, she never developed an interest in any of the more radical philosophies of feminism. Returning the cold shoulder, it was noticeable how few leading feminists took satisfaction from her success, even though she proved to be, in her sphere, the most influential woman of her age, not just in Britain but anywhere in the world.

That she reached the top was seemingly not part of a long-worked-out plan. There is no contradictory evidence to suggest she was being falsely modest when in 1971 she told an interviewer: 'I don't think that in my lifetime there will be a woman prime minister. I am always a realist.'[45] It was not until 1975, the year in which she became the Conservatives' leader, that the equal pay act finally made it illegal to pay women less money for the same work as men; women had only been admitted to the London Stock Exchange two years previously (when, in 1976, Geraldine Bridgewater became the first female trader on the floor of the London Metals Exchange she was met by a chorus of hisses, boos and shouts of 'Get out! Get out! No women allowed, get out! Get OUT!' One trader even kicked her in the shins).[46] Few, indeed, who had watched Thatcher's development at Westminster during the 1960s and early 1970s either identified her as the woman who would be first to reach the top or foresaw that she would espouse a credo that would set both her party and her country on a radically different course during the 1980s.

Until her decision to challenge Edward Heath for the party leadership, she had been a party loyalist, reluctant to depart far from the ideological – or, rather, non-ideological – mainstream. In all her years in Parliament prior to becoming leader, she had only rebelled against the party line once. That was back in 1961, when she forlornly supported the reintroduction of birching for young offenders. It was not until Heath appointed her as his education secretary in 1970 that she started to show more of an independent spirit. Her decision to find minor economies by scrapping free school milk for the over-sevens made her infamous: 'Is Mrs Thatcher human?' asked *The Sun*, before declaring her 'The Most Unpopular Woman in Britain'; the nickname

'Thatcher the Milk Snatcher', coined at the 1971 Labour Party conference, stuck. Yet she had fought off attempts to cut the education budget overall. She even boasted of the spending increases she secured. While she mostly failed, despite her wishes, to prevent local education authorities closing their grammar schools, she succeeded in saving the Open University, which her Cabinet colleagues were adamant should be scrapped. What particularly surprised those same colleagues was when she suddenly aligned herself with Sir Keith Joseph, another high-spending minister who, having overseen social services, underwent a conversion towards budget tightening when the Conservatives fell from power in 1974.

Joseph responded to being freed from the responsibility of government by thinking aloud. In a series of speeches, he began to sketch an alternative philosophy of a smaller state, before blowing his chances in October 1974 by articulating what he regarded as the need for better contraception for badly educated young people 'in social classes 4 and 5', whose permissive behaviour otherwise risked undermining the 'human stock'.[47] In the ensuing uproar, Joseph accepted he was out of the running to succeed Heath, who, having lost three out of four general elections as Tory leader, was facing renewed pressure to justify himself. Thatcher duly turned to Joseph and said: 'Look, Keith, if you're not going to stand, I will, because someone who represents our viewpoint *has* to stand.'[48] With its customary Whiggish distain, *The Economist* dryly observed that she was 'precisely the sort of candidate who ought to be able to stand, and lose, harmlessly'.[49] Indeed, her prospects would almost certainly have been eclipsed if the establishment figure of Sir Edward du Cann, who as chairman of the 1922 Committee led back-bench hostility to Heath, had chosen to risk his City directorships at a moment when his personal finances were tight. Had du Cann thrown his hat into the ring, Thatcher would almost certainly have withdrawn.[50] It is therefore hard to disagree with the assessment of the historian Richard Vinen: 'Thatcher had been almost no one's first choice for the leadership, probably not even her own.'[51]

Heath's campaign organizers assumed the best line of attack was to belittle the woman. They tried to turn her grocer's daughter image against her. At a time when sugar shortages were thought to be imminent, a fictitious claim was spread that she had been spotted in a shop on the Finchley High Road making a bulk purchase of sugar. Journalists were encouraged to ask if she was a secret food hoarder and, humiliatingly, she was forced to invite the cameras into her home so they could inspect her sparse larder. It was all rather pathetic and, denied any front-bench endorsement, Thatcher, almost by default, picked up the support of backbenchers exasperated by Heath's political and personal failings. Beating him by 130 to 119 in the first round of voting, she then had momentum behind her, winning through in a more crowded field of candidates in the second and decisive round. That she pitched her political tent to the right of Heath was clear, but she was still not widely perceived to be advocating an entirely new philosophy. After all, she had sat through Heath's Cabinets without much complaint. She was even lauding Harold Macmillan as her political hero, assuring a television interviewer in February 1975 that the 'marvellous politician' Macmillan 'was working towards the things which I believe in'.[52]

But the second half of the seventies (like, for that matter, the first half) was an excellent time to be in opposition. The Keynesian conventions that accompanied low unemployment and rising living standards came under intense pressure. In place of orderly improvement, corporatist government struggled to cope with rampant inflation and the destruction of savings, the humiliating circumstances of the IMF bail-out, trade union militancy and the massive dissatisfaction and unrest expressed across the public sector. Levels of taxation far exceeded the European average, while comparative competitiveness deteriorated alarmingly. Against these developments, Thatcher resolved to fight.

How much of the Britain created in the thirty years before the seventies she also wanted to sweep away was less clear. Some aspects of the wartime and post-war consensus Thatcher claimed to share. She admired the 1944 Education Act and, having mostly failed to rescue them in the early 1970s, she was now pledged to retain the few remaining grammar schools that were the Butler act's legacy. She even accepted such cornerstones of the post-war welfare state as the Beveridge Report and the 1944 employment white paper – while claiming that their proposals had been perverted by subsequent administrations.[53] With the Attlee government's major act of foreign policy – subscription to NATO and the maintenance of the transatlantic alliance – she was in wholehearted agreement. That she went into the 1979 general election promising a smaller state and tax cuts was not, of itself, distinctively 'Thatcherite'. Successive Conservative leaders had tempted every post-war electorate with these aspirations and inducements. Her proposed assault on trade union power was still quite cautious, her privatization programme extremely limited. On 4 May 1979, as Britain awoke to its first day of the new Conservative government, it seemed Mrs Thatcher was aiming to ensure that the eighties would not be shaped by what she considered as the worst excesses of the seventies. She had won power not with an imaginative and visionary outlook but with a manifesto remarkably similar to Edward Heath's statement of intent in 1970. The difference was her determination to deliver on her promises.

3 THE CENTRE CANNOT HOLD

The Joy of Monetarism

The British economy was to be subjected to the shock therapy of monetarism. But what was monetarism? Simplified explanations portrayed it as a needlessly technical term for the easily understood and long-established tenets of classical liberalism and minimal state interference – the economic doctrine of *laissez-faire*, without the carefree associations cast by a French expression. In public discussion, monetarism came to embody these values as well as the broader ones rebranded for the new decade as 'Thatcherism', for which Nigel Lawson provided the succinct definition: 'a mixture of free markets, financial discipline, firm control over public expenditure, tax cuts, nationalism, "Victorian values" (of the Samuel Smiles self-help variety), privatisation and a dash of populism'.[1] A consequence of equating monetarism with Thatcherism was that Margaret Thatcher continued to be attacked for being in hock to the theory long after its ideologues were mourning the fact that her government had wandered off the monetarist path.

Reducing the size of the state was a product of monetarism but was not the theory itself. Essentially, monetarism gave primacy in economic policy to the control of inflation, believing that if it was kept in check, economic equilibrium would naturally follow. Inflation, it maintained, resulted when too much money chased too few goods. Yet this was hardly a revolutionary observation. The dangers of the cavalier printing of money were well known, both in theory and from the calamitous experience of Germany's Weimar Republic in the 1920s, where it resulted in hyperinflation and the destruction of a whole generation's personal savings, and led to the widespread assumption that the dismal experience was a contributory factor to the rise of Nazism. It did not need a new generation of economists to spring this unsurprising revelation. So, when Sir Geoffrey Howe, whom Margaret Thatcher appointed her Chancellor of the Exchequer, claimed that 'monetarism means curbing the excessive expansion of money and credit', he was not arguing for something that would have astounded his Treasury predecessors.[2] What was different was the single-minded devotion to regarding the quantity of money in the economy as determining the extent of inflation, and, in particular, the belief that it was within the government's grasp to manage the growth of the money supply.

That monetarist theory rested upon this simple belief was a convenience that suited the Thatcher government's wider agenda. The interventionist social and economic policies pursued by successive post-war British governments – rather imprecisely labelled Keynesian, after the economist John Maynard Keynes, whose death in 1946 had denied him the opportunity of commenting on the policies carried out in his name – made the control of demand rather than of the money supply the central task. If the economy looked like entering an inflationary boom, the squeeze was applied by raising taxes and cutting the budget deficit. In tougher times, tax, spending and borrowing disciplines could be relaxed. At its crudest, this led to a jolting 'stop–go' economy, but until the late 1960s it had succeeded in keeping both unemployment and inflation relatively low. By the mid-seventies, however, both were soaring. In this environment, demand-fixing measures to reduce unemployment fuelled inflation, which in turn harmed the economy, creating further job losses and a vicious circle of stagflation (diminishing output and soaring inflation). While the Callaghan government had tried to rein in public spending and prevent the money supply spiralling out of control, it had also attempted to bring down inflation (which had peaked at 27 per cent in 1975) by intervention, giving more subsidies to nationalized industries so that they would not increase prices to customers, and organizing an incomes policy in partnership with the leaders of the TUC. So complicated was the effort to fine-tune economic performance from Whitehall that in the space of the five years between 1974 and 1979 Labour's Chancellor, Denis Healey, had introduced fifteen budgets and mini-budgets. The *idée fixe* of Keynesianism had degenerated into an excuse for Treasury micromanagement and the belief that this still offered the best hope of playing an instrument as diverse and complicated as the British economy. Keynes had anticipated his theories operating in a world of fixed international exchange rates, stable energy costs, modest inflation, containable budget deficits and trade union compliance in ensuring increasing output. None of these preconditions existed during Healey's tenure at the Treasury. Theory and reality had parted company.

In contrast to Healey's multifaceted approach, the claim that control of growth in the money supply should be the central preoccupation of government allowed the Thatcher administration to dismantle complex mechanisms whose combined effect was an increasingly corporatist state. For monetarism offered simplicity. There would be no need to appease the trade unions because, with the abolition of an incomes policy, they would not be asked to frame pay norms across the economy. This was a crucial consideration. If a Labour administration had come unstuck trying to operate an anti-inflationary strategy based upon agreeing wage restraint with their nominal allies in the trade union movement, there was clearly even less chance of their cooperating with a Tory-led incomes policy. In short, that option did not exist, even if Thatcher had believed in it in principle – which she did not. If monetarism and the control of inflation came to be elevated to an all-consuming obsession in the first years of the new Conservative administration, it was for reasons that made perfect sense in the light of Thatcher's interpretation of what had gone wrong in the previous decade. To her and her monetarist friends, inflation did not accompany national decline, it hastened it. An incomes policy aimed at reducing price rises through persuading union members to take wage increases close to or below the inflation rate – in other words to reduce in real terms their standard of living – was doomed to fail. There was no personal incentive to agree to such a cut in living standards, and the effort to enforce it naturally led to strikes for higher pay, which, when successful, only further priced British jobs out of the international market, thereby fostering stagflation. Thus, counter-intuitively, tough incomes policies actually encouraged union militancy and ever higher wage demands. Monetarism offered a way out of government engagement with this vicious circle. Furthermore, if inflation could be controlled by strict monetary policy, there was no requirement to depress prices artificially through subsidies to certain, favoured (usually nationalized) industries. This would leave the free market to determine the price at which producers sold to consumers. And over time, taxation could fall in order to let the market operate more freely, rather than tax rates having to be periodically hiked and lowered in a continuous, and disrupting, cycle of demand management.

That was the theory. The practice was more complicated. Even if inflation was caused by lax control of growth in the money supply, how was that growth to be accurately measured? After all, if it could not be properly measured, government could not know whether it had set appropriate targets. Finding a convincing measure for the money sloshing around in the British economy proved no less difficult than assessing whether controlling demand needed the Chancellor's touch on the accelerator or the brake. Was a narrow definition of money, like Sterling M0 (cash), the best measure? Or would a broader measure, like Sterling M3 (cash and bank deposits) or Sterling M4 (cash and bank deposits and building society deposits), be more appropriate? Even monetarist economists – in fact, especially monetarist economists – could not agree. The broader the category, the more difficult it was for government to control. Sir Geoffrey Howe, who was by training a lawyer, not an economist, used his prerogative as Chancellor to pronounce that the correct measure was Sterling M3. Later, he was not so sure.

Having decided what indicator of money supply growth to watch, the next question was how that growth might be controlled. High interest rates were the obvious tool by which credit, and thus the money supply, could be made more expensive. Howe's policy was to raise interest rates at the same time as he implemented a separate strand of the Tories' agenda – the bringing down of the government's own reliance on credit to fund state investment programmes, by reducing the public sector borrowing requirement (PSBR). The British electorate did not wait long to discover the extent of the new administration's determination to place the war against inflation above other considerations. In June 1979, the month after the election, Howe stood at the dispatch box in the House of Commons to deliver his first budget speech.

He did so at the very moment when it was clear that inflation was again rising back into double digits. Partly, this was for reasons beyond Whitehall's control. The price of oil rose threefold between the beginning of 1978 and the end of 1979. Given that the North Sea rigs were in the process of making Britain self-sufficient, the high price of oil meant large petroleum tax receipts for the Treasury. But it was bad news for British industry and for the cost of living. The re-emergence of inflationary pressure was not purely down to the soaring cost of energy, however. It was also a consequence of political decisions taken during the last months of the Callaghan government. With the approach of a general election, Healey had begun relaxing the tough spending constraints he had previously imposed. The concession of high pay awards to end the Winter of Discontent began to feed through. And Howe had been bequeathed a ticking time bomb by his predecessor's establishment of the Clegg commission on public sector pay. Thatcher had been panicked on the election campaign trail into promising to honour Clegg's recommendations. The pay awards transpired to be high, inflationary and a significant drain on the public purse just when the Treasury was trying to find savings. The pledge, however, could not be rescinded.

Most of all, Sir Geoffrey Howe's 1979 budget demonstrated the contradiction at the heart of the Tories' economic policy. On the one hand, the PSBR could only be reduced by cutting government spending: what the government spent had to cease greatly exceeding what the government raised in revenues. Thus, at least until such time as spending came down significantly, taxes ought to have remained high. Yet the Conservatives had won the election as the defenders of free enterprise. They were the party that wanted to remove the fiscal shackles from the private sector, freeing it to expand and create jobs. With the first signs of a recession already on the horizon, hard-pressed employers pleaded for a lighter tax burden. Indeed, bringing down taxation had been at the heart of the Tories' election campaign. Yet if Howe was to honour the fiscal pledges, he risked upsetting the borrowing targets – and these Thatcher considered intrinsically linked to bringing down inflation. Compounding this problem was the Chancellor's determination to remove other impediments to the free flow of money, such as exchange controls and limits on what banks could lend. Such liberalizations were consistent with the desire to free up the market. They were not consistent with keeping a tight control on credit and the money supply.

Howe's first budget was thus not a consistent policy aimed single-mindedly – as the purest monetarists might have hoped – at attacking the factors that were swelling the money supply. In order to balance the competing demands of curtailing Sterling M3 and encouraging faster economic growth, Howe was forced to push up the cost of credit and to cut public spending even more than if he had been able to leave the tax burden and the armoury of financial controls untouched. This was to compensate for reduced government receipts and the money supply-increasing impact of liberalizations of market regulations. In this way, what British industry gained in lighter taxes it paid for in higher interest rates. This, in turn, pushed up the value of sterling to levels that priced all but the most competitive exports out of the international market. By trying to solve one problem, the Chancellor had created another one.

The monetarist measures were clearly set out. Howe announced he was setting a money supply target of 7 to 11 per cent growth (from its current rate of 13 per cent). The Bank of England's minimum lending rate would rise from 12 to 14 per cent. The PSBR would be cut from 5.5 to 4.5 per cent of national output (measured as GDP). The reduction would be achieved by making about £4 billion of cuts to public spending. The greatest long-term saving came from linking state pensions to price rises. Previously they had been index-linked to whichever of price or wage increases was the higher. Howe's announcement of the switch was interrupted by a furious Labour MP shouting 'That is treasonable!'[3] It was unquestionably a fundamental departure from precedent, with huge consequences for an ageing population. With wages rapidly outpacing prices during the eighties, the cost to the Exchequer of pegging pensions to wages would have been astronomical. The result was relative impoverishment for those dependent solely on the state pension for their income in old age. Nevertheless, it was a switch that successive governments of neither main party found the money to reverse until 2010.

Alongside the squeeze came the incentives. Top rate income tax – to be paid by all those earning over £25,000 a year – was cut from 83 to 60 per cent. This brought Britain's upper-rate taxation to the same level as that in France, although the burden on affluent Britons remained heavier than that placed on wealthy Germans (56 per cent) or in the United States (50 per cent). The cut was met with indignant gasps from the opposition benches, but it could be defended as a revenue-raising measure since it made tax avoidance less attractive and encouraged the diaspora of tax exiles to relocate back to Britain (in consequence, far more revenue was raised through a reduced top tax rate during the 1980s than had been squeezed from the rich in the 1970s). Initially more significant in absolute revenue terms was Howe's announcement that the basic rate of income tax would be cut from 33 to 30 per cent. Reducing the tax grab from pay packets automatically made employees wealthier, thereby encouraging them to make less extravagant wage claims. But the scale of the cut risked widening the budget deficit, necessitating more government borrowing and loosening the monetarist squeeze. To claw back this deficit, Howe massively increased indirect taxes. VAT, which had been at 8 per cent (with a 12.5 per cent marginal upper rate), was raised to a new single rate of 15 per cent. During the election campaign, Howe had denied Labour claims that he would double VAT, and the vast scale of this increase, only a month after the polling stations closed, demonstrated that his denials had been true only as measured against the detail rather than the spirit of the accusation. Unfortunately, the debate about the VAT rise concerned more than the Chancellor's personal probity. Borrowing might be inflationary, but so was a huge VAT surcharge on the cost of many everyday goods. The result added upward pressure to the retail price index, which by July had again passed 15 per cent.

While the struggle to control inflation would prove long and hard, the abolition of exchange controls was secured in an instant. In 1979, Britain had the most stringent exchange controls of any major industrial nation. There were limits on how much foreign investment income could be reinvested abroad. There were restrictions on how much money British citizens could take on holiday or emigrate with. These controls to stop money crossing borders had been introduced as an emergency measure at the outset of the Second World War. But while the threat from the Third Reich had disappeared within six years, the perceived need to protect the British currency had remained throughout the following four decades. The continuation of such controls demonstrated the Treasury's persistent fear of a currency collapse if the free movement of capital was permitted. Not only that, exchange controls provided the government with a means of cajoling British capital holders into investing at home rather than seeking potentially higher returns abroad. It was an active form of financial protectionism and, like import controls or tariff barriers, it was double-edged, for, equally, the controls acted to restrict foreign investment in Britain.

In the space of time it took Howe to make his Commons statement, all exchange controls were dramatically abolished on 23 October 1979, a date that marked the United Kingdom's re-emergence as a principal driver of the process of globalization. The effects were immediate and impacted upon everyday decisions taken by holidaymakers and small-scale investors as well as by banks and major City institutions. For the first time in forty years, Britons were suddenly allowed to open bank accounts in foreign currencies, to buy property abroad without restriction, or to buy overseas shares, gold bullion and commodity futures without limit.

To the Labour opposition it was, in the words of Denis Healey, the shadow Chancellor, 'one more reckless, precipitate and doctrinaire action which the government will regret no sooner than those who go bankrupt as a result'.[4] Howe's decision (backed, rather than encouraged, by Thatcher) was partly of a piece with Conservative thinking on the liberalization of markets. It was also made expedient by the specific circumstances of the moment. Rapidly expanding North Sea oil revenues were dramatically strengthening the value of sterling. This reduced the risk that removing exchange controls would cause the pound's value to go into free fall. Indeed, where the fear of a massive withdrawal of money and a currency collapse had frightened off previous Chancellors who had pondered relaxing exchange controls, suddenly anything that eased the upward pressure on sterling's value seemed a positive outcome. Ending exchange controls did cause capital to exit the country, but far from being a disaster that was a bonus, for without this outflow the balance of payments would have been in even greater surplus because of North Sea oil. That surplus would have pushed the value of sterling so high that British exports would have been rendered wholly uncompetitive in the world market. Even as it was, the combination of anti-inflationary high interest rates and the petro-currency component that North Sea oil brought to sterling was to do immense damage to Britain as an industrial trading nation. Much as successive Labour Party leaders and their Treasury spokesmen lamented this state of affairs, the reality was that throughout the eighties Labour remained committed to reintroducing exchange controls – a policy that, by sending sterling higher still, would have destroyed yet more of British manufacturing's export market and the jobs that went with it.

If Denis Healey and his successors did not understand the counterproductive consequences of maintaining exchange controls for the competitiveness of the currency, then Sir Geoffrey Howe appeared not to have foreseen the extent to which his bold initiative was at odds with his commitment to the strict control of the money supply. Allowing banks to move their sterling lending overseas without restriction effectively made redundant efforts to control the amount of credit they lent within the domestic economy. As Edmund Dell put it: 'Vast flows of capital, far exceeding the value of trade, destabilized exchange rates, forced movements in interest rates, and deprived

governments of much of their remaining control over their domestic economies.'[5] In doing so, the UK moved in the opposite direction from its closest
continental neighbour. In 1981, France's incoming socialist president,
François Mitterrand, introduced sweeping new exchange controls in order
to insulate his country from global money markets. For the City of London,
the liberalization came as an immediate and sustained boost which helped
strengthen its role in the world order of capitalism, which had been threatened since the abandonment of capital controls by the United States in
1974.* Now, the fetters had been removed from British pension fund managers and insurance companies that wanted to expand and diversify their
international investment portfolios. Efforts were made to ensure the revolution was permanent. The Treasury's files on exchange controls were
destroyed, supposedly in order to hamper a future administration that might
try to reimpose them.[6]

The Pain of Monetarism

Whatever the promises of eventual salvation, the early consequences of the
new economic policy were appalling. With strong underlying drivers of
inflation such as rising oil prices and a high public sector wage settlement,
controlling the money supply was easier said than done. Inflation continued
to climb. The response was to borrow more. This created a spiral in which
the further inflation rose, the more the money supply swelled. Howe had
established a guideline growth for Sterling M3 of 8 per cent in 1980–1.
Instead, it grew by 19 per cent. The onset of a recession triggered by the
soaring price of oil pushed up unemployment. This diminished tax returns,
increased benefit pay-outs and unbalanced the budget, thereby ensuring
more government borrowing. In November 1979, with inflation running at
17.4 per cent, Howe responded by raising interest rates (set by the minimum
lending rate) to 17 per cent. The rate had never been higher. Thus Howe
and Thatcher found themselves faced with only unpalatable choices. They
could not long sustain interest rates at such a level without crippling the
economy, and the worse the recession became the greater would be the
ensuing budget deficit. The projected PSBR for 1981–2 of £7.5 billion (3
per cent of GDP) was heading towards £14 billion. The need to finance
such a debt by attracting the necessary loans reduced the scope for reducing
interest rates. It was a vicious circle.

To the Chancellor and prime minister's way of thinking, it seemed the
only way to bring interest rates down was first to reduce the borrowing
requirement. This could be done by putting taxes up. However, reversing

---

* See chapter fourteen.

the tax cuts of the June 1979 budget would be politically humiliating, and businesses would not be greatly helped if the consequence of lopping a few per cent off interest rates was to put a few per cent on their and their employees' tax bills. This left the Cabinet with a grim alternative: cut public spending further. Higher education and local government were hit, as was defence spending, which the Tories had gone into the general election promising to increase by 3 per cent per year. A minor reshuffle in January 1981 removed Francis Pym, who was resisting the cuts, from the Ministry of Defence and installed John Nott, who was prepared to wield the axe. Defence analysts pondered what consequences this would have for the country's role in NATO, particularly for the Royal Navy's role in guarding the North Sea and for the British Army of the Rhine. It was actually in the South Atlantic that the retrenchment would have the greatest consequences. Argentina's military junta made their plans accordingly.*

Cripplingly high interest rates encouraged foreign investors to buy sterling. The result sent the value of the pound soaring, to the detriment of British industry. In the second half of 1980, the pound's value averaged around $2.40. This was close to where it had been at the start of the 1970s, before the collapse of the fixed exchange rate system. Placed in more recent perspective, though, it represented a steep acceleration from nearer $2 in 1979 and was far up from its historic trough of $1.57 during the IMF crisis of 1976. The new, punishing, rate of $2.40 brought about the first blink from the Treasury via the Bank of England. In November 1980, the minimum lending rate fell back to the (still extraordinarily high) level of 14 per cent. This minor cut provided scant and short-term relief. The primacy given to the money supply and the curtailment of borrowing had come at the expense of trying to manage the exchange rate for sterling. The consequences were calamitous for the export market.

The predicament was later set out by Nigel Lawson, who was at that time Financial Secretary to the Treasury: 'We had come to office at a time when the UK economic cycle had peaked and was about to turn down – as for that matter was the world economy – and it would have been much easier to have deferred our attack on the deficit (and indeed on inflation via higher interest rates). But we consciously decided to press ahead, because deferment can become a way of life.'[7] This was, according to taste, either brave or callous. However, the decision to press on with it demonstrated the deepness of the psychological scars left by the Heath government's decision to run away at the first signs of trouble. Even so, many of Lawson's colleagues felt the new determination was foolhardy and that history would have to repeat itself. Indeed, perhaps as much as a majority of the Cabinet believed that the

---

* See chapter six.

only possibility of salvation would come from executing a humiliating U-turn. They now wanted to prioritize staving off the collapse of British industry ahead of controlling inflation. This meant dropping high interest rates so that the exchange rate, rather than the money supply, became the central tool of recovery.

There were historical parallels in Britain's once almost theological commitment to the gold standard. In the nineteenth century, there was an orthodoxy that the currency ought to remain worth a fixed amount in gold. Policy was therefore aimed at not devaluing the currency by increasing supply. This was monetarism Victorian-style. After sterling was forced off the gold standard in the world recession of 1931, governments looked for new ways to manage the exchange rate. From the end of the Second World War until 1971, sterling's value was fixed against the dollar. This proved a tough test in obedience, hence the repeated 'sterling crises' that afflicted post-war British governments, which found that keeping sterling fixed at a particular rate acted as a tail wagging the dog of the rest of economic policy. Freedom from this discipline came in 1972 when, the fixed exchange rate system having collapsed, the decision was taken to let the currency float and find its natural level. For politicians, no longer having to maintain the exchange rate by regular intervention to keep the balance of payments in check proved heady. Sizeable budget deficits were quickly run up in pursuit of boosting demand and increasing welfare funding. Borrowing soared and economic growth faltered. It was at this moment that control of the money supply stepped in to fill the anarchic gap created by the ending of fixed exchange rates. The new discipline seemed even harsher than the old one in terms of cripplingly high exchange rates and interest rates. Indeed, the centrality now given to the interest rate encouraged an unceasing desire to fiddle with it. In 1982, the rate was altered thirty-six times.[8] Nevertheless, when Howe's successor as Chancellor, Nigel Lawson, began the process of shifting the focus of discipline from the money supply back to the exchange rate, first by shadowing the Deutschmark in 1987, which brought back inflation, and three years later through John Major's decision to peg sterling to the European Exchange Rate Mechanism, the resulting recession demonstrated that managing the exchange rate was not necessarily a painless way to squeeze inflation out of the British economy, nor to boost employment.

The clear moment to announce that the monetarist experiment had failed came – and passed – during the length of time it took Sir Geoffrey Howe to deliver his third budget to the House of Commons on 10 March 1981. It took either great self-confidence or reckless insensitivity to stand by the decisions that had been taken and to affirm that they were to be persevered with despite all the evidence pointing to their consequences. The first two years of the Thatcher government had witnessed the greatest fall in industrial production since 1921. Unemployment, which had stood at 1.4 million claimants when the Conservatives came to power, had reached 2.7 million by October 1981 and showed no sign of tailing off. The prospect of three million out of work was a question not of 'if', but 'when'. And 'when' proved to be January 1982. This tally of human despondency created fresh pressures on the national accounts, reducing the scope for interventionist public works projects – even had the Treasury approved of such projects, which it did not. Capital expenditure (spending on the stock and infrastructure of the state), which had represented one fifth of all public spending in 1974, now represented only one tenth. Indeed, for all the cuts Howe and his Treasury team forced through, the exploding cost of supporting the unemployed ensured that total public spending was actually still increasing. It had represented 44 per cent of GDP in 1979 and stood at 47.5 per cent by 1981.

The previous Conservative government had lasted two years before Heath had signalled a full-scale retreat. But Thatcher had so pinned her leadership on not flinching in the face of tough conditions that to repeat her predecessor's surrender could have been as fatal to her survival as standing firm. At her party conference in October 1980, she had delivered the lines, suggested to her by her speechwriter Ronald Millar: 'To those waiting with bated breath for that favourite media catchphrase, the "U-turn", I have only one thing to say. You turn if you want to. The lady's not for turning.'[9]* This was too memorable a catchphrase to permit room for manoeuvre. She was fortunate that, crucially, her Chancellor was equally determined not to flinch. Their only disagreement was over how further fiscal tightening could be achieved during 1981 without putting income tax rates back up. The answer was a sleight of hand, keeping tax rates the same but omitting to raise the thresholds at which they were paid. Given that inflation had nudged 20 per cent in the intervening year, and was still running at 13 per cent in the spring of 1981, this made a significant difference. Higher taxes on alcohol, cigarettes, oil producers and the banks provided the rest of the increase. Much as the 1981 budget was most vigorously attacked for continuing with monetarism, in fact Howe's statement revealed a slight slackening of monetary control, with the increasing grab from tax revenues providing the deflationary discipline.

Twenty days later, 364 economists sent a letter to *The Times* denouncing government policy. They claimed there was 'no basis in economic theory or supporting evidence for the government's belief that by deflating demand they will bring inflation permanently under control' or ensure economic

---

* The playwright Millar was punning on the title of the most famous work of the dramatist Christopher Fry, *The Lady's Not for Burning*.

recovery. By ignoring alternatives to monetarism: 'Present policies will deepen the depression.'[10]

In order to keep the 364 economists in agreement – a historic achievement in itself – the precise alternative course to be followed was not prescribed. Nevertheless, so resounding a refutation could not easily be brushed aside or attributed purely to the self-interest of lecturers whose university budgets were among the targets of the spending squeeze. Initiated by two Cambridge professors, Frank Hahn and Robert Nield, the declaration attracted the support of academics from thirty-six universities and included the signatures of seventy-six present or past professors and five former chief economic advisers to the government. In contrast, the prime minister could not even marshal the support of half of the twenty-two members of her Cabinet.

In reality, Thatcher did not need to listen to her critics to discover that the obsessive focus on the money supply was mistaken. Her new personal economic adviser, Alan Walters, told her as much. 'Bugger Sterling M3!' he supposedly exclaimed, pointing out that 'Sterling is obviously far too high. That can only mean that sterling is scarce.'[11] The 1981 budget succeeded in bringing the PSBR back towards £10 billion, thereby facilitating a welcome depreciation in the value of sterling. Indeed, the day after the budget, interest rates fell by 2 per cent, to 12 per cent. Unfortunately, the relief was a mirage. By October, there was a run on the pound and, in the panic, interest rates were hiked up to 16 per cent. This seemed like a crippling blow to companies still limping along.

The declaration by the 364 economists seemed a withering verdict, delivered at a critical juncture. However, with hindsight, the spring of 1981 proved an inopportune moment to forecast that government policy would 'deepen the depression'. As Nigel Lawson later noted with undisguised glee: 'Their timing was exquisite. The economy embarked on a prolonged phase of vigorous growth almost from the moment the letter was published.'[12] Indeed, the decline in GDP had reached its bottom in the first quarter of 1981, after which recovery – albeit not at a rate to dent the jobless queues – began. Even before this turnaround was evident, the critique of the 364 had been challenged by Patrick Minford, professor of economics at Liverpool University, whose rebuttal in *The Times* earned him a note of thanks from the prime minister.[13] He argued that the eminent academics were more Keynesian than John Maynard Keynes. For while it was true that Keynes had advocated reflation, that was at a time (1932) when the rate of inflation was below zero and the money supply was growing at less than 1 per cent. Thus he had merely been calling for price stability, which was also the Thatcher government's goal – to be achieved through reducing government borrowing. While it was undeniable that the least productive parts of British industry had gone to the wall, the outlook for the survivors was not as bleak as the 364 imagined, for the stock market, sniffing out opportunity before the theorists could, was again increasing the capitalization of even the hardest-hit sectors.[14] Along a particularly dark tunnel, there was a far-off glimmer of light.

'Wets' and 'Dries'

What Keynes might have done thirty-five years after his death was anyone's guess. Yet he was not the only posthumous figure expected to animate the debate. Indeed, much of the tussle over the Thatcher government's first years was conducted through the prism – or at least the labels – of Victorian politics. Thatcher's Conservative opponents repeatedly saluted the memory of Benjamin Disraeli. A reference from Disraeli's 1846 novel *Sybil* to the rich and the poor comprising two nations was invoked by Thatcher's critics in the Tory Reform Group who proclaimed themselves 'One Nation Conservatives'. The clear implication was that Thatcher and her monetarist ideologues were divisive splitters, destroying the fabric of national unity. Disraelian 'Tory paternalism' may have been a somewhat romantic notion, but it provided a convenient bridge between a Merrie England of kind-hearted squires doling out charity to contented, toothless tenants and support for the fundamentals of the post-war welfare state. Appropriating the long-dead Disraeli to their cause was also a means of escaping the 'Heathite' label, with all the connotations of recent failure that it involved. At a deeper level, it fitted better with what really rankled Tory paternalists about Thatcherism.

Sir Ian Gilmour and Christopher Soames struggled to conceal a *de haut en bas* disdain for the *arriviste* Thatcherites who, they believed, were upsetting a settled social order and ruling without recognizing the duty of *noblesse oblige* towards those they stepped over. The critique was perfectly expressed in Gilmour's book *Inside Right*, when he wrote: 'If people are not to be seduced by other attractions, they must at least feel loyalty to the state. Their loyalty will not be deep unless they gain from the state protection and other benefits . . . If the state is not interested in them, why should they be interested in the state? . . . Economic liberalism, because of its starkness and its failure to create a sense of community, is likely to repel people from the rest of liberalism.'[15] By this yardstick, was the prime minister even a Tory? It was not just the neo-Disraelians who thought her worldview far closer to the Victorian liberalism of William Ewart Gladstone. Her favourite American monetarist economist, Milton Friedman, agreed, concluding: 'The thing people do not recognize is that Margaret Thatcher is not in terms of belief a Tory. She is a nineteenth-century Liberal.'[16]

It was, perhaps, an authentically Conservative approach to contemporary problems to turn them into a reflection of the past. Nevertheless, the attempt to fight once again the divisions of the 1880s – or even the 1840s – in the Tory cabinet of the 1980s was historically questionable. So many former Whigs and classical Liberals had defected to the Conservatives between the 1880s and the 1930s, bringing aspects of their beliefs with them, that the modern party had long been a blend of Victorian Toryism and Liberalism in which identifying the separate strands was a specious science. Was not Thatcher's hero, Winston Churchill, the embodiment of how the two traditions had ended up in the same entity? While Thatcher's economic views undoubtedly owed more to the free-trade 'Manchester Liberalism' of John Bright and Richard Cobden, many of her emotional attachments were far removed from their peace-seeking internationalism. Her reverence for the monarchy, the armed forces and the projection of British power, her unease about mass immigration and support for strong punishment for criminal offenders, could scarcely have been more deep-seatedly Tory. In 1981, she stated: 'My politics are based not on some economic theory, but on things I and millions like me were brought up with: an honest day's work for an honest day's pay; live within your means; put by a nest-egg for a rainy day; pay your bills on time; support the police.'[17] Any attempt to deduce whether this made her closer to Asquith or to Bonar Law would have been highly pedantic.

Where she departed from any attempt to wrap herself in traditional Tory sentiment was in her refusal to talk the language of moderation and the imperative of social cohesion. In an unguarded aside to the British ambassador to Iran during a trip to Tehran in 1978, she revealed the extent of her animosity towards those back home who believed searching for consensus was the aim of politics: 'I regard them as Quislings, as traitors.'[18] Yet a year later she put several of the cheerleaders for the line of least resistance in her Cabinet. With the exceptions of Sir Keith Joseph and (surprisingly) Norman St John Stevas, probably no other member of her first Cabinet had voted for her in the deciding ballot for the party leadership in 1975. That she found herself entrusting with major government departments men who had preferred Heath to her was a sign less of her magnanimity than of her weakness. There simply were not enough Conservatives with sufficient experience or standing in the party who shared her outlook.

The easy part had proved to be making sure she did not have to share the Cabinet Room with the great lost leader. Having refused to sit in her shadow Cabinet, Edward Heath had perked up at the prospect of power and wanted to be her Foreign Secretary. He was duly put in his place with the offer of ambassador to Washington – one of the very last places the Grand European wished to end up. He turned it down and resumed his public sulk. But his former supporters (many of them not even former) remained a Cabinet majority: the Foreign Secretary, Lord Carrington, and the Home

Secretary, Willie Whitelaw, were Tories of the old, paternalistic school. The same was true of Francis Pym (defence), Jim Prior (employment), Mark Carlisle (education), Michael Heseltine (environment), Peter Walker (agriculture), Sir Ian Gilmour (Lord Privy Seal), Lord Hailsham (Lord Chancellor) and Lord Soames (Leader of the House of Lords). Those who had come round to Thatcher's view were a minority. Critically, however, she ensured they held the portfolios that determined economic policy. As Chancellor of the Exchequer, Sir Geoffrey Howe was assisted by John Biffen, the Chief Secretary to the Treasury. Thatcher's liberalizing instincts were also shared by her secretary of state for industry, Sir Keith Joseph by John Nott at trade; Patrick Jenkin, who ran social services; David Howell at energy and by Angus Maude, who was Postmaster General. Nigel Lawson, the Financial Secretary to the Treasury, was a significant reinforcement to those who believed in sound finance even though he was not a member of the Cabinet. Thus Jim Prior, as employment secretary, was the only opponent of monetarism with a portfolio intimately involved with economics, and consequently he was the only Heathite on the 'E' committee (the Cabinet committee dealing with economic policy). This, it seems, was not sufficient to entitle him to an invitation to the private Thursday morning confabs that Thatcher scheduled with her monetarist ministers in the first months of her premiership. If this group was to succeed in its objectives, it was necessary to ensure that when the full Cabinet discussed economic policy it was prevented from blocking the fundamentals upon which that policy was being pursued.

Surrounded by her all-male Cabinet, the prime minister stood out in more ways than her sex and her monetarism. Of the twenty-two members of Thatcher's first Cabinet, only three – Thatcher, John Biffen and Peter Walker – had not been educated at public schools.* Peter Walker was the only graduate who had not gone to Oxford or Cambridge. The prime minister's belief in social meritocracy was not the most striking aspect of her Cabinet appointments. Her team included seven Old Etonians, which was one more than had sat in Harold Macmillan's Cabinet. Six were former Guards officers. The Foreign Secretary, Lord Carrington, was a hereditary peer who had served in Harold Macmillan's government, spoke with an exceptionally plummy drawl, and had spent much of the last few years engaged less by front-line politics than by his work for Rio Tinto Zinc. Like eight members of the Cabinet, Lord Carrington had fought in the Second World War, winning the Military Cross for his part in holding the bridge at Nijmegen during the

---

* Walker had gone to Latymer Upper School, at that time a selective direct-grant school, only partially funded by the state, which subsequently went fully independent in the 1970s to avoid the Labour government's determination to turn it into a comprehensive. Biffen had gone to Dr Morgan's Grammar School in Bridgwater, Somerset, which was shut down in the 1970s and replaced by a comprehensive. Only Thatcher's old school managed to retain its status.

Arnhem campaign. Lord Hailsham, who would serve as Lord Chancellor until 1987, sat on the same Woolsack once occupied by his father. Hailsham was born in 1907 and had been in Parliament since winning a bitter by-election in 1938, fought on the issue of Neville Chamberlain's policy of appeasement. While Hailsham was the most venerable figure in a government allegedly committed to disconnecting Britain from its immediate past, even the other leading front-bench ministers enjoyed, on average, a seniority of five to six years over their prime minister. To those who queried her suitability, she seemed handicapped not just by her relative youth but by her supposed inexperience both of life (not having fought in the war) and of government (just three years as education secretary). While she perceived the advantages of not being a natural member of the establishment, her lack of the social links that bound her front bench together – public school, regiment, City firm or gentlemen's club – placed her outside of the *esprit de corps* of her colleagues who could, with sufficient backbone, determine her fate. What helped save her was that widely respected old boys like Hailsham and Whitelaw placed their loyalty to her as prime minister above their doubts about whether she was in the right. Indeed, next to enjoying broad agreement with her Chancellor over the economy, having Willie Whitelaw to smooth over differences with malcontents whose outlook and pastimes he shared proved the most'invaluable shield for Thatcher's back.

The tendency to see intra-Tory differences on policy as dictated by background could be overstated, as could the extent of Thatcher's social iconoclasm. She was, after all, happily married to a man whose social milieu was distinctly old school. Of the five parliamentary private secretaries she selected to serve her directly during the course of her tenure in Downing Street, four were Old Etonians and one (Ian Gow) was a Wykehamist. Nor did an expensive education confer intellectual conformity. Sir Ian Gilmour, Carrington's ultra-Heathite deputy at the Foreign Office, may have been the son of a baronet and a product of Eton and Balliol, but this was exactly the same education as another junior Foreign Office minister, the ultra-Thatcherite Nicholas Ridley, had received. And loftier still, Ridley's father was a peer. Not all the Tory paternalists were quite as grand as they seemed. Peter Walker had made his fortune in the 1970s through the City firm of Slater Walker, whose asset-stripping approach to companies it bought smacked of the very spivvy City activities that Tory paternalism supposedly abhorred. Even in the eyes of many fellow Tory Reform Group members, Michael Heseltine was considered a bit of a social climber (public school – Shrewsbury),[*] who had started out accumulating his fortune by buying and selling property.

---

[*] To a certain sort of Tory paternalist, there was only 'one nation' but seemingly many grades of public school.

For all these subtle gradations, the neo-Disraelians certainly carried an air of social superiority – a posture that succeeded only in provoking the Thatcherites into believing they were up against a tired and effete *ancien régime* from which Britain was in as much need of rescue as from the trade union movement. That Thatcher was more interested in attitude than background was perfectly encapsulated by her estimation of her distinctly Heathite employment secretary. Jim Prior was a successful farmer, with the demeanour of a genial squire. It was a countenance to reassure many Tories. But not the prime minister. He was, she summed up in her memoirs, one of her party's 'false squires', who 'have all the outward show of a John Bull – ruddy face, white hair, bluff manner – but inwardly they are political calculators who see the task of Conservatives as one of retreating gracefully before the left's inevitable advance'.[19] Nothing did more to puncture the Tory paternalists' pretensions to power than the coining of the dismissive public school-speak description of them as 'wets'. The Thatcherites gained the epithet 'dries'. This connoted, by no means inappropriately, a certain humourless asceticism. There was, it may be assumed, nobody drier in manner than the Chancellor, Sir Geoffrey Howe. But in a time of acute challenge, it seemed less dismissive to be marked down as 'dry' than as 'wet'. Both terms stuck and remained the standard appellations for the dividing line in Conservative politics for the rest of the decade. Tellingly, they fell out of use within weeks of Thatcher's political demise.

Thatcher once announced at a Downing Street reception that she was 'the rebel head of an establishment government'.[20] Others close to her described her as 'the only prime minister who moonlit as leader of the opposition'.[21] It was not paranoia but a firm grasp of reality that made her aware that her battle was as much with her own Cabinet as with the Labour Party. Real differences of outlook were sharpened by her naturally combative style for, unfortunately, not all her colleagues enjoyed her love of argument, particularly when conducted in front of other ministers across the Cabinet table. In her argumentative stride, all sense of old-fashioned courtesy disappeared. What she may have thought was knockabout, the recipients thought of as brazen rudeness. Many were not of a generation used to being publicly spoken to by a woman in this way and did not know how to retaliate.[22] For them, the worst part was her schoolgirl-swot approach to argument, trumping their generalities with a seemingly encyclopedic knowledge of highly technical details and statistics. She would ask them a specific question, cutting into their vague response by telling them the answer. By such means, she was able to imply that she was more on top of their department's work than they were. The impression that she was some kind of superwoman shouldering the work of a score of Cabinet ministers was fortified by her ability to cope on a mere four to five hours sleep per night, with just an apple and a vitamin pill for breakfast. This gave her an immense advantage over more elderly men who spent in a state of rejuvenating slumber the time she was sitting bolt upright in bed mastering her ministerial boxes.

While Nigel Lawson conceded the time she put in on her homework 'was a desirable characteristic', it 'could lead to time-wasting attempts to show off her mastery of detail, at the expense of the main business in hand'.[23] Nevertheless, it unquestionably kept her colleagues on their toes. What was more, while she seemed incapable of backing down in an argument or conceding that she might be wrong, she did use the exchanges as a means of deciding what her own position really was, taking on board such points as she had found unanswerable and subsequently adopting them as her own. She did not confine her love of a good scrap to her 'wettest' colleagues. She could be equally demanding of ministers from her own wing of the party. The term 'handbagging' was widely understood by all who trod the corridors of Whitehall. In contrast to her instinctive prickliness and unclubbable attitude towards other members of the Cabinet, she was generally far more sweet-tempered towards her personal advisers and 'courtiers'. The latter, in particular, fulfilled the role of favoured Cavaliers, there to entertain an instinctive Roundhead by providing her with light relief as well as different perspectives. The leaders of this group were her playwright speech-writer Ronald Millar; public relations specialists Gordon Reece and Tim Bell; Bernard Ingham, the bluff, previously Labour-voting, Yorkshire-man, whom she appointed as her press secretary after a two-minute interview; Alistair McAlpine, fine-art collector and party treasurer; and Woodrow Wyatt, newspaper columnist, chairman of the Tote – and former Labour MP. Much as the Tory paternalists thundered about Thatcherism's indifference to the responsibilities of *noblesse oblige*, Thatcher herself could not be faulted for her unstuffiness and was unaffectedly kind and considerate towards her personal staff – drivers, wardrobe assistant, hairdresser and secretaries. The contrast between her thoughtfulness towards them and her indifference to the feelings of her Cabinet colleagues was perhaps most vividly illustrated by an incident during a lunch at the prime ministerial country residence, Chequers, when an armed services girl, standing in as a waitress, slipped and spilt hot soup all over Sir Geoffrey Howe's lap. Thatcher instinctively leapt up, ignoring her scalded Chancellor, to console the girl: 'There, there. Now you mustn't be upset. It's the sort of thing that could happen to anyone.'[24]

There would come a time when Thatcher's lack of concern for Howe's feelings would cost her dear. Nevertheless, there was little indication in the early years of her administration that this would prove the fatal personality clash. Educated at Winchester and Cambridge (but born in the depressed

South Wales area of Port Talbot), Howe had been a QC specializing in labour law and his conversion to monetarism seemed to have sprung less from first principles than from a reaction to the unhappy experience of the Heath government. Perhaps misleadingly, his manner was more that of a technician than a philosopher, let alone an idealist. However, his softly spoken demeanour concealed a determined, obstinate streak which Thatcher eventually tested once too often. It was his inability to come to the point quickly that particularly irritated her. But he was enough of his own man – and his Treasury team was regarded as sufficiently competent – to be allowed to get his way. As Chancellor, he suffered prime ministerial interference but not direction. After all, on the basics, they were broadly in agreement – or thought they were. And such differences as arose during the period were informally smoothed over by Howe's friend Ian Gow, who was also Thatcher's immensely loyal parliamentary private secretary.

Yet it was not to her next-door neighbour in Downing Street that Thatcher first turned for ideas about how to reform the British economy. The irony was that a prime minister with no instinctive respect for or deference towards tenured academics should nonetheless spend so much of her time engaging with intellectuals. Indeed, as the sociologist Paul Hirst put it: 'The first Thatcher government was unique in modern British history: a party led by a clique of intellectuals with a strong commitment to a radical ideology.'[25] This clique was predominantly in Thatcher's circle rather than in her Cabinet. The intellectual godfathers were remote presences indeed – Friedrich von Hayek, author of *The Road to Serfdom* (1944) and *The Constitution of Liberty* (1960), who had won the Nobel Prize for economics in 1974, and Milton Friedman, who had won the same prize two years later and had written the popular book and television series *Free to Choose* (1980). They were remote in the literal sense that both Hayek, an Austrian-born British citizen, and Friedman, an American, were living abroad and only infrequently visited Britain. Scarcity boosted their value to the Tory leader. When either man did visit Britain, often at the bequest of the Institute for Economic Affairs, Thatcher could be spotted listening with the rapt attention of a schoolgirl with a crush. Such was her devotion to Hayek that shortly after becoming party leader she interrupted a speaker delivering a middle-of-the-road homily to a Conservative Research Department meeting by extracting from her bag a thick book, declaiming boldly, 'This is what we believe!' and banging *The Constitution of Liberty* down on the table.[26] Ascribing such significance to any one text, rather in the manner of Chairman Mao's Little Red Book, was certainly not in the Tory tradition, but then one of the most insightful chapters in Hayek's *Constitution* was titled 'Why I am not a Conservative'. Perhaps he was not, but he was still delighted to be made a Companion of Honour by the Queen on Thatcher's recommendation in

1984. Such was his pupil's devotion that only two weeks after she had won the 1979 general election Thatcher wrote a fan letter to Hayek: 'I am very proud to have learnt so much from you over the past few years . . . As one of your keenest supporters, I am determined that we should succeed. If we do so, your contribution to our ultimate victory will have been immense.'[27]

Hayek had taught at Chicago University in the 1950s, alongside Friedman, who remained there until 1977. The Chicago School became the most important bastion for the intellectual assault on Keynesianism. Where Keynes had argued that government could keep unemployment and inflation low by manipulating 'aggregate demand' through public expenditure or tax cuts, the monetarist Friedman maintained that unemployment should be left to find its 'natural' rate. Well-intentioned attempts by the state to drive down unemployment were economically destabilizing and ultimately counterproductive. The Chicago Boys' medicine had been applied by Augusto Pinochet's regime in Chile, successfully applying 'shock therapy' to curb rampant inflation and subsequently addressing the problem of pension reform. But Pinochet's Chile was a right-wing military dictatorship which brooked no compromise and crushed dissent. As such, it was not an example Thatcher could easily hold up as a model for how economic issues could be addressed in pluralist, democratic Britain.

While visits from the Chicago Boys were rare events, their ideas were propagated and applied to British circumstances by a small number of think tanks which enjoyed close access to the prime minister. The Institute for Economic Affairs (IEA) had the greatest pedigree, having been founded in 1957 (when scepticism towards Keynesian demand management was considered the height of eccentricity) by Arthur Seldon and Ralph Harris, two Hayek-admiring economists who had risen from humble backgrounds through the grammar school system and the LSE. In contrast, the Centre for Public Studies (CPS) had been started far more recently, by Sir Keith Joseph, as a response to the perceived disasters of the Heath government. Joseph put his money where his brain was by funding it himself. Harold Macmillan dismissed him as 'the only boring Jew I've ever met'.[28] Coddled by the mementos of world summitry at Birch Grove, Macmillan had perhaps lost his former interest in new ideas, for the CPS played an important part in the lead-up to the 1979 general election by providing intellectual ballast for the direction in which Thatcher sought to take her party in government. Its chairman, Joseph, and its director, Alfred Sherman, shared a Jewish background and an interest in thinking beyond orthodox ideas. But they were different in almost every other respect. Joseph had inherited a baronetcy and a family business, had been educated at Harrow and Oxford and was a Fellow of All Souls, Oxford. Born in Hackney, the son of a Labour councillor, Sherman was an outsider who had started out as a communist and had fought with the International Brigades in the Spanish Civil War, prior to undergoing a conversion – if not on the road to Damascus, then at least while working as an economist in Israel.

Sherman was soon displaying all the zealotry of the convert. When the distinctly High Tory journalist Peregrine Worsthorne once offered him a lift back from a Conservative conference, Sherman spent the length of the walk to the car ranting about the uselessness of the British working class: 'too demoralized by welfare and socialism to be any good for anything'. However, when they reached Worsthorne's car it was to discover it had a flat tyre. Neither man had the slightest idea what to do about a puncture until a passing labourer spotted their plight and kindly changed the tyre for them. Scarcely had the Good Samaritan wished them on their way before Sherman, a stranger to self-parody, resumed his rant: 'As I was saying, absolutely no good, the whole lot of them.'[29] The episode underlined the real nature of the divide at the top of the CPS. While Sherman loathed what he took to be the laziness of the British working man, Joseph knew when a helping hand, rather than a vulgar gesture, needed to be extended, and he had founded a housing association in Paddington to find decent accommodation for tenants who had been at the mercy of unscrupulous landlords. Indeed, Joseph's intellectual torment, torn between what he believed was the right policy and anguish for those who might suffer from it, led to a paralysis of indecision that spoke much for his humanity but blunted his contribution as a practical politician. For a while Sherman was a natural agitator, Joseph was increasingly seen as a tragi-comic figure. Denis Healey mocked him as 'a mixture of Hamlet, Rasputin and Tommy Cooper'.[30] Others settled simply for dubbing him, sometimes affectionately, the 'Mad Monk'. With Joseph's entry into the Cabinet, the chairmanship of the CPS passed to Hugh Thomas, a distinguished historian who also provided Thatcher with unofficial advice on foreign policy. Almost inevitably, Thomas, the historian of the Spanish Civil War, and Sherman, the street fighter who had participated in it, fell out. This led to Sherman's departure from the CPS and a role on the sidelines of Thatcherism to which, with typical curmudgeonliness, he took to finding fault.

The eccentricity of some of their luminaries need not detract from the importance of the work undertaken by think tanks like the IEA and the CPS in bolstering Thatcher's convictions. Aside from the analysis and detail they provided, their contribution was psychological. They showed that the 'dries' were engaged in the world of ideas whereas the 'wets', who had no think tanks worthy of the name,* had nothing to offer beyond wishing Keynes was still alive and attaching themselves to the reputation of Benjamin Disraeli.

---

* The Tory Reform Group published papers and even a magazine, but undertook little detailed, original research.

The 'wet' Sir Ian Gilmour's philosophical musings on the nature of Toryism were insufficiently practical for a leader like Margaret Thatcher. Yet, before her prime ministerial schedule took over her free time, even she had occasionally attended meetings of the Conservative Philosophy Group. Their gatherings were held in the eighteenth-century Lord North Street town house of Jonathan Aitken, an up-and-coming MP and scion of the faded Beaverbrook press empire, whose career mistakes included going out with and then dumping Thatcher's daughter, Carol. The group had been established by the Cambridge don John Casey and the philosopher Roger Scruton, who would prove to be the pre-eminent exponent of High Tory thought during the eighties. The small, traditionally minded Cambridge college of Peterhouse remained its spiritual home, with its dons Edward Norman and Maurice Cowling also to the fore. Cowling rather doubted whether their philosophical ruminations greatly influenced Thatcher's thinking,[31] though the group may have helped construct a bridge between her economic policies and traditional High Tory – as distinct from classical Liberal – thought. Given the widespread hostility towards Thatcherism from the lecturing classes, the Conservative Philosophy Group did provide a degree of academic ammunition for pro-Thatcher newspaper columnists, including the historian Paul Johnson, T. E. Utley in the *Daily Telegraph*, Peregrine Worsthorne in the *Sunday Telegraph* and, in a more whimsical vein, Frank Johnson in *The Times*.

While Thatcher paid little attention to the Whitehall 'think tank', the Central Policy Review Staff, as a source of alternative ideas and did away with it in 1983, she was much more influenced by the rival Downing Street Policy Unit, headed by John Hoskyns and Norman Strauss, two men who had originally been introduced to one another by Alfred Sherman. Hoskyns was tormented by the evidence of his country's decline. His father had been killed fighting in the rearguard that sacrificed itself so that the bulk of the British Expeditionary Force could escape from Dunkirk in 1940. A Wykehamist, Hoskyns had himself held a commission in the army before doing well in the computer business. What he had learned there as a systems analyst he was determined to apply to government. Strauss was a grammar-school boy (the same school as a prominent supporter of monetarism in the *Financial Times*, Samuel Brittan) who had gone into marketing for Unilever. Together, Hoskyns and Strauss shared a twin antipathy for what they took to be the two most powerful institutions that acted as a brake on innovation – the trade unions and the civil service. While others looked to outflank the shop stewards and the Whitehall mandarins through incremental change, Hoskyns and Strauss were obsessed with launching frontal attacks through a confrontational approach summed up in their slogan: 'Escalate for our Lives!'

Hoskyns and Strauss's desire to disable trade union power was shared by a pressure group which, although outside the Conservative Party, was admired by Thatcher and right-wingers generally, if not for its intellectual firepower then at least for its practical vigour. This was the National Association for Freedom – later the Freedom Association (NAFF not being the ideal acronym). It had been set up by the identical twin brothers Ross and Norris McWhirter, whose admiration for individual endeavour and personal goal-setting manifested itself through their being the founding editors of the *Guinness Book of Records* and becoming minor celebrities to a generation of 1970s children as the twins whose extraordinary memory enabled them to answer questions on the BBC show *Record Breakers*. Their organization was particularly concerned with campaigning to end the closed shop, helping and providing legal advice to non-union employees who had found themselves blacklisted. In 1975, the IRA murdered Ross McWhirter. His offence had been to offer a reward for information leading to the arrest of the IRA terror cell that had attempted to blow up the Tory MP Hugh Fraser (who had just stood against both Heath and Thatcher for the Conservative leadership) but instead had killed a passing cancer specialist walking his dog. Norris McWhirter carried on with his brother's campaigning, the terrorists' actions proving a better recruiting sergeant for the Freedom Association than for the IRA. While the legislation the Thatcher government brought in to curb trade union power did not go as far as Strauss, Hoskyns or McWhirter would have wished, with their encouragement it certainly went further than the Cabinet minister responsible, Jim Prior, thought was prudent. Victory there could be measured by the decade's end, with the switch of the Freedom Association's campaigning zeal from facing down trade union muscle to combating the increasing will to power of the European Union, a process Thatcher had meanwhile done so much to advance. Long before that, her failure to adopt her Policy Unit's plans for root and branch reform of the home civil service hastened Hoskyns's departure, in 1983, while Strauss went off to teach management.

Trouble for Tina

Whether in think tanks or Parliament, the harsh realities of office were a dispiriting experience for those who had drawn up wish-lists for action while in opposition. In particular it was the industry secretary, Sir Keith Joseph, who floundered when compelled to bring his ideological thinking into line with the practicalities forced upon him by an economy in decline. In particular, the nationalized industries continued to be a huge drain on resources and demonstrated that while the government might talk the tough language of competition, in reality it was not ready to put the matter to the test. The plight of the nationalized British Steel Corporation was a case in point. Between 1975 and 1980, vastly increased state subsidies (equivalent to £221 for every household in the country) had seemingly muffled rather than stimulated productivity – to the extent that British Steel took double the man-hours to produce a tonne of steel compared with its main European competitors.[32] With mounting losses and facing 52,000 planned job cuts, British Steel's workers responded by going out on strike for the first three months of 1980. There were no cheap solutions. When the government appointed a new tough chairman in the Scots-American Ian MacGregor, the short-term costs of restructuring the industry actually involved yet another increase in the state subsidy. The same story unfolded in the nationalized car industry. Michael Edwardes, the energetic chairman of British Leyland, secured a further £900 million subsidy for the loss-making state-financed car manufacturer. Apart from its Land Rover division, it was reasonably assumed that no foreign buyer wanted to purchase British Leyland, with its disappointing car sales and dreadful strike record. Even Thatcher was not prepared to sanction the scale of job losses in the Midlands that withdrawing the subsidies would have involved. 'No,' she confirmed, she was not 'going to chop you off at the stocking tops'.[33] Hold-ups, handouts – the prime minister at least conjured an arresting image, albeit one that underlined how wretchedly dependent the nationalized industries were on taxpayer support. It was a lamentable situation in which years of pumping state investment into massive corporations had succeeded only in making them so uncompetitive that they could not be expected to survive a matter of months unless they were given yet more subsidy in the hope that, this time, they might somehow turn themselves around. For all his talk of slimming down the state while in opposition, Joseph merely seemed to be writing larger cheques for it once he was in office.

An even greater drubbing was delivered by the miners. In February 1981, the National Coal Board revealed plans to close down some of the most uneconomic pits. With the certainty of a nationwide strike if the plan was pushed through, Thatcher blinked. There were insufficient stockpiles to keep the power stations going during a protracted disruption. Another three-day week beckoned, with the country again reduced to candle power. The National Union of Mineworkers (NUM) could then prove as instrumental in bringing down Thatcher as it had with Heath. Faced with this prospect, the prime minister concluded that a confrontation with the miners could not be won and, therefore, must not be fought. The miners were duly bought off and the subsidizing of uneconomic pits continued. Privately, Thatcher began drawing up plans so that the next time the NUM threatened to plunge the country into darkness the government would be ready with a contingency plan. For the moment, though, it was yet another humiliating defeat.

Was anything going right for the Thatcher government? The party of private enterprise was letting thousands of firms go under, unwilling to assist them by lowering interest rates and encouraging a weaker, more competitive currency for fear that doing so would compromise its money supply strategy. Yet, at the same time, it was prepared to pump vast sums into failing nationalized companies rather than accept the consequences of open competition. At the annual conference of the CBI, its director general, Sir Terence Beckett, declared he was up for 'a bare-knuckle fight' with the government over its economic policy.[34] Such a level of hostility towards a Tory administration from the country's premier business organization was without precedent. There were, nonetheless, three major victories secured during this, the most testing period of the Thatcher government's decade in power, that were to prove among its most significant legacies. The first was the passage of the Housing Act 1980 which, in giving local authority tenants the right to buy their council houses, ensured one of the greatest transfers of property from state to citizens in British history. The passage of legislation aimed at curbing trade union power was also among the most significant acts of Thatcher's first term, largely freeing business from the unofficial walkouts, closed shop, all-union agreements and secondary picketing that had been a central feature of labour relations in the 1970s. The third achievement was the successful control of inflation. An annual rate of 18 per cent in 1980 declined to 8.6 per cent in 1982 and 4.6 per cent in 1983. It had last been that low in 1968. A seemingly rampant dragon had been, if not slain, then at least tamed – and the spectre that had haunted the 1970s, of Weimar or South American-style inflation destroying the nation's savings and potentially bringing down the democratic political system, was averted. Unfortunately, at the time Thatcher remained vulnerable to the charge that the attack on inflation was conducted with such single-minded ferocity that it had caused the collateral damage of a crippled economy and three million on the dole. The old saw was revived about an operation being successful although the patient died.

The difficulty of finding a reliable measure of how the money supply really was growing – let alone whether this was the only cause of inflation – compounded the Treasury's difficulty in determining whether it was administering the correct dosage of purgatives. To monetarism's believers, a plunging inflation rate was proof that the medicine was working and provided encouragement to keep on with it. This attitude only made sceptics even more fearful that the monetarists simply did not know when to ease off and give sickly firms a chance to recover rather than face another, potentially debilitating, onslaught. Appeals for clemency made no sense to Thatcher, who did not see why the chance of a long-lasting victory over inflation should be casually thrown away by those who had never believed – or perhaps understood – the strategy in the first place. Sir Geoffrey Howe coined the uncompromising slogan in defence of persisting with the current policy, which would come to define the monetarist attitude: 'There Is No Alternative.' Shortened to the acronym 'Tina', this obdurate goddess of monetarism naturally attached itself to Thatcher herself.

At the Conservative Party conference in October 1980 the rumblings of dissent abounded. The Leader of the House of Commons, Norman St John Stevas, was heard warning about 'theoreticians living in an abstract world'.[35] St John Stevas, at least, was in the habit of separating his personal regard for Maggie from his imperviousness to 'Tina'. Other 'wets' had reached the point where personalities and policies could no longer be kept apart. Jim Prior looked across at his 'dry' colleagues running economic policy and dismissed them contemptuously: 'None of them had any experience of running a whelk-stall, let alone a decent-sized company.'[36] The parliamentary party as well as the Cabinet were showing increasing signs of being in mutinous mood. On 27 February 1981, Thatcher received a memo from Ian Gow, her loyal parliamentary private secretary, warning her that 'there has been a noticeable deterioration in the morale of our backbenchers'.[37] The last date for a general election was still more than three years away, but the opinion polls suggested the prospect of wholesale slaughter. Backbench tetchiness was, however, less likely to oust the prime minister, or her Chancellor, than a putsch in the Cabinet. The dissidents there had ceased to keep their feelings to themselves, engaging in what Thatcher described as 'the indecent obscurity of leaks to the *Guardian*'.[38] She thought she detected in their attitude a contempt that stretched far beyond the parameters of monetary policy. 'In the eyes of the "wet" Tory establishment,' she later unburdened herself, 'I was not only a woman, but "that woman", someone not just of a different sex, but of a different class, a person with an alarming conviction that the values and virtues of middle England should be brought to bear on the problems which the establishment consensus created.'[39] Speaking the day after the 1981 budget at a lunch for the Young Businessman of the Year (the idea of a businesswoman had seemingly not yet dawned on the event's sponsor, the *Guardian*), Thatcher failed to conceal her contempt for those who, despite wanting higher public spending, criticized the tax rises Howe had felt compelled to introduce. 'What really gets me,' she railed, in words that suggested she was talking specifically about her ministerial colleagues, 'was that they really were saying, "We don't like the expenditure we have agreed, we are unwilling to raise the tax to pay for it. Let us print the money instead." The most immoral path of all. Because what that is saying is let us quietly steal a certain amount from every pound in circulation, let us steal a certain amount from every pound saved in building societies, in national savings, from every person who has been thrifty.'[40]

A paper setting out proposals for further spending restraint in 1982 had the Cabinet in uproar. Only Keith Joseph and the prime minister seemed to think it plausible and further discussion was duly postponed until the autumn. Thus Thatcher went into the summer vacation aware that for her to survive either her Chancellor would have to burn the hair shirt or she would have to cull the leading dissidents in her Cabinet. She chose the latter. In September 1981, a reshuffle was announced that prised away several of the most persistent 'wets' from their ministerial berths. Sir Ian Gilmour did not take well to being sacked and promptly appeared in front of the television cameras to announce that the government was 'steering full speed ahead for the rocks'. It was a bold performance from the ex-Lord Privy Seal, which Thatcher acidly described in her memoirs as resembling 'a flawless imitation of a man who has resigned on principle'. In a further twist of the knife, she added that he 'was to show me the same loyalty from the back benches as he had in government'. Churchill's son-in-law, Christopher Soames, took his sacking with moderately more dignity but no less of a sense of social outrage: 'I got the distinct impression,' Thatcher recalled, 'that he felt the natural order of things was being violated and that he was, in effect, being dismissed by his housemaid.'[41] Other 'wet' casualties took their fate with better grace. Mark Carlisle was asked to vacate education and Jim Prior was persuaded, against his initial inclinations, to run Northern Ireland. These changes came on top of the sacking back in January 1981 of Norman St John Stevas. He had been an early supporter of Thatcher personally and his criticisms had usually been coated in fey and genial good humour, speaking of his boss as 'the blessed Margaret' and 'the Leaderene'. Alas, she was no longer in the mood to be tickled by such whimsy.

It was not just the demotion of the 'wets' but the promotion of the 'dries' that made the reshuffle significant. In Prior's seat as secretary of state for employment now sat Norman Tebbit. The ruddy-faced Tory squire had been replaced by someone with the lean demeanour of a Dickensian poor law commissioner. Hard times were indeed something of which he had had first-hand experience during his working-class childhood. Educated at a selective state school, Tebbit's university had been the RAF, where he had flown Vampire jets before becoming an airline pilot. Never shy about expressing his feelings, he had few doubts that the prime minister was on the right track and that further legislation was necessary to restrain the power of the trade unions. Lord Thorneycroft, the party chairman, who had admitted to suffering from 'rising damp', was replaced by Cecil Parkinson, a rapid promotion from a junior position at the Department of Trade. The son of railway worker, Parkinson was a grammar-school boy who had won a scholarship to Cambridge. His flirtation there with student socialism was now long behind him. His loyalty to Thatcher was complete. Others who, if not necessarily safe in all weathers were at least wax-proofed against wetness, included Norman Fowler, who went to the Department of Social Security, and Nigel Lawson, who, given the Department of Energy, began the process of privatization.

The reshuffle did not make the prime minister safe. She knew she could count on the loyalty of the Home Secretary, Willie Whitelaw, and an unspoken understanding meant that she effectively gave Lord Carrington a free hand to run foreign policy in return for accepting that his world view did not include domestic politics. With Prior immersed in the troubles of Northern Ireland, the two colleagues who might prove the most dangerous to her were Peter Walker and Michael Heseltine. Neither was yet in a position to strike a fatal blow.

Thus it fell to Edward Heath to denounce the government's economic policy from the platform of the party conference in October 1981. It was an extraordinary spectacle, the ex-leader of the Conservative Party publicly declaring his successor was fundamentally in error. Blackpool's serried ranks were treated to a performance that may have reminded more elderly delegates of Khrushchev's 1956 denunciation of Stalin at the Twentieth Congress of the Communist Party. But except in the jowls, Heath was no Khrushchev. He represented not the expectation of a new generation but what the latter regarded as the failure from which escape was being sought. His own mid-term U-turn had not prevented his premiership from ending in ignominious defeat, first at the hands of the miners and soon after from the electorate – twice. It was the memory of those humiliations that helped persuade apprehensive Conservatives to give Thatcher's experiment the continued benefit of the doubt. But that benefit would not continue indefinitely if she carried on regardless and the economy showed few meaningful signs of recovery. In November, she appeared close to despair when privately taking into her confidence the sympathetic editor of the *Sunday Express*, John Junor. Her colleagues were all 'in an utter funk', with only 'Willie, Geoffrey, Cecil and Norman I can count on'.[42] In her memoirs, Thatcher wrote: 'I had said at the beginning of the government, "give me six strong men and true, and I will get through." Very rarely did I have as many as six.'[43]

4 GHOST TOWN

Breadline Britain

At the trough of the recession in 1981, the aggregate valuation of the largest UK companies was lower than it had been, adjusted for inflation, at the time of the British evacuation from Dunkirk in 1940. As Oxford's leading Marxist economics don, Andrew Glyn, pointed out, capitalists had seen more grounds for optimism at the moment the country appeared on the brink of succumbing to Hitler than they did in looking forward to a few more years of Thatcherism.[1]

It was particularly the manufacturing sector that bore the brunt of the bleak expectations. As a share of total UK output, it had already slid from 34 per cent to 30 per cent between 1970 and 1977.[2] Between 1978 and 1981, it fell from 29.3 per cent to 25.0 per cent, its access to affordable credit curtailed by high interest rates and (a related consequence of high interest rates) the soaring sterling exchange rate, which cut into export competitiveness. Manufactures had comprised 83 per cent of total UK exports in 1973, but accounted for only 66 per cent by 1983. Over the same period, manufactured imports rose from 39 per cent to 51 per cent.[3] That the country was no longer the workshop to itself, let alone the world, was made manifest in 1983 when, for the first time on record, the value of manufactures imported exceeded those exported. By then, the share of the workforce engaged in manufacturing was down to 26 per cent, having stood at 35 per cent only a decade earlier. Thereafter, as the economy recovered, the rate of the manufacturing sector's contraction slowed. Indeed, some manufacturing firms that had survived the onslaught of 1979–82 were, or had become, sufficiently lean and competitive to enjoy strong growth. Nevertheless, although total manufacturing output recovered and by the decade's end was 12 per cent higher than its 1979 level, it continued to shrink in proportion to the rest of the economy. By 1989, manufactures represented only 22.2 per cent of national output.[4]

Optimists looking for evidence that traditional manufacturing's contraction was part of a process of economic restructuring in which new technology-driven companies at the higher-value end of the market (though employing fewer staff) represented a brighter future latched on to specific success stories. Technology companies setting up in and around Cambridge's 'science park' caused the area to be referred to as 'Silicon Fen' (while a concentration of electronics firms in central Scotland ensured the inevitable coining of 'Silicon Glen'). During the early eighties, the prospect of Britain seriously rivaling California's Silicon Valley seemed far from ludicrous. In particular, two Cambridge-based companies, Acorn Computers and Sinclair Research, developed home computers at such affordable prices that they all but created the vast domestic market for these products.

In 1980, the Sinclair ZX80 became the world's first computer priced under £100. Even greater success followed with the ZX81 and, in 1982, with the Spectrum, whose first version alone sold into five million homes and became not just the bestselling personal computer in Britain but also helped make Sinclair Research – fleetingly – the market leader in the United States.[5] In 1983, with the prospect of global domination beckoning, Clive Sinclair was given a knighthood. At the same time, his former sales manager and, by then, rival at Acorn, Chris Curry (who, like Sinclair, had not been to university) was reaping the benefits from public funds, Acorn having won the contract to make the BBC Micro in association with the corporation's computer literacy television series. Ignoring the temptation to leave it to the market, the government became so convinced that microcomputers represented Britain's future, and (erroneously) that an ability to understand and write computer programs would become an essential core skill for the next generation, that between 1981 and 1986 the Department of Education heavily subsidized schools' purchasing of, in particular, BBC Micros and the training of teaching staff to go with them. In 1983, Acorn floated, allowing its founders, Chris Curry and his Cambridge-graduate colleague, Herman Hauser, to see a company they had started in 1977 with only £100 of capital increase its value one million-fold. Acorn looked poised to grow into a British Apple.

Unfortunately, it was only Apple's period of commercial difficulties that Acorn soon resembled. In launching the Electron (its rival to the Sinclair Spectrum), it initially proved unable to meet the high demand with supply and then compounded matters by eventually exceeding an appropriate quantity of supply after the demand had evaporated. Sinclair Research faced comparable problems. A licensing agreement in the United States with Timex resulted in delays to the release of an improved Spectrum model and the American market was lost. In 1984, Sir Clive's next computer, the QL, was unveiled for the professional market, potentially offering British competition to the Apple Macintosh launched in the same year. But like the Electron, the QL also suffered supply problems and, additionally, proved to be riddled with glitches. Faith in Sir Clive's entrepreneurial genius was dented further when in 1985 he unveiled the C5, a futuristic-looking tricycle with backup power from an electric battery. With a maximum speed of 15 miles per hour and an inability to conquer going up gradients, the C5 better resembled a luxury-end children's toy than the future of transport. In a matter of months, Sir Clive went from being portrayed as the British economy's great white hope to a national laughing stock.

These commercial misjudgments shattered the ambitions of Britain's two most promising computer companies to become globally dominant in their field. In 1985, Acorn had to be bailed out by the Italian firm, Olivetti, which bought a majority stake but thereafter failed to sustain Acorn as a computer-making company, while Sinclair's computers, sold to Alan Sugar's Amstrad for only £5 million in 1986, ceased production four years later. Flickering brightly from 1981 until 1984, Cambridgeshire's challenge to California had been brief and – in its quirky brilliance and erraticism – all too characteristically British. For all the hopes, what was achieved was never enough to compensate for the decade's job losses in more traditional manufacturing sectors.*

From the vantage point of his new academic post in West Germany, Britain's leading economic historian, Professor Sidney Pollard, surveyed what had been a decade of decline between 1972 and 1982 and lamented: 'After having led the world for two hundred years, Britain is no longer counted among the economically most advanced nations of the world. A wide gap separates her from the rest of industrialized Europe. The difference as measured in national produce per head between Britain and, say, Germany, is now as wide as the difference between Britain and the continent of Africa. One short generation has squandered the inheritance of centuries.'[6] Both Labour and Conservative administrations fell within the scope of Pollard's indictment, though Thatcher's Chancellor had set the scene for his first budget speech, in 1979, by emphasizing how far the country had already sunk by the time the Tories returned to office. 'Only a quarter of a century ago – within the memory of almost every member of this House,' Sir Geoffrey Howe stated:

> the people of the United Kingdom enjoyed higher living standards than the citizens of any of the larger countries of Europe. Amongst the free nations of the world, Britain was then second only to the United States in economic

---

* However, after the eighties ended, Acorn's spin-off company, ARM, was ultimately to justify faith in Cambridge as 'Silicon Fen.' Assisted by Apple's minority shareholding, ARM developed and licensed microchips so efficient that by 2010 they were used in almost all the world's mobile phones and in digital cameras, iPods, iPads and other market-leading handheld devices. By 2012, ARM Holdings, still headquartered in Cambridge, enjoyed a market valuation of almost £8 billion and proved there was a British company that could be a world leader in technology after all.

strength. It is not so today. For example, France and Germany's combined share of world trade in manufactured goods, which in 1954 was almost the same as Britain's alone, is now more than three times as large as ours. The French people now produce half as much again as we do. The Germans produce more than twice as much, and they are moving further ahead all the time.[7]

The visible manifestations of decay were not confined to the factory floor. Summing up cross-Channel differences in 1979 at the end of his term as ambassador in Paris, Sir Nicholas Henderson felt compelled to point out: 'You only have to move about Western Europe nowadays to realize how poor and unproud the British have become in relation to their neighbours. It shows in the look of our towns, in our airports, in our hospitals and in local amenities; it is painfully apparent in our railway system.'[8] Henderson's sense of national inferiority did not improve following his relocation to Washington, DC. In July 1981, he confided to his diary: 'I find that the hopes I entertained exactly two years ago that we might be going to turn over a new leaf under Maggie have been dashed. Our plight is worse than two years ago because we appear to have tried something new and it has failed.'[9]

In terms of urban appearance, the United Kingdom had certainly reached a nadir. The worst of the old brick back-to-back slums, with their high, imprisoning backyard walls and outside privies had been demolished during the three preceding decades, but by the early eighties the 'brave new world' sheen of their prefabricated tower-block replacements was already visibly tarnished, the shoddiness of their construction revealed by uncompromising concrete exteriors streaked by the weather and interiors disintegrating through rising damp. Investment in improving – or demolishing – these failing housing schemes lay years ahead, as, for the most part, did the effort to clean those older buildings that had survived 'comprehensive redevelopment'. In 1980, much of the Victorian civic grandeur – whose proud and ornamental exteriors restoration would subsequently revive – was still veiled in a thick layer of funereal cinders (a deindustrializing economy did at least bring with it cleaner air), while the once majestic proportions of their interiors were too often concealed by the installation of cheap partitions and false ceilings, strip lighting and supposedly protective layers of asbestos.

Unsurprisingly, the urban population voted with its feet. The exodus from Britain's cities was a marked demographic trend by the time Thatcher came to power. Despite continued national population growth during the 1970s, only two of England and Wales's twenty-one largest towns and cities (Plymouth and Dudley) saw an increase in the number of their inhabitants. During the seventies, Greater London suffered a net loss of three quarters of a million citizens. Birmingham, Liverpool and Manchester each leaked over one hundred thousand inhabitants. In Scotland, meanwhile, Glasgow, which

THE SUNDAY TIMES *magazine*

APRIL 27, 1980

HER FIRST YEAR

The iconography of the Iron Lady: Thatcher as national saviour. The putti around her head are her Cabinet colleagues, Sir Geoffrey Howe, Lord Carrington, Willie Whitelaw, Sir Keith Joseph and Jim Prior. A full decade before he made his challenge, Michael Heseltine is already depicted, bottom right, looking impatient.

The Long Hot Summer begins. Police attempting to reclaim Railton Road – Brixton's 'frontline' – from rioters in April 1981.

Thatcher in Thornaby in 1987 launching the Teesside Development Corporation, oblivious to how the image of her walking through a post-industrial wilderness might be interpreted. Her return, a decade later, to admire its rejuvenation as a business park employing 4,500 people failed to conjure an equally enduring image.

Michael Foot limbers up for the 1983 general election campaign.

The 'Gang of Four'. From left to right (literally and politically): Bill Rodgers, Shirley Williams, Roy Jenkins and David Owen. The pretence that they were all equal leaders of their Social Democratic Party did not last long.

Mission Accomplished. HMS *Illustrious* returns to Portsmouth from the Falkland Islands, 17 September 1982.

The Greenham Common women's peace camp helped revive the Campaign for Nuclear Disarmament and became the most enduring protest of the 1980s, so much so that their camp did not close until 2000 – eleven years after the departure of Greenham's last Cruise missiles.

earlier in the century had been the 'second city of the Empire', appeared to be in terminal decline, a city of over one million inhabitants in 1961 was down to nearly 880,000 by 1981. The long process of slum clearance there had hardly transformed the quality of the housing stock. In 1981, 40 per cent of those Glaswegians who remained were graded as being poorly housed. It was difficult to avoid the conclusion that the past twenty years, in which the wrecking ball had been the harbinger of comprehensive redevelopment, had failed to make Britain's cities more attractive places in which to live.

Indeed, planning blight's urban disfiguration left large patches of land – often in the heart even of prosperous cities – as a weed-growing wilderness. At best, these gap sites found a use as car parks – the fate, for instance, until the mid-eighties of a large stretch of what ought to have been prime real estate stretching along Lothian Road at right angles to Edinburgh's celebrated retail boulevard of Princes Street. The city centres of Hull, Nottingham and Bristol still contained sizeable undeveloped sites where German bombs had fallen forty years previously. Incredibly, even in the high-property-value square mile of the City of London, the last bombsite from the Blitz was not developed until 1998. The area of London next to Tower Bridge – one of the most photographed sights in the capital – also remained a gap site, while the long stretch of Docklands on both sides of the Thames beyond the bridge to the east had degenerated into a vast zone of desolation, the rapid decline of the Port of London symbolized by miles of disused warehouses, pocked with broken window panes and bordered by stagnant canals, plugged by boluses of litter. Developers had yet to sell the benefits of warehouse living, a solution that, by the end of the eighties, was to transform the Docklands (and other areas of crumbling Victoriana like it) into a desirable domestic haven for new money. Thirty years on, it is necessary to have recourse to a wide collection of photographs and film footage to appreciate the extent of Britain's urban shabbiness at the moment the seventies gave way to the new decade.

The dishevelment could only be made more depressing by the doubling of unemployment between May 1979 and January 1982, when it passed three million, or one in eight of those of working age. The job losses brought in turn further signs of decay – closed and shuttered shopfronts and factories lying idle. Touring depressed parts of the country, the journalist Beatrix Campbell noticed the extent to which the social landscape had been transformed by unemployment:

> The first thing you see in Sunderland, Coventry or Rotherham is shopping precincts packed with women *and* men. In the middle of a weekday afternoon, men are sitting around on public benches once occupied only by pensioners and mothers, you see denimed youths of nineteen or twenty pushing buggies,

queues of men cashing giros in the same number as women cashing child benefit and old people collecting their pensions.[10]

The explanations for what had gone wrong were as various as the prescriptions for how to put it right. At least those who were politically engaged saw the prospect of ultimate salvation – whether through the Thatcherite medicine eventually working, or it being scrapped by a re-elected Labour government committed to a programme of extensive public spending and tariffs to keep out foreign competition. By contrast, those who concluded that jobs for manual and unskilled workers would never return, because labour-saving automation had effectively abolished an entire stratum of the job market, could only look to the future and despair. A similar mood engulfed those who believed that, regardless of whatever help government gave it, British industry would never return to a position of competitiveness against the low-cost Asia-Pacific economies, and that the first industrial nation was fast becoming the first post-industrial one. The sense of scarcely comprehending bewilderment was most memorably encapsulated in Yosser Hughes, a fictional Liverpudlian, whose plight in Alan Bleasdale's 1982 series of five television plays, *Boys from the Blackstuff*, made him a totem for the times. Unable to come to terms with an environment that could offer him nothing tangible, the increasingly desperate Hughes slipped towards hopelessness, extreme violence and mental disintegration, while endlessly beseeching anyone he thought could help him to 'Gizza' job!'

For the one in eight without jobs, unemployment benefit – at £25 per week or £1,300 per year in 1982 – hardly offered in itself a viable alternative income. In January 1984, ITV's *World in Action* ran an experiment entitled 'For the Benefit of Mr Parris' in which the young Conservative MP, Matthew Parris, was sent to live for a week in the Scotswood area of Newcastle, where the male unemployment rate was 80 per cent, on an unemployed single man's allowance, which by then had reached £26.70. He managed to make his money last five days, which meant he had nothing for the weekend. Without abandoning his view that there was little that government could do to create jobs for which there was no longer a market, Parris admitted that his fellow free-marketeers erred in implying that joblessness was somehow the fault of the unemployed: 'Is there any way you can tell a man that his industry, his job and his family are necessary, even glorious, casualties in the battle to transform the British economy and revolutionize social attitudes – and make him feel good about it?'[11]

In most cases, unemployment benefit was not the only source of income, since three quarters of those on the dole also received supplementary benefit, while a further 1.4 million received supplementary benefit without being on the dole. The growth of top-up benefits to deal with poverty on this scale was a recent phenomenon. In the 1960s and early 1970s, only a quarter of unemployment claimants also received supplementary benefit.[12] While the precise amount of benefit varied according to circumstance, an unemployed couple living together with a child in 1982 might expect to receive £60–65 per week, at a time when those living in straitened circumstances in the Midlands or northern England typically had to find £25–35 per week to cover rent, electricity and gas bills. By being frugal, the family food bill might be kept down to £15, but this left little spare for more expensive, if occasional, items like new clothing and furniture, and almost none for luxuries. A study by the Child Poverty Action Group and the Family Service Unit in 1981 suggested that 80 per cent of those on social security borrowed money to meet their housing and fuel bills – which, in the case of some loan companies, involved repayments at very high rates of interest.[13] By 1985, 9.4 million Britons were living on or below supplementary benefit level, an increase since 1979 of 54 per cent.[14]

After Belgium, the UK's unemployment rate in the early eighties was the highest in the European Community, and by 1982 there were thirty-two dole claimants for every unfilled job vacancy (at the time of the 1979 general election the ratio had been five to one). It was the young who were the hardest hit, with one fifth of the unemployed being under twenty and 40 per cent under twenty-five years old. Regional variation was especially marked, with joblessness nearing 20 per cent in Northern Ireland and standing at around 15 per cent in Scotland and northern England, but remaining well into single figures in parts of the South-East, where the economy was driven primarily by the less depressed service sector rather than by traditional industries. In 1981, almost 13 per cent of manual workers, 9.5 per cent of semi-skilled manual workers and 8.3 per cent of skilled manual workers were registered as unemployed, though only 2.1 per cent of professionals, 3.4 per cent of employers and managers and 4 per cent of other white-collar employees were similarly jobless.[15] The scale and geographical spread of the deprivation made the 1930s the obvious historical reference point, with community support centres, reminiscent of inter-war soup kitchens, opening up to feed and clothe families in unemployment hot spots. Inspired by the hunger marches of the period, and the 1936 Jarrow Crusade in particular, the TUC-supported People's March for Jobs set out from Liverpool on 1 May 1981 and arrived in London thirty days later, its core of five hundred marchers picking up sympathizers en route. Thatcher was no more prepared to receive the delegation than her predecessor in 1936, Stanley Baldwin, and the accompanying 250,000-strong petition demanding government action to cut the dole queues was ignored. In practical terms, the march achieved nothing. The left had reason to find the 1930s analogy alarming, not just because of the social consequences of a return to mass unemployment, but because if there was a political lesson to be learned from that period it was that socialism had failed to win power despite economic misery. In the thirties, as in the eighties, neither unemployment nor the fear of it was evenly spread across the country. Rather, the recession acted to polarize the country between a relatively prosperous (and Conservative-voting) South and the depressed, Labour-voting North, Scotland and Wales. Labour's problem was that deepening resentment against Thatcher in areas that were already Labour heartlands would not be, of itself, sufficient to swing the next election.

For it was these heartlands – almost precisely the same areas as had been hardest hit in the thirties – that bore the brunt a half century later. Armed with a copy of George Orwell's 1937 survey of northern poverty, *The Road to Wigan Pier*, sociologists and commentators naturally sought to examine the strength of the comparison. When the journalist Ian Jack visited Wigan in the autumn of 1982 he found that the industries around which the town had developed no longer existed: the nearby coal seams were exhausted and the cotton mills had closed down. Wigan's two remaining large employers were Tupperware and Heinz, whose vast factory was single-handedly feeding Britain's baked beans habit, at a rate of two thousand tins per minute, and whose three thousand employees could consider themselves the fortunate ones, given that almost 20 per cent of the town's working population was on the dole. For the young, the opportunities for play were curtailed as sharply as those for work. During the 1970s, the town had enjoyed at least one claim to cultural adventure as a centre of the Northern Soul scene, thanks to its famous nightclub the Wigan Casino. On Saturday nights, dolled-up youths from Greater Manchester would catch a late bus or train to Wigan to dance through to Sunday morning (the unusually long opening hours a product of the Wigan Casino's lack of a licence to sell alcohol) at a club that, in 1978, the American magazine *Billboard* had claimed pipped New York's Studio 54 as 'the best disco in the world'. Even this accolade was not enough for it to survive in the harsh environment of the early eighties. The Wigan Casino closed in 1981 and, following a fire, was demolished two years later.

Yet Ian Jack noticed there was little graffiti, litter or obviously antisocial behaviour. Locals proffered a variety of explanations for this, praising the town's strong Roman Catholic tradition (a legacy of nineteenth-century Irish immigration), contrasting it favourably with Liverpool (despite its similar ethnic and religious make-up), and expressing thankfulness that their town had not experienced the wide-scale Pakistani immigration of Bolton and Blackburn. Tory voters might be thin on the ground, but a trip to the local newsagent showed little appetite for left-wing journalism: while the shop made monthly sales of seven copies of *Tribune*, twelve of *Labour Weekly* and thirteen of the *New Statesman*, it was also selling twenty-two copies of *Investors Chronicle* and thirty-six copies of *The Lady*. Neither were arguments for socialism or capitalism remotely as popular as satire, with *Private Eye* selling two hundred copies a month. The most startling demand, though, was for computer magazines, of which the newsagent stocked twenty-five different titles, shifting an impressive 2,500 copies per month.[16] If Wigan was showing signs of social atomization, then the cause could be attributed to its denizens staying at home typing lengthy computer programs into their Sinclair ZX81s as much as to an absence of spare cash to splash out on an evening out. This apparent contradiction between tough times and access to new innovations was not a new one. When Orwell travelled his road to Wigan Pier he noted that 'twenty million people are underfed but literally everyone in England has access to a radio . . . Whole sections of the working class who have been plundered of all they really need are being compensated in part by cheap luxuries which mitigate the surface of life.'[17]

This was not the only continuity in the forty-five years separating the visits to Wigan by George Orwell and Ian Jack. Examining the household spending of the Armitage family – a husband who had been unemployed for two years, his wife and two small children – living on £73.60 per week (£63.10 social security and £10.50 family allowance) in their council house, Jack noted that the breakdown of their weekly budget was not so different from that of a similar Wigan family described by Orwell – albeit Jack conceded: 'Which unemployed Wigan miner in 1937 could have imagined that his unemployed grandson in 1982 would be able to afford a telephone, a washing machine and forty-eight hours of television a week?' Nevertheless, the shopping included a similar absence of fresh fruit (cans of fruit were the substitute), lack of quality meat and an emphasis on carbohydrates, such as pies and cakes. Furthermore, both generations were relying on 'clothing clubs' to dress them, and holidays were all but out of the question. The 28-year-old Mrs Armitage enjoyed reading historical novels, which she borrowed from a stall in Wigan market – paying a deposit, which was partially returned when she handed the book back, and investing her change in the deposit on the next title. She particularly liked Catherine Cookson's novels about life in the Victorian North: 'They make your problems look like nothing,' she pointed out, midway through describing a pit disaster.[18] Whether the Armitages, and those in similar predicaments, were displaying heroic stoicism or a sense of defeatist resignation was open to interpretation, but Jack was left with the distinct impression that Wigan seemed 'about as close to revolt as Weybridge'.[19]

Long Hot Summer – The Brixton and Toxteth Riots

Where mass unemployment created a sense of alienation it could be expected that school-leavers would feel it most intensely. Of the 1.2 million under-24-year-olds on the dole, over six hundred thousand were aged between sixteen and nineteen. There were particular black spots. In Manchester's Moss Side, for instance, the Hytner inquiry found unemployment among nineteen-year-olds exceeded 60 per cent and the rate in other deprived areas was not far behind. Even many of those who were kept active were not actually in full-time employment. One hundred and eighty thousand of them were on the Youth Opportunities Programme (YOP), a government-run scheme for sixteen- to eighteen-year-olds which the Thatcher government had inherited from its Labour predecessor and found itself, through necessity, vastly expanding. From 1983, every unemployed or non-college-/university-going sixteen-year-old was guaranteed a one-year course (two years from 1985) on the YOP's replacement, the Youth Training Scheme (YTS), which offered a mixture of work experience and further education. By 1986, almost one third of school-leavers were joining a YTS scheme rather than going into a job. In an effort to keep idle youths off the streets and to provide them with an alternative to what had formerly been offered by apprenticeships in different industries, the Conservatives found themselves presiding over a vast extension of state oversight. The experience of many on the scheme was that it was more a device for companies to exploit cheap labour than a means of providing the effective on-the-job training it promised; though there was no compulsion to choose a YTS scheme over being on the dole – at least until 1988, when unemployment benefit was finally withdrawn from those of YTS age who refused either to join the scheme or to get a job. As far as the government was concerned, it was better to have young people doing something at least vaguely constructive than sitting around idly claiming unemployment benefit. The most vehement critics were not so sure and considered it merely an elaborate deception, designed for no greater purpose than to massage the jobless statistics.

The spirit of hopelessness animating a large swathe of Britain's youth was never more poignantly expressed than by The Specials, a multi-racial 'ska' band from Coventry, one of the Midlands cities badly hit by the recession. 'Ghost Town' was written by the band's leader, Jerry Dammers, after passing through Glasgow. The relentlessly gloomy, eerie pace and slow reggae beat of the song were accompanied by lyrics that had all of punk's sense of nihilism but with greater poignancy and descriptive power. Ironically, the fracturing of society it described was being replicated within The Specials, the band members scarcely on speaking terms and on the verge of splitting up, their concerts marred by mindless audience violence.

The song was recorded with an accompanying wail, described by Dammers as being 'supposed to sound a bit middle eastern, like a prophecy of doom'.[20] The timing of its release could not have been more portentous, for 'Ghost Town' hit number one in the charts on 11 July. That weekend, Britain's inner cities were engulfed in riots as the anger of the country's youth spilled into an orgy of violence against police and property, with arson, looting and wholesale destruction on an unprecedented scale.

Stone-throwing and street barricades had, of course, become wearily familiar reoccurrences since the outbreak of the Troubles in Northern Ireland, but, aside from the rising tide of Saturday-afternoon football hooliganism, were far from the living memory of those on the mainland. The nearest thing to what became known as the 'long hot summer' of 1981 had been the Nottingham and Notting Hill race riots of 1958. Yet, ugly though those outbreaks were, they had involved little wholesale destruction and, at Notting Hill, only 140 arrests. By comparison, the riots of 1981 were national in scale, broader in cause, far more destructive in effect, and resulted in the arrests of three thousand people. The trouble in 1958 may have disturbed the self-satisfaction of a complacent post-war Britain; that of 1981 seemed to portend a society in crisis and terminal decline.

The first tremors of what was to follow were felt in Bristol in April 1980. There, a drugs raid on the Black and White Café in the city's run-down St Paul's district triggered a night of violent reprisals as the area's mostly West Indian immigrant community fought running battles with the police. Relations between the police and Britain's young immigrant population took a further turn for the worse in January 1981 when thirteen black partygoers died in a fire in Deptford. Two months later, ten thousand protesters marched to register their discontent with the perceived casual manner of the police investigation and anger at the Metropolitan Police's insistence – probably correctly, as subsequent inquiries discovered – that the tragedy was not the result of a racist arson attack. The march's organizers refused to cooperate with the police, and the mood of recrimination among some of those who marched from New Cross to central London was expressed by the throwing of bricks at constables and shop windows.

The anger towards the police felt by immigrant groups was not replicated in the country generally. Despite the periodic exposure of corruption and slipshod practices, the police enjoyed a high reputation. An opinion poll in September 1980 recorded that 71 per cent of respondents thought the police did a good job, and a further 26 per cent thought they did a reasonable job. Only 3 per cent thought they did a bad job. When asked to compare Britain with countries abroad, 83 per cent of those polled named the police as the first reason for taking pride in the country, far outstripping the second reason, tolerance and politeness, at 54 per cent (there was a net negative response to every other comparison between Britain and abroad).[21] For her part, Thatcher had always made it clear that respect for the police was a central tenet of the good society. In the first two years of her government, police officers' basic pay rose by over 50 per cent in absolute terms, an increase particularly marked when placed alongside the squeeze on other areas of the public sector.

Most respondents to opinion polls did not consider themselves likely targets for police harassment. Here, their experience and expectations were markedly different from those of young black people, who in some inner-city areas were disproportionately likely to be arrested on suspicion. A hangover from the vagrancy act of 1824, the 'sus' law allowed police to arrest anyone they suspected might be about to commit an offence, thus making it possible for them to acquire a criminal record without actually having committed a verifiable crime. There was no jury to sift the evidence, merely the say-so of two police officers and the judgement of a magistrate's court, where – in a reversal of the usual presumption of innocence until proved guilty – the defendant was expected to try to disprove the police officers' suspicion (and, in most circumstances, it could hardly be more than a suspicion). Across large parts of the country the charge was seldom brought, but it was still used in London and deployed disproportionately against black suspects (40 per cent of those arrested on suspicion by the Metropolitan Police in 1979 were black; in Lambeth, the figure was 77 per cent), at rates that exceeded the level of reported black street crime.[22] The government had decided to ditch the 'sus' law before the riots broke out, scrapping it in the criminal attempts act of 1981. Nevertheless, the damage was already done and police forces in high-crime areas continued to exercise stop-and-search powers in ways that caused resentment among those who felt themselves picked on because of their colour. Down at the police station, the ordeal could be severe and, on occasion, cross the line into torture. One means of wringing a confession out of a suspect involved forcing him to kneel with his toes against the interview-room skirting-board; pressure was then applied, which would cause excruciating pain to his heels, until he was ready to talk. There were cases of Rastafarians being shorn of their dreadlocks, which would then be pinned up on the noticeboard as a trophy.[23]

The situation was especially fraught in the London borough of Lambeth, where a quarter of the population (and 40 per cent of those under nineteen) were black. The epicentre of Lambeth's black population was Brixton, where over half of black sixteen- to nineteen-years-olds were registered for unemployment benefit. The recession of the early eighties tightened the knots of joblessness and deprivation in Brixton, but did not create them. Rather, the area had experienced decades of relative decline. There were twelve thousand houses deemed unfit for habitation and thousands more marked as sub-standard. Lambeth Council's housing department had eighteen thousand households on its waiting list. Running through Brixton's heart was an especially edgy zone bisected by Railton Road and known to locals as the 'Front Line'. Many of its shops and houses were boarded up. Patchworks of corrugated iron masked dilapidated premises and in the evening young people, mostly black, hung around waiting – not always for long – for something to happen.

Robbery and violent thefts rose by 38 per cent in London between 1976 and 1980, but in Brixton the increase was 138 per cent.[24] It was a spiralling crime wave, which – depending on your outlook – indicated either how ineffective policing was when it did not enjoy local support, or how even more unendurable life would have been for the law-abiding but for the strong police presence in the neighbourhood. By the onset of 1981, 'community policing' was largely in abeyance, having broken down in 1978 when three black members of the Council for Community Relations in Lambeth who happened to be wearing sheepskin coats had been wrongly arrested by police who were looking for a suspect whose principal description was that he was black and was wearing a sheepskin coat. Even without such provocations, part of the problem was that police officers resented the idea that they should discuss their actions with those they regarded as self-appointed political activists who did not necessarily speak for the community they claimed to represent. Indeed, many of those activists did not want to speak to the police: the leaders of almost fifty organizations representing ethnic minorities met in London and drew up a declaration instructing all black and Asian people to refuse to cooperate with the police, either by joining the force, helping out in identity parades or accepting offers to join liaison schemes. Such was the complete breakdown in dialogue that some police officers saw community leaders as more sympathetic to law-breakers than to the law-enforcers. When asked to explain why he had not fore-warned community leaders about a decision to conduct a stop-and-search swoop in Brixton, Commander Leonard Adams explained: 'No good general ever declares his forces in a prelude to any kind of attack.'[25]

It was hardly a novel strategy. Coordinated stop-and-search swoops had been implemented in inner-city areas throughout the 1970s, with constabularies bringing the Special Patrol Group (SPG), whose typically uncompromising and unapologetic attitude undermined any understanding among those stopped without due cause. In the Toxteth area of Liverpool, only 179 of the 3,482 people searched between January and July 1981 were arrested.[26] The plan to cut crime, especially mugging, in Brixton using plain-clothes policemen to stop and search suspects was codenamed Operation Swamp 81. The choice of title was certainly unfortunate. 'Swamp' referred to the all-out, comprehensive penetration of an area, but it had other connotations for those who remembered a passing comment Margaret Thatcher had made in the course of a 1978 interview, when she mentioned the fear some communities had of being 'swamped' by mass immigration. Swamp 81 started on Monday, 6 April 1981, and by the following Friday, 943 people had been questioned. Of these, just over half were black – a high figure, but not proof of explicit racial discrimination given the ethnic profile of Brixton's youth. Of the 943 individuals who were stopped and searched, ninety-three were arrested and seventy-five charged with minor offences. Only one suspect was accused of anything as major as robbery. As a means of targeting serious crime, the operation had clearly been a comprehensive failure. For the 850 people stopped without cause, the intrusive behaviour of the police represented harassment.

Thus, when unseasonably hot weather encouraged large numbers of mostly black young people to mill about Brixton's Front Line on Friday, 10 April, many were in no mood to fraternize with the police. All it needed was a spark to turn surliness into something uglier, and it duly came that evening when two police officers observed a man running from other black assailants and rushed to intervene. The man had a four-inch stab wound, but refused to answer police questions. A crowd gathered and, under the impression that the officers were hassling rather than helping the wounded man, enveloped him and facilitated his getaway. Now surrounded by an angry throng, the police officers radioed for back-up. The wounded man was duly spotted by other officers, who treated his life-threatening wound and called an ambulance. Yet, before it arrived, the crowd had again caught up with him, dragging him away and bundling him off to hospital in a passing car, amid shouts of 'We will look after our own.' The tension continued to mount in the course of the following twenty-four hours, during which an entirely false rumour was circulated that the wounded man had died as a result of police obstruction.

During the Saturday, crowds of white as well as black youths thronged on to the streets of Brixton and shortly after 6 p.m. they began angrily encircling police officers who were busy questioning a taxicab driver. Soon, bricks, stones and bottles were raining down on the police. For the first time in mainland Britain, petrol bombs were thrown. That the police had not foreseen the course events would take was evident from the fact that initially they lacked the riot gear to tackle a crowd that quickly degenerated into a mob. The arrival of properly protected police reinforcements did nothing to cower those who were by now determined on escalating the situation. Barricades were hastily strewn across Railton Road. A police van was set alight. A double-decker bus found itself in the wrong place at the wrong time. Its conductor was assaulted and it was commandeered and driven at the police line. Properties began to be set on fire. This was not entirely indiscriminate. For instance, a pub where black people had not felt welcome was burned to the ground, while the nearby anarchist bookshop, proudly displaying a poster supportive of the Bristol rioters in its window, was left untouched. A school on Effra Road was put to the torch. Fire engines and ambulances were prevented from reaching the burning buildings or treating the injured.

As the rioting and arson attacks intensified, the widespread smashing of shop windows and looting commenced. While television footage and eye-witness testimony showed the majority of the rioters to be black, the looters were more often white. Their opportunism was carried out with disturbing insouciance. One youth was observed breaking into a sports shop and unhurriedly trying on a succession of trainers until he found a pair that suited him.[27] As the police battled to regain control, a reporter from *The Times* captured the scene:

> The only sign of authority was an abandoned fire engine astride the junction, its windows smashed and its wrecked equipment strewn across the road . . . Red-hot debris dripped from a series of burning buildings along both sides of the road. Amid the roaring of the flames and crashing of collapsing buildings, there were screams and shouts. Despite the furnace of heat, figures could be seen running through the smoke, hurling missiles at unseen police.[28]

Where the police found themselves under the most determined assault was in a street off Railton Road. Fearing that lives were in danger as the full fury of the mob closed in, the chief superintendent on Effra Road radioed for urgent back-up: 'We are getting a good hiding and we can't hold out any longer.' Sure enough, his line broke and the mob burst through. Elsewhere, though, the police were beginning to gain the upper hand, progressing in a pincer movement from both ends of Railton Road to quell the epicentre of the insurrection. By 11 p.m., the strong arm of the law was back in control, but only fleetingly, for more trouble flared up on the Sunday and, less seriously, on the Monday as well, before finally petering out. In the space of three days, 450 people had suffered injuries. More than two hundred vehicles had been damaged or destroyed, including four ambulances and nine fire engines. One hundred and forty-five buildings had been damaged, twenty-eight of them wrecked by fire.

Television footage of central Brixton looking like charred remains from the Blitz naturally jolted the country and, when transmitted across the world, helped convince countless more foreigners that Thatcher's experiment in reversing Britain's decline was succeeding only in accelerating it. It was perhaps fortunate that law and order was in the hands of one of the prime minister's most emollient figures, the Home Secretary, Willie Whitelaw, who rushed to appoint an inquiry. Chaired by a suitably independent figure, Lord Scarman, its primary task was to analyse the law and order issues raised. Meanwhile, the Labour Party, while quick to denounce the violence, was equally quick to declare that the riot had been caused by unemployment – a link that Thatcher was understandably keen to dispute. In fact, both Conservative and Labour front benches downplayed the racial aspect in the Brixton riot, pointing out that whites were also involved. Of those charged, 67 per cent were black. It thus fell to Enoch Powell on the political right, and black activist groups on the left, to try and place race back at the centre of the debate.

Believing that Brixton was confirmatory evidence that his infamous 1968 prediction that there would be 'rivers of blood' if mass immigration continued, Powell seized his moment in the Commons, pointedly asking Whitelaw: 'In reflecting upon these events, will the Home Secretary and the government bear in mind, in view of the prospective future increase of the relevant population, that they have seen nothing yet?'[29] When the disturbances duly spread three months later, Powell again suggested that the behaviour of black people was the defining issue, assuring a radio interviewer: 'We have had deprivation, unemployment and all the rest for generations and people have not turned out to wreck their own cities and to attack the police.'[30] The issue of race – or racism – was also central to the case made by many of the most outspoken community leaders. Formed to advise those charged during the riot, the Brixton Defence Committee included members from the Black Women's Group, the Socialist Workers' Party and Blacks Against State Harassment (BASH). It made it clear it would have nothing to do with Scarman and would not cooperate with the state in any way. After bitter internal wrangling, it then expelled its white members, deciding it should be a blacks-only organization.

During what proved to be the long hot summer of trouble, only one riot could be demonstrably shown to have been, in the unambiguous sense of the term, a 'race riot'. On 3 July, three hundred white troublemakers, inspired by the National Front and its culturally related skinhead rock music scene, descended on Southall in west London, ostensibly to attend a gig by their band of choice, The 4-Skins. Southall was home to thirty thousand Asians and had been the scene of violent anti-National Front scuffles in 1979 during which a protester, Blair Peach, had been killed – it was widely rumoured as a result of police heavy-handedness. Rather than be taunted on their own doorstep, Southall's Asian youth massed on the streets to attack the assembling skinheads, who, outnumbered, turned and fled. The police intervened by trying to drive a wedge between the two groups, an action the Asians interpreted as being designed to protect the white extremists from getting the kicking that would otherwise have been their fate. Instead, it was the police who took the brunt of the Asians' fury, suffering over one hundred injuries. The pub where The 4-Skins had been due to perform was burned to the ground.

Coincidentally, on the same evening in another part of the country, police in the run-down Liverpool district of Toxteth tried to apprehend a black man who they thought was making off with a stolen motorbike. In fact, it was his own. The trouble began when his friends, trying to assist his escape, started pelting the police with stones. The following day, 4 July, as more police poured into the area, they were met with a full-scale riot by mobs of black and white youths. There were more than bricks and bottles with which to contend. Among the stolen vehicles driven straight at the police line were a fire engine, a milk float and a cement-mixer. As one police officer was carried out with a six-foot iron railing javelined into his head, the mob could be heard above the shouts and the noise screaming 'Stone the bastards.' As the flames spread, it looked as if they would engulf the Princes Park geriatric hospital and its ninety-six patients had to be swiftly evacuated. As at Brixton, eye-witnesses noted the brazen calmness with which looters operated under cover of the riot, turning up with shopping carts to facilitate their supermarket sweep. 'Refrigerators, dryers, you name it,' reported one observer of the scene, 'I even saw one lady hold up a piece of carpet and ask if anyone knew whether it was 6 ft by 4 ft.'[31]

During the Sunday night, 5 July, 229 police officers were hospitalized by the injuries they sustained trying to regain control of Toxteth. By 2 a.m., the conclusion was reached that they could not achieve it through conventional means. For the first time on Britain's streets, the police resorted to using CS gas to clear a riot. Unsure and not properly trained in what they were doing, they fired cartridges of the gas intended for penetrating doors rather than dispersing crowds, an error that resulted in five injuries. By Monday, Liverpool City Council was requesting that troops be put on stand-by. The government refused. After four days, the police finally brought the situation under some semblance of control. But, in all, the force sustained eight hundred casualties and made over seven hundred arrests. Over one hundred buildings had been destroyed.

While the battle of Toxteth was in full swing, troublemakers in other cities replicated the mayhem. A mixed black and white crowd a thousand strong gathered in Manchester's Moss Side on 8 July and attacked a police station. It was not until 4 a.m. that they were dispersed, and they were back the next day. Having initially tried a softly-softly approach, Manchester police switched to meet the aggression head-on, successfully breaking up the riots through the use of snatch squads jumping from fast-moving police vans – a tactic that had been used in Ulster – and meeting violence with violence. By 11 July, they had regained control, making 241 arrests and suffering twenty-seven injuries. That weekend there were also major incidents in Battersea, Brixton, Dalston, Streatham and Walthamstow in London, and across the country in Aldershot, Bedford, Birmingham's Handsworth district,

Blackburn, Bolton, Cardiff, Chester, Derby, Edinburgh, Ellesmere Port, Halifax, High Wycombe, Huddersfield, Leeds, Leicester, Luton, Newcastle, Nottingham, Portsmouth, Preston, Reading, Sheffield, Southampton, Stockport and Wolverhampton. This involved a lot of copy-cat activity, the disturbances representing an excuse for self-centred hooliganism as well as coherent political protest. A fire-bomb was even thrown at a police car in rural Cirencester. Yet some of the disturbances were the result of specific triggers. A heavy-handed attempt by police to find a bomb-making factory in Brixton succeeded only in ripping through houses lived in by black people and sparking further street riots three months after they had first flared there, resulting in a further forty police injuries and 231 arrests. The scale of the nationwide disorder put pressure on overcrowded prisons. Whitelaw proposed using army camps to hold those detained on charges. He also indicated that the police would be given armoured vehicles if they requested them. The emergency tactics of Ulster's security forces were now being visited upon the mainland.

On the night of 28 July, there was another riot in Toxteth, during which a police van accidentally ran over a disabled white man, the one fatality of the summer of chaos. It proved to be the last rumble of unrest, the riots fizzling out as suddenly as they had ignited. The following day, Charles, Prince of Wales, married Lady Diana Spencer in St Paul's Cathedral and a country that was locked in recrimination and shame showed itself no less overcome with celebration and national pride. Twenty-eight million Britons – more than half the population – watched the 'fairy-tale wedding' (as it was billed) live on television. The worldwide viewing audience topped 750 million. In some towns and cities, neighbourhoods strewn with bricks and broken bottles lay cheek by jowl with streets decked with red, white and blue bunting. Such was the paradox of Britain in the summer of 1981. Alternating between television images of a country engulfed in patriotic pomp and violent circumstance, the rest of the world must have found it perplexing.

One thing became clear as the dust settled: a lot more planning had gone into making their Royal Highnesses' wedding a happy day than had been expended in planning the riots. There had been a fear that rabble-rousers had stirred up and orchestrated the violence. After Brixton's first eruption in April, a gang of black men had taken one journalist, blindfolded on the journey, to see the extent of their amateur bomb-making factory, assuring him: 'There's going to be a lot more, a big lot more, just tell 'em that. We ain't kidding. We goin' burn 'em down, everythin', everywhere.'[32] Newspapers began trying to identify which known political militants had been seen where in the days leading up to the trouble. The government's decision to impose a one-month ban on all processions in London during July aimed at forestalling inflammatory demonstrations and counter-marches between the National Front and the Anti-Nazi League. Yet, while politically motivated activists may have joined the riots, neither subsequent investigations nor the profile of those arrested suggested that known activists were a major presence or that there was any concerted and premeditated plan of attack. In that sense, the trouble was spontaneous.

Societal problems, such as the erosion of the family unit and the diminishing role of discipline in schools, were suggested as causes. Of all the things the rioters lacked, respect for authority was clearly the most evident. It was not just the prime minister who suggested the pernicious legacy of the permissive society. Even Lambeth's Labour MP, John Fraser, suggested family breakdown was among the main causes in Brixton. For most critics of the government, however, unemployment was a more obvious explanation. Sixty per cent of Toxteth's black population was thought to be unemployed; a figure of 70 per cent was posited for Moss Side's black and Asian youth. The majority of those charged during the Brixton and Toxteth riots were unemployed at the time of their arrest, although government ministers preferred to focus on the convictions of those who were in work or, indeed, still at school. As far as Roy Hattersley, Labour's home affairs spokesman, was concerned, there was obviously a link between unemployment, a lack of anything positive to do, and a descent into conflict. As he told the Commons on 16 July: 'I repeat that I do not believe that the principal cause of last week's riots was the conduct of the police. It was the conditions of deprivation and despair in the decaying areas of our old cities.'[33] Those who sought to deny any causation looked callously out of touch. Nevertheless, deprivation struggled to provide a full explanation. After all, unemployment levels were just as severe in areas like South Wales, Tyneside and Strathclyde, which were untouched by rioting. Far worse rates of unemployment and poverty in the 1930s had not produced civil disorder. What the public believed can best be gauged from a nationwide opinion poll conducted by MORI in August. It found that 62 per cent of respondents thought that unemployment had caused the riots, while 26 per cent thought race was the issue and 17 per cent blamed the behaviour of the police. Nevertheless, attributing the cause was not to be confused with condoning the actions. An ORC poll for the *Guardian* showed overwhelming public sympathy for the police, not the rioters.[34]

While the search for the deep-seated reasons focused on socioeconomics, there was no escaping the reality that the spark for the fires of Brixton and Toxteth was not the closure of a particular local workplace but specific police actions that local youths had interpreted as harassment. Indeed, an editorial in the Police Federation's magazine went so far as to blame the resentment of Brixton's black youth on 'the very success of the police measures against crime'.[35] The realities were brought home to Michael Heseltine, the environment secretary, when he toured Liverpool in the aftermath of the Toxteth riots. Crime was clearly rife, yet those speaking for the local community often blamed intrusive policing for the trouble. Relations between police and community were all but non-existent, making it difficult for police officers to identify suspects. Without meaningful inside intelligence, they fell back on trying to find a black suspect by the almost random stopping and searching of black people. The targeting of a specific ethnic group could hardly have been a blunter, or more grossly insensitive, tool of investigation. In response, some vocal community activists wanted the immediate abolition of the police's stop-and-search powers – the Brixton Defence Committee, for instance, wanted the whole area to be a no-go zone for the police. That was hardly practical. More significantly, the Labour Party was moving towards a policy of bringing the police under far greater accountability. In May 1981, Labour gained control of the Greater London Council with Ken Livingstone, an articulate critic of the police, becoming the city's leader. His group won power in the capital with a programme that demanded that the Metropolitan Police be made directly accountable to the GLC and that the Special Patrol Group, the Illegal Immigration Intelligence Unit and Special Branch should all be disbanded. These were not policies to which the Conservative government was likely to give its assent, but the way the Tories' popularity was sliding appeared to indicate that Livingstone's residency at County Hall would last rather longer than Mrs Thatcher's tenure on the other side of Westminster Bridge.

The idea that police racial prejudices might be rife did permeate beyond the far left. First broadcast in November 1980, after the Bristol riot but before Brixton erupted, a celebrated highlight of the BBC satirical sketch show *Not the Nine O'Clock News* featured Rowan Atkinson as a police inspector berating one of his underlings, a Constable Savage, played by Griff Rhys Jones, for arresting the same man, a Mr Winston Codogo, 117 times on a succession of preposterously trumped-up charges. When prompted, Savage improbably claimed not to have noticed whether Mr Cadogo was a black man. The sketch appeared in the same show as featured a gag about the Queen failing to identify the thief who had stolen her handbag, accompanied by a photo of Her Majesty inspecting a guard of black soldiers.

A serious effort to bring closure to the debate was made in November 1981 with the publication of Lord Scarman's inquiry into the Brixton riots. His report acquitted the police of over-reacting in response to the outbreak of trouble and upheld the bravery of officers who 'stood between our society and a total collapse of law and order on the streets'. But it also found fault with the police's lack of transparency, failure to discipline some officers and its unattractiveness to ethnic minorities. It recommended that racist behaviour by police officers should be a sackable offence and called for concerted attempts to enlist ethnic minority recruits. It also proposed new statutory consultative committees for community liaison. Noting that 'by and large, people do not trust the police to investigate the police', Scarman demanded proper independent monitoring of the police complaints procedure. Importantly, he argued that random stop-and-search powers should be better regulated, but not prohibited. While concluding that the riots 'were essentially an outburst of anger and resentment by young black people against the police', Scarman felt compelled to stray into social matters, advising that the 'social context in which policing is carried out could not be ignored'. The government should act to reduce inequality in housing, education and employment, which disfigured urban communities, and it should do so, at least in the short term, by positive discrimination in favour of ethnic minorities. The thrust of Scarman's findings immediately received cross-party support and were applauded by mainstream commentators in the media. It was the Brixton Defence Committee and some local activists, including Lambeth's council leader, Ted Knight, who dismissed Scarman out of hand.

Enacting statutory liaison committees and better complaints procedures was a matter for legislation. More difficult for a government philosophically entranced by the free market was how actively to improve the deprivation that scarred urban life. Michael Heseltine's brief included urban regeneration. He took two and a half weeks out of his Whitehall schedule in July to tramp the streets of Liverpool, partly to show the locals that the government was listening, partly to get a better gauge of realities on the ground. He found a port whose commercial *raison d'être* was much reduced; a city that had once been a magnet for immigration was shrinking and becoming a British Baltimore. A population of 867,000 in 1937 had slid to 610,000 in 1971. During the 1970s, it had lost a further 100,000 residents. Prosperous Liverpudlians had moved to the safety of the suburbs or the surrounding countryside. Local government had proved incapable of finding the means of arresting the decline by making the inner city attractive to new businesses. Talking to ordinary people was at first difficult, as Heseltine resisted the attempts of self-appointed community leaders to monopolize the debate. He was given an armed escort to meet one such source of local power, the Liverpool 8 Defence Committee, an experience he subsequently described as like 'sitting on a powder keg. The wrong gesture, the wrong remark and the whole thing could have exploded.'[36] Only slowly, through visits to youth clubs and community centres, did Heseltine feel he was able to get under the surface of the hostility.

Heseltine persuaded the chairmen of several major financial institutions to join him on a bus ride around the once great gateway to the Atlantic, followed by an effort temporarily to requisition their assistants for regeneration initiatives. Ever at ease in the glare of publicity, Heseltine was open to the charge that he was engaged in a publicity stunt, but by the time his tour was over he was already announcing a list of initiatives, including government grants for better sport facilities and workshops, help for small firms and encouragement for the opening of a northern branch of the Tate Gallery in the dilapidated Albert Docks. With a capable civil servant, Eric Sorensen, effectively acting as an executive for Liverpool's regeneration, Heseltine returned there to check on progress almost once a week throughout his remaining sixteen months as environment secretary. His report for the Cabinet was entitled *It Took a Riot*. Its recommendation for 'substantial additional public resources' to be directed 'to Merseyside and other hard-pressed urban areas to create jobs' ran contrary to the free-market ethos of the prime minister. Nevertheless, making £270 million available for urban redevelopment in 1981–2, Thatcher let her environment secretary continue with his work of making Liverpool a test bed for central government intervention where neither the free market nor left-wing municipal government seemed to offer quick solutions.

Independently of the riots, the government's main response to a decade of urban decay began to be implemented in 1981. Where Heseltine's focus on Merseyside involved state intervention to assist with public–private partnerships, elsewhere the emphasis was more on removing what were identified as the state's barriers to opportunity. This took the form of eleven 'enterprise zones' in deindustrializing centres like Newcastle, Clydebank, Belfast, Swansea and London's Docklands. This status simplified planning rules and exempted development from various tax restrictions. The transformation in the space of a decade of London's Docklands from a desolate wasteland into a desirable residential area and rival financial district to the City was the most visible manifestation of success. The opening in 1988 of Tate Liverpool in the lovingly restored Albert Docks – which immediately became not only a source of local pride but a major international visitor attraction – was testament to the work of the Merseyside Development Corporation and its success in attracting significant investment into a stretch of Liverpool whose purpose had seemingly disappeared in the seventies. The struggling city that missed out was Sheffield. Under David Blunkett's leadership, the steel city's Labour-controlled council refused the government's offer to set up a Sheffield enterprise zone with the dismissive riposte that free enterprise was the problem rather than the solution.

That the government was already working on such plans to attract investment to failing and increasingly post-industrial cities demonstrated that it had not just taken a riot. But for all the public show of defiance and support for the police, the Cabinet was severely shaken by the extent of civil disorder, with Heseltine given more autonomy and money as a result. Two speeches, delivered within hours of each other, at the 1981 Conservative

Party conference, were illustrative. The first was by Heseltine, who warned of the dangers of drawing racist conclusions from what had happened: 'There are no schemes of significant repatriation that have any moral, social or political credibility.'[37] The second was by the employment secretary, Norman Tebbit, who pointed out that when his father had been unemployed in the 1930s, instead of rioting, 'he got on his bike and looked for work'. Interestingly, both performances produced rapturous applause and standing ovations. Thatcher also visited Toxteth, but she delivered a verdict that was closer to the view of her employment secretary on whether it was the state or the individual who had to do something:

> I had been told that some of the young people involved got into trouble through boredom and not having enough to do. But you only had to look at the grounds around these houses with the grass untended, some of it almost waist-high, and the litter, to see this was a false analysis. They had plenty of constructive things to do if they wanted. Instead, I asked myself how people could live in such circumstances without trying to clear up the mess. What was clearly lacking was a sense of pride and personal responsibility – something which the state can easily remove but almost never bring back.[38]

And after three weeks topping the pop charts, The Specials' 'Ghost Town' gave way to Shakin' Stevens's cover version of the amiable 1950s hit 'Green Door'.

The Hunger Strikes

Perhaps it would have been surprising if the decade of unrelenting violence experienced in Northern Ireland, and regularly brought to the mainland in graphic news footage, had not produced some psychological effect upon the politics of protest in England, Scotland or Wales. In the year in which the mainland's riots resulted in one fatality, the Troubles in the Northern Irish corner of the United Kingdom resulted in 113. In order to provide even this level of security in the province, thirteen thousand soldiers were deployed, in addition to the RUC's policing efforts. During the 1970s, over two thousand people were killed in Ulster's political divisions and Thatcher's arrival in Downing Street saw no change of tactics by the Irish republican paramilitaries. On 27 August 1979, the IRA pulled off one of its 'spectaculars', within the space of hours killing eighteen soldiers at Warrenpoint in County Down and blowing up the Queen's cousin Lord Mountbatten, his teenage grandson and two others while they were enjoying a spot of lobster-potting off the Sligo coast. In all, 853 people would be killed as a consequence of the Troubles during the eighties.

There were around four hundred Irish republican prisoners detained in the H-blocks (so called because their layout resembled a letter H) of the Maze prison outside Belfast. In October 1980, the first of these inmates began a series of hunger strikes. The demands were not the generalized wish-list of revolutionary idealists. They were specific and confined to life behind bars, not the society beyond. The republican prisoners demanded the right to wear their own clothes, to have unrestricted freedom of movement within the prison (in effect, to run their own affairs) and to be exempted from doing any work.

Thatcher and her Northern Ireland secretary, Humphrey Atkins, divined a greater motive behind the demands, viewing them as part of an orchestrated IRA campaign to give the terrorists the run of the prison and to win the status of 'political prisoners', incarcerated for their beliefs rather than for violent criminal activity. The government was therefore prepared to make only a partial concession, going as far as permitting the republican inmates to discard their prison clothes in favour of 'civilian-style' (but not their personal) clothing. The notion that they could have the free run of their own prison was firmly rejected.

The terrorists had, in fact, been granted various prison privileges in 1972, which gave them a category and status separate from those of other violent criminals. But the distinction accorded them was revoked by the Labour government in 1976. Two years later, H-block prisoners had begun a dirty protest, smearing their cells with their own excrement. The switch to a hunger strike strategy was altogether more dangerous. Nevertheless, in refusing to bow to the prisoners' demands, the Thatcher Cabinet was acting in line with a May 1980 report by the European Commission on Human Rights which had ruled that the form of detention in the Maze prison was not inhuman and had rejected the prisoners' complaints. Far from being singled out for especially grim or degrading punishment, those incarcerated for terrorist offences enjoyed a significantly laxer regime than British criminals convicted of comparatively minor crimes on the mainland. Nevertheless, the IRA decided to turn the issue into a cause célèbre. In December 1980, one H-block inmate on hunger strike starved himself to the point of going into a coma.

In March 1981, the hunger strikes recommenced with renewed determination and were to continue for a further seven months, during which time ten republican prisoners starved themselves to death. In so far as getting the government to accept that they were political prisoners was their aim, they all died in vain. But as a means of drawing the world's attention to the republican cause, the starvation plan was an undoubted success. Indeed, they had already gained a measure of international awareness from the slow, debilitating suicide of the first H-block prisoner. Bobby Sands was a 27-year-old IRA operative who had served five years of a fourteen-year sentence for possession of a gun fired against RUC officers. Within the H-block, he enjoyed the status of 'Officer Commanding' the republican inmates. With his long hair he could be portrayed as a cross between one of Jesus's disciples and a seventies glam-rock star, but what made him particularly significant was the IRA's decision that he should stand for Parliament, *in absentia*, on an anti-H-Block ticket in the Fermanagh and South Tyrone by-election. A gun-runner facing death was seeking a democratic mandate.

Bobby Sands's campaign not only wrong-footed the government. It placed the main, non-violent, democratic party of Northern Ireland's mostly Catholic nationalist community, the SDLP, in a difficult position. The Fermanagh and South Tyrone constituency had a narrow nationalist major-ity, having previously been held by an Independent Republican, Frank McGuire, the publican primarily famous for his drunkenly shambolic bit-part in the fall of James Callaghan's government in 1979.* If the SDLP chose to forego running its candidate in the by-election created by McGuire's sudden death, it risked tarnishing its anti-terrorist image by stepping aside to ensure an IRA gunman won the seat. Yet, if it contested the constituency, the nationalist vote would be split and an Ulster Unionist candidate would be returned. In this eventuality, the SDLP risked being portrayed as an accomplice of the unionists, joining in the 'persecution' of a young man prepared to make the ultimate sacrifice for his cause. Weighing these two unenviable options, the SDLP decided it would not contest the by-election. Bobby Sands was given a direct run against his unionist opponent. It was a crucial decision, for Sands won the seat by the tight margin of 1,446 votes.

Narrow it might have been, but the victory regenerated the cause of violent republicanism. An incarcerated criminal had been elected to the House of Commons. It was not just the Ulster Unionists who were horri-fied. *The Times* argued in its leader column that the Commons should immediately disqualify him on the grounds that his remaining prison sen-tence exceeded the length of the parliament to which he had been elected.[39] In the event, there was no need to risk anything so questionable. In May 1981, Sands died after sixty-six days of refusing food. Parliament had never experienced one of its elected representatives ending his life in this way before. 'A convicted criminal,' Thatcher told his nominal colleagues in the Commons, 'he chose to take his own life. It was a choice that his organiza-tion did not allow to many of its victims.'[40] This was not how Ulster's enraged nationalist communities saw it. At his funeral, Sands was conveyed by masked paramilitaries in an IRA-decorated coffin and followed by a hundred thousand mourners. His end sparked several days of severe rioting

---

* See pp. 26–28.

in Belfast, resulting in two deaths, a supportive march in Liverpool, and the offering of marks of respect and remembrance all over the world. The extent to which his self-proclaimed martyrdom was a propaganda coup for Irish republicanism could be measured in the dollars American citizens poured into supporting the IRA's front organizations. Their generosity fuelled a gun- and bomb-buying spree. Sands's demise also ensured a by-election which granted him a second victory in death. The replacement candidate, his former agent, even managed to increase Sands's majority.

After another nine inmates had followed Sands's example, the IRA called off its hunger strike campaign on 3 October 1981, in response to the appeals of priests and relatives who pleaded for the lives of those concerned. It had served its publicity purpose. Three days later, Jim Prior, the new Northern Ireland secretary, announced government concessions which included the right of H-block prisoners to wear their own clothes after all. The IRA's response was to intensify its terror campaign. On 10 October, a nail-bomb was detonated on a coach carrying Irish Guards at Chelsea Barracks. Twenty-three soldiers were wounded. Two civilians were ripped apart by the six-inch nails that went flying into them. Days later, there was another fatality from a bomb planted in an Oxford Street Wimpy bar. The following month, the Ulster Unionist MP for Belfast South was shot dead while he was holding a surgery for his constituents.

Amid the escalating violence, Sinn Fein emerged as a major political party and, for the first time since the Troubles began, threatened to supplant the non-violent SDLP as the major nationalist voice in Northern Ireland. The government's response to such developments came in the form of intensifying existing ministerial and official collaboration between Dublin and London, which was duly beefed up and christened the 'Inter-Governmental Council'. This approach assumed that better communication meant enhanced understanding. However, the Irish Republic was also going through a period of instability, with neither Fine Gael's Dr Garret Fitzgerald nor his Fianna Fáil opponent, Charles Haughey, managing to form a long-term administration. Haughey had been dismissed from a previous Irish government in 1970 over allegations of involvement in IRA gun-running. His overconfident announcements about the influence he was bringing to bear upon Mrs Thatcher succeeded only in irritating unionists and, in any case, he quickly showed himself at odds with London's plans for Ulster. What the Northern Ireland secretary, Jim Prior, proposed was a 'rolling devolution' of responsibilities held by Whitehall back to Ulster, with the creation of a Northern Ireland Assembly whose powers would increase the more its rival parties could find agreement to work constructively together. The assembly would be elected by proportional representation in order to prevent the unionist majority achieving an absolute majority. The response from Dublin was as hostile as that from nationalist spokesmen in the province. When elections to the 78-seat body were held in October 1982, the Ulster Unionists and the Democratic Unionists (DUP) won forty-seven seats, the SDLP won fourteen, the non-aligned Alliance Party ten seats and Sinn Fein five. The decision of the Sinn Fein and SDLP members to refuse to take their seats effectively torpedoed the assembly before it had achieved anything. The following year, the unionists also called time on it. Once again, the province's future appeared to have reached an impasse.

It seemed that everywhere the politics of confrontation was triumphing.

5 THE ALTERNATIVE

The Democracy of the Committed

Talk of 'splits' was nothing new in the Labour Party. Internecine bitterness, personal hatreds and heroic principled stands had provided Labour with some of the most dramatic moments in its history – Ramsay MacDonald's breakaway National Labour Party in 1931, the expulsion of Stafford Cripps and Aneurin Bevan in 1939, and the battles of Bevan and Hugh Gaitskell with Labour's unilateral nuclear disarmers in the late fifties and early sixties being only some of the most memorable. Issues and personalities changed, but the essential fault line between committed socialists and liberal progressives remained. Those who regarded Clause Four of the party's constitution as the cornerstone upon which to build in government felt let down by the failure of successive Labour administrations to go more than part of the way towards honouring the solemn commitment dating back to 1917 (and extended in 1929) to ensure the 'common ownership [nationalization] of the means of production, distribution and exchange'. For socialists of this carat, the state was the solution. But it also seemed to be the curse, for whenever Labour politicians actually occupied the offices of state the experience seemed to have a moderating effect on them. Harold Wilson had been elected Labour's leader as a candidate of the left only to move towards the centre when in power. Delegates at the 1973 party conference voted to mandate him to nationalize twenty-five of Britain's biggest companies. He simply ignored the demand. His successor behaved similarly. Given the chance to impose import tariffs and stringent exchange controls during the crisis of 1976, Callaghan instead preferred the public spending cuts demanded by the IMF and implemented by the Chancellor, Denis Healey.

What the left wing interpreted as weakness or betrayal was defended by the party's right wing as sensible and realistic. And in each clash, the latter was able to deploy a winning argument – that the floating voter found a moderate Labour Party more attractive than a red-blooded socialist one. The left could dream, but only the right could govern. It was defeat in 1979 that removed the moderates' aura of electoral success. For, if elections could only be won on the centre ground, how was it that Thatcher, despite being clearly on the right of her party, had landed a 43-seat majority? On this interpretation of events, Labour moderates were complacently misreading the mood. The country was becoming radicalized.

The left's analysis was perceptive in so far as it recognized that the Keynesian legacy had been tarnished by a decade of stagflation and that there was a hunger for new solutions. Thatcher and the monetarist think tanks made the running in the Conservative Party at least partly because they displayed fresh thinking, unlike the Tory 'wets' who suffered from being identified with the failures and retreats of the Heath government. Like the Thatcherites, it was primarily Labour's left that offered dramatic proposals to meet the new challenges presented by a worsening recession and the divisive attitude of the government. By contrast, Labour's moderates appeared to be bereft of ideas, merely offering a return to the policies they had implemented in office during the 1970s and upon which they had lost the 1979 election. Not only was British politics now animated by a level of ideological division greater than at any time since the 1930s, soaring unemployment and the deep unpopularity of the Thatcher government offered the best opportunity that committed socialists were likely to get to overturn the capitalist system. The extraordinary bitterness and hatred that disfigured the Labour Party in the first years of the 1980s owed much to the left's sense that its hour had come and that the possibility of victory must not be frittered away yet again.

The left's strategy to seize control of the Labour Party obviously involved replacing Callaghan with a leader more sympathetic to their way of thinking. But they were plotting more than regicide. What they planned was a revolution, not a palace coup. For not only did they want a new leader, they wanted a new constitution to govern him. Never again should the leader be able to exercise authority in a way that conflicted with the wishes of the rank and file of the Labour movement. In order to achieve this, the left articulated two basic demands. The first was to change the method by which both the leader and deputy leader were elected. This had always been the sole prerogative of the Parliamentary Labour Party (PLP) – in other words, Labour's MPs. Instead, the left believed the leadership should be determined by an electoral college made up of MPs, trade union leaders and constituency activists. The exact proportion of votes accorded to each of these three estates could be debated, but once the arithmetic was settled it should be accepted as final. The second demand concerned who got to write the general election manifesto. The existing system accorded the privilege of laying out the proposed legislative programme to a joint committee of the party leader and the party's governing body, the National Executive Committee (NEC). Experience had shown that in reality this allowed the leadership to have an effective veto over the more radical prose usually proffered by the NEC. The left's demand was that in future only the NEC could frame the election manifesto. A subsequent Labour prime minister and his Cabinet would be bound to implement it, whether they liked it or not.

The revolution was not limited to bending the leader's power to the wider Labour movement's will. The same principle guided the left's demand for the 'mandatory reselection' of all MPs. Under the existing rules, paid-up members of Labour constituency associations (known as the CLPs – constituency Labour parties) could stop their local MP or candidate from standing again at the next election by passing a vote of no confidence in him or her, and if the NEC found no procedural anomaly the local association could then proceed to select a new candidate. However, no-confidence votes were generally difficult to secure unless the MP was guilty of a major personal transgression. Mandatory reselection made it much easier for local activists to ditch their MP on policy rather than personal grounds because it ensured that at least once during each parliament the MP, no matter how spotless his or her reputation, would have to face a new selection contest in which an alternative candidate could compete. The effect of this would be to make MPs less like elected representatives and more like delegates, toeing whatever line the activists in their constituency association demanded of them, for fear they would be deselected if they showed independent judgement of their own. It threatened to turn the traditional Westminster model on its head and usher in activist-led caucus politics.

The underlying demands for an electoral college to determine the leader, for the NEC to write the party manifesto and for mandatory reselection of all MPs were egalitarian and decentralizing and, as such, philosophically attractive to many committed socialists. But it also helped that all three demands would have the effect of increasing the leverage of the left wing over the right wing. The left could not be sure of victory if the leadership election remained in the hands of the Parliamentary Labour Party, where the arithmetic between left, right and those in between was tight. By contrast, the other institutions of the Labour movement were visibly shifting leftwards. Between annual conferences, the party's governing body was the NEC, whose membership was elected by union leaders and constituency associations. Throughout the 1970s, the proportion of moderates and right-wingers on the NEC was whittled down, so that by the decade's end they seldom accounted for more than five out of twenty-nine members. The majority of motions at the annual party conference were determined by trade union leaders who cast block votes proportionate to the size of their union's membership (although only the union leaders, not the members, cast votes in the conference). As the Winter of Discontent demonstrated, the most powerful unions were increasingly led by those with little deference to moderate Labour Party leaders or by those who were too ineffectual to restrain their own more militant subordinates.

The election of Arthur Scargill as president of the National Union of Mineworkers in 1981 was symptomatic of the left's success in winning over the union high command. A similar shift to the left was also apparent in the local constituency associations. In the early 1970s, the Labour Party had seven hundred thousand members nationwide. A large proportion were traditional blue-collar workers, supportive of Labour values without necessarily being energized by the framing of policy initiatives. Disillusion with Labour's record in power during the 1970s caused the national membership to shrink to around two hundred and fifty thousand by the decade's end. Of these, an estimated twenty-five thousand were active participants in their constituency associations and other party bodies. This smaller, tighter group of activists was far more interested in policy formulation and, rather than working in traditional industries, were often teachers, social workers or local government officers with articulate and far more radical views.[1] These were the sort of activists who were most likely to attend MPs' mandatory reselection meetings and to select themselves as delegates to the party conference, where their votes would be counted in the proposed electoral college for the leadership.

Whereas these activists showed extraordinary tenacity and willpower, staying on for meetings that dragged on for hours, moderates increasingly showed little stomach for this attritional form of warfare. They comforted themselves with the knowledge that the left could win as many conference motions or NEC seats as they liked, but ultimately the party leadership – answerable to the parliamentary party if to anyone – would ignore their radical pledges, just as it had in the 1970s. Here was a complacent defence of the status quo, which would be blown away if the left actually managed to rewrite the rules of the constitution. In making their case against the rule changes, moderates were handicapped by the language in which the debate was conducted. The left could speak of wider democratic engagement. The right appeared to be justifying rule by the privileged few in Westminster. When right-wing MPs addressed constituency associations it was potentially injudicious to spell out too bluntly what they really feared – that notionally wider participation would really mean handing over the party to the sort of narrow cadre of hard-left activists who would transform a democratic socialist party into a latter-day cabal of Jacobin tribunes engaged in permanent bloodletting in a search for ever purer ideologues. On this view, the left's agenda amounted not to broad-based participation but to what the left's champion, Tony Benn, approvingly described as 'the democracy of the committed'.

A taste of revolutionary justice was soon being meted out to Labour moderates at party meetings. At a mini-conference to endorse a new NEC policy document on 31 May 1980, Callaghan was bluntly told by one platform delegate to retire to his farm. Healey strode up to make his speech serenaded by shouts of 'Out! Out! Out!' The former Foreign Secretary, David Owen, attempted to defend the retention of nuclear weapons until such time as they could be negotiated away by international agreement and was jeered for his trouble. Dr Owen had spent the previous months arguing that moderates should stay and fight within the party rather than cede it to the left, but his treatment on this and subsequent occasions made him wonder if there was any point in hanging around if all it attracted was abuse.[2] Even greater hostility was meted out at the party conference which began on 29 September in Blackpool. On the opening day, the delegates responded rapturously to Tony Benn who took it upon himself to announce from the platform that the next Labour government would have to abolish the House of Lords 'immediately' (so that Parliament would become unicameral and the will of the Commons could not be challenged or revised). This constitutional innovation was necessary, he declared, because within days of Labour regaining office there would need to be legislation passed granting the state powers of sweeping nationalization, control over financial exchange and 'industrial democracy'. Since this was incompatible with continued membership of the EEC, Britain would quit within weeks of Labour taking office. 'Comrades,' he added, 'this is the very least we must do.'[3]

The comrades loved it. Later that day, it was Shirley Williams's turn, speaking at a meeting of the moderate group, the Campaign for Labour Victory. Despite having recently been one of the Callaghan Cabinet's more popular ministers, Williams had lost her seat at the general election and was enduring her share of vilification from Trotskyite 'entryists' in her constituency association, who were seeking to prevent her from being readopted as a candidate. She met fire with fire, rounding on her denigrators, whose bully-boy tactics she compared to those of the fascists. The shafts of her peroration were, however, aimed directly at the silent majority in her party:

> Too many good men and women in this party have remained silent. Well, the time has come when you had better stick your heads up and come over the parapet, because if you do not start to fight now, you will not have a party that is worth having.[4]

Wherever such people were hiding, it was not on the conference floor. At Blackpool, almost every vote went the left's way: unilateral nuclear disarmament, withdrawal from the EEC, Benn's ideas on mass nationalization and sweeping socialist planning. Mandatory reselection was confirmed, as was the selection of the leadership by an electoral college. There was, however, no agreement on the college's composition. Benn originally wanted 50 per cent for the unions,[5] but was persuaded by his former adviser, Frances

Morrell (deputy leader of the Inner London Education Authority and a member of the Greater London Council), to support a united pitch by the left which would stand a better chance of being adopted: 40 per cent to the unions and 30 per cent each to the MPs and constituencies. When the NEC duly agreed to this division, Callaghan furiously retorted: 'Well, I tell you that the parliamentary party will never accept a leader foisted upon them,' adding for good measure, 'I'll tell you something else, they will never have Tony Benn foisted upon them.' To which Benn snapped back: 'Jim, you speak for yourself and nobody else.'[6] A special conference at Wembley in January 1981 was to determine who would command the big battalions – and with them the destiny of the Labour Party.

On 15 October 1980, less than two weeks after the excitement at Blackpool, Callaghan announced he was resigning the leadership. In doing so, he intended that his successor would be elected under the existing, MPs-only, rules. Although he did not endorse anyone, it was reasonably assumed that Callaghan wanted Denis Healey to succeed him. With his florid cheeks and bushy eyebrows, Healey had one of the most familiar faces in Britain, and he wasted no time in making it clear that he would be running for the top job. Healey combined a competitive, bullying nature towards his colleagues with an affable and amusing turn of phrase in public, of a kind that offered an effective foil to the hectoring and humourless Thatcher. But his efforts as Chancellor of the Exchequer to bring the budget deficit under control by cutting spending and trying to impose a tight anti-inflationary incomes policy had made him a hate figure to the left, whose leader of choice was Tony Benn. Timing, though, was everything – and Benn was dissuaded from standing at a meeting, at his own house, attended by a roll-call of the left's finest tacticians,* who persuaded him that it was still too soon to be sure of victory and that he ought to sit this vote out in favour of another socialist candidate who could garner support from a broader swathe of Labour opinion. This, they concluded, would be Michael Foot.[7] Meanwhile, other left-wingers on the NEC, including Eric Heffer and Neil Kinnock, voted to suspend the election altogether until a more equitable voting procedure could be introduced, but they could not overturn the Parliamentary Labour Party's right to carry on regardless under the existing system. Foiled, some on the left requested that the leadership candidates should announce that they would serve only as a caretaker, pending re-election under the new electoral college rules in January. Such attempts were doomed. Even Foot was content to regard victory under the existing

---

* Vladimir Derer, Geoff Bish, Tony Banks, Victor Schonfield, Stuart Holland, Audrey Wise, Ken Coates, Jo Richardson, Norman Atkinson, Chris Mullin, Reg Race, Frances Morrell, Martin Flannery, Benn's secretary, Julie Clements, and Benn's two sons, Stephen and Hilary.

rules as a sufficient mandate, and when he announced his candidature Benn dismissed 'the whole thing' as 'shabby and calculating'.[8]

Foot was a candidate of the left who promoted a clear socialist agenda on all the main issues. He wanted to nationalize more of British industry, he believed the state should direct comprehensive planning of the economy, he intended to withdraw the country from the EEC and unilaterally scrap its nuclear deterrent. But, unlike Benn, he enjoyed a high reputation at Westminster and cultivated few personal enemies, for Foot was famously courteous to friend and foe alike. He was a man of unimpeachable integrity and intellectual curiosity, whose character commanded respect on both sides of the House of Commons – an institution he continued to hold in esteem, despite the demands for caucus politics of the hard left. Some wavering centre-ground Labour MPs concluded that Foot might be the best compromise candidate. He alone might be able to hold together both wings of the party, whereas Healey's instinctive pugnacity courted all-out civil war. This, indeed, was Healey's great drawback. Like Callaghan, his solace was his family. Politically, he was a loner with few real friends. While he was clearly the candidate who could make Labour re-electable, he was also the man most likely fatally to split the party.

Labour's parliamentarians cast their votes amid rancour and suspicion. The left-wing Labour Coordinating Committee even tried to force every MP to take his or her ballot paper to the local constituency association and, after listening to the opinions of the activists, publicly mark the paper in front of them. The principle of the secret ballot was good enough for the electorate but not, it seems, for the elected. On the first ballot, Healey came out top, with 112 votes to Foot's eighty-three. Two left-wing candidates, John Silkin and Peter Shore, got thirty-eight and thirty-two votes respectively. They dropped out and recommended their supporters to vote for Foot in the second, concluding, ballot. In this contest, announced on 11 November, Foot squeezed home against Healey by 139 to 129. Among the leading moderates, David Owen and Bill Rodgers witnessed each other voting for Healey (no longer MPs, Shirley Williams and Roy Jenkins could not vote), but a subsequent study of voting behaviour has suggested that at least five – and possibly more – of the MPs who subsequently joined the breakaway Social Democratic Party deliberately voted for Foot, knowing that he would be such a disaster that it would stiffen their resolve to quit the party and would encourage others to join them in a new political formation.[9] By such narrow calculations was the fate of the Labour Party in the eighties sealed. After all, if Healey had won the leadership in 1980 and had succeeded in asserting himself over the hard left, it seems improbable that Owen, Rodgers or Williams would have quit the party. Roy Jenkins might have gone ahead regardless and formed his own centre party, but there would have been little rationale for many Labour MPs to join him in a venture that would have seemed little more than a personal vanity project, without traction with the wider electorate.

Yet, it was a moot point whether the likes of Owen, Rodgers and Williams could have successfully bolstered Healey against the foot soldiers of the left. A Healey victory would certainly have been a red rag to the socialist bulls, with the prospect of internecine warfare attending every effort to drag the party back to the centre ground. NEC meetings and conferences would have become even more acrimonious. Healey would certainly have endured a rough relationship with the pipe-smoking Ron Hayward who, as general secretary of the Labour Party since 1972, had showed himself to be a brooding irritant to successive parliamentary leaders. As early as 1974, Hayward was confiding to Anatoly Chernyaev, the Soviet Union's contact man with the British left, that it was his intention to force the Labour leadership to obey conference votes and be subservient to the NEC, and that he was 'committed to developing links with the CPSU'.* Hayward, Chernyaev noted in his diary, 'prepares young people, puts them in the right places, helps them to become prominent'.[10] During the seventies, a steady stream of fellow travellers, from Marxists and Trotskyites to Maoists, joined the Labour Party – even though they did not share its democratic values – as a means of infiltrating it. Their 'entryism' was made possible by the NEC, which, in 1973, had abolished Labour's list of proscribed associations. One group whose adherents were thereafter able to join the party was the Militant Tendency. Militant's roots were in a Trotskyite faction, the Revolutionary Socialist League. Its activists shared with the extremists of the right a vocabulary that was muscular to the point of being overtly violent. The system needed to be 'smashed'. Judges, policemen, Tories, the Labour leadership . . . no distinction needed to be made, for those in power were all the same self-serving betrayers of the working class. 'Winning the streets' was among the ambiguous phrases regularly deployed in an argument suffused with the rhetoric of class war and propagated monthly in their newspaper, *Militant*. Their organizers included Ray Aps and Pat Wall, the latter subsequently becoming an MP and a gift to Tory propagandists. In reality, Militant's roll-call may not have exceeded ten thousand, but this was not insignificant given their energy and indefatigability in a party in which no more than twenty-five thousand members were considered politically active. In this way, Militant became an irritant in many constituencies where moderate MPs were struggling to retain authority. The faction was especially successful in gaining influence over the party's youth section, the Young Socialists, whose national organizer, Andy Bevan, was a Militant member happy to

---

* The Communist Party of the Soviet Union.

announce: 'I am proud to be called a Marxist.'[11] As national youth organizer, Bevan had an office at Labour's headquarters where he remained – while his own youthfulness gradually deserted him – until 1988.

The media, particularly the Tory-supporting newspapers, made much of Militant's destabilizing pugnacity, yet it was not the most successful group within the Labour Party. Less menacing in tone and far more adroit in tactics were the Campaign for Labour Party Democracy (CLPD), the Labour Coordinating Committee and the Rank and File Mobilizing Committee. The common goal of these three groups was to make the party leadership the servant and not the master of the broader Labour movement. Their seer was Vladimir Derer, a grey-haired, bespectacled and rather austere-looking man, who looked older than his sixty years. Derer was a Czech-born admirer of Trotsky who had fled the Nazi occupation of Czechoslovakia in 1939 and sought sanctuary in Britain. By 1964, he had decided that it was through the vehicle of the Labour Party that his adopted country could best be guided to socialism. His wife, a polytechnic lecturer, thought likewise and together Vladimir and Vera Derer had been masterminding the activities of the CLPD from their Golders Green home since 1973. Derer's great insight was that the multitude of left-wing pressure groups, arguing between themselves about often minor differences of policy, were unlikely to achieve any of their ideological goals unless collectively they prioritized changing Labour's constitution so that they could gain control of the party's policy-making apparatus. Despite being run on a shoestring, the CLPD made headway and by 1980 enjoyed the fully paid-up affiliation of four hundred organizations, including 107 constituency parties and 112 trade union branches.[12]

Unhelpfully, the right-wing media indulged in the habit of casually lumping together the various left-wing factions as 'Trots' (Trotskyists) or – a particularly loaded favourite of *The Sun* – 'loony lefties'. This was misleading since they were neither of like mind nor of similar background. While the Militant Tendency tended to be proudly working-class agitators who were generally suspicious of those whose hands were not worn by toil, CLPD activists were often university graduates. Many were intellectuals, at ease in the drawing room of Tony Benn's rather stately, classical-fronted house in Notting Hill (identifiable by its red front door). Although obsessed by processes and constitutional small print, they belonged to the long tradition of pamphleteering, of debate and liberal inquiry. Jon Lansman, a 23-year-old unemployed Cambridge graduate, did much of the CLPD's organizational legwork, churning out commentaries and lobbying those in the Labour movement who were identified as influential figures. The group's coordinators with the trade unions were Peter Willsman, a bearded official with the public sector union NUPE, and Victor Schonfield, a former jazz musician and music critic.

Militant's outspokenness could be as unhelpful to the CLPD's careful preparations as it was menacing to party moderates. Realizing that the cause had to be won step by step, by winning over middle-ground opinion, the CLPD believed the rule change it could get adopted was for Labour MPs to face mandatory reselection only once per parliament. Militant's demand that MPs face yearly reselection seemed exactly the sort of unsubtle, uncompromising approach that risked unravelling the whole initiative. Given the need for discipline, it was a major achievement when Militant agreed to become one of the ten 'rank and file' organizations presenting a united front for the crucial special conference that would frame the new rules for electing the Labour leader.

The conference met at Wembley Arena on 24 January 1981. Realizing that a defence of the prerogatives of MPs no longer impressed party delegates, Labour moderates like the so-called Gang of Three – David Owen, Bill Rodgers and Shirley Williams – sought to outdo the 'rank and filers' in proclaiming the glories of democracy. For while the latter wanted only the activists who attended party conferences to have a vote in leadership elections, the Gang of Three now proposed a far more sweeping enfranchisement – 'one member, one vote', carried out by postal voting. This, it was calculated, would empower the moderate, but all too often silent or apathetic, majority of party members. It seemed a clever move and it was every bit as self-serving for the right as the activist-centric proposals were for the left. This was its problem. The right's transparent motives, belatedly adopted through fear rather than belief, were never likely to win endorsement at Wembley. There, the majority opinion was determined that the left's electoral college model should be adopted. The only question was how the spoils were to be divided. Having been elected under the old rules, Michael Foot remained a committed parliamentarian who saw the dangers of adopting a system by which a leader the MPs did not want could be foisted upon them.[13] To counteract this, he sought to retain half of the votes in the electoral college for his fellow MPs. Meanwhile, the CLPD wanted to maximize the leverage of party activists, and the NEC backed a proposal to give a third each to the politicians, the union leaders and the activists. This did not please the trade union leaders, who were pushing for a larger say for themselves. Their role was especially controversial since the way the votes were weighted effectively ceded massive power to the few general secretaries of the biggest unions. While some of them did not presume to know their members' minds and instigated union-wide ballots to ascertain majority opinion, others followed more opaque methods of consultation. A few scarcely bothered with the inconvenience of taking soundings. In this way, persuading a tiny number of trade union leaders to switch their vote was potentially all that was needed to determine a tight leadership race.

In the event, the block voting of the union leaders proved decisive in ensuring that the conference opted to reward them with 40 per cent of the electoral college and the MPs and the activists with only 30 per cent each. It was the greatest flexing of union muscle since the Winter of Discontent two years before and it emphasized how little contrition the union leaders felt about the power they exercised. Tony Benn was ecstatic at the result, noting in his diary: 'No praise is high enough for the enormous skill of the CLPD, who worked tirelessly to get constituencies and smaller unions to vote for the 40–30–30 option.' As he walked around the hall, he felt a sense of satisfaction: 'I refused all television and radio interviews – except one for the Soviet labour magazine, *Trud*.'[14] The following day, Benn assembled his advisers and began discussing with them the campaign to make him deputy leader.[15] For the Gang of Three, Wembley was the final straw. It meant, as Shirley Williams put it, with only mild exaggeration, that the next Labour prime minister would be elected by 'four trade union barons in a smoke-filled room'.[16] By the time the conference stood to wrap up proceedings with the traditional affirmation of socialist fraternity, the singing of *The Red Flag*, she was nowhere to be seen.

Gang of Four – Bright Dawn over Limehouse

The following day, Williams joined David Owen, Bill Rodgers and Roy Jenkins for a photo shoot outside Owen's house at Limehouse in east London. Like ageing rock stars announcing their band was reforming for a comeback tour, the four grinned at each other, struck poses and quipped with reporters while the photographers snapped away. There was serious purpose, however, behind what the newspapers dubbed the Gang of Four and their Limehouse Declaration. They were calling time on the Labour Party by launching the Council for Social Democracy. Its aim was 'a realignment of British politics', spearheaded by politicians 'who recognize that the drift towards extremism in the Labour party is not compatible with the democratic traditions of the party they joined' and who, they hoped, would be supplemented by 'those from outside politics who believe that the country cannot be saved without changing the sterile and rigid framework into which the British political system has increasingly fallen in the last two decades'. The reference to two decades of failure was especially significant, and somewhat surprising given how prominent a role the four in general, and Roy Jenkins in particular, had played in the politics of those years. Nevertheless, it hit a chord. A full-page advertisement in the *Guardian* on 5 February was answered by twenty-five thousand letters of support and £70,000 in pledges. This was promising, not least because without being able to tap the funding reservoirs of either the trade unions or big business it was the small subscriptions from a critical mass of well-wishers that would bankroll the cause. Emboldened, on 26 March the Gang of Four called a press conference in the Connaught Rooms to announce that their council was to be relaunched as an independent political party, the Social Democratic Party (SDP).

Nothing remotely comparable had happened since 1930 when Oswald Mosley quit the Labour government in order to form the New Party. The example of what had soon degenerated into the British Union of Fascists was hardly one the SDP wished to emulate, and the fact remained that no successful party had been launched nationwide since Labour in 1900. The Gang of Four toyed with various names for their group – including calling it 'New Labour' – but it was 'Social Democrats', with its continental European connotations, that stuck. At the same time, its red, white and blue logo boldly proclaiming the SDP initials seemed patriotic, with a non-partisan appeal to the floating voter. Nevertheless, as Bill Rodgers made clear at the launch: 'We are not a new centre party, we are very plainly a left-of-centre party.'[17]

Despite its claims to novelty, the SDP was a centre-left party committed not to radical change but to the preservation of the post-war consensus. By seeking to replace the first-past-the-post system, which permitted Thatcher and Foot to take their parties in diverging directions, with a system of proportional representation, it hoped to encourage coalition administrations which would gravitate towards centre-ground policies. By condemning 'frequent frontier changes' between the public and private sectors, the Limehouse Declaration made clear that the SDP believed that Labour had settled the proportion of the economy nationalized by the state at about the right level in 1979. Subsequent policy announcements suggested that the tax burden would also remain high by continental standards, and that an SDP government would bring back an incomes policy as its core anti-inflationary strategy. Supportive of continued membership of the European Economic Community and NATO and the retention of an independent nuclear deterrent, the substance of what was dressed up as an exciting new force in British politics seemed remarkably similar to the agenda upon which James Callaghan and Denis Healey had fought the 1979 general election. It was only dual disillusionment with Thatcher's first two years in office and with Labour's lurch to the left that cast the SDP in a light especially favourable to uncommitted voters – for the Social Democrats seemed to offer what Labour might have delivered in the seventies if only the party had not placed its trust in the trade unions and been infiltrated by left-wing activists. The most damning verdict on the new party's philosophical outlook was actually delivered by an academic sympathetic to its intentions, with Ralf Dahrendorf fearing that what the SDP really offered was 'a better yesterday'.

None of the Gang of Four had played a greater role in shaping that land of lost content than Roy Jenkins. As Home Secretary from 1965 to 1967 (and again in 1974–6) he had pushed through the key measures of what he applauded as the 'permissive' society, and his period as Chancellor of the Exchequer, from 1967 to 1970, was widely considered one of the more successful post-war tenures at the Treasury. It was his idealism about Europe that led him to resign the Labour deputy leadership in 1972, over Harold Wilson's tactical opposition to Edward Heath's EEC entry legislation. Jenkins's principled stand did him no favours with the party he still wanted to steer. Badly defeated when he stood for the leadership in 1976, his subsequent disillusion was such that he resigned as an MP in order to become president of the European Commission. It was from Brussels that he began to compare unfavourably Britain's adversarial politics with what he took to be European success through coalition-building. He emphasized this contrast when he delivered the BBC Dimbleby Lecture in November 1979. Entitled 'Home Thoughts from Abroad', it was an appeal for proportional representation to end Britain's 'queasy rides on the ideological big-dipper', and contained Delphic references to how a new moderate party could strengthen 'the radical centre'. His term in Brussels expired at the end of 1980 and he was lined up for a directorship at Morgan Grenfell when, on 29 November of that year, David Owen ventured over to his Oxfordshire country house at East Hendred to sound him out over what those still fighting the losing battle within the Labour Party were formulating. In particular, Owen left Jenkins in no doubt – just in case he entertained his own ideas – that what they proposed was 'not a centre party, but a "Socialist International" party', and that Shirley Williams ought to be its leader.[18] The implication was that Jenkins was welcome to become the fourth member of the Gang of Three – but only on their terms.

As conspiracies go, the Gang's plot to break away from Labour was not long in the planning. Williams, Owen and Rodgers had been in only occasional contact throughout 1980 and it was not until after Foot became leader that they began seriously discussing the logistics of taking a collective leap into the unknown. Until late in the day, Williams dallied with leaving politics altogether – lecturing on the subject seemed a lot less unpleasant. Dining with Jenkins over Christmas, Rodgers assured him he would not leave the Labour Party. Yet that evening, retiring early to bed with a back problem, he changed his mind while reading a biography of George Orwell. It reminded Rodgers of his own late father: 'He was always true to himself, and when I went into the House [of Commons] I remember him saying something about preferring to see me stay on the back benches rather than abandon the things that matter to me . . . That was when I crossed the river.'[19]

Nonetheless, the formation of the SDP naturally fostered allegations that its founders were publicity-seekers with no regard for the party that had given them office. Yet of the Gang of Four, only David Owen had not been nurtured from childhood in Labour's traditions. A Cambridge graduate, it was while training to become a doctor at St Thomas's Hospital that he had been drawn towards Labour politics. From that moment on, he wasted little time, becoming an MP at twenty-eight and only ten years later serving as Callaghan's Foreign Secretary. Bill Rodgers and Shirley Williams had been at Oxford together and had both been secretaries of the Fabian Society. Rodgers had gone on to hold several ministerial offices under Harold Wilson before finally serving in Callaghan's Cabinet as transport secretary. Williams had grown up in a liberal-socialist intellectual environment. Her mother was Vera Brittain, author of *Testament of Youth*. A Labour Party member while still a teenager, Williams fought her first campaign as a Labour candidate when she was just twenty-three. While few might have guessed it from his rather pompous mode of speech and reputation as a *bon viveur*, it was actually Roy Jenkins who enjoyed the most impeccably socialist background. The surname, rather than the accent, was the clue to his South Wales roots. His father, Arthur Jenkins, had gone down the mines aged twelve, before becoming a Labour MP and Clement Attlee's parliamentary private secretary. Arthur Jenkins desperately wanted his intelligent son to get into Oxford, and thanks also to Abersychan Secondary School he did so. At Oxford he emulated another bright Balliol scholar from relatively humble roots, whose biography he subsequently wrote, for, like Herbert Asquith, Jenkins was an active debater in the Oxford Union and graduated with first-class honours. In 1948, he was elected to Parliament, aged twenty-seven.

Between them, the Gang of Four represented great depth of government experience, even though at the time of the party's launch only two of them (Owen and Rodgers) were actually sitting MPs. Their initial stance was that rather than replicating a traditional hierarchy they were to be equal partners in a collective leadership, rather in the manner of a board of directors. Williams defended this approach by claiming that it ought to be the case in politics that 'the days of the paterfamilias are as dead as those of the autocratic employer'.[20] In reality, whatever the quality of the board members, few great companies get by for long without a chief executive and, in July 1982, Roy Jenkins was elected to take the helm.

In the meantime, it was remarkable how little the Gang diverged from a common script, despite their differences in personality. Although the last to join the group, Jenkins was the most senior both in terms of age (he was sixty-one in 1981) and offices held. Leaving Brussels with a generous pension and blessed with a considerable hinterland – friends, wine, books – he could have agreeably spent his retirement writing his admired political biographies or moving into the master's lodge of one of the grander Oxford colleges. Instead, as David Marquand has put it: 'Having been a Westminster parliamentarian to his fingertips, he suddenly found himself appealing, like a latter-day Wilkes or Bright, to a popular constituency, disfranchised by the rules of the Westminster game.'[21] He was a far more popularly recognizable figure than Rodgers, who modestly accepted that he was fourth among equals and was relatively content to be credited for his organizational skills. Owen's happy home life with his American wife contrasted with a detachment from others which was often interpreted as arrogance. His ability was not in doubt; besides being a qualified doctor and pursuing a hectic political career, he had found time to write several books. Owen, it seemed, was the quintessential young man in a hurry, considered vain about his looks and not always quick to realize that his brusque manner gave offence to those he was talking at. Temperamentally, he could scarcely have been more dissimilar from Shirley Williams. Untidy, unpunctual, unpretentious and generous-natured, since losing her seat in 1979 she had divided her time between lecturing at Harvard and, as a divorced mother, bringing up her school-age daughter. Despite her popularity, she seemed indifferent about whether she carried the torch or merely kept it lit for someone else. In the context of the Labour movement, she had always been considered a right-winger, even though many of her sentiments – on immigration and Third World aid, for instance – were solidly part of the liberal-left outlook. As Callaghan's education secretary she had stepped up the comprehensivization of Britain's schools, killing off free selective education in the direct-grant schools and all but succeeding in eliminating the few remaining grammar schools. In some respects, her appeal to the middle class was curious.

No single policy held the Gang of Four more closely together than their approach to Europe. No Labour politician had done more to empower the Common Market (as the EEC – later the European Union – was still widely called) than Jenkins. Not only had Owen and Jenkins helped secure a cross-party Commons majority for Britain's entry in 1972, but as president of the European Commission Jenkins had been instrumental in reversing the creeping 'Gaullism' which protected national interests against Europe-wide measures. In Brussels, Jenkins reasserted the Commission as a political rather than a purely bureaucratic entity, and laid the path for the creation of the European Monetary System, which would eventually lead to a single currency. Arguably, Jenkins's activities in Brussels would prove to have far greater implications for world politics than anything he achieved in British politics. At the time, he enjoyed the full support of Owen, Rodgers and Williams, and it was the Labour Party's lurch back into hostility towards Brussels that inspired the three of them to issue their first joint statement in June 1980, dissociating themselves from party policy and stating that if forced to 'accept a choice between socialism and Europe, we will choose both of them'.[22]

Whatever their attitude to socialism, preserving British integration into Europe was a motivating force for some, though by no means all, of the Labour MPs who defected to the SDP. The new party was launched with the support of thirteen Labour MPs, and by the end of 1982 that number had swelled to twenty-eight. It was understandably a source of annoyance to their ex-comrades that, having been elected as Labour candidates, they did not feel obliged to resign and stand again in by-elections under their new colours. None of them, of course, saw any advantage in taking that risk, preferring to wait until the next general election. Meanwhile, an SDP presence in the House of Lords was built up by the defection of eighteen Labour peers, including a former Foreign Secretary, George Brown. More important were the moderate MPs who stayed put. In this category, Denis Healey was the key sticker. The motivation of those who shared the SDP's political outlook but did not resign the Labour whip varied. Many thought the battle for Labour's soul could eventually be won, or that the SDP would prove a flash in the pan, especially if it could not overcome the arithmetic of a first-past-the-post electoral system. Some simply felt defection would be a betrayal of a party that had been their life and a kick in the teeth to constituency workers who had tirelessly tramped the streets and fed the letterboxes on their behalf. Among moderate-minded Labour MPs, it was generally the older ones with a long tradition of personal involvement in the Labour movement, and who were sponsored by trade unions, who stayed loyal, while younger, more rootless MPs with weaker – or no – links to the unions were more likely to defect.[23]

Where the SDP failed utterly was in broadening its appeal by recruiting Tory 'wets'. A Norfolk backbencher called Christopher Brocklebank-Fowler was the only Conservative MP to defect to them. About a handful of other backbenchers got as far as discussing the circumstances in which they might be tempted to follow him, but none converted talking into walking. SDP luminaries failed to exploit the doubts of these waverers because they lacked the personal links to make the approach – Tory 'wets' had few social connections with what was essentially a platoon of ex-Labour politicians. Similarly, the SDP exuded minimal appeal to the Tory peerage, from which only the Duke of Devonshire eventually defected. In the Commons, none of the Tory 'grandees' – Edward Heath, Sir Ian Gilmour or Jim Prior – was tempted, believing instead that their brand of Conservatism would outlive the brief experiment in Thatcherism. Given that she was clearly doomed, what was the point of jumping ship just before a 'wet' leader replaced her? As Gilmour reassured a fellow 'wet', Julian Critchley, the Tory Party 'is as much ours' as Thatcher's, and 'the Social Democrats can't last – they are not interest-based'.[24] This would prove a shrewd observation and may be assumed to have coloured Gilmour's attitude, despite his and his wife's enduring friendship with Roy Jenkins. Perhaps most importantly, there was no constituency activist movement making life miserable for 'wet' Tories to compare with that undermining Labour moderates. The 'wets' enjoyed a greater sense of tenure in their party and saw less reason to risk their careers by joining a new group which, in any case, described itself as 'left-of-centre'.

Rather than go to the trouble of forming their own party, with all the difficulties of setting up constituency associations, national organizers and fundraising, why did the Gang of Four not just join the Liberal Party? After all, to get anywhere, they would first have to agree an electoral pact with the Liberals so that they did not merely split each other's vote. Perhaps having held many of the great offices of state, the Gang of Four were comfortable with being in power and did not see why they should throw themselves at the mercy of a Liberal Party that had lost every general election since 1910 and which contained no politicians who had ever held office. What was more, Owen, Rodgers and Williams wanted to found a new party that would preserve the agenda and outlook of the sort of Labour Party they had originally joined. They had no desire to be subsumed into an already-established party with its own philosophy, structure and way of doing things. Indeed, it was not as if the philosophy was obviously compatible. The Liberals believed in localism and decentralization of power. The SDP was broadly happy with the current disbursement of authority. Spending years addressing local concerns at council or parish-pump level might provide Liberals with a sense of purpose, but did not represent the big game for Owen, who had reached Foreign Secretary while still in his thirties, or Jenkins, who, having presided over the European Commission, was on social terms with the senior politicians of half the continent. Neither man had much in common with grass-roots Liberal activists, who were the lifeblood of the Liberal Party. On issues like Britain retaining a nuclear deterrent, the Gang of Four was as much at odds with Liberal activists as with Labour ones.

It was in his attitude to the Liberals that Jenkins, nevertheless, stood slightly apart from Owen, Rodgers and Williams. As a sympathetic biographer of Sir Charles Dilke as well as Asquith, Jenkins was the only one of the Gang of Four who had ever shown an interest in or empathy with the Liberal heritage. But Jenkins could not hope to lead the Liberal Party as he might a party of his own. After all, the Liberals already had a youthful and energetic leader in David Steel, who was busy doing his best to restore the fortunes of a party that had courted disaster when its leader, Jeremy Thorpe, was charged with conspiracy to murder his alleged homosexual lover turned blackmailer.* For his part, Steel – whose private member's bill to legalize abortion had become law in 1967 with Jenkins's help – believed Jenkins

---

* Thorpe's acquittal did little to salvage his reputation.

could be far more useful establishing a centre party allied to the Liberals than merely defecting directly.

The Liberals and the SDP needed each other. A Gallup poll in April 1981 showed why an electoral alliance between them was their only hope of securing a decisive number of MPs at the next election. If they fought it separately, the Liberals were on 18 per cent and the SDP on 19 per cent (against the Tories on 30 per cent and Labour on 30.5 per cent). But if they teamed up, a Liberal–SDP alliance attracted 48.5 per cent support, completely overshadowing the Tories on 25.5 per cent and Labour on 24.5 per cent. Reaching agreement on which party should fight which constituency was easier said than done. While many Liberals did not see why their years of carefully nurturing target seats should be cast aside so that some SDP hopeful, with no history of local campaigning, should be offered the prize, their leader offered a less parochial perspective. Steel spoke openly in a party political broadcast of his hope that 'the Social Democrats' valuable experience of government', combined with the Liberals' 'nationwide community campaigning experience', would 'break the mould of a failed political system'.[25] He recognized that a deal with the SDP offered his party the only path out of the electoral doldrums and that if the two parties ran candidates against each other the result would be disaster. Either there was an electoral pact, or a suicide pact. Despite some ill-feeling, Steel got his way and the 'Alliance' was born.

The Donkey-Jacket Tendency

Did the SDP–Liberal Alliance or the Labour Party now offer the best hope of defeating Margaret Thatcher at the next general election? While the media scanned the utterances, even the body language, of the Gang of Four and of David Steel for telltale signs of friction or affection, Labour's destiny rested with Michael Foot and the two men about to slug it out to be his deputy, Denis Healey and Tony Benn. The struggle for the deputy leadership was more than usually significant not just because it was the first to be decided by the new electoral college but because, at the age of sixty-eight, Foot was widely seen as a caretaker leader who, if he did not win the general election, was unlikely to survive long in his post thereafter.

In being one of the greatest orators of his age, Michael Foot sounded like a great leader. But he did not look like one. He had a pinched face, framed by flying buttresses of shocks of white hair. A serious car accident in 1963 had pierced his lungs and broken all his ribs and his left leg, forcing him thereafter to lean on a walking-stick. His eyesight was so poor – an attack of shingles had claimed the sight of one eye in 1976 – that his thick-lensed spectacles came with blinkers attached. The impression of elderliness and infirmity contrasted visibly with the blushered cheeks, coiffured golden mane and primary-colour power suits of his Tory opposite number. Side by side, there was no question which of the two was dressed for business. And it was side by side that a defining image caught them, lined up with wreaths at the Cenotaph on Remembrance Sunday in 1981, Thatcher in a well-tailored dark and sombre coat and Foot in a tartan tie, ill-fitting trousers, rubber-soled shoes and a green motoring coat widely mistaken for a labour-er's donkey-jacket. 'That's a smart, sensible coat for a day like this,' reassured the Queen Mother, kindly.[26] Others were less charitable and assumed, incor-rectly, that the noted peace campaigner was showing disrespect for Britain's war-dead. Such personal dishevelment made him a cartoonist's dream. The satirical magazine *Private Eye* likened him to the scarecrow on children's television, Worzel Gummidge. Warming up the Tory faithful at a 1983 election rally, the comedian Kenny Everett elicited giggles by shouting into the microphone 'Let's bomb Russia!', but got the loudest belly-laugh for exhorting: 'Let's kick Michael Foot's stick away!' Even with the support of the stick, Foot was hardly firmly rooted. Two days after his election as Labour leader, he fell down a flight of stairs, and spent the ensuing weeks hobbling around on crutches with a leg encased in plaster.

If Foot looked like an accident-prone pensioner, he could hardly take offence when critics pointed it out. Yet the personal abuse failed to probe beneath the surface of a deeply thoughtful man. He was born the year before the First World War broke out, into a highly political and remarkably ambi-tious family. His father, Isaac Foot, was a Liberal MP and mayor of Plymouth, so steeped in the struggles of the English civil war and the Whig interpreta-tion of history that he once said he judged a man by which side he would have wanted his ancestor to have fought on at the battle of Marston Moor. The legacy of Oliver Cromwell, the Putney Debates, the Quakers and John Bright informed the household traditions of Nonconformity and protest. Of the five Foot brothers, two became MPs (both reaching the Cabinet) and two received peerages (John as a lawyer and Hugh as a diplomat and Britain's representative at the UN). When, in 1931, Foot went up to Oxford, he did so as a Liberal and, like his elder brothers, Dingle and John, was elected president of the Oxford Union (his brother Hugh was president of the Cambridge Union). Foot's turn at running the prestigious debating society came in 1933, the year that Hitler came to power, and it was the rise of fascism and Foot's exposure to the miseries of poverty while working in Liverpool that converted him to socialism. His journalistic career was launched on *Tribune*, a left-wing journal committed to forging a united front between the Labour and Communist parties. While asthma prevented him from fighting in the Second World War, he used his pen to devastating effect against those who, he believed, had led Britain into it so ill prepared: under the pseudonym 'Cato' he was a co-author of *Guilty Men*, a best-seller that mercilessly savaged Neville Chamberlain and the Conservative old guard (and conveniently ignored Labour's long campaign during the thirties for British disarmament). Foot fell headlong under the troublemaking influence of the greatest press baron of the age, Lord Beaverbrook, and from 1942 served as acting editor of the *Evening Standard* (when he was still only twenty-nine years old) until Beaverbrook finally tired of his efforts to besmirch the Tories with a campaign alleging that they were admirers of Mussolini.

Elected to Parliament in the 1945 post-war Labour landslide, Foot wasted no time in attaching himself to Nye Bevan – whose two-volume biography Foot later wrote and whose Ebbw Vale constituency he inherited in 1960. It was passion and principles that guided Foot's career path, not the attractions of high office. So disregarding was he of the latter's allure that his attacks on his own side in the early 1960s caused him to have the whip withdrawn over his defiance of Hugh Gaitskell's leadership. Unafraid of rocking his mentor's boat, he also parted ways with Bevan in 1957 over unilateral nuclear disarmament. Launched in 1957, with Foot on its executive, the Campaign for Nuclear Disarmament (CND) proved one of his most enduring causes and he was to the fore in the 'Ban the Bomb' marches from Trafalgar Square to Aldermaston. He still found the time to combine Parliament with journalism, writing a column for the Labour-supporting *Daily Herald* from 1944 until 1961 and editing *Tribune* in two stints between 1948 and 1960. In truth, he was a campaigning journalist in politics rather than an administrator obsessed by processes and detail. His Cabinet experience – first as employment secretary and then as Leader of the House between 1974 and 1979 – did not involve any of the big-spending departments but succeeded in demonstrating the depth of his admiration for the trade unions. It took his Cabinet colleagues to dissuade him from trying to criminalize lorry drivers who refused to talk to official pickets. Indeed, quite how deeply he believed in union power became evident when he piloted through closed shop legislation which, for instance, made it difficult for newspaper editors to publish articles by writers who did not wish to join the National Union of Journalists. Those who lacked his belief in collectivist action found it strange, indeed paradoxical, that Foot, the former editor and voice of the outsider, whose heroes included essayists like Jonathan Swift and William Hazlitt, should have championed laws that were anti-individualist and contrary to the most basic notions of freedom of association.

Foot, however, was a deeply paradoxical figure. Despite being a restless intellectual, he showed no sign of questioning uncomplicated views on economic policy that had been framed in the 1930s and which were not revised over the decades that followed. To him, the dismal science represented a zero-sum equation between capital and labour. In this respect, he seemed even less receptive to new ideas than the less intellectual Thatcher, whose thinking had developed from an endorsement of 'Butskellism' to proselytizing for monetarism. The man who spoke with semi-religious reverence of Labour as 'our great Movement' and who railed against social injustice and Tory privilege could nevertheless describe his journalistic mentor, the arch-capitalist Lord Beaverbrook, as someone he 'loved', not 'merely as a friend but as a second father'.[27] Indeed, many of Foot's early philippics against the titans of capitalism were written from a house provided for him on Beaverbrook's estate at Cherkley in Surrey. His rare combination of deep political passion and broad-ranging sympathies was apparent even in the naming of his dog Dizzy after Benjamin Disraeli, a Tory he admired albeit primarily for his outsider status, his radicalism and his novels. Foot's childhood had been spent in a house that allegedly contained fifty thousand books and it was an environment he replicated at his own home in – appropriately – Pilgrim's Lane, Hampstead, where every corner was cluttered with the collection of a dedicated bibliophile. He was equally at ease with normal life and ordinary people. He remained a devoted, and unaffected, fan of Plymouth Argyle FC.

The hope that Foot would prove a more unifying figure than Denis Healey helped secure him the Labour leadership. The prompt defection of the Gang of Four demonstrated how misguided a calculation this had been, but throughout the tumults, insults and accusations aimed at him, Foot did his best to conduct himself without rancour. Unlike many on the left who were unable to contain their rage at the Thatcherite onslaught, he tried to avoid descending into personal attacks on the prime minister. Happily married to the socialist film-maker Jill Craigie, he discovered late in life that three years into their marriage she had been attacked and raped by the writer Arthur Koestler. Asked how he would have acted if he had learned of the attack at the time, Foot responded: 'I don't know. I think I would have written him a letter – something like "our friendship is at an end".'[28] Such punch-pulling moderation seemed at odds with a man whose fragile appearance concealed an extraordinary fighting spirit, deployed with brilliant oratorical effect against his political opponents and reinforced by absolute certainty in the morality of his cause. Truly he was, in the words of his biographer, Kenneth O. Morgan, 'a kind of Methodist Danton'.[29]

It was more Saint-Just, the Jacobin ideologue who held his head like a holy sacrament, that Tony Benn was beginning to resemble. Certain of his own incorruptibility, the justice of his cause and the rightness of harnessing the energy of hard-left activists in the struggle that lay ahead, Benn was not prepared to suppress his talent for factionalism just because Labour now had a leader from his wing of the party. His relationship with Foot got off to an edgy start in their first meeting after Benn joined the shadow Cabinet in January 1981. Foot accused Benn of holding secret convocations with other left-wingers to 'fix votes in advance' on the NEC. When Benn gave an evasive answer, Foot lost his temper and shouted: 'You're a bloody liar.' Benn responded by storming out of the room.[30] Their relationship did not improve, with Foot exasperated by Benn's refusal to regard himself as bound by shadow Cabinet decisions. Benn was far more interested in reaching common positions with his cohorts from the CLPD and regarded the constitutional revolution within the Labour Party to be just started rather than at a satisfactory end. He was as much a hate-figure to the right as was Enoch Powell to the left, but while Powell had taken his tormented talents off to the margins of the Ulster Unionist Party, Benn was far better placed to set the agenda. Extraordinarily for a politician who had never held higher office than secretary of state for industry, the expression 'Bennite' – as in 'a Bennite solution' – entered the popular lexicon. Like Foot, he was another ex-Oxford Union president and scion of a political family. Somewhat embarrassingly, his Liberal-turned-Labour father had, as secretary of state for India in 1930, ordered Gandhi's arrest for civil disobedience. There was no confining the son's lack of deference to the established order. Upon his father's death in 1960, Benn refused to inherit his title as Viscount Stansgate. In doing so, he created a constitutional stand-off which was settled only by the innovation of the right to renounce a peerage. The manner in which the Hon. Anthony Wedgwood Benn, husband of an American socialist millionairess, recast himself as Tony Benn, the people's tribune, evidenced the triumph of his engrained egalitarian instincts over the accident of his birth – as well as demonstrating his recognition that he could not greatly influence the people's party from the House of Lords.

Given the personalities involved and the rival outlooks they championed, the promise of one of the great political set-piece dramas of the decade was assured in September 1981 when Labour's MPs, activists and trade union leaders gathered in Brighton for the annual party conference, where they would elect the deputy leader. The contest was recognized as significant far beyond the limited authority enjoyed by the holder of the office, for it seemed to be a dry-run for Foot's eventual successor. As such, the battle between Tony Benn and Denis Healey was about the soul and the future of the Labour Party. That is why it was so bitter.

The weeks of campaigning stretched relations between the contenders to breaking point. Benn received a standing ovation from a 2,300-strong audience in Newcastle, where he denounced Foot's 'infantile and trivial critique' of socialist dogmatists.[31] Meanwhile, Healey's public meetings were drowned out by booing and hissing. A supportive Labour MP, John Golding, who was with him on the platform in Birmingham, observed the antics of the crowd and concluded that the disruption was 'totally organized. There was chanting, singing and the clenched first. It's like the Hitler Youth.'[32] Healey inflamed passions by misidentifying the CLPD's Jon Lansman as the chore-ographer of the hecklers. This was not the CLPD's style. Rather, Benn's support for causes like the IRA hunger strikers made him popular with a rabble army, some of it with tenuous links to the Labour movement. Benn did call for respect to be shown to both candidates,[33] but, believing the old mantra that there were no enemies on the left, he was in no hurry to turn away support wherever it was to be found.

The public meetings and traded insults were only the warm-up act to the main event, the casting of votes at Brighton. With the block votes of the trade union leaders accounting for 40 per cent of the electorate, a handful of union delegations effectively held the balance of power. The race's also-ran, John Silkin, was eliminated on the first ballot. He had been backed by the Transport and General Workers' Union (TGWU). That this union – the country's biggest – cast its 1.25 million votes for Silkin aptly illustrates the undemocratic nature of the system. A consultation of regional organizers showed that the majority supported Healey, which the union's executive committee interpreted as an endorsement of Benn on the basis of the views of the organizers from the more populous regions. The conference delega-tion then simply ignored both these interpretations of what their members wanted and plumped for Silkin as a compromise candidate.[34] With Silkin removed from the final ballot, the TGWU delegation was forced to decide, in the fevered atmosphere of the conference hall, how to cast its 1.25 million votes. Word went out that they had decided the safest thing to do would be to abstain. It was a decision that appeared to enthrone Healey. As the evening drew towards its theatrical climax, he duly processed into the conference hall exuding a sense of pending triumph. But pride came before a fall. As he settled into his chair, he learned that exactly the sort of 'smoke-filled room' stitch-up of which Shirley Williams had warned would happen under the new voting arrangement. Amid intense lobbying and internal wrangling, the TGWU delegation was persuaded to change its intentions. The union's 1.25 million votes were now being cast for Benn instead. Suddenly the result was too close to call. Across the conference floor and in the surrounding bars and function suites, furious horse-trading was taking place, with both sides rec-ognizing that just a few switched votes could seal their candidate's fate. The future Foreign Secretary and deputy leader, Margaret Beckett, was observed screaming 'Traitors!' at Healey voters.[35] One of those at the tussle's sharp end was Neil Kinnock, an up-and-coming Welsh MP and shadow educa-tion secretary, who had run Foot's leadership campaign. Having stated that he did not have 'any significant disagreements over policy with Tony Benn',[36] Kinnock shocked fellow left-wingers by instead announcing that he would abstain (in part because he disliked Benn's disloyalty towards Foot). Assailed in the conference hall for his apostasy and spat on in the melee beyond, Kinnock endured a torrid week, the low point of which came when he sought a moment's relief in the gents' lavatory of the Grand Hotel. There he found himself standing next to one of Benn's young acolytes, who promptly took a flying kick at him. However, the member for Bedwellty was not a man to be flattened lightly. 'I beat the shit out of him,' the shadow education secretary boasted, 'there was blood and vomit all over the floor.'[37]

Away from the fists flying amid the plumbing and porcelain, Healey remained under the glare of the conference-hall lights, trying to appear unflappable while rethinking the complicated electoral calculations in his head. He knew he could count on the support of the overwhelming majority of MPs. But this advantage was cancelled out by the equal weighting given to the constituency activists, 80 per cent of whom cast their votes for Benn. How was the horse-trading between the union brothers working out? The final result, when it was declared, was met with audible gasps, cheers and shock. Tony Benn had secured 49.574 per cent of the vote. Healey's margin of victory was 0.852 per cent, the statistical equivalent of a hair's breadth.

Breaking the Mould?

Those who assumed the SDP would be the real losers from the battle of Brighton were in for a surprise. While Healey's victory may have persuaded some wavering Labour MPs to give their party a second chance, it was wishful thinking to hope that it would silence the telephones at SDP headquarters. Far from it – having stalled somewhat since the exciting post-launch days, the SDP was about to enjoy a second surge. During the summer, Labour recovered to almost a 10 per cent lead in the opinion polls, while in the race for second place the Tories and the SDP–Liberal Alliance interweaved within two to three points of each other. All this changed during the autumn. Driven both by the Conservatives' failure to bring spiralling unemployment under control and by Labour's internal bloodletting, the Alliance began to move into a comfortable lead. What especially aided its fortunes at this time was a succession of by-elections which allowed it to show its vitality and to garner support as a protest vote against the perceived extremism of the two traditional parties.

During the early eighties, the media still treated by-elections as major political events. Fleet Street pundits and sketch writers enjoyed the opportunity to get out and about in parts of the country that would not otherwise command their attention. Most of all, the BBC invested considerable time, energy and the talents of its by-election specialist Vincent Hanna in turning by-election campaigns into a form of entertainment. Cameras followed the candidates and their front-bench minders around as they solicited votes, kissed babies and dodged the occasional flying egg. Lacking roots and institutional history, the SDP was especially dependent on this sort of publicity to stay in the public eye, and it was fortunate that during 1981 and 1982 they were able to capitalize on a number of by-elections.

The first to come up was in Warrington. Located between Liverpool and Manchester, it was a traditionally northern and working-class constituency, where Labour had enjoyed a 62 per cent share of the vote in 1979. As such, it seemed unfertile ground for a new party to take root. Rather than flunk this challenge, Roy Jenkins courageously stepped forward. There was some doubt that Warrington was really the place for the claret-loving *bon viveur*, but he seemed refreshingly unabashed. 'I have represented one of the most industrial seats in Birmingham for twenty-seven years,' he beamed amiably, 'I believe I had happy relations with them. I certainly won nine elections there.'[38] Still, it was a risk letting him loose on the streets without the protection of a Labour rosette. A much-retold story had it that, as Home Secretary, Jenkins had once visited a prison and attempted to strike up a conversation with an inmate with the guileless salutation: 'How nice to see you here.' Another anecdote maintained that when he stood for the Labour leadership in 1976 his campaign manager told him to go to the Commons bar and buy a wavering fellow Labour MP a pint. He took the instruction literally, leaving the bemused elderly member to sup the beer on his own.[39] It was therefore to the surprise of his detractors that Jenkins proceeded to pound the streets of Warrington with determined vigour, showing himself far more approachable and at ease with ordinary people than the popular caricature of him suggested. When the result was declared, it was a sensation – and not because the Tory candidate lost his deposit. Labour's majority shrunk from over ten thousand to just 1,759. Jenkins had come close to defeating Labour in its own heartland, achieving a swing to the SDP of 23 per cent. It was, as Jenkins admitted from the returning officer's platform, the first time he had lost an election and it was the best result he had ever achieved. No more the insouciant loner in the Gang of Four, he had in the space of a few tumultuous weeks of old-fashioned campaigning made himself the first among its equals.

By the time the next by-election was underway, the Liberal–SDP Alliance was up and running. The electoral pact was overwhelmingly endorsed at the Liberal Party conference in Llandudno in a mood of such heady excitement that David Steel ended his rallying speech with the triumphant assertion (subsequently the butt of much ridicule): 'I have the good fortune to be the first Liberal leader for over half a century who is able to say to you at the end of our annual assembly: go back to your constituencies and prepare for government.'[40] The following month came what seemed like proof of the Boy David's power of prophecy in a by-election fought in the Conservative marginal of Croydon North-West. It was decided that a Liberal would contest it, partly because the candidate already selected, a local activist – complete with beard, if not actually sandals – named Bill Pitt, stubbornly refused blandishments to step aside. When Pitt had been the Liberal candidate there in 1979 he had managed less than 11 per cent of the vote. This time, as the Liberal–SDP Alliance candidate, he won the seat with a 40 per cent share and a majority in excess of three thousand. If the Alliance could win with Bill Pitt, his SDP helpers conceitedly bitched, it could win with anybody.[41]

In November, Crosby came up. A prosperous constituency outside Liverpool, this seemed a rock-solid Conservative seat, even with the difficulties currently battering the party in government. It was far from an ideal seat for Shirley Williams, but aware that, having ducked the opportunity to stand in Warrington, she could not be seen to be running away from another tough challenge, she put herself forward. In doing so, she achieved what was the biggest turnaround in British parliamentary by-election history. A Conservative majority of 19,272 was overturned and Williams, who had spent weeks traversing the constituency to the strains of the soundtrack to *Chariots of Fire*, was sent to Parliament with a majority in excess of five thousand. Little wonder that in her victory speech she announced: 'This is not for us a party but a crusade.'[42] At any rate, it was beginning to take on the aspect of a great American religious revival, offering hope and excitement to all those caught up in it.

Warrington, Croydon and Crosby were three different sorts of seats and the Alliance's level of success in them all suggested its appeal was neither sectional nor regional. Psephologists noted that if a Crosby-style swing was repeated at the next general election, the Parliament returned would consist of 533 Alliance MPs, seventy-eight Labour MPs and four lonely – and doubtless fractious – Conservatives. The mould of British politics looked ready to be smashed to smithereens.

6   THE EMPIRE STRIKES BACK

The Last Good-Old-Fashioned War?

Despite the fact that mainland Britain enjoyed a half-century of generally peaceful conditions after 1945, two of the dramas that best illustrate her changing fortunes over the period were both wars. More than any other event, the 1956 Suez crisis demonstrated that Britain was no longer a front-rank power: the political and economic consequences of trying to secure a Middle Eastern canal and destabilize an Arab dictator were more than the country could manage. Decision-makers and opinion-formers spent the next quarter-century gripped by a sense of wounded pride, impotence and a belief that the task of statecraft was successfully to manage the nation's all too apparent decline. The second defining conflict was the Falklands War of 1982. Logistically and militarily, success in the South Atlantic was more difficult to pull off than at Suez. Yet victory was absolute and the result was an injection of positive thinking into the British psyche that had been quite absent after Suez.

How and why did this rediscovery of British resolve come about? The character of the prime minister was one obvious difference. Resolute, determined, quickly mastering her brief, Thatcher conducted herself during the critical weeks of 1982 in a manner wholly at variance with that of the nervy and neurotic Anthony Eden in 1956. Overcoming the opposition of her Foreign Office and the instincts of much of Whitehall, she did not flinch and was subsequently rewarded by the electorate for showing she was *man* enough for the tough decisions that some of her critics – not least in her own party – seemed temperamentally inclined to funk. There was also the question of the cause. The Falkland Islanders were a quiet, inoffensive folk who had never done anyone any harm. The British objective was as clear as it was limited: to liberate them and their islands from a neo-fascist military junta notorious for murdering those who spoke out against it. As such, the mission had rather more of the cause of righteousness about it than engaging in a deceptive manoeuvre aimed at Middle Eastern regime change.

Nor was this all. Britain was economically weak in 1982, in different but no less serious ways than she had been in 1956. However, a mixture of market liberalization and high interest rates, fortified by increasing oil receipts, ensured she had a floating – but strong – currency. By contrast, Eden's government had found itself trying to support a fixed exchange rate under such daily assault that the run on the pound risked exhausting the Treasury's reserves. This difference leads on to a yet greater consideration. Over Suez, Britain had acted against American wishes and duly discovered that it was subject to that higher power. Washington looked both ways in the first weeks of the Falklands crisis, yet lent valuable logistical assistance to Britain in the critical phase of the war. Thus, while the natural response to victory in the South Atlantic was a renewed sense of national resurgence, one aspect had not changed since 1956 – anything might be possible, so long as the Americans were onside.

Far from being a distant distraction that happened to have major domestic political ramifications, the Falklands War was, first and foremost, a significant military event. Its origins owed more to the preoccupations of the nineteenth century than to the Cold War in that it was about ownership of a territory rather than a contest for ideological supremacy. Notwithstanding the American logistical assistance, it proved to be (at the time of writing) the last major engagement that Britain fought on its own, rather than as merely a partner – and usually a junior partner – in an international coalition. It also marked the end of an era in the manner in which it was fought. The major conflicts in the decades after 1982 were asymmetric, which is to say that they involved a glaring mismatch between one side – for instance, Chechens, Iraqis or Islamist fighters – using low-grade weapons and guerrilla tactics against front-rank military powers deploying cutting-edge technology, overwhelming firepower and unchallenged air supremacy. The battle for the Falklands, in contrast, was between two armed forces using roughly the same quality of weaponry against each other. Indeed, with the exception of the missiles fired from out at sea, the weapons the British and Argentine soldiers aimed at each other were not especially different from those used in the Second World War: artillery shells, mortars, machine guns and even fixed bayonets.[1] Except for what limited satellite imagery the British could beg from the Pentagon and the Argentines from the Soviets,[2] neither side enjoyed the technology to spy from space on what the other was doing. If the combatants on the Falklands wanted to know what was on the other side of the hill, they had to stay camouflaged, sneak up close, get out their binoculars and hope an unseen marksman was not drawing a bead on them.

Nothing could be more mistaken than the notion that the British forces' professional superiority was such that once they had secured a bridgehead on the islands their victory over badly equipped and ill-trained Argentine conscripts would be inevitable. The British troops were fitter and better trained, displayed tighter discipline and used superior radio communications.[3] But that was about the extent of their advantage. Conscripts or not – and many were crack troops – the Argentines possessed the benefit of time to select the most advantageous terrain, to dig in, to lay minefields and to entrench their positions. When battle was first joined, they outnumbered the British by a margin of three to one, a direct inversion of the odds usually deemed necessary to cancel out the advantage of defending rather than attacking. With fresh cargoes being landed at Stanley airport almost until the end of hostilities, they were often better supplied and better fed than the British. To win, all the Argentine troops needed to do was to delay British success beyond the onset of winter, when the weather would make it impossible for the British to remain in the South Atlantic. Thus the British had to secure victory at rapid speed – in reality, about three months – or lose the war. Logistically, the British were in a far weaker position, having to be supplied by a floating, and highly vulnerable, armada of ships thousands of miles from secure bases, in a war zone where, for most of the conflict, it was the Argentine air force that retained the edge in controlling the skies. Indeed, besides Britain's better strategic thinking and superior soldiering, pure luck proved among the deciding factors. If only a few more bombs had detonated when they hit their targets, the British task force could have been crippled. As with the Duke of Wellington's famous assessment of Waterloo, the battle for the Falklands was 'the nearest run thing'. And, for all that, it was no less decisive.

White Flags over Whitehall

How the fate of some windswept and underpopulated islands in the South Atlantic could end up causing a war that claimed a thousand lives was unfathomable to many who were not caught up in its partisan passions. Giving his response to Britain's torpedoing of the Argentine light cruiser *General Belgrano*, the West German minister Heinz Estphal expressed the utter incredulity felt in Bonn. It was, he said, 'inconceivable and incomprehensible' that a fellow European country could have gone to war over such an issue 'shortly before the dawning of the new millennium'.[4] The novelist Jorge Luis Borges described the conflict as 'two bald men fighting over a comb'. With such disdainful impartiality, he stood detached from the long complaints of historical injustice volubly expressed by his Argentine compatriots, successive generations of whom were nurtured on the belief that, by rights, the Falkland Islands were *Las Malvinas*, stolen in an act of British piracy. Ownership of the islands excited no comparable passion in the United Kingdom until Friday, 2 April 1982, when the news that they had been forcibly seized generated a mixture of outrage and bewilderment – and, doubtless, for many a scramble to the atlas to find out where they were located. The cartography showed that, besides smaller outcrops, they comprised two major islands, East and West Falkland, which together were about half the size of Wales. There were one thousand eight hundred inhabitants, half of whom lived in the capital, Port Stanley, and the rest in small villages and scattered settlements spread out across a landscape that was reminiscent of the west coast of Scotland (upon eventually visiting it, Thatcher's husband, Denis, memorably summed it up as 'miles and miles of bugger all'). A further insight into the nature of these distant possessions was offered to those who looked up the design of the Falkland Islands' flag, which featured the Union Jack and a thickly fleeced sheep.

That the islands were a British dependency was long established, albeit a reality legally untested in an international court of arbitration. It is impossible to guess what verdict a UN-backed committee might have come to on the matter, since it would depend on whether it placed the most weight on the islands' history, their geography, the cause of anti-colonialism or the rights of self-determination. As with UN judgements generally, much would doubtless have hinged upon the national composition and ingrained prejudices of those nominated to the relevant committee. Without such adjudication, British possession effectively amounted to nine tenths of the law, an injustice against which Argentina made two main claims. The first was that they legitimately owned *Las Malvinas* before the British stole them, and the second was that the islands were considerably nearer (three hundred miles away) to Argentina than to the UK (eight thousand miles away).

The geographical fact of Argentina's proximity was hardly a clinching argument. If it had been a guiding principle, it would have triggered any number of boundary revisions all over the globe. Indeed, Argentina had been more than happy to dismiss the geographical proximity argument during its 1973 dispute with Uruguay over the island of Martín García. Historically, it was unclear who, if anyone, truly owned the *Malvinas/ Falkland Islands* prior to their becoming a British crown colony, with their own governor, executive and legislative councils, in 1845. Whether the islands were first spotted in the sixteenth century by British or Spanish mariners was disputed, although it was the British who made the first recorded landing, in 1690. There having been no indigenous population, the much-cited issue of colonialism was irrelevant, since uninhabited islands have to be colonized by someone if they are to be settled. The debate therefore descended into an exchange of conflicting claims over who got there first, who got there in larger numbers, and who stayed for the longer period. At the same time as a British settlement was established on West Falkland in 1766, a two-year-old French settlement on East Falkland was ceded to

Spain. By 1811, neither the British nor the Spanish remained on the islands. Five years later, the nascent Argentina gained independence from Spain and in a giant land grab unilaterally laid claim to all of Spain's South American possessions, including what became Uruguay, Paraguay, Bolivia and Chile. When it was made clear that the new state's ambitions also extended as far as the Falkland Islands, the British objected, and in 1833 two Royal Navy vessels turned away an Argentine colonizing party and re-established the British settlement. Thereafter, during the succeeding 149 years, the islands were continuously British, with a population of one thousand eight hundred establishing itself, 95 per cent of whom were originally of British stock and were equally determined to remain British.[5]

The irony was that Britain's Foreign Office did not want the Falkland Islands. Since 1966, diplomats had been trying to find ways round the islanders' obstinate loyalty to their mother country. Good relations with the right-wing Argentine military dictators were seen of being of greater long-term benefit. Britain's trade and investment with the Falklands was a tiny fraction of that with Argentina, leading Whitehall to argue that rapport with Buenos Aires should not be continually hampered by fewer than two thousand, not very economically productive, kelpers and sheep-farmers. After all, what of the business interests of the seventeen thousand British citizens living and working in Argentina? While there was occasional talk that the Falklands might eventually prove their worth if untested analyses of oil deposits in the area were to prove accurate, this was deemed a distant possibility. In so far as it influenced Whitehall's thinking, it was to make the argument for reaching an understanding with Argentina all the more pressing. After all, developing an oil industry in the South Atlantic would be especially difficult if it was obstructed by the only nearby mainland country. With oil, as with everything else, the Falkland Islands were too remote for their inhabitants to have access to regular supplies and easy travel arrangements if Argentina were to cut off all links. Seemingly, the most inexpensive way to prevent such isolation was to appease the despots in Buenos Aires.

Yet, modest though their revenue was, the Falklands were only a minor drain on British resources. In good years, they had even raised more than was spent on them. What was more, the islanders had shown themselves almost embarrassingly grateful for the meagre benefits they got in return for their loyalty. During both world wars, they had pulled together their tiny savings to gift them to Britain's war effort. In the Battle of Britain alone, ten Spitfires were paid for by the kelpers of the South Atlantic. In particular, being British meant they did not have to be ruled either by demagogue populists like the Perons or by the quasi-fascist military juntas that had, on and off, been misruling Argentine territory for over half a century. Fear of such a regime was wholly explicable. Since instigating the 'Dirty War' in

1976, the junta's death squads had murdered eleven thousand Argentine citizens – the euphemistically named 'disappeared' – and were still engaged in murdering dissidents and insurgents when, in 1982, the regime added the Falkland islanders to its list of internal opponents.[6] At the height of the most brutal period of repression, it took the former navy man James Callaghan to put his appeasing diplomats in their place with the outburst: 'I'm not handing over one thousand eight hundred Britons to a gang of f---ing fascists.'[7]

This was the sentiment – if not the precise language – that most resonated with Margaret Thatcher. When advised that it would be courteous to send a friendly message to the new junta of General Leopoldo Galtieri, which had seized power in Argentina in December 1981, she replied icily that she did not send messages 'on the occasion of military takeovers'.[8] Whitehall officials despaired of such an emotional attitude to problem-solving; in November 1980 the Foreign Office revived an idea that had been mooted during the 1970s: Britain would cede sovereignty of the Falklands to Argentina in return for a fifty-year lease-back, which would give the islanders time either to acclimatize to the change or to depart (the latter, incidentally, was easier said than done, because the British Nationality Act 1981 had failed to grant them automatic residency rights in the mother country). Reluctant to be seen to contradict her minister's scheme directly, Thatcher was more than content to let back-bench Tory MPs join with opposition politicians to scupper the lease-back initiative in Parliament. Yet the Foreign Office's inability to secure its preferred measure of appeasement was followed by the failure of the Treasury and the Ministry of Defence to recognize the need to preserve a military commitment in the South Atlantic. The result was a policy of calamitous folly – curtailing Buenos Aires's expectations of a diplomatic settlement while all but stripping the Falkland Islands of their defences. For such was the inescapable conclusion to be drawn from the cuts announced in June 1981 by the defence secretary, John Nott. The Royal Navy was to bear the brunt, reduced from a worldwide role to become little more than a home waters force on anti-submarine patrol. The Chatham dockyards would close and the number of surface ships was to be slashed. Among the vessels to be axed were the aircraft carriers HMS *Hermes* and HMS *Illustrious*, the assault ship HMS *Fearless* – all three of which were to prove essential prerequisites for retaking the Falklands – six destroyers and HMS *Endurance*, which was the sole South Atlantic patrol ship. By itself, the lightly armed *Endurance* could hardly have held up an entire invasion fleet, but it was a useful spy ship and, even more importantly, a symbol of Britain's determination to defend its outpost. Announcing that it was to be scrapped was tantamount to signalling that Britain had lost the will to protect the Falklands.

The news of these defence cuts did not come as a great surprise in Buenos

Aires. Among the principal advocates and planners of a Falklands invasion force was Admiral Jorge Anaya, who derided the British as *maricones*,* a judgement formed while he was naval attaché in London in the mid-1970s. In 1977, Argentina had illegally set up a hut manned by twenty – presumably very cold – personnel on South Thule, the most easterly (and otherwise uninhabited) of the Falkland Islands dependencies. Not only did Britain take no measures to eject them, the then Foreign Secretary, Anthony Crosland, even begged Buenos Aires not to make their presence public.[9] While the Callaghan government did meet the escalating tension by directing a nuclear-powered submarine towards the Falklands, the Argentine junta may not have been aware of the manoeuvre at the time.[10] At any rate, there was no reason to assume this show of willpower would set a precedent: to Latin American eyes, the new Conservative administration seemed to contain at least as many *maricones* as its Labour predecessor.

Where Britain's economic problems brought retrenchment, Argentina's difficulties encouraged assertiveness. With national bankruptcy looming and an inflation rate heading past 130 per cent, the government in Buenos Aires decided what the country needed was the heady distraction of an easy victory. Almost immediately after assuming power, the new junta of General Galtieri, Admiral Anaya and the air force chief, General Lami Dozo, began planning to invade the Falkland Islands and their dependent island of South Georgia, eight hundred miles to the east. Of these intentions, Britain was unaware. The militarist nature of the Argentine regime, the possibility that it might strike before the 150th anniversary of the Falklands becoming a British colony, which would fall in 1983, and the increasingly hostile rhetoric emanating from Buenos Aires were sufficient for Thatcher to minute 'we must make contingency plans' on 5 March 1982,[11] but scarcely represented grounds to divert a significant Royal Navy detachment, which might, in any case, succeed only in exacerbating tension. Reasons to be apprehensive nevertheless continued to mount. During March, more Argentine planes than usual infringed the Falklands' airspace. Another disturbing, but by no means definitive, sign of trouble came on 20 March, when members of the British Atlantic Survey on South Georgia reported that fifty Argentine scrap-metal contractors, some in paramilitary uniforms, had landed and hoisted their national flag at the old whaling station of Leith. The intruders were not the scrap-metal contractors they claimed to be but the vanguard of a detachment of Argentine marines. What London did not know was whether they represented the first wave of a full-scale invasion or were merely a token gesture, comparable to the 1977 landing on South Thule. It was only clear that their presence could not be hushed up – South Georgia was a 110-mile-long

---

* Ineffectual and effeminate (or homosexual) men.

island, not an insignificant dot on the map like South Thule. Either Britain did nothing and effectively showed itself to be content to let intruders take over South Georgia, or an international incident would have to be risked by removing them – if necessary, by force.

The Foreign Office concluded it had no option but to lodge a formal protest and demand that the 'scrap-metal' party leave the island. As a back-up, *Endurance* was ordered to South Georgia with a detachment of Royal Marines on board to assist the intruders' departure. This belated display of martial spirit was to prove one of the most providential decisions of the whole crisis, for it brought matters swiftly to a head, with unexpected consequences. The junta was planning to invade the Falkland Islands in late May (when the onset of the South Atlantic winter would have made it impossible for a British relief force to assemble around the islands for at least six months). It was the sudden crisis over South Georgia that provided the pretext for the junta to act and to do so without further delay. Thus, on 26 March, the junta of Galtieri, Anaya and Lami Dozo brought forward their plans and took the decision to launch the invasion of the Falklands on 2 April. They assumed that Britain possessed neither the will nor the means to get its islands back. And they would have been right about the means if only they had waited – just long enough to meet their original May invasion schedule might have been sufficient; waiting until Nott's defence cuts had been implemented would certainly have delivered victory to the junta. Instead, impetuosity did for yet another dictatorship.

As the subsequent Franks report attested, British intelligence knew nothing of the junta's decision to attack. Not that it would have made much difference if spies had been secreted all round the Casa Rosada – the 'Pink house', Argentina's official presidential residence – for there would have been no time to dispatch a force sufficient to repel the Argentine assault. In the dash to the Falklands, Argentina was always going to get there first. All Whitehall knew for sure was that the situation was critical, that *Endurance* might be fired upon and that a full-scale invasion was at least a possibility. On 29 March, the Ministry of Defence ordered the nuclear submarines HMS *Spartan* and HMS *Splendid* from their Scottish base of Faslane. They would reach the Falklands on 11 April. A story was planted on the front page of *The Times* announcing (erroneously) that another nuclear sub, HMS *Superb*, 'was believed to be on its way' to the Falkland Islands.[12] It was news that came too late to have a deterrent effect. The invasion fleet had already put to sea. A vast armada, supported by the flagship of the Argentine navy, the aircraft carrier *Veinticinco de Mayo*, was within four days of its destination. The Falkland Islands and South Georgia were doomed.

It was late on 30 March that John Nott informed Thatcher that there could be no doubt that there was an Argentine fleet heading straight for the Falklands' capital, Port Stanley. Most of the information Nott was receiving from the Ministry of Defence suggested that Britain could not retake the islands.[13] A national humiliation seemed unavoidable. A country that within living memory had led an empire covering a quarter of the world had sunk to a state in which it could not retake a few windswept islands from a bankrupt and unstable Latin American dictatorship. Had it come to this? Could the British lion really be so utterly toothless? It was at this sombre stage in the discussions that the First Sea Lord, Admiral Sir Henry Leach (having only with difficulty got past a particularly officious policeman), strode purposefully into the room. Standing in his full uniform and determined to prove the senior service's worth against the impending spending cuts, he contradicted every piece of defeatist advice emanating from the Ministry of Defence. There could be no half-measures, he announced. A task force could be assembled over the weekend and could reach the Falklands in three weeks. 'Three days, you mean,' interjected Thatcher, showing herself still an ingénue about war. She was quickly put right. Having to learn quickly on the job, she carefully cross-examined Leach and asked him if he truly believed the islands could be retaken. Leach replied that 'we could and in my judgement, though it is not my business to say so, we should', because: 'If we do not, or if we pussyfoot in our actions and do not achieve complete success, in another few months we shall be living in a different country whose word counts for little.'[14]

That this flourish left Nott unmoved was immaterial.[15] It struck a penetrating chord with the woman who mattered.

Towards the Abyss

'I hope the people realize,' warned the commander of the British task force, Admiral Sir John Fieldhouse, 'that this is the most difficult thing that we have attempted since the Second World War.'[16] Having spent the first fortnight after the Falkland Islands' invasion overseeing developments from the armed forces' headquarters at Northwood in Hertfordshire, Fieldhouse had been flown down to hold his council of war on board the aircraft carrier HMS *Hermes* with the other principal task force commanders, Rear Admiral Sandy Woodward, Commodore Michael Clapp and Brigadier Julian Thompson. By then, 17 April, the task force was off Ascension Island, a British-owned volcanic pimple of land populated by a US airbase. Situated 3,700 miles from Britain and 3,300 miles from the Falklands, Ascension was a crucial mid-point for the task force to rendezvous and take on extra supplies before heading towards its target, ten days' sail away. Suddenly, the prospect of engaging the Argentine forces in a full-scale war had gone from possible to probable. It was a war for which Britain had done no planning whatsoever.

To the hasty decision to send the task force, Thatcher had met with little by way of opposition in the Cabinet (only John Biffen had expressed doubts when it met on 2 April). It was difficult to disagree with the proposition that a South American military junta would be unlikely to respond to diplomatic initiatives unless they came backed up by the threat of arms. If anything was likely to make Galtieri see sense, it would surely be the Royal Navy – in 1982 still the third-largest navy in the world – bearing down upon his increasingly nervous forces. Only if he remained intransigent would the task force find itself going into battle. Yet it was far too dangerous a game to play as a bluff. If much of Whitehall thought Britain could not win the resulting conflict, it was a reasonable assumption that the same calculation was stiffening resolve in the Casa Rosada. What was more, the very act of sending the pride of the British fleet south created its own momentum. Once the armada had assembled off the coast of the Falkland Islands it could not hang around indefinitely while the diplomatic process was drawn out by one tortuous initiative after another. Midsummer in the United Kingdom would be midwinter in the South Atlantic, bringing conditions that would compel the task force to disperse and return home in a tail-between-the-legs withdrawal which could only be interpreted as an admission of failure.

Given the risks involved and the strong hand held by the junta, the incisiveness of Thatcher's response was remarkable and, to some, deeply worrying. Yet there was no time to be squandered in delay, and the task force began to be put together immediately on 2 April, with a mere weekend assigned to completing the herculean task of recalling sailors from leave, making emergency repairs and modifications, getting all the provisions in the right place and the ships ready for a three-month deployment in the South Atlantic. As evidence that at least the Royal Navy, and its civilian contractors, had not succumbed to the much-discussed 'British disease' of laziness and poor management it was definitive. On 5 April, a large crowd gathered along the harbour walls at Portsmouth to watch the first wave of ships, led by the aircraft carriers HMS *Invincible* and HMS *Hermes*, sail out to an uncertain fate. The government's unease about sending the Queen's son, Prince Andrew, a helicopter pilot on board *Invincible*, into a potential war zone was quashed by his mother, who insisted the second in line to the throne wanted to do his duty without fear or favour. A second armada of ships sailed from Gibraltar with Rear Admiral Sandy Woodward, who assumed command of the carrier battle group.

Over the following weeks, the task force built up to full strength with over one hundred ships sailing towards their common target. There were forty-four warships, twenty-two ships of the Royal Fleet Auxiliary and forty-five supporting merchant ships crewed by civilian volunteers. The impressive spectacle hid considerable shortcomings, which hostilities were certain to expose. There were insufficient purpose-built troop-carriers for an operation of this scale, and those forces expected to spearhead the landings, the 2nd and 3rd Battalions of the Parachute Regiment (2 and 3 Para), and some of the Royal Marines' 3rd Commando Brigade, found themselves travelling on the hastily requisitioned P&O cruise liner *Canberra*. Army reinforcements in the shape of 5 Infantry Brigade followed behind on the similarly requisitioned *Queen Elizabeth II*, which sailed from Southampton on 12 May. There was every reason to be nervous. Once the task force came within range of Argentine planes and missiles, the ships would be sitting ducks unless British domination of the skies could be established. Unfortunately, this could not be guaranteed because their destination was far outside the reach of land-based RAF fighters.

The task force would thus be dependent upon whatever aircraft could be packed on to the decks of the carriers. Unfortunately, the Royal Navy's aircraft carrier HMS *Ark Royal* had already been scrapped – a fact of which Leach found Thatcher to be initially ignorant – and the task force was left with what were actually supposed to be helicopter carriers, the 23-year-old HMS *Hermes*, which had to be diverted from the scrapyard, and HMS *Invincible*, which was a third of the size of *Ark Royal* and, despite being only two years old, was already earmarked for sale to the Australians. Argentine jets firing deadly Exocet missiles were not going to be sent packing by a few Royal Navy helicopters, no matter how proficient their piloting. Hopes therefore rested on the brand-new Sea Harrier aircraft of which the navy had just taken delivery. The Sea Harriers' vertical take-off technology meant they could travel on the decks of *Hermes* and *Invincible* – although, problematically, they were so new that many of their pilots were alarmingly short of experience of flying them. It was not even certain whether the Harriers could be flown effectively at night. Truly, it was a journey into the unknown.

Assembling and protecting the ships off the Falklands was difficult enough; actually landing forces to retake the islands was even more problematic. By the end of April, the Argentines had flooded thirteen thousand troops on to the islands, a ratio that equated to seven soldiers for every islander. Whoever held the capital, Port Stanley, effectively held the Falklands, but the task force had to think carefully about the wisdom of mounting a direct assault on a built-up area – partly because that was where Argentine forces, protected by rings of minefields, were most heavily concentrated, and partly because fighting over the capital risked killing rather than liberating the thousand civilian inhabitants.

When the first wave of Argentines had come ashore near Stanley in the early hours of 2 April, they had faced only a detachment of sixty-nine Royal Marines, armed with nothing heavier than a few rocket-launchers, who were deployed to defend Government House on the western outskirts of the capital. By 6.30 a.m., the islands' governor, Rex Hunt, found his radio link with London cut and Government House surrounded by Argentine commandos. For almost three hours, the Royal Marines resisted, keeping up a barrage of fire that kept the invaders at bay. Despite taking out the commandos' officer, Captain Giachino, the marines found themselves pinned down by overwhelming numbers and any attempt at a break-out would risk civilian lives in street-to-street fighting. At 9.25 a.m., with the audible rumble of Argentine armoured vehicles heading towards Government House, Hunt bowed to the inevitable and ordered the marines to cease fire. They were duly taken prisoner, while the governor did his best to keep his dignity, donning full ceremonial uniform before getting into his official car (a London taxicab) to be driven towards the airport and exile. By then, the Argentine flag was fluttering over his capital. That the new occupiers casually assumed they would not be challenged was evident from the commendable speed with which they repatriated to Britain the captive Royal Marines.

South Georgia's turn came the following day, 3 April. The island was defended by twenty-two Royal Marines which HMS *Endurance* had landed on 31 March, and it was via *Endurance* that they received the order to resist the invasion – but 'not resist beyond point where lives might be lost to no avail'. This was a compromise that Nott and the Foreign Secretary, Lord Carrington, had devised in London after successfully dissuading Thatcher whose instinct – surprisingly – was that the marines should lay down their arms without a fight.[17] While the marines took up position, the British Atlantic Survey team huddled for safety in the church at Grytviken. As soon as the invaders came within sight, the Royal Marines opened up, bringing down a Puma helicopter laden with Argentine marines, inflicting other casualties on the assault party and letting rip at an Argentine corvette that was steaming into the harbour. The *Guerrico* was riddled with over one thousand bullets and sufficiently damaged by direct hits from two anti-tank rockets that it beat a hasty retreat back into the ocean. Nevertheless, as with the battle at Government House, the odds made for an unwinnable situation for the marines. For the second time in twenty-four hours, a British force was forced to surrender, leaving South Georgia at the mercy of Alfredo Astiz, a naval officer unaffectionately known in his homeland as *El Ángel Rubio de la Muerte.** Aside from the brutality he had inflicted upon the regime's domestic opponents, he was wanted on an international arrest warrant in Sweden for the disappearance of a seventeen-year-old girl and in France for the murder of two nuns.

Chanting ecstatically '*Las Malvinas son Argentinas*', great crowds surged into Buenos Aires's Plaza de Mayo to greet the news of Argentina's twin

---

* The Blond Angel of Death.

victories. Trafalgar Square was visited by no comparable demonstration for vengeance, the British public's response being restricted to damage to the Argentine embassy's windows from lobbed tins of corned beef. Most of the anger – and the apprehension – was internalized. An opinion poll published on 6 April suggested that 60 per cent of the public blamed Thatcher for the humiliation.[18] Three days previously, she had faced a tense House of Commons, which had been recalled to sit on a Saturday for the first time since the Suez crisis in 1956. No vote was taken then on the course of action, nor on any subsequent occasion during the crisis. Constitutionally, it was not the legislature's prerogative to determine the government's action in an emergency of this kind. In reality, it did not need a formal vote to tabulate the mood of the House: anything short of a resolute statement from the prime minister would have caused a haemorrhage in her standing with Conservative backbenchers. In particular, the speech by the Tory turned Ulster Unionist, Enoch Powell, unnerved her. She had been dubbed the 'Iron Lady', he reminded the House, but it was the coming weeks that would truly show 'of what metal she is made'.[19] There was more than a hint of menace in his suggestion. She had spent the previous day being subjected to a long list prepared by the Foreign Office of all the negative consequences that could flow from a forceful response to Argentina. But she was in no mood for quibbles and prevarications from a department lampooned for being a hotbed of cold feet. 'What was the alternative?' she subsequently summed up her riposte: 'That a common or garden dictator should rule over the Queen's subjects and prevail by fraud and violence? Not while I was prime minister.'[20] Thus it was that she listened to Sir Henry Leach's can-do approach and, without waiting for a more detailed analysis, dispatched a task force on an operation for which no contingency planning existed. In this one headstrong act, the Cabinet committed Britain to a potential military engagement that ran counter not just to John Nott's recently proposed cuts but to every defence review since Harold Wilson's 1967 abandonment of the East of Suez commitments, whereby British strategy assumed a NATO versus Warsaw Pact conflict in the European theatre rather than British-only operations in distant parts of the world.

This sudden about-turn had the backing of the principal opposition parties. The truth was that neither Shirley Williams nor Roy Jenkins was at all at ease with a military response, but they decided to keep quiet and let the more hawkish David Owen (MP for the naval constituency of Plymouth Devonport) speak on behalf of the SDP as events unfolded. Tories who assumed that, as a veteran campaigner for nuclear disarmament, Michael Foot would make the case for pacifism showed only how little they understood a man who had made his name in 1940 with *Guilty Men*, the passionate denunciation of those who had appeased the fascist dictators. While

Labour's defence spokesman, John Silkin, dismissed Galtieri as 'a bargain-basement Mussolini' and accused Thatcher, Carrington and Nott of being the 'three most guilty people' for not foreseeing the turn of events, it was Foot who pronounced the most articulate case for backing up a diplomatic initiative with the dispatch of a task force:

> There is no question in the Falkland Islands of any colonial dependence or anything of the sort. It is a question of people who wish to be associated with this country and who have built their lives on the basis of association with this country. We have a moral duty, a political duty, and every other kind of duty to ensure that it is sustained.[21]

Behind the scenes, however, the Labour leadership was forced to wage its own war against those in its ranks with no desire to unfurl the Union Jack on Margaret Thatcher's behalf. On Labour's NEC, Tony Benn's motion to oppose the dispatch of the task force was lost by the narrow margin of six votes to five. Benn's rejection of any military attempt to reclaim the islands was one of principle, but he also thought it a mistake to 'tie the Labour Party to Thatcher's collapse'. In the succeeding weeks, it was Benn who became the public face of opposition to the war and, in consequence, he received more mail than at any previous time in his career. Some of it, he conceded, was 'vulgar abuse', but most of it was 'overwhelmingly supportive – I suppose coming primarily from middle-class people'. The sack-loads convinced him that the majority of the British public were against going to war, 'but the media are preventing that view becoming apparent'.[22] He was far from being the only Labour left-winger to argue that a military solution was futile. At the first meeting of the left-wing Tribune Group after the crisis began, Benn recorded Robin Cook assuring his colleagues that the islands' loss was a done deal because Argentina was too strong, that 'the position couldn't be reversed, and the Falklanders wouldn't want us back'.[23]

If that was true, then it was the prime minister who looked like becoming an early casualty of the imbroglio. But first – and on the same day on which Cook, the future Labour Foreign Secretary, was rubbishing the idea that the junta could be confronted – it was the current Foreign Secretary who was tendering his resignation after reading the weekend's press, in particular a damning leading article in *The Times*.[24] Two other Foreign Office ministers followed his example. Thatcher allowed them to fall on their broken swords and replaced Carrington with Francis Pym. Like his predecessor, Pym was an Old Etonian veteran of the Second World War (in which he had won the Military Cross). While a 'wet', he had at least shown backbone as well as foresight in arguing against Nott's 1981 cuts to the Royal Navy. When Nott also offered his resignation, Thatcher refused to accept it, not least because it was necessary to her own reputation that the link between the Argentines' actions and recent defence policy was not formally acknowledged.

Although it had endorsed almost without a quibble the task force's dispatch, the Cabinet was too large and unwieldy for the day-to-day crisis management that would now be necessary and much as Thatcher kept it regularly informed – it mostly met twice a week during the campaign – she took the elderly Harold Macmillan's advice that a tight-knit War Cabinet should be formed to direct operations. It met once, and sometimes twice, a day. It comprised Thatcher, Pym, Nott, the Home Secretary, Willie Whitelaw and also Cecil Parkinson, who, as Chancellor of the Duchy of Lancaster and chairman of the Conservative Party, had no obvious reason for being included other than as a Thatcher loyalist upon whom the prime minister might rely in countering any lurch into 'wet' defeatism by her new Foreign Secretary.

In the weeks before the task force reached its destination, the Foreign Office's role was central to the search for a peaceful solution and, if that failed, international acquiescence in a British military operation. The chair of the United Nations Security Council was at that moment held by Zaire (Congo), and any resolution could be vetoed by either of the two communist permanent members, the Soviet Union and China. While the right-wing junta in Buenos Aires was hardly the sort of regime Moscow normally cared to support, the Soviet Union had, despite the vast expanse of its own prairies, become heavily dependent on Argentine grain. Nevertheless, through what can only be adjudged the skilful diplomacy of the British ambassador to the UN, Sir Anthony Parsons – and an urgent telephone call from Thatcher to King Hussein of Jordan – on 3 April, Britain secured the adoption of resolution 502 by ten votes to one (Panama), with four abstentions (China, the Soviet Union, Poland and Spain). The resolution called upon Argentina to remove her forces from the Falklands and enter into diplomatic negotiations for a settlement with Britain. It was cunningly worded, for it focused on Argentina's resort to force rather than the right of British ownership – a far more contentious issue that several 'anti-colonial' Security Council members would not have endorsed. In this respect, the French helpfully persuaded Zaire and Togo to support the resolution and this neutering of Third World opposition may have persuaded the Soviet Union that there was no point in pursuing the matter. Parsons was in no doubt that the resolution represented about as far as the UN could be pushed, warning the Foreign Office in Whitehall: 'We have virtually no support on the substance of the problem. We must bear this closely in mind for the future in the UN context.'[25] With such considerations to the fore, Britain never officially declared war on Argentina. Doing so would have created more legal problems than it was worth, not least given the Cold War impasse on the Security Council where a Soviet veto of British military action would have been certain. Instead, Britain justified its use of force by invoking the UN Charter's article 51, which allows for the 'inherent right of individual or collective self defence'.

On whom could Britain rely in this moment of crisis? Her position was strongly backed by Commonwealth countries like Canada and Australia. New Zealand even volunteered one of its own frigates to free up an additional Royal Navy ship for service in the South Atlantic. Initially, Britain's partners in the European Community were also supportive, introducing economic sanctions which cut off one third of Argentina's export market. It was as the prospect of military action became more likely that Thatcher discovered the depth of this support. In mid-May, Ireland and Italy opted out of the European embargo, while the West German government scarcely concealed its distaste at Britain's determination to back words up with military deeds. No such pacifistic reflexes were shown by the socialist president of France, François Mitterrand. France rushed to provide Britain with details of the armaments and defence systems it had sold to Argentina and worked with British secret agents to prevent Buenos Aires from acquiring any more of the deadly French-made Exocet missiles through third parties (the Israelis and South Africans being especially keen to help Argentina gain a deadly stockpile). Indeed, Nott concluded: 'In so many ways Mitterrand and the French were our greatest allies.'[26]

With colonial possessions of her own in disparate parts of the world, France had no hang-ups about endorsing the fundamentals of Britain's case for ownership of islands eight thousand miles away. It was a difficult outlook for countries without such a tradition to understand. In particular, the republic that had been the first to break away from the British Empire found itself with a dilemma. That the United States did not leap to the defence of its most militarily and politically important ally in NATO struck many in Britain as perverse and as further evidence that the 'special relationship' was a one-way, unrequited crush. Ronald Reagan's administration had taken office in January 1981 and, for all the sentiments it shared with Thatcher, it also saw Galtieri's regime as an ally in the attempt to create an effective anti-communist defence pact in Latin America. In particular, a British–Argentine war risked triggering the break-up of the Rio Treaty. Signed in 1947, this was a key arm of US strategy in the region and was designed to repel Soviet interference thereby allowing any American country to assist any other that was attacked from outside the American continent.

Argentina's staunchest supporters in the Republican administration were Thomas Enders, the State Department under-secretary responsible for South America, and the extraordinarily tough and uncompromising mistress of realpolitik, Jeane Kirkpatrick. The US ambassador to the UN, Kirkpatrick justified her decision to attend a dinner at the Argentine embassy in

Washington a few hours *after* the invasion of the Falklands with the defence: 'Now, if the Argentines own the islands, then moving troops into them is not armed aggression.'[27] Conscious of her Irish nationalist ancestry, Kirkpatrick was sentimentally anti-British. Instructed from Washington to support UN resolution 502, she pointedly excused herself from attending the debate. Reagan found himself trying to balance the United States' competing interests and to prevent serious internal wrangling within his administration. 'It's a very difficult situation for the United States,' he admitted publicly on 6 April, 'because we're friends with both the countries engaged in this dispute.' Becoming an honest broker was one way of avoiding a painful choice, though this created the problem of whether to refer publicly to *Las Malvinas* or the Falklands. With his own ineffable style, the president settled for 'that little ice-cold bunch of land down there'.

The president and his public were not in unison. Despite the damage done to Britain's reputation in the United States by the deaths of the IRA hunger strikers, when asked to make their choice America's press and popular opinion overwhelmingly preferred to cosy up to the English-speaking democracy than to the epaulettes of a quasi-fascist junta. Be that as it may, what clearly was in Reagan's interest was to defuse the row before battle was joined. He dispatched his Secretary of State, Alexander Haig, to try and find a diplomatic solution. Previously NATO's commander-in-chief, General Haig bore the countenance of a stiff, strong, yet rather frustrated soldier, who was serving the president who had crushed his own White House ambitions. From 9 to 19 April, he commuted between London, Buenos Aires and Washington in an effort to find a workable compromise. The United States' efforts to portray itself as a diplomatic intermediary meant it did not impose economic sanctions on Argentina while these talks were ongoing.

The reality, however, was that it was not just a desire to avoid having to choose between allies that pushed the Reagan administration towards trying to broker a peaceful resolution of the conflict. The Pentagon circulated the top US military advice that a war could not be in Britain's best interests because, given the 8,000-mile logistical difficulties and the absence of the ships and aircraft needed to pull it off, it was simply impossible for Britain to win it.[28] She would be humiliated. This made it even more urgent that a formula should be found that would allow Thatcher to call back a task force that she was otherwise sending to its doom. The real headache concerned what to do if no deal could be agreed. In this debate, the cautious, balanced attitude of the State Department, and to some extent of the White House, was aggressively countered by the intelligence community and, in particular, by the actively pro-British defence secretary, Caspar Weinberger. As far as Weinberger was concerned, if Britain was going to fight, then the United

States had a duty to lend every form of military assistance (short of joining the war) in order to give it at least a chance of victory. It was Weinberger who smoothed over difficulties concerning the use of the US airbase on Ascension Island for the British war effort and passed on intercepts of communications between Buenos Aires and its forces on the Falklands. He also ensured that the task force's urgent requests to be supplied with American Sidewinder missiles were met. Fired by the Sea Harriers, the Sidewinders were to prove invaluable in the battles for air supremacy over the South Atlantic.

By 24 April, the task force was not yet ready to mount an assault on the Falklands but was in a position to retake South Georgia. While fruitless diplomatic initiatives continued to grind on concerning the main islands, the War Cabinet saw no reason to squander the opportunity to secure a far less complicated victory in a military operation that would show the Argentines that the task force was not just for show. In the event, the opening manoeuvres of Operation Paraquet started badly when an SAS reconnaissance party had to be airlifted off a glacier and the presence of an Argentine submarine, *Santa Fe*, forced a ship laden with Royal Marines to do an abrupt about-turn. It was shortly after dawn the following day, 25 April, that the task force's luck turned for the better. British helicopters spotted the *Santa Fe* still on the surface and engaged it, repeatedly hitting the sub with missiles and depth charges and causing sufficient damage that it had to limp, semi-crippled, into the harbour at King Edward's Point. On the island, Alfredo Astiz was commanding a 'Sworn to Die' detachment which, instead, reacted to the shelling from three frigates and the landing of Royal Marines by surrendering without firing a shot. It was then that Astiz followed ignominy with infamy: while holding up a white flag and beckoning the marines towards him, he deliberate tried to lure them over a minefield. To his disappointment, the trigger mechanisms had frozen solid. With the job done and no loss of life to report, a message was sent to the Admiralty in Whitehall: 'Be pleased to inform Her Majesty that the White Ensign flies alongside the Union Jack on South Georgia. God Save the Queen.' Thatcher duly strode out of the front door of No. 10 to bring the news to the waiting reporters and rolling cameras assembled in the evening dusk. She rebutted further questions with the rejoinder: 'Just rejoice at that news and congratulate our forces and the marines . . . Rejoice' – a gut expression of relief which her detractors, editing it to 'Rejoice! Rejoice!', later held up as evidence of her jingoistic enthusiasm for war. It was actually Astiz who exceeded what could have been expected from the turn of events – rather than being extradited to France to face a murder charge, the 'Blond Angel of Death' was sent home to Argentina where he was greeted with a hero's welcome.[29]

Those who assumed the easy victory in South Georgia meant Britain was now gung-ho for action did not know the new Foreign Secretary. On 27 April, Francis Pym agreed with Haig a compromise deal which, they both hoped, would avoid war. The terms were that the task force would be recalled and, in return, Argentina would withdraw its Falklands garrison. The islands would then be governed by a tripartite US–Argentine–British 'Special Interim Authority', pending a final settlement. In the meantime, Argentina would gain the right to appoint 'representatives of the resident Argentine population' – a hitherto unknown entity – to the islands' local administration. The proposal made a hazy reference to 'taking into account' the islanders' wishes, but contained no explicit commitment to respect their right to self-determination as the basis for a final settlement. If the Argentine and British governments could not reach a final settlement, the United States would propose and arbitrate a settlement of its own devising. What happened if this proved unacceptable to either Buenos Aires or London was not addressed. There was the potential for years of impasse and non-cooperation, with all the consequences that such uncertainty about the future would create for an inevitably dwindling number of islanders. It was certainly hard to see Argentina's will crumbling during this period, especially if the islands became depopulated and, in effect, ceased to be inhabited by anyone the British Foreign Office would be feel bound to defend.

There can be little doubt that the Foreign Secretary had negotiated away a position that the prime minister herself was unwilling to relinquish. In her memoirs, Thatcher wrote witheringly that Pym's deal would have allowed Galtieri 'to swamp the existing population with Argentinians' during the period of the islands' tripartite administration and, if his proposals had been accepted, she would have resigned.[30] This was no idle boast. Nott's subsequent analysis was that the majority of the Cabinet and also Parliament would have accepted the deal.[31] Such was the lack of faith in Britain's being able to beat Argentina without unacceptable casualties. However, before it got as far as the full Cabinet, let alone Parliament, the Pym–Haig deal had to be approved by the War Cabinet and there Thatcher found she was not alone. Nott, nevertheless, persuaded her to withhold stating her position publicly until the proposal had been formally put to Buenos Aires. It was risky advice, for if the junta accepted the deal then Thatcher would be in trouble. Pym was proposing to advise the Cabinet that if Argentina agreed to it, Britain should also accept it, otherwise 'even friends and allies will wobble'.[32] He hoped that the loss of South Georgia would convince Galtieri to accept the offer of a peaceful way out. But in this Pym proved himself no psychologist of the dictatorial mind. Galtieri was not looking for a way out. On 29 April, he rejected the Pym–Haig proposals, explaining that Argentina could not accept a provisional administration unless the issue of future Argentine sovereignty over the islands was explicit. Where Whitehall offered fudge, Buenos Aires frustratingly demanded clarity. The dispute would thus be settled not by diplomatic contrivances but by the profession of arms. Bowing to the inevitable, Haig abandoned his peace efforts the next day. The United States duly embargoed military exports to Argentina, but decided not to stop all trade or to sever credit for fear it might result in such a massive Argentine default that the world financial system could be imperilled. Sometimes, it paid to be a debtor.

Sink the *Belgrano*!

The end of the Haig mission exposed the task force to imminent attack. It was now within range of about 160 combat aircraft of the Argentine air force, over eighty of which were fully serviced front-line planes. Most flew from bases on the Argentine mainland, which was officially deemed out of bounds for a British strike (although a covert SAS mission on 17 May to destroy Exocet missiles and Super Étendard aircraft at the Rio Grande airbase was only aborted after its reconnaissance helicopter was detected and had to ditch on the Chilean side of the border). The first priority, therefore, was given to disabling the airfield at Port Stanley, the vital strip from which the Argentine garrison was being regularly resupplied. Hostilities on East Falkland duly commenced on 1 May 1982, with an RAF bombing raid, codenamed Operation Black Buck. Armed with 1,000-lb bombs, Vulcan bombers flew from Ascension Island, which, as a 7,860-mile round trip involving ten mid-air refuellings, was the longest-range bombing mission in history. The raid created a neat line of craters, one of which was strategically almost slap bang in the centre of Stanley's runway. This was sufficient to prevent Argentine Skyhawks and Super Étendards from using the strip, but failed to make it totally unusable. Follow-up missions proved less successful. Indeed, during the course of the war, the airfield peninsula was strafed twenty-two times, hit by 218 bombs and shelled by Royal Navy guns 1,200 times. Yet the results of so much ordnance were underwhelming: Argentina remained able to fly in at least limited supplies until almost the very end of the conflict.[33]

Argentine retaliation for the Vulcan raid was immediate, with thirty-five air sorties engaging the task force during the course of 1 May. In this opening joust, the British Sea Harriers came out on top with seven Argentine aircraft shot down and Caspar Weinberger's Sidewinder missiles proving their worth. The Argentine jets' only success was a hit on HMS *Glamorgan*, which sustained superficial damage. Unharmed were the main targets, *Hermes* and *Invincible*. On board these carriers were the twenty Sea Harriers upon which the task force's defence depended. If the carriers were sunk, then so were Britain's chances of regaining the Falklands. Thus it was that the Royal Navy's frigates and destroyers found themselves acting as 'pickets', or decoys, ready to attract enemy fire and, if need be, sacrifice themselves in order to protect the prize targets. Unfortunately, only two of the ships on picket patrol, the Type-22 frigates *Broadsword* and *Brilliant* (later joined by *Battleaxe*), were armed with Sea Wolf missiles capable of intercepting Exocet missiles. The rest were protected by Sea Dart missiles which, while capable of shooting down missiles incoming from a height, were less effective against the low, wave-skimming path of the Exocet. It was the fear of an Exocet strike that rightly exercised the minds of captains and crew alike.

The main theatre of war was the 200 nautical mile total exclusion zone that Britain had drawn in a radius around the Falklands. Any Argentine ships or aircraft intercepted within this zone were deemed to be hostile and a legitimate target. However, a government clarification on 23 April made it clear that the existence of the zone did not preclude action being taken against any hostile threat beyond the twelve-mile limit of Argentina's territorial waters. Thus the Argentine fleet, hovering just outside the total exclusion zone, understood that it also risked attack. To the north of the zone, the Argentine carrier *Veinticinco de Mayo* posed the greatest threat: not only were her aircraft easily within range to sink the two British carriers, but the *Veinticinco de Mayo* was accompanied by three escorts armed with Exocet missiles. Two of the three British nuclear-powered hunter-killer submarines in the area, HMS *Spartan* and HMS *Splendid*, were dispatched to track down the carrier, for while it remained at sea it possessed single-handed the capacity to destroy the entire British operation.

While Rear Admiral Sandy Woodward fretted about the Argentine carrier group to the north of the total exclusion zone, there was also a second enemy formation loitering to the south of it. This consisted of the light cruiser *General Belgrano* and two destroyer escorts. Having survived a previous life in the US Navy at Pearl Harbor, the *Belgrano* was an elderly behemoth, but she was armed with eight 5-inch and fifteen 6-inch guns, whose shells had a 20-mile range. These easily outmatched anything in Woodward's armoury (his Type-42 destroyers had only a single 4.5-inch gun each – less impressive than that of a main battle tank – with a 13.6-mile range),[34] while the *Belgrano*'s two destroyers were armed with eight Exocets each, able to sink a ship twenty-five miles away. If Woodward's carriers and Sea Harriers were to be taken out by air strikes from the *Veinticinco de Mayo*, the *Belgrano* and her escorts could pummel with impunity the remains of the task force, firing from a range at which there could be no retaliation.

Fearing a pincer movement from the carrier group to the north and the cruiser group to the south, Woodward requested permission to attack. While there was still no confirmed fix on the carrier group, the submarine HMS *Conqueror* had the *Belgrano* group in its sights. During 2 May, the *Belgrano* sailed eastwards towards the task force while skirting the outside of the total exclusion zone. It had already begun to change course back towards the west when the War Cabinet (minus Pym, who was away in New York) approved Woodward's request to attack. It would certainly have been less controversial to have withheld permission until the *Belgrano* had crossed into the total exclusion zone. However, Woodward feared that waiting represented too great a risk, since, if the *Belgrano* were about to turn into the zone, she would follow a course over the underwater ridge known as the Burdwood Bank, where *Conqueror* could not easily remain in pursuit without endangering herself. With permission granted, three torpedoes were launched. The first missed. The second hit the cruiser in its bow. The third hit its stern. Rather than pick up survivors, her escort ships scarpered, leaving the *Belgrano* to go down with 323 of her crew.

Shock at the news reverberated around the world, mostly to Britain's disadvantage. President Reagan promptly pleaded with Thatcher to sheathe her sword. The attack confirmed the worst fears of those European countries that were least keen to be associated with Britain's actions. The Irish defence minister denounced Britain as 'the aggressor', while the Austrian Chancellor, Bruno Kreisky, confirmed he was not prepared to support Britain's 'colonial' claim to the islands. Sir Anthony Parsons observed a rapid change in attitudes at the UN, where 'It began to look as though . . . a horrid NATO country [was] clobbering a poor Third World non-aligned state.'[35] In Britain, divisions were drawn between those who assumed that this sort of thing tended to happen in war – the cruiser was hardly on a sightseeing excursion – and those who thought the attack on it represented a needless escalation, especially when the *Belgrano*'s position outside the total exclusion zone was admitted. The controversy that this last point generated in Britain was rather lost on the Argentines, whose defence ministry later affirmed that the sinking was 'a legal act of war'.[36] There were certainly no qualms in the offices of *The Sun* at the time. The editor, Kelvin MacKenzie, and a small group of staff were trying to bring out their newspaper in the midst of an eleven-day strike by the National Union of Journalists. The features editor, Wendy Henry, reacted to the breaking news by shouting 'Gotcha!' – a coarse sentiment that MacKenzie duly immortalized on the paper's front page. In fact, the most notorious headline in British newspaper history only lasted as long as the first edition. As reports began to suggest that there might have been serious loss of life, even MacKenzie had second thoughts and replaced 'Gotcha!' with the less offensive – though more inaccurate – 'Did 1200 Argies Drown?'[37] But it was the reflex action that caused the trouble and, for many, summed up everything that was distasteful about Rupert Murdoch's right-wing tabloid.

Distasteful or not, the sinking of the *Belgrano* ended the threat from the

Argentine surface fleet. Greatly alarmed, the *Veinticinco de Mayo* hastily returned to the safety of her port, where she cowered impotently for the rest of the war. This was a huge blow to Argentina's fighting effectiveness. Only the submarine *San Luis* remained on the loose and, evading detection, fired torpedoes – which missed – at the frigates *Arrow* and *Alacrity* on 11 May. It is hard to reach any other conclusion than that the *Belgrano*'s demise was one of the turning points of the conflict which, at a stroke, all but removed one of Argentina's three armed services from the battle. Of course, it did nothing to lessen the threat posed by the other two Argentine services and, two days later, on 4 May, Argentine Super Étendard jets spotted HMS *Sheffield*. Despite being on picket duty, the Type-42 destroyer was caught unawares, her radar temporarily inoperable while she was transmitting satellite communication messages. The ship's chefs were busy deep-frying potatoes when the Exocet missile ripped through the hull, engulfing the vessel in fire and killing twenty. Reduced to a burned-out hulk, *Sheffield* floated lifelessly for a bit and then sank, the first Royal Navy warship to be lost since the Second World War. 'In military terms, the Falklands war is turning into a worse fiasco than Suez,' the *New Statesman*'s political editor, Peter Kellner, hastily pronounced. Other commentators on the left were equally quick to interpret *Sheffield*'s fate as proof that Britain should no longer risk pretending to be a medium-rank power. The eminent professor of politics Bernard Crick denounced 'the narrowly legal doctrine of sovereignty' which had ensured only 'atavistic routes of patriotic death when our last shred of power lies in our reputation for diplomatic and political skill'. If ever there was a time to subsume Britain within the greater pulling power of the European Community, Crick was certain this was it.[38]

In the mind of the Scottish Labour MP Tam Dalyell, patriotic death was the conscious policy of a government genuinely wanting to give war a chance. Dalyell was an independent-minded Old Etonian socialist who had resigned from the shadow cabinet because of Foot's support for the war (Foot even endorsed the decision to torpedo the *Belgrano*). Dalyell began a lengthy campaign in which he claimed, as he put it in a speech to the House of Commons, that Thatcher 'coldly and deliberately, gave the orders to sink the *Belgrano*, in the knowledge that an honourable peace was on offer and in the expectation – all too justified – that the *Conqueror*'s torpedoes would torpedo the peace negotiations', which, at that moment, were being organized by the Peruvian government.[39] That Thatcher deliberately engineered a war that killed a thousand servicemen was a serious charge and that it gained some traction was evidence of just how loathsome many judged their prime minister to be. It rested upon a number of assumptions. The first was that the War Cabinet should have disregarded the opinion of the carrier group commander, Sandy Woodward, that the *Belgrano* presented an extreme danger to the task force. The reality was that the previous day British signals intelligence had intercepted a message sent from the Argentine admiralty to the *Belgrano* ordering it to attack the task force.[40] Indeed, no less an authority than the *Belgrano*'s captain, Hector Bonzo, later testified that his ship was poised to go on the offensive when it was hit.[41] Dalyell's second assertion was that but for the sinking (and ignoring the *Belgrano*'s aggressive intent), the conflict was containable. Here, the MP for Linlithgow perhaps took a more sanguine view than the crew of HMS *Glamorgan*, which Argentine Mirage jets had struck and attempted to sink only two days before the *Belgrano* met its fate. Third, Dalyell's conspiracy theory rested upon an assumption, unsupported by the testimonies of the diplomats closest to the negotiations, that Thatcher ordered the *Belgrano*'s sinking because she feared the Peruvian plan was about to secure peace. At the time the War Cabinet gave its approval to sink the *Belgrano*, it had not even seen the detail of any such plan.

What was true was that the Argentines were able to cite the *Belgrano*'s sinking as a reason for turning down the Peruvian initiative. In reality, the plan was similar to the Pym–Haig proposals of 27 April, which Buenos Aires had already rejected. The Peruvian deal called for both sides to withdraw their forces and proposed 'the immediate introduction of [a] contact group composed of Brazil, Peru, the Federal Republic of Germany and the United States into the Falkland Islands', which would have ultimate authority to administer the islands, pending a final settlement. There was another vaguely phrased acknowledgement of the islanders 'aspirations and interests', but not of their right to self-determination.[42] Far from ensuring this initiative was shelved, the *Belgrano*'s sinking led to the government in Lima intensifying its efforts. What was more, with international opinion increasingly hostile to Britain after the loss of the *Belgrano*, on 5 May the War Cabinet – including Pym and, more surprisingly, Thatcher – was even, with qualifications, minded to accept the Peruvian deal.[43] The full Cabinet was all but unanimous in supporting the proposal, with only Michael Heseltine and Lord Hailsham adopting a more hawkish posture.

It was Argentina that again rejected this compromise, the junta calculating that its position would be strengthened if negotiations could instead be passed to – and drawn out by – the UN. Alexander Haig's assessment was that the Argentines 'believe that time is on their side, that Britain's diplomatic support will dwindle and that with the onset of winter in the South Atlantic and possibly the sinking of another ship, we [the Americans] will buckle'.[44] With the failure of the Peruvian plan, efforts to broker peace were duly taken up by the UN secretary general, Javier Pérez de Cuéllar. This development presented particular difficulties for Thatcher. Britain could not be seen to disregard the efforts of the UN secretary general for fear of putting herself in the wrong as far as international opinion was concerned, but every additional week spent in negotiation threatened to push back the date for a ground invasion beyond what the deteriorating weather would permit. Pym and Pérez de Cuéllar worked together on a proposal that envisaged putting the islands beyond the reach of either interested party by handing them over – at least in the short term – to the UN's jurisdiction. However doubtful it is that Thatcher would have acquiesced to this solution, her energy secretary, Nigel Lawson, later wrote that he thought it would have been supported by the majority of the Cabinet. In the event, the question – and the consequent prospect of Thatcher's resignation – never arose, because on 19 May the Argentine junta rejected the plan. As far as Buenos Aires was concerned, '*Las Malvinas son Argentinas*', and not the property of an international and diffusely accountable talking-shop based in New York. Demonstrating a level of dogged fortitude that even Neville Chamberlain lacked, Pym refused to see the latest rejection as a reason to stop searching for a formula. When he made it clear that he wanted to try again, his colleagues finally told him enough was enough. Argentina was never going to agree to anything that did not cede it sovereignty as a precondition. Diplomacy had failed and the weather would soon be turning for the worse. It was time to get a move on with the forcible liberation of the islands.

The following day, the debate in the House of Commons presented few problems for the government. In defiance of their party whip, opposition came from only thirty-three Labour MPs, led by Tony Benn, Tam Dalyell and Dame Judith Hart. Writing in his diary, Benn despaired at the rest of his colleagues, in particular what he described as that 'old Tory warmonger' James Callaghan, offering 'absolutely naked support for Mrs Thatcher'.[45] Meanwhile, the failure of two Tory 'wets', Ray Whitney and Sir Anthony Meyer, to follow their leader was easily swept aside as the action of a couple of eccentric backbenchers with past careers in the diplomatic service. In her Commons speech, Thatcher adopted a Churchillian mantle in which the crisis was an instalment in the great narrative of history: 'Britain has a responsibility towards the islands to restore their democratic way of life. She has a duty towards the whole world to show that aggression will not succeed, and to uphold the cause of freedom.'[46] What was most evident was the extent to which the British public, at first apprehensive and resentful, was swinging determinedly behind military action. An opinion poll for the *Sunday Times* on 2 May (conducted before either the *Belgrano* or the *Sheffield* was hit) showed as many as 60 per cent opposed to reclaiming the islands at the cost of the lives of British servicemen. Confidence in the cause came only with confidence in the prospect of success – a clear example of how opinion is moulded by leaders who lead rather than react to what market research tells them is the popular will. By the time the diplomatic channels were exhausted, support for war had hardened and become far more unconditional. Opinion polls suggested 55 per cent supported the war on 20 May, and 76 per cent the following day. Indeed, far from being fair-weather fighters, by then, 53 per cent of respondents agreed that even heavy casualties were a price worth paying for retaking the islands.

In retrospect, it was the stance of *The Sun* as the newspaper most stridently committed to a military response that came to be seen as the embodiment of this strengthening desire to risk all in combat – going, in one easy move, from bingo to jingo. To the prospect of a peace proposal, *The Sun* responded with the memorable headline 'Stick It Up Your Junta'. A spoof reader offer, promoted with the promise 'Kill an Argie and Win a Metro', was actually the fantasy of *Private Eye* magazine, but it not unfairly satirized the glib tone with which *The Sun* went to war. Yet the tabloid's ill-concealed excitement at the prospect of giving some Latin Americans a good hiding found few echoes elsewhere in the media. Its Labour-supporting rival, the *Daily Mirror* (which still claimed over ten million readers) opposed the war. Unease widely pervaded the broadsheet column inches. The *Financial Times* argued against dispatching the task force, lecturing that Britain should not defend an 'anachronism' but instead adapt to the modern world – an international solution should be found, perhaps by turning the islanders into wards of the UN.[47] Where the *FT*'s opposition was technocratic, the *Guardian* was passionate and outspoken. In the judgement of its celebrated columnist Peter Jenkins: 'We should have no wish to become the Israelis of Western Europe.'[48] Even keener to turn the other cheek was the influential left-leaning weekly magazine, the *New Statesman*. It splashed its front cover with a close-up photograph of a somewhat demonic-looking Thatcher, across which ran the indictment 'THE WARMONGER'. It was not the quasi-fascist junta in Buenos Aires against which the magazine's editor, Bruce Page, riled but 'the thing we still have to call our government – the United Kingdom state . . . so long as it has its dominion over us it will betray us – and make us pay the price of betrayal in our own best blood'.[49] Among the daily broadsheets, only the *Daily Telegraph* and *The Times* unambiguously backed going to war from the first. A much-cited *Times* leading article, 'We Are All Falklanders Now', written by its editor, Charles Douglas-Home, pointed out that the junta well knew how to handle its opponents – 'the disappeared ones' – and that now 'it intends to make a whole island people – the Falklanders – disappear'.[50] There was, nevertheless, no unified line from the Murdoch press. The *Sunday Times* was far less hawkish, warning that a military operation to retake the islands was 'a short cut to bloody disaster'.[51]

Getting accurate news quickly from the South Atlantic was extremely difficult. Journalists travelling with the task force could only send back their reports via the Royal Navy's ship-to-shore transmission system, and copy was often officially vetted as many as four times before being released for publication, usually several days later.[52] Nevertheless, the Falklands War was the last major conflict in which newspaper reports provided more immediate news than television coverage. The war zone was outside of any broadcaster's satellite coverage so video footage had to be flown to Ascension Island from where it could be fed back to London, a process that could take twenty-three days to reach British television screens (three days longer than it took newspaper readers to find out the fate of the Charge of the Light Brigade in 1854).[53] There were no 'impartial' journalists from non-combatant countries able to get anywhere near the war zone, and the slowness with which the Ministry of Defence cleared British journalists' reports inevitably left the BBC seeking other sources of information. This led to them citing 'Argentine claims' against 'British claims' in a manner that suggested the latter were no more credible than the former, an attempt at even-handedness that *The Sun* and some Tory backbenchers found offensive. *The Sun*, in particular, identified 'traitors in our midst' in the BBC and the Labour Party, in a campaign that risked degenerating into a witch hunt. Perhaps most memorable of all was the starring role accorded to a Ministry of Defence civil servant, Ian McDonald, who was conscripted to read out, in slow, measured, sonorous tones, the official version of events, in a manner that harked back to the Reithian dawn of broadcasting. The contrast could not have been greater with the rolling news programmes and live satellite link-ups that provided instant coverage of the Gulf War less than nine years later.

White Flags over Stanley

General Mario Menéndez had dispatched his Argentine army to three main areas. The most diffusely distributed were spread across West Falkland. While there was only a small population of islanders to be guarded on this island, garrisoning it prevented the British task force from using it as a ground base from which to launch operations against the real prize, East Falkland. Menéndez's far larger East Falkland garrison consisted of a 1,100-strong force at Goose Green, a village with an airstrip on a narrow isthmus connecting the two halves of the island, and almost ten thousand troops deployed across the approaches to Port Stanley. This concentration of strength at the key strategic points made far more sense than a scattered dispersal all over the island. The most obvious line of attack by the British would be an amphibious assault near Stanley in an effort to seize quickly both the all-important airport, through which Argentine supplies arrived, and the capital itself, thereby forcing a speedy Argentine surrender. Of course, it was the obviousness of such a plan that made it so risky. The

British would be landing on mine-strewn beaches, raked by Argentine firing positions, all but on top of a numerically superior defending force which could use the buildings of the capital – and perhaps its inhabitants – as cover. However, the alternative landing grounds also had their drawbacks, and this led Menéndez to assume that an assault on, or near, Stanley remained the most likely prospect. After all, the early Argentine experience of East Falkland's boggy hinterland suggested that much of it was impassable to massed forces, even if conveyed by tracked vehicles.

For this reason, the Argentines left unguarded the area where the British decided to land. San Carlos Bay was a barren settlement on the western side of East Falkland, approached by sea through Falkland Sound, the deep-water channel that separated the two main islands. Certainly, it was a good spot to park an invasion fleet. The problem was what to do once the troops got ashore. From San Carlos, Stanley was fifty miles away, not in itself an insurmountable distance but for the fact that there was no road, nor even a proper track for most of the way. The terrain that would have to be crossed was wholly unsuitable for carting heavy loads on even the most robust of four-wheel drives – what the peat bogs did not lay claim to, the rocky outcrops and boulders surely would. The British plan, therefore, was to overcome these obstacles by ferrying the heavy loads by helicopter. The plan envisaged that Chinook helicopters, which were being brought on board a container ship, *Atlantic Conveyor*, would do the job, but even with these there would scarcely be sufficient numbers to ferry enough artillery pieces and ammunition to hammer the Argentine positions embedded in the ring of hills guarding Stanley. If – as transpired – the Chinooks never arrived, the fallback was to use Sea King helicopters, at the risk of enormous strain on a tiny number of aircraft and pilots. It would take around seventy-four Sea King sorties just to move into position a single six-gun battery with men and enough ammunition for a single night's firing.[54]

The commander of land forces, Major General Jeremy Moore, was firming up plans with Admiral Fieldhouse at Northwood and would not arrive at the Falklands until 30 May. On the spot, the landings were directed by Commander Michael Clapp and Brigadier Julian Thompson of the Royal Marines. Alarmingly, history offered no precedent for a successful amphibious operation without air superiority, and this the British did not have. To try and mitigate the worst of this disadvantage, on 14 May a 45-strong SAS raiding party had landed on Pebble Island off West Falkland, where they launched a hit-and-run mission against the airfield, knocking out an Argentine radar station and eleven aircraft. Given its proximity to Falkland Sound, the airfield would have posed an especially grave threat to the invasion fleet sailing towards San Carlos Bay. As it happened, the Argentines did not make the connection. The other worry was that the Argentines might have mined the approaches to the landing ground. There was only one way to find out. In the night darkness of 20 May, HMS *Yarmouth*, followed by eighteen ships carrying five battalions of men, sailed silently and with all lights out into Falkland Sound and began their approach towards San Carlos Bay. With no available minesweepers, it fell to the frigate HMS *Alacrity* to test the waters. It hit no mines. One after another, the other ships followed. And again no mines were struck. A gap in the Argentine defences had been probed and was about to be opened wide.

The men were ferried to the shore in landing craft almost identical to those that had hit the Normandy beaches on D-Day, thirty-eight years previously. By mid-morning, the bridgehead was established. The crucial element of surprise had been gained, even though a company of crack Argentine troops had moved up from Goose Green on a reconnaissance mission, observed the landings and managed to bring down two Gazelle helicopters before beating a retreat. As each hour passed, the prospect of the massed Argentine army arriving to drive the landing party back into the sea diminished. The day before the operation commenced, Sir Frank Cooper, the permanent under-secretary at the Ministry of Defence, consciously misled the British press into reporting that the most likely form of attack would be not the establishment of a single bridgehead but a series of smash-and-grab raids. Picking up on these reports, the Argentines could not be sure whether the landing at San Carlos represented the major thrust of an invasion or merely a diversionary tactic, intended to lure them into a trap.

When it came, the counter-punch was delivered not by Argentina's soldiers but by its airmen. All available Sea Harriers were deployed to screen the skies around San Carlos Bay, but there were not enough to protect the fleet from wave after wave of attacks. Waiting their turn to unload and unable to manoeuvre in the narrow straits of Falkland Sound, the ships were sitting ducks, trying to repel air strikes with machine guns strapped to their deck sides. Most vulnerable of all was the huge, easily identifiable, cruise liner *Canberra*, which brought four thousand troops to what was about to be christened 'Bomb Alley'. The surrounding hills provided a partial shield since they hampered the Argentine pilots' vision and ensured they could only lock on to their target at the very last minute before releasing their load. But even this was a mixed blessing because the hills prevented radar operating properly, giving the ships very little warning of an incoming attack. While Rapier batteries were quickly established on the surrounding rises, they proved unsuitable to the terrain and the low-level flight paths against which the missiles had to be manually directed. By coming in low, the Argentine pilots successfully dodged much of the missile barrage, though they often failed to prime their bombs accurately to take account of the shorter drop. Had they got their priming calculations right, the damage inflicted would have been potentially game-changing. Likewise, had they been able to hit the ships ferrying the troops to the beachhead rather than the frigates on picket patrol, the amphibious operation would certainly have ended in catastrophe. How close this came to happening was demonstrated on the fourth day of the landings, when Argentine Skyhawks attacked the logistical support ships: a 1,000-lb bomb struck *Sir Galahad* and two others hit *Sir Lancelot*. None of the three bombs exploded and, in *Sir Lancelot*'s case, it took a tense twenty-two hours to extract the most inaccessible of the bombs from the wreckage and lower it safely over the side. That these bombs did not go off was one of the war's hinges of fate, upon which depended the lives of three hundred men of the Commando Logistics Regiment and the Royal Corps of Transport, along with vital stores and provisions for the ground campaign.

By then, it was mostly the frigates that had taken the brunt of the Argentine assault, which began, as soon as the landings were confirmed, on 21 May. Strafed by cannon from Dagger jets, HMS *Brilliant* managed to carry on. Three more Daggers strafed HMS *Antrim* with forty cannon shells and hit her with a 1,000-lb bomb. Fortunately, the latter failed to explode and was defused, but the damage to the frigate's capabilities, including her radar, was enough to make her virtually inoperable and she was reduced to the role of decoy duty. The same fate befell HMS *Argonaut*, which was hit below the waterline by two 1,000-lb bombs. Again, the bombs were defused, but not before the damage they had wrought had claimed two lives and left the ship, without power, effectively crippled. HMS *Ardent* was less fortunate. One of the two bombs that careered into her hull exploded, killing twenty-two men on board. What remote chance she had of surviving this assault was removed when a second wave of Skyhawks bombed her again. Belching fire and smoke, she took her time to sink, but go down she did. By the end of the first day, *Yarmouth* and *Plymouth* were the only escorts in San Carlos Water that remained undamaged. While the Argentine air force had lost six planes in the attacks, if they could keep up their strike rate then they could yet claim victory. The problem for the British, as the military historian Hugh Bicheno has put it, was 'a reversal of the usual charge that armed forces prepare to fight the last war. The Royal Navy was, albeit inadequately, prepared to fight World War III – it simply was not equipped for the World War II-style, low-level bombing attacks it faced around San Carlos.'[55]

Nevertheless, five battalions were safely brought ashore in the first twenty-four hours and they began furiously digging in in order to defend their toehold. Over the following days, many more men and much more materiel needed to be landed if this vanguard was ever going to be able to break out of the beachhead. It was the weather that intervened to save them on the second day, 22 May, with low cloud cover preventing Argentine sorties. But the skies cleared the following day and the attacks recommenced. This time

HMS *Antelope* was hit twice by bombs which failed to explode. The reprieve was short-lived, though. That night one of the devices went off, killing a bomb-disposal expert who was valiantly trying to defuse it. The order to abandon ship was made just in time, for the fire soon ignited the magazine, the resulting fireball turning *Antelope* into a firework display that lit up the night sky. Charred and mangled beyond recognition, she went down the next day. As her cracked hull slowly sank beneath the waves it closed up into a V-sign. It could hardly stand for victory, so it was interpreted as a parting gesture to the Argentines.

Back at command headquarters at Northwood in Hertfordshire, it was not just the loss of ships that was causing concern. There, Admiral Fieldhouse was impatient at the slowness with which Brigadier Thompson was getting his forces away from the San Carlos beachhead. From an 8,000-mile distance, the logistics doubtless looked easier than they did to those clinging to the windswept turf of East Falkland. Yet, whatever the hurdles, Fieldhouse was impatient for them to be cleared, believing that they were not greater than those that would be introduced by further delay. There was a twofold rationale for moving on and scoring a quick and striking victory: getting bogged down in an apparent stalemate would encourage the UN to intervene with new demands for an extremely inconvenient ceasefire; and there was the danger of Argentina air-dropping reinforcements in Lafonia (the southern part of the island and perfect terrain for a mass parachute landing). Lafonia was connected to the rest of East Falkland by a narrow isthmus where there was an airstrip and two settlements, Goose Green and Darwin, already garrisoned by one thousand one hundred Argentine troops. Potentially, they could sever the lines of communication of a British advance on Stanley. Indeed, if Thompson did not get a move on there was even the possibility that the Goose Green force could strike up towards San Carlos and drive the bridgehead-holders back into the sea. Thompson thought otherwise. His instinct was that diverting troops for a frontal assault on Goose Green, a well-defended position, was more trouble than it was worth. A raid could disable its airstrip, after which the garrison could be bottled in on the isthmus by a relatively small detachment of troops, leaving the main thrusts to get on with the more urgent objective of marching across East Falkland towards Stanley. This holding strategy, however, was overruled. On 25 May, Buenos Aires sent messages to Stanley, ordering General Menéndez to move from the defensive to the offensive and to drive the British back. The following day, Fieldhouse ordered Thompson to attack Goose Green.[56]

Thompson's apprehension was understandable. Supported by heavy artillery, the Argentine garrison was dug in, protected by carefully laid minefields and benefiting from the natural advantages provided by a series of ridges and by the narrowness of the isthmus, which limited the routes through which they could be attacked. They outnumbered by almost two to one the six hundred men of 2 Para assigned to make the assault. With initially no air support and only two mortars, 2 Para could only bring whatever firepower they could carry on their backs. There was not much margin for error and disaster might not just rebound on the paratroopers alone, for the fighting could spill into the settlement of Goose Green itself, threatening the lives of 112 islanders whom the Argentines had locked up and were holding hostage in a community hall. To make matters even worse, an unforgivable slip-up back in London imperilled the whole endeavour. Eighteen hours prior to the designated launch of the attack, loose talk emanating from the Ministry of Defence had led the BBC World Service to broadcast the speculation that 2 Para was massing for an assault on the Goose Green and Darwin area. Both the Paras and the Argentines heard the broadcast. The former were incandescent that their cover had been blown. By a stroke of luck, the latter may have incorrectly assumed that the BBC was spreading deliberate misinformation. Nevertheless, they were ready and waiting for 2 Para when, under the cover of early morning darkness of 28 May, the assault was launched.

Lieutenant Colonel H. Jones, 2 Para's commanding officer, was forced to alter his plans at short notice as his orders changed and the size of the opposition was adjusted alarmingly upwards by a covert SAS patrol tasked with watching enemy movements. The attack began towards Darwin with supporting shelling provided by HMS *Arrow*, firing from off the coast in Grantham Sound. Far from running away, the Argentine defenders proved difficult to dislodge and showed themselves determined to stage, at worst, a fighting retreat. As dawn broke, the Paras were well short of their objectives while communications were hampered by their radio batteries running low. They were also already short of ammunition for their two mortars. The morning attack on Darwin Hill especially was hampered by well-sited Argentine machine-gun nests deployed along a ridge. A hail of gunfire forced back the Paras' assault, killing three. His offensive stalling and finding himself pinned down in a gorse gully, 'Colonel H', as Jones was popularly known, decided to lead by example and restore some momentum. With the exhortation 'Come on "A" Company, get your skirts off,' he rose up, sprinted round the spur of the hill, stopping briefly only to reload his submachine gun and proceeded to charge an entrenched machine-gun post. Hit once, he picked himself back up and carried on before being shot down only yards from his objective.[57] It had been a headstrong and reckless action by a commanding officer which in less desperate circumstances would have been a needless sacrifice. But it demonstrated the real meaning of leadership and as 'A' Company surged forward, valuable ground was gained from which they could at last direct their anti-tank rockets accurately. At this, the

Argentine resistance crumbled and the defenders began to emerge from their trenches with their hands in the air. Darwin Hill was captured.

From there, the Paras had no option but to press on, advancing towards the Goose Green airfield with bayonets fixed. On Jones's death, Major Chris Keeble took command, after first briefly finding a spot to kneel in prayer. The battle had now been going on for fourteen hours and the fighting remained as intense as on the ridges around Darwin. Closing in on Goose Green, a Para officer thought he saw a white flag being fluttered. Advancing to accept the surrender, he was shot dead. The whole incident may have been a genuine misunderstanding, a product of the confusion of battle rather than a deliberate attempt to abuse the laws of war. Nevertheless, the intense gun battle that followed generated a false rumour that the enraged Paras had stopped taking prisoners and killed fifty Argentines holed up in the school-house. This massacre story was later disproved and the reality of the 'white flag' incident was six deaths – three British, three Argentine.[58] But the battle was not yet over. The lifting of the cloud cover invited air strikes. First, Argentine Pucaras swooped over and dropped napalm, only to miss their target. Sea Harriers followed, attacking the Argentine gun emplacements. The Paras were by now low on ammunition and exhausted through lack of sleep, but they had to push the Argentines back to the last remaining objective, the settlement of Goose Green itself. Enemy artillery was placed next to houses and Major Keeble presumed that a direct bombardment risked killing the islanders. While preparing to attack, he first gave the Argentine commander, Lieutenant Colonel Piaggi, the option of surrender. Sensibly, Piaggi took it and by mid-afternoon on 29 May the battle of Goose Green had ended with the freeing of the local inhabitants from the community hall, where for the past twenty-nine days they had been imprisoned in grim conditions. 2 Para had lost sixteen men – additionally, a Royal Engineers commando and a helicopter pilot were killed during the operation – and suffered a further thirty-six wounded. Colonel H. Jones was awarded a posthumous Victoria Cross and became the most famous British hero of the campaign. Argentine casualties were around fifty dead and over ninety wounded, with 961 taken prisoner. The gamble had resulted in an overwhelming victory, albeit one that had demonstrated that the Argentines would stand and fight, and fight tenaciously. Brash assertions back home about cowardly Latin American conscripts were misplaced. Here was a formidable foe that was even prepared to unleash napalm if necessary.

It was as well that there was good news to report from Goose Green because there was exceptionally bad news emanating from other fronts. During the mid-afternoon of 25 May – Argentina's national day – Argentine Skyhawks had spotted the Type-42 destroyer HMS *Coventry* on picket duty off Pebble Island. With devastating precision, three 1,000-lb bombs hit her and exploded in her hull. She went down in fifteen minutes, with the loss of nineteen lives. An hour later, two Super Étendards spotted the 15,000-ton freighter *Atlantic Conveyor* to the north of East Falkland. She was attacked and sunk with all but two of her complement of helicopters, as well as tents for 4,500 men. Her captain, Ian North, went down with his ship and was among twelve of her crew who perished in the bitterly cold water. The loss of the *Atlantic Conveyor* created a huge logistical problem for the land campaign. Brigadier Thompson could no longer rely on a sizeable fleet of helicopters to ferry his men over boggy terrain – men who, with the loss of their tents, could expect to endure some teeth-chatteringly cold nights out in the open.

With helicopter support so greatly depleted, only the bare necessities of heavy gear could be airlifted. For the soldiers, there was now no option but to 'yomp' on foot across East Falkland, carrying everything they could on their backs. Their advance on Stanley took the form of a pincer movement: assisted by the Special Boat Service, which secured Teal Inlet, 3 Para took the northern pincer, while 2 Para and the 5th Infantry Brigade took the southern pincer. Yomping from Goose Green, 2 Para took unopposed the settlements of Fitzroy and Bluff Cove on the eastern coast, south of Stanley. There, the Welsh Guards, together with much heavy ammunition, could be landed by sea. On 8 June, they lay off Bluff Cove awaiting disembarkation from the ships *Sir Tristram* and *Sir Galahad*. The order to begin coming ashore was delayed by technical and logistical problems, as well as by disputes over exactly what should be unloaded where. It was to prove a fatal hesitation during a brief moment of acute vulnerability: the Rapier missile defences on the coast were not yet up and running properly and the nearest Sea Harriers were off chasing a formation of Argentine aircraft that had just hit HMS *Plymouth* with four bombs (all of which failed to explode). Thus the two troop-laden ships were sitting ducks when Argentine Skyhawks came screaming over the horizon. Moments after three bombs struck *Sir Galahad*, fire and smoke tore through the ship as on-board ammunition exploded in a fireball. Two bombs hit *Sir Tristam*, which also caught fire, albeit less fiercely. A third attack hit and sank a landing craft, killing five. In all, the attacks killed forty-nine men (thirty-nine of them Welsh Guards), with a further 115 injured, some with appalling burns.

The toll would have been far worse but for the bravery of Royal Navy helicopter pilots who all but flew into the flames to rescue men and intelligently used the down-wind from their rotors to blow imperilled life-rafts away from the burning wrecks. News of the disaster was broadcast in London, but not the number of casualties, fuelling rumours that the loss of life and limb was catastrophic. Media talking-heads conjectured that as many as nine hundred troops might have been killed or wounded, which, had it been true, would have dealt a potentially fatal blow to the task force. Even four days after the attack, figures of two hundred and twenty dead and four hundred wounded were still being widely, if unofficially, reported. The anguish this caused at home was balanced by the intentional false hope it gave to the Argentines that the assault on the Stanley perimeter had either been called off or at least seriously delayed, restoring to the British the element of surprise.

The final assault was planned by Major General Jeremy Moore, who was at last on the island and in full control of land forces. Having taken the northern pincer from San Carlos via Teal Inlet, 42 Commando was in position on Mount Kent, an important strategic height which an advance SAS detachment had already been staking out for some days. It enabled them to direct accurate shelling from out at sea by HMS *Alacrity*. The assistance of Royal Navy marksmanship was especially helpful given that the land artillery pieces the British were dragging into position were – thanks to the helicopter shortage – supplied with only five hundred rounds each, half of what had been requested as necessary for the job. Nonetheless, the pounding of the Argentine army day and night over 10 and 11 June was merciless. Not that the firing was all one way. Having fired 261 shells on to enemy positions on the hills of Two Sisters, HMS *Glamorgan* got a little too close and came within shore-based Exocet range. She was hit on her port side but managed to extinguish the fires and make it back out to rejoin the carrier group, having suffered thirteen deaths in the explosion and gaining the admiration of Sandy Woodward, who signalled: 'While I am very sad at the casualty list, I am glad to note that you are the first warship in the world to survive an Exocet attack.'[59]

For the men on the ground, the attack was perilous. The advantage of attacking at night-time was to some extent mitigated by the fact the Argentine defenders had better night-vision equipment than the British. The approaches were littered with minefields which needed to be navigated, while the hills themselves were natural fortresses, with rocks and boulders providing strong positions for the dug-in defenders, who had well-sited machine-gun posts. Late at night on 11 June, 3 Para attacked Mount Longdon, 45 Commando went in on Two Sisters, and 42 Commando assaulted Mount Harriet. On Mount Harriet, the ruse of a feint attack successfully misdirected the defenders' attention and they were duly outflanked and hit from the rear. For the loss of two dead and another twenty wounded, 42 Commando took over three hundred men prisoner. On Longdon, the battle was especially intense and lasted ten hours. With his platoon commander wounded and his men pinned down by an Argentine machine-gun nest, Sergeant Ian McKay led a break-out. His compatriots falling around him, McKay charged on alone, taking out the nest with grenades before collapsing dead from his wounds.

He was to be the second posthumous VC of the campaign, and one of eighteen Britons killed in the capture of Mount Longdon. A further four fell taking Two Sisters.

As dawn broke, 3 Para remained in a vulnerable position with firing on Longdon coming from Argentine artillery on Mount Tumbledown. Briefly, the British paused while fresh ammunition was brought up, before the next big push was launched in the darkness of the early hours of 14 June. With bayonets fixed, the Scots Guards moved in to dislodge seven hundred Argentine marines (far tougher nuts to crack than nervous conscripts) from the rocks and crags of Tumbledown. The conditions were atrocious, with the Scots advancing into a blizzard and some of their opponents audibly singing patriotic songs as they fired their machine guns. Yet the attack succeeded, for the loss of eight Scots Guards. Elsewhere the picture was mixed. When the Gurkhas advanced on Mount William it was to find – to their apparent disappointment – that the defenders had already fled. On Sapper Hill, however, marines from 40 Commando, supporting the Welsh Guards, were dropped too close to Argentine positions, ensuring a tough firefight before the defenders gave up. Unlike the rest of the surrounding terrain, the approach to Wireless Ridge was suitable for light tanks, and these, along with further naval gunnery, assisted 2 Para's attack. The defenders' resolve faltered after their counter-attack at Moody Brook was beaten back. Finally, with the capture of Sapper Hill, the Argentines were driven from all the high ground surrounding Stanley. An orderly retreat was turning into the disarray of a rout to such an extent that the British stopped firing. For the Argentines, the position was now desperate. Despite the last hurrah over Bluff Cove, their air force was shot to pieces and could no longer deliver the air superiority of old, and with almost everywhere now within range of British guns, the last chance of resupply from Stanley airport had gone. General Menéndez had two options, fight house to house in Stanley, risking hundreds of civilian lives in what could now only be a futile show of defiance, or seek terms to bring the nightmare to an end.

Moore sent Menéndez the message: 'I call on you . . . as one military man to another, to lay down your arms now, with honour to avoid unnecessary bloodshed.'[60] Meanwhile, 2 Para was ordered to halt by the racecourse on the outskirts of Stanley. Not considering himself bound by the order, the *Evening Standard* journalist travelling with them, Max Hastings, proceeded on his own into the capital and thereby took the battle honour of the Upland Goose Hotel. There he found the proprietor, who assured him: 'We never doubted for a moment that the British would come, we have just been waiting for the moment.' Hastings reflected that 'it was like liberating an English suburban golf club'.[61]

With order among his troops in Stanley finally breaking down, Menéndez was in no doubt that he could not fight his way out. Getting a call through to Buenos Aires, he had a difficult conversation with Galtieri who, having taken to drink, was, in the manner of the Führerbunker, sending imaginary divisions back into the struggle. Eventually, with the president at last convinced that resistance was not a serious option, Menéndez agreed to the British terms for unconditional surrender (though those precise words were excised in order to appease Argentine sensitivities) on both East and West Falkland – the latter an important point since West Falkland was still in Argentine hands. Although dated 14 June, it was actually shortly after midnight that Menéndez signed the instrument of surrender in Moore's presence. After their seventy-four days as the 'liberators' of *Las Malvinas*, over eleven thousand Argentine troops were ordered on to the Stanley airport isthmus, where they laid down their weapons. Moore signalled London: 'The Falkland Islands are once more under the government desired by their inhabitants. God Save the Queen.'[62] Back home, first reports of a 'ceasefire' started intruding on television broadcasts of the Football World Cup final between Italy and West Germany (both Argentina and England had been knocked out in the second round, without meeting). In the dark remained many of the islanders who, under curfew, were trapped in their homes and unsure what was going on. A group was huddled together in a large store room when a British officer walked through the door and said: 'Hullo, I'm Jeremy Moore. Sorry it's taken rather a long time to get here.' He was met by a spontaneous volley of cheering, while some simply burst into tears.[63]

He had arrived not a moment too soon. The British artillery was running out of shells. The ships were low on ammunition for their 4.5-inch guns. Of the complement of Sea Harriers, only half were still airworthy. The weather was getting worse by the moment: off the coast, a force-ten storm was making coordinated activity extremely difficult for the ships of the task force. The exercise had ended in total victory – a result much international expert opinion had dismissed only weeks earlier. But the margin was, until the last moment, perilously close. The Argentine air force had fought its finest hour and if only it had managed to sink one of the aircraft carriers or a major troopship, or even if a few more of the bombs it had dropped had gone off, then the greatest strategic gamble in late twentieth-century British history would have ended up being cited as proof that the country really was a shadow of its former self. Thatcher rode her luck – of that there was no doubt – and on this occasion fortune favoured her bravery. When the campaign ended on 20 June with the eleven-strong Argentine base on South Thule peacefully surrendering to HMS *Endurance*, the audit recorded that the war had killed 255 British servicemen and injured a further 777, sunk six ships and damaged ten more. Seven hundred and forty-six Argentines had lost their lives in a blow to national prestige so great that it produced the unintended consequence of overthrowing military rule in Buenos Aires and bringing democracy to the country. As distinct from the war at sea, the ground war had killed 177 British and 279 Argentines. Three Falkland islanders had been killed in Stanley when a British shell fell short of its target, a sad mishap that did little to dent the normally undemonstrative islanders' outpouring of joy at their liberation. The financial costs of fighting the war and paying for the subsequent reconstruction, and the need to station a large garrison on the islands to deter any future attempt at invasion or sabotage, were vast – by 1988, the total bill was already heading towards £4 billion.[64] Less easy to quantify would have been the cost to Britain's reputation and her role as the senior European partner in NATO at a time of Cold War tension if she had conceded she was not up to reversing Argentina's aggression.

To opponents of the war in Britain and, indeed, to those disturbed by anything that smacked of a returning sense of national assertiveness, the scenes of jubilation at the victory were, as Tony Benn put it, 'utterly distressing'.[65] He found Michael Foot's expression of satisfaction at the success of the campaign, and the compliment he paid the prime minister, 'odious and excessive'.[66] The conflict coincided with the historic first visit of a pope to Britain, and on 29 May, while the battle of Goose Green was drawing towards its denouement, the contrasting image was beamed across the television networks of Pope John Paul II attending a service at Canterbury Cathedral. Neither his nor anyone else's prayers for peace were answered except through force of arms. Vast crowds lined the banks of naval towns to cheer the returning warriors and wave Union Jacks, and these displays of semi-delirious patriotic exuberance – and relief – came to represent popular opinion far more memorably than the placard-waving protesters who had marched on 23 May and 6 June. The Campaign for Nuclear Disarmament had tried to draw together those opposed to the war with those alarmed at the possibility of nuclear Armageddon – at one rally, the CND vice president, Professor Mike Pentz, prophesied that Thatcher would surely launch a nuclear strike on Argentina if Prince Andrew was harmed. Surprisingly, when it came to the victory march through the City of London in October, it was Thatcher, rather than the prince's mother, who took the salute.

Cast as the new Boudicca, or even Britannia, Thatcher could be forgiven her sense of pride in British arms and satisfaction in her own role, even if her annoyance at the Archbishop of Canterbury's prayers for the Argentines displayed a vindictive streak. She ought to have been reminded that the archbishop, unlike herself, had actually fought in a war and had been decorated with the Military Cross. Nevertheless, her outward display of Churchillian resolve was not the whole story. She had let Pym pursue the chimera of diplomatic solutions far beyond what she personally felt was workable. Those working closely with her during the crisis attested that news of British casualties regularly reduced her to tears.[67] She made a point of writing personally to the families of every dead serviceman, starting a tradition that her successors were to follow. Publicly, however, her role was easier to explain. Her toughness in war had been vindicated and, by implication, so it would be in domestic matters too. Her own position in the country and in the Cabinet was immeasurably strengthened. The assumption was that the 'wets' would never have seen the crisis through to its conclusion. This was, of course, a simplification: two monetarist 'dries', the Foreign Office minister Nicholas Ridley and the defence secretary, John Nott, had played their part in unintentionally fostering the Argentine belief that Britain wanted rid of, or would not defend, the islands. But the perception was clear: hard decisions were not taken by 'wets'. Ironically, those most affected by this perception were the generation of Cabinet ministers who had fought in the Second World War, their authority duly seeping away to a younger, post-war generation (Parkinson, Lawson, John Moore, Tebbit) of Thatcher loyalists (plus the independently minded Heseltine), who appeared likely to represent the party's future.

The grandest conclusion was, however, drawn by the prime minister herself. In July 1982, she summed up at a Conservative rally at Cheltenham Racecourse what she believed to be the legacy of the Falkands:

> When we started out, there were the waverers and the faint-hearts. The people who thought that Britain could no longer seize the initiative for herself.
>
> The people who thought we could no longer do the great things which we once did. Those who believed that our decline was irreversible – that we could never again be what we were . . .
>
> Well, they were wrong . . .
>
> We have ceased to be a nation in retreat.
>
> We have instead a new-found confidence – born in the economic battles at home and tested and found true eight thousand miles away.[68]

7 RESURRECTION

The Resolute Approach

'The issue is Thatcher,' declared *The Economist* at the beginning of the 1983 general election campaign.[1] That this looked likely to play into the Tories' hands would have seemed all but unimaginable a year and a half earlier. A Gallup poll in October 1981 had put Thatcher's approval rating at 24 per cent – the lowest ever recorded for a prime minister.[2] At that time, with the surge of the SDP and its formation of the Alliance with the Liberals, it seemed a racing certainty that Britain's two-party system was over. Political and constitutional experts like David Butler and Vernon Bogdanor began writing books with titles like *Governing Without a Majority* and *Multi-Party Politics and the Constitution*. The task of government would be especially difficult given how far polarized the two main parties had become and, consequently, how difficult it would be for the Alliance to sustain a coalition with either of them. Nobody factored in the unforeseeable – that a war in the South Atlantic would be viewed as vindicating a woman who – literally – stuck to her guns in the face of terrible odds. It made her the embodiment of what she began describing as the 'resolute approach'.[3]

Yet while the 'Falklands factor' might explain the scale of the Conservative Party's landslide in the June 1983 general election, it was not exclusively the reason why the party won a majority. The opinion polls suggested that, on the eve of General Galtieri's desperate bid for glory in April 1982, the Tories' fortunes were already recovering. Unemployment was continuing its rise, albeit at a slower rate. The black spots of deprivation were not shrinking, but neither were they growing. Those still with jobs had reason to start to feel secure. Consumer confidence was returning and, for the employed, living standards were rising. The economy was turning round and inflation seemed almost conquered, offering Thatcher grounds for claiming her policies were being proven right. Just before the Falklands were invaded, Labour, the Alliance and the Conservatives were all but tied on the same opinion poll rating. Yet it was the Conservatives who drew most cheer from this, for the trend was in their direction: having bottomed out in the autumn of 1981, their ratings had thereafter been on a continuous upward slope, while the two opposition parties had seemingly peaked and were in decline. With two years to go before an election had to be held, the final result was not predetermined, even if a hung parliament remained the most likely possibility.

While it is certainly conceivable that the Conservatives might have sneaked a second term on the back of modest economic recovery, Labour 'extremism' and a divided opposition, it was the Falklands that transformed Thatcher into their prime electoral asset. In a 'Ten reasons to vote Conservative' leaflet issued during the campaign, the final, tenth, point read simply: 'Mrs Thatcher'. The flyer's reverse listed 'Mr Foot' as the concluding reason for not voting Labour. Vigour and vitality were pitched against infirmity and impotence. The principal parties seldom mentioned the Falklands War directly during the election campaign – and when it was raised, it was more often clumsily brought up by Labour. Yet it scarcely needed to be discussed, for it self-evidently represented a fundamental change in perceptions both of Britain's fortunes and of its warrior-queen prime minister. In 1979, Britons were the least optimistic out of thirty-one nationalities sampled by Gallup. By 1983, they were the eighth most optimistic.[4]

For her part, Thatcher resisted the temptation to call a snap general election to get the most out of the post-Falklands bounce in her popularity. Doing so in the autumn of 1982, just over midway into a term of office, would have looked scandalously opportunistic. In any case, there were good tactical reasons for delaying into the summer of 1983. The Conservatives had won in 1979 on old constituency boundaries that were advantageous to Labour. The Boundary Commission was at work trying to iron out some of the iniquities in a redrawing which, it was estimated, would add thirty seats to the Conservatives. These changes came into effect in March 1983. Positive local election results at the beginning of May made up Thatcher's mind and the general election was called for 9 June.

In one of his least astute judgements, the *Guardian*'s political correspondent, Peter Jenkins, concluded that the Conservatives' manifesto demonstrated that 'Thatcherism is dead – at least for the present.'[5] In fact, *The Challenge of our Times*, drafted by Adam Ridley (Sir Geoffrey Howe's political adviser) and Ferdinand Mount (head of the Policy Unit at No. 10), succinctly set out the stall for extending Thatcherism far beyond its core monetarist values of sticking to the current economic policies, prioritizing the fight to keep inflation down and further reductions in income tax. It heralded the next wave of ideas – ones that Thatcher had scarcely dreamt of when in opposition but which the conquest of inflation and the chipping away of trade union privileges had created an opportunity to purse. Thus the manifesto announced the intention to roll back the state's control of major sections of the economy, with the privatization (in whole or in part) of British Telecom, British

Airways, British Steel, British Shipbuilders and Rolls-Royce. Furthermore, the assault would be taken into the Labour heartland: union leaders were to be elected by secret ballot and Labour's municipal fiefdoms were to be broken up, with the Greater London Council and six metropolitan authorities abolished and power returned to borough and district level. The balance between central and local government would be shifted, with what became known as 'rate capping' introduced to prevent high-spending (Labour) councils setting very high local tax rates. This was an effort to remove the fiscal burden from ratepayers, but at the cost of making local government less responsible for its own actions – with consequences that should have been foreseen.[6]

For radicalism, these proposals were exceeded only by the Labour manifesto. This document was clumsily structured, the inevitable consequence of its having been drafted by the party's National Executive Committee, which presented it to the shadow Cabinet as a fait accompli rather than as a rough copy awaiting discussion and amendment. But its ideas were startlingly bold. It promised unilateral nuclear disarmament and Britain's withdrawal from the European Community. The country would be protected from the winds of competition through a form of siege economy. For politicians who claimed to be international socialists, the outlook was surprisingly compatible with that of age-old zealots for 'little England', ready to close the national drawbridge and defend the moat against the challenging world beyond. Market forces were to be curtailed. Quotas and tariffs would be imposed to restrict imports. Exchange controls were to be brought back to curb the international flow of capital and the major clearing banks were threatened that if they refused to 'cooperate with us fully . . . we shall stand ready to take one or more of them into public ownership'. State planning of the economy would return, with a new corporatist Department of Economic and Industrial Planning, tasked with drawing up and implementing a five-year plan. The limited privatization that had taken place already would be reversed. Indeed, sweeping new nationalizations were deemed essential. Electronics and pharmaceutical companies were to be largely nationalized, along with 'other important sectors, as required in the national interest'. For many businessmen, this last promise seemed alarmingly vague, its broad sweep all but an enabling act to allow the state to seize any profitable private business at will. Private health care would be stopped in its tracks. Private schools would be stripped of charitable status and 'integrated' into the local authority sector 'where necessary'.[7] This sounded close to abolition through indirect means. In contrast, trade unions would regain their former powers and privileges. The manifesto's official title was *The New Hope for Britain*, but the description by which it was to be remembered was provided by the Labour MP Gerald Kaufman: 'the longest suicide note in history'.

The remarkable scale of the Labour manifesto's ambitions provided easy targets for the Tory campaign, which rushed out an advert, 'Like your manifesto, Comrade' – pointing out eleven areas of common policy between the Labour Party and Communist Party manifestos, including the reintroduction of exchange controls, withdrawal from the Common Market, the abolition of parents' right to choose their children's schools and opposition to secret ballots in union leadership elections. Detailed opinion polling suggested that it was on defence that the Conservatives enjoyed the greatest lead over Labour (plus 38 per cent) and that they were almost as far ahead on 'inflation and prices' (plus 35 per cent) as well. But much depended upon how the question was phrased. The party of defence was only 13 per cent ahead on 'nuclear disarmament' (perhaps because many respondents were not even sure they agreed with the proposition), and while Labour was 16 per cent ahead on 'the NHS' it was only 2 per cent ahead on 'hospitals', and 13 per cent ahead on 'unemployment' but just 7 per cent on 'jobs'.[8]

Almost everything was slicker about the Tories' campaign, from the adverts devised by Saatchi & Saatchi to the attitude and demeanour of the party chairman, Cecil Parkinson, a northern grammar-school boy who embodied the aspirational generation with which Thatcher wanted to be associated. Indeed, Parkinson represented the social changes she was bringing to her party (he was certainly a contrast to the previous chairman, the Old Etonian amateur watercolourist, Lord Thorneycroft) and was tipped to be Thatcher's next Foreign Secretary – until he informed her that he had got his former personal secretary, Sara Keays, pregnant (after the election Thatcher made him *only* secretary of state for trade and industry, but he felt obliged to resign amid the popular uproar that followed the revelations about his 'love-child'). Such mishaps were for the future – the only moment during the campaign when the choreographed performance almost came unstuck was in a television encounter organized by the BBC's *Nationwide* programme which allowed viewers, linked up by camera from regional studios, to put questions to the leaders. Thatcher found herself aggressively cross-questioned by a Cirencester housewife, Mrs Diana Gould, who refused to believe her claims that the torpedoing of the *Belgrano* was not also intended to sink the Peruvian peace deal, despite Thatcher's protestation that the details of the proposal were not even known to London at the time the order was given. Catching out the prime minister on one factual slip – Thatcher had contested Mrs Gould's opening statement that the *Belgrano* was 'sailing away from the Falklands' – the questioner made the prime minister appear temporarily flustered and evasive. The professional interrogators found her less flappable. The reality, however, was that raising the Falklands War remained a risky strategy for her tormentors and backfired on two Labour politicians who did so. On 1 June, Denis Healey claimed Thatcher's response to the conflict was one of 'glorying in slaughter'; while on the eve of the poll, Neil Kinnock, responding to a heckle from someone in a television audience that Thatcher 'had guts', retorted sharply: 'And it's a pity that people had to leave theirs on Goose Green in order to prove it.' At this provocation, the defence secretary, Michael Heseltine, leapt in, describing Kinnock as 'the self-appointed king of the gutter of politics', to which Kinnock retorted: 'If I was in the gutter, and I ain't, he is looking at me from the sewer.' It was not quite Oscar Wilde. Somewhat archly, Thatcher tried to rise above it with: 'I think in politics, as in life, some things are best left unsaid.'[9]

Yet, the abuse directed towards the prime minister was as nothing compared to the derisive jibes aimed at the Labour leader. The press had a field day as one ineptly organized rally merged seamlessly into another and Foot's colleagues croaked in the effort to hit the same notes of a common melody. Even before the campaign had begun, Bernard Levin, the famously acerbic columnist of *The Times*, was dismissing Foot as 'lurching between disaster and calamity with all the skill and aplomb of a one-legged tightrope-walker', a man 'unable to make his own shadow cabinet appointments or indeed to blow his nose in public without his trousers falling down'.[10] The attacks became sharper in the weeks leading up to polling day. Never ashamed to kick a man when he was down, *The Sun* ran an unflattering picture of Foot shambling along on a morning walk with the headline 'DO YOU SERIOUSLY WANT THIS OLD MAN TO RUN BRITAIN?'

An NOP opinion poll suggested only 19 per cent of the electorate was 'satisfied' with the Labour leader. By contrast, 50 per cent of respondents were satisfied with Thatcher. Albeit narrowly, the winner in the personality contest was actually the Liberal leader, David Steel (52 per cent satisfaction). His problem was that the Alliance had a split personality, since he was only its co-leader along with the SDP's Roy Jenkins, a politician deemed less of an asset (30 per cent satisfied with his performance).[11] To the frequently posed question of who would be the Alliance's prime minister if it won the election, the official explanation – that it would be the leader of whichever of the two parties had the most MPs – meant that voters did not know in advance of polling day which of the two men would end up in Downing Street. An attempt at clarity had been made at the end of April 1983 when it was agreed that Jenkins – who, unlike Steel, had experience of office – was 'prime minister designate', but Steel was put in charge of the Alliance's election campaign. This recipe for confusion and contradiction was given the title the 'Partnership of Principle'. By the end of May, 78 per cent of opinion poll respondents were expressing the view that 'the Alliance should be clearer about who is leading it'.[12]

This irritation was symptomatic of greater difficulties and tensions within a force that had until recently seemed poised to 'break the mould' of British politics. The SDP–Liberal Alliance had ended 1981 with a vast opinion poll lead, Gallup tallying its support at over 50 per cent, more than 20 per cent clear of both Labour and the Conservatives. It was a sensational position to be in and well beyond the reasonable expectations of the four ex-Labour ministers who had posed for photos on a cold morning in Limehouse eleven months earlier. Yet here was the Alliance at the start of the 1983 election campaign with opinion poll figures of 18 per cent, languishing badly in third place behind Labour, whose support was firming up at around 30 per cent.[13] How had the euphoria evaporated so quickly?

The Falklands War was a contributory factor, but was not the cause. The truth was that Alliance support had been sliding for months before the islands made the news. It was not that any catastrophic mistakes had been made. There were some modest signs of friction within the Gang of Four (although no more than in the Cabinet or shadow cabinet) and it looked unimpressive that SDP MPs could not agree a united line over whether or not they supported Norman Tebbit's legislation to curtail the closed shop and other restrictive practices. Yet such differences were more interesting to Westminster obsessives than to the average floating voter, for whom the new party held the greatest appeal. More significant was that the Alliance had become an established fact and was therefore no longer a news story as of right. There was no need for the media to dispatch a camera team every time Shirley Williams stepped deftly from a railway carriage on to a station platform or Roy Jenkins emerged well satisfied from a working lunch. Their diminishing novelty value coincided with the two traditional parties sharpening up their performance. For the Tories this came on the back of better economic conditions, while Labour's improved poll ratings may have owed something to the hard left's decision to consolidate its position and to offer Foot its backing, rather than to stir up further trouble after Tony Benn's narrow defeat for the deputy leadership.

The SDP needed a leader who would take responsibility rather than pronouncing through the politburo of the Gang of Four. As a military hawk, David Owen cut a dash during the Falklands conflict, in contrast to Williams and Jenkins, neither of whom could convincingly feign excitement about hoisting the Union Jack in a distant part of the world. It was the parliamentary sketch writer, Frank Johnson, who most adroitly ridiculed Jenkins's attitude when describing him poised to make a Commons intervention as the Royal Navy sailed towards danger: 'Like Switzerland, he is prosperous, comfortable, civilized and almost entirely landlocked. His only previous contact with the high seas has been in various good fish restaurants.'[14] Jenkins had only been returned to Parliament the week before the Falklands were invaded, in a by-election at Glasgow Hillhead. The victory there, though

tangible, was not unqualified because, unlike the avalanches of votes garnered by Bill Pitt in Croydon and Shirley Williams in Crosby, Jenkins had
won with only 33 per cent of the vote in a constituency which, although
Conservative-held for decades, had a social profile almost tailor-made for
SDP success – with its neoclassical terraces inhabited by university lecturers
and other public sector professionals, it was thought to comprise the best-
educated electorate in Britain. Nevertheless, in July 1982 it was the
61-year-old Jenkins, not his hungrier and younger rival, Owen, who won
the ballot of SDP members to become the party's leader. Having been
Home Secretary, Chancellor of the Exchequer and president of the European
Commission, Jenkins clearly possessed the experience and temperament to
administer the country, but his talents equipped him neither for mastering a
House of Commons that had become far rowdier since his days in the
Labour Cabinet nor for the sound-bite culture of the modern media. Too
often a simple question elicited from him a complicated, and often unclear,
answer. As a man who claimed never to have lunched alone, he failed to
convey natural understanding for families struggling on the breadline, even
though his intentions towards them were plainly benevolent. Problematically,
benevolence seemed like the posture of an eighteenth-century Tory squire
rather than a modern politician. He was, in the concise summary of one
increasingly disillusioned SDP MP, 'a soft man in tough times'.[15]

Subsequent by-elections suggested the SDP was proving itself to be a
busted flush.[16] Nevertheless, for the general election campaign the media
gave the Alliance only slightly less airtime than the two major parties, and
this level of free publicity was invaluable. As it became clear that Labour's
campaign was unwinding, opinion polls started showing Alliance support
creeping up towards the mid-20 per cent range. What the new force in
British politics was actually offering was really more of the old policies that
had been tried by the Labour governments of Harold Wilson and Jim
Callaghan, but without the desire to bolster the privileges of the trade union
high command. The joint Liberal–SDP manifesto promised to cut unemployment by borrowing money to pay for public works schemes. The
nationalized industries would remain. In place of monetarism, the government would seek to control inflation by arbitrating fixed pay levels with the
unions and principal business leaders. A pay and prices commission would be
reconstituted to order companies not to increase their employees' pay above
nationally determined levels. The Inland Revenue would gain powers to
impose a 'counter-inflation tax' to penalize businesses that paid salaries
according to the market rate rather than government directive.[17]

While it was the Labour manifesto that subsequent commentators have
identified as marking a historical dead-end for socialism, the less frequently
analysed Alliance manifesto provided equally strong evidence that the centre

ground was also committed to government-directed policies. Gaining a supportive hearing from the press proved relatively easy. Many key columnists like Polly Toynbee in the *Guardian*, Anthony Sampson in the *Observer* and even the *Daily Mirror*'s agony aunt, Marjory Proops, were active supporters. Tony Benn grumbled that the BBC was an 'agency of the SDP'.[18] If the subsequent 'New Labour' party of Tony Blair could stand accused of being too obsessed with public relations, it is easy to see how the 1983 election had taught hard lessons about the consequences of being insufficiently media-friendly. Of the seventeen national newspapers, only two – the *Daily Mirror* and *Sunday Mirror* – endorsed Labour. The *Mail*, *Express*, *Telegraph* and *The Times* all ran editorials urging a Conservative vote (although subsequent market research suggested a third of *Times* readers ignored the paper's advice and voted for the Alliance). The *Financial Times* failed to appear during the later stages of the campaign because of a strike by its printers. The greatest surprise was that, while an estimated 40 per cent plus of *Guardian* readers voted for the Alliance, the newspaper of the white-collar public sector employee ran a somewhat equivocal editorial lamenting the way the voting system would not reflect the Alliance's true level of support and hoping that the Tories would be denied a landslide. The paper did, however, show where its heart was by condemning Thatcher's 'profound corner-shop caution' and 'profound, doctrinaire stupidity'.[19] For less subtlety, newspaper readers were directed to the front pages of the two main tabloids. The 3.3 million buyers of the *Daily Mirror* were greeted on the morning of the election with the full-page headline 'STOP THE WASTE OF OUR NATION . . . for your job, your children and your future, Vote Labour'; while the 4.2 million who bought *The Sun* were treated to the punchier 'VOTE FOR MAGGIE', decorated with a cartoon of her as Britannia. The country's third-biggest-selling newspaper, the *Daily Express*, settled for 'NOW IS THE HOUR. MAGGIE IS OUR MAN.'[20]

The course of the campaign showed a shift in votes between the two main opposition parties rather than between them and the Tories. Perhaps due to the ease of predicting which party would win, turnout, at nearly 73 per cent, was a few pips below the average for the preceding twenty years, although close to the proportion of the electorate who had cast their ballots in the famous contest of 1945. And it was to Clement Attlee's finest hour that the statisticians returned on the morning of 10 June 1983 when the results showed the Conservatives had won by the greatest landslide since that first post-war election, with 397 seats to 209 for Labour and only twenty-three for the Alliance (others made up twenty-one seats). This increased the Tory parliamentary majority from forty-three to 144. Whereas the electorate had voted to change the incumbent in 1970, February 1974, and 1979, this time it had opted to stay with the devil it knew. For Thatcher personally it

Special Relationship. Thatcher, Reagan and Lucky in the White House's Rose Garden, April 1985 (*above*). The popular impression that Thatcher was the President's poodle belied their heated private arguments, not least over abolishing nuclear weapons, but provided rich comic material for the puppet satirists of ITV's *Spitting Image* (*below*).

With synthesizers replacing electric guitars and shirts and velvet supplanting denim, pop drifted from rebellion to ostentation. 1981 found Andy McCluskey and Paul Humphreys of Orchestral Manoeuvres in the Dark (*top left*) singing about Joan of Arc while resembling the lead characters of that year's hit television serial, *Brideshead Revisited* (*top right*). (*Below*) The New Romantic look would not have appeared out of place at a 1920s party thrown by the 'Bright Young Things'.

Nutty Boys and Salford Lads. With twenty consecutive top twenty hits in the charts between 1979 and 1985, Madness (*above*) could reasonably claim to be *the* band of that period, though it was The Smiths (*below*) who ultimately found themselves compared to The Beatles.

(*Above*) Wembley, 13 July 1985: the most spectacular charity appeal in history is watched by 74,000 in the stadium and more than 1.4 billion on television. (*Below*) Bob Geldof whispers in Prince Charles's ear while Princess Diana focusses on the music. Behind her, rock royalty's David Bowie confers with Brian May and Roger Taylor of Queen.

was a triumph, as she became the first twentieth-century Conservative prime minister to win two successive working majorities. The contrast with Michael Foot, who had steered his party to its worst result since 1935, was stark. Recognizing the hopelessness of his situation, he announced his intention to stand down in time for a new leader to be selected in the autumn.

Nevertheless, while Labour had undeniably suffered a disaster, the Conservatives had scarcely swept all before them. Due to the growth of three-party politics, they had won a fractionally smaller share of the vote than four years earlier, down from 43.9 per cent to 42.4 per cent. Not since 1922 had they won an election on so small a share, their increase in seats coming as a consequence of a far greater lead (14.8 per cent) over Labour – a lead even exceeding that which Attlee had secured over Churchill in 1945 and which had not been bettered in nearly half a century. In the sense that they had failed to convince a majority of the electorate to vote for them, the Conservatives fell short, as had every post-war government; but in terms of showing themselves to be vastly preferred over their two main opponents, they had secured an extraordinarily firm mandate. With a 27.6 per cent share of the vote (down almost 10 percentage points from last time), Labour had narrowly avoided the ignominy of coming third. A late push took the Alliance to 25.4 per cent, and the fact that this translated into so few seats only made them more determined to proclaim the iniquities of the first-past-the-post electoral system. The age-old Liberal Party, with seventeen MPs, had done better than the newfangled SDP, which had won only six seats. Of the one Tory and thirteen Labour MPs who had defected to the SDP at its launch in March 1981, only four were returned to Parliament. Indeed, out of the ten who lost their seats, just one managed even to come second. Shirley Williams lost Crosby, the seat she had won in such spectacular fashion only a year and a half earlier. Bill Rodgers was defeated in Stockton. At Westminster, the Gang of Four was now a two-man band – each of whom harboured suspicions about the other. In every respect but their actual share of the national vote, the Alliance had endured an exceedingly disappointing night and Jenkins, like Foot, recognized it was time to surrender the leadership. Given that David Owen was the only other MP with sufficient experience for the job, he assumed the reins unopposed. It was necessarily a coronation rather than a contest and, as such, it made the Limehouse Declaration's assertion that Labour had drifted away from its 'democratic traditions' ring rather hollow. But in the circumstances, what else could the SDP do?

When the House of Commons reassembled, the new boys included Tony Blair (aged thirty), Gordon Brown (aged thirty-two) and, the youngest member returned, the 23-year-old SDP MP for Ross, Cromarty and Skye, Charles Kennedy. The frequent gripe that politicians should have more experience of the real world once again ran up against the reality that ambitious people who go far in their chosen profession start at it while they are young. This was not the only unshaken reality. Ethnically, the chamber was still entirely white. There had been eighteen candidates from ethnic minorities (eight Alliance, six Labour, four Conservative), none of whom was elected. This was scarcely regarded as peculiar. After all, there had not been a non-white MP since 1929. It was, nonetheless, a postscript to a campaign in which the Conservatives' most controversial advert had depicted a black man in a suit with the slogan 'Labour Says He's Black, Tories Say He's British'. Despite the domination of the Iron Lady, it was also still predominantly a man's domain. The number of female MPs crept up only from nineteen to twenty-three (thirteen Tory, ten Labour, zero Alliance), an increase from 3 to 4 per cent of honourable members. In other respects, the traditional affinities and backgrounds of the MPs had changed little. Of Labour's 209 members, 123 were sponsored by trade unions. Fourteen per cent were public schoolboys (two of them Old Etonians), as against 70 per cent of Tories, among whom were forty-nine Old Etonians.[21]

The casualty list hit the Labour Party profoundly, the most prominent victim being Tony Benn in Bristol East (though he returned the following year courtesy of a by-election in Chesterfield). Outside London, the party was all but wiped out in southern England, its survivors clinging to the heartlands of central Scotland, South Wales and northern England. This made Labour politicians almost exclusively the representatives of Britain's most deprived areas and, conversely, the Tories were equally dominant where prosperity was returning. Scarcely before had British democracy been quite so starkly divided between the party of the haves and the party of the have-nots, with all the inevitable consequences this produced for mutual incomprehension. However, haves and have-nots had ceased to be proxy terms for middle class and working class in the broader sense. Nationally, the working class had swung by 3 per cent from Labour to Conservative – a statistic that masked what was really the fracturing of the class, with skilled workers moving decisively to the Conservatives but unskilled workers (and those among the unemployed who voted) sticking overwhelmingly with Labour.[22] In this sense, the traditional class–voting relationship was breaking down. Thatcher's message of aspiration – or, to its critics, greed – appealed particularly to the more affluent C1 and C2 categories of the working class.

While the emergence of the Alliance as a third party with nationwide appeal further unsettled traditional voting patterns, the minor parties fared poorly. Neither the Welsh nor Scottish nationalists made any headway, each returning just two MPs to Westminster. Furthermore, the polarized stances of the two main parties cut the small extremist parties out of the market. Seemingly in terminal decline, the National Front and its breakaway British

National Party between them won a not very grand total of 41,686 votes nationwide, while the Communists sank to 11,606 votes and the Trotskyite factionalists of the Workers' Revolutionary Party a mere 3,643 – despite the best efforts of its most prominent supporter and former candidate, the actress Vanessa Redgrave. With the Conservatives determined to roll back the state, Labour promising to push it ever onwards, and the Alliance offering a safe haven for 1970s-style corporatist Keynesianism, voters could hardly protest at the lack of clear choices available among the electable candidates.

Recovery

'Landslides don't on the whole produce successful governments,' had been the courageously expressed opinion of the Foreign Secretary, Francis Pym, when he appeared on the BBC's *Question Time* programme shortly before the country went to the polls. If by that he meant they encouraged prime ministers to ignore the search for consensus and to dispense with cautious or contrary colleagues, then his judgement was quickly shown to be sound. The day after the election, Thatcher summoned him to Downing Street and delivered the brutally direct greeting: 'Francis, I want a new Foreign Secretary.'[23] His government career terminated, Pym trudged back to the back benches. Yet, those who feared that giving the prime minister such a majority would only encourage her to wring the remaining 'wets' out of office and impose an even more restrictive form of monetarism were in for a surprise. Thatcher responded on the morrow of her triumph by keeping in the Cabinet such potential troublemakers as Michael Heseltine, Jim Prior and Peter Walker. What was more, with Sir Geoffrey Howe assuming Pym's Foreign Office responsibilities, the Treasury passed from a man with the temperament of a Puritan to one with the air of a Cavalier.

Upon offering Nigel Lawson the job, Thatcher managed to restrict herself to making only one demand – that he get a haircut. She did not think it seemly for a Chancellor of the Exchequer to look too carefree. He submitted to a token trim before rebelling by letting his locks grow back to their previous length. Lawson, after all, was a man of considerable self-assurance, whose will was further fortified by the knowledge that the bare facts of Howe's tenure scarcely represented a hard act to follow. The scale of the recession, by curbing tax receipts and boosting welfare payments, had increased rather than diminished the state's size. The intention had been to reduce public spending by 4 per cent in four years. The reality had been an increase of 6 per cent. Despite cutting the rates at which income tax was levied, the total tax burden (excluding North Sea oil revenue) had jumped during Howe's tenure from 35.5 per cent to over 38 per cent.[24] Unemployment stood at three million and, incredibly, was still rising.

On the positive side, apparent victory over inflation could certainly be trumpeted, even if it was achieved only through a mixture of design and accident. Hitting the targets for money supply growth had proved mostly beyond the Treasury's ability. It transpired to be the fall in world commodity prices, as well as the tight monetary policy, that brought inflationary pressure under control. During 1986, inflation fell to 3.4 per cent, which represented the lowest level for nineteen years. With the economy growing again, Lawson could take comfort from the thought that Howe had endured the worst of it and that better times lay ahead. Aside from unemployment, most of the key indicators were heading in the right direction. The one advantage of Britain's manufacturing sector being leaner was that it was fitter: in the previous year its productivity had soared by 12.5 per cent, ensuring that those firms that had survived the deluge were well placed to benefit both from returning domestic consumer confidence and from a falling exchange rate, which boosted exports. Assisted by soaring North Sea oil production, the balance of payments was improving and returning a £4 billion current account surplus. Thus the prospects for removing the regulatory and fiscal burdens on business and individuals had not looked so favourable for well over a decade. Though large parts of the country would reap scant gain from it, the 'Lawson boom' was about to take off.

If unemployment was to be brought down in the long term, then it was clearly going to take more than the plethora of training schemes that were being established. To Lawson, the key was to reduce the burdens on business. Although some mitigating allowances were scrapped, corporation tax was reduced from 50 per cent in 1983 to 35 per cent in 1986. The cost of National Insurance contributions to companies and their lower-paid employees also fell, thereby reducing the expense of hiring labour. While indirect taxes on spending continued to rise, a renewed effort was made to bring down income tax, since Lawson held that lower direct taxes, unlike lower indirect taxes, encouraged saving and investment. Lawson's 1984 budget lifted 850,000 low-paid workers out of paying any income tax at all. Even so, it was not until the budget of 1986 that the basic rate of income tax was brought down for the first time in seven years, and that was only a 1 per cent drop, to 29 per cent. Meanwhile, Lawson's cuts to public spending transpired to be cuts in the rate of increase rather than in absolute terms. Where there was clear success in sticking to the rhetoric was in the continuing reduction in the PSBR, which by 1985/6 had fallen to 1.5 per cent of GDP, its lowest level since 1970/1. In consequence, the cost of interest payments on government debt fell.

While the British economy had slipped into recession ahead of its major competitors, it also emerged out of it ahead of them. By 1986, economic growth was outstripping all of the country's principal European competitors.

It was, of course, a boom that appeared more impressive because it was ascending out of a period of stagnation. The relaxations on austerity measures were risked only because of the pain that had previously been applied in order to drive inflation down to acceptable levels, emphasizing the extent to which control of inflation was seen as the prerequisite. Meanwhile, the boost in consumer demand had been stimulated back in July 1982 when Howe had abolished hire-purchase controls. Returning confidence and easier credit helped get the country spending again. Banks lent £934 million, out of £2.09 billion turnover, on credit card accounts in 1980. These sums began to multiply to the extent that by the decade's end, they were lending £6.6 billion on credit cards, on £20 billion turnover. In fact, compared to the highly leveraged first decade of the twenty-first century, borrowing money remained expensive throughout the eighties. But at the time it seemed that a climate of easy credit was emerging, which contrasted with the prime minister's strictures about the need to save and put something aside. Along with ever greater mortgages to support a soaring property market, the consequences represented a financial revolution.*

The expansion of credit had obvious consequences for monetary policy. Lawson announced in his 1985 Mansion House speech that he was effectively giving up on Sterling M3 as the Treasury's primary money supply indicator. It had continued to exceed its targets even when interest rates went back up. While still searching (vainly) for something better, Lawson promoted the importance of Sterling M0, a narrower definition of the money supply which sought to quantify the amount of cash held by the public along with the till money held in banks. He also announced that 'the other good and early guide to changing financial conditions is the exchange rate'.[25]

For disciplined monetarists in the Cabinet, like Nicholas Ridley, it seemed the Chancellor was suddenly preaching heresy.[26] For the previous six years, the Treasury had largely left the exchange rate to the whim of the markets, seeing it first soar in the early days of high interest rates and oil receipts, and then dive by the middle of the decade to a point where it almost reached parity with the dollar. Now, Lawson was arguing that managing the exchange rate was useful not just in order to create greater stability for trade but also as a tool of Treasury policy. It could hardly be questioned that seismic changes in sterling's value were of no consequence. Together with soaring receipts from North Sea oil, the high interest rates that had accompanied the tight monetary squeeze at the beginning of the decade had helped price British exports out of international markets, adding to the woes of the manufacturing sector in particular. Sterling had stood at $2.45 in October 1980. But

---

* See chapter fourteen.

from then onwards it began to slide. By April 1983, it had slumped to $1.54, reaching an all-time low of $1.05 in February 1985. Previously hard-put exporters of goods and services rejoiced at the opportunity to swamp foreign markets, allowing UK manufacturing output finally to exceed its level of the eve of recession in 1979.

The explanation for the currency's rapid depreciation lay only partly with the relaxation of interest rates – much reduced though they were, at 12 per cent in July and 9.5 per cent in December of 1984 they were hardly negligible. The primary explanation lay less in London than in Washington. Having contracted in 1982, the US economy bounced back and during 1984 soared by over 6 per cent. It was a rate of expansion that, when combined with high interest rates, ensured an overvalued dollar. In February 1985, it took concerted action by the Bank of England and the European and Japanese central banks to head off the immediate prospect of a 1:1 sterling–dollar exchange rate. This was a temporary respite, for the over-strong dollar remained a problem that risked overshadowing world economic recovery. With American exports being priced out of the markets, the mood in Congress turned vengeful and introspective, with concerted demands for protectionist tariffs – a response no more attractive to Reagan than it was to the free-trader of Downing Street.

The prospect of a descent into protectionism was headed off in September 1985 when Lawson and his fellow US, French, German and Japanese finance ministers convened their informal G5 group of major capitalist nations and agreed the 'Plaza Accord'. Japan promised to remove its impediments to foreign imports, while the US accepted its responsibility both to cut its dramatically widening budget deficit and to intervene to prop up the value of the other G5 currencies against the dollar. For Britain's part, Lawson agreed to carry on his dual policy of balancing the budget and removing market restrictions.[27] It was the markets' reaction to the Plaza Accord that would be the true test of whether the solidarity between finance ministries was taken seriously. As was hoped, the dollar began to slide to a more competitive rate and the calls for protectionism diminished. Narrowly avoiding parity, sterling appreciated against the dollar throughout 1986 (but slid against the Deutschmark). Most significant from the British economic perspective was that the episode strengthened Lawson's belief in an internationally managed exchange rate – taking him first into a furtive policy of shadowing the Deutschmark and then, when that failed, into a deadly dispute with his next-door neighbour over taking sterling into the European Exchange Rate Mechanism. It was a divide that would do much to seal his fate and, eventually, that of the Conservatives' claim to economic competence.

Thatcher had long maintained that unemployment would fall once inflation was slain. This proved to be the case, though the time lag between the creation of relatively stable prices and job creation demonstrated that it was no simple or direct equation. The proportion of the workforce that was unemployed increased – albeit at ever slower rates – in almost every month of the Conservative government until the summer of 1986. But when the fall eventually came, it was dramatic in scale, plunging in the following three years as precipitously as it had risen between 1980 and 1982. During 1989, it was down to 6.3 per cent, a level last seen in 1980. The damage, however, had already been done, particularly to the long-term unemployed and the disfigured communities they inhabited. What was more, pockets of high joblessness remained in the hardest-hit areas. Even in 1989, the unemployment rate remained at 10 per cent in the north of England, over 9 per cent in Scotland and over 7 per cent in Wales. In Northern Ireland, it was 15 per cent.

The scale and seeming immovability of three million on the dole was also the reason why a political party committed to cutting both public spending and the overall burden of taxation achieved neither goal. Excluding the effects of North Sea oil, the tax burden as a proportion of GDP had risen from nearly 35 per cent in 1979 to over 39 per cent in 1981/2 and though it was sliding below 37 per cent when Thatcher fell from power in 1990, this was still more than 2 per cent higher than when she had arrived in Downing Street. Looked at from the angle of marginal tax rates, and including National Insurance surcharges, the record looked better – falling over the decade from 53 per cent to 44.5 per cent, though hardly justifying the rhetoric of creating an economy invigorated by low taxation.[28] The real effort to cut the tax burden came in the three years after 1986, when unemployment finally took a dive and general government expenditure (which included debt repayment but excluded proceeds from privatization), which had soared towards 47 per cent of GDP between 1982 and 1985, plummeted below 40 per cent by 1989 as growth in the private sector roared ahead.

That the government in the second half of the eighties belatedly looked like delivering its promises on taxation and the size of the state emphasized what it might have been able to achieve if unemployment had not cast its dark shadow over public spending in the first half of the decade. During the entire lifetime of the Thatcher government between 1979 and 1990, the British economy (as expressed by GDP) grew by almost one quarter (23.3 per cent). After the effects of inflation are taken into account, the state still spent nearly 13 per cent more at the end of the eighties than it had done at the end of the seventies, even though the amount represented a proportionately smaller share of the total economy due to the greater rise in private sector activity. Within the overall increase, priorities had changed markedly. The burden created by unemployment, social change and an ageing population was underlined by the expansion of the social security budget by almost one third (31.8 per cent) and the sums spent on employment and training schemes by exactly one third. This continued the long-term trend by which the welfare state assumed the lion's share of state expenditure: 43 per cent of total government spending in 1951/2, 47 per cent in 1971/2, 52 per cent in 1981/2, and 56 per cent in 1987/8.[29] During the eighties, spending on the National Health Service also increased by almost one third, though because the costs brought about by more old people, higher expectations from medicine and the expense of new treatments and equipment were greater than the general rate of inflation, rising levels of health spending did not translate precisely into better hospitals or shorter waiting lists – hence the ongoing popular assumption that the Conservatives under-resourced the NHS, and the widening gap between health spending in the UK as a proportion of GDP and the higher levels of its major European competitors. It was in the area of other formerly expensive calls on the public purse that the government really did make serious cuts. Privatization and an end to widespread industrial subsidies ensured the trade and industry department's budget fell by 38.2 per cent in real terms, while with the end of the council house building programme the housing budget fell by more than three quarters (67 per cent) over the decade.[30]

For all the transatlantic comparisons made between Thatcher and Reagan, the Treasury had a far more Victorian attitude towards matching taxation with spending in order to balance the budget than did its American counterpart. At the core of 'Reaganomics' was a belief in the Laffer curve – a theory popularized in the mid-1970s and (rather imprecisely) attributed to the economist Arthur Laffer, which held that there was an optimal rate at which taxation gathered the maximum amount of revenue. Setting a higher rate was seen as self-defeating, because the corresponding disincentive to make money would yield less tax revenue. Where that optimal point was located remained a matter for debate, though the 'supply-side' economists were in no doubt that it lay at a point considerably lower than had been set during the 1970s, a conviction that ensured that (unlike in the more hesitant UK) American marginal tax rates were slashed by one quarter between 1981 and 1984. The total tax revenue raised did indeed increase, but so did government spending. The result was spiralling US national debt. Where Thatcher and her Chancellor believed that taxes should not fall until spending and borrowing constraints had balanced the budget, Reagan fell back on the claim that if US taxes were raised in order to cut the deficit, Congress would merely find additional ways of spending the money rather than reducing the debt.[31] In contrast, by the time of his 1987 budget, Nigel Lawson was able to boast not only that the PSBR had fallen below £4 billion, or 1 per cent of GDP, but that in the coming year there would be a PSDR, or public sector debt repayment, whereby the government would actually repay some of its debts out of an overall budget surplus of nearly £3.5 billion. As the international edition of *The Economist* pointed out, 'such an outcome could hardly have been dreamt of in 1979'.[32] That a British government was finally repaying debt rather than acquiring more of it exemplified what Thatcherism owed to Gladstonian Liberalism. It also proved to be a fleeting moment, rather than a new dawn, in the nation's financial history, as the legacy was duly squandered. Indeed, the scale of the deficits run up in the first decade of the twenty-first century, alongside the increasing tax burden needed to cover the interest payments, highlights how Gordon Brown's strategy differed from that both of Nigel Lawson and of Lawson's American counterparts – managing to bequeath the debts of Reaganomics without delivering the corresponding fiscal stimulus.

The North Sea Oil Bonanza . . . and Where It Went

That the British state was in a position to fund for several years the unemployment benefits of three million jobless and to support millions more dependent on low incomes and unfunded pensions, while at the same time cutting the budget deficit, certainly seemed remarkable. But it was made possible because of a stroke of geological good fortune which allowed the Thatcher government to use up the tax proceeds from North Sea oil in a short-term dash to balance the books. It was a petroleum bounty that had not been available to the Labour administrations of Harold Wilson and James Callaghan, and it existed only on a much diminished basis for the successive Major, Blair and Brown governments which followed in the twenty years after 1990. As such, it poses the question whether the Thatcher government's claim to have turned round the British economy was really just a quick fix, achieved by squandering oil proceeds which would have been better invested for the long-term benefit of future generations.

It is easy to see why those who had struggled to turn the British economy around in the 1960s and seventies looked on enviously at Thatcher's good luck in coming to power at the very moment that North Sea oil production soared. In the mid-1960s, Britain had been on the verge of bankruptcy, with sterling propped up only through emergency financial guarantees from Washington. Even this lifeline did not prevent the politically damaging devaluation of 1967. Now, oil could be used to prop up Conservative plans in the same way that American financial support underwrote Labour's expansion of the state in the sixties. Whatever Thatcher's strategic desire to walk arm in arm with Reagan, 'black gold' proffered what no British government had been able to enjoy since the outbreak of the Second World War – an end to economic dependency upon the United States.

The North Sea certainly seemed to turn the British economy's reliance on petrol from a curse into a blessing – though, as it soon transpired, something of a mixed one. The soaring price of oil, compounding the industrial unrest of 1973, was a factor in bringing down Edward Heath's government in 1974. At the outset of Thatcher's first term, disagreement between members of the oil-producing cartel OPEC risked turning the screw a second time. The Islamist revolution that deposed the Shah of Iran was quickly followed in 1980 by the outbreak of a bitter and protracted war between two major OPEC members, Iran and its neighbour Iraq. The consequence was a three-fold hike in the world oil price, which threatened Western economies with ever higher energy costs and mounting inflationary pressures. For competitors like France, Germany and Italy, this was unequivocally bad news. But the United Kingdom was fast turning into as much a producer as a consumer of the valuable commodity, becoming for the first time in its history a net exporter of oil in 1981. The only major Western economy to be self-sufficient in oil, by 1983 Britain was producing 60 per cent more than it was consuming.[33] Against the higher price paid by industry and by motorists at the petrol pumps came the advantage of swelling Treasury coffers, since (in the short term at least) the higher the price, the greater the taxable profit.

Whether the taxman's gain was more important than the consumer's loss was questionable, given that oil revenue helped fund the unemployment benefits that were a consequence of higher energy costs burdening industry and putting employees out of work. The addition to the cost of living also increased hardship. As described in chapter three, an inflation rate heading back beyond 20 per cent was countered by a tight monetary squeeze. The accompanying high interest rates pushed up the value of sterling, a currency that soaring oil production in the North Sea was already helping to over-value. The consequence was an uncompetitively high exchange rate. As the chairman of the car manufacturer British Leyland, Michael Edwardes, put it in his South African twang to delegates at the CBI conference in 1980: 'If the Cabinet do not have the wit and imagination to reconcile our industrial needs with the fact of North Sea oil, they would do better to leave the bloody stuff in the ground.'

Oil had been struck in the North Sea in 1969. Over the two following years, the discovery of the Forties and Brent fields in British territorial waters suggested that deposits existed in such quantities as to be worth the vast cost of extracting them from up to 9,000 feet below the seabed. With regal ceremony, the first pipeline to bring oil ashore from the Forties field was turned on in 1975. In the ensuing decade, Scottish and northern English shipyards became the sites of gargantuan oil platform construction work, in what the commentator Andrew Marr has described as 'the most extraordinary civil engineering project in Britain since the Victorians began the railways in the

1840s'.[34] Between 1980 and 1985, around 6 per cent of total UK fixed investment was being spent on oil and gas extraction. Thus those who lamented the failure to repair the crumbling infrastructure of early eighties Britain only saw part of the picture. Huge private investment was going into yards in remote Highland locations like Nigg Bay and Ardersier, where whole workforces were brought to build a new offshore infrastructure to power the country's future prosperity. The United Kingdom had become the first industrial nation at the end of the eighteenth century, thanks to innovation and the accessibility of vast local supplies of coal. Twice blessed – or so it seemed – the same country was now able to supplant its diminishing coal reserves by bringing up from even greater depths the energy source powering the modern age.

The comparison between oil and coal shaped the government's attitude to the industry's development. To Thatcherite minds, the post-war history of the coal industry – nationalized, heavily subsidized, over-manned, inefficient, wholly unionized, strike-prone, its politicized union leaders proving a perpetual thorn in the side of Conservative administrations – demonstrated precisely what path the oil industry needed to avoid. Instead of state control, international capital flowed in and American expertise was decisive in bringing projects to fruition. By the beginning of the eighties, there were twenty platforms and over twenty thousand workers out in the North Sea working on the rigs. Those who toiled there needed to be tough as they were marooned on an elevated and windswept pad above crashing waves in conditions aptly described as akin to 'outer space with bad weather'. It was not deemed an environment for women, consisting as it did of hard, manual labour and off-shift immersion in the culture of the canteen and the porn video. Typically, the men were employed by contractors rather than directly by the oil companies. The absence of trade unions certainly suited management, but was also acceptable to some of the workers who tended to be hard-headed and individualist by nature. Many of the most experienced among them had previously worked in the oilfields of the Middle East and were prepared to accept the risks and long hours for the large sums of money being offered to them, particularly in the most dangerous jobs like deep-sea diving. Thus, in terms of rewards, rig workers were far removed from coal miners. What was more, offshore workers who did agitate to be represented by a trade union were speedily sacked.

Danger, risk-taking, big rewards, tough management, individualist attitudes . . . to admirers and critics alike, the rush to make money from the North Sea had a Wild West feel to it. This was not an industry that the Thatcher government wanted to turn into a state-run monopoly. In any case, the moment to confine the oilfields to a single nationalized corporation, perhaps on the lines of Norway's Statoil, had already passed by the time the Tories came to power in 1979. Given that previous governments had already welcomed multinational companies into the North Sea, it was hardly a serious option to seize their assets and endure years of litigation and billion-pound compensation pay-outs. Rather, what was at issue was the degree to which it was in the national interest for Whitehall to direct and control development.

The state had two principal means of intervention. The first was through British Petroleum (BP), in which the state had acquired a controlling stake in 1914 and had the right to appoint two of the directors to its board. Thus the government could, if it wished, seek to use its leverage to make BP sub-servient to its own agenda for North Sea oil exploration and extraction. However, no previous government had interfered with the company's com-mercial independence in this way, and enacting any policy that retarded BP's commercial imperatives and share price would risk undermining it in rela-tion to other, foreign-owned, competitors. The second agent of state intervention was the British National Oil Corporation (BNOC), the wholly state-owned company set up in 1975 by the then energy secretary, Tony Benn. It held direct stakes in oilfields and enjoyed the right to buy back 51 per cent of any private company's oilfield production. However, while ini-tially holding on to the buy-back rights as a means of trying to ensure price stability, the government soon decided to sell the majority of its stake in BNOC's exploration and production operations. When the company – duly christened Britoil – was floated in 1982, it raised £500 million for the Treasury. Given the sums later generated, this may not seem much, but at the time it represented the largest privatization in the modern world.

By 1988, Britoil was being taken over by BP, which, in turn, had ceased to have the Treasury as its major shareholder. In 1977, the Callaghan gov-ernment had started selling off its shares in BP as a means of raising £564 million of emergency cash to satisfy the country's IMF creditors. Though it no longer had the IMF to worry about, the Thatcher government intensified the process, divesting itself of its holding in BP in several stages, finally selling all but a token fraction of its remaining 31.7 per cent share in 1987. While BP was still smaller than Shell or the American market leader, Exxon (whose Esso logo was a familiar sight along Britain's major roads), it under-went rapid expansion during the eighties under the chairmanship of Sir Peter Walters, thanks to the output from the Forties field and its oil interests in Alaska. This was a far better outcome than could have been foreseen at the beginning of the decade, when BP had suffered the nationalization of its assets in Iran and Nigeria. Nevertheless, whatever the case for the Treasury selling off its stake in BP, its timing was disastrous – the share floatation went ahead just days after the Stock Market crashed on 'Black Monday', 19 October 1987. As the British government moved out, the Kuwaiti government moved in, with its sovereign wealth fund quickly buying more than a 20 per cent share at a knock-down price, sufficient to give the Gulf emirate effective control of the company's future direction. Responding to political pressure, the Treasury found itself calling in the Monopolies and Mergers Commission. In October 1988, the commission duly concluded that the Kuwaiti acquisition was against the national interest. The emirate was restricted to owning less than 10 per cent of the company. In oil, at least, the question of foreign takeovers could not yet be left entirely to the market.

Nigel Lawson, first as energy secretary from 1981 to 1983 and thereafter as Chancellor of the Exchequer until 1989, was the dominant figure in this process. He believed in principle that the decisions of great British companies should not be directed by government departments. But, like all residents of 11 Downing Street with immediate commitments to honour, he was also motivated by a short-term desire to maximize the money coming into the state coffers. Selling the government's share in BP raised £6 billion. Together with the proceeds from floating Britoil and from privatizing British Gas, which raised almost £5.5 billion in 1986, it ensured that a majority of all the proceeds raised for the Treasury through privatization in the 1980s came from selling off North Sea energy companies.[35]

Even more money was to be made from taxing the oil companies directly. The 1979 price hike following the Iranian revolution had a positive knock-on effect for North Sea companies, encouraging the maximizing of production and making exploring new oilfields economically justifiable. In addition to corporation tax, a special tax on oil company profits, petroleum revenue tax, was introduced by the Labour government in 1975, although the size of the companies' initial development costs (which could be subtracted from profits) prevented much tax revenue being generated. By 1980, this was no longer the case: profitability was soaring ahead, offering a tax bonanza for the Treasury. The first three budgets of the Thatcher government pushed the petroleum revenue tax rate to 75 per cent in 1982, by which time there was also an additional supplementary petroleum duty. During 1983, Lawson at the Department of Energy argued with Howe at the Treasury that such high rates were ultimately counterproductive. Lawson won this debate, the tax burden was gently eased and, sure enough, by encouraging even higher output, tax receipts actually went up. By 1982/3, the Treasury's coffers were being filled with nearly £8 billion from North Sea taxes, equivalent to almost 8.5 per cent of all tax revenue; and by 1984/5, the North Sea's £22 billion income brought in £12 billion for the Treasury, equivalent to 8 per cent of all tax revenue. Such was the significance of these figures that double the amount of revenue was being raised from taxing North Sea oil and gas output than was being raised through corporation tax on all other business sectors put together.[36]

By 1983, two million barrels of oil per day were being pumped from the North Sea, with technological advances in oil platform construction making extraction feasible from ever deeper waters. Offshore and on, about seventy thousand people in the UK were employed directly by the oil industry, with a further twenty thousand jobs indirectly dependent upon it.[37] The majority were located in Grampian region, with house prices in the granite city of Aberdeen soaring to levels that would have been unimaginable before the oil men arrived. Britain's largest oil port became Sullom Voe, which brought jobs and prosperity to the Shetland Islands (this was certainly appropriate, for had not a cash-strapped Scandinavian monarch in the fifteenth century pawned the islands as part of his daughter's dowry to the King of Scots, the massive Brent oilfield would have been in Norwegian waters). While the daily heroics that brought up the oil may scarcely have troubled the imagination of many Britons, it gave renewed pride and purpose to a Scotland where the outlook for those engaged in the traditional heavy industries and in coal mining looked bleak. These were years in which the prospects from oil loomed so great in the Scottish consciousness that the opening credits for *Reporting Scotland*, BBC 1's main regional news programme north of the border, featured an oil rig, its flare boom burning bright, within the stylized outline of Scotland. It was a dynamic new image to replace the familiar hills, glens and tartan clichés that had long symbolized the nation.

Given that the oilfields would have been overwhelmingly within the waters of an independent Scotland it was hardly surprising that the Scottish National Party was the immediate political beneficiary of the discovery of North Sea oil in the 1970s. But the party's momentum was checked by the lost referendum on devolving power in 1979, and by a dismal showing in the ensuing general election which reduced the SNP to two MPs and produced an internal split between its leadership and left-wing activists. The party fared no better at the polls in 1983, despite a campaign that included a cartoon of a sinisterly grinning Thatcher with Dracula fangs dripping oil alongside the caption 'No Wonder She's Laughing. She's Got Scotland's Oil.' The message may have resonated, but the solution did not. At least until such time as a Scottish Parliament existed, the obvious way for Scots to get Thatcher out of their lives was to vote Labour in Westminster elections. The 1987 general election merely took the SNP parliamentary tally to three. Nevertheless, the cry of 'It's Scotland's oil' remained a potent one. Nervous of a nationalist backlash, Nigel Lawson only allowed BP to acquire the Scottish-based Britoil in 1988 if it promised to keep a headquarters in Glasgow and to endow several Scottish universities.

Given how much faith was placed in North Sea oil's ability to fuel an economic renaissance, it stimulated notably little response from novelists or dramatists. No British version of J. R. Ewing hit prime-time television –

Dallas did not have a windier equivalent called *Aberdeen*. Even for Scottish viewers, the only major television programme to come regularly from the city at the centre of the oil boom was a hardy perennial series for horticulturalists called *The Beechgrove Garden*. The British film industry was only slightly more attuned to the moment, its one successful foray into the oil phenomenon coming in 1983 with a David Puttnam-produced latter-day Ealing Comedy by the Scottish writer–director, Bill Forsyth. *Local Hero* told the tale of a fictional Scottish fishing village that a Texas oil firm hoped to buy in order to build a refinery on the site – the plot twist being that some of the jaded villagers are keen to sell and make a quick buck, and it is the oil company rep sent to negotiate the terms who ends up seeking to preserve the village and its gentle way of life.

In reality, the golden egg was about to crack. North Sea oil production peaked in 1985 at 953 million barrels per year, which, together with gas, represented 4.6 per cent of world oil production and nearly 5 per cent of the United Kingdom's total GDP. But in early 1986 the international price of oil collapsed as quickly as it had soared seven years earlier. The immediate cause was the further fracturing of the OPEC cartel and the relaxation of its production-fixing quota system. The market responded predictably to the oversupply of a commodity by discounting its value. The price of oil dived from \$30 per barrel in November 1985 to \$10 in April 1986.[38] Presciently, the Department for Energy had in March 1985 dispensed with BNOC's remaining role of buying other companies' North Sea oil at quarterly fixed prices before selling it on. Given how violently the price was about to plummet, the effort to shore it up by such means would have been doomed and an expensive waste of taxpayers' money. At such moments, the market was beyond direction and the winding up of BNOC was merely a further example of the government's determination to distance itself from direct involvement in the North Sea industry.

The crash's consequences were felt immediately. During 1986, the value of British North Sea oil production halved from £20 billion to under £10 billion, with drilling being cut by 40 per cent.[39] Twenty thousand jobs were lost as offshore workers were laid off, onshore platform and supply construction contracts were cut, and companies merged or went under. Compounding the bad news, tragedy awaited some of those still going out to the rigs. On 6 November 1986, forty-five men were killed when a Chinook helicopter taking offshore workers back to the Shetland Islands crashed. Even worse was to follow. On 6 July 1988, 110 miles off the coast of Aberdeen, a gas-condensate pipe exploded because a valve on a pump had not been correctly replaced on the Piper Alpha platform. The rig, owned by an American company, Occidental, was responsible for bringing onshore 10 per cent of the UK's North Sea oil. Within twenty minutes, the pressurized gas pipeline burst under the heat of the explosion, spewing forth a fireball powered by the release of 3 tonnes of gas per second, equivalent to one and a half times the entire British gas consumption at that moment. Subjected to 1,000-°C heat, the platform buckled and crashed into the sea. Of the 226 personnel who had been aboard, 167 died. Seven George Medals were awarded – some posthumously – to those who had risked all to rescue desperate men. When the Cullen inquiry detailed what had gone wrong, it revealed not only specific errors on Piper Alpha but more general systemic failings in a culture of lax rig safety procedures. In the zeal to extract 'black gold', unacceptable shortcuts had been taken.

The Piper Alpha disaster came to symbolize the end of a dream of instant and trouble-free riches which had begun to fade two years previously with the price crash. The diminished price for oil decimated profit margins and discouraged further exploration. This in turn forced the Treasury to cut its tax rates in an attempt to induce new activity. Yet even by 1989, production was still, at 90 million tonnes, only one third down on its 1985 peak. Worldwide, there was still oversupply, and one result of the years of high prices was the promotion of greater fuel efficiency, which succeeded in cutting demand. For every dollar that the price per barrel fell, about £500 million was lost in tax receipts to the Treasury. By 1992, the North Sea's income stood at almost half its 1985 level – £11.7 billion, yielding merely £2.2 billion in tax. The age in which oil had been a major factor in propping up sterling and cutting borrowing was all but over. For her part, Thatcher struck an optimistic note, claiming that falling prices were for the best. As she reassured a conference of Conservative activists in March 1986: 'Those who thought the oil price explosion of the 1970s did harm to our industry and slowed our growth rate were right. Falling oil prices are, on the whole, good news . . . Industry's costs are being cut. All this is a bit like a tax cut.'[40] Despite being the wife of a former director of Burmah oil, the North Sea boom had never captured the prime minister's imagination even though, until the crash, it was a crucial ingredient in her objective of bringing the budget into balance. Indeed, the phenomenon received only the most passing of mentions in her 900-page memoirs.

What should have been done with the oil revenue? The prime minister's ex-Cabinet colleague, Sir Ian Gilmour, lamented that 'North Sea oil could have been used to finance a massive increase of investment in industry and in the infrastructure', leaving 'industry restructured and made more competitive'.[41] It was a view that ran wholly counter to Thatcher's notion that what British industry needed to become more competitive was fuller exposure to market forces, rather than easier access to Treasury handouts. She interpreted the case for using oil revenue for the 'restructuring of industry' as merely an effort to involve the state again in picking winners, a policy practiced without conspicuous success by Harold Wilson's government. Thatcher probably doubted her own ministers would be adept pickers of which companies and projects to back; she was certainly not keen that a fund might still be fructifying for a future Labour administration to spend as it pleased, perhaps propping up dying blue-collar industries at the behest of the trade union movement. Put bluntly, she did not want the revenue raised from oil wells redirected back down coal mines. Entrepreneurs should look to banks and the stock market – nothing she had seen in the workings of government convinced her that civil servants were better than capitalists at indentifying where there was a return to be made from an investment. Consequently, Thatcher continued the policy of the Callaghan government which, during a Cabinet meeting in February 1978, had determined that the oil revenue should instead go into general Treasury funds, thereby leaving the Chancellor free to decide the disbursement between current public spending, investment, debt repayment and tax cuts.

The failure to answer the question of what the country would do once the oil eventually ran out raises the proposition that it would have been better to ensure that that day was postponed for as long as possible. Drawing out the life of the oilfields would have meant Whitehall enacting a 'depletion policy' by intervening to slow down the rate of extraction. Such a policy was pursued by the other major North Sea oil nation, Norway, through its state-owned company Statoil. Curtailing rather than permitting an unbridled production boom between 1979 and 1982 would have removed some of the upwards pressure on sterling, making it less of a petro-currency at exactly the moment that the high exchange rate was pricing British industry out of export markets. However, the Treasury's hands were tied during the crucial period of sterling's appreciation because of a binding commitment the Labour government had made in 1974 to the oil companies promising not to enforce major extraction restrictions until 1982 – the date, as it transpired, by which the worst of the recession had passed. Although Nigel Lawson then extended the guarantee until 1985, after that point there was no need for a Whitehall diktat to enforce reduced extraction rates because the market, in the shape of the oil price crash, had achieved the same end. Indeed, the low price for oil in the years after 1985 suggested that, far from squandering future revenue, the Treasury had maximized petroleum revenue tax at exactly the right moment. This was a happy accident – though one brought about only because the government refused to bow to the contemporary wisdom that delaying the rate of extraction made sense because oil could only continue to appreciate in value, especially as it became scarcer world-wide. It was not until the first decade of the twenty-first century that the oil price really appreciated again, by which time government policy was switch-ing to the promotion of greener, non-carbon energy sources. Thus, it is possible that British 'short-termist' attitudes in the early eighties actually allowed the most value to be extracted from the asset.

Nevertheless, should that value have been invested for the future rather than spent at the time? Norway's experience offered an example of how North Sea oil might have been carefully managed and its revenue directed to long-term aims. In truth, the Norwegian approach was as much a product of common sense as of Scandinavian socialist planning. After all, the destabilizing effect of North Sea oil production on a diverse and sizeable economy of fifty-six million Britons was as nothing to the distortion that unrestricted production would have brought to a nation of four million Norwegians. For Oslo, the *laissez-faire* approach was never a viable option: either the oil stock was carefully managed or it would grotesquely and detrimentally unbalance the national economy. Nevertheless, proportionate to the size of the economy, Norway's oil production during the eighties was vastly greater than that of the UK – by 1990, it was even outstripping the UK's production in absolute as well as relative terms.[42] Investment in the country's infrastructure greatly increased the number of Norwegians on the public sector payroll but did not boost the numbers engaged in the industrial sector. Despite considerable investment from oil proceeds, the proportion of Norwegians employed by industry shrank significantly below that of the UK, to 17 per cent of the workforce by 1990. To confuse matters for comparative purposes, Norway's government was Conservative between 1981 and 1986 and combined a managed depletion policy and economic investment with the tax cuts and financial deregulation favoured in Britain. When the oil price collapse brought Norway's Conservative experiment to a halt in 1986 – with the country's budget deficit still running at 15 per cent – the incoming Labour administration partly reversed the country's market-liberalizing policies.[43]

The essential difference was that both Norway's left- and right-wing governments established a legacy from oil that the Thatcher years failed to bequeath. Norway used part of its North Sea oil revenue to create what by 2008 had reached a 2 trillion kroner (£200 billion) national pension fund. If Britain had likewise invested in government bonds over the same timescale, it could have multiplied to around £450 billion (equivalent to Britain's total tax revenues for 2007/8), which could have been used, as in Norway, to help pay for the long-term burden of an ageing population.[44] Whereas oil-producing nations such as Saudi Arabia, the constituent states of the United Arab Emirates, and Kuwait channelled their oil proceeds into sovereign wealth funds, which became huge investment organizations taking major shares in prize foreign assets (including British ones), the UK instead chose the short-term option, addressing the immediate need to reduce taxation (and to pay for a vastly larger section of society on unemployment benefit) while seeking also to balance the budget.

Resurrection

But even short-term fixes have longer-term consequences. The extent to which lower taxes generated enterprise and stimulated growth, while impossible to measure accurately, cannot be discounted as a factor in the country's above-average economic performance when measured against European competitors over the succeeding thirty years (having suffered a growth rate below the European average over the preceding thirty years). Without the oil revenue, tax levels on both producers and consumers would inevitably have been higher, or else the Thatcher government would have been forced to introduce far more stringent spending cuts. In 1979, even basic rate tax-payers surrendered 33 per cent of their earnings to income tax. By 1990, they were losing only one quarter rather than one third of their wages to income tax, while higher earners had seen a transformative fall in the tax on their incomes from 83 per cent to 40 per cent. Burdens were also removed from business, with corporation tax slashed from 52 to 34 per cent. Lower taxes gave Britons, whether as employers or employees, more money to save or spend as they chose. Much of this ended up fuelling the property market, creating a distortion of its own and channelling savings into one of the less productive sectors of the economy. But the property market was not the only destination for this new wealth. While the Thatcher government left no Norwegian-style pension fund or Kuwaiti sovereign wealth investment arm as a legacy from the oil bounty, it could claim to have used it towards creating the conditions in which private pension funds were able to generate vast sums for those in search of a comfortable retirement. Indeed, the contribution of British oil companies to the stock market was extensive, ensuring that in the twenty years following the eighties pension funds relied heavily on BP as one of their core equity holdings. Of the £70 billion the top 100 FTSE companies paid out in dividends in 2009, £10 billion came from BP.[45] It was private earnings from the North Sea that helped create one of the undoubted turnarounds of the eighties – the burgeoning stock of the UK's net overseas assets, which by 1986 had reached almost £110 billion (up from £12 billion in 1979), giving the British economy a portfolio of foreign assets on a scale it had not enjoyed since the sell-offs necessitated for national survival in the Second World War. By the late eighties, only Japan had a higher level of overseas assets.

Britain's national finances in 1979 were sufficiently precarious for both the outgoing Labour and incoming Conservative governments to conclude that oil proceeds were a necessary lifeline for the present, rather than the future. What was not foreseen was the extent to which a serious recession would send revenue from other sources of taxation plummeting, using up far more of the oil revenue – necessarily, but unproductively – in providing welfare benefits. From this point on, analysis becomes overwhelmed by conflicting counter-factual propositions. Charges that the economic crisis was one of Thatcherism's own making typically hypothesize that the call on the public purse would ultimately have been less if the government had tried to stimulate economic growth rather than hike up interest rates to clamp down on inflation. Stimulating demand and printing money were arguably viable when the Brown and Cameron governments tried it during the recession of 2008–12 because, at least at the start of the process, there was minimal existing inflation to worry about. Indeed, the fear was that without quantitative easing there would have been deflation. But Britain in 1980 was already struggling with a 20 per cent inflation rate. Pump-priming an economy at such a moment risked a Latin American-style inflationary explosion, making money worthless, wiping out savings and precipitating economic collapse – which would ultimately also have lengthened the unemployment queues. Even if the government had somehow managed to keep a lid on inflation while borrowing vastly more money to keep the economy buoyant, the proposition that Thatcher should have been more prudent and far-sighted with the oil revenue is undermined if, in the same breath, the case is made that she should also have borrowed far more money. Given that borrowing is taxation deferred, the return on oil investments would have been clawed back by the debt interest to be repaid on an increased budget deficit.

Whereas oil revenue could have been ring-fenced to create a £450 billion sovereign wealth fund over the next quarter-century, this would have left a gaping hole in the government finances in the meantime. Assuming no other changes, the removal of oil revenue from government receipts would have left a public sector net debt equivalent to around 50 per cent of GDP by 1990, instead of the actual figure of just under 30 per cent. Projecting further onwards, this would have left a public sector net debt which was about 32 per cent higher by 2008 than actually transpired – the equivalent of a £450 billion shortfall which would have needed plugging by additional borrowing.[46] Thus the potential long-term gains and losses that had to be considered in assessing whether to use the oil revenue to meet immediate needs or to create a long-term investment fund were more closely aligned than might at first be imagined. The reality of the United Kingdom's failure to make the most of its good fortune in the North Sea was that it could only invest it wisely for the future by risking ruin in the meantime.

8 TWO TRIBES

Protest and Survive

In the autumn of 1983, the world came uncomfortably close to annihilation. From the Kremlin there were unmistakably jumpy spasms triggered by fears that efforts to probe Soviet early warning systems prefigured an American nuclear first strike. 'Reagan is unpredictable,' judged Yuri Andropov, who combined the leadership of the world's other superpower with being bedridden with terminal kidney failure. 'You should expect anything from him.'[1] With these apprehensions clouding in, on 1 September 1983, Soviet jets shot down a South Korean Boeing 747 civil airliner that had inadvertently strayed into the USSR's airspace over the Sea of Japan. All 269 passengers were killed (of whom sixty-two were American and two were British). Particularly disastrously for international relations, one of the dead was a US congressman. After initially denying the incident had happened, the Soviet government swiftly changed tack, covertly recovered and concealed the flight recorders, publicly denounced the United States for the provocation and refused to apologize for the deaths. Three weeks later, on 26 September 1983, the Soviets' early warning system showed up what appeared to be a reckless act of retaliation: the United States had launched five nuclear missiles that were heading straight towards the Soviet Union.

The correct procedure was to check if other command centres were reporting the same formation and then seek Andropov's response. Rather than follow procedures, Lieutenant Colonel Stanislav Petrov, the duty officer at the early warning command centre that had spotted the incoming threat, reasoned to himself that the expected US pre-emptive strike ought to have consisted of far more than five incoming missiles. He spent what were potentially the few minutes available gambling – correctly, as it turned out – that it was a glitch in the satellite system. Thus he did not raise the alarm and Andropov's permission to launch a nuclear response was not sought. It cannot be confidently asserted that Petrov's caution was all that prevented nuclear Armageddon. Nevertheless, it was a tense incident with catastrophic potential. For his display of personal initiative, Petrov received neither reward nor promotion and instead found himself reassigned. He took early retirement and suffered a nervous breakdown.

Within days of this scare, Warsaw Pact forces were put on full alert when, on 2 November, a massive NATO exercise, codenamed Able Archer, was assessed – incorrectly – not as the practice drill it claimed to be but as potentially the cover for a full-scale attack. A cause for particular suspicion was that the exercise involved a simulated nuclear response and the active participation in the procedure of Margaret Thatcher and West Germany's Chancellor, Helmut Kohl, using new launch encryptions. Not until the exercise finished ten days later did the Soviet high command breathe a sigh of relief.[2] Of Petrov's dilemma, the West – as the United States and its allies were then collectively known (when not calling themselves the 'Free World') – learned nothing until the 1990s when the collapse of the USSR brought forth a gush of disclosures. Through Britain's KGB double agent, Oleg Gordievsky, Ronald Reagan did, however, learn just how dangerously twitchy the Soviet Politburo had been while Able Archer went through its paces.[3] The revelation left the president, according to his national security adviser, in a state of 'genuine anxiety'.[4] It was a state felt by millions across Britain, Europe and beyond who, while in ignorance of the particular incidents of September and November 1983, feared that the mistaking of a rare cloud formation for incoming missiles or military manoeuvres for the real thing was precisely the sort of dangerous mishap that made the world an unsafe place, when its fate was in the hands of two superpowers with sufficient nuclear weapons to blow up the planet but insufficient trust in each other to be sure what the other intended. Indeed, there was not only a lack of trust but a breakdown of communication. Apart from an unofficial visit to Moscow by the 91-year-old former wartime ambassador to the USSR, W. Averell Harriman, in June 1983, Andropov did not hold a single serious discussion with a senior American official during his fifteen months as leader. Reagan was in his second term of office before he met his Soviet counterpart.[5]

The non-meeting of minds was one thing – but, as a consequence, Margaret Thatcher believed that if anything had prevented a third world war, the missiles had done so. Although its MAD acronym was unfortunate, 'mutually assured destruction' explained why the Soviet Union would think hard before attacking the West, whether with nuclear or conventional arms, given the threat of being wiped out by nuclear retaliation. The Soviets may not be trustworthy, but Thatcher gambled that they were not suicidal. Her views on social issues and economic policies changed and developed over the course of her parliamentary career, but she resiliently clung to her certainty that the only language the old men of the Politburo understood was strength – and that the chief danger would come from uncertainty, especially if they thought they could get away with probing NATO's resolve. The sober reality of the Cold War was one of the constant, unchanging features of the world as she understood it, and in the new US president, Ronald Reagan, she believed she had an ally with a similarly steadfast view as to where the main threat resided.

It was because of the seemingly immutable nature of the Cold War that for most of the 1980s the politics of 'defence' in public discourse was all but shorthand for 'nuclear weapons'. The Falklands War had been a wholly unexpected incident which demonstrated to Britain the value of sizeable conventional forces and the continued possession of the world's third-largest fleet (even though it was the Royal Navy that fared least well out of the three services from government spending priorities during the Thatcher years, despite defence secretary Michael Heseltine's reversal of the worst of the cuts planned in 1981 by his predecessor, John Nott). Yet for all its drama and 'lessons', the war in the South Atlantic did not reverse the East of Suez decision of 1967, which effectively acknowledged that Britain's role was to guard the North Sea and defend Western Europe from potential Soviet attack, not to maintain a presence all over the globe. In this sense, the Falkland Islands were an exception – made so by the fact that they were populated by British kith and kin. In other circumstances, Thatcher was – in the language of a previous age – more a proponent of the 'Continental Commitment' than the 'Blue Water School'. Her government had the same priorities as the Callaghan government it replaced: to maintain Britain's role as second in command of NATO and to station a sizeable British Army of the Rhine (BAOR) in West Germany, ready to stand in the way of a Soviet attack there. The third priority was one that Callaghan also shared, but had yet to take the final decision on when he fell from office. That was the policy to keep and modernize the British independent nuclear deterrent. This last, exceptionally expensive, spending commitment, which saw Polaris replaced by Trident, was to prove highly contentious. However, while scrapping it was a goal of those campaigning for unilateral nuclear disarmament, it was not the British nuclear arsenal but rather the siting of American ground-launched, nuclear-armed cruise missiles on British soil that became the principal focus of popular alarm. The result was the extraordinary phenom-enon of the women's peace camp at Greenham Common and the dramatic rise in support for the previously all but moribund Campaign for Nuclear Disarmament (CND).

In 1979, CND had scarcely three thousand members. The popularity it had enjoyed in the six years that followed its foundation in 1957 – when its 'Ban the Bomb' marches between Trafalgar Square and the nuclear research establishment at Aldermaston had attracted great attention and widespread support among intellectuals, clergymen, journalists and commentators – had almost entirely ebbed away. From 1980 onwards, however, it enjoyed a dramatic and remarkable resurgence. By 1982, its membership had risen tenfold, to forty thousand, and this figure greatly underestimated the strength of its support by excluding the tens of thousands more associated with it through affiliated peace groups. During 1983, CND's membership reached 100,000. The popularity of its monthly magazine, *Sanity*, was such that it was sold in branches of W. H. Smith alongside the *New Statesman* and the *Spectator*. CND's chair, Joan Ruddock, and general secretary, the Catholic clergyman Monsignor Bruce Kent, became nationally recognized figures. Nor was it the sort of organization whose members supported it quietly and discreetly. At a time when wearing lapel badges was back in fashion, the distinctive, circular CND badge quickly became the adornment of choice for those committed to the cause, as well as signifying a more general youthful statement of distrust of authority. On 1 April 1983, just two months before the general election was to be held, seventy thousand people formed a 14-mile-long human chain between the nuclear establishments at Aldermaston and Burghfield and the airbase at Greenham Common, where cruise missiles were expected to be deployed later in the year. Then, on 22 October, on a day of massive peace protests across Western Europe, where the collective number of participants was calculated in millions, CND organized its biggest demonstration in Britain with well over a quarter of a million supporters bringing central London to standstill.

The movement's most strategically significant victory was the conversion of the main opposition party to its cause. Delegates at the 1982 Labour Party conference had committed Labour to unilateral nuclear disarmament – scrapping Britain's independent nuclear weapons and 'closing down all nuclear bases, British and American, on British soil or in British waters',[6] regardless of whether the Soviet Union did likewise. While this stance appeared to have been one of the many factors that had contributed to Labour's drubbing in the 1983 general election, the possibility that the party might win a subsequent general election on the back of other issues and then implement its unilateral strategy as soon it came to power clearly disturbed those who saw the weapons as a deterrent. Michael Foot's departure as Labour leader changed little. His replacement, Neil Kinnock, reaffirmed his party's commitment to British unilateralism.

The re-emergence of the anti-nuclear campaign caught the government by surprise and, scrambling to counter it, Thatcher chose one of her Cabinet's most able communicators, Michael Heseltine, as her new defence secretary in January 1983. He was certainly adept at news management. On the day the Greenham–Aldermaston–Burghfield human chain was formed, he contrived his own publicity spoiler, arriving back just in time from West Berlin where, he announced, he had seen the real peace-keepers at work facing the barbed wire, watchtowers, machine-gun posts and concrete slabs of the

Berlin Wall. Heseltine was soon the human lightning conductor in the storms that followed. With political activism returning to the campuses, he found himself regularly bundled around the country's university lecture halls while anti-nuclear protesters (as well as other groups) tried to prevent him from addressing Conservative students by jostling, throwing eggs, a brick and even, on one occasion, swinging a baby in front of his fast-moving police support car.[7] For students coming to applaud rather than harass the new defence minister – who quickly attracted the nickname 'Tarzan' – his assailants seemed at best naive and at worst all but fellow travellers. The Federation of Conservative Students helped distribute both its own posters and those designed and funded by other 'pro-defence' organizations. One showed the CND symbol breaking up and morphing into the Soviet hammer and sickle. Heseltine arranged for the links some leading CND activists had with far-left and Marxist organizations to be publicized – an action that was met with fury but no litigation. In 1983, MI5 began tapping the telephone of John Cox, who was both one of CND's vice chairmen and a member of the national executive of the Communist Party of Great Britain. The warrant for the tap was revoked in 1985 when it became clear to the security service that 'members of the CPGB were not manipulating CND or exercising decisive influence within it'.[8]

CND's resurgence was driven by the deteriorating relations between the two superpowers. The period of détente between Washington and Moscow which had accompanied the long-drawn-out strategic arms limitation talks (SALT II) had effectively collapsed even before Ronald Reagan became president in January 1981. What was to be dubbed the 'Second Cold War' began on Christmas Eve 1979, when Soviet forces invaded Afghanistan. Then, on 13 December 1981, the communist regime in Warsaw imposed martial law, plunging Poland into a state of emergency which lasted until 1983. At the time, the actions of Poland's General Jaruzelski were presumed to be motivated by fear that unless he cracked down on the Solidarity trade union, the first in Eastern Europe to be free of state control, the Soviet Union would invade Poland and restore a firmer totalitarian grip – though later archival revelations suggest that, in fact, Jaruzelski may actually have invited a Soviet invasion. Regardless of whether Jaruzelski was trying to head off or encourage Soviet repression, East–West relations rapidly deteriorated. All means of communication between Poland and the outside world were severed, the phone lines cut, the borders sealed and curfews imposed during which transgressors risking being – and were – shot. Dissidents, including the Solidarity leader, Lech Wałęsa, were imprisoned without trial. For the moment, it appeared that Polish resistance had been broken, though Wałęsa was aware that, morally, he was winning the showdown just by enduring it. 'This is the moment of your defeat,' he assured the secret policemen who came to arrest him. 'These are the last nails in the coffin of communism.' For nothing had stirred the Polish conscience more deeply than the elevation of the Polish Karol Wojtyła as the first non-Italian pontiff for four hundred and fifty years. On his triumphant return to his officially atheist homeland in 1979, vast crowds, chanting 'We want God! We want God!', had greeted the new pope, John Paul II. He urged them not to be afraid. It was a dangerous message for, on 13 May 1981, he was shot in St Peter's Square. Only six weeks earlier there had been an attempt on Reagan's life and, as with the pope, the subsequent course of events was profoundly affected by the successful removal of the bullet. But while Reagan's would-be assassin was a deranged 26-year-old with a perverse notion of how to express his unrequited love for the teenage actress Jodie Foster, the motive behind the Turk sent to murder the pope was suspected to be altogether more political. Mehmet Ali Ağca appeared to have links to the Bulgarian intelligence service and through it – it was widely assumed, though never proven – to Moscow.

In these months of trepidation, the greatest causes of tension – and of protest in Britain – came from two interlinked decisions taken before either the Soviet invasion of Afghanistan, the crackdown in Poland, or the assassination attempts on the US president and the pope. The first was the Soviet deployment of the SS-20, an intermediate-range nuclear missile. It was aimed at targets across Western Europe and it was especially difficult to track its deployment because the missiles could be moved around on trucks and hidden in forests. The second decision followed in December 1979, when NATO ministers decided to respond by basing 464 cruise and 106 Pershing II intermediate-range nuclear missiles in Britain, West Germany, Italy and the Netherlands. These missiles were so fast and so accurate that they were designed – at least in theory – to pinpoint and destroy the Soviets' nuclear command system before it had time to launch a retaliatory strike. The intention was that Britain would become America's 'unsinkable aircraft carrier'[9] – home to 160 cruise missiles, each of which would have four times the destructive power of the atomic bomb that levelled Hiroshima.

Until these new missiles arrived in 1983, the only European-based nuclear weapons that could hit the Soviet Union were air-launched from an ageing and far from invulnerable fleet of British Vulcan bombers and US F-111 jets. Of course, long-range intercontinental ballistic missiles (ICBMs) could be fired all the way from the United States, but this raised the question of whether an American president would risk turning his own country into a target for massive nuclear retaliation if the limited-range SS-20s were only raining down upon selected targets in Western Europe. Thus cruise (and the shorter-range Pershing II, which was deployed in West Germany) were intended to send a signal to the Kremlin that it could not attack Western

Europe without the certainty of nuclear retaliation, and that NATO could respond at whatever level and scale the Warsaw Pact chose: battlefield nuclear weapons would be met with battlefield nuclear weapons, medium-range missiles with medium-range missiles, ICBMs with ICBMs. What was more, if the forces of the Warsaw Pact were to invade Western Europe using only conventional weapons, their vast advantage in numbers, and a three to one superiority in tanks, would likely ensure their success. However, while NATO promised it would not attack first, it pointedly refused to promise that, if attacked, it would not be the first to respond with nuclear weapons. The medium-range nuclear arsenal was therefore deemed imperative to make up for Western Europe's shortfall in conventional forces. Efforts by the Kremlin to offer significant arms reductions in return for cancelling the cruise and Pershing deployments were destined to fail for this reason – as well as because the Soviet offer did not include longer-range SS-20s, some of which were based beyond the Urals and could reach Western Europe while remaining beyond the range of a pre-emptive strike by cruise and Pershing. Prior to the cruise and Pershing deployment, Soviet nuclear missiles outnumbered NATO's in the European theatre by a margin of three to one. Neither Thatcher nor Reagan – nor any of the other major European leaders – was greatly tempted by a Soviet offer that, while reducing the absolute numbers on both sides, essentially left the imbalance in place. What Reagan offered, in a proposal he announced in November 1981, was the complete removal of all Soviet and US intermediate-range nuclear missiles from Europe: the intention to deploy cruise and Pershing II would be cancelled in return for Moscow scrapping its SS-20s as well as its SS-4s and SS-5s. This initiative, for what promised to be the abolition of an entire class of nuclear weapons, was labelled the 'zero option'. But with the Kremlin's refusal to consider so comprehensive a deal, Britain prepared for the arrival of cruise.

As the date drew nearer, the campaign to oppose the cruise missile deployment intensified. Polaris, Britain's own nuclear deterrent, was carried in submarines under the sea and, unlike land-based nuclear missiles, was almost invulnerable to a Soviet first strike – and equally inaccessible to protesters (even to those who turned up outside the submarines' base on the Gare Loch). In contrast, the cruise missiles had a wholly landlocked base, Greenham Common, in the extremely accessible home county of Berkshire. What's more, they were American missiles, operated by the American armed forces, and therefore a focus for anti-American sentiment which had strengthened markedly since the election of Ronald Reagan, whose critics depicted him as a gun-toting cowboy (a role he had played in his days as a Hollywood actor). Those who feared the worst from him were not reassured by his description in March 1983 of the Soviet Union as the 'evil empire', nor by the ill-judged joke he made during an off-air soundcheck for his weekly radio address in August the following year: 'My fellow Americans, I am pleased to tell you today that I've signed legislation that will outlaw Russia forever. We begin bombing in five minutes.'

While the British government welcomed cruise as a sign that, if the Warsaw Pact attacked Western Europe, the continent would not be left to its fate by a United States seeking to save itself, opponents turned the argument on its head. They maintained that the deployment of cruise meant that for the United States a nuclear war would not mean mutually assured destruction, because a Republican administration in Washington might be prepared to respond to Soviet aggression by turning Europe into a nuclear wasteland in an intermediate-range missile exchange, while the air that Americans breathed remained uncontaminated. Reagan could prove careless with European lives if he did not have to worry about those of his own citizens. Might he even use Greenham Common to launch a pre-emptive first strike on the Soviet Union?

This concern could easily have been addressed by the British government insisting upon a 'dual key', which would prevent the United States from launching the cruise missiles without British authority. Washington had offered Britain a dual-key arrangement if it agreed to pay for the missiles.[10] But if they remained under American ownership, then the owner alone would have the sole right to fire them. To Thatcher, this seemed perfectly reasonable. Always one for a saving, she did not want the additional cost of buying the missiles – she trusted US intentions and, additionally, did not want to create an awkward situation for West Germany's incoming Chancellor, Helmut Kohl, who was insistent that West Germany should not have a dual key on the Pershing II missiles, precisely because his country had renounced its own nuclear ambitions (while being happy to host America's nuclear arsenal).[11] Her desire to help Kohl and, more especially, her unclouded faith in Reagan put her at odds with her own electorate. She was embarrassed when Reagan repaid her faith in October 1983 by launching an invasion of the troubled Commonwealth Caribbean island of Grenada without properly forewarning her, in an operation the United Nations General Assembly condemned as a 'fragrant violation of international law and of the independence, sovereignty and territorial integrity of that state'.[12] Privately, Thatcher was furious with Reagan.[13] Nevertheless, she still insisted that Britain did not need a finger on the cruise trigger. Unimpressed, an opinion poll in November 1983 suggested 94 per cent of Britons wanted a dual key.[14]

It was in that month that the cruise missiles arrived at Greenham Common airbase, two miles from Newbury, where for the past two years a women's 'peace camp' had sprawled along the perimeter fence. The idea had all but come accidentally. Led by Ann Pettitt and Helen John, a group of thirty-six women (and four men) from South Wales calling themselves 'Women for Life on Earth' had organized a Cardiff to Greenham Common march in August 1981 and on reaching the base ten days later, on 5 September, had chained themselves to the perimeter fence. Having made their suffragette-style point, the original intention had been to go home again. But, infuriated by the derisive attitude of the airbase's commander, some of them opted to stay. As weeks passed into months and publicity for their vigil developed, they attracted followers and assistance from a broadening pool of well-wishers. Indeed, the breadth of support risked undermining their parallel commitment to feminism. To defend this, they announced that they preferred to communicate only with female journalists and officials and, when it came to legal action, engaged only female lawyers. In February 1982, they expelled the small number of men who had joined them. Partly, this was the ultimate expression of the feminist ethos uniting the women, but it was also out of a desire to ensure the protest stayed peaceful – to limit the targets for police brutality, as well as in anticipation of the innate aggressiveness of the Y-chromosome. Tellingly, the peace camp's two rules were 'non-violence' and 'no men overnight'.[15]

The dilemma for hostile newspaper reporting was whether to portray the peace women as lesbians or as truant wives and mothers. In reality, the two positions were not necessarily contradictory – as was shown by Helen John, who left a husband and five children in South Wales in order to remain at Greenham, where she began an affair with another woman. While the same-sex arrangements put many women off, the reality was later expressed by another mainstay of the camp, Rebecca Johnson, who pointed out that 'Greenham wouldn't have existed much beyond the first couple of years if it hadn't been for the lesbians', because it was they who, being less likely to have dependents to care for, were most able to commit to years of on-site protest.[16] They were also more likely to be at ease in a women-only commune.

As a foil to the increasingly bold make-up and power-dressing that was defining mainstream women's fashion at the time, the hippy demeanour of the Greenham women provided the decade's most startling aesthetic contrast. To its admirers, their peace camp was a symbol of female empowerment and an energizing example of civil activism over supine political apathy – an apathy that appeared to sedate millions even when the future of the planet was at stake. But while the camp attracted women from grandmothers to housewives to students, the face it offered to the outside world was too narrowly drawn, in its woolly-hatted, make-up-free apotheosis, to appeal to the sex as a whole, let alone to blokes. Heseltine's subsequent assessment was: 'The Greenham women were their own worst enemies, in that no matter how much people sympathized with parts of their message, they found no inclination to identify with the messengers.'[17] Equally, the sacrifice of creature comforts attracted both admiration and repulsion. Abuse from drunken local youths was accompanied by animosity from local residents who resented having their common turned into a squalid shanty town. Besides tents, the women lived in makeshift 'benders' of transparent plastic sheeting propped up by poles and branches. Some local pubs and shops began refusing to serve the women, who, often having gone for weeks without washing facilities and proper sanitation, were accused of nauseating regular customers. Newbury was treated to protest marches festooned with banners declaiming '"Peace Women" You Disgust Us' and 'Clean Up and Get Out'. From May 1982, Newbury District Council began trying to evict the women from the land it owned, but found itself unable to prevent them from moving to other stretches around the base. Indeed, the eviction attempts proved propaganda coups for the women, who were seen peacefully resisting the bulldozers employed to raze their encampments. They also realized that taking repeated legal actions against their tormentors bought valuable time while their lawyers argued that they were legitimately disporting themselves on common ground.

Given the conditions and the provocations, the women's staying power was remarkable. Spirits were kept up by huddling around the camp fire to sing such numbers as 'I Am a Witness to Your War Crimes', 'Take the Toys from the Boys' and, a particular favourite, 'You Can't Kill the Spirit / She is Like a Mountain, Old and Strong'. The various camps constructed around the airbase's exit gates quickly developed their own traditions. One was strictly vegan and some were militantly lesbian, while others welcomed the women's children or catered for religious groups like the Quakers. The protesters ranged from those who stayed for a day to those who stayed for nineteen years. This, too, was both a strength and a weakness. Resisting hierarchical power structures, the women tried to make their decisions in as egalitarian a way as possible, which inevitably led to resentment when those who had been there for years were contradicted by those who were just staying for the weekend. Arguments raged over whether anyone should be allowed to smoke a joint in the comfort of their own bender, with Helen John arguing that it was just the sort of illegal activity that threatened the credibility of the protest.[18] Breaking the law was not done lightly and months passed before the women cut through the fence and trespassed where the missile silos were being built, on New Year's Day 1983. Without apparent irony, the women were charged with 'breaching the peace'. When, in August 1982, a group of them attempted to occupy a sentry-box and were bound over to keep the peace for a year by Newbury magistrates, they refused to agree to do so and found themselves spending a fortnight in Holloway prison.

The frequent bolt-cutter attacks on the fence and the attempted break-ins that followed proved to be no more than an irritant to those charged with keeping the base secure, though they were potentially dangerous antics: the missile silos had armed guards and the prospect of a moving target – potentially unidentifiable in the dark as a woman, a saboteur or a spy – risked unintentionally creating an Emily Davison-style martyr for the cause. Perhaps this was one reason why the guards had the sense not to shoot. Far more successful from the perspective of gaining publicity were the mass protests. The most spectacular of these came on Sunday, 12 December 1982, when between thirty and fifty thousand women held hands to enclose the entire nine-mile perimeter in an 'Embrace the Base' demonstration. Many carried candles and torches and festooned the wire fencing with flowers and teddy bears. The press coverage of this intensely symbolic act varied according to the stance of the newspaper. The *Daily Express*'s line was 'Russian TV cameras roll as 30,000 women ring missile base in anti-nuclear protest'.[19]

Publicity of whatever kind was one thing, either changing the mind of the government or, failing that, simply changing the government was quite another. The reality was that the women's appeal was entirely lost on the Cabinet and the alternative, the Labour Party, remained in the electoral doldrums, many of its more 'moderate' supporters actually regarding its commitment to unilateral nuclear disarmament as a cause of its distress. When, in May 1983, the polling company NOP asked respondents whether 'Britain should give up its nuclear arms even if other countries do not give them up', only 16 per cent answered in the affirmative. Among Conservative and Alliance voters, opposition to unilateralism was overwhelming. Even almost 60 per cent of Labour voters opposed it.[20]

Meanwhile, the optimistic hope among the women campaigners that they could physically prevent the cruise missiles from arriving exemplified the amateurishness of their approach. The planned date and arrangements for the missiles' arrival were leaked to the *Guardian* by Sarah Tisdall, a clerical worker at the Foreign Office. The *Guardian* printed its scoop and Tisdall was subsequently identified and ended up serving four months in jail for breaching the Official Secrets Act. Yet even such disclosures failed to halt the weapons' delivery. The government merely changed the date. On 14 November 1983, having spent months planning for the moment when they would prevent the deadly arsenal's arrival, the peace women were obliviously sitting round a carrot and broccoli stew when they heard on the radio that the missiles were in place behind them.

Rather than pack up and go home, the women switched tactics. They may not have prevented the weapons from coming but they were determined to disrupt their deployment on manoeuvres (like the SS-20s, cruise missiles could be mounted on lorries and, if need be, fired from untargeted locations). By making life difficult in this way, the protesters hoped to persuade potentially less resolute European governments to renege on their own commitment to accept the missiles for fear of encouraging similar unrest. Military convoys taking the missile launchers on practice manoeuvres out on Salisbury Plain had to run the gauntlet of women trying to block the gates. When the convoys invariably got out of the base – the women often omitted to block side exits – they found their every movement being monitored by 'Cruisewatch' volunteers who lay in wait, morning, noon and night, trying to follow them, disrupt their passage and announce that they had discovered where the 'secret' launch sites were located. The Cruisewatchers kept in contact by Citizens' Band radio, alerting each other to a convoy with the signal 'Calling all herbs, calling all herbs!'[21] Their success was not in preventing the practice deployments but in causing irritation to their organizers, keeping the authorities alert to the danger of road accidents, and encouraging the fear that if the Cruisewatch monitors kept lists of the missile launchers' destinations, the information could be leaked – potentially even to the Soviets.

No such obstruction was attempted – not least because it would not have been tolerated – in the Soviet Union. Nevertheless, in May 1983, a deputation of the Greenham women arrived in Moscow. They hoped to impress upon the Soviet authorities how passionately they desired to end the arms race. The result, however, was a propaganda coup neither for the women nor for the Kremlin. By turning up with Olga Medvedkova, a Russian dissident well known to the KGB, the women demonstrated in equal measure their courage and their naivety about the regime's attitude to dissent. Far from being treated as serious players in search of a solution to the arms race, they received instead a distinctly cool reception from the wary, state-appointed, vice chairman of the Soviet Peace Committee.[22] Long subjected to the trite jibe that they should go and take their protest to Russia, the women had finally done so – and come back perplexed.

However, while they had no political success to show for their pains, their role in helping to shape the cultural agenda of the times was far more apparent. This victory was particularly in evidence in youth and popular culture, and was not confined to Britain. Nicole, a German teenage singer, dominated the 1982 Eurovision Song Contest with 'A Little Peace', a sweet and/ or trite plea for world harmony which reached number one in the British charts (in succession to 'Ebony and Ivory', Paul McCartney and Stevie Wonder's appeal for racial harmony). If not explicitly about nuclear arms, it was hardly a request for deadlier weapons. Another German female pop singer, Nena, had even greater success in February 1984 when her '99 Red Balloons' (an English-language version of her German hit '*99 Luftballons*') raced to number one in Britain and stayed there for three weeks. The

English-language version was far more explicitly an attack on militarism than the German original, with references to 'Captain Kirk' and 'the president's on the line' implying that the Americans' gung-ho attitude was the main worry (the single's release coincided with the deployment of Pershing II in West Germany). Nevertheless, both versions had the same theme, that in the jumpy, fear-driven world of the arms race even innocent children's balloons could inadvertently trigger a nuclear war[23] – a point with which the Soviet Lieutenant Colonel Stanislav Petrov could doubtless have empathized.

Among British bands, Frankie Goes to Hollywood was by far the most prominent of those spinning anti-arms race messages from the turntables. Released in the summer of 1984 (though written a couple of years earlier) the lyrics of 'Two Tribes' were given visual amplification by an accompanying pop video in which actors playing Reagan and the new Soviet leader, Konstantin Chernenko, slugged it out in a boxing ring, egged on by a crowd which included other world leaders. It topped the charts for nine weeks. It was mixed with an introduction featuring an early warning siren and the core message was repeated on the B-side of the single, the band's cover version of the pacifist anthem 'War, What is it Good For?' Even a mainstream supergroup like Queen was to be found belting out in 'Hammer to Fall' an anthem that appeared to suggest that surrendering would be a rather less painful means of heading off the looming menace of a nuclear mushroom cloud. This was the most significant period for protest songs since the 1960s (the success of Band Aid's 1984 Ethiopian famine appeal song, 'Do They Know It's Christmas?' encouraging the belief that music actually could save lives). Nothing compared with it in the quarter-century that followed.

As if the decibels of pop protest were not enough, the nuclear rearmers also had to contend with what they took to be the more formal indoctrination of youth: by 1983, a third of schools in Labour-controlled education authorities had 'peace studies' on the curriculum. This was part of a process by which Labour, though unable to win power at the national level, used the tools at its disposal to win hearts and minds at a local level where it continued to control town halls in inner-city areas. Launched in Manchester in 1980, Labour councils rushed to declare their areas 'nuclear-free zones'. By this, they meant that the council pledged to permit no nuclear activity – whether the passing through of weapons or waste, or even the undertaking of civil defence exercises – on their patch. Whether residents felt they could sleep safer in their beds because an SS-20 would career instead into a neighbouring Tory-held local authority was doubtful, even if the idea caused hilarity among those who thought nuclear-free zones tokenistic and ridiculous. In reality, these initiatives represented practical expressions of dissent since Labour councillors were capable of mustering around the subject – and thereby provided further reasons, as far as the Conservative government was concerned, for clipping the wings of local government.

Whatever their views on the sense or otherwise of unilateral nuclear disarmament, the public's concern about atomic war could not be easily assuaged. The government had unintentionally helped fuel concern in 1980 by sending to every household a copy of an official leaflet, *Protect and Survive*, which, while striving to offer useful advice on how to barricade your home in order to sit out a nuclear winter, succeeded only in instilling readers with a sense of the makeshift hopelessness of living off stored tins of processed food while the world outside had been blitzed and contaminated beyond repair. In 1984, the BBC broadcast *Threads,* a harrowing drama about life in Sheffield before, during and after a nuclear attack, showing how society would disintegrate. The scene of milk bottles melting in the heat of the explosion proved particularly stark and memorable. Emboldened, the corporation also finally screened *The War Game*, which portrayed, as if in a series of television news reports, the descent into nuclear war and its effects on Rochester (supposedly hit by a stray Soviet missile). *The War Game* was broadcast twenty years after it had been originally made as a Wednesday Play and then left in the can for fear of causing upset – to viewers and to the Wilson government. To the fear of nuclear war was added the suggestion that corporate and state vested interests were actively driving Britain towards the precipice. In 1985, the BBC screened the thriller series *Edge of Darkness*. Scripted by *The Italian Job* and *Z-Cars* writer Troy Kennedy Martin, the plot concerned a central character, played by Bob Peck, who uncovers a giant conspiracy by the nuclear power industry, backed by the security services. Equally sinister machinations were implied in the denouement of *A Very British Coup*, a play by the Labour politician Chris Mullin, when in 1988 it was made into a series by Channel 4. In the drama, 'Harry Perkins', the leader of the Labour Party, wins a general election on a promise to remove nuclear arms from Britain. The final seconds of the last episode conclude with a BBC news voice-over on the morning after the election, calmly announcing a takeover by the military.

Fictional conspiracy theories coalesced with real-life suspicions following the murder in 1984 of Hilda Murrell. The 78-year-old peace campaigner had been due to present a paper, 'An Ordinary Citizen's View of Radioactive Waste Management', to the inquiry into the Sizewell nuclear plant when her Shropshire house was burgled by an assailant who stole some money, sexually abused her and bundled her into her car, before leaving her for dead in a ditch with multiple stab wounds. A campaign began to prove that this horrific crime was the work of the security services. Motives ranged from an attempt to silence a peace campaigner to the belief – propagated by the tirelessly suspicious Labour MP Tam Dalyell – that she knew something about the sinking of the *General Belgrano* (her nephew was an intelligence officer who was wrongly assumed to have given the order for the Argentine cruiser's sinking). The raping and bludgeoning to death of an elderly woman would certainly have marked a new low for MI5, and it was indicative of what some anti-nuclear protesters believed was the nature of the state they were up against that many suspected it was the sorry truth. Aside from extensive newspaper coverage, the conspiracy spawned three television documentaries, two books, two debates in Parliament and several stage plays. To considerably less interest or publicity, in 2005 DNA evidence led to the conviction of Andrew George for the crime. Far from being an agent of the 'secret state', he was, at the time he murdered Murrell, a sixteen-year-old builder's labourer.

Protect and Survive

In Ronald Reagan, CND had found a perfect, if unwitting, recruiting agent. The perception that the Republican president's aggressive rhetoric was raising, rather than lowering, East–West tensions was instilled in those who derided or chose to ignore the flip side of his policy – the 'zero option', which, had the Soviets accepted it, would have removed all intermediate-range nuclear missiles from Europe. Reagan, it was certainly true, lent himself readily to crude caricature. His attention to detail was famously absent, his folksy charm, which he had in abundance, merely confirming those not under its spell in their belief that he was a simpleton, incapable of grasping the nuances that prevented an extremely dangerous situation from ending in catastrophe. His utterances did little to undermine Europe's sense of intellectual superiority to a New World run by a former Hollywood actor. The puppet-based satirical television show *Spitting Image*, which began broadcasting in 1984, regularly featured a sketch entitled 'The President's Brain Is Missing'. From such satire, the colourless, unsmiling, out-of-touch, fatally ill men who wielded power in the Kremlin got off lightly. They were distant, inscrutable entities whose ruthlessness was not doubted but who were at least given the benefit of the doubt in matters of intelligence.

With no sign that communism would lose its hold (indeed, in whole areas of the world, like Africa and Central America, it was still spreading), a broad consensus of informed Western opinion held that the task of statesmanship was not to risk taking Moscow's leaders to the limit of their endurance, but rather to find ways of lowering tension by recognizing the division of the world into 'free' and communist as an immutable fact of life. Such assumptions, culminating in the arms limitation talks of the 1970s, had motivated earlier efforts at détente. What appeared frightening about Reagan was that he showed scant regard for the pieties of détente, which, shortly before running for the presidency, he had dismissed as 'what a farmer has with his turkey – until Thanksgiving Day'.[24] To his thinking, détente merely kept the Cold War alive by freezing it at a particular moment – and, what was more, a moment that he calculated gave the optimum strategic advantage to the Soviet Union. If there was to be genuine progress, then it would come only through breaking the deadlock – by creating a totally new strategic paradigm. Aghast at the risks implied, the president's critics took this to mean nuclear brinkmanship.

Thatcher's public embrace of most things American and of Reagan in particular naturally created the impression that British and US attitudes to nuclear escalation were identical. As the National Union of Mineworkers' leader, Arthur Scargill, put it on a goodwill trip to Moscow in 1983, the greatest threat to world peace came from that 'most dangerous duo, President Ray-Gun and the plutonium blonde, Margaret Thatcher'.[25] The reality was rather different. For while Thatcher saw the continued possession of nuclear weapons as a necessity for as long as the Soviet Union posed a threat, Reagan was less sanguine about the peace-keeping propensities of mutually assured destruction. Thatcher wanted cruise missiles on British soil because she believed having them there would make the Warsaw Pact wary about using its superiority in conventional forces to attack Western Europe. Reagan, in contrast, genuinely saw the missiles' deployment as a bargaining chip designed to counter the SS-20 menace – and one that could be removed on both sides if his 'zero option' was accepted by Moscow. Disagreement on this fundamental point was laid bare during a meeting at Camp David in December 1984 when Thatcher, listening to Reagan's optimistic assessment of the prospects for a nuclear-free world, cut in with what she regarded as a necessary home truth, that it would be 'unwise' to 'abandon a deterrence system that has prevented both nuclear and conventional war. Moreover, if we ever reach the stage of abolishing all nuclear weapons, this would make conventional, biological or chemical war more likely.'[26] At a White House seminar on arms control which Thatcher had attended with Reagan and the high command of the US State and Defense departments in July 1984, she had demanded to know whether, if the nuclear arsenal was bargained away or made redundant, the NATO powers would be prepared to fund the massively increased cost of making their conventional forces in Europe equal to those of the Warsaw Pact. Reagan had replied, somewhat vaguely, that such would be the assumption.[27] Thatcher, however, was clearly unconvinced. She had maintained James Callaghan's commitment to increase British defence spending by 3 per cent per year each year until 1986. This was painful enough, even if it only actually increased the defence budget's share of GDP from 4.7 per cent to 4.9 per cent between 1980 and 1986. She certainly did not want to have to unbalance her budget in order vastly to expand the British armed forces when equivalent deterrence could be had from cruise, courtesy of the American taxpayer. What especially alerted Thatcher to Reagan's unsoundness in nuclear matters was his announcement, on 23 March 1983, of the Strategic Defense Initiative (SDI). The prime minister could be forgiven her testiness. With SDI, Reagan was proposing a fundamental change in the West's strategy without first consulting either her or any other NATO partner. In doing so, he was also choosing to ignore the widespread scepticism about the feasibility of his new pet project that was felt throughout much of the Pentagon. Undaunted, Reagan pushed on. SDI – quickly dubbed 'Star Wars' in mocking deference to the president's supposed sci-fi fantasy/Hollywood world view – envisaged launching into space a network of lasers or particle-beam weapons which would zap incoming nuclear missiles, thereby creating a defensive shield. If it worked – an almighty 'if' – it would make redundant all the existing stock of nuclear ballistic missiles. Reagan's tone on the matter resonated idealism. He even spoke of sharing the technology, once it was perfected, with the Soviet Union. Of course, the actual likelihood of the United States freely giving away its invention in this way was largely discounted, not least in Moscow. Thatcher, however, responded to the suggestion not with suspicion but with horror, for she thought it insane for the US 'to throw away a hard-won lead in technology by making it internationally available'.[28] If SDI succeeded, then the fear of mutually assured destruction would cease to maintain the balance of power – or, rather, the balance of fear – between the two superpowers. That was a prospect to which Thatcher and Reagan responded quite differently.

Always reluctant to make public a breach in the 'special relationship', even when she felt taken for granted, Thatcher preferred to voice her disquiet to the president personally and privately. She was thus irritated when her new Foreign Secretary, Sir Geoffrey Howe, publicly blurted out British concerns that reliance on SDI risked imbuing Washington with a 'Maginot mentality' – in effect, a potentially false sense of security which would encourage American disengagement from the active defence of Western Europe. During her visit to Reagan at Camp David in December 1984, she tried to dissuade him from placing blind faith in such a protective shield. 'In the past,' she pointed out, 'scientific genius had always developed a counter-system. Even if an SDI system proved 95 per cent successful – a significant success rate – over 60 million people will still die from those weapons that got through.' She bullied him into announcing publicly that he would pursue a system that aimed at 'military balance, not superiority' with the Soviet arsenal.[29] With this assurance, Thatcher felt able to sublimate her fears and support its development. Given how much Reagan was committed to it, it was clearly going to happen, regardless of what Downing Street thought.

That being so, there was also the small matter of securing for Britain a share of the massive US investment in SDI research and development. In return for Thatcher's advocacy, the first collaborative contracts were signed in 1985, resulting in an injection of about $150 million into British companies and institutions over the following fifteen years.[30]

Even while it struggled to get past its theoretical stage, the prospect of SDI shook up the assumptions of both sides in the nuclear debate, forcing them to re-examine the entrenched dogmas that they had been respectively parroting for years. Those, like Thatcher, who had argued that mutually assured destruction had successfully kept the peace found themselves – at least publicly – backing a technological advance that threatened to undermine the assumptions upon which MAD rested. Much as she might remind both houses of the US Congress, when given the honour of addressing them in April 1985, that the West's 'task was not merely to prevent nuclear war, but to prevent conventional war as well',[31] she really feared that Reagan would unintentionally make the latter more likely, whether through negotiation or through over-reliance on the power of his space-age lasers. The anti-nuclear campaigners were no less challenged by the US president's potentially game-changing initiative. Having long argued that MAD offered no guarantee of peace, they now feared that by eliminating it, SDI would create an even greater danger – offering America protection from the consequences of nuclear war and making its president more gung-ho about threatening his enemies. In fact, it was unclear whether SDI really would put an end to MAD. Potentially, the extension of the arms race into space might spark even more cripplingly expensive research and development on a new era of nuclear missiles that could evade being zapped from outer orbit, a point that Thatcher had grasped in her argument with Reagan at Camp David as fully as had the spokespersons of CND.

This was a point also grasped in the Kremlin. During the early 1980s, the USSR's economy stagnated. Manufacturing little that the Western world wanted to buy, its balance of payments was sustained by its oil and gas sector, which by 1984 was accounting for more than half of all exports – a dependence that had dire consequences when the international price of oil collapsed in 1985. Meanwhile, socialist central planning had failed to stimulate and drive innovation in new sectors of the economy. Particularly alarming was the widening technology gap between East and West. In developing the 'information age', Western, and especially United States, companies were progressing by leaps and bounds. By contrast, a communist-controlled economy in which the free exchange of ideas and information was anathema was not structured in a way that made the same sort of advances in information technology possible. Nor was the United States going to supply the information – an embargo on exporting high technology to the Soviet

Union and its allies accentuated the gap between the 'free' and communist blocs. The best that could be hoped was that Soviet agents could steal the West's technology, but even this prospect necessarily involved the USSR always being several steps behind US developments. That Washington was now planning a vast new technological leap that risked making the entire Soviet nuclear arsenal redundant was understandably greeted as disastrous news in Moscow. The USA had the economic vibrancy to shoulder the burden of starting a whole new level of the arms race from space, but the USSR did not. Just trying to keep pace with America ensured that the defence budget was consuming, by some estimates, towards one quarter of Soviet GDP, which was an unsustainable level in an economy that had already gone into reverse and was only one sixth the size of that of the United States.[32] Upon entering the White House, Reagan had initiated a five-year target to raise defence spending to $1.6 trillion, the greatest peace-time expansion in US history. While his spending surge took defence spending as a proportion of US GDP from 4.9 per cent in 1980 to 6.1 per cent in 1985, this was still a far more affordable burden than that which was crippling the USSR. Against this background, it seemed that to keep pace with Reagan's latest Star Wars escalation the Soviets had but two stark choices – end the arms race by throwing in the towel, or free up the Soviet economy and society so that it could compete in technological advances at this higher level. Both options threatened the future of communism.

In the short term, the Kremlin's response appeared to confirm the fears of those who believed SDI was a disastrous provocation, since all hopes of a new round of arms limitation talks fell through. Neither intellectuals, commentators, generals nor politicians in Britain (or the USA) properly understood the extent to which the massive increases in defence spending heralded by SDI would put more pressure on the USSR than it could endure. Yet the speed with which Reagan's announcement heralded change at the top in Moscow and brought about efforts to 'reform' communism – which ultimately proved fatal to its survival – was remarkable. As early as 1992, Soviet diplomats of the experience of Vladimir Lukin were admitting: 'It is clear that SDI accelerated our catastrophe by at least five years.'[33] In 1993, a decade after the president announced his intent, Thatcher admitted in her memoirs that, having originally 'differed sharply' with Reagan over SDI, not least because she thought a nuclear weapon-free world was 'neither attainable nor even desirable', she had been wrong. 'Looking back,' she had come to realize, 'Reagan's original decision on SDI was the single most important of his presidency.'[34] She wrote that appreciation in the same year in which Bill Clinton's administration effectively wound up the programme, without it ever having worked. Never had the threat, rather than the reality, of US know-how achieved so much. With hindsight, too, it is perhaps surprising that so admiring a fan of capitalism as Margaret Thatcher should have underestimated the capacity of the United States to shoulder the cost of ratcheting up the arms race and overestimated communism's ability to keep pace. As she said during a UN press conference in October 1985: 'I do not think the communist bloc will change in my lifetime.'[35] Then again, she had once made similarly gloomy prophecies about the prospects of a woman in Downing Street.

Cold Thaw

During the mid-1980s, Britain assumed a political significance in the diplomacy of the Cold War that went beyond its traditional role as the second most senior power in NATO. The primary reason was not the continued possession of the British nuclear arsenal, which was scarcely considered in the bilateral poker game played out in 1986 and 1987 between the United States and the Soviet Union. France's *Force de Frappe* was equally incidental to the main event. Both countries were bit-players in the stakes of global obliteration. But unlike François Mitterrand, Thatcher found herself in an especially influential position when the only Soviet politician with whom she had succeeded in cultivating a good relationship took over the reins in Moscow. It was not that Thatcher became an indispensible intermediary between Ronald Reagan and Mikhail Gorbachev, a role for which neither superpower leader had need, but rather that she was now more than America's staunchest ally, she was also the European leader the Kremlin took most seriously. Neither Edward Heath nor John Major enjoyed anything like the same authority at the White House or the Kremlin, let alone at both addresses. Unlike the 'Iron Lady', neither man proved capable of developing the necessary personal rapport, or of slipping naturally into a show-stealing, actress-like display when in the presence of more powerful men.

Understandably, Thatcher made much of the fact that she had identified the potential of Gorbachev before others had done so. It was undoubtedly helpful for Reagan to be able to make approaches to the Kremlin after 1985 without fear of alienating Republican hardliners by being able to point out that no less a cold warrior than Maggie Thatcher had led the way. In fact, she had even tried her hand with Gorbachev's predecessor, Konstantin Chernenko, at a time when Washington was still struggling to build meaningful communication with the Kremlin, and the disappointing results had underlined how much personal chemistry it would take for something worthwhile to develop.

Admittedly, with Yuri Andropov there was little that could have been done. His past – he had been head of the KGB for a remarkably long time, from 1967 to 1982 – was even more intimidating than his demeanour: a cold face, framed by square, hard-rimmed spectacles. Bedridden with kidney failure for twelve of his fifteen months in power, he finally slipped into eternity in February 1984. Taking his funeral to be an opportunity, Thatcher decided to attend and while in Moscow was introduced to his successor. Aged seventy-two, the white-haired Chernenko was actually the same age as the dyed-haired Reagan, though physically he seemed to belong to a far more distant decade. Not trusted to talk extempore, he attempted to mumble a monologue by reading from a succession of prompt cards containing a compendium of hackneyed clichés about the importance of dialogue. When Thatcher attempted to join it, Chernenko looked confused and turned helplessly to his foreign minister, Andrei Gromyko. With this despairing effort eliciting nothing of importance, the new leader tried to say something friendly off the cuff. Alarm stealing across his countenance, Gromyko, who was clearly fearful of what indiscretion might come next, immediately indicated the audience was at an end.[36] Succinctly, Thatcher later summed up: 'I was unimpressed.'[37]

But where she was unable to make an impression with the ailing Chernenko, she succeeded with Mikhail Gorbachev, the coming man in the Politburo, when he accepted an invitation to visit Thatcher at Chequers in December 1984. The two quickly dispensed with pleasantries and got down to a series of frank and wide-ranging arguments, to each other's immense satisfaction (and to the strain of their respective interpreters). Sensitive to his delicate position in the Soviet succession, Gorbachev offered no hostages to fortune, but Thatcher immediately warmed to his easy, approachable style and ability to think on his feet and debate issues rather than retreat into parroting predetermined official statements.[38] He certainly seemed more modern-minded, a trait evinced by the fact he brought his wife, Raisa, with him (by contrast, the first confirmation that there was a Mrs Chernenko was when she turned up at her husband's funeral). The favourable verdict on Gorbachev was not one given purely with hindsight. As soon as he had left Chequers (nearly an hour and a half behind schedule), Thatcher presciently announced to the world that Mr Gorbachev was a man she 'could do business with'. According to Reagan's National Security Advisor, she then wrote to Reagan to tell him that 'the overriding impression left was that the Russians are genuinely fearful of the immense cost of having to keep up with a further American technological advance' and that, consequently, they were preparing the ground for negotiating significant arms reductions.[39] Her endorsement of the Kremlin's coming man was quickly picked up on when, upon Chernenko's death on 10 March 1985, the communist that the Western world would embrace as 'Gorby' assumed power.

If he thought he was in for an immediate improvement in Anglo-Soviet relations, then he was quickly disabused. Fearing his treason was about to be uncovered, the KGB agent Oleg Gordievsky had defected to Britain, bringing his secrets with him. Armed with his information, Britain identified and expelled thirty-one Soviet spies. In retaliation, thirty-one Britons were duly expelled from the USSR. But this proved to be no more than a blip, for it quickly became evident that both sides were actively seeking to mend fences. During 1986, Anglo-Soviet deals were done on trade and finance, ending outstanding claims relating back to the period of the Bolshevik revolution and thereby making possible serious Russian investment in the City of London. In March 1987, Thatcher visited Moscow for four days of lengthy talks with Gorbachev, during which she characteristically gave as good as she got, again trading punches with her favourite communist sparring partner. Gorbachev's memoirs are not liberally laced with gushy effusions and his comments about Thatcher maintain a characteristically respectful tone. 'Easy,' he conceded, she might not have been. 'Still one must admit that in a number of cases she was able to substantiate her charges with facts, which eventually led us to review and criticize some of our own approaches.'[40] As the Western leader with the greatest influence over Reagan, she was clearly deemed the one who mattered most. To her, this was a justification of her transatlantic attitude.

The clearest barometer that the Soviet Union was undergoing a new openness – *glasnost* – was when Thatcher was not merely accorded a fifty-minute interview on state television but that it was broadcast unedited despite the fact it contained her characteristically unflinching criticisms of communism. Rather than accept the offer of making a long speech to camera, she asked to be subjected to the questions of a three-man interviewing panel. It quickly became clear that a lifetime of soliciting officially worded statements had not prepared the three interviewers for the easy freedom with which this woman tossed up and fired back ideas like tennis balls, seamlessly covering economics, contrasting philosophies, nuclear escalation (which she blamed on the Soviet deployment of the SS-20s) and the practical realities of her own public and private life. Touring the drab streets, she decked herself up in a fur hat and expensively tailored coat and was duly surrounded by ordinary Russians mobbing her with undisguised adulation. This was new (she certainly wasn't welcomed this enthusiastically back home) and not something any of the greying and fattening men who led the other European countries could have pulled off. She met dissidents like Andrei Sakharov and lit a candle for freedom of conscience in a Russian Orthodox church – previously unthinkable parts of an official tour. History was being made, with the member for Finchley, dressed like a tsarina, attempting to steal the show. Even her most entrenched critics in the British press pack trailing her admitted that she alone of her European contemporaries had star quality.[41]

Yet hers could only be a supporting role. The speed with which Reagan and Gorbachev began to discuss nuclear disarmament was bewildering to hawks and doves alike. The two men had their first face-to-face negotiations in Geneva in November 1985. The personal chemistry worked, even though the talks broke up without a deal. Reagan's commitment to persevering with SDI prevented an agreement. Yet SDI remained the West's trump card. Even though the Star Wars shield did not yet exist – and some wondered whether it would ever be technically possible – the prospect of it was sufficient to scare the Soviets into increasingly desperate offers to conclude a far more comprehensive deal than had ever been on the table during the détente of the 1970s. What, back then, had been dubbed SALT (strategic arms *limitation* talks) now enjoyed the acronym START (strategic arms *reduction* talks). The difference was one of substance, not just semantics. Certainly, it was Reagan's good fortune to have a counterpart in Gorbachev. But it was Gorbachev's good fortune to be negotiating with what the leading historian of the Cold War, John Lewis Gaddis, has described as 'the only nuclear abolitionist ever to have been president of the United States'.[42] Unlike Thatcher, Reagan was genuinely motivated by a desire to ban the bomb. Because he did not share their tactics, CND supporters failed utterly to comprehend that he shared their goal. They had taken his threats to the Soviet Union at face value, but never his olive branches. Yet, as Kenneth Adelman, then director of the US Arms Control and Disarmament Agency, later conceded, the more National Security Council meetings he attended with the president, 'the more I was surprised that for an anti-Communist hawk, how anti-nuclear he was. He would make comments that seemed to me to come from the far left rather than from the far right . . . many times [Reagan] would pop out with "Let's abolish all nuclear weapons", to the clear consternation of his advisors.'[43]

By the time Reagan and Gorbachev met in Reykjavik in October 1986, their minds had been further focused by a terrible disaster. On 26 April 1986, the Chernobyl nuclear power plant in the Ukraine exploded. In the efforts to contain the catastrophe, heroes were made. But the causes of the disaster went to the heart of what was wrong with a secretive command economy, as Gorbachev was quick to recognize, and reinforced more widespread fears that nuclear power represented a threat rather than security. When the two leaders met in Iceland's capital, Gorbachev was ready, as his predecessors had not been, to see if Reagan's 'zero option' offer was genuine. He discovered that it was – the president really did want to eliminate all intermediate-range nuclear missiles from Europe. In addition, Gorbachev suggested cutting all Soviet and US strategic missiles by half. Reagan trumped him by suggesting the abolition of the two superpowers' entire arsenal of intercontinental ballistic missiles by 1996, at which time:

He and Gorbachev would come to Iceland, and each of them would bring the last nuclear missile from each country with them. Then they would give a tremendous party for the whole world . . . The president . . . would be very old by then and Gorbachev would not recognize him. The president would say, 'Hello Mikhail.' And Gorbachev would say, 'Ron, is it you?' And then they would destroy the last missile.[44]

After forty years of holding the world in thrall to a nuclear Armageddon and funding countless proxy wars against one another all over the globe (American funds were at that very moment being channelled to the mujahideen to repel the Soviet occupation of Afghanistan), was this to be the uplifting end to the story? Gorbachev's courage to face hard realities and Reagan's Hollywood ability – so long derided by the peace movement – to dream beyond reality seemed a transformative combination.

Thatcher was aghast. In 1986, Reagan had advocated a ban on all new ballistic missiles, a proposal that would have axed her Trident-purchasing programme, upon which the future of the whole post-Polaris 'independent' British nuclear deterrent rested. Thatcher wrote to Reagan to protest. But his efforts to mollify her were now shown to be a fleeting nicety, for he put the idea back on the table at Reykjavik. When Thatcher learned what the 'leader of the Free World' was ready to sacrifice, it was, as she later put it, 'as if there had been an earthquake beneath my feet'.[45] She was amenable to halving the number of strategic nuclear weapons in five years, but horrified at the prospect of abolishing them all within a decade and signing away the next generation of Britain's nuclear deterrent, without British agreement. (Although the British deterrent was outside the remit of the Reykjavik discussions, it would not survive if the Americans stopped manufacturing it – unless Britain wanted the vast expense of developing its own system, or buying one from the French.) Britain retained its ability to buy Trident thanks to the SDI, which Thatcher had originally disparaged. For the initiative that had done so much to bring matters to a head was still standing in the way of a US–Soviet agreement. Ignoring – or disbelieving – Reagan's offer to share the technology, Gorbachev made the deal conditional on SDI's non-deployment. The president promised not to deploy it for ten years but refused, as he put it, 'to sign an agreement that would deny to me and future presidents the right to test and deploy defences against nuclear weapons' – from whichever emerging nuclear power they might emanate.[46] Upon this sticking point, the deal collapsed.

In Britain (beyond Whitehall), there was palpable disappointment that a once-in-a-lifetime opportunity to end the arms race had been scuppered because the American president's obsession with his Star Wars fantasy had obscured his grasp of what could be attained on the ground. To Thatcher, the breakdown of the Reykjavik summit was a relief and she flew out to Camp David in November to seek reassurance that the president had not become a peacenik – only to leave with a joint statement that, while appearing to safeguard Trident's future, was nevertheless far closer to Reagan's doctrine of disarmament than to her own of deterrence.[47] Reykjavik, however, was not the end. Gorbachev remained desperate and returned for a third summit – via a stopover in London to take soundings from Thatcher – in Washington in December 1987. There, on 8 December, Reagan and Gorbachev signed the Intermediate-Range Nuclear Forces (INF) Treaty, which put into practice the 'zero option' that Reagan had offered shortly after becoming president in 1981. The US would remove all cruise and Pershing II missiles from Europe if the Soviet Union did likewise with its SS-20s and other comparable missiles. For the first time, an entire class of nuclear weapons – those of intermediate (300- to 3000-mile) range – would be abolished.

In compliance with the treaty's terms, the cruise missiles began leaving Greenham Common on 1 August 1989, and from the second (not fully operational) base at Molesworth the following month. They were bound for Arizona, where they were to be destroyed. Soviet inspectors were formally welcomed to Greenham and allowed to poke around the silos and verify that the missiles truly were being confined to history. Satisfied, they joined their former foes for some traditional conviviality down at The Coach and Horses in nearby Midgham. The women peace protesters did not join them. Andrew Brookes, who was RAF operational commander at Greenham (1989–91), noted that 'when the last missiles came to be flown out, some women tried to lie down on the runway to prevent the airlifter from taking off. Just being there had become their life.'[48]

Truly, it was a bewildering moment for the Greenham women. Their objective had been achieved but, incomprehensibly, by those they continued to distrust and despise. One of the stalwarts of the camp, Ann Pettitt, defended the purpose of the protest as an attempt 'to gatecrash a bunch of nobodies into a private party at which the future of the world was being decided'. Doing so made Greenham women 'one of the globally recognized symbols of the eighties'.[49] Nevertheless, the reality was that they had never been admitted to the party. The summits that ensured cruise's removal and elimination succeeded as a result of the very power politics the women abhorred. They were not even mentioned when Reagan and Gorbachev published their memoirs, and had they managed to gatecrash The Coach and Horses they would doubtless have found that the US and Soviet military men toasting peace and prosperity displayed much more empathy for each other than towards the peace protesters. When the US air force vacated Greenham in September 1992, some of the women packed up and went home – a remote place after so long away from it. Others found excuses for staying on, much to the irritation of local residents who were desperate to reclaim their common. Still singing 'You Can't Kill the Spirit', the women's protest outlived the cause. The last of them finally packed away their benders for good on 5 September 2000, nineteen years after their protest began and eleven years after the cruise missiles left the base.

Thatcher also had to readjust to the collapsing moral certainties of her changed world. As she admitted after leaving Downing Street: 'I had always disliked the original INF "zero option", because I felt that these weapons made up for Western Europe's unpreparedness to face a sudden, massive attack by the Warsaw Pact; I had gone along with it in the hope that the Soviets would never accept.'[50] Her defence of nuclear weapons had been predicated on her belief that they prevented a conventional war. But she – along with received opinion – assumed the Warsaw Pact would remain armed and belligerent, with massed tank divisions awaiting the command to push west through the Fulda Gap and on to the Rhine. What was not comprehended was that the Kremlin had lost the will to fight, lost even the will to uphold the 'Brezhnev doctrine' and defend Marxism–Leninism wherever it was wilting. Had the West but recognized the fact, the doctrine had actually died in 1981 when the Kremlin preferred to let the Polish authorities crush the Solidarity movement rather than do the dirty work itself. That this reluctance to get involved was the reality was publicly admitted only when Gorbachev stood before the UN General Assembly on 7 December 1988 and announced that the Soviet Union would unilaterally cut half a million soldiers from its commitment to the Warsaw Pact. It was an unmistakable signal that Moscow would not prop up floundering communist regimes. The division of Europe would not be sustained through force. Communism really was about to throw in the towel.

9 CULTURE SHOCK

Paying the Piper

In 1981, the National Theatre on London's South Bank rejected Pearl Assurance's £750,000 sponsorship offer because, it announced, 'It seems to us wrong to be into a position where we had to have private sponsorship to do the job we are paid to do by public money.'[1] The notion that major cultural entities would have to start engaging in fundraising on top of – or even instead of – relying on state subsidies was seemingly not to be countenanced. Between the 1940s (when the taxpayer-funded Arts Council of Great Britain was formed) and the 1970s, the state had become so pre-eminently the cultural patron that private sector funding had largely withered away. In 1976, the total amount raised from the latter was a derisory £750,000.[2] Without needing to be legally nationalized, a large sector of British culture had become as dependent on state handouts as British Steel or the National Coal Board.

When the Conservatives returned to power in 1979, the arts community had little inkling of just how fundamentally their expectations of entitlement to state support were about to be challenged. The National Theatre's director, Sir Peter Hall, fed up with his staff going on strike for the fifth time in four years, in disputes that had cost up to £500,000 a time in lost revenue, had even broken the habit of a lifetime by voting Conservative in the general election.[3] Given that Thatcher's first arts minister, the exuberant, opera-loving Norman St John Stevas, had promised that there would be 'no candle-end economics in the arts', Hall and his colleagues could be forgiven for having subsequently felt duped. Compared to the amount of taxpayers' money directed down the coal mines (£300 million of additional subsidy in 1981 alone, on top of £2.5 billion over the preceding seven years), the total government subsidy to the arts in 1981 (£180 million, of which £80 million was distributed through the Arts Council) was but a small drag on government finances, especially since the arts had an estimated turnover of £900 million and employed over two hundred thousand people.[4] But the sector was no less immune to public spending cuts for that. Among the bodies that consequently proved unable to survive the loss of grants was the D'Oyly

Carte Opera Company, which, having performed Gilbert and Sullivan for over one hundred years, folded in 1982 (though it was briefly resurrected at the end of the decade).

Alongside the government's immediate goal of including the arts budget in the drive to cut overall public spending was a more general philosophical attitude that held dependency on state subsidy – in whatever field of activity – to be harmful. Indeed, the apostles of Thatcherism might have better defended themselves from the charges of cultural vandalism if they had pointed out that the Arts Council's first chairman, John Maynard Keynes, had envisaged that his new body should exist to 'prime the pump of private spending' in the arts, not to replace it. Since he saw its work as funding capital outlays for new venues and guaranteeing loans, rather than providing long-term subsidies for running costs and performances, Keynes had even imagined that the Arts Council's role would diminish over time.[5] Despite the allegations that would be levied against them, none of Thatcher's arts ministers were ever Keynesian enough, judged by his own vision. Even after five years of Tory-imposed belt-tightening, the Arts Council was still able to subsidize the average seat at the opera by £19, dance by £7.50 and theatre by £2.80.[6] Despite widespread suspicions in the creative sector, no plan to abolish the Arts Council was seriously considered. Its budget, which had been £63 million when Thatcher came to power, reached £176 million by the time of her fall, which, even allowing for inflation, represented a real-terms increase. In addition, local authorities boosted their arts budgets from £80 million in 1979 to £200 million in 1989, with local theatres being a particular beneficiary.

However, an overall increase in funding over a ten-year time frame concealed significant real-terms cuts in the early eighties. It was in this period that the leaders of the arts developed a virulent hostility towards Thatcher which had still not healed thirty years later. This antagonism was not just a consequence of the failure to fund specific projects; it was manifest in the charge that Thatcherism encouraged materialism and commercialism, forces that were inimical to true – or at least challenging – art. Furthermore, the prime minister was depicted as the living embodiment of this vulgarity – a provincial-minded woman, wedded to reductive housewife economics, who, like Oscar Wilde's description of a cynic, knew the price of everything and the value of nothing. This distaste was most evident in the response to her ministers' call for the arts to look to alternative, private sources of funding and, in particular, to corporate sponsorship. The policy was supported by Sir William Rees-Mogg, whom the government appointed chairman of the Arts Council in 1982 after fourteen years editing *The Times*, and especially by the Arts Council's new secretary general, Luke Rittner. Although selected through a process of open competition, the appointment in 1983 of Rittner, who had been running the Association for Business Sponsorship of the Arts (ABSA) for the past seven years, divided the Arts Council's board and alarmed the wider cultural community, which assumed that – as a 32-year-old with minimal school qualifications, taking over from the 65-year-old Sir Roy Shaw – all he would bring was knowledge of the tastes of businessmen rather than a real appreciation of art for art's sake. Rittner arrived at the Arts Council to find his staff welcoming him with a letter they had signed attesting that they would work for him because he was their boss but not out of any respect for him.[7]

In fact, unlike any of his predecessors, Rittner had actually worked in the arts, having trained as an actor and been both stage manager and administrative director of the Bath Festival. While the recession of the early eighties was an inopportune moment to be going in search of additional funds, by 1983 the sums being successfully solicited reached £13 million, a vast improvement on the position when Rittner's fundraising efforts at ABSA had begun in 1976. In an effort to reassure those who feared that private fundraising would merely be self-defeating if it ensured smaller state subsidies, in 1984 the government agreed to a business sponsorship incentive scheme whereby, for every £1 of corporate money raised, the state pledged to provide a further £1. By the time Rittner stood down from the Arts Council in 1990, the corporate funds raised had topped £30 million.[8] The trend continued thereafter. In its first decade, the business sponsorship incentive scheme raised £74 million for the arts.[9]

For some commentators, corporate sponsorship was by its nature tainted. The prominent art critic Richard Cork worried that the consequence would be to stifle risk-taking, since major corporations would want to be associated with the tried, tested and popular art of the great masters, rather than punting on more controversial, contemporary work.[10] Yet if the state was not prepared to underwrite every new exhibition or concert season, it was unclear where better alternatives lay. Norman St John Stevas had tried to get the banks to fund a £500 million national endowment for the arts, but the plan had foundered, not least because one of the principles of corporate sponsorship was to link a company's support to a particular event rather than merely to donate indiscriminately. Instead, as the decade progressed, American Express, Mobil and even Carlsberg proved willing to part-finance major exhibitions. The oil company Amoco supported Welsh National Opera. Tobacco companies were especially generous – and controversial – patrons: the eagle-eyed among the audience spotted that the colour of the Philharmonia Orchestra's music stands resembled that on the cigarette packets of their sponsor, Gallaher. To raised eyebrows from those who regarded art as the antithesis of commerce, the V&A opened the Toshiba Gallery.

Bang!

It was necessity more than open-mindedness that drove much of this push by arts administrators for private sector money. The national museums (which were government-funded through the Museums and Galleries Commission) saw their total revenue fall in real terms by 3.2 per cent between 1979 and 1988, while state funding of their purchase grants fell by one third over the period – an even more grievous cut given that soaring auction prices were making acquisitions more costly.[11] Faced with these reductions in their core funding, other options had to be considered. The tradition (briefly interrupted in the early 1970s) of free entry to major museums and galleries was undermined in 1984 when the National Maritime Museum in Greenwich began charging admission fees. The Natural History and Science Museums followed suit. In 1985, the V&A started suggesting a £2 'voluntary donation' from visitors – a move that was widely interpreted as preying on visitors' sense of guilt at being seen as freeloaders, when the museum ought to have been welcoming in those who, regardless of means, sought cultural enlightenment. Some who were unencumbered by guilt took to wandering through the building sporting the lapel badge 'I Didn't Pay at the V&A'. To those offended by the intrusion of commercial imperatives, the museum added insult to injury by enlisting the Tory-patronized Saatchi & Saatchi to devise an advertising campaign which went under the slogan 'V&A: an ace caff with quite a nice museum attached'. Since the great national museums were already primarily taxpayer-funded, there was also the question of the ethics of making taxpayers effectively pay twice for the privilege of seeing artefacts that had been bought by or gifted to the nation. The British Museum, National Gallery and Tate Gallery held out against charging. The attendance statistics did much to bolster their stand, for between 1984 and 1988 the British Museum's admission figures rose by around 20 per cent, while the V&A's fell by 31 per cent.

While the arts minister, Lord Gowrie, discussed with the V&A's director, Sir Roy Strong, how to encourage a new age of philanthropy from 'the "new" classes [to] pay for art and not to regard it any more as part of the state handout',[12] those producing the art worried more about the consequences should such efforts succeed. Despite its critical successes, the Royal Court Theatre in Sloane Square was among the institutions facing a difficult future without finding new sources of revenue beyond its ticket sales and state subsidy. Yet on its council Hanif Kureishi 'voiced his concern at the acceptance of the need for commercial sponsorship and its recruitment of people who represented the kind of society to which the [theatre] was opposed'. He was supported by his fellow board member and playwright, Caryl Churchill, who attacked the 'impetus by the government towards the privatization of theatre', and 'called for a concerted rejection of private sponsorship because of the intrinsic inequalities which the system promotes, and because of the level of control which it gives to business organizations whose values are ultimately those of Thatcherism'.[13]

Art had to be true to itself. Nevertheless, it seemed doubtful tactics for its champions to combine unrelenting and often extremely personal attacks on the prime minister with continual demands that her government give them more money. While the *Guardian*'s seasoned theatre critic, Michael Billington, maintained that 'through its mixture of moral bullying and punitive cutbacks Thatcherism stifled intellectual debate',[14] the near-universality of the arts establishment's revulsion also made meaningful dialogue with Thatcher's supporters difficult, helping ensure that they would retreat into a caricature assumption that the arts lobby was irredeemably contemptuous of the very enterprise culture that provided its subsidies. Here was a non-meeting of minds, eloquently displayed in the attitude of one of decade's most successful theatre and opera directors, Dr Jonathan Miller. To him, Thatcher was 'loathsome, repulsive in almost every way', with all her 'odious suburban gentility and sentimental, saccharine patriotism, catering to the worst elements of commuter idiocy . . . Why hate her? It's the same as why the bulk of the human race is hostile to typhoid.'[15] In 1986, Harold Pinter and his wife, the biographer Lady Antonia Fraser, along with John Mortimer and his wife, Penny, formed a group of dramatists and writers dedicated to discussing how they might hasten Thatcher's downfall. Calling themselves the 20th June Group, the obvious analogy was with the 20th July Plot of 1944 when Claus von Stauffenberg and the German resistance attempted to assassinate Hitler. In the event, the Pinter putsch did not even manage to plant a metaphorical bomb beneath Thatcher's Cabinet table, busying itself instead with dinner invitations to her regime's celebrity dissidents. As a dramatic conceit this might have worked well in one of Pinter's plays. Undeterred, he assured the press: 'We have a precise agenda and we're going to meet again and again until *they* break all the windows and drag us out.' In fact, Pinter's Georgian town house was never at risk of assault from the agents of the state. As another 20th June Group habitué, David Hare, later conceded: 'There was something preposterously enjoyable about the notion of Mr Mortimer's portly frame, or Lady Antonia's gracious person, being squeezed through the windows of Campden Hill Square.'[16]

The depiction of Thatcher as a philistine – perhaps in part because she was not interested in the avant garde – was harshly drawn. She admired the sculptor Henry Moore (even attending his memorial service in 1986), read poetry, attended the opera out of choice rather than duty, and devoted time and money to building up her private collections of porcelain and ancient Chinese scrolls. In 1988, she convinced the Cabinet of the need to spend in excess of £200 million acquiring for Britain the Thyssen art collection (which included major works by Holbein, Caravaggio, Cézanne, Degas and

Van Gogh), only to be thwarted in the attempt by Spain. Despite their limitations, her cultural interests ran deeper than either the two prime ministers (Wilson and Callaghan) who preceded her, or the two (Major and Blair) who followed her.[17] When she lunched with the Arts Council's national council (the first prime minister to do so), she demonstrated an impressive knowledge of issues and individuals.[18] Yet the suspicion that she had never renounced the commercial outlook of the Midlands grocer's shop clung to her, ensuring condescending derision from the arbiters of taste. It made little difference that she had a few (mostly ageing) admirers in literary and artistic circles – in particular, Philip Larkin and the Angry Young Man (retired) Kingsley Amis. More importantly, not one of the decade's truly significant books, films or theatre dramas unambiguously saluted the principles of Thatcherism. Instead, as the playwright Howard Brenton saw it: 'Thatcherism, like all authoritarian dogmas, was brightly coloured. Writers were trying to get at the darkness, the social cruelty and suffering behind the numbingly neo-bright phrases – "the right to choose", "freedom under the law", "rolling back the state".'[19] This lack of comprehension in the output of the country's cultural leaders towards the thrice election-winning political leader was one of the most extraordinary disconnections of the era, for it meant that eleven years passed in which no literary or dramatic art consciously celebrated the guiding spirit of the age.

On stage, screen and page, the prime minister became the embodiment of what was wrong – or had gone wrong – with Britain. As the film historian Leonard Quart has pointed out, this was a level of personalized abuse generally absent on the other side of the Atlantic, because the social–political points American directors like Richard Pearce in *Country* (1984) and Spike Lee in *Do the Right Thing* (1989) were trying to make were delivered without 'barbed and contemptuous remarks aimed explicitly at Ronald Reagan'.[20] Yet in Mike Leigh's *High Hopes* (1988), 'Thatcher' is the name Cyril, the kind-hearted socialist, gives to his cactus, in a film that mercilessly parodies the blundering social aspirations of his sister and her used-car salesman husband, as well as the selfish behaviour of a snooty 'yuppie' couple who have bought and renovated a former council house next to Cyril's elderly mother. Though it was the supposed blasphemy towards Islam contained in *The Satanic Verses* (1988) that forced its author, Salman Rushdie, to seek round-the-clock protection from her government, Thatcher was portrayed in the offending book as 'Mrs Torture'. In *Paradise Postponed* (1985), John Mortimer's paean to the post-war dream, the loathsome despoiler and man-on-the-make is the Thatcherite Tory MP Leslie Titmuss. And while one of the decade's most celebrated novels, *Money* (1984), by Martin Amis, was not explicitly an attack on the prime minister and her policies, its withering portrait of the corrupting influence of materialism and self-gratification upon

John Self, a vulgar and crude maker of commercials, exposed the shallowness of the world the Tories were supposedly encouraging.

The theme unifying many of these and other works was an attack on the destabilizing consequences of upward social mobility, especially when self-advancement happened without regard for those left behind. Those who did well in finance, advertising, public relations, property and sales were particular targets for the arts sector's assumption that success in these eighties growth areas was unearned and unmerited. As John Self discovered, such apparently easy wealth was a chimera. For all the arts community's loathing of the newly moneyed in Thatcher's Britain, it was the character of the corporate raider, Gordon Gekko, played by Michael Douglas in Oliver Stone's Hollywood film *Wall Street*, that most satisfyingly embodied all that was regarded as wrong with getting rich quick. Gekko's indifference to the social consequences of the hostile takeovers he engineers in pursuit of his belief that 'greed, for lack of a better word, is good', provides a morality tale. The real message — delivered in the film's penultimate line by the blue-collar father of Bud Fox, the trader who has been sucked into Gekko's world, as he drives his son to court to answer for his crimes — is that it is better to 'create instead of living off the buying and selling of others'.

Made in 1987 and released in Britain in April of the following year, *Wall Street* lent the phrase 'greed is good' to the entire decade. Caryl Churchill's 1987 play *Serious Money* was the nearest British equivalent. Its opening at the Royal Court Theatre was well timed, coming in the aftermath of the Big Bang deregulation that had 'democratized' the City and the arrests of the 'Guinness Four' on charges of fraudulently manipulating Guinness's share price during its takeover of Distillers. Churchill's comic satire on market amorality and insider-dealing, performed in rhyming couplets, featured crudely stereotypical characterization and a plot whose central riddle (the mysterious death of futures-trader, Jake Todd) is not resolved. City traders are depicted as repulsive, foul-mouthed alcoholics, whose ties and suits mask the reality that they are uneducated barrow boys (in the derogatory term of the period, 'oiks') now rubbing shoulders with the 'old money' that had previously ruled the Square Mile. A public relations expert persuades Corman, the corporate raider, of the self-serving benefits of sponsoring the arts: 'Theatre for power, opera for decadence / String quartets bearing your name for sensitivity and elegance'; and an Ian Dury-composed chorus jubilantly hails another Thatcher election victory: 'Five more glorious years, five more glorious years / We're saved from the valley of tears for five more glorious years / Pissed and promiscuous the money's ridiculous . . . (etc. etc.) five more glorious years.' Undaunted by its condemnatory intent, genuine City traders were among the most vocally enthusiastic regulars in the audience, hooting, cheering and crying 'hear! hear!' whenever their stage caricatures and values were being portrayed at their most venal. These unscripted interventions reached a crescendo on two evenings when the investment banks Morgan Stanley and Shearson Lehman Brothers bought every seat in the house as a works outing for their employees. Whether their laughter and applause subverted or confirmed the playwright's earnest indictment was necessarily a matter of opinion, but the Royal Court's finances were improved by the corporate buy-out of the auditorium for these performances, the theatre's management deciding that 'everybody attending would be given a letter outlining sponsorship opportunities'.[21] At the time, Churchill did not find the irony amusing, though on the long view she at least had the last laugh over the bankers from Lehman Brothers.

Where 'new rich' barbarians were welcomed at theatreland's gates, the results were transformative, though often still contentious. The Old Vic was rescued and restored by Ed Mirvish, owner of Honest Ed's department store in Toronto, who bought the theatre in 1982 for £550,000 and spent a further £4 million renovating it. Commercially, the most enduring successes of the period were Andrew Lloyd Webber's musicals. *Cats* opened in 1981 and ran for twenty-one years, while *Starlight Express* (1984), *Phantom of the Opera* (1987) and *Aspects of Love* (1989) also proved extremely popular – all, apart from *Phantom*, directed by Trevor Nunn. There was no overt political message attached to these performances, unless interpretation was stretched as far as Michael Billington's assertion that the onstage struggles of individuals seeking to fulfil their dreams represented the espousal of a right-wing rejection of collectivism. On such a reading, much of the Western literary canon would need reclassifying as right-wing. It was more the fact that they represented middlebrow culture, composed by someone who contributed music for the Conservatives' 1987 general election campaign, that reinforced the prejudices of those who believed popularity was as inseparable from cultural debasement as subsidy was from serious art. Yet for all that Billington feared that Lloyd Webber's crowd-pleasers were 'Thatcherism in action',[22] there was no escaping the fact that they helped ensure that the West End overtook Broadway as the place where new musicals were premiered and promoted, with all the resulting box office receipts and investment that this brought to the London stage. Indeed, the Lloyd Weber-composed and Cameron Mackintosh-produced musicals not only dominated the West End, they led a 'British invasion' of Broadway, almost entirely eclipsing the American musical, which had for so long been dominant in its own backyard. Now, it was musicals composed, directed, produced, choreographed and performed by Britons that conquered stages across the Western world.

For most of the decade, the concern that this great renaissance of British musicals would ultimately make it more difficult for serious drama to find a platform seemed remote. After all, under Sir Peter Hall's directorial tenure, the National Theatre remained unafraid to court controversy. Howard Brenton's *The Romans in Britain* (1980) memorably involved a Roman soldier sodomizing an Ancient Briton (Brenton's metaphor for the modern British 'occupation' of Northern Ireland). The scene became a court case two years later when the anti-smut campaigner Mary Whitehouse unsuccessfully brought a private prosecution for gross indecency. In 1985, the National hosted another of Brenton's dramatic parables. Co-written with David Hare, *Pravda* concerned the dire consequences when a right-wing South African tabloid owner, Lambert La Roux (played by Anthony Hopkins), bought and transformed a well-respected British broadsheet newspaper and sacked its ineffectual editor, Elliot Fruit-Norton. The obvious target was Rupert Murdoch, the Australian-born owner of *The Sun*, who had rescued *The Times* from closure in 1981. Having dispatched his wife to the National to watch *Pravda*, the press magnate batted off inquiries by declaring, through grins, that the *Daily Mirror*'s owner, Robert Maxwell, might find it actionable.[23] Fruit-Norton was assumed to be artistic revenge on Sir William Rees-Mogg, who had followed editing *The Times* with implementing the government's budget constraints as chairman of the Arts Council.

By the time the curtain lifted on *Pravda*, the National Theatre's relations with the Arts Council were fraught. Having achieved commercial success with Richard Eyre's direction of *Guys and Dolls* in 1981, Sir Peter Hall hoped to repeat the formula three years later with a new musical, *Jean Seberg*. Costs overran by £132,000 and the resulting flop was described by the critic Bernard Levin as 'one of the most frightful stagefuls of junk ever seen in London'.[24] With his theatre's deficit nearing £500,000,[25] Hall went to the arts minister, Lord Gowrie, demanding an additional £1 million on top of the existing state subsidy. When Gowrie refused, Hall called the press to the foyer of the Olivier Theatre where he mounted a coffee table to announce 'bluntly' that 'the Arts Council has betrayed the National Theatre'.[26] Jobs would have to be cut and the National's smallest auditorium, the Cottesloe, would close. In the event, the Cottesloe was reprieved when the Labour-controlled Greater London Council increased its grant by an additional £350,000. Other saviours were found too: having spurned larger offers only four years previously, by 1985 the National was bringing in an additional £250,000 through corporate sponsorship.

While the most vocal members of the arts lobby petitioned relentlessly for more state support for London's national institutions, a parallel complaint held that the capital actually enjoyed a disproportionate subsidy compared to the rest of the country. This was acknowledged by the Arts Council's 1984 policy paper, *The Glory of the Garden*. Claiming that 'we live as two artistic nations – London and everywhere else', the document sought 'the largest single programme of devolution in the history of the Arts Council . . . a step back from centralized bureaucracy as a mode of administering the arts in Great Britain'. Jonathan Miller immediately charged that the real aim was political, 'to extinguish voices which, in the view of the Arts Council, are inimical to the political views of this particular government'.[27] In reality, there was nothing obviously Thatcherite about ensuring that £6 million was diverted from London to enhance the patronage powers of twelve regional Arts Council grant-awarding bodies. Hopes were entertained that eastern England could acquire its own world-class orchestra, by inducing one of London's four main orchestras to relocate as the price of retaining its subsidy. But the orchestras proved adept at finding ways to stay put, and the move never came to pass. Although the decade ended with the closure of the twenty-year-old Kent Opera, which was unable to survive without the tax-payer's benefaction, elsewhere in the country there were significant artistic achievements. Glyndebourne prospered without seeking government grants or compromising standards. Under the baton of Simon Rattle, the City of Birmingham Symphony Orchestra achieved international recognition. Sadler's Wells Royal Ballet took up residency at the Birmingham Hippodrome in 1987 and moved there permanently in 1990, becoming the Birmingham Royal Ballet. The combined efforts of private sector sponsorship and public sector funding through the Arts Council, the Museums and Galleries Commission and the National Heritage Memorial Fund (which the government set up in 1980 to safeguard art and architecture), together with increasing local government grants, helped unblock the cultural bottleneck of the capital city. In 1984, the Scottish National Gallery of Modern Art in Edinburgh moved from cramped surroundings into the spacious and impos-ing classical building of an abandoned private school, and in 1988 the National Gallery of Scotland benefited from an extensive renovation. Long in the planning, the Burrell Collection finally opened in its own purpose-built museum in Glasgow parkland in 1983. Enhanced as part of the 'Glasgow's Miles Better' campaign, the city's reward came in 1990 when it became European City of Culture and its Royal Concert Hall opened. Nor was Glasgow the only provincial city where investment in culture was iden-tified as a route out of industrial decline. Having been established by the government in 1981, the Merseyside Development Corporation did more than seek out investors in Liverpool's business future. Tate Liverpool was opened in 1988 as the centrepiece of the corporation's redevelopment and restoration of the previously derelict mid-nineteenth-century warehouses of the Albert Dock. With its collection of British and international modern art, it quickly became a major visitor attraction.

The vast sums pumped into the cultural infrastructure with the launch of the National Lottery in 1994 came to overshadow the scale of eighties investment, the considerable extent of which tended to be masked in public debate at the time by the focus on the shortfall between what the state offered and what the arts lobby demanded. Even the opening of the Clore Gallery, a new wing of the Tate to house its collection of Turners in 1987, provided an occasion for its chairman, the architect Richard Rogers, to launch an attack on government funding in front of the Queen – despite the £1.8 million of public funds that had gone into building the wing.[28] A further £6 million had been provided as a legacy from the foundation of Sir Charles Clore, whose money had come from the Sears retail empire which he had expanded through an unrelenting policy of company takeovers.

While the Thatcher government hoped that encouraging a new generation of Clores – their private wealth helpfully taxed at a more lenient rate – would ensure the greatest outpouring of arts philanthropy since the Victorian age (of which the Tate was itself an example), one of the most visible cultural consequences of the new money was the soaring value of art at auction. When, in 1984, Sotheby's sold Turner's *Seascape Folkestone* so that Colin and Alan Clark, the sons of the art historian Kenneth Clark, could pay their late father's considerable tax bill, it fetched the then world record-breaking price of £7.37 million. It soon looked like a bargain. Four years later, Christie's had pushed the record sale price up to £24.75 million for Van Gogh's *Sunflowers*. Within eight months, even that had been trumped by a Van Gogh painting of irises. Between 1979 and 1989, the auction prices for Impressionist works rose by 974 per cent.[29] Victorian art also came back into fashion. As with the financial markets in the City, so with the art market – London's old institutions adapted quickly and successfully to becoming the favoured trading place for international investors on a scale that dwarfed what had gone before. Some of the critics who had spent the decade berating the lack of money in the arts did not seem much happier when the money did roll in. 'Old-fashioned love of art could increasingly be replaced by hunger for investment,' worried Richard Cork. Worse, it could infect more than just the purchasers, for 'this emphasis on monetary value alone meant that museum visitors, confronted by a great painting, would be tempted to regard it simply as a multi-million-dollar banknote framed on the wall'.[30]

Contrary to the fears, the assumption that new money only chased old art was quickly disproved. The record for a living artist reached $20.68 million in November 1989 when Sotheby's in New York sold De Kooning's abstract work *Interchange* to a Japanese collector. At one stage, when the bidding had stalled at $1.7 million, a Swedish bidder audaciously upped the ante and got the price moving again by shouting '$6 million dollars!'[31] High-end art had joined private equity finance as the preserve of international risk-takers, unafraid to play 'chicken' when bidding for trophy assets. What was more, the new giants of financial success and excess were keen to sponsor as well as to buy. The Turner Prize was launched in 1984 for 'the person who, in the opinion of the jury, has made the greatest contribution to art in Britain in the previous twelve months'. By 1987, the prize was being underwritten by Drexel Burnham Lambert, the US investment bank at the centre of a take-over mania using the sort of methods that Gordon Gekko would have endorsed in *Wall Street*. In 1985, Charles Saatchi, whose firm of Saatchi & Saatchi had become the most famous name in British advertising and held the Conservative Party account, opened with his wife, Doris, the Saatchi Gallery in a converted paint factory off London's Abbey Road. It became the showcase for the Young British Artists (YBAs) of the nineties, many of whom in the mid-eighties were about to enrol as students at Goldsmith's College and for whom Saatchi's early promotion of contemporary American art would provide a source of inspiration. In both the creative enmity it spurred and the sponsorship and patronage it generated, Thatcherism defined the culture of its times.

Next Programme Follows Shortly

In 1979, Britain had only three television channels and, on average, 70 per cent of viewers were tuned to ITV.* A decade later, broadcasting was undergoing a transformation, with four terrestrial channels supplemented by a plethora of subscription channels reaching homes through cable and satellite. The transformation was made possible by technological advances. At the start of the eighties, a household wanting to receive images directly from satellites in space would have needed a 10-foot-diameter dish, but by 1989 a dish scarcely the size of a dustbin lid would suffice. But while improving technology made satellite TV a practical proposition, it did not mean there was any consensus that it was desirable – prophesiers of 'more is worse' warned that greater. choice would diminish standards and Americanize British culture. Having waxed enthusiastically about the 'white heat' of a coming technological revolution in 1963, former Labour prime minister Harold Wilson chaired a committee on future developments in broadcasting in 1979 and duly warned the Commons that Britain would shortly be subjected to 'a foreign cultural invasion through the satellite', which would undermine the quality of the BBC and the advertising revenue of ITV – a prospect summed up in the next day's *Daily Express* front page as 'TV PIRATES FROM SPACE'.[32]

Such were not the attitudes of the Thatcher government, which, ignoring

---

* Except between August and October of that year, when strike action forced ITV off the air for ten weeks.

calls to preserve the status quo, introduced permissive legislation encouraging new companies to enter the broadcasting market. This expansion might not have happened had Labour been in power. The media policy adopted by Labour's National Executive Committee in 1982 pledged to block any channel that relied on subscription charges, because 'we believe that all citizens should receive an equal public service regardless of wealth and geographical location'.[33] The problem with this stance was that the costs of starting up a satellite broadcasting company on a scale to compete with existing terrestrial broadcasters proved to be far beyond what advertising revenue alone could generate, hence the need to charge for the service.

There was little sign of this ideological fault line during the passage of the Broadcasting Act 1980, which led to the creation of Channel 4. Rather, there was broad cross-party consensus towards establishing the first national television channel since BBC 2's launch in 1964. In September 1979, the new Home Secretary, Willie Whitelaw, expressed the Conservative government's ambition for Channel 4 to broadcast 'programmes appealing to and, we hope, stimulating tastes and interests not adequately provided for on the existing channels'.[34] While this could be taken to mean offering the microphone to racial, sexual or political minority groups, the criteria were sensibly not spelt out. It would be publicly owned, via the Independent Broadcasting Authority (IBA), which as the state regulator of commercial television was ultimately answerable to the Home Office, but funded by the fifteen regional companies that comprised the ITV network, which, in turn, would recoup the cost by selling its advertising space in their own regions. In other respects, Channel 4 was intended to stimulate greater competition; it would commission programmes rather than make them itself. This dependence upon independent production companies encouraged free-marketeers to hope that, by diversifying the number of television's content providers, not only might a more entrepreneurial spirit animate the industry but the trade unions' grip on it might be slackened. The greatest controversy prior to Channel 4's launch was caused by the Conservatives' reneging on a promise to establish the fourth channel in Wales as a Welsh-language broadcaster, a decision that sparked in the principality a campaign against paying the licence fee, attacks on transmitters, and even a threat by Plaid Cymru's president, Gwynfor Evans, to go on hunger strike until the government caved in. This it duly did, and the Welsh-language S4C was launched the day before Channel 4 went live.

On the eve of launch, Channel 4's chief executive, Jeremy Isaacs, assumed the austere public service mantle of the BBC's first director general, insisting that 'Channel 4 is the last Reithian Channel! Reithian!'[35] What Sir John Reith would have made of the opening schedule on 2 November 1982 can only be imagined: it began with the anagram-themed quiz show *Countdown* before moving on to *Brookside*, a soap opera set in suburban Liverpool, while the centrepiece of the evening schedule was the first Film on Four, *Walter*, directed by Stephen Frears and starring Ian McKellen as a mentally disabled man, and including scenes of homosexual molestation in a psychiatric ward. These first offerings set the tone for what was to follow: the critically acclaimed *Walter* demonstrated the channel's determination to tackle subject matter that mainstream entertainment had generally avoided, while *Brookside* and *Countdown* retained large audiences over the next twenty years, the latter still occupying its mid-afternoon slot thirty years later. As it transpired, the most embarrassing failure in the early weeks was less with the programmes than the commercials – of which there were insufficient to fill the time slots allocated to them. The refusal of the actors' union, Equity, to permit the screening of any adverts featuring professional actors until their repeat performance fees had been improved ensured that only a few amateurish sales pitches were aired, followed by light music and a test card assuring viewers that the 'next programme follows shortly'.

Assessing the channel's success depended upon how the viewing figures were interpreted. Its remit to cater for non-mainstream tastes necessarily ensured that it could scarcely hope to appeal as broadly as the well-established fare offered by the BBC and ITV. That it managed to attract 23 million viewers per week was therefore an achievement, albeit modified by the reality that few watched for more than short periods, hence its average share of total weekly television viewing was only 4 per cent (its lowest recorded share came in the week following Christmas 1982 when it managed just a 2.8 per cent share). It was on this basis that *The Sun* began taunting it as 'The Channel that Nobody Watches'. While many of its early programmes failed to attract a discernible following, a few did capture the imagination – in particular, *Treasure Hunt*, though this was attributed to the trailing cameraman's rear-angle shots of Anneka Rice leaping energetically from helicopters in search of hidden clues, while from a distant studio semi-sedentary contestants ungraciously urged her to get a move on. It was not the new channel's dabbling in the sort of game shows that could easily have appeared on ITV that embroiled it in controversy so much as its endeavours to honour the remit to accommodate marginalized or alternative tastes. When it was revealed that New Year's Day 1983 would be marked with *One in Five* – a show for gay people – the right-wing Tory MP John Carlisle went so far as to argue that this was grounds for shutting the broadcaster down: 'The channel is an offence to public taste and decency,' the member for Luton West protested, 'and should be drummed off the air forthwith.'[36] In the event, the programme's viewing figures – at 858,000 – represented somewhat less than one fifth of the population, though they were nevertheless sufficient to ensure that Jeremy Isaacs was collared during a dinner at the

German embassy by the employment secretary, Norman Tebbit, who assured him: 'You've got it all wrong, you know, doing all these pro-grammes for homosexuals and such. Parliament never meant that sort of thing. The different interests you are supposed to cater for are not like that at all. Golf and sailing and fishing. Hobbies. That's what we intended.'[37]

Whatever the intentions of the politicians who legislated it into life, Channel 4 demonstrated a preparedness to push boundaries that the BBC and ITV had preferred only to brush against. In doing so, it remained accountable for what it broadcast to the IBA, against whom Mary Whitehouse unsuccessfully brought a prosecution for dereliction of duty when it permit-ted the channel to screen the violent borstal drama *Scum*, which had originally been commissioned – and then dropped – by the BBC. In particular, Channel 4 pioneered showing X-rated/certificate 18 films on national tele-vision, albeit restricting the range to those with artistic pretentions. These included Derek Jarman's discordant vision of punk Britain in *Jubilee* and the unapologetic homoeroticism of his *Sebastiane*, which the IBA permitted on condition that Channel 4 electronically inserted a masking strip over the film's one erect penis. There was no covering up blasphemy, however, and the regulator initially banned Monty Python's *Life of Brian* from being shown. Eventually, Jeremy Isaacs came up with a means of showing films that some viewers might find offensive when he devised a small red triangle to appear continuously in the top left-hand corner of the screen to symbolize that the film contained adult content. Initially, the triangle also appeared in the TV listings, but was soon removed when it became clear that it was encouraging higher viewing figures than would otherwise have been expected – the only rational explanation for why almost 2.4 million people switched on after midnight to watch *Themroc*, a French film about cave-dwellers with no dialogue, which in September 1986 became the first film to be branded with the mark of Isaacs. Having proved the law of unintended consequences, the experiment was discontinued the following year.

Meanwhile, the widely anticipated arrival of major new competition from cable and satellite technology failed to materialize. In the United States, cable had taken off and expectations were similarly raised in Britain when the Broadcasting Act 1980 removed the legal restriction that required cable companies to carry only BBC and ITV. The immediate results met neither the investors' expectations nor the fears of the nation's cultural and moral guardians. There was little interest in a channel owned by the *Daily Mirror*'s proprietor, Robert Maxwell, nor even for Premiere, a film channel backed by the main Hollywood studios. The other option was Satellite Television plc, which was set up by Brian Haynes, a former producer at Thames Television. Despite its name, the size of the dishes necessary to receive it meant that its miniscule British audience watched it through cable (what followers it did attract were mainly in West Germany and the Netherlands). Its claim to represent the future was undermined by its preference for screening repeats – though reruns of *Please Sir!* were the inevitable consequence of a business model that relied on advertising revenue (scrambler technology was still insufficiently advanced to make a subscription service impregnable) for a channel with a tiny audience. In 1983, with its debts mounting and its start-up capital exhausted, Satellite Television was not an attractive proposition, which was why Rupert Murdoch was able to buy a majority stake in it for £1 (plus its debts). His thinking was simple: 'When it was suggested to have a second ITV, they went for an upmarket choice – Channel 4, and this simply extended the monopoly. This was, I believed, enormously vulnerable to attack. So all the time, I was looking for a way of giving the public an alternative.'[38] But after four years of owning Sky (as it was renamed), and with its accumulated losses exceeding £10 million, it was still far from clear that the great newspaper proprietor had much more idea what to do with satellite TV than had Brian Haynes. When the IBA rejected Murdoch's bid for the sole franchise it was offering to a national direct satellite broadcaster, it seemed he had backed a loser.

The lead ought to have come from Murdoch's bête noir, the BBC, which in 1982 had been allocated two satellite channels. However, the corporation regarded the expense as greater than the opportunity and withdrew from the race. Instead, in 1986 the IBA awarded the franchise – and with it a monopoly – to British Satellite Broadcasting (BSB), a consortium originally comprising Granada, Anglia Television, Pearson, Virgin Records and Alan Sugar's company, Amstrad. BSB had not only seen off Murdoch but DBS UK, a consortium that included Michael Green of Carlton Television, London Weekend Television (which shared with Thames the ITV franchise in London) and Saatchi & Saatchi. Where DBS UK had so underestimated the expense of a satellite operation that they imagined they could offer an advertising-funded free-to-air service, BSB recognized that quality and profitability would come only by perfecting subscription television encryption. The start-up costs, after all, were enormous, with BSB (under-)estimating that it would need to raise at least £450 million of high-risk capital, a sum that made it second only to Eurotunnel as the largest private sector start-up in British history. Thus the security of knowing it had the sole franchise to operate was vital. But in granting the right to a monopoly, the IBA had made conditions, tying BSB to using a new microchip transmitting system, D-MAC. Championed by both the British government and the European Commission, D-MAC was being devised by IBA technicians to offer the high-definition picture quality that was thought to be necessary to trump encroaching Japanese competition and to set the standard for the future. Unfortunately, it was also costly and time-consuming to perfect, thereby delaying BSB's launch from the intended date of September 1989 to April 1990. An additional regulatory condition was that BSB had to pay £170 million to construct and launch its own Marcopolo satellites. These satellites had little spare capacity for adding extra channels. As Michael Grade, who was then at London Weekend Television, subsequently put it: 'It was incredible regulatory and government intervention that told them which satellite to use, how to do it, what they wanted. You can't run a business, a new start-up business, on the basis of civil servants and politicians telling you what the structure is going to be.'[39] It was exactly the sort of prescriptive culture that Murdoch scented an opportunity to undermine.

In the time it took for D-MAC to be perfected and Marcopolo to launch, Murdoch had found a quicker, cheaper way of breaking the monopoly BSB imagined it enjoyed. For £54 million he took out a ten-year rental on Astra, a privately financed European satellite, launched from French Guiana. Its PAL transmission was less advanced than D-MAC, though it had the advantage of being tried, tested and ready. Astra also offered the prospect of relatively easy expansion, since it had vastly more space than Marcopolo to add extra channels whenever the demand was found for them. Since Astra's owners were registered in Luxembourg, Murdoch did not need to apply to the IBA for a licence, since the latter's remit did not run to foreign frequencies and satellites. At a stroke, the BSB monopoly had been breached; Sky was the new Radio Caroline, broadcasting from beyond national regulatory jurisdiction. Although the Broadcasting Act 1980 prevented national newspaper owners or non-Europeans from owning more than 20 per cent of a British television company – requirements Murdoch failed to meet on both counts – these stipulations had not been extended to include broadcasting from medium-power, foreign-registered satellites like Astra. Despite petitioning from BSB, the government failed to extend them when the legislation was updated in 1990. Given that it had expected a monopoly in return for adhering to the expensive regulations foisted upon it, BSB was understandably aggrieved. But the Thatcher administration had built its reputation as a promoter of competition, not a restrictor of it; the prime minister admired what Murdoch had done to remove trade union power in the newspaper industry and was grateful for *The Sun*'s political endorsement. It fell to the House of Lords to consider an amendment that would have extended the restrictions on ownership to include Sky. Willie (by then Lord) Whitelaw weighed in to assure his fellow peers that Sky News would 'waken up both the BBC and ITN',[40] and despite the contempt Murdoch had regularly voiced towards the British establishment, their Lordships turned the other cheek. He was free to continue breaching the walls from the outside.

With Alan Sugar switching sides so that Amstrad manufactured the Sky dishes and Richard Branson's Virgin speedily offloading its stake in BSB, the

battle for what the press predictably dubbed 'Star Wars' became exceptionally bitter. The difference in tone and attitude was starkly apparent to anyone
visiting their rival headquarters. Sky inhabited a glorified shed, hurriedly
erected without thought to aesthetics or grandeur, on a nondescript industrial estate near Heathrow airport. Alcohol was banned but smoking was
unrestricted. BSB occupied Marco Polo House, a shiny new glass and marble
temple of postmodern triumphalism just off the Thames at Battersea.
Smoking was banned but wine cabinets were unrestricted. At Sky, company
cars were banned; at BSB even an executive's mother-in-law was given
one.[41] The difference in management was equally stark. Having portrayed
Sky as the opponent of cultural elitism, an unpretentious liberating force that
would give the public what it wanted, Murdoch was not going to entrust it
to Englishmen. Sky's senior management was disproportionately Australian,
while the executive chairman was Andrew Neil, the hard-working, non-
deferential Scot who was simultaneously editing Murdoch's *Sunday Times*.
At Marco Polo House, BSB's chief executive was Anthony Simonds-
Gooding, the Anglo-Irish, Ampleforth-educated grandson of a big-game
hunter. Popular with his staff, his career had been in marketing, first with the
drinks firm Whitbread (he had run Heineken's 'refreshes the parts other
beers cannot reach' campaign) and then as a global executive at Saatchi &
Saatchi. The more Sky positioned itself as the great cultural emancipator, the
more Simonds-Gooding effectively disparaged it as the moving images
edition of the *News of the World*. Yet it was not really quite the struggle for
the soul of national culture that either side claimed. The reality was more
prosaic, because the victor would be determined less by whether the offering
was upmarket or downmarket than by such pressing considerations as speed
and ease of product availability and the resources required to sign up the
most popular films for its movie channel. Ultimately, it was Hollywood, not
home-grown production values, that both sides really believed would prove
the biggest draw. In that sense, British tradition had already lost the culture
war, regardless of who won 'Star Wars'. With Sky and BSB trying to outbid
each other for the rights to each of the seven major studios' films, they ended
up committing themselves to forking out $1.2 billion for Hollywood movies
over the next five years. The auction's real winner was Los Angeles.

In the race to launch first, Murdoch trounced Simonds-Gooding. Sky had
a fifteen-month head start, going live on 5 February 1989 with a four-
channel network (Sky One, Sky News, Sky Movies, Eurosport). Yet this
advantage was partly lost by supply problems which limited the availability
of dishes for sale. At £300 for a start-up kit, their cost was hardly negligible
for the low to middle market at which they were aimed. With only ten
thousand sold by July, Sky may have been broadcasting but hardly anyone
was watching. The joke went round that Salman Rushdie had found a

hiding place from his would-be assassins as a Sky presenter. Those who did sign up discovered that much of the output consisted of American imports and minor sporting events. The tiny viewing figures (not that *The Sun* took to describing it as 'The Channel Nobody is Watching') were disastrous for advertising revenue, which was the only source of income until February 1990 when the encryption technology was finally perfected to enable Sky to charge its viewers. Tempers frayed and executives came and went with bewildering speed. Eventually, in September 1990, Murdoch brought in Sam Chisholm, another abrasive Australian with a default dislike of the British establishment matched with a fierce determination to cut costs. At the same time, a change of strategy meant that a direct sales team supplanted high-street retailers as the main distributors of start-up kits. Sky became available through monthly rental, without any upfront charges for the receiver equipment. This significantly boosted the number of Sky dishes in evidence, particularly on housing estates (doubtless a factor in ensuring that middle-class neighbourhoods self-consciously eschewed them). BSB finally went on air in April, with five channels and some already familiar faces from terrestrial television, including Sir Robin Day and Selina Scott. Their salaries were greater than their viewing figures. While Sky dishes were now easily obtainable, supply problems dogged BSB's far more discreet, diamond-shaped 'squarial'. 'It's smart to be square,' ran the promotional slogan – to little effect, since six months after going live scarcely 120,000 squarials had been sold (by which time Sky had 750,000 subscribers). Given that the two technologies were not compatible, the public seemed wary about investing in either dish or squarial until it was clear which would ultimately triumph – a hesitancy that, logically, could only ensure that neither did. Such nervousness was understandable, since choosing the wrong system would leave them with a useless technology – as Betamax purchasers had discovered in the battle of the video systems scarcely seven years earlier.

For all the promise of more choice, by the summer of 1990 it looked as if Britain's satellite experiment would end with both rivals bludgeoned to extinction. BSB was haemorrhaging £8 million per week, with accumulated debts that by the autumn were heading towards £1 billion. Yet, for Sky's employees the news that they were only blowing £2 million a week was little consolation. Murdoch had backed his entire company – including *The Sun* and *The Times* as well as his American assets – on Sky succeeding. He found himself desperately pleading with 130 different banks to reschedule the $8.2 billion debt (equivalent to the national debt of Ecuador) with which his company, News Corporation, was now saddled – for to add to Sky's drain on its resources, News Corp had bought *TV Guide* in the United States for $3 billion. With these debts maturing, and unable to secure sufficient bridging loans unless he could convince lenders that he had a plan to plug the losses, Murdoch's empire stood on the brink of collapse. He needed to sign an armistice every bit as much as did the consortium that owned BSB, a reality made explicit by the speed with which the warring parties silenced their guns. Secret talks got under way and on 2 November 1990, without the involvement of either Simonds-Gooding (who was enjoying a family holiday in Ireland) or the IBA regulator, the two companies agreed a fifty-fifty merger. The new company would be called British Sky Broadcasting (BSkyB), but would trade as Sky. It was soon apparent that the merger was, as the shortened title suggested, rather more of a takeover than a fusion of equals. Given that the former BSB holding was split between the major members of the consortium, News Corp was by far the biggest shareholder in the new company, and its executives took over most of the leading roles (a bewildered Simonds-Gooding was curtly informed not to turn up at Marco Polo House – his belongings would be sent on to him). The BSB channels were ditched or submerged into those offered by Sky; the Astra satellite and PAL were kept, the Marcopolo satellite and D-MAC were ditched. The dish had trumped the squarial.

The alarm and outrage stretched beyond the owners of redundant receiving equipment who found themselves urgently seeking a refund or an upgrade. The IBA considered taking legal action to block the merger on the grounds that BSB had breached its contractual obligations, only to decide that forcing BSB to stand alone would hasten its collapse. This calculation was not made by the opposition front bench. Condemning the 'Skyjack', Labour's broadcasting spokesman, Robin Corbett, announced his party was 'totally opposed to a satellite monopoly, particularly when controlled by a non-EC national [Murdoch]'.[42] In reality, the Monopolies and Mergers Commission was never likely to block the creation of BSkyB since its 1 per cent share of the UK's television audience was scarcely a stranglehold. To have reached even that meagre level of penetration, BSB and Sky had between them spent around £1.25 billion, which was the equivalent of what the annual licence fee generated for all BBC television and radio nationwide.[43] 'They had simply spent themselves into oblivion, all of them,' concluded Sky's Sam Chisholm. 'The truth was that both businesses were conceptual failures . . . it hadn't just been a failure, it had been an appalling failure.'[44] The merger helped ensure that two months later Murdoch was able to reschedule his debts, but the turnaround in Sky's fortunes was far from immediate or certain. Salvation did eventually come, though less from screening Hollywood movies than from showing the English Premier League. Sky's £304 million winning bid for the football rights in 1992 demonstrated that satellite television could indeed compete with terrestrial television, with results that were to prove as profound for broadcasting as for football.

None of these consequences was yet evident when the eighties ended. In output and audience, neither the BBC nor ITV had changed radically over the decade. The government's requirement that they both commission at least one quarter of their programmes from independent production companies did not take effect until 1990. There was much that caused irritation to Downing Street, particularly Thames Television's *Death on the Rock* documentary looking into the circumstances in which three IRA terrorists were shot dead in Gibraltar by the SAS in 1988, but it was the BBC's continuous tone and corporate culture that irritated Thatcher throughout her time in office. The most serious breakdown in relations came in 1986 over an episode of *Secret Society* in which the investigative reporter Duncan Campbell revealed the existence of Project Zircon, a secret satellite that spied on the Soviet Union, which, he alleged, the government had concealed from the public accounts committee (though the project had actually been cancelled).[45] Special Branch duly searched the offices of BBC Scotland and the *New Statesman* magazine, as well as Campbell's home, for evidence of illegally obtained state documents. With an injunction issued and fearing prosecution under the Official Secrets Act, the BBC's director general, Alasdair Milne, postponed broadcasting the programme (it was eventually shown in 1988). For Milne it was but the latest in a series of controversies that had pitted him against the government, and he was forced out in January 1987 when the board of governors, led by its new chairman, Marmaduke Hussey, made it clear they had lost faith in him.

While many within the corporation – and beyond – identified Hussey as a man brought in by the government to clip the BBC's wings, he nevertheless rejected the demand of the Conservative Party chairman, Norman Tebbit, for an investigation into what Tebbit claimed was the BBC's biased reporting of the United States' air strikes against Colonel Gaddafi's Libya. Such was Conservative Central Office's ongoing anxiety that in 1987 it established a unit specifically tasked with monitoring BBC output for signs of anti-Tory bias – a move that made the party look as obsessed with perceived slights from the BBC as was the Labour leadership with the unabashed assaults of Murdoch's *Sun* newspaper. Tory suspicions were heightened when the corporation suddenly cancelled Ian Curteis's *The Falklands Play*, to which it had committed a £1 million production budget and a three-hour prime-time BBC 1 slot, scheduled for April 1987. According to Curteis, the BBC demanded script changes to remove scenes of Thatcher appearing distressed by news of British loss of life and to create new dialogue between Cabinet ministers to show that the prosecution of the Falklands War was actually linked to party political and electoral calculations rather than principles of national sovereignty.[46] For its part, the BBC claimed the cancellation was to safeguard against the possibility that Thatcher might call a general election at the very time a play was portraying her in a sympathetic light. The corporation duly went ahead with filming Charles Wood's *Tumbledown*, a drama about a soldier (played by Colin Firth) crippled, mentally debilitated and disillusioned by his experiences of fighting in the Falklands conflict.

Thatcher summed up her feelings, in November 1990, in a comment to a foreign dignitary she was showing out of Downing Street just as Rupert Murdoch was arriving to inform her that Sky would have to merge with BSB. 'Here is Mr Murdoch,' she announced, 'who gives us Sky News, the only unbiased news in the UK.'[47] By then, she had been foiled in her efforts to make the BBC at least partly dependent on advertising revenue rather than the licence fee alone. Chaired by Professor Alan Peacock, the committee the government set up to look into the matter issued a report in July 1986 recommending that the licence fee should stay. Though Thatcher's attitude towards a national institution like the BBC appeared too iconoclastic even for many Conservatives, Labour was moving towards the opposite extreme and pondering aloud whether it should get rid of commercial television altogether: 'If advertising was replaced by an expanded licence fee (perhaps moderated by direct taxation) there would be a wide range of immediate benefits,' the shadow arts minister, Norman Buchan, assured the Peacock committee, since it 'would open the way for new mechanisms of accountability and responsiveness'.[48] Instead, the government reluctantly accepted that the BBC should remain advert-free and even rejected the Peacock committee's majority view that both Radio 1 and Radio 2 should be privatized.

It was an irony that, despite having been established to advise on the BBC's future funding, the Peacock committee's report ultimately had a greater effect on the complexion of ITV, recommending that its regional franchises should be put out to competitive tender. Among the minority on the committee who dissented from the proposal was the former *Guardian* editor, Alistair Hetherington, who warned that 'it would be difficult to choose between a company with a long and good record of programming and one with no track record in television but plenty of money'.[49] For Labour, Norman Buchan went from the specific to the philosophical, contending that civilization 'cannot be left in the hands of the profit makers'.[50] To free-marketeers, however, the mysterious fashion in which the IBA decided which regional companies should retain or lose their ITV franchises was ripe for change. Here, they came across opposition that was so determined it even included prominent profit-makers. With endorsement from popular entertainers, including Rowan Atkinson and Esther Rantzen, the Campaign for Quality Television was launched with the intention of ensuring that there should be a regulatory quality threshold, rather than the franchise being awarded to the highest bidder in a blind auction. To this, the government made a modest concession, with the Broadcasting Act 1990 permitting the highest bid to be blocked if, 'in exceptional circumstances', the quality offered was perceived to be unacceptably low. When the auction was held in 1991, a number of bidders were duly disqualified by this stipulation, but even Thatcher was among those unhappy at some of the winners and losers, writing to Bruce Gyngell, TV-am's chairman, that she was 'heartbroken' that his company had lost its franchise, especially since 'I am only too painfully aware that I was responsible for the legislation.'[51] The longer-term consequences of the act were an unprecedented spate of mergers and consolidations of regional stations, to the extent that the merger of Carlton and Granada in 2004 brought all the regions of England and Wales under one parent company (in 1990 there had still been eleven separate companies). Thames was among the once mighty station franchise-holders that duly carved out a future as independent production companies, vying to have their programmes commissioned, though even in this role Thames found itself subsumed into a pan-European media conglomerate. Thatcher may have hoped that the enhanced competition would be felt most profoundly by the BBC. Yet the arrival of Sky, followed by new digital channels and the internet, proved to have far more transformative consequences for the nation's main commercial channel, where consolidation appeared the only solution to the pressures of globalized capitalism. Having commanded 70 per cent of the audience in 1980, ITV's share had fallen below 20 per cent thirty years later.

You Have Been Watching

How was British culture in the eighties shaped and reflected by television? There was much to repel those who identified the spirit of the age as superficial, consumerist and unserious. As if to confirm such prejudices, *The Price Is Right* became popular by unapologetically embracing all three attributes. With a near-delirious studio audience roaring on contestants invited by the presenter Leslie Crowther to 'Come on Down!' the show had the audacity to offer prizes for demonstrating no particular skill beyond an ability to guess the price of consumer durables. Avarice was its own reward. Yet what at the time looked like a vulgar celebration of materialism and the workings of the free market, assumes an altogether gentler complexion when viewed from the perspective of a quarter-century later. The evident excitement of *The Price Is Right*'s contestants at scooping the prize of a portable colour television or an exercise-bike suggested how little their lives were dominated by the sort of material possessions taken for granted by scoffing critics of more affluent means. In 1988 – four years after Central Television launched *The*

Price Is Right – the IBA issued new regulations that raised the maximum that could be offered on game shows to an average of £1,750 per show.[52] Whoever wanted to be a millionaire was not going to get rich quick by being an eighties game-show contestant.

The Price Is Right was a clone of an American prime-time show and a continuing debate throughout the period concerned the extent to which the presumed superiority of British television was being threatened by American imports and their perceived lowbrow values. British quality was measured by the artistry of its television dramas, especially literary adaptations, though transatlantic differences were no less stark in the social milieux depicted by rival soap operas. Two American soaps proved especially popular: *Dallas* (1978–91) and *Dynasty* (1982–91). In November 1980, twenty-one million Britons watched to find out who had shot *Dallas*'s anti-hero, J. R. Ewing, in an episode that was heavily reported not only in the tabloid press but even on the BBC's nine o'clock news. What *Dallas* and *Dynasty* shared was an escapist glimpse into the lives of the super-wealthy. In contrast, the British soaps continued to inhabit the environment of more ordinary communities. This remained the case not only for ITV's long-established *Coronation Street*, *Emmerdale Farm* and *Crossroads* (the latter discontinued in 1988), but also for the decade's two newcomers. Where Channel 4's Merseyside-based *Brookside* differed from the established British soaps was that it tackled contentious and even political subjects which they had tended to avoid, such as unemployment, strike action, domestic violence, homosexuality and Aids. Three years later, BBC 1 finally decided that it also needed to attract the mass audience that a successful soap would offer and launched *EastEnders*, which by the end of 1985 was attracting an audience of twenty-two million. The mansions and power-dressing paraded in *Dynasty* were nowhere to be seen in *EastEnders*, though both soaps placed family relationships at the heart of their stories. Rather, for *EastEnders*, as for *Coronation Street*, the traditional 'local' was where much of the social interaction took place and the London-based series essentially continued with the format of its Salford equivalent – although a little grittier in that the character of 'Dirty Den' Watts, a pub landlord of compelling menace, was played by an actor, Leslie Grantham, who had served time for murder. More than half the UK's population watched the Christmas 1986 episode in which he served his on-screen wife with divorce papers.

Two months before this kitchen-sink *coup de théâtre*, the BBC bought in from Australia a new lunchtime soap called *Neighbours*. Set in a classless, unpretentiously comfortable Melbourne suburb, it was distinct from the socially stratified habitats of the British and American alternatives, appealing especially to young people (the pop stars Kylie Minogue and Jason Donovan first became famous in it) and to those attracted by its sunny and generally optimistic outlook. *Neighbours* exemplified a trend in the eighties whereby Australian cultural exports became as natural a part of British television scheduling as American ones. In 1989, ITV felt it needed an Australian soap of its own and bought *Home and Away*. Among the performers who benefited from the new appetite for all things Antipodean was the comedian Paul Hogan – first through his own television show on Channel 4 and subsequently through the film *Crocodile Dundee*, while his promotion of Castlemaine XXXX coincided with a pronounced boom in British sales of Australian lager alongside those of Australian wine.

Britain's most influential Australian (albeit a US citizen for business reasons after 1985) still found little to his liking. In delivering the MacTaggart lecture at the 1989 Edinburgh Television Festival, Rupert Murdoch revelled in the opportunity to portray himself as the country's emancipator from a stultifying form of cultural imperialism that the BBC and ITV/Channel 4 sustained under the guise of the reputed world-class quality of their programme-making. 'In the values that it exudes, British television has been an integral part of the British disease,' the media proprietor claimed. Obsessed with class, most drama was 'run by the costume department' and 'the socially mobile are portrayed as uncaring, businessmen as crooks, money-making is to be despised . . . To the British establishment with its dislike of money-making and its notion that public service is the preserve of paternalists,' he laid down the challenge 'that anybody who within the law of the land provides a service that the public wants at a price they can afford is providing a public service'. Murdoch, of course, had his own Sky network to promote and an interest in disparaging the old guard it sought to displace. Yet he had identified a deep-seated prejudice that pervaded British, but not American or Australian, television. With the exception of *Howard's Way* (a BBC drama serial about a man who invested his redundancy pay in his own yacht-building company), it was noticeable that the output of the four terrestrial channels replicated the decade's serious theatre, cinema and literature in depicting negatively entrepreneurs and the socially mobile.

There were elements of disdain for those 'on the make' even in the decade's comedy. Harry Enfield created the character of an unpleasant plasterer, whose cash-in-hand employment ensured that he had 'loadsamoney' and who invited the less fortunate to 'look at my wad!' The comedian got the idea from observing Tottenham Hotspur fans holding aloft £10 notes to taunt the supporters of visiting teams from the depressed north. Thanks to Enfield's popularizing of the expression, during 1988 'loadsamoney' became a catchphrase to describe a far broader range of southerners who were doing well out of the economic boom, and was even briefly taken up by Neil Kinnock as a term to indict Thatcherism – though accusing the Tories of helping ordinary people to get rich quick was a questionable vote-winning strategy. A somewhat more generous view of the small businessman was offered by the BBC comedy *Only Fools and Horses*, which, in terms of viewing figures, became the most successful sitcom in British history. Beginning in 1981 and continuing throughout the decade, it was set on a Peckham housing estate, where the essentially warm-hearted market-trader, 'Del Boy' Trotter, continues to reassure his younger brother that 'this time next year we'll be millionaires' – even though, in reality, Trotter's Independent Traders deals in little beyond selling faulty or stolen goods to gullible punters. A similar portrayal of the small businessman as an, albeit endearing, minor con-man was Arthur Daley in Thames Television's hit comedy *Minder*. In dress and tone, Daley actually resembled a post-war spiv (appropriately, since he was played by George Cole, the 'Flash Harry' spiv of the 1950s St Trinian's films), for whom the eighties offered renewed opportunities to pursue 'a nice little earner'. Daley imagined this made him an entrepreneur, whereas actually he was, like Del Boy, engaged in little more than conceiving scams or offloading 'hot' merchandise. *Only Fools and Horses* and *Minder* gently mocked small businessmen with big ideas because their interpretation of the free market owed much to the black market, while the portrayals of Arthur Daley and Del Boy were affectionate partly because their rags-to-riches schemes usually backfired. An honest and successful nouveau-riche businessman ultimately coming to the aid of an 'old-money' establishment widow provided the plot of *To the Manor Born*, a sitcom that ran from 1979 to 1981, but this owed more to the outgoing decade in which it was conceived, when the 83 per cent top rate of income tax and 75 per cent death duties almost made the wealthy into victims capable of attracting an audience's sympathy. As the eighties gathered momentum and making money became identified with the tenets of Thatcherism, upward social mobility came to be portrayed as a route not to salvation but, at the very least, to self-delusion.

Murdoch's assessment of British broadcasting bias may have contained some truth, but his suggestion that he offered a brighter, more democratic, alternative did not go unchallenged. A large portion of Sky1's output consisted of American imports and to an establishment (though not anti-Murdoch) figure like Sir William Rees-Mogg, 'international market forces', while generally much preferable to national monopoly, 'tend to break down national culture', threatening a 'McDonald's culture in which television provides the international fast food of the mind'.[53] This was putting it strongly since only the most superficial viewing of, say, *The Simpsons* – which Murdoch's Sky brought to British audiences in 1989 – could have mistaken it for unintelligent or culturally indistinct. Yet the equation of American imports with undemanding content remained a popular perception nonetheless. The other issue was that the impressive back-catalogue of English literature meant that, unless adaptations were to stop, British television's costume departments were going to be kept busy. Backward-looking they may have been, but literary adaptations continued to provide many of the most critically acclaimed programmes, a reality that inevitably made those who disparaged them look more like philistines than prosecutors of a cultural critique. For the BBC, Alan Plater adapted two of Anthony Trollope's novels as *The Barchester Chronicles* (1982) and four years later crafted *Fortunes of War* from the novels of Olivia Manning, starring two promising young actors, Kenneth Branagh and Emma Thompson. Yet the successful literary adaptation was by no means the preserve of the BBC. Granada Television scored a critical and commercial hit with its version of Paul Scott's 'Raj Quartet', *The Jewel in the Crown* (1984), which, while set in the last years of British imperial power, was hardly a glorification of it. Granada's greatest triumph, however, had come three years previously with its eleven-part adaptation of Evelyn Waugh's *Brideshead Revisited*. Directed by Charles Sturridge, *Brideshead* represented a watershed in British television drama not for its aristocratic subject matter, but for bringing to the small screen the superior filming techniques and production values of the big screen. Despite the availability of videotape in the 1970s, the legacy of live broadcast drama meant that interior scenes were still shot on over-lit studio sets. *Brideshead* let in the natural light of real locations, ensuring that television drama never looked as amateur and 'stagey' again. These developments were put to good use in another of the decade's popular genres, the adaptation of crime novels. Agatha Christie's Miss Marple was given a new lease of life by the BBC in 1984 and ITV did likewise for Hercule Poirot five years later. Dispensing with the old-fashioned costumes but retaining the historic backdrop of Oxford, ITV's run of *Inspector Morse*, which began in 1987, took Colin Dexter's creation not just to fifteen million viewers in the UK but to seventy-five million in the rest of the world, while attracting scriptwriters of the stamp of Anthony Minghella, Julian Mitchell and Charles Wood.

Given these successes, it was surprising that critics devoted so much ink to grumbling about the decline of the television play. The charge had some validity if defined so narrowly as to focus purely on the one-off dramas – often concerned with contemporary social issues – that during the 1970s had been showcased by the BBC's Plays for Today. The Play for Today format ended in 1984, its theatre-style stage sets looking dated compared with the more realistic production techniques ushered in by *Brideshead*. The lamentations were, in any case, misplaced. Far from dying during the eighties, the television play expanded into multi-episode serials (which, hour for hour, were more cost-effective to produce) or was given the full cinematic treatment through Channel 4's Film on Four commissions. If the balance between confronting serious subjects and providing mere entertainment tipped towards the latter, the quality of the former stood comparison with the best of the previous decade, as Alan Bleasdale's *Boys from the Blackstuff* attested.* Nor did increasingly sophisticated technical expertise invariably sideline an emphasis on quality scripts. Devoid of any artifice beyond the actor looking into the camera as if it were a trusted friend, Alan Bennett's dramatic monologues exemplified the triumph of the spoken word over visual effects. What became Bennett's *Talking Heads* series in 1988 actually began six years earlier with Patricia Routledge's performance in *A Woman of No Importance*. *Talking Heads'* themes of loneliness and loss were conveyed either in Bennett's own mournful tones or those of actresses who conveyed the playwright's particular talent for giving voice to women disappointed by life.

In contrast, drama was less successful at exploring the strong female role model that – despite leading feminists' scorn for her – the prime minister embodied in politics. It was not until 1990, the year of Thatcher's fall, that Thames Television finally got round to producing a sitcom, *No Job for a Lady*, about a new female MP in the man's world of Westminster. It succeeded neither as comedy nor as commentary. Despite the advances made by women in the seventies, television still preferred to feature strong women from the 1940s. Set in a Japanese prisoner-of-war camp, *Tenko* (1981–5) proved a success despite the initial fears of BBC programmers that an all-female lead cast (looking necessarily bedraggled) would not draw a sufficiently broad audience. The series was devised by Lavinia Warner and co-written by Jill Hymen, who, between drafting scripts for *Howard's Way*, repeated the resilient women in wartime formula for LWT's drama series about female secret agents, *Wish Me Luck* (1987–9). It could not be said that the corporation led by example. In 1985, only 8 per cent of BBC departmental heads and senior producers were female and only 14 per cent of mid-evening programmes featured female lead characters.[54] Although the BBC did mount an ambitious adaptation of Fay Weldon's *The Life and Loves of a She-Devil*, in which a wife wreaks revenge on her adulterous husband and his romantic novelist lover, generally the decade's most prominent women on television were either news presenters or, increasingly, comediennes like Dawn French, Jennifer Saunders and Victoria Wood.

During the early eighties, comedy was heavily stratified between two different approaches to making people laugh. Mainstream acts cracking timeless and – apart from those wearisomely perpetuating racial stereotypes – mostly inoffensive jokes about human relationships suddenly had competition from 'alternative comedy', which was edgier and less concerned with following the sort of time-honoured comic structure that inevitably concluded in a

---

* See p. 82.

punchline. In particular, alternative comedy was more than happy to cause offence and was concerned to address, rather than ignore, contemporary socio-political issues. This movement's graduating academy was the Comedy Store, which opened in London in 1979. Offering a live venue for stand-up and an audience merciless in rooting out performers likely to be disabled by stage-fright, the Comedy Store's formula spawned imitators across the country. Among the comedians most committed to stand-up as a protest against all forms of conservatism was Ben Elton, whose radical political agenda could scarcely have differed more from that of his uncle, Geoffrey Elton, at the time Cambridge's Regius Professor of Modern History. Having studied at Manchester, Ben Elton was, like so many alternative comedians of the period, a product of university but not of Oxbridge. This generation was thus distinct both from the comic innovators of the previous decade, like the Oxbridge-educated Monty Python team, and from a new brand of adult humour emanating from the depressed housing estates of Tyneside. The latter's new testament was *Viz*, which started off as a cheaply produced comic-strip magazine sustained by money its creator, Chris Donald, had invested from the enterprise allowance scheme which the government had established to offer funds to unemployed people trying to set up their own businesses. Where archetypal alternative comedians had a limited range of political targets – Thatcher representing the bull's eye – in a brand of left-wing invective that became known, confusingly, as 'right-on', *Viz*'s lack of political and cultural discernment was truly anarchic. Resembling the *Beano*, but with Geordie dialect and expletives, it mocked those that the 'right-on' comedians did not care to touch: *Viz*'s regular cast of ridiculous characters included a humourless lesbian feminist campaigner called Millie Tant and a couple of man-hungry nightclub-goers called The Fat Slags. By 1989, the magazine was selling a million copies per issue.

A rude and crude adult comic on this scale was unprecedented – *Viz*'s circulation reached more than ten times that managed even at the peak of *Oz*'s notoriety in the early seventies – and it soon spurred many inferior imitators. Meanwhile, alternative comedy seemed more like the natural progression from the satire boom of the 1960s, replacing the whimsy of that period with angry diatribes and drawing from a pool of talent that stretched beyond those who already knew each other from term time on the banks of the Cam or Isis. For all this, the Oxbridge graduate satirists were far from falling out of fashion. Among the familiar names in British entertainment during the eighties were such ex-Cambridge Footlights luminaries as Emma Thompson, Clive Anderson, Griff Rhys Jones, Stephen Fry and Hugh Laurie, and Oxford Revue alumni Rowan Atkinson, Mel Smith and Richard Curtis. Joined by the Australian comedienne Pamela Stephenson, Atkinson, Smith and Rhys Jones became the stars of *Not the Nine O'Clock News*, a fast-paced BBC 2 sketch show mixing topical satire with traditional comic material. Produced by John Lloyd and Sean Hardie, *Not the Nine o'Clock News* (whose working title had, revealingly, been *Sacred Cows*) survived an indifferent first series in 1979 to become over the following three years a cult programme, spawning best-selling spin-off books and record albums. Lloyd's intention was that his comic foursome would go on to become the new Pythons. Atkinson, however, wanted to move on with ideas of his own, finding even greater success as the lead in four series of *Blackadder* between 1983 and 1989, a historical romp from the Middle Ages to the First World War, which Lloyd produced and Atkinson wrote in collaboration with Richard Curtis and Ben Elton. Besides performing in their own two-man show, Rhys Jones and Smith formed a production company, TalkBack, which created many of the most popular comedies of the following decade and eventually merged with Thames Television – in itself an extraordinary affirmation of the business of laughter.

What was remarkable was less the achievements of all these new approaches to comedy than the resilience of traditional mainstream family entertainment in the face of the challenge. The television ratings battle was still regularly won by comedy shows that had started in the seventies and shown little inclination to develop over time. Never straying from its cosy, middle-class, suburban setting, *Terry and June*, which had begun as *Happy Ever After* in 1974, kept its ten-million-strong audience through to its final series in 1987. Having started their run in 1971, Ronnie Corbett and Ronnie Barker – *The Two Ronnies* – continued to serve up light double-entendre and sing songs in fancy dress until finally bidding goodnight from one another in 1987. While the alternative comedy circuit railed against Thatcher, *The Two Ronnies* offered a gentle spoof serial, *The Worm that Turned* (1980), in which a nation of downtrodden men is subjugated by a female police state run from fortress-like headquarters in 'Barbara Castle' by a blonde bombshell – 'a woman with an iron will and underwear to match' (played by Diana Dors). Whether this was a satire on Thatcher or feminism, or merely an excuse to feature leggy girls goose-stepping in leather hot pants, was left to the viewers' imagination. Whichever way, it was very popular. It was not the only example of slapstick fascism. Having co-created *Dad's Army* fourteen years earlier, David Croft came up with further wartime capers, albeit relocated to occupied France, in *'Allo 'Allo* in 1982 with both the Germans and the Resistance inheriting the amiable incompetence of Captain Mainwaring's platoon. The gulf between the approach to humour promoted by the Comedy Store and that being scripted by David Croft and Jeremy Lloyd (who were also responsible for the holiday camp sitcom *Hi Di Hi!*) could be summed up in one of the recurring themes of *'Allo 'Allo*, where copies of a stolen painting, *The Fallen Madonna with the Big Boobies*, were rolled up in an ill-concealed sausage.

Contrary to some expectations, the spirit of variety was not entirely snuffed out by the sudden deaths of Tommy Cooper and Eric Morecambe within weeks of each other in 1984. Its endurance owed much to Russ Abbott and the double acts Little and Large and Cannon and Ball. When, in 1980, Tommy Cannon and Bobby Ball appeared at the 3,200-seat Blackpool Opera House, their two shows a day were sold out for eighteen weeks. End-of-the-pier humour it might have been, but the duo were in such demand that ITV commissioned ten series from them between 1979 and 1990, which attracted audience figures of fifteen million.[55] With such appeal, Cannon and Ball could reasonably claim to have inherited the mantle of Morecambe and Wise as the most enduring successes of British comedy in the eighties. They did so without smut, profanity or topicality. For all the energy and cultural significance of the alternative comedians and their anti-establishment jibes, it seemed that predominantly working-class audiences still mostly preferred the apolitical, non-divisive humour of slapstick and mother-in-law jokes. More pointedly still, some who did like a bit of socio-political comment opted for the far from 'right-on' observations of Jim Davidson, Freddie Starr and even (though he was no longer deemed fit for television) Bernard Manning.

The Thatcher era, with its readily identifiable and easily caricatured politicians, could scarcely have escaped the satirists' attention whatever the input of the alternative comedy scene. In the ITV series *The New Statesman*, Rik Mayall's portrayal of Alan B'Stard, a pathologically amoral Conservative MP, was launched three months after Thatcher won her third term in 1987. Although a comic grotesque, B'Stard seemed to represent everything that was assumed to be venal and arrogant about young right-wing politicians, interpreting their leader's gospel of self-reliance as an excuse to do as they pleased. From the moment of its launch in 1984, the most innovative and successful television political satire was ITV's *Spitting Image*, a technically accomplished puppet show, which mercilessly parodied Britain's leading politicians, royal family and celebrities, while also taking particular relish in exposing the supposed brainlessness of President Reagan. The latex puppets created by Peter Fluck and Roger Law were undoubtedly an appropriate means of satirizing a House of Commons whose raucous and vitriolic exchanges retained the pugnacious temper of a Punch and Judy show. For its first three years, *Spitting Image* was produced by John Lloyd, fresh from *Not the Nine O'Clock News*, who later reflected: 'I can't remember in my lifetime a government that was disliked as much, so certainly it came at the right time.'[56] Donning men's suits and chomping on Churchillian cigars, the wild-eyed Thatcher was shown as determined and demented. Her closest Cabinet supporter, Norman Tebbit, appeared as a skinhead hooligan, violently enforcing her will. Whatever the intention, it was certainly debatable whether portraying the prime minister and her henchman as brutal, ruthless and strong-willed was as damaging to their reputations as depicting their opponents as gormless and incompetent buffoons. The Labour leader, Neil Kinnock, was represented as a vacuous windbag, while the puppet of his deputy, Roy Hattersley, constantly sprayed spittle from its mouth when speaking. The Alliance was treated equally disrespectfully: the Liberal leader, David Steel, so loathed being depicted as a tiny head protruding from the breast-pocket of a dominant and vain David Owen that he even discussed with Owen what measures they might take to avoid reinforcing the popular impression.[57] In contrast, the masculine depiction of Thatcher only pandered to the well-worn joke that she was the only man in the Cabinet. Perhaps the most famous sketch involved her taking her colleagues out to dinner. Having chosen raw steak for herself, she replies to the waitress's enquiry 'And what about the vegetables?' by gazing at her Cabinet and announcing: 'Oh, they'll have the same as me.'

Comedy of this kind – as of most kinds – was not to the prime minister's taste. According to her press secretary, she turned the television off whenever *Spitting Image* came on.[58] She did, however, make time to watch *Yes Minister* (1980–4), a BBC sitcom about an ingénue Cabinet minister, Jim Hacker, whose efforts to initiate change are constantly outmanoeuvred by his department's senior civil servants, who are invariably interested only in defending the status quo against reform of any kind. '*Yes Minister* is my favourite programme,' trilled the prime minister. 'Its closely observed portrayal of what goes on in the corridors of power has given me pure joy'.[59] Both it and its sequel, *Yes, Prime Minister* (1986–8), proclaimed no party political standpoint, though its concurrence with a Conservative administration promising to cut bureaucratic red tape and confront Whitehall's 'management of decline' ethos naturally ensured an association with the party in power. Thus it was that the actor Paul Eddington, who played Jim Hacker, noted: 'Whenever I meet a Cabinet minister I get treated as a colleague, while the opposition regard me with suspicion.'[60] The depiction of the well-intentioned man at the mercy of officialdom was hardly novel, having been central to the plots of the Ealing comedies of the 1940s – though those, too, were interpreted as conveying an anti-socialist message. More detached verdicts concluded that whether or not Jim Hacker's tribulations represented Thatcherite propaganda was not the point. From across the Atlantic, *Variety* offered the perspective of American idealism by showing surprise that a series that presented a 'pretty cynical view of politics . . . seems to have struck a chord in Britain, where the program is popularly regarded as being accurate'. Nearer to home, another critic put it succinctly: '*Yes, Prime Minister* could only happen in a country which had stopped taking itself seriously.'[61]

The British Are Coming . . . and Going

In 1981, *Chariots of Fire* became the first British film since *Oliver!* in 1968 to win the Academy Award for best picture. When its scriptwriter, Colin Welland, received one of the film's four Oscars, he concluded his words of thanks by startling his Hollywood audience with the roar: 'The British are coming!' Perhaps an American auditorium was not the place for a Briton to revive a famous War of Independence warning about approaching redcoats. Yet given the stereotypical British national characteristic of repressed emotion, his pride and lack of reserve seemed refreshing. For all that, the boast was rather bewildering. If the past decade was anything to go by, the British were nowhere near taking on Hollywood. Yet for a brief and tantalizing moment, Welland's prophecy looked as if it might indeed be spectacularly prescient. Complete with its three hundred thousand extras, *Gandhi*, directed by Richard Attenborough, won the best picture Oscar in 1982. In 1984, a runner-up was yet another British film, *The Killing Fields*, which, like *Chariots of Fire* and another commercial and critical success, *Local Hero*, was produced by David Puttnam and made by the British production company Goldcrest. With other significant films planned and Goldcrest becoming increasingly ambitious, it appeared that a return to the nation's finest cinematic hours of the 1940s was within grasp. But just as this prospect appeared tangible, Welland's appropriation of a war-cry from 1775 proved unhappily double-edged. Goldcrest's 1985 film about that transatlantic showdown, *Revolution*, boasted as director *Chariots of Fire*'s Hugh Hudson and starred Al Pacino, but it was released prematurely and flopped so spectacularly that it all but brought down Goldcrest with it. Instead of orchestrating the great British film revival, Hudson's talents were diverted to making – admittedly highly artistic – advertisements for Benson & Hedges, British Airways and Neil Kinnock's 1987 general election campaign. Puttnam moved to Hollywood for a brief and bruising tenure as chief executive of Columbia Pictures. Meanwhile, the number of home-made feature films collapsed back to the level of the dog days at the start of the decade: thirty-two in 1980, up to eighty in 1985 and down to twenty-seven by 1989.[62] It was 1996 before another (at least nominally) British film, *The English Patient*, won the Oscar for best picture.

That the great British film renaissance lasted for half of the eighties was, in the long perspective, a story of business failure. However, anyone gifted with hindsight at the end of the seventies might easily have concluded that such a period of success represented a minor triumph. During that decade, output had become concentrated around the increasingly exhausted humour of the *Carry On* films (which ended in 1978) and equally low-budget horror films and sex romps. Racking up a record for the longest continual showing at a West End cinema, it was scarcely a source of professional pride that *The Mousetrap* of the British film industry was David Sullivan's dismal soft porn effort *Come Play with Me*, which opened in 1977 and was still showing to full houses in 1981, a full two years after its star, Mary Millington, had taken her own life. The hope that mainstream entertainment would be kept afloat by Lew Grade's company ITC effectively ended with its involvement in *Raise the Titanic!* – a disaster movie in every sense of the term which left Grade famously quipping that it would have been cheaper to lower the Atlantic. The ship that became a metaphor had seemingly added British cinema to its incident log.

Where it had been expected that ITC would solve the conundrum of why a country that made popular television drama and comedy programmes could no longer translate that success into film-making, a partial solution was instead offered by the launch of Channel 4 in 1982. Its board was persuaded by the dramatist Stephen Poliakoff that the channel should have a film development arm which would finance, or part-finance, films, and Channel 4 would enjoy the screening rights. To this end, the channel's fiction commissioning editor, David Rose, was given an initial £6 million budget with which to get twenty films made. Working out at £300,000 per production, this was not much of a fighting fund, but the success ratio was such that the sums soon burgeoned. In the eleven years following its launch, Channel Four Films invested almost £100 million in 273 films and demonstrated that decent box-office takings in the cinemas could follow, as well as precede, exposure on television. [63]

Besides the roller-coasting fortunes of Goldcrest, Channel Four Films was a central component of the home-grown industry's run of accomplishments in the eighties. With support from the British Film Institute, it was behind the intriguing/perplexing Restoration-era drama *The Draughtsman's Contract* (1982), which brought to public attention the talents of its director, Peter Greenaway, and the composer responsible for its neo-baroque soundtrack, Michael Nyman. Their collaboration continued with *A Zed and Two Noughts* (1985), *Drowning by Numbers* (1988) and *The Cook, the Thief, his Wife and her Lover* (1989). Greenaway was a maker of 'animated paintings' and the last film's art-house sex and nudity proved internationally enticing. Other successful British films of the eighties that Channel 4's film arm helped develop included Richard Eyre's *The Ploughman's Lunch* (1983), a critical dissection of the romantic and social ambitions of a journalist covering the modern Conservative Party, written by Ian McEwan; *A Private Function* (1984), the Alan Bennett-scripted comedy about rationing; and *Letter to Brezhnev* (1985), in which two girls seek romance with a couple of visiting Soviet sailors in the hope of escaping their prospect-free existence in eighties Liverpool. It was also Channel Four Films that funded *My Beautiful Launderette* (1985), which, being set in the British-Asian community and featuring interracial sex (both straight and gay), white racist thuggery, an Asian girl flashing her breasts, and – perhaps no less controversially – an Asian businessman extolling Thatcherism, had failed to find a backer for its £650,000 budget. Channel 4's punt on Hanif Kureishi's script proved shrewd and the film became the first major success for a new production company, Working Title, which went on to become the most significant creative force behind British cinema over the following quarter-century.

In particular, Channel Four Films helped fund a genre indelibly associated with British cinema in the eighties. What these films had in common was an Edwardian or inter-war setting and a plot involving characters attempting, with varying levels of success, to overcome social or sexual inhibitions and the persistence of class constraints. A preponderance of stiff upper lips and floppy public schoolboy haircuts was shown off to good effect in visually splendid settings, further enhanced by beautiful cinematography. The popularity of the genre had been firmly established by the great successes of 1981, *Chariots of Fire* and the eleven-part television series *Brideshead Revisited*. It was subsequently indulged by several Channel 4-funded films, including *Another Country* (1984), Julian Mitchell's inter-war boarding-school drama, which helped launch the careers of Rupert Everett and Colin Firth, and *A Month in the Country* (1987), which starred Firth alongside another emerging talent, Kenneth Branagh. The (partially) Channel 4-funded film that really caught the popular imagination, however, was *A Room With a View* (1985). Starring Helena Bonham-Carter, it was the first of three adaptations of E. M. Forster's novels by the producer–director partnership of Ismail Merchant and James Ivory, whose films came to epitomize the style so effectively that the Merchant–Ivory tag became synonymous with the entire genre. Indeed, the Merchant–Ivory vision of Englishness attracted such recognition that it could easily be forgotten that neither producer nor director was actually English. Besides lush period settings, good-looking leads, public school education and old-fashioned social constraints, the genre was distinctive for its sympathetic portrayal of homosexuality. Whether active, repressed or hinted at, gay men were central characters in *Brideshead Revisited*, *Another Country*, *A Month in the Country* and the Merchant–Ivory film *Maurice* (1987), which cast Hugh Grant in his first major role. The problem was that the intended message of all these films – that love and emotion should conquer traditional norms and mores – got diluted by the sumptuous and aesthetically pleasing nature of the production, ensuring that the films ended up indulging and celebrating the look and feel of a stultifying social order. This might explain their appeal to otherwise conservative and nostalgic audiences and the consequent dislike for such 'heritage' films on the part of liberal-leaning critics, who might otherwise have endorsed their message of social and sexual liberation. It was certainly the case that their popularity coincided with one of the eighties' most striking cultural phenomena, the admiration for old-fashioned class distinctions and dress sense embodied by the Sloane Rangers.*

While the Sloane Ranger paraded the values of 'old money', the young upwardly mobile – 'yuppies' for short – were the *arrivistes* on the lookout for new wealth. Sharing the attitude pervading theatre and literature, British film-makers did not trouble to portray this aspirational culture in a positive light. The lacuna was filled by Hollywood, where the overlooked wise guy who seeks a just reward for having a clever idea was always an essential component of the American Dream. Among the social-aspiration films that Hollywood successfully exported to Britain were *Trading Places* and *Risky Business*, which were both released in 1983, and *The Secret of my Success* in 1987. There was no British equivalent to the roles played in these upbeat comedies by Eddie Murphy, Tom Cruise and Michael J. Fox. Indeed, it is noticeable that in eighties British films, black tie is worn in the context of class-based historical costume dramas, while in the Hollywood films being made at the same time the tuxedo continually pops up in contemporary settings and is worn as a badge of modern smartness by young and old alike, regardless of the social circumstances in which they find themselves at the start of the movie. Denied aspirational role models by their own cinema, Britain's yuppies therefore found affirmation either in the cinema of Reagan's America or in the one sector of their own country's creative arts that did actively seek to glamorize those 'on the make', namely the pop music industry.

The different transatlantic attitudes towards those moving onwards and upwards was also evident in the 'rites of passage' genre. Aside from *Gregory's Girl* (1981), Bill Forsyth's engaging teen comedy of first love in a drab Scottish new town, British film-makers conceded the rich vein of adolescent anxiety to Hollywood. What cinema offered the eighties generation of British teenagers thus transpired to be the growing pains of white, middle-class adolescents going to school in the American Midwest. The profitability of youthful and family-friendly franchises had been ably demonstrated by *Star Wars* in 1977, and in the eighties by its two sequels, along with the Indiana Jones movies. Introducing the 'Brat Pack' stars, John Hughes's indulgent and sentimental 'coming of age' films *Sixteen Candles* (1984), *The Breakfast Club* (1985), *Pretty in Pink* (1986) and *Ferris Bueller's Day Off* (1986), alongside Joel Schumaker's tale of Georgetown graduates in *St Elmo's Fire* (1985), were box-office hits on both sides of the Atlantic. Even in their country of origin there were those who despaired at their success, the American film magazine *Variety* reviewing *The Breakfast Club* with the ostentatious lament: 'When the causes of the Decline of Western Civilization

---

* See p. 414.

are finally writ, Hollywood will surely have to answer why it turned one of man's most significant art forms over to the self-gratification of high-school-ers.'[64] Yet unlike the most tiresome sequels of the period's youth franchises, which may be summed up by the release in 1989 of *Friday the 13th, Part Eight*, the Brat Pack films were at least gently kooky, wry and charming. In this respect, they were distinct from the one British cult classic of the period, *Withnail & I*, whose student-age audience was drawn to its powerful themes of drink, drugs, friendship, the passing of youth and the fear of failure.

The contrast between the backing and resources offered to Brat Pack film-maker John Hughes and to *Withnail*'s writer–director Bruce Robinson well demonstrated the gulf between the Hollywood studios and those at Pinewood and Shepperton. Having written the Oscar-nominated script for *The Killing Fields*, Robinson was hardly an unknown figure in the British film industry. Furthermore, *Withnail & I* was to be made by Handmade Films, which George Harrison, the former Beatle, had set up in 1979 initially to produce two financially troubled productions, Monty Python's *Life of Brian* and *The Long Good Friday*, and thereafter the equally acclaimed *Mona Lisa* (1986). For all this impressive pedigree, almost everything about the making of *Withnail* was shambolic. Robinson had never directed before and announced on his first day of filming that he did not really know what he was doing. The lead actors were Richard E. Grant, who had only done one small television part before, and Paul McGann, who had television experience but was untried in feature films. As the dimly lit tale of two 'resting' actors at the end of the 1960s took shape, the American executive producer, Denis O'Brien, thought *Withnail* unfunny. Failing in his aim of shutting it down, he tried to limit the damage by cutting its budget to the bare minimum. Ultimately, it cost £1.1 million to make with Robinson, who threatened to quit several times, paying for some of the scenes out of his own pocket. It took the better part of a year to find a distributor. At its launch in 1987, it went largely unnoticed, taking only £500,000 at the box office, and was pulled from cinemas after a fortnight. Only later, and through the haphazard process of word of mouth, did it come to be recognized as one of the jewels of British comedy and regularly cited among the nation's best films of all time.[65] Of course, its quirky Britishness meant it could never have been made by Hollywood, but then, despite everything in its favour, it was nearly not made in Britain either. If it was this difficult to succeed with a peerless script, what hope was there for anything less? Robinson's subsequent directorial work flopped, while Handmade got into financial difficulties and was sold at a knock-down price in 1994.

Handmade's plight, like that of Goldcrest, showed that there was insufficient financial depth to sustain a production company that risked at least one expensive failure (*Shanghai Surprise* did for Handmade what *Revolution* did for Goldcrest). In the space of a few months between 1985 and 1986, most of the British film industry's remaining advantages were swept away. A combination of the strong dollar and a generous tax structure had lured American investment into British films. From 1979 until 1986, film investors had enjoyed a first-year capital allowance which was, in effect, a tax write-off. This tax break was ended in 1985. Investment (much of it American) in British films, which had hit a record £300 million in 1985, fell to £126.5 million in 1988 and by the decade's end was down to a paltry £64.5 million.[66] Part of the rapid decline may be attributed to the depreciating exchange rate for the dollar and to the international Plaza Accord of 1985, rather than to anything specific to the British film industry, though the removal of the tax break clearly did not make British investment easier. Other factors were also significant. In 1986, one of the most important native investors, Thorn–EMI was bought by the Cannon Group, which was owned by the Israeli cousins Yoram Globus and Menahem Golan. Since Thorn–EMI owned 40 per cent of all British cinema screens, as well as Elstree Studios, the takeover had great significance, though the trade and industry secretary, Paul Channon, saw insufficient grounds to refer the matter to the Monopolies and Mergers Commission. In retrospect, this was unfortunate: Cannon was actually nearing bankruptcy and would face investigation in the United States for presenting misleading accounts. As part of the terms of its rescue by Pathé, Cannon asset-stripped its British acquisition, with predictable consequences for the domestic film industry.

Hanging over all these developments was a vast social change manifest in the shutting down of the cinemas. Television's advent had made it inevitable that British cinema-going would decline significantly from its post-war peak (1,635 million admissions in 1946). But the extraordinary boom in home video machine ownership in the early eighties accelerated the trend. One fifth of households owned one by the end of 1982 and more than half did so by 1987. With the number of cinemas contracting quickly and some towns finding themselves no longer served by any picture house, admissions sank to forty-three million during 1984. However, not all the videos being watched in homes would necessarily have been viewed in cinemas. Unlike cinema films, videos carried no age-restricted classifications, leading to a boom in what the press dubbed 'video nasties' – most infamously the rape-revenge flick *I Spit on Your Grave*. In an editorial headlined 'Rape of our children's minds', the *Daily Mail* charged that 'Britain fought the last World War against Hitler to defeat a creed so perverted that it spawned such horrors in awful truth. Now the nation allows our own children to be nurtured on these perverted horrors and on any permutation of them under the guise of "entertainment".'[67] In 1984, the law was duly changed to extend the British Board of Film Classification's remit to cover videos and it established a list of

seventy-four prohibited titles, among them *The Evil Dead*, which ha(
the most rented video of 1983. Whether family-friendly or not, the p..i.er-
ence for watching films at home instead of in cinemas seemed irreversible
unless urgent action was to be taken. Since the 1950s, the Eady Levy had
taken a statutory cut of all cinema box-office receipts, which various government agencies then passed on as a subsidy to those producing British-registered
films. In 1985, the government concluded that the levy was increasingly
funding distribution rather than production, while acting as a tax on already
hard-pressed cinemas. The levy was abolished, along with the government's
subsidy-distributing body, the National Film Finance Corporation.

Thereafter, cinema-going, as distinct from film-making, made a partial
recovery. Cinema admissions went back up to 94.5 million in 1989 and
continued to climb thereafter. The Eady Levy's scrapping may only have
made a small contribution to this turnaround; other factors included the
waning sense of novelty in home video watching and the construction of
new, often out-of-town, American-style multiplexes which increased screen
choice and combined cinema with other youth-oriented facilities like
ten-pin bowling and fast-food restaurants. The government, meanwhile,
drew the same enmity from film-makers as it did from the other sectors of
the creative arts. It was hardly surprising that resentment should be expressed
at Britain's lack of state support, given the extent to which it was still available in other European countries. There, film was viewed less as a commercial
enterprise than as a cultural treasure, which required protection from the
very market forces that the Thatcherites believed offered the only viable
means of funding films (like other cultural creations, such as books and
newspapers) in the long term. Both sides found arguments to back up their
principles. Subsidies had failed in the seventies to save the British film industry from producing both low-quality and loss-making movies; and the same
was true of attempts to reintroduce tax breaks and distribute funds through
government quangos in the first decade of the twenty-first century. The
occasional British successes of the 1990s and 2000s were largely the product
of American funding and were only British in the sense that British talent
helped make them. This was not really a fundamental change, but a historic
continuity that pre-dated the eighties: in 1967, 90 per cent of the finance for
British film production was American.[68] In other areas of the arts, the
Thatcher government was able to claim it had created an economic climate
in which lower taxes on wealthy individuals and corporations had encouraged a significant increase in philanthropy and sponsorship for the arts. It was
a significant cultural shift to which home-grown film finance remained
largely impervious. The United Kingdom remained essentially unchanged
from its status in 1979 – a country of significant film-makers in search of a
significant film industry.

10 STYLE OVER SUBSTANCE?

After Modernism

In eighties Britain, a surprisingly violent cultural battleground proved to be a tussle over architecture. Across the visual, literary and performing arts, strong and at times vitriolic dissent was expressed against Thatcherite attitudes. The political and cultural agendas occupied different, exclusive and mutually antagonistic spaces. Architecture was the artistic exception. There, the defenders of the post-war consensus lost their cultural predominance and were thrown into retreat by an insurrection mounted from inside as well as outside their profession. The assault brought together conservatives with a big as well as a small 'c' who succeeded in their aim of breaking up the monopoly of modernism.

Sent reeling by these counter-revolutionary forces, the immediate response of architectural progressives was to blame their defeat on the Prince of Wales, whose interference seemed to them a misuse of royal influence so egregious that it bordered on the unconstitutional.[1] They accused Prince Charles of whipping up the popular press and untutored opinion to foist timid traditionalism upon the architectural profession's innovators. Unsurprisingly, His Royal Highness became a hate figure to those who, having spent at least six years in training, deeply resented having their work insulted by a public figure whose only qualification was that he was the heir in a hereditary monarchy. However, the allegation of elitism cut both ways. The prince's attack wounded its target precisely because he skilfully articulated the contempt that a large section – perceived to be the overwhelming majority – of the population supposedly felt for those who had shaped the post-war built environment. What was more, the lofty condescension the architectural profession meted out to this princely-led peasants' revolt only reinforced the belief that they were indeed an insulated and haughty club, from whom it took constant pressure to extract so much as a whimper of contrition for even the most egregiously dispiriting creations.

Few cultural ideologies have swept aside their competition more completely than modernism. Its central tenets were inflexible and uncompromising: the design and appearance of a building must express the industrial means of its production; form must follow function; decoration, unless serving some useful purpose, was unacceptable. Le Corbusier had pronounced that a house was a 'machine for living in' and machines had no use for artifice that concealed the beauty of pure form and design. To those who remained unconverted, modernism resembled a puritanical religion, obsessed with 'purity' or 'integrity' of design and 'honesty' towards materials – language that suggested the art of building was one giant fight against such immoralities as historical reference, debased 'homeliness', pastiche or a sense of place. Between the 1940s and the 1970s, this modernist ideology determined the aesthetics of the capitalist West as completely as Marxism–Leninism framed the only officially recognized mode of thought in communist societies. Save for some war-damage repair work and the occasional extension to a boarding school or a venerable college, scarcely a single public building of importance was erected in Britain in the thirty years after 1945 that did not conform to the modernist mantra. The movement's theorists argued that this monopoly was not the triumph of their particular style but rather a victory *over* style. After all, from the 1840s to the 1940s, British architecture had been a continuous style war – classical, Gothic revival, Greek revival, Ruskin-inspired Venetian Gothic, Arts and Crafts, art nouveau, art deco and so on. Modernism's rejection of non-functional decoration very abruptly and effectively ended this fashion show of fancy dresses. The extent to which modernism's monopoly over expression was finally challenged in the 1980s may be gauged by the diversity of styles that suddenly jostled, often self-consciously, for attention during the decade: high-tech, neoclassical, vernacular, postmodern. Having disappeared for forty years, style – with or without substance – was back.

While it was the Prince of Wales's chastisements from 1984 onwards that particularly irked modernist architects, he was the follower rather than the setter of a trend. The intellectual case against the modernist monoculture had been ably and succinctly made in 1977 by the Cambridge art historian, David Watkin, whose *Morality and Architecture* drew what, for modernists, were uncomfortable parallels with the Victorian moral self-certainties of the Gothic revivalists. For the lay person, opposition to modern developments bulldozing their way through charming old terraces and communities was perhaps most poignantly expressed by the poet laureate, John Betjeman. During the 1970s, the conservation movement had begun to fight back against the developers as popular anger mounted at modernism's unsubtle building materials, insensitivity to setting and 'futurist' priority for cars over pedestrians. What was more, modernism had sown the seeds of its own destruction. Its lack of interest in the skills of the craftsman bequeathed mass-produced, prefabricated methods of construction with materials that were ill adapted to the British climate. The result, too often, was buildings that fell apart. The functional quickly ceased to function.

Nevertheless, this failure of practicality and the growing chorus of critics played only a part in modernist architecture's retreat during the eighties. Like so much else in the decade, the main cause was the preference of private enterprise over the state. The spending restraints imposed first by the Callaghan government and continued under Thatcher massively restrained the public sector's role as the great patron of modern architecture. Since the Second World War, national and particularly local government had sponsored vast building programmes as the welfare state took shape in steel frames and concrete. Huge housing estates as well as new schools and hospitals were needed. With local councils adjudicating on the appropriateness of their own schemes, the demolition of whole town centres was sanctioned, to be replaced with new amenities, civic centres and offices for the burgeoning bureaucracy. Local authority bodies like the London County Council architects' department became giant employers of like-minded modernists who were given the chance to master comprehensive redevelopment. Modernism was a neat solution on economic grounds, since it promised easy-to-assemble and relatively cheap construction techniques which allowed councils to do more for less. Its historically liberated form also appealed at a visceral level to those who looked at the presumed elitist manifestations of the country's class-ridden past with distaste and could not wait to replace them with a more egalitarian industrial aesthetic. Now, central government's efforts to balance its budgets withdrew the grants that were needed for local government to continue in this fashion. In 1979, the multi-storey concrete Alexandra Road complex in Camden proved to be the end of the road. It was the last of Britain's vast housing estates to come out of a local authority planners' department.

Denied a ready public sector patron naturally sympathetic to modernist design, architects were now at the mercy of commercial tastes. While there had long been a market in speculative office blocks, architects found themselves being commissioned to design shops, bars and restaurants – jobs that in the 1960s would have been considered beneath a self-regarding architect's dignity. Yet Julyan Wickham's work on the City of London chain of Corney & Barrow wine bars and the Kensington Place restaurant in Notting Hill Gate exemplified all that was best in the marriage of architecture and interior design, demonstrating that identifiably modern spaces could – in the vogue of the decade – be luxurious rather than utilitarian. Other architects chose to work alongside conservation projects, producing harmonious new works together with extensions and improved facilities whose intent was not to replace the past but to give it new vitality. Thirty years later, such an approach might not seem very remarkable, but in the early eighties it was tantamount to gross insubordination since it ran counter to the modernist creed that the test of a great building was that it fitted perfectly its purpose, and once that purpose had gone there was no longer any point in maintaining the building.

Liberated from such shibboleths, disused and derelict industrial buildings like the Albert Docks in Liverpool and London's Docklands were converted into expensive office, retail and residential accommodation, where previously they would have been visited only by the wrecking ball. Importantly for architects, the revitalization of these newly fashionable areas also ensured the commissioning of new structures. Along the Thames, the endeavours of Piers Gough's CZWG practice to introduce innovative, quirky additions to the gaps at China Wharf near Butler's Wharf caught the imagination sufficiently to appear on the cover of the London telephone directory – an extraordinary achievement for a block of offices and flats only one year old.[2] The development exemplified the new spirit in architecture: uniformity was out, eclecticism was in.

The notion that art involved a search for ultimate truths was mocked by such a mishmash of styles and reference points and by the introduction of humorous touches. Yet while the replacement of local authority patronage by the private sector dealt a numbing blow to the austere modernist language that had ruled previously, it also provided the money for a new form of modern architecture – high-tech – whose masters included Richard Rogers, Norman Foster and Michael Hopkins. From a distance, high-tech architecture seemed like an industrial look for an increasingly post-industrial Britain. Examined more closely, the shiny elements revealed a commitment to technology and innovation that, as a symbol of the age, ought to have delighted the prime minister herself.

In some respects, high-tech designers had digested the lessons of modernism better than the modernists themselves: their buildings truly were machines for living, their form stressing how the building worked, with features made out of those functioning parts – like pipes and cables – that even sixties modernists had tended to hide from view. Unlike the standard sixties constructions though, high-tech architecture necessitated both expertise and expense, since cheap prefabrication and poor materials would quickly transform the cutting-edge to the cheap and tatty. It was a style ideal for wealthy private sector companies seeking to draw attention to themselves. It was not for clients who could ill afford large maintenance costs, like Britain's public sector.

For high-tech, the top of the market was reached when the HSBC skyscraper by the British architect Norman Foster was completed in Hong

Kong in 1986. It was an extraordinary office tower, rising as if on giant cranes with struts providing powerful cross-bracing for the floors. At £800 million, it was in absolute terms the most expensive building that had ever been built. More significant from mainland Britain's perspective was Richard Rogers's Lloyd's Building in the City of London, also finished in 1986. Coming in at £186 million, it almost seemed like a bargain by comparison. That price tag was misleading, however: it had significant long-term over-heads, for if not kept in pristine condition it would soon have resembled an inner-city oil rig. Twelve storeys of open-plan offices rose as galleries around a magnificent atrium whose appearance referenced Joseph Paxton's Crystal Palace. With Lloyd's, Richard Rogers had produced not just a machine for working in but the closest an insurance clerk could get to pacing around inside a human body. Its functioning organs were on full outward display: shining pipes resembled arteries and veins, while prominent ducts and exhaust pipes acted as a respiratory system and extracted waste. Instead of their usual position at the core of a building, lifts – made of glass – shot up and down the exterior, providing a constant sense of drama to a building alive with incident. It was, of course, too over-animated for some tastes. 'Poor old Lloyd's,' sighed one underwriter when he looked at his shiny new office, 'after three hundred years . . . we started off in a coffee-house and finished up in a coffee percolator.'[3] But the nods to the past remained. As a *pièce de résistance*, an original eighteenth-century dining room designed by Robert Adam was reassembled on the eleventh floor. Completed in the year of Big Bang, if any structure in Thatcher's Britain might be singled out as the icon of the age, the Lloyd's Building was surely it.

Conservatism in 1980s architecture, nevertheless, typically manifested itself in something rather less of the moment, for it was also the decade in which neoclassicism was resurrected from the doldrums in which it had lan-guished for the previous forty years. That a classical revival was under way was apparent as early as 1981 with the first major exhibition of the work of Quinlan Terry. Terry was a pupil of Raymond Erith who, almost alone among the architectural profession of the 1950s and 1960s, had persevered with Georgian classicism. Indeed, believing that the classical orders were divinely ordained, Terry was perhaps even more certain of the rectitude of his own stylistic preference than were the modernists of theirs.[4] He, too, was a fundamentalist, reluctant to compromise. Prolific throughout the eighties, much of this tweed-suited classicist's work involved designing country houses, a process critics sneered at as the nouveau riche's efforts to acquire the trappings of 'old money' through the buying of fake heritage. Terry's commissions included a summer house at Michael Heseltine's stately pile in Oxfordshire. An obvious choice, no doubt, for a man sniffed at for being a social arriviste who 'bought all his own furniture'.[5]

That Quinlan Terry's classicism found favour with those with private fortunes to spend confirmed the suspicions of dissidents who viewed the Thatcher phenomenon as a reactionary rather than a revolutionary process. At the peak of the Callaghan government's high taxation policies in the 1970s, Terry had designed a classical column in the grounds of the Hampshire home of Lord McAlpine (subsequently the Conservative Party's deputy chairman) bearing a Latin inscription that, translated, read: 'This monument was built with a large sum of money that would otherwise have fallen sooner or later into the hands of the tax-gatherers.'[6] It was to Terry that Margaret Thatcher, supposedly careful with the taxpayers' money, turned when commissioning the restoration of the three state drawing rooms at 10 Downing Street in 1988. Few architects of any age receive such important political commissions, and the result was an elaboration of William Kent's original eighteenth-century interiors. After viewing the refit, the former resident, Harold Macmillan, mumbled archly that it reminded him of Claridge's.

Terry nonetheless proved to be more than a mere eccentric catering for a select right-wing clientele with expensive, if not progressive, tastes. That neoclassicism was again becoming a serious artistic movement was demonstrated by the major public buildings commissions reaching his bucolic Dedham Vale practice. At Downing College, Cambridge, he built additions to William Wilkins's original Greek-classical campus, including a Greek revival library and the Howard Building, which continued Wilkins's elegant restraint on one side only to give way to a fussy version of Palladianism on the other. Those who could get beyond the stylistic assertions were forced to conclude that as a lecture and concert hall it worked perfectly, with excellent acoustics.[7] Terry had been chosen by the college not just because he worked within the classical medium but because his use of traditional materials meant fewer long-term maintenance problems – elsewhere in Cambridge, modernist buildings were already beginning to fall apart, landing the university with huge repair bills. Terry used practical arguments for traditional building materials, emphasizing their durability and energy-saving properties. In doing so he proved unusually ahead of his time, anticipating the environmental concerns that hit the building industry in the early twenty-first century.[8]

Terry's most significant commission proved to be the redevelopment of the Riverside at Richmond between 1983 and 1988. Fronting on to the river Thames, it was a prime – perhaps *the* prime – site in the affluent borough, a site that, all too tellingly, had suffered years of planning blight and decay. Restoring some of the pre-existing buildings and adding his own, Terry created an extraordinary complex for office, residential and recreational uses. Part Georgian, part Italianate eighteenth century in inspiration, had it existed when Canaletto passed by in the 1740s it would surely have provided subject matter for one of his canvases. Rising confidently from the riverbank, it was a composition in warm red and yellow brick and stucco plastering, with stone detailing, columns, an internal courtyard and even a fountain. Critics leapt to point out its dishonesty, for it was an elaborate fake in which classical facades concealed modern office interiors and the neo-Georgian sash windows were pushed shut when the air conditioning was switched on. These compromises to the modern world were not Terry's own preferences but requirements forced upon him by the developers' brief. Unperturbed by the dishonesty of aesthetic compromise, the development proved noticeably popular with the public, who took to it as a pleasing and in-keeping addition to their elegantly old-fashioned neighbourhood and the perfect backdrop to a riverbank promenade. Not just popular with locals, it proved to be one of a relatively small number of eighties buildings that attracted large numbers of tourists from almost the moment the scaffolding came down.

The Prince of Wales's admiration for the classical pretensions of Richmond's Riverside was, of course, reason enough for the architectural establishment to hate it. Their distinctly non-deferential animosity towards the heir to the throne had been aroused by a speech he delivered at the 150th anniversary dinner of the Royal Institute of British Architects (RIBA) at Hampton Court Palace in May 1984. Rather than pander to the mood of self-congratulation, the prince threw oratorical stink bombs, chastising what he saw as the profession's forty years of arrogant disregard for place, scale and the public's wishes. The particular target for his ire was the striking and una-bashedly modernist design that Ahrends, Burton and Koralek (ABK) had proposed for the extension to the National Gallery in Trafalgar Square. He likened it to 'a carbuncle on the face of an old and much-loved friend'.[9]

The 'carbuncle' reference was a potent phrase which left the RIBA audi-ence spluttering at their guest speaker's impertinence. With that one royal sentence, ABK's scheme for the National Gallery extension was wrecked. Emboldened by his success in speaking truth unto power, Prince Charles intervened again three years later in an effort to scupper proposals for a site considered even more sensitive than Trafalgar Square. This was Paternoster Square, the area surrounding St Paul's Cathedral. Reduced to rubble by the Luftwaffe, it had been rebuilt after the war with utilitarian office blocks of such breathtaking banality that they had daily tested the ingenuity of photog-raphers trying to get Sir Christopher Wren's baroque masterpiece in the picture and the encroaching slab blocks out of it. The laity's excitement that the dismal offices were to be demolished soon subsided when the replace-ment proposals by Arup Associates turned out to show little more regard for the historic setting. 'Surely here,' protested the prince in another widely reported speech, 'if anywhere, was the time and place to sacrifice some

profit, if need be, for generosity of vision, for elegance, for dignity; for buildings which would raise our spirits and our faith in commercial enterprise, and
prove that capitalism can have a human face.'[10] He backed up his words with
support for an alternative scheme – John Simpson's Georgian-style reworking of the area in elegant brick, which followed more closely the old medieval
street plan. The London *Evening Standard* and public opinion, when asked to
consider the two alternatives, weighed in heavily in support of Simpson's
scheme. In 1988, a slightly chastened Arup submitted redrawn plans which,
while modern in execution, at least made a passing semi-classical nod to the
setting. But it was still not contrition enough. This plan, too, fell by the
wayside. The prince on the warpath had claimed a second scalp.

By now, Charles was making the most noteworthy royal intervention in
British life since Edward VIII had opted to marry the woman he loved. It
seemed that scarcely a major new development could proceed without being
weighed against what His Royal Highness/popular opinion – the two were
generally conflated – either thought or could be presumed to think. More
precise elaboration on the heir to the throne's opinions was provided in
October 1988 when six million viewers watched him broadcast his ninety-
minute *Vision of Britain* on BBC 1's Omnibus programme. Its themes were
expanded as a major exhibition at the Victoria and Albert Museum the following year, complete with a ten-point manifesto and an accompanying
book. His request list included the restoration of the human scale in domestic building (ascending according to the structure's public importance), the
rediscovery of a sense of enclosure and intimacy, the use of local building
materials, visually pleasing decoration and a respect for setting. The past was
to be learned from, not discarded in pursuit of 'abstract principles'. The
exhibition attracted packed crowds, with most of those who left comments
supporting the prince's agenda, while his accompanying book was a best-
seller. At a time when architecture books rarely had a first print-run in excess
of three thousand, Prince Charles's was two hundred thousand.[11] Having
caught the popular mood, the prince's sentiments were picked up and
echoed by the prime minister. Thatcher devoted an entire section of her
1987 party conference speech to lambasting the 'folly . . . incredible folly' of
'the planners [who] cut the heart out of our cities. They swept aside the
familiar city centres that had grown up over the centuries. They replaced
them with a wedge of tower blocks and linking expressways, interspersed
with token patches of grass and a few windswept piazzas, where pedestrians
fear to tread.' To this she added the accusation of a left-wing political
agenda, which the prince had been unable to articulate: that the planners'
creation of the 'urban utopia' without 'a pub or corner shop . . . snuffed out
any spark of local enterprise. And they made people entirely dependent on
the local authorities and the services they chose to provide.'[12]

Realizing the ground was slipping from under them, the modernists mounted a desperate rearguard action. The designer of the new British Library, Colin St John Wilson, and the influential critic Martin Pawley compared their future sovereign to Hitler, claiming he had a Nazi approach to aesthetics. For good measure, Pawley added an unflattering comparison to Pol Pot.[13] At a slightly more elevated level, in 1989, RIBA's president, Maxwell Hutchinson, wrote a short book *The Prince of Wales, Right or Wrong?: An Architect Replies*. Needless to say, the architect found the prince wrong, with Hutchinson thundering that 'the intervention of the Prince of Wales has made honourable that which would have been considered cowardly half a century ago: the renunciation of the new in favour of the old'.[14] Hutchinson was an engaging interlocutor whose personal preference for archaic three-piece quality tailoring sat ill with his argument for functional modernity. Yet so admiring of the latter was he that he even compared St Paul's Cathedral unfavourably with Denys Lasdun's concrete National Theatre on the South Bank, which, being more honest to its design, was therefore a better building. Clearly, between the architectural old guard and popular opinion there was to be little meeting of minds. But it was clear which of the two entities considered itself to be on the defensive. At any rate, Pawley may have compared the Prince of Wales to a succession of homicidal dictators, but he owed his job as architecture critic of the *Guardian* to him. It was in response to the new-found public interest in architecture following the prince's intervention that the newspaper created the position.[15]

Po-Mo – The Spirit of the Age

The rout of the modernists was never more evident than in the long, forlorn campaign of the property developer Peter Palumbo to have a skyscraper erected at No. 1 Poultry, adjacent to the Mansion House, right in the very heart of the City of London. The glass slab had been designed back in 1958 by Mies van der Rohe, its sleek, if unimaginative, lines closely resembling his Seagram Building in New York. Despite Palumbo's team of experts who earnestly espoused the need for Britain to gain a posthumous gift from the world-renowned master of glass and steel – 'international' chic – two separate public inquiries rejected the plan. Yet the result was not a reprieve for the Venetian Gothic Victorian building that the conservationists wished to preserve on the site. After a long fight, it eventually fell victim to Palumbo's next proposal, a building as strikingly different from Mies's vast glass slab as could be imagined. Rather than a skyscraper, Palumbo promoted a ground-scraping complex of offices, shops and restaurant roof gardens designed by James Stirling. It was not another post-dated exercise in modernism but an essay in postmodernism – perhaps the most recognizable building style of Thatcher's Britain.

Postmodernism (Po-Mo for short) was not just synonymous with Thatcherism because of its ubiquity during the eighties. It was an unashamedly commercial style, displaying just the sort of brash transatlantic characteristics of style over substance that the decade's critics found so irksome. Where the modernists had offered sober truths in untreated concrete, the postmodernists proffered humour and a riot of polychromatic frontages. Po-Mo offices regularly boasted clip-on facades of polished, but extremely thin, granite panels bolted to a steel frame. This superficiality – in effect, architectural wallpaper – was attacked by both extremes. Prince Charles thought it looked cheap and failed to use traditional materials, while the modernists continued to regard any form of exterior frippery, be it cheap or expensive, as deceitful. In reality, postmodernist structures were often erected using similar techniques to sixties buildings and were merely employing different outer-surface materials for that most modernist of structural devices, the curtain wall hung from the steel frame. Drawing the inevitable conclusion that appearance was therefore more important than reality, recladding sixties buildings with the new shiny surfaces became a vogue. Cash-strapped local councils joined the fashion. Recognizing that rebuilding Britain's failing housing estates was beyond their budget, it was a much quicker fix to just stick Po-Mo's exterior decor and bright colours on to sixties concrete slab blocks. The result was cheap and cheerful – the 'regenerated' housing estates coming to resemble a pale and sickly old man given several sessions on a sun-lounger in order to create an impression of rosy good health.

Since postmodernism's departure from modernism was more on the surface than deep-rooted, the real differences were of tone and temperament. While the architects of the sixties imagined their austere, 'honest', egalitarian structures were in the spirit of the age, those growing up in that decade were imbued with a sense of irony and lack of deference and exposed to the influences of garish advertising and pop art. By the eighties, this generation had come of age and Po-Mo was the result. Vulgarity abounded in this reaction against modernism's puritan strictures, and when all subtlety was abandoned the results were not so much amusing as plain silly. Terry Farrell's TV-am headquarters by Camden Lock resembled a 1930s corrugated-metal Hollywood film lot, complete with giant egg cups to symbolize its occupants' early morning broadcasting role. Uninhibited, showy and impolite – these were more good reasons for the Prince of Wales, with his emphasis on aesthetic good manners, to dislike the style.

Worse, when Po-Mo adopted classical motifs it succeeded only in parodying them. Writing the soundtracks for Peter Greenaway's films during the eighties, the composer Michael Nyman showed himself an exponent of borrowed baroque themes, clipped and orchestrated to a minimalist score. Po-Mo architecture followed a similar rhythm, in which the minimalist structures of the modernist movement were erected with baroque shoulder padding. Strength and bulk were finessed with the addition of extremely basic triangular porticoes and baubles the size of giant cannonballs. It was like the Blenheim Palace architecture of Sir John Vanburgh, but built from Lego. Status symbolism was most in evidence in the huge entrances which all but proclaimed to those who passed in: 'You Have Arrived.' Not for eighties Po-Mo the obscure, unassertive entrances of sixties public sector commissions, whose outward declamations were so coy that signposts with arrows were needed to indicate to visitors where the front door might be. With Po-Mo's great monuments to bombast, there was never much doubt.

It was a postmodern take on classicism, rather than the scholarly exercises in the ancient orders by the likes of Quinlan Terry or John Simpson that the Prince of Wales favoured, that won the battle of Trafalgar Square. While the prince's intervention scuppered the insensitive ABK proposal, the National Gallery's Sainsbury Wing ended up being designed by postmodernism's American pioneers Venturi-Scott Brown. Impressed by the symbolic expressions of Las Vegas's casino architecture, Robert Venturi advocated a 'decorated shed' approach to building, contradicting Mies van der Rohe's famous 'less is more' dictum with his own retaliatory sound bite: 'Less is a bore.' Begun in 1987 and completed four years later, the Sainsbury Wing was in the words of the Po-Mo writer and practitioner Charles Jencks 'the most accomplished pluralist building in London'.[16] It was this very pluralism that united the straighter-laced classicists and modernists in condemnation, equally unamused by Venturi's playful decorative references. These included such heresies as switching classical orders, a cornice that unaccountably petered out, and the stone facade facing Trafalgar Square being exposed as no more than a thin screen by the sheet-glass outer wall of its connecting elevation. Here, indeed, was a classically decorated shed whose theoretical postures may have insulted purists but which succeeded in its purpose as a gallery.

Away from the showpiece commissions, postmodernism also made its presence felt in domestic architecture, and its contribution to the urban landscape was at least jollier than the typically rain-stained grey monotonies erected during the previous forty years. Yellow or warm-cream brick was preferred, providing good cheer with darker-coloured brick bandings deployed to reduce the sense of mass. Nautical touches – familiar to British design in the 1930s – came back into fashion. Portholes punctured Cascades, Piers Gough's whimsical brick-fronted block of flats on the Isle of Dogs. Elsewhere, small square windows, often with blue frames, were in vogue as were prow (V-shaped) windows. Like an acute variant on the oriel window, these protrusions provided articulation to the elevation of buildings and were a particular feature of James Stirling's Clore Wing of the Tate Gallery.* Beside the ubiquitous, cheap-looking, clip-on thin stone panels used to face Po-Mo office buildings, there were occasional triumphs. In Berkeley Square, Lansdowne House (tellingly, the head office of one of the period's most emblematic companies, the advertising firm Saatchi & Saatchi) featured panels cut and mounted to create edges and shadows in an overall effect reminiscent of art deco – unquestionably the historic style that Po-Mo most closely resembled.

The atrium was another common feature of eighties office design. Technological advance and the deregulation of the financial markets created a need for offices with large, open-plan dealing floors. As a result, the width of office buildings expanded. A central atrium provided an obvious solution, penetrating the bulk and letting in natural light to those working in the heart of the building. An atrium also created a magisterially soaring reception area, heightening the occupants' sense of self-importance and projecting the impression of grandeur. A device used for transatlantic shopping malls thus became the customary feature of the successful British company headquarters. Where there was not the space or money for an atrium, atrium-shaped windows were fitted on eighties office buildings across the country. As with so many other architectural developments during the decade, it was in London that the most successful – and least cheaply imitative – examples were built. Immediately following the Big Bang deregulation of 1986, the area of the City around Liverpool Street Station became a giant building site from which rose the Broadgate complex, offering the rapidly expanding financial institutions the floor space and office environment they needed. Alongside Broadgate Street, the practice of Skidmore, Owings and Merrill (SOM) erected a line of offices in the transatlantic Po-Mo style, their oppressive mass broken up by different colours, shiny granite panels and vast atrium-shaped windows. Arup Associates was responsible for the offices around the Broadgate Arena, with atria providing internal light, but displaying a different approach to the outward appearance by hanging the polished clip-on panels more clearly beyond the glass frontages so as to remove any doubt that they had a structural, load-bearing significance. Such a rejection of artifice might have appeased even the most recusant modernist. Broadgate's significance, though, was not just that it provided a lot of suitable office space, but rather the claim it could make to be one of the most successful examples of modern urban-space design. What might in the 1960s have become an empty, windswept piazza was instead given life and drama by a

---

* Subsequently renamed Tate Britain.

colonnaded amphitheatre. Artfully draped with hanging greenery, it providing tiers of spectator-lined bars, cafes and places to sit and eat a lunchtime
sandwich around a forum that in winter became an ice rink. Here was somewhere to sunbathe, picnic, relax with friends – a village green for the
international capitalist community.

In the last three years of the eighties, the City's available office space
increased by one third. Surprisingly, this vast expansion took place after the
Stock Market crash of 1987, not before it. It was in this supposedly post-
party atmosphere that the world's largest property development, Canary
Wharf, began rising from the disused wasteland of East London's Docklands.
As at Broadgate, SOM produced the Canary Wharf master plan. The centrepiece was One Canada Square, a fifty-storey, stainless-steel-clad tower
resembling a shiny Ancient Egyptian obelisk. Designed by the American
architect Cesar Pelli, it was, at its completion, the tallest tower in Europe and
was visible from thirty miles away. Canary Wharf had few discernible reference points to indigenous culture. The look was more reminiscent of
Chicago or Toronto. This was not just because the architects were commissioned by the Canadian property developers Olympia & York. Rather, it
was symptomatic of a style that was essentially an American import to Britain,
designed to appeal to the borderless priorities of international capital. Indeed,
Po-Mo buildings were much more ubiquitous in Britain and America during
the Thatcher/Reagan years than in continental Europe. Yet not only were
such symbols of 'yuppie' confidence as Broadgate and Canary Wharf constructed after the crash of 1987, Thatcher was no longer in Downing Street
when they were completed. The most virile architectural statement of eighties money-making, Pelli's tower at Canary Wharf, was not finished until
1991, when John Major was in Downing Street, the country in the pit of
recession and Olympia & York poised to file for bankruptcy, ruined by what
suddenly – if prematurely – looked like *folie de grandeur*.

The quintessential styles of the eighties were killed off by the recession
that hit the construction industry in the early nineties. When James Stirling's
No. 1 Poultry building in the City was belatedly erected in 1997, it already
seemed curiously out of date, its heavy Po-Mo motifs belonging to an aesthetic crushed under the weight of its own self-parody. One of the most
accomplished of the eighties Po-Mo architects, Terry Farrell, produced
works at the decade's end that included two extraordinary additions to the
banks of the Thames – the new MI6 building (resembling an art deco
version of the temples of Luxor) and the office development of Embankment
Place, whose curved arches rose above the platforms of Charing Cross
Station like the front radiator grille of a 1920s sports car. It was assumed that
Farrell would dominate the British architectural scene in the nineties, but
instead he spent much of it working in Hong Kong. By the time his focus

returned to Britain, minimalism was back at the forefront of design and the near-ubiquitous architect of the age was the high-tech modernist Norman Foster.

So, Po-Mo proved to be a short-lived phenomenon, instantly identifiable as the veneer of Thatcherism. Similarly, the neoclassicists, while continuing to find a niche in the twenty years that followed, failed to realize their critics' foreboding that they would succeed in turning back Britain's architectural clock. Poundbury, Prince Charles's instantly traditional village bordering Dorchester in Dorset, was admired by some, ridiculed by others, but closely imitated by none. It is therefore tempting to see the great architectural brou-haha of the eighties as representing not so much the beginning of new aesthetic trends as a brief excursion down a cul-de-sac. In reality, the intel-lectual substance of the period survived better than the passing styles. For the eighties bequeathed a renewed interest in urbanism. This was an approach to town planning that took into account setting and sought to achieve harmony between old and new by recreating, instead of breaking up, traditional street-scapes and spaces. The emphasis was no longer on riding roughshod over the past with flyovers and massively insensitive stand-alone buildings that made no attempt to respect their historic setting. 'Concrete jungles' ceased to be acceptable, the worst forms of prefabrication and system-building were rejected. In place of the modernists' comprehensive redevelopment, context was prized, old buildings adapted rather than demolished, vernacular touches encouraged in new designs and the scale and mixed-use variety of the street restored. What the eighties taught urban planners was that the architect was not God: new structures did not exist just to be admired in isolation, lifted straight from the plan and imposed upon their surroundings, but were rather a part of a greater whole whose development was organic and reflective of a sense of community. This counter-revolution may not have gone as far as the Prince of Wales dreamt it might, yet in this quiet way the profession's conservatives won a considerable victory over four decades of progressive theory and self-belief.

11 ELECTRIC BAROQUE

Are 'Friends' Electric?

Pop music in the eighties was shaped by three technological advances and by one economic shift within the music industry. The heavy reliance upon the synthesizer rather than the electric guitar gave many of the decade's biggest hits a signature sound that came to be intrinsically associated with the period. Two other technologies mastered were the pop video and the compact disc, both of which changed modes of presentation and delivery. Meanwhile, those seeking an alternative to the mainstream performers and ethos marketed and promoted by the major music companies benefited from a shift in distribution networks which transformed small independent labels servicing niche tastes through mail-order sales into a significant presence on the high street.

Besides these innovations, the eighties marked an ending as much as a beginning in pop music. The effective swansong of vinyl records coincided with the last days in which singles were bought in vast quantities. In 1981, for instance, Altered Images could sell almost four hundred thousand copies of their chirpy jump-around single 'Happy Birthday' and still not reach number one in the charts. Twenty years later, a song that racked up thirty thousand sales could easily expect to top the charts in any one week – an achievement no longer guaranteed to bring in its wake even modest fame, let alone fortune. By contrast, during the eighties, singles chart positions were still taken seriously by listeners and producers alike. Dedicated fans followed their favourite bands' progression through the charts with the same reverence that football supporters' monitored their teams' standing in the league, as if reaching number one was as significant as lifting the cup. The same football-like tribalism extended to youth fashion, with record buyers aping the look of their chosen bands (or 'movements') to an extent that was no longer publicly evident in the two succeeding decades.

Besides the charts, the other mighty – but vulnerable – eighties pop music institution was the BBC. As the broadcaster of Radio 1 and the television shows *Top of the Pops* and (for chart non-obsessives) *The Old Grey Whistle Test*, the corporation exercised extraordinary influence over what music got broadcast nationwide. Over ten million viewers watched *Top of the Pops* every Thursday evening – an eighties family ritual that declined towards the decade's end, then went into terminal collapse, ceasing altogether in 2006. The BBC's only serious terrestrial competition arrived in 1982 with Channel 4's edgier *The Tube*, and it was not until the American pop video channel MTV launched in Britain in 1987 that the real shift in pop broadcasting took hold. Certainly, the proliferation of local commercial radio stations during the 1970s meant that competitive forces were more active in radio throughout the eighties. But even on that medium, the BBC's monopoly of nationwide channels lasted until 1990, when a broadcasting act finally made it possible for the first independent stations – Virgin Radio, Talksport and Classic FM – to enter the market (and of those, only Virgin was pop-oriented). Thus the deregulating spirit of Thatcherism came late to the airwaves and was initially controversial among those who equated choice with diminishing standards – the grounds upon which the Labour Party opposed the Broadcasting Act 1990.

Synth-pop, the most distinctive sound of the eighties, had its origins in the previous decade's musical experimentation. In the months before its withdrawal in 1972, Stanley Kubrick's film version of *A Clockwork Orange* had provided a fleeting image of a future dystopia with its distinctive synthesizer music soundtrack accompanying a concrete-jungle setting – an oppressive estate built on the Le Corbusian principle of 'machines for living'. The estate was actually Thamesmead, though it might easily have been mistaken for the brutalist housing schemes of Sheffield, where Phil Oakey and Martyn Ware formed an experimental group called The Future which subsequently became The Human League. The debt to *A Clockwork Orange* (both the film and Anthony Burgess's book) was obvious, providing the title 'The Dignity of Labour' for the group's second twelve-inch single and also the name Heaven 17 for the breakaway band that Ware was to form following his break with Oakey. But the musically progressive attitude of the original line-up was, if anything, even more aptly conveyed by their first choice of name, The Future. For the tone of the new movement was established by futurism's obsession with technological advance as a means of driving changes that disregarded previous forms of instrumentation and composition. The resulting sound represented not a revival, or reworking, of something that had gone before in pop, but rather a genuine effort to craft something new. And it was timely, for just at the moment that a generation of British teenagers was being introduced to the computer age, either through the BBC Micro in the classroom or their own personal Sinclair ZX Spectrum in the bedroom, a new wave of British groups came up with a computerized futuristic sound for pop music as well.

Synthesizers allowed for processed sounds to be struck from a keyboard. In the seventies they had been large modular blocks whose switches and wires protruded like a 1920s telephone exchange. Unwieldy and expensive, they were used by prog-rock bands to provide typically over-elaborate keyboard breaks in between equally overwrought electric guitar riffs. British composers who mastered the equipment, like Rick Wakeman and Mike Oldfield, used them to create soundscapes that celebrated the Knights of the Round Table or English folk melodies. More significant for those who would make the sound their own in the eighties was the influence from Europe – where the Italian Giorgio Moroder deployed synths to create disco rhythms and the German group Kraftwerk, whose 1977 album *Trans-Europe Express* used only electronic instruments, fashioned a modern, future-oriented look of sharp-cut suits in contrast to the long-haired rocker aesthetic dominating the seventies in Britain. Critically, by the end of that decade innovation and economics had brought the price of the equipment within the grasp of aspiring bands. By 1980, a quality synth – far smaller and more portable than the early contraptions – could be bought for £200, making electronic keyboards no more expensive than some electric guitars. In consequence, the 'do-it-yourself' attitude that had animated the untrained, unschooled, working-class punk bands could now be adopted by those who, while equally making it up as they went along, did not share the Sex Pistols' nihilistic denial of a fulfilling future.

It was a pasty-faced, cold, unsmiling loner with Asperger's syndrome who took the synth sound to the top of the charts in May 1979. The front man for the Tubeway Army was Gary Numan, who had changed his surname from Webb better to convey his sense of being a futurist being. His blood-drained, asexual appearance suited the tone of his hit single 'Are "Friends" Electric?' which was about the cyborgs of a Philip K. Dick-influenced science-fiction novel he had once contemplated writing. His lyrics were those of the isolated outsider, remote from human interaction, a sentiment reinforced by the follow-up hit 'Cars'. Influenced by the novels of J. G. Ballard, this was futurism spoken – for Numan did not do anything as conventional as sing. Rather, he delivered his lyrics in a robotic monotone, unsmiling and, by avoiding gesticulation, consciously conjuring up all the stage presence of a semi-automated mannequin.

With his album *The Pleasure Principle*, Numan created pop music without any of its traditional instruments. Drums were replaced by pre-programmed drum machines, with the orchestral accompaniment created by Moog synthesizers. Gone was the emblem of rock and roll, the electric guitar. In total, Numan's sales exceeded ten million. Yet while his minimalist compositional approach was ultimately stultifying, other acts quickly demonstrated the new genre's adaptability. At exactly the moment that 'Are "Friends"

Electric?' was topping the charts, a Liverpudlian 'new-wave' duo, Orchestral Manoeuvres in the Dark, released their first (appropriately titled) single 'Electricity'. Guitar-free synth music you could dance to had arrived, and during 1981 it transformed pop. Depeche Mode, formed only the previous year in Basildon, had their breakthrough single 'New Life', while the Christmas number one (ultimately selling nearly 1.4 million copies) was the Human League's 'Don't You Want Me'. A ballad about a relationship splitting up that could nonetheless be played on the dance floor and supported by a memorable video whose conceit was to be a video of the group shooting the video. *Dare*, the accompanying album, sold five million records.

At its most basic, synth-pop produced a tinny sound, as if someone had electronically tampered with a glockenspiel and added a drum machine to keep a constant, simple and unvarying beat. The music critics generally hated the pretentious new arrival, not least because they saw it as a rejection of the honest, unapologetically working-class, drum- and guitar-playing acts of the sixties and seventies. Programming synthesizers lacked the energetic physical activity, let alone dexterity, of former days when groups were more properly called bands. Some of the electronic pop upstarts were even wearing suits and crisp, buttoned-up shirts, as if they aspired to be in the professional classes rather than staying true to the blue-collar spirit of denim and rock. Depeche Mode's infectiously poppy 1981 release 'I Just Can't Get Enough' prompted the *Melody Maker* review: 'I can, you will.'[1] Nor was the hostility merely a matter of taste or prejudice. In 1982, with electronic pop dominating the charts, the Musicians' Union took against Numan, Depeche Mode, et al., fearing their synth sound would put 'genuine' instrument-playing musicians out of a job. With Canute-like effectuality, the union tried to issue guidelines insisting that the use of synthesizers for recording sessions and public performance had to be restricted.

If the point of culture had been merely job creation, then the union's concerns would have seemed well placed. Typically, a rock band had four, five or even six members. However, the variety of sounds the synths produced cut down the number of performers needed to front a group. This made duos a common line-up for electro-pop, usually with the extrovert performer singing while the more reticent partner loitered in the background like a computer technician, twiddling knobs and dispassionately hitting the occasional key. Exemplifying this division of labour were Annie Lennox and Dave Stewart of The Eurythmics (commercially the most successful duo in British pop history), Soft Cell's Marc Almond and Dave Ball, and the Pet Shop Boys, Neil Tennant and Chris Lowe. Depeche Mode's Vince Clarke proceeded to be one half of a couple of duos, teaming up first with the singer Alison Moyet to form Yazoo and then with Andy Bell in

Erasure. Meanwhile, synth-pop developed beyond its initial, amateurish efforts, which had appeared to place greater emphasis on the imperative to sound futuristic than to produce catchy tunes. Assisted by ever improving technology, the sound became lusher and more varied. And the lyrics became more meaningful. Depeche Mode started writing songs about greed, racial prejudice and teenage suicide. Soft Cell particularly dispelled the notion that electronic music was lightweight by introducing overtones of sleaze, darkness and despair. Their first hit, a cover version of a half-forgotten sixties soul classic, 'Tainted Love', turned into the world's best-selling song in 1981, going to number one in seventeen countries and lasting a (then) record-breaking forty-three weeks in the US charts. Whatever might be happening to heavy industry's order books, British synth-pop was exporting all over the world.

In fact, fewer band members performing on stage did not actually mean a reduced payroll creating the music. Complex electronic scores called upon considerable technical expertise, necessitating especially long sessions in the recording studio and helping to ensure that the producer could be as important as the singer/songwriters to the sound of a finished album. By 1984, synth-pop's most sought-after producer was Trevor Horn. Fittingly, Horn had burst upon the scene as one half of The Buggles, whose 1979 hit 'Video Killed the Radio Star' contained the prophetic line about how the new technologies would change the medium. After this one-hit wonder (it was number one in sixteen countries), Horn moved from performing to producing. For ABC's *Lexicon of Love* album he assembled a team of programmers alongside the orchestral arranger, Anne Dudley. Produced by Horn, this team formed Art of Noise, a project – rather than a group, in the conventional sense of the term – whose use of sampling and indifference to vocals as lyrics anticipated the dance genre that came to dominate the late eighties and nineties. Yet however ahead of its time Art of Noise might have been, it was another early signing to Horn's label, ZTT,* that really caught the popular imagination. This was a Liverpool band which, having sensibly ditched the name Hollycaust, opted instead to reference Sinatra with the title Frankie Goes to Hollywood.

Horn produced Frankie Goes to Hollywood to such an extent that by the time the completed version of the debut single 'Relax' was finished it contained no trace of any of the actual group's original instrument-playing (besides vocals, their only intrusion on to the completed mix came in the form a sampled recording of them jumping into a swimming pool). Admitting that 'there was no actual playing by the band', Horn nevertheless sought to

---

* ZTT stood for 'Zang Tuum Tumb' from a 1913 Italian Futurist manifesto which described the sound of battle . . . obviously.

qualify the producer's decisive input by observing, 'but the whole *feeling* came from the band'.[2] Released in October 1983, 'Relax' took three months before it became a hit, despite airtime on the BBC. Just as it had crawled into the top ten, the Radio 1 DJ Mike Read spotted that the lyrics were sexually suggestive and promptly ejected the record while it was playing live on his morning show. The surprise was more that it had failed to stir anyone at Broadcasting House earlier (the band had even appeared on *Top of the Pops* the previous week). But once the alarm was raised, Read's Reithian efforts to protect his listeners from what appears to be advice about avoiding premature ejaculation received almost immediate endorsement with a BBC-wide prohibition. The perhaps inevitable consequence was to turn the single into a cause célèbre and a massive hit: it stayed at number one for five weeks in January and February 1984, during which time *Top of the Pops* was embarrassingly unable to play the top of the pops.

Having worked with Malcolm McLaren on the latter's innovative *Duck Rock* album, Trevor Horn had come to appreciate his talent for engineering the sort of publicity that had propelled the Sex Pistols to the front pages of the tabloid press as prize exhibits in the debate over the state of the nation. At ZTT, the role of turning five Liverpudlian wannabes into an exhilarating/dispiriting expression of the zeitgeist fell to Paul Morley, who had already made his name as a *New Musical Express* journalist. Morley oversaw the 'Relax' record cover (the images of sperm and nipple-twisting rather confirming Mike Read's categorizing of the work as 'overtly obscene'). Morley's real moment of inspiration, though, came when he took Katharine Hamnett's idea of sloganized T-shirts and designed a white T-shirt with the slogan in bold black lettering 'FRANKIE SAY RELAX'. During the summer of 1984, Frankie T-shirts were being paraded up and down the nation's town and city centres, spouting forth on all manner of topical issues, including 'FRANKIE SAY WAR! HIDE YOURSELF' and 'FRANKIE SAY ARM THE UNEMPLOYED'.

Frankie Goes to Hollywood's first three singles, 'Relax', 'Two Tribes' and 'The Power of Love' all went to number one, making them the first band to have achieved that feat since Gerry and the Pacemakers twenty-one years previously. This was quite something for a five-man group, two of whose members (Holly Johnson and Paul Rutherford) were unabashedly gay just at the moment when Aids was creating the panic of the age. Devoid of coyness, the 'Relax' video featured Johnson being carried on a rickshaw into a fetish club where he proceeded to toy with a tiger and ride another man. It, too, fell foul of the BBC. Nevertheless, as a purely gay sado-masochist ensemble, Frankie Goes to Hollywood might have enjoyed no more than novelty status. Instead, Morley's promotional skills and the video for 'Two Tribes', in which Ronald Reagan and Konstantin Chernenko lookalikes slugged it out in a boxing ring,* ensured that the band addressed two urgent popular apprehensions of pending annihilation in their first couple of releases. The result was Britain's seventh and twenty-second highest-selling hit singles of all time.

Perhaps this sort of glory was always destined to be fleeting – there is a limit to how many contemporary issues one group can address without standing accused of exploiting grave events in pursuit of chart position. Indeed, as contemporaries of Nena (whose anti-nuclear arms warning, '99 Red Balloons', supplanted 'Relax' at the top of the charts) and Live Aid, Frankie Goes to Hollywood were as much joining the protest bandwagon as driving it. But for a brief mid-decade moment, pop reclaimed its role as a revolutionary youth movement for social and political change. During 1985, with continuing sales of their album *Welcome to the Pleasure Dome* suggesting no diminution in their popular appeal, the group turned down Morley's efforts to market them as The Beatles of the eighties with a feature film aimed at their further promotion – even though Martin Amis was being lined up as scriptwriter and Nicholas Roeg as director. Feeding on their association with impending doom, the film would have cast them as survivors in a post-apocalyptic world.[3] Instead, the group wanted to be masters of their own fate. Content to let Trevor Horn guide their ascent, reaching the summit had dimmed their enthusiasm for continuing to submit to his mentoring, rather as the Sex Pistols had similarly tired of Malcolm McLaren's manipulative style of management. A determination to play live and perform their own music began a process of loss of direction and splits which was speedily followed by a disappointing second album in 1986 and, for Holly Johnson, the onset of an all-consuming legal tussle to be freed from ZTT's stingy contractual obligations. The legal battle was eventually won, but not before the creative momentum had been squandered. Ultimately, without Horn's elaborate and expensive production techniques, Frankie was going nowhere.

Ridicule Is Nothing to Be Scared of

If the pop music of the first half of the eighties had recycled historical categorizations, then 'Relax' would have been an exemplar of modern baroque. This lavish and exhibitionist, bombastic yet effeminate, style had become mainstream by 1983 and naturally suited uncompromisingly exuberant 'out and proud' gay performers like Holly Johnson and Soft Cell's Marc Almond, as well as the far less sexually assertive cross-dresser Boy George, who three times topped the charts. While the lead singer of Culture Club dressed like

---

* See p. 209.

a girl, the suit-wearing Annie Lennox, with her dyed, short hair, emerged as Britain's first successful androgynous female pop star. Indeed, gender-bending was a common look for this electro-pop baroque and could hardly have been better exemplified than by Phil Oakey's haircut, one half of which appeared to belong to a man and the other half to a woman. This seemed an appropriate fashion to accompany a form of music-making that did not involve muscular guitar strumming and drum banging; so wide-spread became the poser-in-make-up look that it did not even necessarily connote homosexuality. After all, it had sprung not just from the seventies glam-rock school of Marc Bolan and David Bowie but also from the decidedly un-camp borstal of punk.

Styling himself Adam Ant, Stuart Goddard was a former art-college punk who had come under the tutelage of Malcolm McLaren. It proved a short-lived association (McLaren lured away Adam's fellow Ants to join the fourteen-year-old Annabella Lwin in Bow Wow Wow, a Burundi-beat band which he hoped would ensure his next lucrative outrage), but it still lasted long enough for McLaren to help shape the romantic-hero appearance that subsequently propelled Adam Ant to prominence. The punk warpaint and earrings were kept, but in place of ripped jeans and safety pins the singer was dressed as if his horse had bolted during the Charge of the Light Brigade. Successive hits came made-to-measure with even more absurd historical costumes: among them a highwayman for 'Stand and Deliver' and a Regency dandy for 'Prince Charming'. The 'Prince Charming' video featured the pop star strutting around a ballroom and intoning 'ridicule is nothing to be scared of', while striking a succession of ludicrously mannered poses, accom-panied by Diana Dors as a fairy godmother. Catchy though Adam and the Ants' music may have been, it was hard not to conclude that the tone was established more by the accompanying visual spectacle than by purely aural considerations.

Yet Adam Ant was far from being alone in blending the aesthetics of punk with those of David Bowie to imbue pop with a theatrical, almost panto-mime, essence. The pioneers of this movement were dubbed the New Romantics, taking punk's spirit of exhibitionism, self-expression and rejec-tion of conformist attitudes and dress sense, while emphatically ditching its accompanying promotion of aggressive, antisocial and crude behaviour. The movement had begun in a small Covent Garden club which opened in 1979, called Blitz. Its doorman was Steve Strange, who determined whose look was sufficiently to his liking to be worthy of entry. Strange's preference was generally for the outlandishly dressed, and the 'Blitz Kids' were often either students at the nearby St Martin's College of Art or shop assistants and clerical workers escaping the tedium of routine by dressing up at night like punks who had somehow either been invited to a 1920s party thrown by the

Bright Young Things or wandered into the Weimar cabaret of a Christopher Isherwood novel. Boys hopeful of gaining entry donned Ruritanian uniforms and other camp fopperies, girls arrived as if ready to strike a pose for Tamara de Lempicka. Exemplifying the gender-bending trend, both sexes slapped on unsubtle quantities of make-up, the definitive look involving geisha-white foundation to create a facial blank canvas on to which dramatic expressions − a raised eyebrow, a frown − or a beauty spot or a circle of rouge could be painted. The chosen few who made it inside found a not-yet-famous George O'Dowd (Boy George) working as a cloakroom attendant dressed either in ecclesiastical drag or as a geisha. The dance floor resonated to the synth-pop sounds favoured by the resident DJ, Rusty Egan, a former drummer with punk bands whose friendship with Strange had started when he lent him his sofa only to find the dosser bringing his extensive travelling wardrobe with him. As Egan later reminisced: 'The song that became the anthem of the club was "Heroes" by Bowie. "Just for one day" you could dress up and be more than what Britain had to offer you.'[4]

Egan and Strange formed their own band, Visage, which in November 1980 scored a hit that helped establish the classic New Romantic sound nationwide. Co-written with Midge Ure and Billy Currie (who would both soon find fame in Ultravox), 'Fade to Grey' was electro-pop at its purest, its art-house pretentiousness assisted by seductive-sounding backing vocals in French. No less (and perhaps more) important, the accompanying video made the powdered face, eyeliner and spiky hairsprayed coiffure of the New Romantic style familiar beyond the confines of the Blitz Club, to *Top of the Pops* viewers across the length and breadth of the country. For the visual splendour and art-pop glamour of the New Romantic groups perfectly suited promotion through music videos, a medium that was only beginning to establish itself and which New Romanticism was now to play such a part in developing. The time was right not least because there was an abundance of creative talent available which, unable to find work in the declining film industry, either had to make exceptionally artistic television adverts or else work on advertisements' natural spin-offs − pop videos.

The distinctive style of the early eighties' British pop video was fundamentally shaped by two directors, David Mallet and the Australian-born, London-domiciled, Russell Mulcahy. Mallet's credits included the extraordinary, discordantly coloured dreamscape accompanying David Bowie's 'Ashes to Ashes' (1980) in which something close to the visual language of Ingmar Bergman's *The Seventh Seal* was reproduced: Bowie, dressed as a clown, is followed by a dark-caped retinue − one of them Steve Strange − pushed onwards by a big digger towards a beach with a black sky. The memorable result represented a considerable artistic achievement given that the necessary post-production technology was in its infancy. It certainly set the bar for pretentiousness – equalled by Mulcachy, who directed The Buggles' futuristic 'Video Killed the Radio Star' (1979), a film-noir setting for the members of Ultravox to tread the moonlit cobbles of Covent Garden (incongruously) singing 'Vienna' (1981), a boater-clad Elton John prancing around the French Riviera to 'I'm Still Standing' (1983), Duran Duran sailing a luxury yacht in 'Rio' (1982) or spinning round on windmills and dodging flying savages in 'Wild Boys' (1984) – the last requiring a set so elaborate that it took up a large part of Pinewood Studios and a $1 million budget. With lesser talents seeking to mimic these videotape masterpieces, the overblown results were ably parodied in the 1982 *Not the Nine O'Clock News* sketch 'Nice Video, Shame about the Song' – a pop video for the imaginary band Lufthansa Terminal, featuring a lake on fire, a stately home, sword-wielding cavaliers, leggy female Nazis and Mallet-esque colour manipulation. In truth, the spoof was no more ridiculous than the video Mulcachy directed that year for Bonnie Tyler's number-one hit 'Total Eclipse of the Heart', in which the back-lit, husky-throated, blonde singer walked dreamily through the dorms of a public school (actually a defunct Victorian Gothic lunatic asylum), while the boys raised black-tie toasts to each other, donned boating jackets, sang in choral surplices, took communal showers and, less explicably, flung themselves about while dancing in karate kit. This was not rock and roll as anyone serious had previously portrayed it.

Instead, the expensive production values that these videos brought to pop turned a medium that had once been a means of working-class expression into a form of dramatic spectacle that aspired to high opera and was certainly as expensive to choreograph. According to taste, this was a betrayal of pop's proletarian roots – to say nothing of punk's cheap 'do-it-yourself' ethos – or a triumphal manifestation of how consumerism and aspiration could make aristocrats of anyone (so long as they had a major record label behind them). Now it was pop stars who performed in dinner jackets (their black bow ties fixed around wing-collars – soft collars being momentarily deemed *too* ordinary) and swung on chandeliers as if they were Oxford undergraduates applying for membership of the Bullingdon Club. Bryan Ferry performed attired as if he was out for a balmy evening stroll along the Promenade des Anglais – a long way from his working-class childhood in Tyne and Wear. Removed from their industrial Sheffield roots, the band ABC did a promo shoot for 'All of My Heart' dressed as country squires and performed the video for 'The Look of Love' in the sort of striped blazers and straw boaters that might have made it into the stewards' enclosure at the Henley Royal Regatta. The video for the atmospheric, nostalgic 'Souvenir' by the electro-pop group Orchestral Manoeuvres in the Dark (OMD) involved tracking shots of the band's two front men, Paul Humphreys and Andy McCluskey, driving a classic convertible sports car around the park at Blenheim Palace, interspersed with footage of Humphreys looking dreamily thoughtful by the Palladian temples of Stowe public school. It was as if these two lads from the Wirral were aping Evelyn Waugh's Sebastian Flyte and Charles Ryder, just at the moment when Granada Television's screen adaptation of *Brideshead Revisited* had brought the privileged friends back into the public consciousness. Whether the conversion of bands from gritty and depressed parts of the country into glamorous toffs was subversive to Britain's class structure or subservient to it depended upon the critic's sense of irony.

More prosaically, promoting pop through images of luxury, stately homes, swimming pools, the Riviera and other exotic destinations may have had almost as much to do with aping recent iconic adverts for products such as Martini. Imagery and lyrics were, in any case, not always in sync. With the noticeable exception of the loner Gary Numan, pop acts openly endorsing Thatcherism were hard to find. Yet even a Sheffield-bred band like Heaven 17 – responsible for the anti-Reagan '(We Don't Need this) Fascist Groove Thang' and other left-wing sentiments – was content to embody the new go-getting spirit of the age. For their 1981 *Penthouse and Pavement* album cover they were drawn as 'yuppies' in City suits agreeing a business deal. Even allowing for a measure of tongue-in-cheek, the impression was of a band embracing the white-collar world and work ethic, tapping on their electronic instruments with the same money-making intent as bankers sitting at their computer keyboards. As Heaven 17's leader, Martyn Ware, explained, this portrayal was really trying to say: 'Let's get rid of all this hypocrisy of "We're artists, we don't care about the money." Let's strip the facade bare and have a look at what's underneath – handshakes, signing contracts, busy-ness.'[5]

Money for Nothing

The baroque bombast of Britain's electro-pop and New Romantic groups drove the country's greatest cultural export during the eighties, with the United States proving the most receptive market. There, the 'English haircut bands', as they were pejoratively termed, filled the void created by disco's decline as the natural alternative to the aggressively heterosexual blue-collar rock scene. Even more than at home, it was in America that the British mastery of pop's visual dimension proved decisive, because the music video channel MTV (which did not arrive in the UK until 1987) was launched in the US in 1981 just as the New Romantic movement was gathering momentum. The video chosen to open the new channel was, appropriately, the Trevor Horn composition 'Video Killed the Radio Star'. Such was the creative superiority – and quantity – of British pop videos at the time that three quarters of those aired in MTV's early years were for

British groups.[6] This was certainly a factor in the extraordinarily successful promotion of Britain's youth culture across the Atlantic: by 1983, British pop groups had secured 35 per cent of the US *Billboard* singles and album charts, and at times made up the majority of top ten acts,[7] an unprecedented level of penetration which exceeded even the glory days of The Beatles and has not come close to being equalled since. Aware that something was in the air, in November 1983 *Rolling Stone* magazine emblazoned its front cover with the headline: 'ENGLAND SWINGS: Great Britain invades America's music and style. Again.' The accompanying portrait of a demurely smiling Boy George provided the double-entendre to the nature of English 'swinging'.

The supposedly 'un-American' effeminacy of the New Romantic groups naturally triggered a backlash from the same quarter that had castigated disco in the seventies. Hard rock was the resistance force. Yet even here, it was British acts like Iron Maiden, Def Leppard and Saxon that took a significant share of the American market as exponents of heavy metal's 'new wave', with the emphasis firmly on power chords, a quick tempo and nods to folk-loric mysticism and manly barbarism. Tellingly, when the Rob Reiner-directed, American spoof 'rockumentary' *This Is Spinal Tap* was released in 1984, the eponymous fictional heavy metal band were British rockers touring America to promote their album *Smell the Glove*. By the second half of the eighties, the joke was beginning to rebound, with American adolescents turning away from imported guitar strummers in favour of the burgeoning heavy metal scene centred on Los Angeles and its headline bands, Metallica and Mötley Crüe. Nor could acts that originated in Barnsley (Saxon) or Leyton (Iron Maiden) convincingly tap the home-town rock environment of which Bruce Springsteen became the undisputed champion with his 1984 tribute to American blue-collar values, *Born in the USA*.

Whether as headbangers or haircut bands, the British invasion discernibly faltered during the second half of the decade, a precursor to its devastating defeat in the nineties when its share of the American market fell towards 5 per cent. One explanation was that British pop, which had been so innova-tive between 1978 and 1984, simply ran out of steam mid-decade. Aside from the enduring success of the Eurythmics' lead singer, Annie Lennox, Britain produced no equivalent to such American female superstars of com-mercial pop as Madonna, Cyndi Lauper, Belinda Carlisle and The Bangles (indeed it was not until the 1996 breakthrough of The Spice Girls that British female acts really achieved sustained success). What was more, the music scene in the US was undergoing a revolution of its own, with the rise of contemporary R&B, hip hop and rap. These African-American street responses inherited rock's 'tell it like it is' lack of deference, crafting an attitude and delivering a message with which the predominantly white bands from Britain could hardly compete for authenticity. Nevertheless, capturing the trend just as it was surging in popularity was the 1983 album *Duck Rock* on which Malcolm McLaren, in an unlikely collaboration with Trevor Horn, travelled to Soweto and New York for inspiration and came back not just with the cheerful hop, skip and jump of 'Double Dutch' but, more importantly, 'Buffalo Gals'. The latter, featuring scratching and hip hop (with break-dancing by Rock Steady Crew on the accompanying video), was a portent of a revolution in the making, one in which Britain would subsequently play little part beyond second-rate imitation.

Instead, the revolution sweeping British music was more of a technological than a compositional nature. In the first half of the decade, vinyl records remained the most popular format, with the traditional 7-inch single being supplemented by the 10-inch EP, the latter especially useful for extended remixes. The subsequent assault on vinyl came from two quarters. The launch of the Sony Walkman, a pocket cassette player with earphones, made viable relatively discreet listening to music on the move. The ease for the listener had repercussions for everyone else inhabiting the public space. To commuters and passers-by offended by the fashion – much exaggerated by the press – for blasting music from a large portable cassette player (nicknamed a 'ghetto blaster') nonchalantly slung over the shoulder or carried under the arm, the Walkman offered at least modest relief, even if its earphones still leaked low but irritating emissions of tinny-sounding noise. Meanwhile, during 1983, compact discs (CDs) and their players started appearing on British high streets. Yet until sales reached a critical mass, album releases continued to be recorded on analogue equipment. What made Dire Straits' *Brothers in Arms* (1985) album special was that it was digitally recorded and produced as a CD first, and in traditional formats second. The result was an international blockbuster and the first CD to sell a million copies, after which the transition to CD purchasing intensified across the country. Three million CD sales in 1985 became 41.7 million in 1987, the year in which the format overtook the LP record. Nevertheless, cassettes were still the most popular music medium.[8]

By then, the British market had also come under the spell of another craze – the compilation album. The concept was hardly new, but until the early eighties the appeal of compilation albums had been limited by internecine wrangling between rival record companies and licensing restrictions that ensured that, for instance, the *Top of the Pops* albums were actually largely the work of session musicians rather than the original artists. This changed in the run-up to Christmas 1983 with the release of *Now That's What I Call Music!* Behind the *Now!* concept was the Virgin Records boss, Richard Branson, who appropriated the title from a vintage advertising campaign for Danish bacon. Featuring artists from his own Virgin label as well as the other leading British record company, EMI, the original *Now!* double album contained thirty tracks, eleven of which had topped the charts. For fans of mainstream pop, this was a treasure trove of riches and the start of a series that duly became one of the most successful and enduring brands in British pop history. The compilation concept even proved capable of being shrunk from album to single format, with two disc jockeys from Rotherham – marketing themselves as Jive Bunny and the Mastermixers – responsible for a string of hits that were no more than segments of Glenn Miller and 1950s rock-'n'-roll classics stitched artlessly together with the bonding agent of a drum machine. It was a sign of mainstream pop's declining creativity that Jive Bunny followed in the footsteps of Gerry and the Pacemakers and Frankie Goes to Hollywood in topping the charts with their first three releases. To add insult to injury, they came within a week of providing the parting number one of the eighties.

Instead, that honour fell to another derivative performance – a reworking of Band Aid's 'Do They Know It's Christmas?' As a tribute to the period's most celebrated attempt to improve the lives of the less fortunate (and to keep the charity money flowing), there was much to be said for the decade ending on this recurring note. Unfortunately, it did so with a version of the song that, put together by the leading producers of the moment, Stock Aitken Waterman (SAW), represented the formulaic and predictable sound to which mainstream British pop had degenerated by the eighties' end. The success of the producing trio of Mike Stock, Matt Aitken and Pete Waterman had begun with Dead or Alive's 1984 hit 'You Spin Round (Like a Record)', though their period of chart dominance only really took off in 1987. Four number ones for SAW acts in that year were followed by an astonishing seven chart-toppers in 1989. This magic touch led to their business being dubbed the 'Hit Factory' – a double-edged compliment since it also conveyed connotations of an assembly-line approach to the craft of music-making. In a similar vein, though rather more flatteringly, the trio's ability to knock out hits also garnered comparisons with Tin Pan Alley. The comparison was one of product as much as song-writing method. The songs, albeit carried along by a typically eighties quick-tempo drum-machine beat, retained the feel of 1950s skiffle tunes, complete with a wholesome quality to the performers selected to be SAW's ventriloquists. A world away from the rude intrusions of punk and heavy metal, the blazer-wearing Rick Astley gave voice to old-fashioned, clean-living sentiments of uncomplicated fidelity and romantic constancy. Jason Donovan and Kylie Minogue had already attracted a considerable television following as the fresh-faced love interest in *Neighbours*, the Australian soap opera that had been airing on BBC 1 since 1986, and Kylie proved to be the only one of

SAW's signings with the staying power not only to outlive the Hit Factory but to move on to greater stardom beyond. Apart from Jason, Kylie and the already established girl band Bananarama, those whom SAW promoted were not obviously burdened with talent or innate charisma. In this respect, SAW's acts foreshadowed the reality-television celebrity scene that all but defined popular culture in the first decade of the twenty-first century. While punk had encouraged the idea that anyone could stand up and perform, regardless of training or technical ability, there was at least the presumption that they would make the effort themselves. The Hit Factory relieved them of this burden, since the producers chose whom they wanted, provided them with a look and a song to sing, marketed them and then dropped them back into the obscurity from which they had been plucked. Such instant and brief gratification helped ensure that by the late eighties, SAW's label, PWL, had become the largest independent record label in the country. The commercial rather than artistic imperative seemed the only objective – which to its enemies perfectly encapsulated what they believed to be the essence of Thatcherism. The embodiment of all that was dispiriting came when SAW, hoping to repeat their early success with Mel & Kim, signed another couple of sisters, The Reynolds Girls. The song written for the two permed-haired Liverpudlian teenagers had as its hook the refrain 'I'd rather Jack than Fleetwood Mac', and was billed as a youthful rebuke to radio stations' preference for playing well-established bands. When performed live, the protest might have carried more weight if the Girls had not had to mime the words.

The Rise and Fall of the Indies

There was another way of doing things. Although PWL was an independent label, the highly commercial, unchallenging music it promoted might as well have come from one of the major record corporations, like EMI, CBS or PolyGram. Yet while so many of those who took pop seriously despaired of the alleged taste-debasing power of the 'majors', the reality was that the 1980s were also a golden age for 'indie' music. The latter tended to persevere with the traditional instruments of drum kits and electric guitars rather than newfangled synthesizers and drum machines. Where the New Romantics paraded like cockatoos in colourful, shiny clothing and puffed-up, hairsprayed coiffures, those signed to independent labels were more likely to be wrapped up against the cold in unpretentious, shapeless garb – drab, dowdy and unapologetically ordinary – or, in the case of the Goths, heavily made-up in funereal style. This was part of a conscious rejection of the optimism implicit in synth-pop's embrace of futurism. Indie bands tended to be pessimistic and backward-looking, siding with the millions who felt marginalized by the onward march of Thatcherism rather than with those flaunting the fact they were doing very nicely out of it. In particular, the indie bands helped perpetuate folk music's legacy of meaningful lyrics rather than the predictable boy-meets-girl simplicities of the mainstream acts. For their focus was on the craft of writing songs with 'something to say' and embodied the supposed purity of impoverished idealists struggling for their art against those who had sold out to corporate money, with its glib cheerfulness, heavy marketing and ostentatiously expensive promotional videos.

Perhaps inevitably, the more the majors took their signings in one direction the more the indies reacted in the opposite direction, with the resulting polarization defining and reinforcing the boundaries of creativity. Yet even among the indies there was a sharp divide between groups whose motivation appeared to be the articulation of socio-political statements and others for whom a catchy hook was a greater priority. There were also two different types of indie label. Until the late seventies, successful indies, like Virgin and Island Records, were supported by funding and distribution deals with the majors. Independent record companies that also had their own distribution networks enjoyed a fringe existence. The company that did most to transform the prospects of this latter category was Rough Trade, and in doing so it helped broaden the market for indie music generally. When Rough Trade started (initially as a shop with a mail-order business in London's then tatty Notting Hill) in 1976, there were about a dozen independent labels in existence. Four years later, there were hundreds. It seemed a genuinely alternative approach to the established 'music business' was under way.

Rough Trade was co-founded by Geoff Travis, a Cambridge graduate who had spent time on his uncle's kibbutz in Israel. Travis ensured that what was technically a private company was nevertheless run like a collective, with democratic decision-making and equal pay for all employees. Even some of the aspirant band members staved off poverty by working on the shop floor and, when the time came for them to release a record, they benefited from the support, advice and mail-order service that the shop provided to get their cheaply produced recordings to a wider audience. In this they were also helped by the open-minded enthusiasm and eclectic tastes of the BBC broadcaster John Peel, whose show on Radio 1 offered those lucky enough to catch his ear the prospect of nationwide attention. The agreements signed after Travis launched the Rough Trade label in 1978 typically involved a fifty-fifty share of the profits with the bands (after manufacture, distribution and promotion costs) and, again unlike the majors, left ownership of the master tapes with the bands rather than the record company. What was more, instead of the indentured labour-like conditions that the majors offered, whereby signatories would be paid large advances in return for being locked into multi-album deals which effectively committed them to meet commercial as much as artistic imperatives, Travis was generally happy to limit his bands' liability to one album at a time and gave them the freedom to follow their own creative path without interference.

The obvious problem with this model was that while notional royalties were potentially considerably better than the usual 10–11 per cent (minus costs) offered by the majors, groups got smaller advances for single-album contracts than for multi-album deals, and inevitably some acts concluded that a little creative compromise was a small price to pay for long-term financial security. Stiff Little Fingers, Cabaret Voltaire and Scritti Politti were among those for whom Rough Trade proved merely a calling card to bigger labels. Their choice was between 'selling out' completely to the major music corporations or switching to indie labels that collaborated with the majors on distribution and other expensively capitalist aspects of the trade. Foremost among the more wordly indies was Island Records. Its founder, Chris Blackwell, having enjoyed an affluent adolescence split between Jamaica and Harrow School, had started off his extraordinary enterprise roughing it as an importer of ska music, before branching out in the seventies with prog-rock bands as well as Cat Stevens and, most lucratively of all, Bob Marley and the Wailers – a signing that all but catapulted reggae from the embrace of the Afro-Caribbean community into the British mass market. Blackwell's eclectic taste and ability to invest in winners was validated again in 1980 when he signed U2, an Irish rock group that had been turned down by every label it had approached and would proceed to take three years before justifying Island's faith with the release of *War*. Thereafter, U2 became one of the most successful bands of the eighties and beyond. Technically, Blackwell's company was ill named because, far from being an isolated outcrop, its reach extended to partnerships with a range of other labels. It was Island that provided the financial support for Trevor Horn to launch ZTT, having already effectively rescued another seminal indie label, Stiff Records. In 1983, Stiff repaid the compliment: with Island having made the injudicious decision to expand into the film-making industry and in need of money, Stiff's co-founder, Dave Robinson, offered funds and Island acquired half of Stiff's back catalogue while Robinson became Island's managing director.

Stiff's rise from trawling through unpromising pub-rock acts to collaboration with a company of Island's standing was built upon success first with Ian Dury and then, crucially, through its signing of Madness, the band responsible for more top-twenty chart hits than any other in the eighties. Madness consisted of seven lads, scarcely out of adolescence, from north London, who enjoyed larking around and playing the music they liked. For them, the formative influence was Jamaican ska, which 2-Tone acts like The Specials had imbued with punk-like fury to create the perfect staccato tunes to which their (mostly white and male) following could bullishly stomp around. Indeed, getting feet moving at live performances was what the music was primarily about, not spending months in the recording studio to craft an over-mastered album that was unplayable on a cramped, beer-stained stage.[9] The additional element came with the accompanying fashion, which harked back to the pre-reggae/pre-hippie 1960s 'rude-boy' look of Jamaican youths and to the British mods: sharp, tailored suits, thin ties, braces, white socks, sunglasses and even pork-pie hats. It was a revivalist style given a timely boost in 1979 by the success of Paul Weller's sharply dressed group The Jam and the release of the film version of *Quadrophenia*, set amid the seaside scuffles of Mods and Rockers fourteen years earlier.

Madness took many of 2-Tone's elements with them when they signed to Stiff Records in 1979, but before long their music had evolved beyond its ska roots into an uncategorizable and consequently timeless pop, whose appeal crossed the generation gap and bridged the deep divides separating the period's rival tribes. Perhaps their own definition of it as the 'nutty sound' could not easily be bettered. Whereas The Specials were racially mixed, rooted in the economic and social problems of the Midlands and committed to writing serious, urgently political songs like 'Ghost Town',* Madness (though appearing at several centre-left benefit gigs) conveyed all the apolitical, carefree good cheer of seven white lads from the greasy spoon and tatty pub end of Camden Town enjoying a good knees-up. The song-writing duties were shared among them – although, while the public quickly recognized the lead vocalist, Suggs (real name Graham McPherson), as the front man, it was the Hornsey art college drop-out Mike Barson, on key-boards, who was the more prolific composer. There was a hint of 1930s music hall about Madness, seeking out laughs by dancing in a silly and un-cool way, even performing a signature 'train' shuffle which resembled the conga for the non-spatially aware. Such exuberance was retained for their low-budget but inventive videos, from the flying saxophonist in 'Baggy Trousers' to the group donning pith helmets and Eighth Army uniforms for 'Night Boat to Cairo'. Old-fashioned and nostalgic at a time when the cultural running was being made by the electro-pop futurists, Madness's emphatic Englishness and unapologetic love of the simple pleasures and mores of working-class culture were equally the antithesis of the operatic pop baroque of the narcissistic, image-conscious New Romantics.

Yet while some of the band's lyrics might just as easily have been croaked out by the then popular pub-piano act Chas 'n' Dave, only the most super-ficial listener could have mistaken Madness for being asinine. True, there was none of the overt, almost preachy, socio-political commentary of The

---

* See chapter four.

Specials' Jerry Dammers (son of a vicar) or The Jam's Paul Weller (son of a taxi driver). Suggs (abandoned as a toddler by his drug-addict father, left school with two O-levels) sang wry, sometimes funny and often poignant observations about the struggles of ordinary life, self-effacingly explaining: 'You should write songs about things you understand.'[10] 'Our House' was a celebration of living in a terrace, exalting if not exactly the property-owning democracy then at least the traditional notion of an Englishman's home as his castle, while 'Baggy Trousers' offered a nostalgic reflection on the missed opportunities of schooldays. Not all the songs came wrapped in such cosy conservatism. 'Embarrassment' was about the social ostracism of having a mixed-race child. 'Cardiac Arrest' described an overworked, white-collar professional having a heart attack on his morning commute. 'House of Fun' – which reached number one in the charts – was obliquely about a blushing youth attempting to buy his first packet of condoms. The BBC, which two years later would ban Frankie Goes to Hollywood's 'Relax' because of its sexual connotations, showed no such qualms about promoting a double-entendre-laden song about prophylactics, though it effectively dropped 'Cardiac Arrest' from its playlist out of sensitivity towards the Radio 1 DJ Peter Powell, who had recently lost a relative.[11]

These were songs and subjects in the tradition of Ray Davies of The Kinks or even Flanders and Swann. And with them, between 1979 and 1985, Madness had twenty consecutive top-twenty hits; indeed, of the seven years over which the band existed, four of them were spent with a single in the charts.* Yet, remarkable though this level of consistency was, it was not the nutty boys of Camden Town but four Mancunians in a traditional guitar and drum four-piece who secured the period's most enduring critical acclaim. At its most hyperbolic, this led to The Smiths being spoken of in the same breath as The Beatles. Although there were some comparisons to be made between the respective song-writing partnerships of Lennon and McCartney and Morrissey and Marr, it was a difficult analogy to sustain. While The Beatles were an international phenomenon, The Smiths, despite tours to the United States, were primarily for domestic consumption: a British band speaking to British adolescents. Musically, they were not innovators, and while guitar bands of the next decade like Oasis cited them as an influence, their legacy produced few noteworthy imitators. Although they thought of themselves as essentially a traditional 'singles' band, they never remotely equalled Madness's success with the format. Despite recording over seventy songs and releasing eighteen of them as singles during a career of less than five years, no Smiths' single climbed higher than number ten in the charts, nor did they produce a song that came to define their age. Rather,

* See Appendix.

The Smiths' appeal was demonstrated by the success of their four studio albums, which reached, respectively, numbers two, one, two and two in the album charts between February 1984 and August 1987.

More than any of their contemporaries, it was The Smiths who epitomized and helped prop up the indie music business – as was evident from the sector's troubled fortunes after the group eventually walked out on it. Rough Trade had been close to bankruptcy when in 1983 The Smiths' twenty-year-old guitarist and song-writer, Johnny Marr, approached Geoff Travis with a demo tape. Travis's offer of a £22,000 advance stretched to the limit the sums he was prepared to commit to new acts, but it proved sufficient. Though the one-year-old band was already attracting interest from other A&R men, their decision to sign with Rough Trade was a clear vote of confidence in the ability of a supposedly non-commercial label to propel the four Mancunians to the top – where, with remarkable self-confidence, they already believed they belonged. And thanks to the ensuing album sales, they proceeded to help keep Rough Trade afloat at a time when a host of unsuccessful signings had risked its future. It was a salvation for which many other independent labels – including Factory Records – were grateful, given their own dependence on Rough Trade distribution.

Of course, to speak of The Smiths' significance purely in business terms is to miss their point. Johnny Marr was an admirer of the song-crafting skills of Leiber and Stoller, and the chord changes and complexity of his compositions returned rock to a period before its subjugation to the primitive impulses of punk. That The Smiths broadened the parameters of rock music's message was largely the work of the band's singer, front man and lyricist, Morrissey. Preferring to be known only by his surname, Steven Patrick Morrissey was an unemployed writer of such underappreciated tomes as *Exit Smiling* (a digest of Hollywood's also-rans) when Marr first approached him to join his band. As Marr reflected five years later: 'On the face of it we wanted to ditch everything that people superficially think is rock 'n' roll – leather trousers and long hair and drugs – but the most important aspect of rock 'n' roll, the gang mentality, with something exclusive to say and the arrogance, was our forte and still is.'[12] This credo forced Marr to suffer for his art, as he later admitted: 'All through that time what I wanted to talk about was clothes, football and smoking pot. I felt I had to keep that side away in a sense because it wasn't what the group was about.'[13] The discipline was less of a struggle for the bookish loner Morrissey, whose very un-rock-'n'-roll stage persona involved sporting a rockabilly quiff and NHS glasses, throwing gladioli at the crowd and breaking into the sort of falsetto warble that was wholly at odds with what was expected from northern guitar bands.

The doctrine of Morrissey and Marr rejected the overbearing posturing of traditional rock groups no less than the pretentious art-college posing of the synth-pop duos and New Romantic dandies. Calling their band The Smiths was a conscious declaration of ordinariness, and they were even reluctant to accompany their singles with videos – though they eventually relented, and even called upon the directorial talents of Derek Jarman, video never became a core component of their promotion. They disarmed the testosterone-charged rebelliousness of rock with Morrissey's reflective lyrics about the unheroic loneliness and isolation of adolescence. This individualism countered rock's presumption that youth stood proudly united behind one side of society's great generational dividing line. 'A child of punk with all the rage and enmity turned inwards,' Morrissey ensured, in one critic's assessment, that 'where their predecessors celebrated fun, danger, passion and excitement, The Smiths were about despair, disgust, boredom and, at their most proactive, panic'.[14] Such expressions of inadequacy and resignation were a startling retort to rock's two decades of glorifying sex, licence and gratification. Despite concerted attempts by journalists to label him as homosexual, Morrissey maintained that he was an asexual celibate. Influenced by northern, female-oriented, 'kitchen-sink' dramas like Shelagh Delaney's *A Taste of Honey*, he was the Alan Bennett of pop.

It was not a tone applauded by those who dismissed The Smiths as 'miserablists'. The categorization was understandable given lyrics such as those in 'I Know It's Over', 'Asleep' and 'There is a Light that Never Goes Out' that meditated upon doom and even suicide. Yet these dark sentiments were balanced by Morrissey's flashes of acerbic, Oscar Wilde-like wit and by Marr's usually jaunty guitar tempo. Far from wallowing in unremitting gloom, few eighties albums spanned the complete emotional spectrum as fully, or successfully, as The Smiths' most celebrated work, *The Queen is Dead*. Nor did Morrissey's introspection blunt his desire to sing about broader themes. The band's most successful single, 'Panic', with its incitement to string-up DJs, was inspired by the experience of listening to Radio 1 when its news report of the Chernobyl nuclear plant explosion was followed by Wham's bullishly trite 'I'm Your Man'. 'Panic' made it on to the Radio 1 playlist only to fall foul of some music journalists: with an imaginative leap, *Melody Maker* condemned it as the racist sentiments of a white 'indie' band disparaging black culture. Rarely quick to walk away from a confrontation, Morrissey responded by suggesting that it was actually reggae, 'the most racist music in the entire world', that ought to be the target of those critical of glorifications of racial supremacy.[15] Like John Lennon before him, his outspokenness kept him at the forefront of the music press, proffering comments that appeared to justify the IRA's murderous assault on the 1984 Conservative Party conference – 'The sorrow of the Brighton bombing is that Thatcher escaped unscathed'[16] – and even violence against all those, including high-street butchers, who harmed animals. Seemingly untroubled by the paradox of his support for violence against those he accused of violence, the aggressiveness of Morrissey's outbursts was softened by the wistful, unprepossessing tone in which he expressed himself. His indifference to mainstream opinion even led him to sneer at Band Aid, archly musing on the 'absolutely tuneless' single 'Do They Know It's Christmas?': 'One can have a great concern for the people of Ethiopia, but it's another thing to inflict daily torture on the people of England.'[17] And gullible, liberal-minded juries were the target of his lyrics in 'Sweet and Tender Hooligan'.

It was a mixture of business and personal pressures that tore The Smiths apart. The band consisted of four members, only two of whose signatures appeared on the contracts. Rough Trade may have been run like a collective, but that was not the model Morrissey and Marr adopted for their own group. Indeed, for all Morrissey's and Marr's disdain for Thatcherism, in matters of labour law they practised its most ruthless aspects when defending their own business dealings and self-interest. They treated bass guitarist Andy Rourke and drummer Mike Joyce as if they were session artists, to be hired and fired at will (as Rourke discovered when he was briefly sacked for succumbing to heroin addiction). Managers were also a disposable commodity, which meant that with Morrissey increasingly failing to turn up for commitments if he did not feel like it, the burden fell on Marr, who, to make matters worse, was drinking heavily as a means of dealing with the pressures of touring. Much of the irritation was taken out on Rough Trade and rumours that the band was scouting around for a new label caused Geoff Travis to take the precaution of a High Court injunction to stop them breaching their contract. This delayed the release of *The Queen is Dead* and, despite increasing the group's advance, Travis found himself rewarded by being parodied on the rumbustious track 'Frankly Mr Shankly'. Despairing of Travis's continued funding of uncommercial bands, Marr felt Rough Trade had not adapted to the success of its greatest signing, complaining: 'We've grown to major status while the label is still stuck with the more negative aspects of the independent scene.'[18] In an act that diehard indie supporters judged a betrayal, The Smiths duly signed to the corporate giant EMI – only to find Travis unwilling to be bought off from releasing their last Rough Trade studio album, *Strangeways, Here We Come*. As it was about to be released in August 1987, Marr decided he needed a break, a decision that, in the ensuing acrimony, triggered his walking out on the band just as it appeared to be near the peak of its creative powers and acclaim. Thereafter, Morrissey and Marr did not speak to one another until at least 1996, when they found themselves defending (in vain) in the High Court the paltry royalties they had assigned the two other band members. Marr performed with other bands and Morrissey proceeded on to a successful solo career, but neither proved individually capable of holding the popular and critical attention to which they had laid claim as The Smiths.

The break-up of The Smiths coincided with the declining fortunes of many of the most important indie labels. Having enjoyed a 40 per cent share of the market at their eighties peak, the indies now found themselves stretched to their limits and facing renewed competition from the majors, which, in the sincerest form of flattery, were setting up their own specialist labels. At Rough Trade, the workers' collective structure that Travis had developed broke down in 1987, to be replaced by a more businesslike, capitalist model. Four years later, the company mishandled its cash flow and went into administration, taking others in its wake. Stiff Records had collapsed in debt in 1986, the same year in which Madness split up after having unsuccessfully opted to set up their own label, Zarjazz. In 1989, Chris Blackwell sold Island Records to the music goliath PolyGram for $272 million. Though Blackwell continued to run his own Island A&R fiefdom within the corporation, an age in which independent labels self-consciously held their own against, rather than as part of, the majors was passing, and those that promoted the 'Britpop' bands of the nineties did so using commercial methods that were virtually indistinguishable from the way the majors operated. The defeat for those seeking an alternative way of producing music was also psychological. Indie music had confronted but failed to topple the political as much as the business establishment. In the run-up to the 1987 general election, Paul Weller and Billy Bragg organized a series of concerts by leading indie bands, supported by a troupe of alternative comedians, under the banner 'Red Wedge'. The intention was to mobilize the youth vote to return Labour to power. The sound and fury were considerable, but the general election result dealt a withering blow to pop as a medium of political protest. The eighties were drawing to a close and radical musicians had failed to paint it red. Indie music duly went in search of a new focus and in doing so rediscovered hedonism and, in its wake, the embrace of some unrepentantly pro-free-market entrepreneurs.

Welcome to the Acid House

Dance music had survived the demise of seventies disco. Within the pop mainstream the genre was carried forward by The Pet Shop Boys, a duo consisting of Martin Lowe and Neil Tennant, who ensured that the synth-pop of the first half of the eighties continued to resonate across dance floors in the second half. Enthused with Tennant's essentially sad and wistful lyrics – which he spoke rather than sang – the sensibilities of Ivor Novello and Noël Coward were duly brought to the world of Roland drum machines. Indeed, Tennant was a rare case of a former pop music journalist who turned out to be a better performer than critic. In the midst of the 'yuppie' boom of 1986 (though the song was actually written three years previously), the intended irony of 'Opportunities (Let's Make Lots of Money)' was lost on those who thought it the definitive anthem of the good times and the track that embodied Thatcherism's apex as satisfyingly as The Specials' 'Ghost Town' had intoned its nadir five years earlier. While The Pet Shop Boys conjured up a version of art-house pop whose lyrical subtleties went over the heads of City brokers and secretaries postprandially bopping to its jaunty tempo, elsewhere dance music was being taken in a different, more rugged, direction. The centre for these developments was Manchester, an increasingly post-industrial city endeavouring to recast itself as a place for cultural renewal through its dance clubs; as the home no longer of manufacturing production lines but of Factory Records, it was increasingly the destination for students and youthful pleasure-seekers, where jobs might be scarce by day but where the night-time economy kept the city alive and vibrant.

The impresario of Manchester's transformation through clubbing was Tony Wilson. Educated at a Salford Catholic grammar school and – as he was rarely slow to point out to those who doubted his genius – Cambridge University, Wilson was twenty-eight when in 1978 he founded Factory Records. Such was his commitment to artistic freedom that he was happy to sign groups without Factory securing any ownership rights over their music. Immediate success with Joy Division was cut short with the suicide of its lead, Ian Curtis, in 1980, but the band's other members stuck with Factory, promptly forming New Order and proceeding to innovate in dance music, fusing it with elements of electronic and alternative rock. Where the traditional 7-inch single had constrained dance to a tight format designed for pop's three- or four-minute formula, the growing popularity of 12-inch records perfectly suited longer musical explorations in which the essence of a song could be remixed and extended, its complexities pared down and the prominence of the underlying bass line enhanced as the motor of the tune. In 1983, New Order released a landmark dance track which laid claim to being the world's biggest-selling 12-inch record. Its tone established by an opening beat reminiscent of the tapping of Morse code, 'Blue Monday' owed much to the group's exposure to the sounds of the New York club scene. There, as well as in Detroit and Chicago, innovative DJs were experimenting with new dance rhythms in predominantly gay and drug-fuelled clubs, creating a genre that became known as 'house' (after a Chicago club called the Warehouse). Much of New Order's profits from 'Blue Monday' were duly channelled into Factory Records' efforts to create a Chicago Warehouse-style club in Manchester. Established in a disused yacht showroom in a tired part of the city, its 'industrial' decor framed by its trademark yellow- and black-striped factory hazard warnings and the stains from a leaky roof, the venture was named, somewhat absurdly, The Haçienda. 'For any real form of substantive youth culture to thrive in a city, there has to be a place to go, somewhere to meet,' Wilson enthused. 'The Haçienda had to be built.'[19] With the racist comedian Bernard Manning hired to do some curtain-raising stand-up, there was certainly nothing about its opening night in May 1982 to suggest the club would end up as one of the period's most significant pop venues, and in its early days it was primarily a venue for live bands rather than dance mixes. This began to change in 1984 when Mike Pickering became one of its resident DJs, drawing in a broader clientele by bringing together the city's student and local youth populations to an extent that had not previously been seen. Slowly gathering momentum (though still losing money), by 1987 the Haçienda had achieved primacy as Britain's secular cathedral of house music. It would soon have competition. That autumn, two DJs, Paul Oakenfold and Danny Rampling, took what proved to be an enlightening holiday to the Mediterranean party island of Ibiza and brought its house anthems to London at their respective clubs, Spectrum and Shoom. By the spring of 1988, house had become the sound of Britain's dance culture.

The pace of house music was set by a pumping bass line, typically at 120 beats per minute. Words were kept to a minimum and often consisted of no more than sampled out-takes from other recordings, extracted from their original context and remixed to create new lyrics. As one of the Haçienda's DJs, Dave Haslam, put it, house's contribution to music was 'to reinvent the instrumental, stripping music to rhythms, electronic noise, samples. It was refreshing to escape the prosaic verse-chorus-verse-chorus-guitar solo formula of rock music and enter a realm of noises, bleeps and electronic echoes from the ether.'[20] This was never likely to appeal to those who continued to see music as a formal song-writing craft and for whom these 'noises, bleeps and electronic echoes' resembled nothing more poignant than the interplay of competing burglar alarms. Furthermore, setting pilfered out-takes of other artists' material to a unifying rhythm was how Jive Bunny and the Mastermixers had conquered the singles charts, much to the derision and despair of the serious music press. House played the same game while managing to retain an urgent, cutting-edge appeal that was wholly beyond the likes of Jive Bunny. Where the latter crammed as many 1950s tunes as possible into four minutes of musical grand larceny – unintentionally proving that the flip side of Mies van der Rohe's famous dictum was equally true and that more was less – the real master mixers showed that sampling could produce expansive rather than reductive results, weaving anthems to which clubbers could dance all night long.

The synth-pop pioneers of the early eighties had demonstrated how new technology made it possible for two people to front a group even though they were devoid of musical training and incapable of playing instruments that required the dexterity of more than one finger at a time. House took this approach to its ultimate conclusion since it could be made by one person with a computer able to sample sounds, resulting in relatively cheap-to-produce 12-inch records rather than albums. This, in turn, saved on the expense of time-consuming hours in a studio assisted by a platoon of producers, technicians and session musicians. Punk's 'do-it-yourself' ethos lived on. Nor did the creative process end with a finished product booming out from a sound system. Rather than just playing the discs to the assembled clubbers, DJs became live performers, extemporizing by scratching and mixing competing rhythms on two record turntables in a search for musical fusion. In this way, house was not a pre-made and packaged commodity but a living entity, with its DJ interpreters becoming as famous – or more famous – than the names on the label. It was the last great innovation in eighties popular music and, crucially, one that was still in vogue twenty years later.

The other house ingredient was drugs and the stimulant of choice was MDMA, commonly known as Ecstasy. The relationship of rock'n'roll with drugs was as time honoured as it was with sex, but while drug-taking was standard procedure for pop stars it was not necessarily a prerequisite for listening to their work. Of course it was perfectly possible to spend hours on end dancing in the required trance-like state with arms exultantly raised in the air to the repetitive beats of house without taking drugs, but taking Ecstasy both kept up the energy levels and made the experience more explicable. Though some MDMA users suffered unpleasant side effects, it mostly produced the euphoric state that gave it its Ecstasy soubriquet. In particular, it was perceived as a 'happy drug', which encouraged a state of togetherness and human empathy among the dancers, moving to the beat as a mass of joyful individuals, rather than encouraging the proprietorial exclusivity of pairing into couples. Although MDMA had been a 'class A' illegal substance in the United Kingdom since 1977 – a full decade before it became widely available – its users believed it to be harmless, or at least no more harmful than legal stimulants like alcohol and tobacco. 'Popping an E' was as simple as swallowing a paracetamol tablet and involved none of the off-putting needles and other paraphernalia of hard drugs like heroin. During 1987, house became increasingly referred to as 'acid house' or 'rave' (terms that were technically sub-genres) as its association with Ecstasy became more overt and the drug's suppliers raced to meet a demand running into the millions for an illegal product which just three years earlier had been experienced in Britain by only a few West End bohemians. Not since the smell of marijuana had drifted from the hippie festivals of the late sixties had law-breaking been so inextricably entwined with youthful expression and, like Woodstock's long-haired joint-smokers, acid-house ravers talked as if they too were discovering, through 'E', a new age of Aquarius.

The sudden surge in Ecstasy use caught the forces of law and order off-guard. The government's anti-drugs campaign, built around the 'Heroin Screws You Up' message and the dangers of spreading Aids from sharing needles, had scarcely considered the potential appeal of MDMA. At first, the police had no idea how to react to hundreds – and then thousands – of clubbers behaving peculiarly. When crowds spilled out on to the Charing Cross Road after a new acid-house club, The Trip at the Astoria, finished for the night at 3 a.m., they were still in a euphoric state, continuing their partying by dancing on the roofs of parked cars. Police were at a loss how to move them on – for the blaring of police sirens captivated them into dancing to their importunate beat. But the craze would soon claim casualties, pitching clubbers against coppers. The first Ecstasy fatality, in June 1988, could be put down to misadventure since the 21-year-old victim, Ian Larcombe, had been so incautious as to take eighteen pills at once. More disturbing was the death of Janet Mayes three months later after swallowing only two pills. By then, the press had latched on to what they assumed was an especially dangerous youth trend. 'You will hallucinate. For example, if you don't like spiders you'll start seeing giant ones,' cautioned *The Sun*'s medical correspondent, Vernon Coleman. 'There's a good chance you'll end up in a mental hospital for life . . . If you're young enough there's a good chance you'll be sexually assaulted while under the influence. You may not even know until a few days or weeks later.'[21] For the tens of thousands who had started using Ecstasy without experiencing the side effects of arachnophobia or vague recollections of having been raped, such hysterical scaremongering seemed risible.

The reality was that neither Ecstasy's users nor its critics really knew what they were talking about. The drug's rise had been so sudden that there were no unimpeachable evaluations of its more distant effects. Whether it might cause long-term brain damage – as a 1985 American study, based on laboratory animals, suggested – remained conjecture. The only clear short-term consequence was the comedown, which induced in users feelings of listlessness and depression that could last into mid-week. The drug was not medically addictive, though repeated use caused the body to acclimatize to its effects, thereby encouraging ever greater quantities to be consumed, sometimes topped up with other, far more risky, drugs. There was also the danger that as large criminal syndicates moved in to meet the soaring demand so pure MDMA might be adulterated with other questionable substances. Another problem was that taking 'E' stimulated its users to dance beyond their physical limits and could bring on the effects of heatstroke. This could be combated by drinking water, but some drank so much that they brought on death by doing so. In these ways, Ecstasy risked leading users into genuine medical harm, but for most clubbers during the summer of 1988 the ratio of fatalities to pills popped did not seem to suggest the dangers were excessive.

For the police, the greatest public order threat came not from the taking of a drug whose effect was generally to make its users less aggressive, but from the noise, nuisance and dangers to life and limb caused by a craze that had quickly spread beyond licensed clubs to impromptu raves in disused warehouses, barns and even – as the summer weather took hold – fields in the middle of the countryside. At least in licensed establishments there were restricted opening hours and a legally accountable management, but no such controls existed to contain the unlicensed raves, with all the potential for trouble and calamity that this could entail. Some events were held in warehouses without proper fire-safety equipment or unbolted fire exits, and the possibility of arson from criminal gangs over thwarted drug deals, as well as accidental mishaps, risked turning the covert venues into death-traps. Undaunted, promotors organized illegal events and launched premium-rate phone lines and pirate radio stations to spread the word about where partygoers should assemble (often a motorway service station), from where they would be given the secret of the rave's real location. Typically, convoys of cars carrying young ravers circled the M25 (which had only been completed i.1 1986) following a series of directions to industrial estates or distant fields which, despite the encroaching darkness, were surreally identified by an ethereal haze of light and an echoing thump-thump-thump-thump. Some farmers and warehouse owners were happy to make a quick, cash-in-hand profit for lending out their underused property for a night's revels. Others did so under false pretences, having been led to believe it was to be used for a film-shoot, pop video or some other venture necessitating lorries, lights and stage equipment.

For rave organizers there were initially easy profits to be made from charging between £10 and £20 admission to several thousand partygoers in return for a relatively modest outlay on a giant sound system, some colourful projections and an invariably inadequate number of portable loos. It was not difficult to paint these young men (as they predominantly were) as the unacceptable face of Thatcherism – spivvish entrepreneurs indifferent to the law and to any consequences that might stand in the way of their rush to cash in on optimistic and perhaps naive youngsters. The promoters came from a range of backgrounds, but the most prominent among them conformed to this caricature. Branded by the *Daily Mirror* the 'Acid House King', Tony Colston-Hayter was a young, middle-class, comprehensive-school-educated entrepreneur and gambler. Establishing his rave empire under the title 'Sunrise', he ensured that its profits went through its grandly named parent company Transatlantic Corporation, which was registered in the tax haven of the Virgin Islands. Among the other leading rave organizers were two public schoolboys, Quentin 'Tintin' Chambers and Jeremy Taylor, the latter of whom had been jointly running the 'Gatecrasher Balls' for school-age Sloane Rangers since 1983. Progressing from helping privileged under-age children get smashed on fizz, Taylor's shift to hosting raves for a drug-fuelled generation of clubbers showed his adeptness at moving with the times. The suggestion that such young men were examples of what happened when Thatcherism ran riot gained further credence when Colston-Hayter appointed a 22-year-old libertarian named Paul Staines as Sunrise's public relations executive. Having been a Federation of Conservative Students activist while at Humberside College of Higher Education, Staines certainly had unimpeachable credentials as an individualist. He combined his advocacy of illegal raves with work as a researcher for free-market think tanks, including the Adam Smith Institute and the Committee for a Free Britain. The latter was run by David Hart, a maverick multi-millionaire on the outer reaches of Thatcher's circle of admirers/advisers, who during 1984 had helped direct funds to those trying to break the miners' strike. Sharing Hart's parallel causes of promoting liberty for entrepreneurs and combating the threat from global communism, Staines drew comparisons between left-wing authoritarianism abroad and the refusal of the government to let its citizens do as they pleased at home. 'My credibility was slowly going down in politics,' he later mused. 'One minute I would be on News at One saying "there's no drugs at these parties", and the next minute I'm supposed to be talking about civil war in Angola.'[22]

Such concerns were far removed from the essentially communitarian spirit animating young rave-goers. Acid-house music did not contain enough lyrics to convey a message, let alone a political one, but the general mood replicated the disconnect from conventional society that had been at the core of the Woodstock generation's outlook. First the middle months of 1988 and then those of 1989 were referred to as a 'second summer of love'. The chilled and funky 'Pacific State' by 808 State and Black Box's altogether higher energy 'Ride on Time' were the tracks most associated with that second summer, which – ideal for open-air raves – was unusually warm and balmy (May 1989 was the hottest for three hundred years). The accompanying dress sense of baggy T-shirts and jeans or tracksuits and trainers could scarcely have been further removed from the sharp suits, primary colours and shoulder pads of corporate Britain; the ravers' logo of a smiley face in the shape of a little round pill was self-explanatory.

The illegal raves of the 'second summer of love' ranged from those resembling little more than a barn dance with drugs to the spectacular events laid on by Sunrise where twenty thousand ticket-only fun-seekers were treated to laser displays, enveloping puffs of artificial smoke, giant projection screens, bouncy castles, Ferris wheels and big dippers. The overall effect was like a cross between a rock festival, a fun fair and a May ball at one of Cambridge's less pretentious colleges. The police's Pay Party Unit, established to combat the craze, was led by Chief Superintendent Ken Tappenden, a veteran of law enforcement during the miners' strike. He deployed two hundred officers across the country to gather intelligence on where parties were being organized and by whom. This went as far as watching and tracking the movements of scaffolding contractors and private security firms used by the principal event planners in the hope of identifying the location of their next job. Realizing they were being tailed, promoters responded by sending one convoy of lorries in one direction and, after the police had headed off in pursuit, sending out a further convoy to the real party location. When the police successfully identified where a rave was being held, they set up roadblocks to prevent those hoping to attend from doing so. On 1 July 1989, the police closed off a twenty-mile stretch of the M4 to frustrate those trying to get to the Energy party run by Taylor and Chambers in Membury, Berkshire. Three weeks later, an effort to cordon off the whole area around Heston services in order to stop another Energy rave in a warehouse narrowly avoided causing loss of life when the partygoers dodged the police cordon by parking their cars on the hard shoulder and running across a six-lane motorway to gain access to the event. The sheer weight of numbers made containment extremely difficult, but the picture it created of drug-crazed teenagers so under the spell that they would leg it across a motorway to get their fix of acid house naturally alarmed those who found the movement perplexing and disconcerting.

Worse was to follow. On 30 September, sixteen police officers were injured when their efforts to intervene at a rave in Reigate were rebuffed by the event's security guards, who attacked them with CS gas and Rottweilers. Eventually, more than fifty arrests were made, but the scenes – which were caught by television news cameras – of effectively a private army in combat with the police further undermined the credibility of the event organizers as harmless purveyors of youth entertainment. The environment minister, Virginia Bottomley, responded by stating it was 'intolerable that peaceful citizens should be terrorized' by the noise, mess and disruption of raves and that the government was urgently looking to find ways of cracking down on their organizers, including three-month jail sentences and confiscation of profits.

It was certainly proving difficult to bring rave organizers to book under existing laws. After Sunrise's Colston-Hayter had been charged with organizing an illegal party, his lawyers secured his acquittal by arguing that because he had issued membership cards with the tickets, his events were, in fact, private parties. Lawyers also managed to undermine the roadblock policy by challenging the right of police to prevent individuals from peacefully walking down certain lanes. For their part, the rave organizers were also unhappy with the law as it stood since they believed it hindered their efforts to run a legitimate business. Better to make the case against outmoded licensing restrictions, Paul Staines set up Freedom to Party, a pressure group backed by several of the main rave organizers. He launched it in October 1989 at the Conservative Party conference in Blackpool. Colston-Hayter chipped in with the observation: 'Maggie should be proud of us, we're a product of enterprise culture.'[23] Sadly for him, it was not the sort of enterprise that appealed to the prime minister. Staines may have seen a parallel between young people being free to party wherever, whenever and however they liked and the protests simultaneously taking place in Eastern Europe. There, communist citizens were showing they were no longer afraid of their authoritarian police states in a peaceful but nonetheless revolutionary movement which was about to shatter the Berlin Wall. But the analogy seemed rather strained to those not immersed in rave culture: the television pictures of East Germans defying the Stasi and demanding the right to visit relations in West Germany were of an altogether profounder nature than the preoccupation of British youth with getting high on Ecstasy and partying all night. Calling for stiffer penalties, the *Daily Mail* lectured that 'acid house is a facade for dealing in drugs of the worst sort on a massive scale. It is a cynical attempt to trap young people into drug dependency under the guise of friendly pop music events.'[24] The Conservative and Labour front benches were united in their condemnation of raves and supported the private member's bill introduced by the Conservative MP Graham Bright which became law in July as the Entertainments (Increased Penalties) Act 1990. It sanctioned fines of up to £20,000 and six months in prison for illegal rave organizers.

Bright's act reached the statute books at the moment the conflict was turning decisively against the rave organizers. In the early hours of 21 July 1990, a mass arrest took place on a scale that had few parallels in the history of British law enforcement. Organizers of the Love Decade rave broke into a large shed in a village on the outskirts of Leeds. Once the shed was full, they effectively barricaded their customers inside by parking a van behind the doors so that the police would have to force an entry. This the police nevertheless managed to do and in the ensuing melee made 836 arrests. Elsewhere, police tactics were also finally having an effect. Posing as rave organizers, they had started disseminating details of bogus rave locations to pirate radio stations. Increasingly, partygoers did not know whether their journey would end in a successful night out, or in a cul-de-sac with a policeman at the end of it telling them it was late and well past their bedtime. The initial excitement of trying to outsmart the police became wearisome as the police increasingly proved to be one step ahead, transforming the long drive in search of a party into a wild goose chase. Meanwhile, the organizers found they had more dangerous enemies to worry about than the local constabulary. The drug that was fuelling their customers' appetite for dancing was also making their own business empires precarious. Comprehending the profits that were being made, major drug dealers started making demands for a cut. This often took the form of the criminals' enforcers and local football hooligans offering 'protection' to those organizing parties on 'their patch' in return for money, along with the hint that all might not go well if the offer was rejected. Jeremy Taylor hired a posse of ex-SAS soldiers to keep him from harm – a precaution to which he had never had to resort when organizing the 'Gatecrasher Balls' for teenagers in tuxedos and taffeta. The threat to their livelihoods from gangsters as well as judges convinced the organizers that their window of opportunity was closing fast. Colston-Hayter duly returned to his other career as a gambler, and Jeremy Taylor went off to run Noel Edmonds's Crinkley Bottom theme park. Paul Staines became a professional blackjack player, then a hedge-fund manager, before declaring himself bankrupt. He subsequently established himself as the controversial political blogger Guido Fawkes.[25]

The illegal rave scene had been crushed, its defeat made manifest when the police felt able to close down the Pay Party Unit in September 1991. But the war had been won against unlicensed parties, not against Ecstasy or rave music. While Graham Bright's act cracked down on illicit raves, at the same time a more liberal attitude to licensing hours ensured that all-night dancing to house music could be enjoyed at established clubs instead. These extended entertainment licences paved the way in the 1990s for vast new clubs like the Ministry of Sound in Vauxhall to become global brands. House lost its rebel edge and became overtly commercial (the Ministry of Sound was owned by the son of Lord Palumbo, the ex-chairman of the Arts Council). The popularity of Ecstasy endured. It was impossible to quantify even loosely how many MDMA and derivative pills were being popped by the mid-1990s, with regularly quoted but unverifiable estimates suggesting half a million taken every weekend; that half of British youth had taken drugs and that the dance scene – legal and illegal – was worth £1.8 billion a year and thus on a par with the nation's newspaper and book publishing industries. At any rate, Customs and Excise's records suggested a rise of 4,000 per cent in foreign Ecstasy coming into the UK between 1990 and 1995.[26] As an exercise in creating a market from almost nothing, and then successfully meeting soaring demand, it was a story of commercial success that many multinational corporations might have struggled to replicate. Instead, it was made possible by organized crime's increasing focus on the narcotics trade as a source of profits. Ultimately, no other phenomenon in eighties pop culture rivalled the long-term influence of house music.

Madchester

Drugs and music were the twin motors of Manchester's continued prominence as the country's pop capital in the last days of the eighties. And it was primarily drugs, too, that brought the experiment in urban renewal through clubbing to the brink of destruction. By 1989, Tony Wilson's prophecy that the city's cultural renaissance needed his flagship club as its focus appeared to be well founded, with the Haçienda continuing to pack in clubbers and musicians and its fame established across the country. Unfortunately for its backers – principally Wilson's Factory Records via its most famous signing, New Order – the Haçienda returned great profits not to its owners but to Manchester's drug barons. After all, it was difficult to make money from customers who, having taken their 'happy pill' before arriving (or in a quiet corner of the club), proceeded to drink little more than water at the Haçienda's bar. But, in the meantime, salvation appeared to be at hand from a band Wilson had spotted in the club and signed to Factory. Led by brothers Shaun and Paul Ryder, The Happy Mondays consisted of six scruffily dressed Salford lads who combined the guitar aggression of alternative rock with the cheap hedonism of house. Posturing and staggering around on stage was part of their appeal (a freedom enabled by their being able to turn the switch on pre-recorded material). Indeed, beyond shaking maracas, jiving around artlessly was virtually all that Bez (Mark Berry) was able to bring to their live concerts, thereby blurring the distinction between performer and audience, stage and floor. But there was more to The Happy Mondays than freaky dancing. For those seeking 'authenticity', they appeared to be the genuine article. Ravaged by late nights of vodka and drugs, Paul and Shaun Ryder cut the dishevelled figures of delinquents who might as easily hot-wire a parked car as make era-defining music. This was part of their appeal, taking a trainer-kick to the flimsy partition between art and real life.

Bogusly claiming to vote Conservative as part of his mission to shock, Shaun Ryder identified himself as one of Thatcher's children in ways that would have mystified her: 'We dealt [drugs]. They called us criminals, but the way we saw it, we were enterprising business people. She laid the cards out and people had no choice but to play the game.'[27] Yet, unlike so many eighties indie acts, the Mondays were not remotely interested in politics, nor in being moulded into a glamorous brand like the decade's more overtly commercial stars. A section of the music press identified this as representing the most exciting shake-up to record industry complacency since the anarchic snarls of The Sex Pistols in the Queen's silver jubilee year of 1977. In the United States in the meantime, rap and hip hop had dared to speak unvarnished truths to power. By comparison, British mainstream acts appeared either banal or, in the case of master-songwriters like Morrissey and Marr, arch and straining to be clever. In contrast, Shaun Ryder's vibing lyrics – mostly disconnected ramblings about street life and tripping – offered a sort of rap for scallies, accompanied by rock and house instrumentals. Not everyone got it: a giant consignment of Kit Kats was sent to The Happy Mondays' office after the manufacturer, Rowntree's, mistook a photo of Shaun Ryder lovingly unwrapping the chocolate bar's silver foil as a good publicity opportunity.[28]

It was The Happy Mondays who popularized two terms that came to represent their place and time – 'Madchester' and 'Twenty-Four-Hour Party People'. During 1989 and 1990, the city, its bands and its clubs led the way for British pop culture. Another Manchester band, The Stone Roses, spiced house with funk and psychedelia, conjuring up the sort of sound that might have emanated from The Beatles if they had stayed together and settled in San Francisco. What came to be considered Madchester's defining moment took place on 27 May 1990 at a concert The Stone Roses performed on Spike Island in the Mersey estuary in front of almost thirty thousand (appropriately stoned) young people, many of whom struggled to hear much of the music projected out from an inadequate PA system, but for whom the occasion's significance became magnified in the memory.

Perhaps the Spike Island concert came to be shrouded in so much nostalgia not because it was the start of a new experience but, in retrospect, because it marked the beginning of its end. With international recognition assumed to be merely round the corner, The Stone Roses tried to dump their indie label for a major, only to find that legal action by the jilted Silvertone Records prevented their follow-up album coming out until 1994, by which time they had drifted from their Madchester moorings and utterly lost their bearings. The downfall of The Happy Mondays was – all too inevitably – less prosaic. Paul and Shaun Ryder became heroin addicts and Factory Records sent them with the rest of the band to Barbados (an island deemed not to be awash with heroin) to record their fourth album. Unfortunately, Barbados – as the Mondays soon discovered – was flooded with crack cocaine. When the band ran out of money, they sold the furniture in the recording studio to fund their new habit. 'The real trouble was that I wasn't interested in writing any music,' Shaun Ryder explained, without evident self-reproach. 'I had no ideas. I went over there and just totally enjoyed myself.'[29] By the time he and his band-mates were plucked from the island, the album's recording costs had spiralled towards £400,000 and the producers had not yet managed to coax Ryder into contributing any vocals to it. Unsurprisingly, the album's release had to be delayed and it was

not very good even when it was finally turned into something vaguely sale-
able in 1992. Besides marking the downturn in The Happy Mondays'
creative fortunes, it destroyed what was left of the finances of Factory
Records. As New Order's Bernard Sumner saw it, the fault lay less with the
irresponsible behaviour of the pop stars than with those who indulged it:
'No one should have allowed the Mondays to spend nearly so much, but
money was never a major concern at Factory. With Tony [Wilson], the
artists always got what they wanted.'[30] It was an approach that had resulted
in some of the most important pop music of the period, but which had in it
the seeds of its own destruction. Damaged also by the failure of New Order
to produce a new hit album in time and by an ill-judged move to expensive
new offices, Factory went into receivership. Its dream for Manchester was
also turning sour as the city's drug gangs settled their turf wars by drawing
firearms. Though it finally shut its doors six years later, the Haçienda never
fully recovered after shootings forced its temporary closure in January 1991,
when Tony Wilson issued a clear statement: 'We are quite simply sick and
tired of dealing with instances of personal violence.'[31] In 1992, the club's
security bill alone came to £375,000. On one occasion, the head of security
was chased through the club by a disaffected youth wielding a sub-machine
gun, escaping summary execution near the fire exit only because the Uzi
jammed.

Madchester, it seemed, was aptly named. Yet ultimately even its creative
successes, while commanding a nationwide following, had struggled to be
heard far beyond. Unlike the New Romantics or the new waves of synth-
pop and heavy metal, Madchester never deeply penetrated the American
market, which, during the 1990s, moved from the happy hedonism of house
to the depressive wails of grunge. The nineties were not to be an age in
which global pop culture was primarily shaped in the United Kingdom.
Specific bands succeeded, but not whole movements. Having cornered one
third of music sales in the United States during the early and mid-eighties,
British acts struggled to account for more than a few per cent during the following decade. The eighties had been a special – and not to be readily
repeated – era in British pop history.

12   MORAL PANIC

No Such Thing as Society

None of Thatcherism's critics coined a phrase more damning or suggestive of its corrosive consequences than her own claim that 'there is no such thing as society'. The extraordinary assertion suggested that the fracturing of traditional patterns of community was not a regrettable by-product of government policy or a mysterious consequence of the modern world, but rather the deliberate goal of a prime minister committed to the triumph of the unencumbered individual. The outcry that followed her statement could hardly have been louder if she had quoted approvingly the assertion of the occultist Aleister Crowley that to 'do what thou wilt shall be the whole of the law'. Twenty years later, when Thatcher's statement was still regularly being cited as the fitting epitaph for her effect on national life, the Conservative politician turned journalist Matthew Parris suggested it was actually 'one of her few really interesting remarks'.[1] By a few months, it anticipated the April 1988 release in the UK of the film *Wall Street* which spawned the catchphrase 'greed is good', and together the two pronouncements captured the popular imagination as the embodiment of the age's selfish materialist values.

Thatcher's most memorable philosophical musing was made during the course of an interview with *Woman's Own* and was published by the glossy magazine in October 1987, four months after she had won her third successive general election. The transcript of her conversation with the interviewer, Douglas Keay, shows that her actual words were considerably more nuanced than was implied when the quotation was shorn of its context. The prime minister was discussing her fear that too many people were inclined to look at their predicament and conclude 'I have a problem, it is the government's job to cope with it!' – whereas in reality 'life is a reciprocal business and people have got the entitlements too much in mind without the obligations, because there is no such thing as an entitlement unless someone has first met an obligation'. Unemployment benefit, she thought, was there to help the jobless while they looked for work, but was not an alternative to finding work, because: 'It is your neighbour who is supplying it and if you can earn your own living then really you have a duty to do it and you will feel very much better!' It was to those who believed they had a right to live at the expense of others without offering anything in return that she warned: 'There is no such thing as society. There is a living tapestry of men and women and people and the beauty of that tapestry and the quality of our lives will depend upon how much each of us is prepared to take responsibility for ourselves and each of us is prepared to turn round and help by our own efforts those who are unfortunate.'[2]

Developing the theme that it was voluntary organizations and good-neighbourliness that made life better, Thatcher went on to profess that her favourite charity was the National Society for the Prevention of Cruelty to Children because, despite the strides that had been made in material welfare, too many young people had been shown nothing but cruelty at home. 'For those children it is difficult to say: "You are responsible for your behaviour!" because they just have not had a chance.'[3] This was not far removed from a similar point made in 2006 by David Cameron, which his Labour opponents mockingly paraphrased as 'hug a hoodie'. But, back in 1987, the surrounding threads of Thatcher's tapestry were successfully unpicked by the efforts of her critics to identify the denial of social obligations as her political mission. The damage to her reputation had been done by the time, six years later, she attempted to clarify what she had meant: 'Society was not an abstraction, separate from the men and women who composed it . . . the error to which I was objecting was the confusion of society with the state as the helper of first resort.'[4] What she could not satisfactorily answer was why the accusation that she wished to destroy society had gained such traction. Doing so would have necessitated going to the core of what fuelled popular apprehensions about social change in the 1980s. These concerns stemmed from what might vaguely be termed the weakening of a social contract – the tangible results of which were a widening gulf between rich and poor, rising crime rates, along with football hooliganism and antisocial behaviour, a perceived decline in community spirit, and the undermining of 'family values' and responsibilities.

There was consensus on neither the causes nor the consequences of these social changes. In the foreground stood unemployment as a major source of poverty and the undermining of human relationships. Given the anxiety joblessness created, alongside feelings of social exclusion and purposelessness, it defied common sense to imagine there was no correlation with growing signs of social fragmentation. By the middle of the decade, seven out of every ten convicts going to prison were registered unemployed.[5] Communities that had been built around one or two dominant employers – such as a coal mine or a single large factory – were disproportionately affected when that employer shut down, plunging the whole community into a state of helplessness. In particular, male unemployment inevitably undermined the traditional patriarchal model of the man finding purpose as the family's principal wage-earner. The surprise would surely have been if such shocks had not strained human relationships and led to an increase in antisocial behaviour. However, establishing a direct correlation was not easy. As Thatcher was quick to point out, unemployment (peaking at 11 per cent of the workforce in 1986) was half that of the 1930s (22 per cent in 1932),* yet the thirties coincided with historically low levels of family breakdown and, by later standards, remarkably little crime.[6] According to this critique, it was cultural change rather than economic hardship that had intervened to breed modern social ills. The blame could thus be laid on the culture of the 'permissive sixties' – and, by implication, at the door of the liberal left. Into this debate, the American social scientist Charles Murray imported a term that became shorthand for a sector of society that, having become dependent upon welfare benefits, had supposedly given up on the prospect of reintegrating into the workplace and seeking self-improvement – the 'underclass'. It was a new term for what previous generations had described as the 'feckless' and the Victorians had depicted as the 'undeserving poor'. The fear was that the underclass was becoming so entrenched that it would prove impervious to the opportunities presented to the rest of society by returning economic growth.

The Thatcher years were particularly anxious ones for those whose outlook valued the presumed stability offered by conventional family structures. For them, alternative ways of living posed a challenge and the evidence of social atomization represented their consequence. Some – but not all – of the statistics appeared to bear out the charge that the decisive shift had actually taken place before Thatcherism took hold. The level of marital break-up, for instance, suggested that the eighties confirmed, rather than accelerated or reversed, the trend of the previous two decades. The divorce rate had soared during the sixties and seventies: in England and Wales there were 37,657 petitions for divorce between 1961–5 and 162,481 in 1976–80 – an increase of 331 per cent, which far outstripped the population increase of scarcely 5 per cent per decade. After rising modestly in the first half of the eighties, the numbers getting divorced then gently slid to 152,360 between 1986 and 1990, a fall of over 6 per cent from ten years earlier.[7] This decline was only slightly exacerbated by proportionately fewer marriages being contracted.[8] The essential point, however, was that, although the period of steady ascent in the divorce rate had come to an end, it remained close to its all-time peak. No such plateaus were reached in the growing levels either of illegitimate births or of abortions. Here, it was the eighties that witnessed the great change in behaviour, with births outside marriage accounting for 12 per cent

---

* Though different means of calculating entitlement between the 1930s and 1980s made an exact comparison between the two rates misleading.

of all births in 1981 but over 26 per cent by 1989 (the rate continued to soar thereafter and had reached 46 per cent by 2009).[9] Neither the easier availability of contraception nor the destigmatizing of illegitimacy reduced the number of terminations carried out. The rate of legal abortions in England and Wales during the late seventies ran at a little over 110,000 per year, but reached 160,000 per year in the late eighties.[10] The exception was in Northern Ireland, where abortion remained illegal.

In the meantime, the nature of the family had undergone a transformation. By 1984, there were nearly a million one-parent families in the UK. The incidence of divorce was one reason, the numbers of births outside a stable relationship another. Single mothers who had never shared a household with a partner became a significant group in society (rising by 168 per cent from 160,000 in 1981 to 430,000 in 1991).[11] The social assumptions upon which Beveridge's version of the welfare state had been founded – of an average household in which the husband was the breadwinner for a wife and child – now appeared to belong to a bygone age: an age that had been dismembered by the shrinking number of breadwinning partners, whether because of widespread joblessness or because, out of personal choice, they were no longer partners. For some single mothers, friends or relatives provided the support necessary to allow them to hold down at least a part-time job, but for many others dependency upon supplementary benefits became a way of life – and, to the Treasury, a cause for alarm. Thatcher's intention that absentee fathers should not escape paying their share to the mothers of their children was not realized until the Child Support Act 1991 was introduced, which only reached the statute book after she had fallen from office. The only working mother to become prime minister, her understanding of why many mothers might prefer to stay at home to bring up their children was nonetheless sufficiently strong for her to reject proposals that would have introduced a tax allowance for childcare. There was disappointment for those who wanted the sticks and carrots of taxes and benefits to be used in a way designed to recreate the environment of the 1950s. Tax breaks to support marriage ran up against Nigel Lawson's desire to simplify the tax system, and it was not until 1988 that some of the income tax penalties operating against marriage began to be reduced. Husbands and wives were finally taxed independently in 1990.

Despite these years of major social change, there was in eighties Britain nothing remotely comparable to the campaign for 'family values' that so energized the conservative movement in Reagan's America. The Cabinet was populated by politicians who had either endorsed (with whatever level of enthusiasm) many of the measures that created the 'permissive society' in the sixties or had long since come to accept them as irreversible. In 1967, Thatcher had voted in favour of legalizing both homosexuality and abortion and she was not minded to reverse either move while in Downing Street, though she did allow Section 28's inoperable attempt to stop local councils from actively promoting gay relationships.* Nor had she any intention of reversing the legislation that had made divorce easier (though married to a divorcee she had voted against the liberalization in 1968, concerned by what she took to be its implications for deserted wives and families).[12] Nevertheless, divorce was made easier in 1984 by the passage of the Matrimonial and Family Proceedings Act, which reduced the minimum length of time between marriage and filing for divorce from three years to one year. Thereafter, Thatcher was keen to keep the divorce law as it stood, which was why she did not look favourably upon the Law Commission's November 1990 recommendations for the introduction of 'no-fault' divorce.[13] The greatest threat to the scope of the abortion law came not from government ministers but from a private member's bill introduced in 1988 by the Liberal Democrat MP David Alton, which attracted sufficient cross-party support to gain a second reading before being talked out of time. Even that only envisaged preventing the relatively small proportion of terminations that took place after eighteen weeks, which it hoped to make the new upper limit in place of the existing twenty-eight weeks. As for contraception, Whitehall was certainly not going to do anything to reduce the effectiveness of the fight against Aids and teenage pregnancy. The courts were similarly robust. In 1985, Victoria Gillick, a mother of ten, lost her protracted legal battle to stop doctors prescribing contraceptives to under-16-year-olds unless they had parental consent – though the British Social Attitudes survey did suggest a majority of the population backed her stance.[14]

Law and Disorder

There could be few clearer signs of a fractured society than soaring rates of crime, and in this respect the eighties brought an alarming breakdown of order. In England and Wales, the number of indictable criminal offences notified to the police rose by 52 per cent in the decade between 1979 and 1989, from over 2.5 million to over 3.8 million. The single biggest category, theft and handling stolen goods, rose by 42 per cent, while violence against the person increased by 86 per cent and sexual offences rose by 36 per cent. In Scotland, total offences rose by one third. Only in Northern Ireland was the increase, at one tenth, noticeably more modest.[15] Even more alarming was the implication of the British Crime Survey that the number of reported offences hugely underestimated the real level of crime.

As with changes in the structure of the family, there was no consensus on

---

* See p. 330.

which factors were driving criminal activity. If theft was a response to job losses, were sexual offences equally attributable to socio-economic factors? To Thatcher, of course, the link was neither proven nor, if it did exist, justifiable. Blame was more properly directed not at the state but at a state of mind channelled by social and political radicals towards scepticism and disrespect towards institutions, authority and discipline. 'We are reaping what was sown in the sixties,' Thatcher told a meeting of party delegates in March 1982. 'The fashionable theories and permissive claptrap set the scene for a society in which the old virtues of discipline and self-restraint were denigrated.'[16] She was still on this theme five years later, assuring the party conference that 'civilized society doesn't just happen. It has to be sustained by standards widely accepted and upheld' – which was why 'when left-wing councils and left-wing teachers criticize the police they give moral sanction to the criminally inclined'.[17] 'We Conservatives know,' she told her last party conference as leader, 'even if many sociologists don't, that crime is not a sickness to be cured – it's a temptation to be resisted, a threat to be deterred, an evil to be punished.'[18]

One identifiable stimulant of this counter-culture originated from beyond the limits of national sovereignty. In January 1979, an Islamic revolution deposed the shah in Tehran, causing a temporary spike in opium production while power changed hands and opponents of the new regime whose bank accounts had been frozen sought out alternative means of accessing money. Then, in December that year, the Soviet Union invaded Afghanistan, only to be met by resistance funded partly from the proceeds of the country's swiftly expanding opium crop. The result was the swamping of the West with cheap and easily available heroin. During 1979, the price of one gram of heroin fell from £200 to £50, and it continued to slide thereafter. Heroin users multiplied and by 1984 were estimated to number fifty thousand Britons.[19] With nothing better to occupy their time, addicts sought oblivion in the 'shooting galleries' of housing estates in Glasgow, Edinburgh, Manchester and other pockets of deprivation. To fund their addiction, they turned to street crime and burglary, since disproportionately heroin addicts were, or had become, unemployed – and in danger of becoming unemployable. In this respect, the fights against crime, drugs and the sense of purposeless were clearly intertwined.

The opinion polls suggested that regardless of where the public looked for the causes of crime, they overwhelmingly preferred the Conservatives' solutions to those offered by Labour or the SDP–Liberal Alliance. The impression that Labour was not greatly exercised by the evident crime wave was reinforced by the party's 1983 election manifesto, which proposed various measures to hold the police to greater account and to improve conditions for prisoners, while downgrading the tackling of criminality to a couple of sketchily imprecise generalities which read suspiciously like afterthoughts.[20] Particularly for those on the left of the party, restraining the forces of law and order sometimes appeared to be the priority. 'The police are one of the most worrying aspects of society and have become a very political organization indeed,' claimed one of the left's standard-bearers and leader of the Greater London Council, Ken Livingstone.[21] Certainly, the police had personal cause to be thankful that there was a Conservative government in office which was busy greatly expanding their numbers and dramatically increasing their pay. In other measures designed at getting tough with criminals, a new prison-building programme was instituted and the Criminal Justice Act 1988 sought to lengthen some prison terms by giving the Attorney General the power to appeal against supposedly over-lenient sentences. At the same time, the legislation tried to deal more sensitively with those who were victims of crime, offering compensation as well as better protection for children in court proceedings and privacy in child-abuse cases.

The public pronouncements of the prime minister and the rhetoric at successive Conservative Party conferences left little doubt that the Tories were the self-styled party of law and order. The reality was more complex. While Thatcher could be labelled as, at least by instinct, a hanger and flogger, she had actually long ceased to regard bringing back the birch as practical politics (nevertheless, she did vote against scrapping corporal punishment in state schools when, on a free vote, Parliament decided, by a majority of one, to end the practice in November 1986). Even the proposal for the restoration of capital punishment, which she supported, was restricted to those found guilty of terrorism or killing police officers, and would therefore not have impinged upon the vast majority of homicide cases. When it was debated in the Commons, soon after the Conservatives came to power, in July 1979, MPs rejected the proposal by 362 to 243 (among Tory MPs the vote was 228 in favour and ninety-four against, the latter group including the Home Secretary, Willie Whitelaw). Despite occasional calls to give all police officers the protection of firearms, the government preferred to keep Britain's streets as the only ones in Western Europe routinely policed by an unarmed force.

These were not the only differences between tough talk and more nuanced action. Conviction rates did not remotely correspond with the level of crimes being perpetrated. By 1985, only 22 per cent of notified robberies were cleared up.[22] The numbers found guilty of indictable offences increased during the first half of the decade, only to fall so sharply after 1985 that in England and Wales there were nearly seventy-three thousand fewer sentences handed down in 1989 than in 1979 – despite the intervening rise in crimes committed.[23] The ratio of prisoners to the level of criminal convictions was lower during the eighties than in any previous decade of the twentieth century.[24] The Home Office expressed the desire that judges should not impose custodial sentences on those responsible for non-violent burglaries because of the fear that putting such (usually) young offenders in prison, however briefly, merely enrolled them in an academy of crime and brutality which would make their rehabilitation less, rather than more, likely. This attitude was particularly prevalent when Douglas Hurd was Home Secretary, between 1985 and 1989, since he regarded the increase in the average annual prison population in England and Wales from 42,220 to 46,000 over the previous five years as a sign of policy failure rather than of success – though it was only by the end of his Home Office tenure that his efforts to reduce custodial sentences began to have an effect.[25] By contrast, it was during the nineties that the governments of first John Major and then Tony Blair actively propounded a 'prison works' strategy to reverse the comparatively liberal attitude of the eighties. A far cry from the 1985 statistics that had alarmed Douglas Hurd, by 2008 the prison population exceeded eighty thousand. This was a shift of policy that coincided with – whether or not it engineered – the falling crime rates experienced in Britain, the United States and most other industrialized Western countries at the end of the century.

Policing in the eighties was far from confined to detecting and preventing individual criminal acts. In contrast to the relative civic order of the post-war period, policing had also come to be about dealing with displays of drunken rowdiness in town centres – the decade gave birth to the term 'lager lout' – as well as controlling violent mass protest and outbursts of potent thuggery. The rise of football hooliganism provided one test, the containment of political rallies and industrial disputes that turned to violence another. The pitched battles fought during the 1984 miners' strike and the 1986 'siege' of Rupert Murdoch's newspaper printing plant at Wapping are discussed in the next chapter. In the year between those two conflicts between management and unions, there was a return of full-scale urban uprisings whose distinctive feature was racial tension and whose target was the police. The rioting in several English inner-city areas in the autumn of 1985 was a reminder that the cinders of the 'long hot summer' of 1981 had not been fully extinguished.

Events began on 9 September in the Lozells area of Handsworth in west Birmingham, when the arrest of a suspected drug trafficker triggered a violent response from local youths – mostly black – who began attacking the police and engaging in widespread looting and arson, which culminated in the burning to death of two Asian shopkeepers in their post office. An even wider breakdown of order took place on 28 September, when a bungled police raid in Brixton resulted in the accidental shooting of the mother of Michael Groce, an armed robber who days previously had evaded capture by sticking a gun into the apprehending policeman's mouth. The rumour quickly spread that Mrs Groce had been killed (she had, in fact, been crippled by the shot), inciting fury among those in the black community who saw this as just the most grievous instance of how the police's prejudices had remained untouched by the lessons of the Scarman report. A crowd of local black youths responded by attacking the nearby police station with Molotov cocktails. The efforts of a black priest to pacify the mob through a loudhailer had to be abandoned when he, too, came under a shower of fire-bombs. As news of the disturbances spread, the mostly black rioters were joined by white thugs, alongside agitators from the Revolutionary Communist Party and the anarchist group Class War. Shops were ransacked and set ablaze, as was a block of flats on Gresham Road and the Conservative Club on Effra Road. In the ensuing battle, a freelance photo-journalist working for the *Sunday Telegraph* was set upon by looters and beaten up so severely that he died from head injuries, and two 23-year-old white girls (one reportedly an MP's daughter) were raped by black youths, one in her house, the other openly in the street.[26] Fifty-three people were injured and 230 arrested.

Three days later, riots broke out again in Toxteth, following the charging of four black youths over a stabbing incident. Then, on 6 October, the trouble moved to the Broadwater Farm estate in Tottenham, in north London, ignited by similar circumstances to those that had sparked the trouble in Brixton. In the trauma of a police raid on her home, the (black) mother of a man suspected of possessing stolen goods suffered a heart attack and died. Within hours, the housing estate had erupted, with mostly black youths – joined by some whites, who were described as 'skinheads' – engaging in widespread looting and assaults on police lines. With its grim, forbidding concrete gantries and elevated walkways, Broadwater Farm proved the ideal citadel from which to lob concrete blocks and petrol bombs at those struggling to restore order below. For the first time in the century, rioters were armed with guns. One police officer was shot in the abdomen and two others were also treated for gunshot wounds. The firing seemed indiscriminate, with a BBC cameraman shot in the eye and a Press Association reporter receiving multiple pellet wounds. A blaze was started by the petrol-bombing of a shop and when firefighters arrived to tackle the flames they, too, came under attack. As the police moved forwards in an effort to protect the firefighters, one officer, PC Keith Blakelock, tripped and stumbled to the ground. He was immediately set upon by a mob wielding knives and a machete. Lacerated by forty-two blows, the helpless Blakelock was hacked to death – the first serving policeman to be killed in a mainland British riot since 1833. In total, the night's carnage produced over two hundred and twenty injuries, two hundred of which were to police officers.[27] 'This is not England,' a bewildered police officer told the BBC. 'This is just madness.

My men are being used as target practice.' No sooner had the riot been quelled than Bernie Grant, the Labour leader of Haringey council, addressed a rally outside Tottenham town hall where he explained what he took to be the views of local youths, that 'the police were to blame for what happened on Sunday night and what they got was a bloody good hiding. There is no way I am going to condemn the actions of the youth on Sunday night.'[28] His desire to be associated with the rioters' actions was greeted with cheers from the crowd and widespread condemnation beyond. Grant, who had recently become Britain's first black council leader, was two years later elected as the country's first black MP.

The Home Secretary, Douglas Hurd, promised to 'get tough' with those who were responsible for 'the lawlessness which has broken out amongst ethnic communities in inner-city areas'.[29] But the legacy of the riots also brought changes to police procedures. In the hope of avoiding repetition of the incompetence that had left Cherry Groce paralysed, CID detectives lost the right to carry guns, with firearms use henceforth restricted to designated trained units within the police force. At the same time, the Home Secretary found his hard words about lawlessness among ethnic communities equally applicable to white youths attracted to the sub-culture of football hooliganism. The sport had long attracted sporadic off-pitch episodes of rowdy – and on rare occasions even violent – behaviour, though during the seventies such outbursts had become more frequent and necessitated the erection of pens on the terraces in order to prevent opposing factions from attacking one another or surging on to the pitch. Such measures sought to contain the behaviour. Preventing it at source was more difficult. The 'English disease' became a common phrase on both sides of the Straits of Dover, reflecting the manner in which the nation's hooligans were distinguishing themselves among their European rivals by the extent and savagery of their antics.

Called in by the government in 1985 to investigate safety and trouble at football grounds, the High Court judge Sir Oliver Popplewell noted that hooliganism was by no means confined to those who had been hardened by the dispiriting experience of unemployment and poverty into becoming antisocial yobs. Rather, many 'often hold down good jobs during the week, dress stylishly and detach themselves from those fans with club scarves who travel on official coaches or trains. They plan their violence as a recreation in itself to which football is secondary or a mere background.'[30] Buttoned-up shirts with cashmere V-neck sweaters was one look that distinguished the premeditated hooligan, though some went as far as wearing Italian-made suits. Generically designated 'casuals', they adopted monikers specific to their chosen club. In London, Chelsea had its Headhunters, Millwall its Bushwhackers and West Ham the ICF (Inter-City Firm), so called because its members preferred to travel in the relative comfort of InterCity125 trains

– they took to issuing printed ICF calling cards to their victims as they attacked them. In Birmingham there were City's Zulus and Aston Villa's multi-racial C-Crew and Steamers. In Edinburgh, Hibernian had the CCS (Capital City Service) and Hearts the CSF (Casual Soccer Firm). Like the Bank Holiday seaside fisticuffs between Mods and Rockers of twenty years previously, and given Popplewell's finding that most were in full-time employment, this seemed to be more about finding an identity distinct from the mundane and conventional working environment than a consequence of exclusion from that world. While the organized violence was overwhelmingly perpetrated between whites, the verbal hostility mouthed towards black players on the pitch (who had been rare in top-flight football until the eighties) and the involvement of far-right agitators among some casual groups added a racist dimension. The cultural influence of Ulster's paramilitary organizations was particularly evident in Scotland, where sectarianism distinguished the two main clubs in Glasgow and, to a lesser extent, in Edinburgh. Like all fashions, copycat behaviour drove the football firms' style and formation. Scenes of disorder and violence from the Troubles in Northern Ireland, which were a regular feature of television news coverage throughout the seventies and eighties, supplemented by inner-city riots and strikes that turned into pitched battles with the police, may well have been factors indirectly influencing the hooligan mentality.

Thus it was that escalating levels of injury and death appeared to incite further aggression among those competing to top the league for raw masculinity. On 11 May 1985, the same day on which a discarded cigarette caused a fire to sweep through the aged wooden stand at Bradford City football ground, killing fifty-six spectators and injuring 255 more, Leeds United hooligans rioted at Birmingham City's ground – in the melee, 125 arrests were made and a wall tipped over, killing a boy. Less than three weeks later, on 29 May, just as the European Cup final was about to start in the decrepit Heysel stadium in Brussels, Liverpool fans attending the match followed up their opening barrage of projectiles with an all-out assault on Juventus fans, smashing through the segregating barriers and charging into the Juventus end of the ground. As the Italian fans tried to flee, a crush developed and a wall collapsed, killing thirty-nine of them and injuring six hundred more. Despite what had just been witnessed, officials were so fearful of what might happen if they cancelled the game that they let it go ahead, providing the players with a police escort on and off the pitch. With Thatcher's encouragement, the Football Association announced a ban for the rest of the season on English clubs participating in European competition, an admission of shame and defeat that failed to head off stiffer penalties from UEFA, which duly banned all English clubs from Europe until the 1990/1 season (with the punishment of an extra year for Liverpool). The ban did not affect the

English national team. The carnage at the Heysel stadium appeared not to have had any sobering effect on the two hundred and fifty England fans arrested for going on the rampage in four German cities during the European Championships in June 1988.

The worst tragedy of the decade followed on 15 April 1989 at the Hillsborough ground in Sheffield during an FA Cup semi-final tie, when ninety-six Liverpool fans were crushed to death. Violence was not the cause – the number of late arrivals panicked the police into opening turnstiles that were meant to be shut, creating an unanticipated flow of five thousand supporters who were not properly directed towards where there was still space in the stand. They therefore pushed into an already packed area, causing suffocation. Much as human error was the cause, the regular experience of having to deal with hooliganism had a bearing on the horrifying turn of events, for it was the need to contain and separate supporters that had necessitated the pens that confined and crushed the fans; and when many of those scrambling for their lives tried to climb over the perimeter fence, some police officers failed to comprehend what was happening and initially assumed they were hooligans intent on a pitch invasion. In an effort to deflect blame, police officers proceeded to doctor witness statements and propagate the myth (duly spread by *The Sun*) that the tragedy was spurred by drunk and unruly Liverpool fans. Yet if the real lessons were learned by those responsible for crowd control, the same could not be said of those who remained bent on violence. Four weeks after the shocking scenes at Hillsborough, the police were back in action trying to separate Birmingham City and Crystal Palace fans fighting on the Selhurst Park terraces, the City fans taking advantage of a low perimeter fence to invade the pitch and disrupt the match for half an hour until dispersed by a police cavalry charge.

Among the traits by which Britain's first female prime minister distinguished herself from her predecessors and successors was that she never feigned an interest in football. But finding a cure for the 'English disease' was for her an absolute priority. The Scottish precedent (introduced in 1980) of banning alcohol within grounds was extended to England and Wales, with the Public Order Act 1986 empowering courts to prevent identified individuals from entering grounds. Further legislation in 1989 allowed for convicted hooligans to be banned from going to international matches. A more drastic policy initiative was sparked by events in March 1985 when Millwall hooligans ran amok at Luton Town, partially wrecking one of the Kenilworth Road stands in a riot that injured more than thirty police officers, one of them almost fatally. Rather than risk a repetition, Luton Town responded by restricting home matches to its own supporters, who would have to apply for membership/identity cards. These could be denied to troublemakers. It represented an extreme response which seemed explicable only in the context of the Popplewell report's warning that unless hooligan-ism was crushed, 'football may not be able to continue in its present form much longer'. There was much to be said against the proposal, which would clearly deter the uncommitted match-goer (perhaps the least inclined to violence), and it failed to address the ease with which those denied identity cards could merely organize their violence in the surrounding streets – where many of the clashes took place. Brushing aside doubters within the FA and her own Cabinet (including Douglas Hurd), Thatcher became con-vinced that a mandatory identity card-based national membership scheme for all football supporters was the answer. The enabling legislation was rushed through Parliament in 1989, only to be successfully derailed by the Taylor report, called in response to the Hillsborough disaster, which in January 1990 argued powerfully that the scheme was not a solution.

Where Taylor and Thatcher were agreed was upon the need to upgrade the often dilapidated grounds. The process of rebuilding had begun following the devastating fire at Bradford City. Crumbling facilities and dishevelled ter-racing had failed to keep pace with raised expectations of comfort in family life and, it was felt, represented one reason why attendances had been in long-term decline, creating an atmosphere that discouraged attendance by women and young families with their (presumed) moderating influence. Public lava-tories that were as primitive as they were scarce meant that, as the Taylor report put it, 'urinating against walls or even on the terraces has become endemic', which 'directly lowers standards of conduct'.[31] Overcoming objec-tions that removing standing-only terraces would diminish the atmosphere, the government acted on the Taylor report's recommendation that all grounds in the top two English and Scottish leagues should convert to seating-only stadiums, where each ticket-holder would have an assigned seat. This involved a major investment by clubs, enabled by the timely interjection of a vast new revenue stream from the sale of the Premiership's television rights to Rupert Murdoch's Sky TV. Combined with better policing methods, advance intel-ligence and the use of CCTV at grounds to identify troublemakers, the 'English disease' was severely diminished – though not eliminated – in the following years, while new international investment following from the Sky deal transformed the feel, commercialism and culture of football.

Don't Die of Ignorance

Acquired Immune Deficiency Syndrome began to affect Los Angeles' gay male community at the beginning of the decade and the first – extremely sketchy – discussion of its pneumonia-like symptoms appeared in the medical journal *Morbidity and Mortality Weekly* in July 1981. About four hundred and fifty Aids-related deaths had occurred in the United States by 1983 and it was not until 1984 that American and French doctors isolated the HIV virus. By then the disease had already arrived on British shores, having claimed its first victim, Terrence Higgins, a 37-year-old computer programmer, on 4 July 1982. Five months after his passing, a group of Higgins's friends founded a group in his name to raise funds for research into the still-mysterious disease.

In tandem with research, there was an urgent need for education about the risks. Widespread public attention was not engaged until the broadcast in April 1983 of a BBC Horizon documentary entitled *Killer in the Village*. Shortly thereafter, on 1 May, a *Mail on Sunday* headline warned of a 'gay plague' – a contagious phrase with biblical overtones which quickly embedded itself in the public consciousness, defining both who was primarily affected by the disease and, by implication, who was responsible for its spread. But what was initially transmitted through male gay sex was clearly not going to be confined to gay men, unless it was assumed that none of them ever also slept with a woman. Haemophiliacs were also showing symptoms and the revelation that their infection came from Aids-contaminated blood used by the NHS for transfusions caused further alarm (by the autumn of 1989, ninety-nine haemophiliacs had died and more than a thousand were HIV-positive),[32] tinged with anger that the sexual behaviour of gay men had endangered the lives of others. Calling for the screening of gay men who wanted to give blood (the Home Office subsequently called only for 'promiscuous' gay men to abstain from giving blood), a leader in *The Times* of November 1984 stated: 'The infection's origins and means of propagation excites repugnance, moral and physical, at promiscuous male homosexuality – conduct which, tolerable in private circumstances, has with the advent of "gay liberation" become advertised, even glorified, as acceptable public conduct.'[33]

Despite the efforts of the government's chief medical officer to reassure the public, fear that infection could be spread through non-sexual contact intensified. Sufferers were the object of fear as much as pity, as the desire to protect immediate friends and family from the threatened pandemic clouded objective – let alone compassionate – judgement. In the autumn of 1985, one third of children at a Hampshire primary school were withdrawn from classes by their parents when it emerged that one of their classmates, a nine-year-old haemophiliac, had been accidentally transfused with Aids-contaminated blood. The following year, an Aids sufferer was identified and was banned from swimming pools in Caernarfon and Cardiff until such time as the Sports Council for Wales was satisfied that he, and those like him, presented no risk.[34] Such callousness was dispiriting, yet it was hardly inexplicable given the limits of knowledge at the time. After all, the disease was spreading rapidly. No cure existed. It was not unreasonable to assume that the medical authorities lacked a full understanding of how Aids could be transmitted. If it could be passed on through contaminated blood, then perhaps even fleeting contact with someone with a small cut could prove deadly? The Church of England found itself offering guidance on the celebration of the Eucharist because there was disquiet about whether someone with a cold sore might unintentionally infect a communion cup and wipe out an entire parish. Health workers and prison guards were particularly uneasy about the occupational hazards they believed they might face. Some newspapers managed to strike a balance between compassionate coverage and articulating the scarcely comprehending fears of their readers. Highlighting 'Sarah's tragedy', the *Daily Express* reported: 'She is 23, intelligent and pretty. She has never slept around or used drugs. Today she is dying of Aids. Is anyone safe now?' There was a less nuanced tone at *The Sun*: 'Have You Got Aids? Ten Ways to Find Out' ran one feature which, listing tiredness, weight loss, diarrhoea and a sore mouth, succeeded only in adding to the panic.[35] Some articles were not only uninhibitedly sensational and factually misleading but plain wrong. Even as late as 1989, *The Sun* ran with the claim that Aids could not be passed on through heterosexual sex.[36] On this point, it was forced to climb down, though it remained indignant at complaints about its continuing references to homosexuals as 'poofs'. However, to blame irresponsible or shoddy journalism entirely for stoking public anxiety would be to focus far too narrowly on who was disseminating information. Those in positions of authority at the time were reduced to making educated guesses which proved grossly inaccurate. In January 1985, for instance, the Royal College of Nursing forecast that by 1991 there would be one million Aids sufferers in the UK.[37] Extrapolating such a rate appeared to spell doom for the human race unless a cure could be found. 'I can assure you that half of the boys in this room will be dead in thirty years' time because of what you think is a laughing matter,' one Edinburgh schoolmaster admonished his class, when a pupil responded to the announcement of an Aids prevention lecture by striking a limp-wristed posture.[38] At any rate, the Edinburgh tradition of young people going up to the Royal Mile to greet the New Year by sharing drinks and kissing strangers all but ceased that Hogmanay, given the concern that traces of blood in saliva could potentially deliver the kiss of death. The combined threats to human life on earth from Aids and nuclear Armageddon made the mid-eighties a period disfigured by fear.

Within the UK, twenty-nine cases of Aids had been recorded by the end of 1983, 106 by 1984, 271 by 1985 and 610 by 1986.[39] A breakdown of the country's 1,762 Aids cases in October 1988 showed that 87 per cent of them – 1,532 in all – had been contracted though homosexual acts. By comparison, the other causes remained small in scale: 123 cases through contaminated blood given to haemophiliacs, sixty-nine through heterosexual activity and thirty-eight though sharing of contaminated needles by intravenous drug users.[40] The following year took the total up to 2,296, which, for all its seri-ousness, was nevertheless far short of the earlier predictions of one million sufferers within the next two years. While heading towards epidemic pro-portions across sub-Saharan Africa, Aids was failing to spread at the expected rate in the First World. One factor, of course, was the change in sexual behaviour engendered by education about the disease and screening among the communities most at risk. In 1987, HIV testing was introduced across the country and needle-exchange centres were established to protect intra-venous drug users. That the UK's rate of transmission was significantly less than that of France suggested that the speed with which action had been taken was a significant factor.[41]

Preventive measures – which included supplying heroin addicts with the means of delivering one health risk in order to save them contracting and spreading another – demonstrated the extent to which the government had determined upon drastic action. By contrast, in December 1986 the head of the Roman Catholic Church in England and Wales, Cardinal Basil Hume, warned of a 'moral Chernobyl'. Far from offering 'tacit acceptance', he maintained that using condoms represented 'a counsel of despair' because sex belonged exclusively within marriage and otherwise abstinence offered the only means of combating the disease.[42] When the BBC tried to promote Aids awareness among the young, Monsignor Vincent Nichols (Hume's successor but one) accused the corporation of 'disregarding moral principles' by promoting condom use under the slogan 'Play Safe'.[43] Endorsement of self-discipline also came from 'God's copper', as the tabloid press had taken to calling the chief constable of Manchester police, James Anderton. He condemned those most at risk from Aids – homosexuals and users of drugs and prostitutes – as the authors of their own misfortune: 'as the years go by, I see ever increasing numbers of them swirling around in a human cesspit of their own making', adding, 'why do homosexuals freely engage in sodomy and other obnoxious sexual practices, knowing the dangers involved? . . . Why is this question not asked of these people?'[44] Treading the little-worn path from Methodist lay preacher to Roman Catholic convert, Anderton claimed his opinions were guided by his faith; and although he was censured by the Association of Chief Police Officers (of which he was president), Manchester police stations were deluged with telephone calls from the public voicing support for him. *The Sun* joined the plaudits, recommending: 'What Britain needs is more men like James Anderton – and fewer gay terrorists holding the decent members of society to ransom.'[45] As late as 1988, the British Social Attitudes survey suggested that two thirds of the population believed the government's Aids campaign should go beyond health advice and issue moral strictures against some sexual practices.[46]

Thatcher, however, chose to ignore the advice of the social and religious commentator Malcolm Muggeridge who wrote to her advocating bringing the anti-smut campaigner Mary Whitehouse into the Cabinet to articulate the response to the crisis.[47] Much as the prime minister instinctively found distasteful the sending of leaflets discussing 'anal sex' to every home in the land, she accepted the judgement of her health secretary, Norman Fowler, and health minister, Tony Newton, that an uninhibited explanation of the risks and preventive measures should be the priority. Fowler and Newton also secured an increase to their department's budget for Aids publicity from £2.5 million to £20 million. The government's first major campaign was launched in March 1986 and gave practical – as opposed to moral – advice. In November, a special Cabinet committee, chaired by the deputy prime minister, Willie Whitelaw, began coordinating government action, discussing the threat from Aids in tones previously reserved for war and terrorism. Among the ideas muted (before being dropped) was for the health secretary to deliver a broadcast to the nation. Two weeks later, an emergency debate in the Commons revealed considerable cross-party support for the approach adopted by Fowler and Whitelaw's Cabinet committee. In the New Year, the official leaflet went out to the nation's twenty-three million households. It recommended the use of condoms and advised against sharing needles for injecting drugs, counselling parents to discuss these precautions with their family, because 'whether you approve of it or not, many teenagers do have sex and some may experiment with drugs. Even if you think your children don't, they will need advice because they may have friends who encourage them to.' It went on to offer reassurance that the virus could not be passed on through shaking hands, kissing, sharing cups and cutlery or from public baths or lavatory seats.[48] The leaflet, entitled 'Don't Die of Ignorance', was supported by an intensive advertising campaign which ran across billboards, television (the BBC as well as ITV and Channel 4) and in cinemas, relaying the hard-hitting message alongside imposing images of icebergs whose great bulk lay concealed beneath the surface and giant tombstones chiselled with the word 'Aids'.

While the government was at pains to instil the message that protecting against the virus was everyone's responsibility, the disease naturally returned homosexuality to the forefront of national attention. Lesbianism had always escaped the restrictions of statute law, while sex between consenting men over the age of twenty-one had been legal in England and Wales since 1967. But it had remained illegal in Scotland and Northern Ireland, where public opinion had prevented the reform's extension. It took the Criminal Justice (Scotland) Act 1980 to legalize it in Scotland and, following a ruling of the European Court of Human Rights in Strasbourg, the government legislated to decriminalize male gay acts in Ulster in 1982. Throughout the realm, the law continued to prosecute men under the age of twenty-one who had gay sex, for which there were over two thousand arrests between 1988 and 1991 alone.[49] Popular apprehensions were hardly likely to be allayed by the spread of Aids. A British Social Attitudes survey suggested the proportion of those believing homosexual relationships were either always or mostly wrong had risen from almost two thirds in 1983 to three quarters of the population by 1988. Only 10 per cent of Scots stated that they thought there was nothing wrong with homosexuality.[50]

In 1976, what became the Lesbian and Gay Christian Movement was founded by two Anglican priests, Richard Kirker and Peter Elers, the latter having escaped with a mild admonishment for performing a service of blessing – interpreted as a symbolic wedding – for two lesbian couples. In February 1981, Elers and another vicar, Robert Lewis, testified to their sexuality before the Church of England's General Synod. Both clergymen continued to enjoy the support of their parishioners and efforts to pass con-demnatory motions were sidelined by the synod. Already poised for possible schism over the issue of female ordination, the Archbishop of Canterbury, Robert Runcie, was particularly keen to avoid opening a new avenue for division, though he did express his personal sentiment that homosexuals ought not simply to be condemned as sinners but treated with greater under-standing, as if they were disabled – because the disabled could often 'obtain a degree of self-giving and compassion which are denied to those not simi-larly afflicted'. He thought it acceptable for clergymen to campaign for gay liberation, but they could not remain ordained if the zeal of their campaign was to the detriment of their other duties.[51] In November 1987, the General Synod passed a motion that gay sex – along with fornication and adultery – fell 'short of the ideal' and therefore necessitated repentance, while rejecting another motion calling for homosexual clergy to be removed from their posts.

Meanwhile, gay politicians remained reticent about 'coming out'. The revelation in the mid-seventies that the Labour MP Maureen Colquhoun had left her family for another woman was quickly followed by an attempt to deselect her by her constituency party. She was reinstated, only to lose her seat in the 1979 general election. That George Thomas, the Speaker of the House until 1983, was gay remained unknown beyond a few trusted friends. It was a private life the Methodist lay preacher was prepared to protect even at the expense of paying off blackmailers.[52] Speaking briefly during the Commons debate in October 1982 which legalized homosexual acts in Northern Ireland, Matthew Parris made clear he supported the measure 'strongly and personally . . . with all my heart', a choice of words to which no deeper meaning was accorded at the time. As Parris later confessed: 'Not the whips, not my parliamentary colleagues and not the press, but anxiety about my constituency and all the good people there who had taken me on trust and worked for me: this was what in the end held me back from making myself plain.' The following year, after Parris had spoken at an Oxford Union debate in favour of gay rights, a whip tried to offer him well-intentioned advice: 'I don't believe in God. But I don't shout about it. I don't feel the need to add it to my election address at general elections – special box, bold type: *Your Conservative candidate does not believe in God . . .* It's private.'[53]

The Bermondsey by-election of February 1983 demonstrated both the perils of making an issue out of gay rights and the level of innuendo to which a candidate suspected of homosexuality could be subjected. The local Labour party had adopted as their candidate Peter Tatchell. The young agitator's views were controversial, for besides gay rights he was also an opponent of the monarchy and had written about the case for 'direct action' beyond Parliament. But he was defending a majority of almost twelve thousand and there was not much chance of a constituency in a deprived stretch of south-east London returning a Tory. Tatchell was nevertheless persuaded by the Labour Party not to confirm his sexual orientation – though given the pub-licity, nudges and winks to which he was subjected during the campaign, staying in the closet hardly offered much shelter. The attention of the tabloid press, for whom Tatchell was the embodiment of everything that had gone wrong with Labour, was supplemented by the smear tactics of local Liberal activists campaigning for their candidate, Simon Hughes.[54] Badges were produced with the boast 'I have been kissed by Peter Tatchell', while Hughes's campaign literature announced that he offered 'the Straight Choice' against his Labour opponent. Anonymous leaflets were also widely circu-lated with a picture of Her Majesty and a photograph of a particularly effeminate-looking Tatchell alongside the question 'Which Queen Will You Vote For?' The result was an unwanted post-war record for Labour: a swing away from the party of 44 per cent and a 9,319 Liberal majority. Having won the seat, 'the Straight Choice' did not admit to his own bisexu-ality until twenty-four years later, by which time he was president of the Liberal Democrats.

In such circumstances, it was courageous of the Labour MP Chris Smith to become, in November 1984, the first politician to 'out' himself. His example spurred no immediate imitators, even though within three years he was appointed to the shadow Treasury team. Instead, in June 1986 scandal exposed the right-wing Conservative MP for Billericay, Harvey Proctor, whose participation in spanking parties with, among others, a seventeen-year-old rent boy, ended his parliamentary career with a prosecution and a fine for gross indecency. The actor Michael Cashman's portrayal of an alto-gether more committed gay relationship – the first of its kind to be aired on

British television – featured in *EastEnders* in 1987. Cashman duly found himself joining Sir Ian McKellen and other prominent campaigners in opposing a measure that came to epitomize the counter-attack against gay rights. In doing so, Cashman and McKellen were instrumental in establishing the gay pressure group Stonewall. The *casus belli* was the stocking in some libraries of *Jenny Lives with Eric and Martin*, a picture-book for primary school children about a young girl living happily with her father and his boyfriend. Having received little attention on its publication in 1981, the book suddenly became – at least in terms of public notoriety – the *Lady Chatterley's Lover* of 1987. For those like the arts minister, Richard Luce, there seemed to be an extraordinary double standard operating whereby the Labour-controlled councils that intentionally stocked children's libraries with books 'which seemed positively to advocate homosexuality' were usually the same authorities that simultaneously banned books 'which had given generations of children great pleasure because they were allegedly "racist" or "sexist"'.[55] While no legal mechanism existed to save Biggles or the Famous Five from becoming proscribed reading in Labour-run libraries, two Conservative backbenchers, David Wilshire and Dame Jill Knight, took it upon themselves to retaliate by banning the likes of *Jenny Lives with Eric and Martin*. They did so by tabling an amendment – Section 28 – to the local government bill which stipulated that local authorities 'shall not intentionally promote homosexuality' nor 'promote the teaching in any maintained school of the acceptability of homosexuality as a pretended family relationship'. The measure passed with government support, even though legally it was effectively unworkable because the difference between providing information upon – as distinct from promoting – homosexuality was not easily definable, and the government had made clear that it did not apply to educational material in the fight to contain Aids. The expectation of the Tory backbencher Peter Bruinvels (who duly lost his seat in the 1987 general election) that it would 'help outlaw' homosexuality, 'and the rest will be done by Aids', proved far from prescient.[56] No prosecutions under Section 28 had been brought by the time of its repeal in 2003. What was intended as a totem of Tory support for family values and opposition to the supposed 'misuse' of local ratepayers' money by left-wing councils managed only to garner sympathy for the gay rights cause. A law directed specifically against a named minority smacked of vilification and contributed towards the perception that the Conservatives were not the party of civil liberties.

Faith, Hope and Charity

In 1975, the Archbishop of Canterbury, Donald Coggan, issued a 'call to the nation' beseeching Britons to consider the sort of society in which they wished to live and to embrace the need for spiritual renewal. Fleetingly, there was a response, followed by a murmur and then silence. Understandably, Coggan's successor, Robert Runcie, was not encouraged to come up with an encore. Holding together a Church of England whose unity risked fracture over the extent of its engagement with secular attitudes, rather than a comprehensive reassertion of the spiritual over the secular, encapsulated Runcie's tenure at Canterbury, which ran from 1980 to 1991, almost contemporaneously with Thatcher's premiership. In his politics as in expounding his personal theology, Runcie's tone was undemonstrative and, as such, suited to the task of conciliation. This unceasing search for consensus – not least where little of it could be discerned – represented a very different approach from that of Thatcher, whom he had first met in 1946 when both were members of the Oxford University Conservative Association (though only one of them also had a subscription to the University's Labour Club). Some controversial issues he safely navigated. The issue of homosexual clergymen was deferred rather than defused. The pronouncement of the General Synod's standing committee in February 1981 against re-examining the prohibition on church weddings for divorced persons kept another contentious matter off the agenda, though – after a struggle with the ecclesiastical committee of Parliament – being divorced ceased to be a bar to ordination in 1990. Calming the debate over ordaining women clergy proved altogether more difficult.

That the church could proceed, in principle, towards examining how women might be ordained as priests had been affirmed by the General Synod in 1975. The practical difficulty of finding the necessary majority for any such scheme explained why no enabling legislation ensued. In July 1979, the Movement for the Ordination of Women was founded with the Bishop of Manchester, Stanley Booth-Clibborn, as moderator. Battle lines were drawn by the formation of its two opposing forces, Women Against the Ordination of Women and the Association for the Apostolic Ministry. These 'antis' found a champion in Graham Leonard, the traditionalist whom Thatcher appointed in 1981 as Bishop of London, even though the prime minister also expressed her personal support for women's ordination. Among the clerics duly outraged at her effrontery in straying beyond the temporal realm was the Bishop of Leicester, who slapped her down with the retort: 'I do not recall that she has studied theology.'[57] In reality, the theological nature of the debate was complicated by practical politics – in particular, what provision would be made for dissenting clergy. Ordaining women could only hinder ecumenical approaches towards the Roman Catholic Church. Indeed, if the dissenting vicars could not be appeased, the prospect lay open for a sizeable defection to Rome. Eventually, in 1987, all three houses of the General Synod got as far as passing a motion that would enable a definitive vote to be taken on women's ordination.* It was a sign of how much persuasion and inducement remained necessary in order to secure reform that a further five years elapsed before the vote was finally held, in November 1992, with victory for female ordination then secured by a margin so narrow that if two members of the laity had voted the other way the necessary two thirds majority would not have been reached.

The consequences of the 1992 vote lie outside the remit of any study of the eighties, but even without women priests the hopes of those seeking greater unity between the two principal Christian churches rested more at a symbolic than a theological level. The encouraging signs that the final report of the Anglican–Roman Catholic International Commission claimed to discern in September 1981 lasted less than twenty-four hours before being disowned by a press release from the Vatican's Congregation for the Doctrine of the Faith, under Cardinal Ratzinger.† When, the following May, Pope John Paul II became the first pontiff to visit Britain, it seemed it was the Old Faith that had the greatest opportunity for renewal. After 450 years of Italian-born popes, the descent upon the Gatwick tarmac of the charismatic Pole, who had survived an assassination attempt only twelve months earlier and who embodied his homeland's struggle for freedom from martial law and communist ideology, resonated beyond the direct enthusiasm of the faithful. The trip had nearly been cancelled at the last moment by the outbreak of the Falklands War in April, with the Vatican's apprehensions assuaged only by the scheduling of a counterbalancing trip to Argentina and the agreement that the pope would meet Queen Elizabeth but not the prime minister. The enduring image of the trip was provided by pope and archbishop kneeling together in prayer before the tomb of St Thomas à Becket in Canterbury Cathedral, though the most extraordinary testament to the pontiff's appeal came in Glasgow's Bellahouston Park where three hundred thousand people (almost 40 per cent of the entire Catholic population of Scotland) turned up for mass. Yet for all such displays, when reduced to the accountancy ledger, the best the Roman Catholic Church could achieve in Britain during the eighties was a congregation declining at a gentler rate than the protestant competition. The pope was no more able to reverse the trend with his visit than was the American evangelical preacher Billy Graham with his Mission England tour of the summer of 1984. Over one million people crowded into the enclosures of the nation's football grounds to hear Graham interpret the gospels, in a series of events of which the only enduring legacy was a new hymn-book, *Mission Praise*. Only the Pentecostal Church, which drew its congregations disproportionately from the Afro-Caribbean community,

---

* The Bishops voted by 28 to 21, clergy by 137 to 102, laity by 134 to 93.
† The future Pope Benedict XVI.

ended the eighties with more members than it started with – by which time only 11.7 per cent of Britons were still attending church at least once a week.

Thatcher was reluctant to introduce God into contemporary politics – another feature of the manner in which her brand of conservatism lacked the unabashed religious self-certainty then animating the right-wing Republican revival in the United States. 'I do not like talking about religion because people will misinterpret,' she confided to the broadcaster David Frost when he tried, with only limited success, to steer an interview for breakfast-time television on to the nature of her faith. Privately, while in Downing Street she snatched moments of relaxation by slowly working her way through the Old Testament, along with commentaries by such diverse theologians as Cardinal Hume; C. S. Lewis; the former Archbishop of York, Stuart Blanch; and the Chief Rabbi, Immanuel Jakobovits (whom she elevated to the House of Lords).[58] Despite this, outside the Orthodox Jewish community she struggled to find much support for her political agenda from religious figures. A lack of choice ensured that only one of her appointments to various bishoprics – Bill Westwood at Peterborough – was considered sympathetic to her politics. The donnish David Jenkins, whom she appointed Bishop of Durham in 1984, was a persistent critic of her politics, particularly over the miners' strike. While Thatcher decided to ignore the provocation, her energy secretary, Peter Walker, was so affronted by the bishop's pronouncement that the government 'did not seem to care for the unemployed' that he sent Jenkins a seven-page letter pointing out that, 'as somebody whose father was an unemployed factory worker in the 1930s', he was only too aware of 'the despair of unemployment' and that 'I know of no problem which so dominates the thinking and the anxieties of myself and the government' – before going on to take issue with the bishop's condemnation of Britain's retaking of the Falklands and his attack on increased spending on law and order.[59] Jenkins was no better at restoring harmony when addressing matters theological, succeeding in dividing his own parish by questioning the virgin birth and raising the possibility that Jesus's resurrection might not have been physically manifest but just 'a conjuring trick with bones'.[60] In May 1988, Thatcher did make one sustained effort to explain the compatibility of her outlook with scripture, a piece of evangelism that fell upon the stony ground of the General Assembly of the Church of Scotland. For the most part, she chose to leave it to less reverential Tories to tell clergymen offering political instruction to set their own house in order first.

Money was the root of serious misunderstanding between church and state during the eighties. The perceived greed of those doing well and the despair of those doing without provoked a succession of pulpit denunciations of the government's economic policies. Hardship in an age of materialism, and Thatcherism's assumed responsibility for both, fostered the most sustained political engagement by clerics since the nuclear bomb had brought dog-collars to the front rank of CND a quarter of a century previously (and the Cold War did so again during the cruise missile deployment in 1983, although, despite the arguments for Britain's unilateral nuclear disarmament put forward in the paper of its working party, *The Church and the Bomb*, the General Synod did vote, albeit narrowly, in favour of deterrence). Thatcher, oblivious to complaints that the rich getting richer made for a less equal society, not only saw no inconsistency between wealth and doing good, but regarded it almost as a prerequisite, pointing out to the interviewer Brian Walden in 1980: 'No one would remember the Good Samaritan if he'd only had good intentions; he had money as well.'[61] The collective riposte to government policy came from *Faith in the City*, a report into inner-city deprivation compiled by senior Anglican churchmen and published in December 1985. Many of its recommendations concerned what the church could do to improve its social outreach, but it was its advice to the government that contained the contentious material. While carefully eschewing a party political line, its assertion that 'too much emphasis is being given to individualism and not enough to collective obligation', while calling on clergy to 'get involved' in the debate about the government's 'dogmatic and inflexible macro-economic stance' because it was creating 'unacceptable' levels of unemployment, left little doubt that Thatcherism was weighed in the balance and found wanting. *Faith in the City* called for higher government grants to the voluntary sector, more public sector jobs to be created in areas where the private sector was absent, and higher public spending on capital investment and services, especially education and local services, 'even if it meant more taxes or borrowing'.[62]

The irony was that at the very moment the Church of England was calling for increased state spending, it was itself engaged in one of the most speculative forms of capitalism. This was because its shrinking income from declining congregations was no longer sufficient to meet the church's high levels of expenditure, particularly the ever rising pensions bill. Anglican clergymen typically had relatively little experience of making money – perhaps one reason why they found it difficult to empathize with the enterprise culture Thatcher saw as the road to salvation – and showed little interest in where the financial subsidies came from that sustained their own livelihoods and their parishes. The reality was that, to meet the shortfall, the Church Commissioners opted to finance high-risk commercial property developments, mostly raising the proceeds through borrowing, which rose from a total of £11 million in 1986 to £518 million in 1990 – just as the property market collapsed. The subsequent parliamentary inquiry into the losses was damning, finding 'complacency about the loss of up to £800 million of the

Commissioners' capital base' and stating that they had 'foolishly speculated' and had 'failed to comply with normal accounting practices that are a legal requirement in the commercial world thereby creating a misleading impression of the church's finances'.[63] Thatcher was too preoccupied with her own problems by that time to remind the clergy of her 'dogmatic and inflexible macro-economic stance' about living within one's means, but with clerical stipends cut and the Commissioners ending all parsonage refurbishments as part of emergency austerity measures, the message nevertheless reached the vicarage during 1990 and 1991. Not that the legacy was especially Thatcherite: within a year the church was turning to the state for a bail-out, in the guise of its church and cathedral repair bill being subsidized by English Heritage and the National Heritage Memorial Fund.

If society's ills were to be healed through enterprise and philanthropy, it would be necessary for rejuvenated mechanisms and voluntary bodies to flourish where previously the state's monopolistic tendencies had squeezed out private provision. In the United States, church-based charity continued to provide a major conduit through which individual wealth could be directed towards community projects. Problematically for the United Kingdom during the eighties, the same process was hindered by the diminishing congregations and collection plates of organized religion. Since it scarcely existed as a social construct, organized atheism was clearly not going to assume the obligation – the membership of the British Humanist Society remained comfortably within the low thousands. Other organizations and structures would have to be built up. In encouraging individual endeavour, government did take steps to remove barriers to benefactors. Legislation in 1980 and 1986 made charitable covenants more attractive, while gifts to charity were exempted from stamp duty in 1982 and from inheritance tax the following year. Further tax relief for donations followed in 1986. However, in terms of ensuring that voluntary bodies were efficient and well run, the response was tardy. Until it was updated in 1992, the law failed adequately to regulate charities. There was no obligation for registered organizations to submit their accounts to the Charity Commission and only one tenth of the 171,434 registered charities existing in 1990 bothered to do so voluntarily.[64] War on Want was so ineptly run that when it went insolvent in 1990 it was under the impression that it had £1 million in the bank, whereas in reality it owed its bank over £40,000.[65]

On a positive note, the number of registered charities rose by a quarter over the decade and the sums they distributed increased significantly as well.[66] Most of these organizations remained small in scale and narrow in purpose. In terms of income, the sector continued to be dominated by the top two hundred registered charities; taking account of inflation, their real income continued to increase during the eighties at roughly the same rate as it had done in the seventies and would do in the nineties – an increase that, more tellingly, also grew as a proportion of GDP. As to how they raised their money over the decade, what they received from fees charged for their services and from funding via government bodies nearly equalled the amount they raised through voluntary donations, so the equation was not a zero-sum equation of the state simply bowing out so that the voluntary sector could take over.[67] Among the most successful bodies during the eighties was the National Trust, whose membership more than doubled to well over two million.[68] As with the arts, the voluntary sector was encouraged to seek out corporate sponsors and donations. The top two hundred corporate donors increased their philanthropy by 50 per cent in real terms between 1979 and 1987,[69] though given the low base from which this sector was growing, the amount remained but a fraction of total charitable income. This was despite the efforts of Sir Hector Laing, the Thatcher-admiring chairman of United Biscuits, who in 1986 set up the Per Cent Club whose business members promised to contribute at least 0.5 per cent of pre-tax profits (or to institute 'money-in-kind' staff secondments) towards community projects.

The age's most prominent charity impresario transpired to be neither a clergyman nor a captain of industry but a pop singer. In 1984, famine in Ethiopia worsened significantly; searing images were broadcast on the BBC news, with Michael Buerk reporting a disaster of what he called 'biblical' proportions. The footage of dying children strapped to their emaciated mothers, who had walked for days in the vain hope of finding food and shelter, profoundly affected Bob Geldof, the Irish-born, British-domiciled, lead singer of The Boomtown Rats. Outraged by the inadequacy of the response, Geldof teamed up with Midge Ure, lead singer of Ultravox, and quickly enlisted forty-three of the most prominent British pop stars of the moment to perform a hastily written charity single, 'Do They Know It's Christmas?' Released at the end of November to raise funds and awareness of the Ethiopians' plight, it spent five weeks at number one in the charts, during which time it sold more copies (3.5 million) than any other single up to that point in British pop history. Neither Ure nor Geldof were under any illusion that this could be more than a token response to the enormity of the famine. On 13 July 1985, they put on what at the time was the most spectacular charity appeal in history.

Live Aid, as the event was billed, had antecedents, most notably the 1972 Concert for Bangladesh. What made it remarkable, however, was the majestic scale of its ambition. In the space of little over a month, Geldof, with help from Ure and the promoter Harvey Goldsmith, organized a continuous sixteen-hour live event which was held simultaneously at Wembley stadium in London and the JFK stadium in Philadelphia. To succeed, it relied upon precision timing (warning lights alerted the bands when they were about to have the power shut off if they did not wrap up their performances). In particular, it was made viable by satellite technology, which enabled the transatlantic spectacular (with additional contributions from other parts of the world) to be shown in real time across more than one hundred and fifty countries – even in communist states. With a few notable exceptions, Geldof managed to cajole the biggest pop acts of the period to appear without a fee, which was all the more remarkable given the shortness of notice and the reality that – at least until that moment – Geldof was scarcely a rock star of international renown. Come the day, there were a few technical hiccups when the sound or the live feed momentarily faltered, but given the extent to which the technology was being pushed to its limits, the most ambitious world television event that had ever been attempted could only be regarded as a remarkable success. A conjectured 1.4 to 1.9 billion of the world's five billion inhabitants supposedly watched the concert – which, if true, implied few television sets could have been tuned to much else.

What the global audience witnessed included seventy-four thousand young people filling Wembley – a mere six weeks after the Heysel stadium disaster had brought disgrace to English football crowds – and responding with wild cheering to the arrival of the Prince and Princess of Wales, accompanied by the first act on stage, the Coldstream Guards, who played the national anthem, followed, appropriately enough, by Status Quo. The most memorable performance was delivered by Queen, whose lead singer, Freddie Mercury, bestrode the stage with such self-confidence that he even successfully engaged in a *pas de deux* with the cameraman busy filming him. Thanks to a seat on the Concorde supersonic jet, Phil Collins performed in mid-afternoon at Wembley and then less than ten hours later in Philadelphia. The real star, of course, was Geldof, who found himself being serenaded by the Wembley crowd with a spontaneous chorus of 'For He's a Jolly Good Fellow'. Geldof, who remained apprehensive that the event was failing in its primary function and was under the impression that scarcely more than £1 million had been raised, fired off expletives of outrage during a backstage live interview. However, the final sum raised exceeded £50 million, and considerably more in the longer term. What Live Aid did not do was – in the repeated refrain of 'Do They Know It's Christmas?' – 'feed the world'. It did not even end the suffering in Ethiopia, where news reports better conveyed the natural disaster than the extent to which it had been man-made by the collectivization policy of the Marxist Mengistu regime in Addis Ababa and its conflict with Eritrean and Tigrayan insurrectionists. Some of the aid ended up partly funding the war, which, together with the politically motivated resettlement programme, significantly added to the death toll.[70] But more than any single event of the eighties – or, indeed, of the last quarter of the twentieth century – 13 July 1985 encapsulated how youthful idealism and modern technology could be harnessed in the *effort* to do good. And it was at an event primarily organized in London that the embodiment of borderless, common humanity was fleetingly glimpsed.

Liberty, Equality, Fraternity?

One pop concert did not a world of plenty make. But Live Aid caught the popular imagination and spawned imitators. Comic Relief was launched in 1985 and in 1988 Red Nose Day began with a live seven-hour 'telethon' on BBC 1 in which comedians and television celebrities performed silly acts as a means of raising money for Africa. The first Red Nose Day raised £15 million and the formula thereafter became a television staple, with related events springing up in schools, workplaces, sports and social clubs throughout the country. The scale of this and other events (most notably the London Marathon, which was founded by Chris Brasher and John Disley in 1981 and became the world's largest annual charity fundraising event, securing £500 million for 'good causes' in its first thirty years) did not suggest the eighties was marked by a greater degree of self-centredness than prior decades – though, of course, it could always be argued that the occasional charitable gift or sponsored run is insufficient as an indicator of more altruistic attitudes in society. Indeed, while the size of donations increased, the proportion of the population who undertook regular voluntary work did not markedly change between 1981 and 1992.[71] The motivations of those who did give their time and money can only be guessed. Some may have been prompted to share the personal wealth that greater opportunities and lower taxes had afforded them. Others may have participated as a conscious rebuke to what they perceived as state-sponsored selfishness or indifference to those in need. The British Social Attitudes survey found that the percentage of the public who agreed with the statement 'the government ought to help more and not rely on charity to raise needed money' increased from 80 to 88 per cent during Thatcher's premiership.[72] When she enthused about 'Victorian values' she was thinking of the great benevolence of Victorian philanthropists. To many listeners, though, the term doubtless conjured images of paupers and poor law commissioners, for charity was simultaneously evidence both of a sense of social obligation and of the failure to stamp out inequality.

Even the most optimistic observer of the eighties could hardly describe it as a period of relative political and social harmony, though the same generalization would surely have been no less applicable to the years of strife and industrial disputes, rancour and punk rock that had distinguished the seventies, against which Thatcherism had positioned itself as the cure. Not since her 1979 misattribution to St Francis of Assisi had the prime minister articulated the value of harmony – other than on her own terms. The fear of nuclear war and the spread of Aids, the ongoing terror campaigns in and from Northern Ireland, the public drunkenness of 'lager louts', strife on the football terraces and between police and disaffected youths, particularly those from ethnic communities, the pit villages divided over the 1984 miners' strike and the assault on the collective bargaining powers of the unions which defined one stratum of working-class solidarity, unprecedented levels of crime and family fragmentation, the lack of opportunities for those without skills or jobs to apply for – all represented challenges to the notion that the kingdom was united in anything other than name. Most of all, the division was evident among leading opinion-formers and in Parliament – in the almost polar opposite prescriptions for national recovery set out by the two main parties, whose policies were further apart than at any time since the 1930s.

Yet in ways that were as least as profound if less newsworthy, the country was actually becoming more integrated. From the 1940s to the 1970s, grammar schools had offered a challenging and highly academic education to about one quarter of children over the age of eleven, leaving the majority of adolescents to stick to the basics in secondary modern schools. Swept away during the late 1960s and the 1970s – even while Thatcher looked on in dismay and impotence as Heath's education secretary – the grammar school sector had been all but wiped out (except in Kent, Buckinghamshire, Lincolnshire and Northern Ireland) by the eighties, and did not make a comeback. Whether this was good or bad for education and social mobility remained contentious given the disappointing performance of so many of the successor comprehensive schools, but in terms of removing a clear delineating barrier in education the result was clear-cut. Unlike the previous forty years, nine out of ten teenagers growing up in the eighties shared a common adolescent institutional experience. What they learned would thereafter be made more uniform too. The Education Reform Act 1988 (which took full effect in England four years later) replaced state schools' freedom to teach what they liked with a national curriculum.

At the same time, single-sex education was all but confined to the private sector. Even there, it was during the eighties that boys-only public schools ceased to be the majority even among the elite institutions affiliated to the Headmasters' Conference, as the numbers admitting girls – either just to the sixth form or throughout – proliferated. Segregation also broke down in higher education, with single-sex university halls of residence becoming rarities. Male and female students at Glasgow University had separate student unions until 1980. Until that point, female guests to the (all-male) Glasgow University Union were confined to socializing in an inauspicious annexe, leaving the main building's Scots baronial splendour to the tender mercies of male bonding. Although a dwindling number of all-female institutions remained, Oxford's last all-male college went co-ed in 1985, and Cambridge's last bastion of testosterone in tweed, Magdalene, followed suit three years later. Unimaginable to a previous generation of oarsmen, even the Boat Race went mixed – at any rate, to the extent that in 1981 Sue Brown became the first of a new generation of female coxes to steer her men to victory. Where other universities had led in seeking a more balanced admissions' policy, the two most venerable institutions followed, and during the decade the proportion of female undergraduates at Oxford increased from 30 to 43 per cent and at Cambridge from 28 to 40 per cent.[73] In contrast to the undergraduate experience, however, among the dons the gender imbalance remained starkly evident.

Between men and women who did find work, life after formal education had ended also involved less segregation. Great focus was placed at the time on the emasculating effect of the dwindling number of jobs in heavy industry and mining, and it was not unreasonable to assume – as commentators regularly did – that some of the displays of thuggish behaviour were a psychological reaction to the identity crisis this loss of association, as much as status, brought about. But looked at from another perspective, the decade's increasing opportunities to work in the offices of the service sector, rather than on the factory floor or in the shipyard, not only shifted society's once iron division between white-collar and blue-collar decisively in favour of the former, it was instrumental in breaking down the workplace division of the sexes. What was more, it was women who were increasingly donning the white collars. In 1975, women comprised 4 per cent of trainee bank managers. By 1989, they represented a quarter – the same proportion as among the country's accountants. Half of lawyers were women by the decade's end. It was in middle management (one in ten) and senior executives (one in fifty) that women had not yet made the decisive advance.[74]

The process of dismantling the divide between the sexes was also evident in the social life that followed the day job. The Sex Discrimination Act 1975 outlawed licensed premises that either did not serve women or else corralled them in their own designated lounges, and during the eighties pubs continued to become more inclusive in their ambience and clientele as brewers and landlords sought to create an environment that would appeal to accelerating female spending power and the reality that – with greater integration in the work place – social networks were becoming equally integrated. At no previous stage in the twentieth century had the places where Britons worked and socialized been so open to both the sexes. In this regard, an important rider needs to be made to the assertion that the country was becoming more socially fractured.

13 THE WORKERS, UNITED, WILL NEVER BE DEFEATED

Which Side Are You On? – The Miners' Strike

'There is a class conflict, we do live in a class society,' Arthur Scargill, who was about to become president of the National Union of Mineworkers, reassured readers of the magazine *Marxism Today* in April 1981. In keeping with Marx's teaching, Scargill regarded sociology as a binary discipline: 'There are two classes in our society – those who own and control the means of production, distribution and exchange and those who work by hand and by brain. There is no middle class as is suggested by those academics and intellectuals who would like to stratify society.'[1] The son of a miner and the husband of a miner's daughter, Scargill was immersed in the politics and culture of the collieries. Yet for him, the task of running the NUM extended beyond defending the narrow interests of his union's members. It was also to awaken all workers to the false consciousness that led them to cooperate with capitalism and its institutions. Suitably led, they would recognize that it was within their power to become the masters. As he elucidated: 'The only way in which we can achieve socialism, in the first instance, is by involving in mass struggle workers for an alternative economic policy now, but one that does not include or involve worker's control, seats on boards of management, or worker participation' – because such collaboration risked contaminating the revolutionary purity of those sucked into it. Rather: 'I am for the trade union movement itself exercising power, exercising authority and compelling management, be it private or nationalized, to do certain things in terms of investment, planning, extension and development in the same way that we've been able to do on wages and conditions, for many, many years.'[2]

The boldness of Scargill's vision was conveyed in his telling description of socialism as something reachable in 'the first instance'. The real destination was something that particularly worried Thatcher, who was in no doubt that the NUM was now led by those who regarded 'the institutions of democracy' as 'no more than tiresome obstacles on the long march to a Marxist Utopia'.[3] In reality, Scargill's socio-political theories had shifted from Marxism–Leninism towards syndicalism, but even in public he scarcely dissented from Thatcher's interpretation of his revolutionary motives, assuring the NUM conference in July 1983 that because of the Tories' landslide victory in the general election the previous month, extra-parliamentary action was 'the only course open to the working class and the labour movement'.[4] From 1973 onwards, every Home Secretary, Labour or Conservative, had renewed the warrants necessary to allow MI5 to tap Scargill's telephone – a fact of which he seemed to be aware, occasionally shouting abuse down the phone to those he rightly assumed were eavesdropping.[5] Even senior 'wet' Conservatives who despaired of their prime minister's instinctive desire to stimulate argument harboured a fear-sharpened loathing of Scargill and the threat they believed he posed to constitutional government.

The Barnsley-born son of a lifelong communist, whom he followed down the local mine at the age of fifteen, Scargill had spent seven years in the Young Communist League before joining the Labour Party in 1962. As a Yorkshire NUM militant, he had led the decisive action of the 1972 miners' strike, picketing and closing down the Saltley coke works, that hastened Edward Heath's Conservative government's capitulation to a 27 per cent pay demand. His role in persuading the NUM to strike all over again in January 1974 forced Heath to initiate a partial shutdown of the country's energy supplies by instituting a three-day week and calling a snap general election, which, amid signs of a country descending into chaos, the Tories duly – if narrowly – lost. The incoming Labour government moved quickly to sue for peace with the NUM. Scargill was nevertheless incredulous that after becoming prime minister Callaghan 'once again tried to reform the capitalist system' and thereby missed the opportunity of pending national bankruptcy in 1976 to announce 'we take into common ownership the means of production, distribution and exchange'.[6] But he bided his time and when, in February 1981, the Thatcher government attempted to close twenty-three of the most seriously loss-making pits, he demanded a miners' strike with immediate effect. In Whitehall there was every reason to panic. At that moment, four fifths of the electricity output of the state-run Central Electricity Generating Board was generated by coal-fired power stations.[7] Without sufficient stockpiles to see off a prolonged cut to energy supplies, Thatcher felt obliged to surrender rather than risk repeating the fate of the last Tory administration. As Scargill crowed: 'The very fact that miners, within thirty-six hours of 40,000 of them coming out on strike, were able to change a government's course as far as pit closures were concerned is a clear demonstration that it can be done.'8

What Scargill insufficiently comprehended was the extent to which those in Whitehall felt they had now been drubbed once too often and that such humiliation could not be allowed to happen again. While the miners embraced their dynamic and relatively youthful champion (at forty-four he was young to be leading a union), electing Scargill NUM president with 70 per cent of the vote in November 1981, Thatcher recognized that the next time the miners threatened to switch the country's lights off, the government needed to have a back-up supply to keep them on. MISC 57, a secret Cabinet committee, chaired by the civil servant Peter Gregson, was set up with a remit to draw up contingency plans. One answer was to build more nuclear power stations. About 14 per cent of the United Kingdom's energy supplies were coming from nuclear energy in the early eighties, but it would take a long time before new plants could be built – far longer than the expected date of the next miners' strike – and in the meantime not nearly enough nuclear energy could be supplied to fill the gap left by coal. This left two other options: to convert more of the existing power stations to burn oil (a much more expensive option than letting them burn coal), or to stockpile coal in order to endure a long strike. When the Heath government had gone for broke with the three-day week in January 1974, coal stocks had been down to 15 million tonnes. By 1984, stocks had been built up to 48.7 million tonnes, which represented careful husbandry considering that coal production had been cut by a quarter because of the NUM's imposition of an overtime ban (by such means the union, rather than the management, exercised the muscle effectively to decide maximum output).

Two appointments in the aftermath of the 1983 general election victory suggested Thatcher was readying herself for the inevitable showdown. The first was her new energy secretary. Peter Walker was an adept politician and a personable communicator. Although a leading Tory 'wet', he was, as Heath's former trade and industry secretary, not disposed to be sentimental towards the miners' cause. The second was the announcement that the new chairman of the National Coal Board (NCB) – the management body of the nationalized coal mines – was to be the abrasive, seventy-year-old Scots-American, Ian MacGregor. His record, like his verbal brevity, spoke for itself. In his previous job, running the nationalized steel industry, he had cut British Steel's workforce from 166,000 to 71,000 between 1979 and 1983 and its annual losses from £1.8 billion to £256 million.

When it came to coal, subsidy could circumvent market economics but not geological realities. Exhaustion of seams and successive rationalizations, even during periods of greatly increased investment, had shrunk the coal industry from 700,000 employees in 980 pits at the time the collieries were nationalized in 1946 to 184,000 employees in 174 pits at the beginning of 1984. Even the 1974–9 Labour government, which considered it expedient to keep the miners satisfied, found it necessary to close thirty-two pits. Despite this contraction, a 1983 report by the Monopolies and Mergers Commission suggested that three quarters of the country's pits were loss-making. Thus the mines received an annual subsidy from taxpayers of £1.3 billion and still managed to record an annual loss of £250 million, with production targets (even when hit by overtime bans) greater than the market for coal and surplus quantities remaining unsold. There was, however, nothing uniquely British about this state of affairs. Indeed, the main foreign coal industries, including those of Britain's partners in the European Community, were similarly – and even less productively – bankrolled by their taxpayers. Thus making British coal mining more cost-effective would not necessarily secure it a future when it was traded against the subsidized extraction of other nations. There were other concerns, such as the security of the energy supply (an argument undercut by the NUM's record of indus-trial action), but the substantive issue was whether prolonging the slow death of a finite industry by out-subsidizing the heavily subsidized competition represented a worthwhile return on taxpayers' resources.

The impartial logic of the market offered little comfort to those miners who believed they had a right to work and that without the pithead wheels turning, no prospect existed for them to find alternative employment. According to this assessment of their future, miners would be dependent on the state whatever happened: Whitehall's choice was either to subsidize them, at ever greater cost, to dig out ever thinning seams of coal, or simply to pay them welfare benefits to do nothing. The options were succinctly expressed by the slogan the NUM would soon adopt: 'Coal Not Dole'. Mining communities were just that, and to remove the mine would be to kill the community. To those who regarded pit village life as insular and its appeal as unfathomable – particularly when a pit village, without a pit, had lost its rationale – to up sticks and move to an area where more jobs were available seemed the obvious solution. But mining was not a skill easily transferred to most new trades, especially not to the developing technologi-cal and white-collar job market. That eight hundred pits had closed or merged over the past forty years without an overall diminution in the living standards of mining areas ought to have assuaged the worst fears of those who saw the next round of colliery closures as a callous assault on a way of life. Between 1960 and 1968, 346,000 miners had opted for voluntary redundancy, a figure that towered over the numbers who would quit the collieries during the eighties. But these previous contractions had coincided – at least until the 1970s – with a relative ease of finding other suitable jobs. Those were in short supply in the Britain of 1984. Thus the example of their forefathers who had severed their bonds to find new work elsewhere held no more traction than the bicycle ridden by Norman Tebbit's job-seeking father. Culturally, there remained a chasm between a government on one side talking the language of change, innovation, moving on and social mobility and, on the other side, miners whose sense of identity – expressed through their banners, social clubs, galas, commemoration of past struggles and loyalty to their union – was built upon venerating themselves as the embodiment of the British working class. To aspire to becoming something 'other' was to betray this heritage and its values. The miners were the real conservatives.

At the beginning of March 1984, Ian MacGregor proposed cutting the mining workforce by 44,000 with the loss of around twenty pits. This was not out of line with the long-term trend. Indeed, it was less than the number of pit closures presided over by the last Labour government. Nor did the terms and conditions suggest that either the NCB or Peter Walker was looking to provoke a strike over this issue at this time. Far from presenting the miners with as stark a prospect as possible in the hope of goading them into a strike, the terms were intended to minimize that risk. No previous generation of miners had been offered anything comparable. All mine workers between the ages of twenty-one and fifty who took up the offer would be given a voluntary redundancy payment as a lump sum, at a rate of £1,000 for every year of employment. For those who had worked twenty or thirty years, this represented a pay-off equivalent to the price of a house, given that property prices in mining villages were considerably lower than the country's average of £34,000 in 1985. But staying in an area deprived of the primary employer, upon which other local businesses were dependent, was hardly a prospect to be grasped with unbridled joy. What was more, there could be no guarantee that – as in the past, so in the future – more closures would not be announced in subsequent years. MacGregor may not, as Scargill claimed, have already drawn up a secret hit list of other pits to close, but the logic of his ambition ultimately to make the coal industry profitable implied that those scheduled for closure by 1985 would not be the last. If a stand were not made now, then might it not be too late to maintain coal mining as a major industry? When, on 5 March 1984, miners at the first pit named for imminent closure, Cortonwood in South Yorkshire, walked out and called on other Yorkshire collieries to join them, they discovered a groundswell of support from other NUM branches. In fact, Cortonwood exemplified the problems afflicting the industry: its coal was sold for £47 per tonne, despite costing £64 per tonne to excavate. News of its closure was nonetheless greeted with alarm and anger. Declarations of solidarity from the NUM leadership in Yorkshire and Scotland were followed by Durham and Kent, turning Cortonwood's struggle into a nationwide showdown for the future of the industry. By 12 March, about half of Britain's 184,000 miners were on strike.

The NUM's national executive was faced with a dilemma. To be constitutional, an official nationwide strike necessitated holding a ballot of all the union's members. An alternative strategy was to let the strike develop where support for it was greatest and then use flying pickets (strikers from one area bussed into another) to persuade, or intimidate, non-striking areas into joining the action. In this way, a countrywide strike could be instigated without having to hold a vote to ensure it enjoyed majority support. There were obvious objections to such a strategy. Calling a nationwide strike without seeking a nationwide mandate patently lacked democratic legitimacy, and allowed the NCB and the government to claim that the strike was being spread through coercion, rather than with the genuine support of most miners. Subsequent opinion polls suggested that 88 per cent of the public thought a ballot should have been held,[9] and the issue caused a rift with Neil Kinnock, who had succeeded Michael Foot as leader of the Labour Party in October 1983, who forlornly pleaded with Scargill to seek a proper mandate. Had a ballot confirmed the support of most miners for the strike, the likelihood is that far fewer miners would have persisted in turning up for work. Furthermore, the use of flying pickets to shut down pits where men were still working would almost inevitably ensure confrontation and violence if those labelled 'scabs' were physically prevented from exercising their right to work. It was also liable to be classified as 'secondary action' (picketing by those not directly employed at the plant in question), which the Conservatives had made illegal in the Employment Act 1980. While it would prove impractical for the police to arrest thousands of pickets at any one time, legislation in 1982 had made unions liable for damages if the courts found that their officials had promoted unlawful action. By not calling a national ballot, Scargill adopted a risky strategy. By relying on flying pickets to persuade or intimidate those intent on continuing to work, he was embarking upon a collision course with the police and the courts.

At a tactical level, the NUM leadership's reasoning was understandable. Three times between 1982 and 1983 Scargill had called for a strike and three times his members, when balloted, had rebuffed that call. Now that a major strike was under way, it was risky to hold a vote the result of which might go against the action. On 19 March, eight NUM areas in the Midlands, the North-East and the North-West took matters into their own hands and balloted their members on whether to join the strike. These ballots involved 70,000 miners, 50,000 of whom voted against joining the strike. In Nottinghamshire, the scale of the rejection (73 per cent to 27 per cent) was overwhelming. The problem was that it was the least militant areas that had held the ballots, and so the result could not be extrapolated to South

Yorkshire, Scotland, South Wales or Kent. An opinion poll of miners on 31 March suggested that if Scargill had held a national ballot he would probably have won it – respondents favouring striking by 51 per cent to 34 per cent.[10] But he could not have been totally confident of the result and chose not to risk it. As the NUM's vice president, the Scottish communist Mick McGahey, put it: 'We shall not be constitutionalized out of a strike.'[11]

The battleground was the Midlands coalfields. Nottinghamshire, with 31,000 non-striking miners and forty-two pits still operating, quickly felt the full force of flying pickets from South Yorkshire and beyond, as the NUM endeavoured to coordinate its invasion of the dissident county. To ensure they kept their troops in the field, the NUM only distributed strike pay to those who actively joined the picket lines. The Social Security Act 1980 had prevented strikers from claiming welfare benefits while a dispute lasted (although their families could still claim benefits), consequently, signing up for picket duty became a vital source of income for tens of thousands of strikers. The opposing forces, meanwhile, were also coordinating their response. MISC 57 had anticipated the NUM's strategy and concluded that leaving the country's fifty-two police forces to deal individually with a nationally coordinated picketing offensive would put intolerable strain upon constabularies in the key areas. To meet the challenge, the police established a National Reporting Centre to organize the call-up of reserves from around the country to police the picketing. As well as meeting the manpower needs, bringing in police officers from outside the community they served also made sense given rising tensions in the insurgent pit villages. However, there was a clear risk that by deploying the police in this manner they would be seen to have become a centralized and politicized tool of the Tory government. The establishment of roadblocks to turn back busloads of flying pickets intent on besieging working collieries was particularly contentious. The alternative, though, was to accept that the law prohibiting secondary picketing was inoperable and that individuals and companies were to be left to the mercy of organized gangs from outside the area who were intent on preventing them lawfully going about their business. The balance between being seen to uphold the liberty of workers without becoming state-run strike-breakers was a difficult one to achieve, and as the dispute intensified the number of complaints about police partisanship multiplied. Scargill's wife, Anne, was one of many non-violent protesters whose experience of being arrested and treated disrespectfully by police officers, only to have the courts subsequently dismiss the charges, diminished what respect they had previously had for the British bobby.[12] Twelve months in which thousands of people from one community traded insults, blows and court appearances with the forces of law and order could only have a corrosive effect on relations between the two entities.

Nevertheless, that the confrontations could not safely go unpoliced was evident as early as 15 March with the first fatality of the dispute, when a flying picket was struck by a brick during scuffles between working and striking miners in Nottinghamshire, though it was never discovered from which side the deadly projectile had been thrown. By the time the strike entered its second month, one thousand miners had been arrested. The NUM's strategy was not confined to trying to shut down the remaining operating pits, for it also sought to sever the means by which the stockpiled coal could be supplied to power plants and steelworks. The aim was to engineer national economic collapse in order to ensure the surrender of the NCB and the government. At the strike's commencement, the NUM had agreed to allow steelworks to be supplied with the minimum level of coke necessary to stop irreparable damage being done to their blast furnaces, while still seeking to make them inoperable as producers of steel during the lifetime of the strike. Mothballing the steel industry particularly strained relations between the miners' union and that of the steel workers, the Iron and Steel Trades Confederation (ISTC), which refused to respond to Scargill's call to join the strike. Without coke to fuel the foundries, job lay-offs at British Steel were inevitable and the ISTC's leader, Bill Sirs, concluded that being abused as a 'scab' was preferable to shrivelling the size of his own union membership. Scargill was contemptuous of Sirs's lack of syndicalist fraternity, believing that such self-centredness demonstrated only how the working class could never triumph over the boss class unless it stuck together.

Indeed, it was Scargill's efforts to stop supplies reaching the steel plants that caused the single worst violent incident in a British industrial dispute since the war.[13] The scene of the battle was the Orgreave coke works south of Sheffield. Hoping to repeat his 1972 triumph at Saltley, Scargill declared an all-out blockade of the plant on 29 May in an attempt to prevent its products being transferred forty miles down the road to the British Steel works at Scunthorpe. The first day saw serious disorder as 2,500 police officers, using truncheons, riot shields and horses, moved in to prevent 6,000 flying pickets from blocking the exits from the plant. The police operation was successful in so far as it allowed the initial convoy of thirty-five lorries, their windscreens protected with wire mesh against the projectiles hurled at them, to drive the coke safely from Orgreave to Scunthorpe. The failure to disrupt the supply prompted Scargill to call for a redoubling of the besiegers' efforts, calling on 'the whole trade union movement' to descend on Orgreave, and to condemn the law and order operation as comparable to 'an actual police state tantamount to something you are used to seeing in Chile or Bolivia'.[14] On 30 May, while attempting to marshal his pickets for another salvo, Scargill was arrested and charged with obstruction. Over the following days, the scuffles became less ferocious until what proved to be the all-out assault of 18 June.

A battle between Ancient Britons and Romans, a scene from the English civil war, the Peterloo massacre . . . there was a choice of historical analogies for the passionate, if disorganized, throng of pickets, mostly topless or in T-shirts, who threw themselves upon the lines of smartly uniformed police officers at Orgreave, on the same hot summer day on which – in another England – the Queen's landau trundled along in front of the cheering ranks of top hats at Royal Ascot. At Orgreave, the reception for the horses was rather different, with the pickets – as if at Agincourt – driving a line of angled stakes into the ground to repel the anticipated cavalry charge. As battle commenced, it was the pickets who had the momentum. Their 6,500 men, outnumbering their opponents by nearly two to one, surged forward in an effort to swamp the police lines deployed to protect the approaches to the coke works. Under the pressure, one of the police lines buckled and appeared to be on the brink of being overwhelmed. Three times, mounted reinforcements were sent in to drive the onslaught back. As one picket observed: 'The long riot shields parted and out rode fourteen mounted police straight into the pickets. As they did, police in the line beat on their riot shields with truncheons, creating a wall of noise which was meant to intimidate and frighten. It was more than simply a noise, it was a declaration that we were facing an army which had declared war on us.'[15]

With the pickets' initial assault wilting under the ferocity of the counter-attack – 'When you've got half a ton of horse being ridden at you, you don't hang about'[16] – hand-to-hand fighting broke out, before lulling and then flaring up again. The engagement was being fought in open coun-tryside, which suited those who could gallop better than those who could run. To avoid being outflanked on the grassy expanse of common ground, Scargill's infantry fell back to a stronger defensive position along the dry moat of a steep railway embankment, forded only by a narrow bridge. As the police pushed on towards this redoubt, they came under a hail of projectiles – not only bricks, bottles and jagged glass but also iron bars which were used as javelins to spear them. The battle for the railway bridge lasted nearly two hours before the position was taken. Among those injured as the officers stormed across was Scargill who, caught close to the thick of the fighting, received a gash to the back of his head. He claimed the injury was caused by a blow from a riot shield; the police maintained that during the pushing and shoving he slipped off the top of the embankment and banged his head on a railway sleeper below. Either way, the sight of him being led away to an ambulance to receive treatment was greeted by police cheers.[17] The blow to the strikers' cause was greater. While the siege of Orgreave was not lifted until 21 July, the encounter had long since been decisively won by the forces trying to keep open supplies to Britain's steel industry. Despite the boast of the *Socialist Worker* placards held aloft by the pickets, they would not repeat the famous victory at Saltley. Strategically, Scargill had blundered, drawing more and more of his manpower into a battle on terrain of his opponents' choosing. For the forlorn effort to bring the Orgreave coke works to a halt had diverted thousands of flying pickets away from the main theatre of operations – the Nottinghamshire collieries supplying the coal upon which the government's ability to endure depended.

In any case, Orgreave was not the steel industry's only supplier of coke. Imports also provided a lifeline. To show solidarity with the miners, the leadership of the country's biggest union, the TGWU, called a national dock strike on 9 July. The action risked paralysing the ports and, with it, the country's international trade (digging for the Channel Tunnel did not start until 1988 and it was 1994 before the link opened). The response, however, was disappointing. Liverpool and Southampton docks were shut, but the others remained open because the dockers proved unenthusiastic about risking their own livelihoods – or, at the very least, the survival of the restrictive practices of the National Dock Labour Scheme – merely for the sake of the miners. Having failed in its objectives, the dock strike was suspended on 20 July, only to flare up again in mid-August when TGWU members refused to unload imported coke brought into the Hunterston ore terminal on the Firth of Clyde. The coke was intended for the Ravenscraig steelworks on the outskirts of Motherwell. One of the world's largest hot-strip steel mills, Ravenscraig's mighty furnaces risked irreversible damage if deprived of the coke to fuel them for long, and the prospect of taking action on behalf of the miners at the cost of sabotaging one of Scotland's most important heavy industries placed the Labour movement in a quandary. When British Steel turned to non-TGWU members to unload the coke at Hunterston, in clear contravention of the terms of the National Dock Labour Scheme, the TGWU called a strike, only to have to abort it for lack of support. Had trade unionists not been divided and Britain's ports been successfully paralysed, the trade and industry secretary, Norman Tebbit, was in no doubt that the Cabinet would have been forced to surrender to the miners.[18]

This was far from being the only moment when the strike might have speedily moved from deadlock to resolution. The perception that neither MacGregor nor Scargill was interested in any result short of the unconditional surrender of the other masked several clear opportunities to settle the dispute on terms that, while falling short of Scargill's insistence that the pit closure plan must be scrapped, did involve strategic compromises by management. The first round of substantive talks between the two sides, on 23 May, broke down because Scargill regarded 'exhaustion' as the only grounds for closing a pit, whereas MacGregor deemed 'uneconomic' to be sufficient; but the gulf between these two words narrowed during further talks in mid-July and in particular on 9 September, when MacGregor appeared to be prepared to keep open loss-making collieries that might still be 'beneficially developed'. Taken at face value, this was a significant climbdown by the NCB, since 'beneficially developed' could potentially embrace all but the most exhausted pits. The NCB's offer of 13 September also involved a 5.2 per cent pay rise and up to £800 million of increased investment in the surviving collieries. Miners from closing pits would be eligible for job transfers to the surviving pits if they did not want to take voluntary redundancy. For Scargill, however, 'beneficially developed' was still not good enough. In despair, one trade unionist close to the talks, John Lyons, the general secretary of the Engineers' and Managers' Association, believed that the miners' had been offered '95 per cent of what they were after', only for Scargill to walk away.[19]

Within days, it seemed his stubbornness might pay off. On 28 September, a decision to strike by members of the small NACODS union – the National Association of Colliery Overmen, Deputies and Shotfirers, who were responsible for underground pit safety – briefly posed a direct threat to those mines that were still working, since the presence of the supervisors was a precondition of their remit to operate. The NCB's failure to appease this small but vital group of specialists enraged the prime minister. 'The management of the NCB could indeed have brought the government down,' she later claimed, still fuming, 'the future of the government at that moment was in their hands.'[20] Acting speedily, she brought pressure to bear on MacGregor to ensure the NACODS members' terms for remaining at work were met. Given the stakes involved, it was a small price to pay. Had Scargill seized this moment to announce that the NUM was willing to settle for similar terms, the miners' strike might have concluded with a deal that amounted to a partial victory for the NUM. But the president was not for turning.

Scargill appeared to believe his own rhetoric that, as summer drew on towards autumn, time was on his side. The electricity generating stations would not need the greatest supplies during the warmest months (and from this perspective, launching a strike in March rather than September had hardly been opportune), and it would be during the colder months ahead when the government and its dwindling stockpiles would come under the greatest pressure. In order to appease those miners still working, coal-fired power stations were not using imported coal, and in Whitehall conflicting reports were being received as to exactly how long the stand-off could continue before the power supply faltered. The question for the NUM was how long the pit villages could stick out the fight without proper wage-earners.

Farmers and allotment owners awoke to discover their root crops had been dug up in the night. Desperate men were seen climbing slag heaps to scavenge for coal, a dangerous activity which resulted in the deaths of three teenagers. Yet, despite evident signs of hardship, a reporter from *The Times* found that the mood in the South Yorkshire pit village of Rossington remained buoyant at the end of the first one hundred days of the strike. Not one of the 1,500 employed at the nearby mine had returned to work, despite families 'surviving on bread, potatoes and a community spirit revived by prolonged austerity'. Most had mortgages.[21] In Rossington, as elsewhere, extended families, charities and the union helped provide the basic necessities. Soup kitchens were opened and the number of children eligible for free school meals multiplied. Local shopkeepers, aware that the closure of the colliery would mean the end of significant disposable cash in the village, took a long-term view when it came to offering discounts to customers struggling to afford the price on the label. Like the overwhelming majority of the country's 174 pits, Rossington was not earmarked for closure (it survived, in a reduced form, until 2007) and its display of solidarity with those that did face the axe actually risked being counterproductive. Accumulations of coal dust caused by the pit lying idle for months created a risk of spontaneous combustion, resulting in one of the faces having to be cemented off, leaving behind equipment worth £2 million and a large coal seam which could never be retrieved.[22] The longer the strike endured, the more dangerous the idle coal seams became and the first closures to follow the strike's end were of pits that had become unsafe.

Beset by such worries, the resilience of the strike-supporting communities was remarkable. Nevertheless, there was also a less attractive side to this pulling together, manifested by the intimidation meted out to those who broke ranks. This took various forms, from violent assaults on miners who indicated their intention to return to work, verbal threats to their wives and children, refusal to serve them in shops and pubs (or 'blacking' of those businesses that did serve them), to social ostracization, not just for the moment but for as long as they remained in the area. To be labelled a 'scab' in a small community was to be cast out as a pariah. The decision of the NUM's national executive on 11 July to set up a star chamber to discipline miners whose actions it classified 'detrimental to the interest of the union' did nothing to heal the divisions and was, from the NUM's perspective, self-defeating, for it helped spur the creation of the rival Nottinghamshire-based Union of Democratic Mineworkers, ending forever the closed shop monopoly the NUM had enjoyed as the nationwide representative of miners' interests.

The most calamitous expression of hatred towards those who chose to cross the picket lines took place on 30 November, when two strikers leaned

(*Above*) The efforts in June 1984 by striking miners to blockade a British Steel coking plant resulted in a pitched battle with the police at Orgreave where, the previous month, the miners' leader, Arthur Scargill (*below*), had been arrested … but not silenced.

(*Above*) Frankie Goes to Hollywood's songs about sex and nuclear war turned mid-eighties anxieties into chart success. (*Below*) Their 'Frankie Say Relax!' T-shirts popularized a fashion for slogan clothing, worn by mainstream acts like Wham! ...

... and by the designer who inspired them, Katharine Hamnett, when meeting the Prime Minister. Thatcher pointed out that it was Cruise, not Pershing, missiles that were being based in Britain and wondered if she had come to the right place, 'which,' Hamnett recounted, 'I thought was rather rude as she had invited me'.

No slogan carried more punch than the government's Aids awareness campaign.

Cambridge May Ball 'survivors'. The eighties' encouragement of 'new money' did little to dispel the visibility or volubility of 'reactionary chic'. The decade's best-selling trade book was *The Official Sloane Ranger Handbook*.

Young Sloanes got their teenage kicks at the Gatecrasher Balls, organized by up-and-coming entrepreneurs, Jeremy Taylor (*left*) and Eddie Davenport (*right*). Taylor subsequently ran raves. Davenport subsequently went to prison.

over a road bridge and dropped a concrete slab on to a taxi carrying a miner returning to work at the Merthyr Vale colliery. Missing its intended target, the slab killed the taxi driver. When, in May 1985, a couple of months after the strike ended, the two miners found guilty of the crime were sentenced, seven hundred of Merthyr Vale's miners stopped work to show solidarity with them and to appeal – successfully – for their convictions to be reduced from murder to manslaughter.[23] On 8 November 1984, three weeks before the fatal slab was hurled, the first miner turned back up for work at Cortonwood, the colliery where the strike had begun. He needed intensive police protection because the local community lined the route, hurling abuse at him with an intensity that gave grounds for fearing they might actually lynch him if given the chance. How such scenes were interpreted depended, of course, on the viewer's perspective. Was it the brave stand of the individual against the mentality of the mob? Or was it an example of the selfishness of Thatcherite individualism rejecting obligations to a wider society? Was it simply the philosophy of desperation, the degradation of a man reduced to betraying his class and his instincts in order to scrape a living? To the prime minister, the answer was clear. As she put it to her party's conference: '"Scabs" their former workmates call them. Scabs? They are lions!'[24]

While the government's public stance was to maintain that it was a matter for the NCB and NUM, rather than the Department of Energy, to agree a settlement, there was never any doubt as to the result Thatcher was seeking. Controversy flared over remarks she made in July to a private meeting of back-bench Tory MPs: she drew a parallel between the Argentine junta during the Falklands War, whom she dubbed 'the enemy without', and the NUM leadership, who were 'the enemy within, much more difficult to fight, [and] just as dangerous to liberty'.[25] Did the prime minister really think she was dealing with an insurgency? The official historian of MI5 describes as 'fanciful' the accusation that the security service tapped the phones of a wide range of NUM and other trade union officials. His research supported the contention that surveillance, for which individual Home Office warrants were a prerequisite, was conducted in accordance with MI5's charter and 'limited to leading communist and Trotskyist militants and those judged to have close links with them'. This brought active communists like Mick McGahey within the remit, and also Scargill, who was included as 'an unaffiliated subversive'. Wider allegations of security service 'dirty tricks' – including highly placed 'moles' within the union – have not been substantiated.[26] At the time she made it, Thatcher's 'enemy within' jibe drew a furious rebuke from Neil Kinnock, who protested: 'Any prime minister of Britain who confuses a fascist dictator who invades British sovereign territory with British trade unions and with miners, I think is not fit to govern this country.'[27] A more elegiac response came from one of her predecessors when in November the ninety-year-old Harold Macmillan finally took up his seat in the House of Lords. Taking the title of Earl of Stockton (the depressed constituency he had represented in the 1930s), he chose in his maiden speech in the chamber to pronounce: 'It breaks my heart to see what is happening in our country today. A terrible strike is being carried on by the best men in the world. They beat the Kaiser's army and they beat Hitler's army. They never gave in. The strike is pointless and endless. We cannot afford action of this kind . . . I can only describe as wicked the hatred that has been introduced.'[28] His perspective was a world – or at least a couple of generations – away from that of Thatcher, whose memoirs included the observation: 'The sheer viciousness of what was done [by striking to non-striking miners] provides a useful antidote to some of the more romantic talk about the spirit of the mining communities.'[29]

Scargill certainly worried about an enemy within, reserving especial rage for those in the Labour movement whose supportive words were not backed by decisive actions. When the TUC's new general secretary, Norman Willis, addressed a miners' rally in Aberavon on 14 November, his condemnation of acts of violence was met with furious jeers. Sitting beside him on the plat-form, Scargill looked on impassively while a hangman's noose was dangled threateningly above Willis's head. What the NUM wanted from the TUC was summed up by Mick McGahey: 'No scab coal. No crossing picket lines. No use of oil. Stop industry.'[30] The son of a man who had been a prominent communist organizer of the 1926 General Strike, McGahey was calling for a repeat effort to paralyse the economy. However, the TUC recognized the legal dangers of calling for sympathetic action, given the likelihood that this would involve activities that the courts could construe as illegal secondary picketing. The penalties for unions minded to ignore the law included sequestration of their assets. In August, two Yorkshire miners (their legal fees financed by David Hart, a maverick Thatcher-admiring businessman) had taken the Yorkshire NUM to court for calling an 'official' strike without a ballot, in contravention of the union's own constitution. In October, the High Court ruled in the two miners' favour. Reprimanded for refusing even to turn up for the court hearing, Scargill was fined £1,000, and the NUM was fined £20,000. His own fine paid by an anonymous well-wisher, Scargill ordered that his union should not pay its fine. In the judgement of Mr Justice Nicolls, the union thereby 'decided to regard itself as above the law, and to make this plain repeatedly, emphatically and publicly',[31] and he ordered that, being in contempt of court, it should have its nearly £11 million of assets sequestered until it recanted – which it refused to do.

In principle, the sequestration left the NUM endeavouring to sustain a strike without any money. In practice, only £8,500 of assets was initially seized. Having foreseen the likelihood of sequestration, the union had squir-reled away the vast majority of its assets in various international bank accounts. What the sequestration did ensure was that henceforth it would have to raise money through various 'front' organizations, and it was to these that campaigners and other trade unions contributed. Cash was preferred because it could be handed covertly to NUM officials without the courts being readily able to trace and seize it. The downside of this practice was its unaccountability, fostering subsequent allegations of misappropriation. One source of covert funding was the communist-controlled French trade union, the CGT, which handed over unmarked bags of cash (this was not just to evade the British courts but also to circumvent the French socialist govern-ment's exchange controls, which prevented significant sums of money leaving France). The CGT was not the only foreign fundraiser. The NUM's general secretary, Peter Heathfield, was given a plastic bag with $96,000 in cash which had been raised by communist Czechoslovak and Bulgarian trade unions. Another source was the Soviet Union. Scargill secretly entered into negotiations with two Soviet diplomats at the TUC annual conference and on 12 October the Soviet Communist Party's central committee agreed that one million roubles (about $1.2 million), raised from Russian trade union funds, should be sent to the NUM. Unfortunately, the Soviets' efforts to place the money in the NUM's secret Swiss bank account were thwarted when the bank, suspecting a money-laundering operation, refused to accept it – in the process drawing attention to the existence of this clandestine hidey-hole. With the payment delayed, Scargill appealed again to the Soviets, on 28 December, for £10–20 million, pointing out that the strike was costing £300,000 per week to fight. On 12 February, $1.1 million was duly channelled from the Soviet Union to an account in Dublin in the name of the Miners' Defence and Aid Fund, which was a effectively a front for the NUM.[32]

Accepting 'Moscow gold' from the totalitarian regime of Konstantin Chernenko might have seemed like the sort of cheap anti-Scargill smear propagated by the more stridently Tory-supporting newspapers. But this was no 'Zinoviev letter'; it was true. What was particularly surprising was that the solicitations to Moscow continued even after opprobrium had been heaped on the NUM when its covert links with Libya's despotic regime were revealed. British–Libyan diplomatic relations had been severed in April 1984 after Yvonne Fletcher, a young policewoman on duty during a protest, was killed by shots fired from the Libyan embassy in St James's Square, London. Unperturbed, six months later, Scargill sent a member of the NUM executive, Roger Windsor, to Libya surreptitiously to solicit funds from the country's dictator, Colonel Gaddafi. Scargill was led to believe that Gaddafi – whose commitment to international terrorism included arming the IRA

– would donate around £1 million. If the sum reportedly proffered – £163,000 in cash – was accurate, then he may have felt short-changed.[33] Worse, the meeting was supposed to be secret, a detail evidently not fully grasped in Tripoli, where state-run television broadcast footage from inside the tent of the NUM's plenipotentiary kissing Gaddafi's cheeks. Having been hot on Roger Windsor's trail itself, the *Sunday Times* revealed the assignation on 28 October. Scarcely more than a fortnight previously, the Provisional IRA had attempted to murder the prime minister and her Cabinet by detonating a bomb in Brighton's Grand Hotel, and unconnected though the two events were, the timing of the Tripoli mission was particularly unfortunate in view of Libya's known links with terrorism.

The Brighton bombing came just as hopes of renewed talks to settle the miners' dispute were heightening. Indeed, it was a last minute decision by the energy secretary, Peter Walker, to remain in London to handle possible avenues for negotiation rather than to travel to Brighton for the party conference that led him to offer his hotel room to the deputy chief whip, Sir Anthony Berry. When the bomb exploded, Berry was killed in the room. Walker's escape was a fortunate one, as was that of the prime minister herself, who was unscathed despite the wrecking of her bathroom. The front of the hotel was blown out, causing a partial collapse. After several hours, Norman Tebbit was painstakingly pulled from the rubble. His wife was paralysed from the neck down for the rest of her life. The chief whip, John Wakeham, remained unconscious for days and his wife was one of the five fatalities. Thatcher's sense of resolution and calmness in the face of danger shone through, as did the fragile threads by which she remained prime minister (the wreckage in her bathroom was sufficient either to have killed her or to have condemned her to Margaret Tebbit's fate). As the IRA's press statement put it: 'Today we were unlucky, but remember we only have to be lucky once. You will have to be lucky always.'

Throughout the autumn, the miners' strike continued, though the slow yet continual drift back of employees to their pits encouraged the perception that momentum was slipping away from the strikers. The NCB's offer of financial sweeteners to coax miners to return to work, including back-pay and a Christmas bonus, began to have an effect. Opinion polls suggested that the public's sympathies, which in the summer had been fairly evenly balanced between the two sides, were by the winter overwhelmingly on the side of the management.[34] As if oblivious, Scargill remained defiant, as was evident when his rhetorical flair was deployed to rally his men at a gathering in Porthcawl:

Can you say to your son or daughter: in 1984 I took part in the greatest struggle in trade union history? I fought to save your pit. I fought to save the jobs.

I fought to save this community. And in doing so, I preserved my dignity as a human being and as a member of the finest trade union in the world. I'm proud to lead you. The miners, united, will never be defeated.[35]

It was only when there were rumours of imminent peace talks that the numbers of returnees slackened off, there being little point in suffering the ostracism of being labelled a 'scab' if the strike was about to end anyway. Having envisaged the TUC's role as being one of offering unquestioning support for the NUM, Scargill was uneasy at the organization's determination to try and broker a deal on the miners' behalf. In the event, the TUC almost saved the day for the NUM. When, on 30 January 1985, Norman Willis led his delegation to meet the NCB negotiators it might have looked as if the latter's choice of venue, the Ritz Hotel, was intended to rub in how little the managers were suffering compared with the strikers. If so, the psychological advantage was quickly squandered, for Ian MacGregor's style of negotiating transpired to be as soft as the hotel furnishings. On 12 February, his inattention to detail almost ensured that he agreed terms to end the dispute whereby only pits 'deemed exhausted' would be closed – the criterion for which Scargill had long held out. Not only was this far removed from the previous criterion of 'uneconomic', the draft document failed to make clear who – the NCB, the NUM, or an outside arbitrator – had the right to determine what level of depletion qualified as 'exhausted'. Could the NCB chairman really have talked tough for eleven months only to concede defeat at the moment his opponents were on their knees? It was as MacGregor was about to sign his name to the draft agreement that a copy was sent to Peter Walker at the Department of Energy. Appalled at what he read, Walker sent a minute to MacGregor angrily protesting: 'I would have thought that we could have been consulted on the wording of any paper which was going to form the final agreement with the TUC and through them the NUM.'[36] MacGregor was ordered to keep the cap on his pen and to stall for time while the government substituted new terms for him to settle the dispute. This intervention demonstrated who was ultimately in charge, though the fact that MacGregor had proceeded to the brink of agreement without consulting Walker was extraordinary – even if it was consistent with the government's persistent, if disingenuous, protestations that settling the dispute was not its responsibility but that of the NCB and the NUM.

The visit of Norman Willis and his seven-man deputation to meet the prime minister in Downing Street on 19 February represented a rare invitation for the TUC, and a tactical defeat for Scargill who was expected to respond to, rather than determine, the terms of the debate. Willis's pitch was that the NUM should concede the NCB's right to manage the coal industry but that 'uneconomic' was not, of itself, sufficient grounds for closing pits.

Where there was dispute over a colliery's future, a new independent review procedure should adjudicate. The following day the NUM held a meeting with the NCB during which MacGregor presented a final clarification (this time with the government's choice of words) acknowledging the independent review body's role. Offered these terms, Scargill dismissed them out of hand.

Facts on the ground were making the NUM president's intransigence a flight from reality. On 27 February, the NCB claimed that 93,000 miners were reporting for work, which, if true, was more than were still out on strike. The exact figure was disputed, though evidence that support for the strike was dwindling was irrefutable, especially since even in such previously militant areas as South Wales there was talk of a mass return to work, regardless of whether a national agreement was concluded. On 3 March, with angry protesters outside shouting 'We're not going back! We're not going back!', the NUM executive met at Congress House, the TUC's headquarters, to look again at the terms that had been offered. Efforts to contact the government in the hope of extracting further concessions were thwarted. Neither Peter Walker nor anyone else in a position of authority at the NCB would answer the telephone.

Having run out of options, the union's executive decided to vote on whether to call off the strike, only to divide eleven for, eleven against. Despite finding himself with the casting vote, Scargill abstained. Always determined to assert his leadership during the fifty-one weeks of conflict, the president chose to abdicate – to avoid responsibility at the vital hour of defeat. It fell to the NUM's delegates' conference to break the executive's impasse. With Scargill refusing to make clear where he stood on a solution, but still insisting he would not sign the document the TUC had negotiated, the options were reduced to voting either to maintain the strike or else to call it off without accepting any negotiated terms. It was a sign of the state of mind moulded by the struggle that returning to work without an agreement was deemed more honourable than accepting the concessions that were on the table. The delegates voted by 170 to nineteen against staying out on strike, and by ninety-eight to ninety-one to return to work without an agreement. With this declaration, the strike was over and the victory for the NCB, and the government, overwhelming – a reality Scargill rhetorically circumvented by announcing that 'the greatest achievement is the struggle itself'. Then he walked up to Willis's office in Congress House where John Monks was on hand to offer him tea and sympathy. 'How are you feeling, Arthur?' asked Monks. With Robespierrean incorruptibility, Scargill replied: 'Pure. I feel pure.'[37]

The strike's costs were colossal. Around ten thousand individuals had been arrested and twenty thousand people – strikers, strike-breakers and police – sustained injuries. The expense of policing the dispute was put at £20 million, while the direct cost to the country of the strike was estimated at £2.75 billion. If the overall effect on national output were included, the figure probably exceeded £5 billion.[38] Many of the miners did their best to return to work on 5 March with their heads held high, banners unfurled, brass bands playing, though there was no question that they were a beaten army, marching towards oblivion. The NUM could hardly expect to label its members in Nottinghamshire, Derbyshire and Leicestershire 'scabs' and expect to regain their loyalty. As a result, the NUM's ability to represent every miner in the country was lost, its monopoly challenged by the new Midlands-based rival, the Union of Democratic Mineworkers. Even without this schism, eleven months of fruitless struggle had drained what power the NUM might conceivably have had to resist a far swifter dissolution of the collieries in the years ahead.

That there would be far more pit closures than the number announced in March 1984 was the one prediction Scargill got right. The damage done to mines which became unsafe through lying idle for the strike's duration widened the hit list – one more example of how the NUM's strategy had proved counterproductive. But in most cases, the safety of the seams was not the principal factor. Much of the country's market for coal was secure only for so long as the Central Electricity Generating Board remained a nationalized entity. In 1990, the process of its privatization began and it was no longer required to buy the fuel it needed to fire up its power plants from British coal mines at more than the market rate. The consequence was a new round of pit closures. With this contraction, much of the rationale for keeping British coal mining as a nationalized industry disappeared. By the time of its privatization in 1994, its workforce stood at a mere 25,000 with only fifteen deep mines still in operation. By 2011, five deep mines remained.

In place of home-hewn coal, Russian gas and Middle Eastern oil helped fuel Britain's power plants. These sources did not require subsidy from British taxpayers, though whether they would always prove more politically reliable than the NUM remained to be seen. However, the contraction and privatization of Britain's coal industry did not end the call on the taxpayer to subsidize energy generation. Nuclear power brought relatively low running costs along with the considerable expense of eventually decommissioning the plants. This required Treasury grants, as did the spread of wind-farms and other green technologies. Ultimately, if Thatcher and her free-market economics had not confronted the NUM in the eighties, environmental pressure groups – many of them decidedly anti-free market – would have done so in the 1990s and early 2000s. Instead of Ian MacGregor and Peter Walker tolling the mining industry's death knell in 1984, the Labour government of

Tony Blair would have been forced to do so because of its determination to sign the 1997 Kyoto Protocol. The international agreement signed at Kyoto committed Britain to reduce its fossil-fuel emissions – and hence its coal-fired power plants – in the belief that doing so would help combat climate change, a decree wholly at odds with maintaining a sizeable mining industry. If Scargill had triumphed in 1984, he would have humbled and perhaps destroyed Thatcher's reputation. But he would not have secured a long-term future for British coal mining.

The End of the Street – Revolution at Wapping

The defeat of the miners' strike broke 'not just a strike, but a spell'.[39] The verdict of Norman Tebbit was shared by Margaret Thatcher, who concluded in her memoirs that 'from 1982 to 1985 the conventional wisdom was that Britain could only be governed with the consent of the trade unions. No government could really resist, still less defeat a major strike; in particular a strike by the miners' union . . . That day had now come and gone.'[40] Scargill's humbling certainly came to be associated with a turning point in industrial relations after which the trade unions never again enjoyed the same self-confidence or engendered comparable loyalty or loathing. The reality was less clear-cut and was certainly not apparent to many on the left at the time. Ever optimistic about the course of historical determinism, Tony Benn believed the forces of conservatism had suffered a pyrrhic victory: 'The miners' strike was the greatest piece of radicalization I've seen,' he declared, 'there have never been as many socialists in the country in my lifetime. We're only halfway between Dunkirk and D-Day.'[41] It was certainly true that the miners' return to work in March 1985 had not reduced British syndicalism to a sullen acquiescence towards the Tories and the free market. A violent 51-week strike by the miners was quickly followed by a vicious 54-week disruption by print workers.

In some respects, the two disputes were very different in character. One concerned a nationalized industry, the other a trade that had always been in private ownership. The miners' strategy was to bring the government either to its knees or to the negotiating table by turning off Britain's power supply; the ambition of the printers was merely to shut down Britain's most popular newspapers and hurt the media proprietor Rupert Murdoch in the pocket. The miners were fighting to prevent pits from closing and irrevocably ending an entire way of life. Less far-sightedly, the printers were campaigning to ensure their industry continued to use outdated technology and inefficient practices in order to maximize the numbers employed in it. Yet while the two disputes were certainly different in motivation, they were similar in the character of their prosecution. Both were critical to British society. For while the fate of the miners' strike cleared the way for the privatization of coal and other major 'old' industries, the printers' strike determined what role the unions would play in the 'new' technology-driven enterprises, of which the media hoped to become a shining example.

Scarcely any sector of the economy endured poorer industrial relations than 'Fleet Street', as the country's national newspapers were collectively known – the term deriving from the proximity of their operations to the central London street where presses had clattered out books, broadsheets, handbills and periodicals since the time of Caxton. Indeed, Fleet Street was central London's last remaining manufacturing industry of any size. A closed shop effectively prevented non-union members from working in the print halls, and by the early eighties two unions, the National Graphical Association (NGA) and the Society of Graphical and Allied Trades (SOGAT), predominated. The former largely comprised those engaged in typesetting and printing the newspapers, the latter represented those distributing the papers or in clerical and ancillary roles. In turn, the two unions boasted sub-divisions known as 'chapels', presided over by a shop steward rejoicing in the paternalistic title of 'Father of the Chapel'. The implied deference was appropriate, since most employees could expect him (the concept of chapel mothers did not exist) to be their daily contact point on terms and conditions. In this way, chapel fathers operated as a parallel chain of command to management. Indeed, the print hall was effectively rendered out of bounds for many of those nominally running the newspaper from the office upstairs. During the early eighties, the future editor of *The Times*, Peter Stothard, only once took the lift from the journalists' floor to the print floor. 'I was greeted by grown men pretending to be monkeys in a zoo. I did not go back. Many managers, I discovered, had rarely entered the alien territory which they were vainly charged to control.'[42]

For those it embraced, the benefits of this set-up were overwhelming. Since the employers could not select anyone to whom the union denied a membership card, a career printing national newspapers became almost a hereditary occupation through which favoured (biological) fathers passed jobs on to their sons. The result was a print hall populated predominantly from the East End of London, almost wholly white and male. Given the power of patronage in their gift, chapel fathers generally expected, and received, deference. In particular, the Byzantine complexity of the chapel structure, each with its own demarcation rules, made management–union negotiations a protracted and tortuous exercise which successfully ground to a halt efforts at innovation and improvement to the newspaper itself. Tellingly, the print and picture quality of most Fleet Street newspapers had only marginally improved in forty years, despite the fact that competing media, like television, had made huge technical advances over the same period. At Times Newspapers Ltd alone, there were fifty-four chapels, each needing consultation before a significant proposal could be enacted and each capable of bringing production to a standstill if it did not get what it wanted. This represented serious power. If a wildcat strike stopped production for a few hours at a car plant or shipyard, there was always the possibility of making up the shortfall in successive days without supply to the salesrooms being seriously compromised. In contrast, a newspaper that did not hit the news-stands in the morning had no marketable value if it appeared twenty-four hours later. In this way, the chapel fathers successfully held the newspaper managements to ransom, since it was usually cheaper to accept their demands than lose an entire edition's revenue. Even so, in the ten years between January 1976 and January 1986, strikes and stoppages sabotaged Fleet Street and prevented the publication of 296 million copies of *The Sun*, 104 million copies of the *Sunday Times* (an extraordinary figure given that it only came out once per week), 96.5 million copies of *The Times* and 38 million copies of the *News of the World*.[43] Other newspapers – and their readers – suffered similar woes.

Up in the office of *The Times* in 1985, a journalist's basic salary was £15,050 per year. Below, in the bowels of the building, the same journalist's article would be run off the press by a production worker on £18,000. Furthermore, salaries of up to £40,000 per year were within the grasp of skilled compositors, all NGA members, operating machinery that appeared to be inspired, if not designed, by W. Heath Robinson. In 1978, Times Newspapers' management had tried to replace its linotype machines (patented in 1889) with computers which would have permitted journalists to type their articles directly into the newspaper's database. When the unions refused to cooperate, *The Times* and *Sunday Times* were shut down for a year, until November 1979, at which point the management conceded defeat and in 1981 sold both newspapers to Rupert Murdoch. The Australian-born owner of *The Sun* and *News of the World* was the only serious bidder to promise to keep the 196-year-old *Times* going (the other bidder, the *Daily Mail*'s owner, Lord Rothermere, indicated he wanted the *Sunday Times* but, given its losses, would not guarantee to keep *The Times* as a viable entity).[44] At first, Murdoch proved no more capable of outwitting the chapel fathers than the previous owners. The NGA insisted that it would only allow the new computers if access to them was restricted to its own members. Journalists were members of a different trade union, the National Union of Journalists. The answer was 'double-key stroking' – journalists would type up their articles and then hand them to NGA members who would retype them on their computer terminals. The duplication was ludicrous and often involved additional typing errors creeping into the paper. Day in, day out, Fleet Street's newspapers chastised politicians and drew their readers' attention to what was wrong with modern Britain, while being too fearful of the unions to put their own house in order.

For the newspaper proprietors, there was one advantage to this arrangement. The cost and hassle of owning a newspaper was so great that it discouraged potential competition from entering the market. Thus, the restrictive practices of the unions effectively turned Fleet Street into an unofficial cartel for the proprietors. The victim, of course, was the customer. An attempt to break this stranglehold was not risked until March 1986 when Eddy Shah started a mid-market tabloid called *Today* and in doing so became the first Fleet Street outsider to launch a national daily since the Communist Party's *Daily Worker* in 1930.*

Eddy Shah was in the distinctive predicament of being both a self-made man and the fourth cousin of the Aga Khan. His background defied categorization within the traditional British class structure. All that could be said was that, as the son of an English-Irish mother and a Persian-Indian father, he was hardly the conventional grandee of the fourth estate. A rebellious temperament and a disrupted schooling which took him from Karachi to Gordonstoun to various schools in Sussex without his ever taking an A-level, was followed by a stint as a stagehand and a spell selling advertising space for a local newspaper before he scraped together the money to launch a local free-sheet of his own. It was not until 1983 that he came to national prominence because of his attempts to employ non-union members at what had become the Messenger Group of local newspapers in Warrington. Rather than see its closed shop breached, the NGA picketed the plant and, in an effort to ruin Shah, halted production at the *Daily Mirror* in London until its owners promised to divest themselves of their 49 per cent stake in the Messenger Group, and then proceeded to shut down all Fleet Street newspapers on 27 November 1983. Two days later, the Warrington plant was attacked by four thousand pickets who set fire to buildings and, until the timely arrival of police reinforcements, seemed intent on razing the entire Messenger plant to the ground, despite the fact Shah and his staff were trapped inside. What lifted the siege of Warrington was the police demonstrating – as they would thereafter do with the miners – a willingness to intervene to protect employees from violent intimidation, and also the application by the courts of the terms of the Employment Act 1980 against secondary picketing. The NGA's assets were temporarily sequestered until it agreed to obey the law. Having won the opening encounter in Warrington, Shah aimed for a far greater prize, trying to circumvent Fleet Street's restrictions by printing *Today*, via a satellite link, at several regional printing plants, with the help of electricians from the Electrical, Electronic,

---

* The *Daily Worker* was renamed the *Morning Star* in 1966.

Telecommunications and Plumbing Union (EETPU). Breaking ranks with the rest of organized labour, EETPU's general secretary, Eric Hammond, secured his members' participation in return for a no-strike guarantee and an agreement that modern computers would be used, including 'direct input' from journalists. There would be no 'double-key stroking' or other so-called 'Spanish practices'. With lower production costs and access to new technology that was still being denied to Fleet Street, *Today* promised to shake up the media. 'We're going after an industry that's just ripe to be taken,' said Shah bullishly. 'It needs just one guy.'[45] The results, however, suggested otherwise. Although it led the way with colour printing, the quality was disappointing and produced almost comically blurred pictures. Initial sales of one million stood at half that number by the end of the first month. With circulation well below his business projections, Shah quickly ran out of money and in June, only three months after its launch, *Today*'s imminent demise was deferred only by its being sold to Tiny Rowland's Lonhro conglomerate, which also owned the *Observer*. The following year, Rowland, unable to turn around its fortunes, sold *Today* on to Rupert Murdoch, whose purchase secured the paper an eight-year stay of execution. Shah's sale of the paper and its eventual, if protracted, demise demonstrated the toughness of the market and the difficulty for an outsider intent on reshaping it.

Ultimately, it was Murdoch, rather than Shah, who possessed the guile, tenacity and money necessary to transform the country's newspaper industry. In 1977, Murdoch bought an eleven-acre site of dilapidated and disused London Docklands in Wapping, on the north shore of the Thames, just beyond the Tower of London. There, he built a vast, airy printing hall, with modern presses. It cost £72 million and in May 1983 negotiations commenced with the print unions as a precursor to moving production of *The Sun* and the *News of the World* – whose cramped and antiquated print room in Bouverie Street, off Fleet Street, had long ceased to be adequate – to Wapping. Nineteen months later, in December 1984, the unions were still refusing to relocate the short distance to Wapping unless they could transfer their existing over-manning and restrictive practices there, reminding Murdoch's chief negotiator, with evident pride, that 'the *Daily Telegraph*'s press room lay idle for eight years waiting on our union's agreement'. One SOGAT representative was even blunter: 'When will you get it through your thick heads,' he postured, 'we will never let you use it, you may as well put a match to it – or we'll do it for you.'[46] The unions, however, were picking on the wrong proprietor. Concluding that there was no way Wapping's presses were ever going to start spinning with the NGA and SOGAT dictating the terms, in February 1985 Murdoch and a small, hand-picked team of executives began planning a covert operation. Codenamed

'Project X', it involved using employees who were not members of either the NGA or SOGAT to print all four of the company's national newspapers at Wapping. If the plan succeeded, the power of the traditional Fleet Street print unions would be circumvented and newspapers could finally be run by their managements without the constant threat of disruption.

Success depended upon the utmost secrecy. If the NGA or SOGAT realized what was being planned at Wapping before the presses were ready to roll, they could bring production to a standstill at Murdoch's Bouverie Street and Gray's Inn Road (home of *The Times* and *Sunday Times*) print halls in the meantime. The loss of revenue would cripple him, forcing his capitulation. Thus, during the twelve months it would take to transform Wapping to be ready not just to print four newspapers but also to house offices for their journalists, a cover story had to be concocted to explain the signs of activity there. The pretence was that it was being fitted up to produce a new evening newspaper, to be called the *London Post*, on which, when it was ready, new positions would be offered to NGA and SOGAT members. The reality was very different. As Eddy Shah had done before him, Murdoch concluded a deal with Eric Hammond to have members of EETPU get Wapping up and running. Hammond saw this as an opportunity to create jobs for his members and to show that moderate unions need not necessarily be antipathetic to the new technology-driven sectors of the economy. Having endured successive TUC conferences where delegates took delight in shouting him down whenever he tried to address them, Hammond was in no mood to be lectured about fraternity from those he believed were actually wrecking trade unionism with their militancy. Recruiting electricians in London was deemed too risky, in case they talked about their work, so they were hired in Southampton and daily bussed eighty miles to Wapping and back. This was not the only long and circuitous route. The Atex computer mainframes which would transform how national newspapers were edited and produced were bought in Boston but shipped in unmarked boxes via Paris to throw off the scent any print union sympathizers monitoring such a surprisingly large purchase. They were then assembled in London by an all-American team working in the utmost secrecy from an unprepossessing shed in Woolwich licensed to a cover company called Caprilord Ltd.

Even though every precaution had been taken, by September rumours had reached SOGAT's new general secretary, Brenda Dean, that dummy print-runs were being rolled off at Wapping. The revelation made a mockery of the claims of Murdoch's management that there were only a few electricians there doing a bit of wiring. Dean immediately suggested strike action to bring Murdoch's four newspapers to a standstill, only to find other members of her executive convinced there was no cause for alarm. In the face of such insouciance, Dean was incredulous, vainly protesting: 'Fleet

Street stops at the drop of a hat for absolutely bugger all . . . What's wrong with you all? Now's the time to strike!'[47] She was right, it would have been the time. And the time passed. Instead, the NGA and SOGAT got their timing and their tactics catastrophically wrong. On 21 January 1986, in the face of redundancy threats, ballots recorded over 80 per cent of both unions' members demanding that Murdoch's company, News International, guarantee them 'jobs for life' – otherwise they would strike. Murdoch could scarcely believe his luck. The unions were making their most outlandish demand just at the moment his shadow workforce at Wapping had confirmed that the new presses were ready to roll. The siege of Wapping was about to begin. At St Bride's, the Fleet Street 'journalists' church', an emergency all-night vigil was held for the future of the newspaper industry.

Late in the evening of Saturday, 25 January, Wapping's presses began printing the following day's *Sunday Times* and *News of the World*. Many journalists recognized this as an exciting moment to break free from the restrictions that had so often prevented their articles from being printed. For the first time, they enjoyed direct input of their copy. The objective was a bold one. As one *Sunday Times* journalists later put it: 'How many other industries have gone from the equivalent of steam to microchip in a week, without interrupting production?'[48] Not all found this advance so invigorating. Among employees who did not turn up for work were those obeying an edict from the National Union of Journalists forbidding them to 'enter the Wapping plant' or to operate the new technology – the union having thrown in its lot with the printers in a display of workers' solidarity. Other absentees simply wanted to record their irritation that, in springing such a major surprise at the last moment, neither their editors nor News International's management had had the courtesy to take them into their confidence about the proposed move. It offended their professional pride – though if Murdoch had managed to keep his secret after first announcing it to his journalists, it would certainly have made for a world-exclusive. Whatever their feelings about management's tactics and the project's aims, most regarded moving to the physical location of Wapping with as much enthusiasm as a posting to Siberia. The regeneration of London's Docklands had scarcely begun. There were no quality bars, shops or restaurants – unlike the Fleet Street with which journalists were so cosily familiar. What was more, the Wapping plant, which included the offices and print hall for *The Times*, the *Sunday Times*, *The Sun* and the *News of the World*, was a forbidding fortress with twelve-foot railings topped by razor wire, security cameras and guard-dog patrols. It quickly became clear that the aesthetics of the concentration camp would form a necessary protection from the besieging army beyond. It hardly made for a happy and welcoming work environment.

What those who did answer the call to work discovered on the opening nights was terrifying. NGA and SOGAT pickets, joined by hundreds, and often thousands, of sympathizers (perhaps also motivated by a desire for vengeance against newspapers that had opposed the miners' strike), gathered outside in an effort to block all the exits and prevent the newspapers leaving the plant. *The Times* journalist Tim Austin recalled the scene on the first night as his paper was ready to be dispatched:

> We stood behind the fence and watched the trucks lining up behind the gate, revving. There were hordes of baying pickets. The noise was fantastic. A huge police presence. The whole area was floodlit. Cries of 'Scabs! Scabs! Bastards!' The police were confident their line would hold for the trucks to get out. You could see the driver in the first lorry. He had obviously psyched himself up. The potential for him being damaged severely was pretty clear. They opened the gates and he just put his foot down. I've never seen a lorry accelerate so quickly. By the time he got to the gatehouse he must have been doing thirty miles an hour. If he was going to kill somebody, too bad. He wanted to get out.[49]

Days turned into weeks, over which the siege intensified. Staff were given an ever-changing telephone number to call that would let them know where and when special buses with wire mesh over the windows and drawn curtains would pick them up and take them in and out of the compound, in order to protect them and conceal their identities. Those who travelled in by car were at risk of having their vehicles vandalized. Those who went in on foot got covered in spit. *The Times*'s property correspondent survived a smashed beer-glass thrust at his jugular. In particular, senior management needed personal protection. Their principal collaborators were equally in danger: Eric Hammond escaped the abuse being hurled at him in the street by walking into the TUC's Congress House for a scheduled meeting of its general council, only to find himself being kicked and punched by several union officials inside the TUC's foyer.

It was perhaps surprising that trade unionists, having only the previous year seen how the NUM's use of flying pickets and physical menace had failed to shut down the working pits of the Midlands, should imagine the strategy would succeed in East London. However, the calculation second time around seemed a more favourable one: while striking miners had never marshalled sufficient numbers simultaneously to close all the working pits, there was only one Wapping plant to shut down. On the other hand, a single target was also easier to defend, and the police were deployed in sufficient numbers to keep its exits unblocked. In particular, SOGAT and the NGA went on strike under the misapprehension that Wapping lacked the capacity to print sufficient numbers of newspapers. It possessed only forty-eight presses whereas, at its old premises, a full *Sunday Times* print-run had necessitated all ninety presses. The seeming shortfall was bridged by the ability of Wapping's electricians to print double the number of copies per hour that the NGA members had managed to produce. Indeed, the ability of Wapping's 670 production staff to print four newspapers begged questions about how efficiently the 5,500 NGA and SOGAT members had worked prior to January 1986. Other newspaper proprietors also noticed the difference. Inexplicably, it was taking 6,800 employees to produce the *Daily* and *Sunday Express*, despite those titles having a fraction of the combined circulation of Wapping's output. In April, Murdoch offered the unions a deal. If they called off their strike, he would give them *The Times*'s old offices and print hall in Gray's Inn Road, compete with all its presses. Suggesting they use it to start up their own newspaper, Murdoch announced: 'This is the opportunity for the TUC to achieve their ambition and at the same time employ the people who previously worked at the plant. It allows the trade union movement the start-up capital free of charge with no interest charges round their neck.'[50] 'We put print workers before print works,' came Norman Willis's disingenuous reply. 'Our priority has to be people not property.'[51] The chance to test the market for a new pro-Labour newspaper produced by 5,500 print union members was hastily passed up.

Instead, the unions persisted in believing they could defeat Murdoch through a unified campaign of picket lines, blackings and boycotts. Most wholesale workers were SOGAT members, who were instructed by Brenda Dean to 'black' – to refuse to handle – all Murdoch titles. Only those in Glasgow, Coventry and Liverpool obeyed her command. Worse, the blacking call to those not directly employed by News International was a clear breach of secondary picketing legislation, and when Dean persisted her contempt of court caused SOGAT's £17 million of assets to be sequestered. This caused hardship – and resentment – among the union's 213,000 provincial members, who could not receive pensions and other benefits because of the union's action in defence of the 4,500 members demanding 'jobs for life' in London. The courts released the money in May when Dean purged her contempt. Other efforts to black Murdoch titles also fell flat. In order to prevent the National Union of Railwaymen refusing to transport his newspapers, Murdoch switched to road haulage. When the TGWU's general secretary, Ron Todd, ordered his members not to drive the lorries, he was met with the same response that Dean had received from the wholesalers. Regardless of appeals for union solidarity, the majority of SOGAT and TGWU members showed no desire to imperil their own jobs for the sake of printers in London, most of whom had long enjoyed far higher pay than themselves. The least successful blacking campaign was launched by Neil Kinnock, who called for a boycott of all of Murdoch's newspapers – only to find that their circulation increased during the period of his *fatwa*. Even less satisfactorily, the Labour leader's announcement that neither he nor his colleagues would have any dealings whatsoever with papers that accounted for a quarter of national circulation – including refusing to brief them or to give them stories – made it even more difficult for Labour to get its point across.

In rejecting Murdoch's £58 million redundancy package (offering them between £2,000 and £30,000 each, depending on length of employment), and with the failure of the boycotts and the secondary action, the strikers' options narrowed and the picketing of 'Fortress Wapping' intensified. On the night of 2 June, News International's warehouse in Deptford, where newsprint for its papers was being stored, was fire-bombed, incinerating the building and causing the biggest fire London had witnessed since the Blitz. It took a fireboat pumping 26,000 gallons of water from the Thames every three minutes to prevent the flames spreading to a nearby housing estate. The culprits were never identified. Throughout the summer and across the country, depots for lorries engaged in conveying the newspapers were repeatedly broken into and the trucks and vans smashed up.

Tempers were also fraying within the two main unions. Aged only forty-four when the strike started, Brenda Dean was the first woman to run a major British trade union. Sporting a bouffant hair-do which resembled that of the prime minister (though she might have preferred comparison to Barbara Castle), Dean was softly spoken and well dressed, and the antithesis of the right-wing press's caricature of a female Labour activist. By sex, background (she was from Greater Manchester) and temperament, she was equally far removed from the London print chapels, which failed to conceal their resentment at some woman from outside their area running their union. Her priority was the low-paid SOGAT members, often female cleaners and junior office staff, who were the clear victims of the dispute – another reason for the suspicion and animosity shown towards her by the more misogynistically minded chapel fathers. As the dispute reached its first anniversary, Dean could see the battle was lost. The majority of her sacked members had found new jobs – which, paradoxically, made them more resistant to agreeing a deal, believing there was nothing to be lost by holding out for more. In the meantime, the Wapping picket line was attracting political activists and hooligans who were not directly involved in the dispute but who saw it as a cause over which to attack a Tory-supporting newspaper company and its guardians, the police force. The conflict's worst night of violence came on 24 January 1987, which saw 12,500 demonstrators descend upon Wapping, many throwing petrol bombs and hurling sharpened railings, stringing wire across the road to maim the police horses, and almost succeeding in smashing down the gates to the plant. There were seventy injuries and sixty-seven arrests (of which, tellingly, only thirteen were of print workers).

For Dean, it was the final straw. She booked a flight on Concorde and met Murdoch's negotiator in New York. There they agreed that because the scale of the protests exceeded the legal stipulation of no more than six pickets at an entrance, News International should take SOGAT to court and, under threat of massive fines and the sequestration once again of its assets, Dean would then be in a position to persuade the union's national executive to call off the strike. This she achieved on 5 February. It was pointless the NGA continuing without its nominal ally, so it, too, came to heel, calling off the strike two days later. There was little to show for the struggle. The print unions' defeat proved as protracted and emphatic as that suffered by the NUM. The final audit included one death, almost 1,500 arrests, 574 injured police officers and over one thousand violent attacks on drivers and vehicles. Not a single edition of any of Murdoch's papers printed at Wapping had been stopped. Nor, in the succeeding quarter-century, did industrial action prevent a single edition of any of his papers reaching the news-stands. 'Collective action' had been smashed.

The subsequent absence of strikes was only one manifestation of the 'Wapping revolution'. Management had gained a hitherto unknown level of flexibility, being finally free to employ whoever it liked, to deploy whatever technology it could afford, and to make whatever changes it wished to the size, style and print-runs of its papers without tortuous and potentially unsuccessful negotiations with truculent chapel fathers. More pages were added, production quality improved markedly and colour photography became common by the decade's end. It was Murdoch's gamble that made these changes possible and he was the first to reap the rewards, his British newspapers' operating income increasing from £38.4 million in 1985 to £150.2 million two years later.[52] His company, News International, was the London Stock Exchange's best-performing major listing in 1987, and the revenue helped fund his expansion into the American film and television market, turning him into a global media presence and providing funds for his next big idea for Britain – Sky TV.

The benefits were also reaped by Murdoch's competitors. As even the celebrated *Guardian* journalist Hugo Young felt compelled to concede: 'What [Murdoch] did for the economics of newspaper publishing, by killing the power of the worst-led trade unions in modern history, has benefited every journalist, advertiser and reader.'[53] In the post-Wapping euphoria, a range of new national newspapers started, including the unashamedly vulgar and unserious tabloid *Sunday Sport*, the earnest left-wing tabloid *News on Sunday* (pre-launch slogan: 'No tits, but a lot of balls') and the highbrow broadsheet, the *Sunday Correspondent*. The last two quickly folded. However, in October 1986, former journalists from the *Daily Telegraph* launched the *Independent*, which was quickly perceived as a rival to *The Times*. They had begun planning the new broadsheet before Murdoch's Wapping experiment commenced and their paper would have launched regardless of it. Nevertheless, it was hard to envisage how the *Independent* could have survived if it had been subjected to the union culture that Wapping helpfully blew away. Long-established competitors reaped the same advantages. Using money made from the flotation of Reuters (in which all the newspapers had shares), they, too, expanded, building new press halls and enjoying their new-found managerial freedom. Those that kept unions were now able to bind them to agreements, including no-strike clauses, that restricted their actions in ways that would have been unimaginable without the ability to invoke the salutary warning of Wapping. Most of them de-recognized the National Union of Journalists.

Besides the print and journalists' unions, there were three losers in this process. The first was the *Daily Telegraph*'s elderly and rather reticent owner, Lord Hartwell, who miscalculated the cost of a massive new print hall in Docklands and, finding himself overstretched, was forced to sell his newspaper inheritance to a new buccaneering style of Conservative – a Canadian called Conrad Black. The second was Eric Hammond, whose vital early help for Murdoch was not repaid by a deal recognizing EETPU bargaining rights at Wapping, News International having come to the conclusion that it could operate perfectly happily without deals with unions. The third was old Fleet Street itself. The move to bigger premises in new locations, mostly in London's Docklands, ended forever the press's geographical association with 'the street of adventure' (or, pejoratively, 'the street of shame') in a severing of historic ties that aroused sentimental feelings among those who remembered with fondness its cosy cheek-by-jowl collegiality, clubbishness and heavy drinking – a culture that soon came to be deemed unprofessional in the new media world of blinking computer screens, corporate presentations, audited expense accounts and employee–management relations conducted through a department of human resources.

On the Waterfront

The newspaper companies were among the first major businesses to relocate to Docklands, an area of London's East End which in 1981 – when the last of the Port of London's up-river docks closed – looked more devastated and derelict than it had done after seventy-six consecutive nights of bombing by the Luftwaffe in 1941. Indeed, 'the world's busiest inland port' had recovered remarkably quickly from its wartime pummelling and in 1964 had recorded its highest-ever volume of trade, its wharves and cranes lining the Thames as far up-river as St Paul's Cathedral. From that pinnacle, the descent was swift. Docklands was not suitable for newly designed large container ships which necessitated deep-water terminals like those constructed at Tilbury and Felixstowe. In 1969, the basin of London Docks was filled in, eventually becoming the Wapping site of Murdoch's newspapers. In 1980, the piling up of barrels of rum and crates of bananas on the quayside at Canary Wharf ceased with the shutting of the West India Dock, a closure that effectively ended economic activity on the formerly bustling Isle of Dogs. In the space of sixteen years, the tidal approach to one of the world's great cities was transformed from a hive of activity into a desolate wasteland.

What was to be done with this bleak prospect? 'I believe that this is the decade that London will become Europe's capital,' prophesied Harold Shand, the fictional East End gangster with hopes of becoming a serious property entrepreneur in the 1980 film *The Long Good Friday*. 'Having cleared away the outdated, we've got mile after mile, acre after acre of land for our future prosperity.'[54] Shand's big idea was to bring in American mafia money to transform the Docklands as the site for a future Olympic Games. He was rather ahead of his time in suggesting the ultimate sporting event could pay its way by driving urban regeneration given the contemporary examples of Montreal (1976) and Moscow (1980). Nevertheless, the government shared Shand's optimism that the sheer scale of desolation actually created an opportunity to build afresh and in doing so to showcase an entirely different vision for Britain's future prosperity. In 1981, the environment secretary, Michael Heseltine, set up the London Docklands Development Corporation with a brief to spearhead regeneration, and the following year the area was designated one of several new 'enterprise zones', where private enterprise was lured with minimal planning restrictions, a 100 per cent capital allowance against corporation tax and ten years' exemption from paying local business rates.

In addition to these *laissez-faire* efforts to unfetter capitalism, considerable public money was also committed. There was, after all, little hope of turning the area into a new financial centre to rival the City without an efficient transport link between the two. A start was made with the Docklands Light Railway, which began taking fares in 1987, only three years after construction had begun. Newspapers were not the only media companies to decamp along its route. At Canary Wharf, Limehouse Studios became home to one of the decade's major independent television studios. The sheer pace of change sealed its fate, however, for it fell victim, a mere five years after opening, to the wrecking ball because its location lay in the way of a far grander project. This was the vast new financial district funded by the

Canadian property developer Olympia & York. The project featured what became the tallest skyscraper in Europe. At fifty floors, One Canada Square (more generally known as the Canary Wharf Tower) was visible from thirty miles away and, after much internal debate, was clad in steel as an acknowledgement of Britain's industrial past. The future it offered was very different: international investment funding an entirely speculative development in the belief that international financial and media institutions, attracted by Thatcherism's lighter regulatory touch, could be enticed to move in. Thatcher was among the dignitaries who braved its summit for the topping-out ceremony on 8 November 1990. Though she did not know it, she had only another twenty days left as prime minister. Indeed, the immediate fate of the obelisk-shaped tower appeared to mock all the hopes that she, as well as Canary Wharf's promoters, had placed in financial and property-based speculation. When the tower opened the following year, almost all its floors remained un-let and Olympia & York went bankrupt with debts of $20 billion. It was not until 1999 (when the extension of the Jubilee line improved accessibility) that the tower became fully occupied, and it was only in the first decade of the twenty-first century that Canary Wharf was recognized as one of the great success stories of the eighties – even if the financial institutions it housed would prove no more immune to risk than the generations of seafaring enterprises that had connected the old Port of London to the sinews of global trade.

Docklands was the perfect example of a part of Britain that was transformed during the eighties from a place where 'visible' earnings were made by trading goods and raw materials into a location for the generation of 'invisible' earnings from financial and allied services. The domestic consumer boom of the second half of the decade increased the demand for imports of goods that Britain either no longer made or else made at a higher price than most customers wished to pay, worsening the trade balance significantly in spite of the supposedly counterbalancing inflow from 'invisibles'. But whether imported or exported, goods continued to pass through the country's remaining ports and it was there that the third and final great eighties tussle with traditional trade union power was fought.

Throughout the months of strife in the coalfields and disorder outside Fortress Wapping, the most restrictive union practice of all, the National Dock Labour Scheme, continued to operate in sixty-three major British ports – including Tilbury, Liverpool, Southampton, Hull, Cardiff, the Forth and the Clyde – affecting the profitability of 150 firms and the rights of over nine thousand workers. Introduced by Attlee's government in 1947, the scheme's objective was to end the insecurity the country's dockers suffered through being employed as casual labour, since the quantity of goods to be loaded or unloaded could vary considerably from day to day. It solved the problem by, in effect, guaranteeing them employment regardless of whether there was work to be done. Assigned half the seats on the National Dock Labour Board, TGWU representatives enjoyed the statutory privilege of being able to block any management proposal that involved job losses. It was also in the gift of the TGWU – the largest trade union in the Western world – to determine who was employed in the docks and to adjudicate on matters of discipline. Unsurprisingly, sackings were rare when the decision was taken by a union rather than an employer. The most spectacular decoupling between market forces and the payroll was manifest in the way the scheme operated when a dock closed down. In this eventuality, registered dockers were entitled to choose either a £25,000 severance payment or transfer to a dock that was still operational, the latter being legally compelled to employ them even if there was no work to be undertaken.

Given these burdens, it was hardly surprising that docks did close down, their business migrating either to Felixstowe and Dover (which were outside the scheme and were able to deploy flexible labour) or to other European entrepôts such as Antwerp and Rotterdam. While many registered dockers opted for the severance pay-out, the weight of having to support those who applied to the remaining docks undermined the latter's competitiveness. What was more, the scheme had not even bought industrial peace. Union militancy in the docks remained high. Terrified of taking on the TGWU, Edward Heath's government had even strengthened the scheme's terms in order to buy off a potentially crippling strike in 1972, and stoppages, official and unofficial, continued to plague productivity. If the Thatcher government was up for a fight, it could only abolish the scheme by repealing the 1947 act. Yet while several Cabinet ministers, including Nick Ridley, Tom King and Nigel Lawson, believed the immediate aftermath of the defeats of the mining and print unions represented exactly the psychological moment to revoke the dock scheme, Thatcher hesitated.[55] There were only so many long and bruising strikes a country could endure in almost continuous succession, and the dockers had the ability to sever most of the major arteries of the country's international trade. As a consequence, the National Dock Labour Scheme almost survived the eighties intact.

Finally, Thatcher was persuaded to risk a confrontation, though the terms she countenanced demonstrated how keen she was to buy off the dockers rather than fight them to the death. In return for losing their registered status under the scheme, they would each receive a payment of £35,000. The sweetener's cost to the taxpayer exceeded £300 million. The probability that the dockers would nonetheless reject the offer remained high, and the government's plans were undertaken in great secrecy because forewarning the dockers of the scheme's imminent demise risked giving them time to plan a coordinated response. Among the precautions taken was the identification of small harbours where goods might be loaded and unloaded in the event of a strike paralysing the major ports for months. One particularly incendiary proposal involved flying in foreign dockers to undertake the work. Announced on 6 April 1989, the repeal act became law on 6 July. The speed with which it was rushed through Parliament caught the dockers off-guard; for while some stopped working unilaterally, it took time for the TGWU to organize the necessary strike ballot, not least because of delays caused by having to fight off – successfully – legal action by the dock employers. As a result, by the time the strike started officially, the dockers were manning picket lines in defence of a scheme that no longer existed. This was not the basis for fighting a sustained campaign and, fearing the sack and the prospect of losing the £35,000 pay-out, a return to work by dockers at Tilbury triggered similar capitulations in other ports. Its effectiveness shattered, in August the strike was called off. Except in Liverpool, where the port owners continued to recognize the TGWU in return for agreeing major redundancies (the showdown would not come there until 1995), union power in Britain's ports was shattered. Docks became again a place for casual and contract labour. However, as the government had anticipated, greater productivity attracted back to Britain trade that had been diverted to European ports – breathing life back into docks from Bristol to the Forth, Sheerness to the Tees, whose future in the late eighties had seemed imperilled.

United They Stand?

If judged purely by the number and scale of strikes and stoppages called, the eighties clearly transformed the country's industrial relations. Less than four million days were being lost to strikes in the second half of the decade, compared with over fourteen million when Edward Heath was prime minister. What was more, Thatcher's period of office not only reversed the militancy of the previous decade, it set the economy on course for even fewer strikes in the nineties. By 1997, strike activity was at its lowest level since records began in 1891, and the historically low incidence of disputes continued through the first decade of the twenty-first century, reaching a new recorded low of 157,000 days lost in 2005.[56] While other Western countries also experienced reduced levels of industrial action during this period, it was in Britain that the fall was most marked: by the nineties, the number of days lost per British employee was less than half the European Union average.[57] A country that when Thatcher came to power was internationally notorious for being strike-torn became, within a short period of time, a model of industrial peace. The statistics in Table 1 speak for themselves:

Table 1. Industrial Disputes in the UK[58]

Year	Number of strikes	Workers involved	Days lost
1970–3 (average)	2,917	1,573,000	14,077,000
1975–9 (average)	2,345	1,658,000	11,663,000
1980–4 (average)	1,363	1,298,000	10,486,000
1985–9 (average)	895	783,000	3,939,000
1990–9 (average)	274	223,000	824,000

The most obvious explanation was that the eighties coincided with the start of a continual decline in trade union membership. In 1979, the year of the Winter of Discontent, membership stood at an all-time peak of 13.2 million. By 1990, it was down to 9.8 million, and heading below 7 million by the beginning of the 2010s, a thirty-year decline that took union membership from over half the workforce down to less than a quarter.[59] Not only did 'organized labour' shrink in absolute numbers, it was especially hard hit by the privatization of – and job losses in – formerly nationalized industries where militancy had been especially strong.

Market forces were not the only factor. In particular, the Thatcher government's legislation transformed the way in which strikes could be organized, investing the courts with powers to fine unions that transgressed the letter of the new laws. James Prior's Employment Act 1980 ensured picket lines were legal only if they were manned by workers employed by the company at the heart of the dispute and took place at that company's premises. 'Sympathetic' action by other unions and their members was thereby illegal. The Employment Act 1982 made disobeying these picketing requirements no longer an option. Unions knowingly doing so could be fined and if they refused to accept liability, they risked having their assets sequestered until they purged their contempt of court. Piloted through the Commons by Norman Tebbit, the Trade Union Act 1984 made it illegal for union leaders to call their members out on strike without first putting the matter to a secret ballot. Had Tebbit's law reached the statute book in time, the requirement to hold a ballot would have ensured either that the miners' strike enjoyed far wider support, or that it did not happen at all.

The miners' and printers' strikes demonstrated the effectualness of legislation designed to make picketing primarily a force for persuasion rather than coercion. Nottinghamshire's working collieries might have been overrun but for the ability of the police to turn back flying pickets. Fear of their being classified as 'secondary action' restricted the deeds of sympathetic unions. Sequestration of assets hampered the NUM's activities and, ultimately, dealt the *coup de grâce* to SOGAT. Nonetheless, though such measures were deployed in some of the most important strikes, it would be an overstatement to suggest that they became the standard means of restoring the whip hand to management. With the number of strikes running at about one thousand per year between 1983 and 1987, the combined figure of 114 court injunctions against unions during this period showed both the high level of union compliance with the law – despite the fact that it was not until 1986 that the TUC dropped its opposition to pre-strike ballots – and the reluctance of employers to turn to the courts to undermine those with whom they were in dispute.[60]

Judging union power purely through the number and severity of strikes provides a telling, but limited, picture. Neither government policies nor union activities were single-mindedly focused upon this one weapon in the armoury of syndicalism. The limiting of union influence went far further. In particular, doing away with an incomes policy meant that there was no longer a need for government ministers to negotiate pay norms with union leaders – indeed, no need to engage the unions in policy decisions at all. The whole structure of corporatism – which had enticed Heath's administration almost as much as Wilson's and Callaghan's – was dismantled. Since 1962, the National Economic Development Council (known as 'Neddy') had brought ministers and civil servants together with representatives of British business and the unions to outline plans for economic growth. Without taking the trouble to abolish it (a task left to her successor in 1992), Thatcher made sure Neddy became an irrelevance. Its convocations became occasional, with government ministers often represented by their understudies. In 1989, the TUC was even deprived of its right to chose the union representation on the council – insult being added to injury when the government decided Eric Hammond, whose union was by then not even affiliated to the TUC, should attend. In truth, there was almost nothing that mainstream union leaders were likely to propose that did not conflict with Thatcher's determination to make the labour market more flexible as a primary means of reducing the burdens on job creation. Openly sidelined, union leaders were disabused of the notion that they were still regarded as partners in policy formation – just as those among them who tried to use strikes to recreate the dynamic of the Heath years or the Winter of Discontent until their demands were met were forced to think again. In these ways, Thatcher finally provided the answer to the question 'Who Governs?' which her hapless Conservative predecessor had fatally put to the electorate back in 1974.

Other, more specific union practices and prerogatives also came under attack. Strongly promoted by Michael Foot's Employment Protection Act 1975, the closed shop forced those employers it embraced to hire only members of a specified union. Intended as a means of securing strong collective bargaining, the closed shop was a major restriction on management's ability to choose whoever it considered the best talent for a job, and it forced applicants to join a particular union rather than to enjoy the possibility of freedom from – as well as of – association. Indeed, under Foot's legislation it was a legal requirement to sack employees who tried to leave the union to which they were assigned. The Employment Act 1980 began to undermine this effort to create a union monopoly by making the continuation of the closed shop conditional on an overwhelming endorsement (the threshold was 80 per cent in a secret ballot) by employees in the companies where it operated. This stipulation, and the declining numbers of jobs in traditional areas of the economy where the closed shop was most entrenched, ensured that during the eighties the number of employees subject to closed shop terms of employment fell from 4.5 million to under half a million. Dismissal for refusing to join a union was made illegal in 1988 and the closed shop was done away with altogether four years later.

At the same time, the practice highlighted by the Wapping revolution and the abolition of the National Dock Labour Scheme of companies de-recognizing unions in the workplace, while salutary to those it affected, failed to become commonplace across the economy as a whole. Between 1980 and 1988 there were only fifty-six such instances.[61] In the longer term, the threat to unions' influence came less from losing their grip in private companies where previously they had enjoyed a presence than from failing to gain a toehold in modern, emerging enterprises. Only one third of companies set up after 1980 recognized unions.[62] Particularly contentious within the trade union movement was the belief among reform-minded general secretaries like Eric Hammond of the EETPU that signing single-union, no-strike agreements with companies represented a viable way of ensuring a union presence in the future (despite his failure to make a deal stick at Wapping). Single-union deals were not the closed shop by any other name since employees were not bound to join the union. The idea of denying the right to strike was anathema to traditional union leaders, who thought it worth fighting a civil war over within the union movement. This had unfortunate consequences when, in March 1988, the TGWU's efforts to scupper a single-union deal negotiated between the Amalgamated Engineering Union and Ford caused the car manufacturer to cancel its plans to create a thousand jobs in Dundee. Spanish workers benefited instead. Regardless, the TUC's general council pressed ahead with its campaign against the single-union protagonists, suspending EETPU as a precursor to an overwhelming vote by conference delegates in September 1988 to expel the union and its 330,000 members from the TUC.

Excommunicating Hammond did nothing to solve the problem of the continuing slide in union membership and the associated decline of collective bargaining in the workplace. The privatization of monopolistic state-owned industries and utilities into separate companies further disrupted the ability of unions to achieve nationwide collective pay bargaining. It was partly in an effort to redress this process that an accelerated pace of mergers created a handful of super-unions which aimed to speak as the unchallenged representatives of the workers across entire sectors of the economy. These mergers were driven not just by a belief that security came in numbers, but by a recognition that the pace of economic and technological change was undermining many skills, while increased job flexibility offered choice as well as potential insecurity. Consequently, the old-fashioned demarcation between proudly independent skilled labourers keen to protect their apprenticeships and craft-guild traditions from one another no longer corresponded to the realities of the workplace. The largest mergers did not take place until the nineties, but the creation of the GMB from the Amalgamated Society of Boilermakers, Shipwrights, Blacksmiths and Structural Workers – more sensibly known as 'the boilermakers' – and the General and Municipal Workers' Union in 1982 set an example which was followed in 1988 by the formation of the Manufacturing, Science and Finance Union,* which merged unions representing foremen, skilled workers, technicians and white-collar employees, predominantly in the engineering, research, health and insurance sectors.

The unions also sought salvation from another driver of cooperation and integration – Brussels. At the same 1988 TUC conference that expelled Eric Hammond, delegates gave a rapturous welcome to the president of the European Commission, Jacques Delors. The French socialist outlined his proposal for a European Social Charter to standardize employment law throughout the European Community, guaranteeing the right of all workers to collective bargaining and worker representation in management decision-making. 'Social Europe', it seemed, could rescue British syndicalism from the straitjacket imposed upon it by Westminster. In return for the promise of salvation, Delors received more than a standing ovation – he won converts from a movement that had until that point widely regarded the European project as capitalist dogma.

Twelve days after Delors charmed the conference-goers in Bournemouth, Thatcher crossed the English Channel in the opposite direction to deliver a speech in the Belgian city of Bruges that put beyond doubt her disenchantment with the regulatory, centralizing mission of European integration. A new enemy had been indentified, but this time, as she advanced to confront it, the prime minister would not have all her army marching behind her. Finally, her enemies saw their chance.

---

* Subsequent mergers changed the name first to Amicus and later to Unite.

14 CREATIVE DESTRUCTION

Rolling Back the State

The biggest privatization the world had ever seen was scheduled for November 1984. There was good reason to anticipate its failure. The problems extended far beyond estimating the scale of British Telecom's notional future profits. It was not even easy to work out how it generated its existing income. Since 1912, the Post Office had enjoyed a monopoly of telephone provision and operation throughout the country. Wholly state-owned, British Telecom's independence from the Post Office only dated from 1981, and when the Department of Trade and Industry first looked into whether a successful privatization was possible it discovered that BT's accounts were so vague that it was unclear which parts of the business were profitable and which were not.[1] Without shareholders to answer to or competition to fear, such basic accountancy was seemingly a low priority. Certainly, the patience of the customer was severely tried. Private homes wishing to have a telephone were put on a waiting list. Routinely, installation could take three months or more. Businesses were also hindered by the inability to meet demand with supply. In the early eighties, the ambition of stockbroking firms to do more of their share-trading by telephone was handicapped because BT proved unable to install sufficient lines even within an area as confined as the Square Mile. The comedian John Cleese popularized the joke that the reason public telephone boxes were routinely out of order was not because they were vandalized but rather that they were vandalized because they were out of order.

That the prevailing culture might change alarmed those who saw no reason to challenge the existing system. BT's unions led the campaign to prevent the privatization and Labour articulated the parliamentary opposition, the party's trade and industry spokesman, Peter Shore, condemning 'the folly of attempting to privatize this large, profitable and extremely innovative and successful public enterprise'.[2] Moreover, even experienced capitalists doubted whether offering shares in 50.2 per cent of such a vast entity was a sensible idea. Ahead of the proposed flotation, the Chancellor of the Exchequer, Nigel Lawson, attended a private dinner party with leading industrialists and financiers from the City of London. The venue was a penthouse suite at the top of the Dorchester Hotel with panoramic views across the rooftops in one direction and of the vast, verdant expanse of Hyde Park in the other. Around the dinner table, the vision remained conventionally myopic. With a solitary exception, every one of the experts present assured Lawson that 'the privatization was impossible: the capital market simply was not large enough to absorb it'.[3] The contrary voice was Martin Jacomb, who, as the vice chairman of Kleinwort Benson, the merchant bank handling the flotation, had a vested interest in talking up its prospects.

It was easy to see why BT might be considered too big to sell. In the United States the recent break-up and sale of AT&T for $500 million had set the record for the industry. By comparison, selling half of BT would net nearly £4 billion – if enough buyers could be found at the asking price of 130 pence per share. No stock market anywhere in the world had handled an equity issue of this size. Undaunted by much of the City's apparent self-doubt, the government pressed ahead. Offering local authority tenants the right to buy their council houses had proved one of the most significant policies of Thatcher's first term in office, the take-up having greatly exceeded expectations. Anthony Eden's phrase about creating a 'property-owning democracy' was revived, and if those of modest means could be persuaded to invest in property then the possibility presented itself that millions of them might also start buying shares in companies. A massive advertising campaign was launched, targeting not the main institutional investors but private individuals and, in particular, potential first-timers with no previous experience of dabbling in the stock market. The share offer opened on 20 November with 39 per cent of the shares specifically restricted to individual purchasers (permitted one application each) and only 50 pence of the 130 pence needed as a down payment. The offer was five times oversubscribed and the 2.3 million Britons whose applications were successful watched gleefully as the share price almost doubled within hours of dealing beginning on the Stock Exchange floor.[4]

In the space of weeks, the conventional wisdom that the flotation would flop morphed into the accusation that its success was so preordained that the government's opening price represented either an incompetent or a cynical undervaluation. Those who feared the whole promotion was little more than an incitement to greed had their suspicions confirmed when among those caught illegally trying to make multiple personal applications (by using variations on their names) was the Conservative MP Keith Best. Forced to resign his seat, the future chief executive of the Immigration Advisory

Service managed to have his four-month jail sentence overturned in return for an increased fine of £4,500. More significantly, the fact that 5 per cent of the country's adult population had legitimately bought BT shares almost doubled the number of people in Britain who owned shares. 'We are seeing,' declared the jubilant Chancellor, 'the birth of people's capitalism.' Thatcher admired the sentiment if not the phraseology, which she thought smacked of Marxism–Leninism. She duly amended it to 'popular capitalism'.[5] This was to be the new focus for her political mission, now that inflation seemed to have been conquered and the trade unions confronted. Explicitly linking the sale of council houses with that of nationalized entities, she ebulliently assured her 1986 party conference: 'The great political reform of the last century was to enable more and more people to have a vote. Now the great Tory reform of this century is to enable more and more people to own property. Popular capitalism is nothing less than a crusade to enfranchise the many in the economic life of the nation.'[6]

The campaign for the vote certainly took longer to bring about. For, if hardly occurring by accident, the rolling back of the state during the eighties was nonetheless the result neither of lengthy planning on the part of government nor of a mass movement clamouring for it. As Nigel Lawson subsequently put it, although Keith Joseph, Geoffrey Howe and he saw privatization as an intrinsic part of a future Tory government, 'little detailed work had been done on the subject in opposition' because of 'Margaret's understandable fear of frightening the floating voter'.[7] With the controversial exception of the steel industry, during the 1950s and 1960s the nationalization of the major public utilities, as well as the railways, British airlines and other major industries, had ceased to be politically contentious, regardless of varying levels of dissatisfaction with the service they provided. The timidity with which the Conservatives approached the issue was evident when Edward Heath's Conservative administration contented itself with privatizing a chain of state-owned pubs in Carlisle. Indeed, in taking the troubled Rolls-Royce from receivership into state ownership, Heath actually extended the reach of nationalization, a process that continued after 1974 when the incoming Labour government took control of the aerospace and shipbuilding industries, along with the country's major car manufacturer, British Leyland. When the Conservatives returned to power in 1979, their manifesto promised only to privatize aerospace, shipbuilding and the National Freight Corporation. The rest would remain in the hands of the state.

Although the Conservatives moved beyond their manifesto pledges during their first term in office, the privatizations attempted offered no certain template for more radical and comprehensive action thereafter. An effort to sell British Airways had to be abandoned. When the state sold half of Cable & Wireless in October 1981 (since the 1940s it had been part of the Post Office), £224 million of shares were bought – more than had ever previously been paid for a company that was effectively new to the London Stock Exchange. Providing an accurate valuation proved especially difficult. The state offered its shares in the pharmaceutical company Amersham International at far too cheap a price in February 1982, thereby making only £71 million on a company whose real value the market soon found to be far higher. Then, nine months later, the government got the offer price wrong again – but in the opposite direction – when floating 51 per cent of its shares in the state oil corporation, Britoil. At £549 million this had set the (soon to be repeatedly broken) record for 'the largest privatization the world had ever known',[8] but it coincided with two disincentives for investors – a gloomy forecast for future oil prices, and the medium-term threat that if Labour won the next election it would honour its pledge to renationalize the company at its sale price (indeed, Tony Benn was insisting that the state should seize back assets that had been sold without paying the current owners any compensation whatsoever).[9] In consequence, the Britoil flotation was badly undersubscribed. This was potentially a serious setback. If investors were nervous about buying into assets as lucrative as North Sea oil, what hope was there that they would want to buy less obviously profitable sectors of the state-run economy? So much of a shot in the dark was privatization considered in 1982 that even some of those who would later regard it as accepted orthodoxy were initially sceptical. On the eve of the Britoil flotation, the leading article in *The Times* questioned the wisdom of 'transferring ownership from twenty million taxpayers to a few hundred thousand shareholders, simply to raise a relatively small amount of money'.[10]

The relatively small amount from this first phase of privatization, between 1981 and 1983, was £1.4 billion for the Treasury and £25 million for the City institutions that advised on and handled the sales.[11] By contrast, it was the huge scale of the success of BT's sale, which brought in £3.9 billion for the Treasury, that emboldened the government to be considerably more ambitious. The biggest sale of all was of British Gas, whose flotation in December 1986 swelled Treasury coffers by £5.4 billion. The promotional advertising campaign again targeted small investors, its catchphrase 'If you see Sid . . . Tell him!' embedding itself sufficiently into the popular consciousness for 'Sids' to become a term for the new generation of share-buyers. Then, in February 1987, British Airways was sold for £900 million. In contrast to the other major state holdings, the airline had been identified for privatization as early as 1979, only for its sale to be cancelled because of fears about its future profitability and worries that it would lose a legal case (eventually settled out of court) concerning the alleged market-rigging methods deployed to destroy its youthful British competitor Laker Airways. With the evaporation of these clouds from its horizon, BA's share offer was eleven times oversubscribed and more than 90 per cent of the airline's employees bought shares in the company – ignoring the advice of their union to boycott the sale. In May 1987, Rolls-Royce was sold for £1.3 billion, followed two months later by the British Airports Authority for nearly the same amount again. In December 1988, six hundred thousand people applied to buy shares in British Steel – previously a persistent recipient of taxpayer subsidy – when it was privatized, raising £2.5 billion. A year later the sale of the ten regional water authorities brought in over £5 billion.

Some privatizations could be justified on the grounds that they helped unleash competition where previously there had been none – and the sort of customer service that could be expected from complacency nurtured through monopoly. BT, for instance, gained competition, on a small scale, first from Mercury and subsequently from other communications providers. Yet it was not competition alone that brought improvements – not least because the extent of the competition created was often highly limited. In privatizing some of the major public utilities, the government was not so much destroying monopoly providers as shifting them from state to private sector ownership. In these cases, the state created new independent bodies – among them Oftel for the telecoms industry and the National Rivers Authority for the water providers – to prevent the abuse of monopoly and to limit price rises by imposing formulas linked to productivity gains and the retail price index. Whatever the limitations of this approach to consumer protection, it ensured better than some nationalizations had done that those responsible for setting the standards were autonomous from those running the services (or, in the case of Whitehall departments, were removed from conflicting political pressures). As far as the utilities were concerned, the clearest gain came in the access privatization gave them to fresh investment. By the mid-eighties, the utilities were facing considerable expenses in maintaining and enhancing their infrastructure. In particular, the water authorities were endeavouring to operate through crumbling Victorian drains and faced enormous costs if a European Community drinking water directive from 1980 was to be implemented. Given that the government was focused on trying to bring down the public sector borrowing requirement and to balance a budget threatened by the rising cost of unemployment benefits, there was little appetite in Whitehall for making this level of investment. Letting the utilities turn to the capital markets to raise the money they needed therefore relieved the taxpayer of a significant cost and freed the utilities from the corset of Treasury restraint. One of the clearest examples of this came with the vastly increased levels of investment in water and sewage treatment that followed the water authorities' sale to the private sector. Ironically, this was also the privatization that was most contentious, with opinion polls suggesting that more than three quarters of the electorate opposed the change (the share offer was oversubscribed all the same).[12]

For the Treasury, there were huge one-off windfalls to be scooped by selling the nationalized industries and utilities. However, even some Conservatives questioned the way in which the windfalls were treated as current account disposable income. This was the point the Earl of Stockton (the former prime minister, Harold Macmillan) attempted to make in a speech to the 'wets' of the Tory Reform Group in November 1985, though the subtlety of his argument was undermined by his arch reference to 'selling the family silver', a quip that was seized upon both by his Thatcherite detractors and by those on the left who tried to interpret his remarks to imply that he imagined the nationalized industries were assets on a par with an aristocratic family's Canalettos.[13] Regarding investment as essentially a task for the private sector rather than Whitehall, the use of privatization windfalls to balance the budget and to make possible tax cuts seemed perfectly acceptable to the current generation of government ministers. For them, privatization brought an additional political benefit because it ensured that the state no longer had to be directly involved in pay bargaining and other negotiations with the trade unions, whose members were no longer state employees. An entire branch of post-war corporatism withered and, with it, the influence of the unions upon government strategic and spending priorities.

That the nationalized sector's preparation for privatization involved extensive job-culling demonstrated both the extent of over-manning that had been tolerated by state-owned entities at the taxpayer's expense, and the ruthless prioritizing of commercial imperatives once shareholders assumed ultimate ownership (albeit moderated by the consumer protection directives of the regulators). One argument was that the state was disposing of assets that were capable of bringing in long-term net revenue. In the case of the already profitable BT, the state did retain a minority share until 1993. Generally though, it was only the discipline of being made ready for the market that brought profitability to the denationalizing sector. The financial accounts for the period prior to this process painted a depressing picture. By 1982, the nationalized industries had cost £40 billion in grants and capital write-offs, the taxpayer having contributed £94 billion in investment – for which the Treasury's return on investment averaged minus 1 per cent.[14] Despite this record, the principle of state ownership retained its adherents. The Labour Party promised to renationalize those companies that had been privatized – though 'nationalization' had been rebranded as 'social ownership' by the time Labour's 1987 election manifesto promised also to 'take a socially owned stake in high-tech industries'.[15] This desire to renationalize, however phrased, ultimately foundered on economic reality, since buying back controlling stakes in privatized companies that had subsequently become highly profitable would have all but crippled the Exchequer. The Bennite solution of the state simply seizing for itself the existing private shareholdings was not seriously entertained – such expropriation without compensation would have triggered a titanic battle through the courts. Other realities also imposed themselves, since in some cases the rationale for renationalization soon seemed to belong with the imperatives of a bygone age. With customers benefiting from prices being driven down by growing international airline competition and from the birth of 'budget airlines', where was the social utility in the state owning British Airways? Similar arguments applied to British Telecom. The necessity of keeping all telecommunications in the hands of a sub-department of the Post Office had ceased to resonate among customers choosing from a wide array of mobile phone and internet providers at the beginning of the twenty-first century.

Ultimately, the Conservatives' privatization programme during the eighties did more than disturb Westminster's settled consensus of the previous quarter-century and replace it with a new consensus for the succeeding quarter-century. It led the way for a global movement of economic change. What Thatcher's government pioneered, other Western or westernized nation states watched and then followed – and if imitation is the sincerest form of flattery, then there was little else achieved in Britain during the eighties that gained such widespread international admiration. It was a process that also created lucrative spin-offs for those British banks (especially Rothschild's), accountants and lawyers who had worked on domestic privatizations and were able to sell their experience as advisers on foreign flotations.

Within the UK, many of the so-called 'Sids' opted to cash in on their shares by selling them almost immediately (the proportion of individuals holding BT shares, for instance, falling from 39 per cent to 29 per cent by June 1985).[16] The majority, however, held on to their investment, and between 1979 and 1989 the number of the nation's shareholders rose from two million to twelve million, an increase in only a decade from 7 per cent to 29 per cent of the adult public. Nevertheless, it was scarcely evident that this shift indicated a new culture of 'popular capitalism' gripping three in ten of the electorate and encouraging them to take an active interest in investing in enterprise. That level of immersion in trading remained a minority pursuit. Rather, it was through investing in unit trusts or private pensions that most individuals were dependent on the movements of the stock market for income, and in this respect they were remote actors whose stakes were handled by large institutional investors. It was these entities that, by the decade's end, held four fifths of the UK's equities.[17]

Furthermore, the scale of the sell-offs, though considerable, needs to put in context. The UK's capital stock had been 44 per cent state-owned in

1979, and even after the world record-shattering privatizations it was still 30 per cent state-owned in 1989. The state had certainly been rolled back from running the commanding heights of industry, but when the service sector was included the UK was still very much a mixed economy. While at the time of Thatcher's fall from power the railways and mines continued to be state-run (John Major's government privatizing the former in 1993 and the latter in 1994), far more significant in terms of size, budget and workforce was the fact that the entire National Health Service and over 90 per cent of the education sector remained firmly in public ownership – a seemingly settled consensus that was to continue unchanged over the succeeding quarter-century regardless of which party was in power. In this respect, *laissez-faire*'s limits remained clearly demarcated.

A Tale of Two Cities

'La "City", un îlot de prospérité dans un ocean d'austérité,' summarized a 1982 headline in the newspaper *Nice-Matin*, highlighting these relative concepts for the benefit of its readers on the Côte d'Azur.[18] The starkness of the contrast between Britain's financial sector in the City of London and the country's struggling industrial base beyond was no less evident to commentators closer to home. Yet for all the apparent display of good times in the Square Mile, there was not one 'City' to be found there but two. The brash *prospérité* of the one masked the reality that the other was increasingly marginal to world finance and was facing a momentous decision. If it carried on without reform it could accept a perhaps comfortable but nevertheless long-term relative decline. Alternatively, it could risk the unleashing of international competitive forces. These might either restore London to its Victorian glory as the centre of global capitalism, or else sweep away the great stockbroking companies and merchant banks whose names were synonymous with British finance. Few at the time suggested a further possibility – that the City's future prosperity and the disappearance of these proud firms might not be mutually exclusive.

The City at risk was that of the securities markets, where investment decisions were made through the trade in shares. At its heart was the London Stock Exchange, with a history dating back to the deals concluded in seventeenth-century coffee shops and an ethos summed up in a motto that when translated meant 'my word is my bond'. The Stock Exchange not only provided the physical trading floor for the buying and selling of shares, it also determined who could participate in the activity. Its rules effectively excluded foreign membership. It was this criterion, rather than any innate native genius for finance, that explained why all of the more than two hundred broking and jobbing firms that were members of the Stock Exchange were

British-owned. This did not, of course, prevent foreign institutions from buying shares, but in 1983 their contribution still represented under 10 per cent of the Stock Exchange's turnover.[19] Primarily, it was a place for British institutions to invest in British companies. One consequence of this intro-spection was that, compared to Wall Street, the City's securities market was seriously under-capitalized. In 1982, the $500 million made in trading by the US investment bank Salomon Brothers exceeded the total profits made by all the member firms of the Stock Exchange put together.[20]

As one side of the City looked inwards, another gazed outwards. This second City was focused not upon the Stock Exchange but upon interna-tional bond and currency markets. By its nature it was less burdened by tradition, not least because so much of its success was of recent minting. In 1963, John F. Kennedy's administration had tried to discourage American firms from exporting capital by imposing an interest equalization tax on the purchase of foreign securities. The émigré financier Siegmund Warburg recognized this as London's opportunity and he pioneered a 'eurodollar' market to take advantage of the large post-war surplus of dollars still held by investors (in part, a legacy of the Marshall Plan). This new market allowed for bonds to be traded in a different currency from that used domestically by the government or company issuing them. In the eleven years during which Kennedy's tax operated, a bond market that might otherwise have been based in Wall Street instead took root in the City. It allowed London to compensate for the two factors – the loss of empire and the end of sterling as an international reserve currency – that seemed otherwise to be condemning it to second- or even third-rate status as a world financial centre. Once estab-lished in this new market, the City proved able to see off belated competition; London-issued eurobonds became the primary denomination in which international bonds were traded, and the London market became the world's largest source of capital. By the early eighties, the City's turnover from this eurobond market dwarfed that of the Stock Exchange and was a major factor in encouraging foreign banks to increase their presence in the Square Mile. Related activities developed in tandem. It helped that London was located in an ideal time zone which spanned the New York, Paris, Frankfurt, Rome, Hong Kong and Tokyo markets. That London became by far the world's most significant marketplace for currency dealing in such a relatively short period of time was nonetheless remarkable and, more importantly, it showed no signs of abating in the face of competition. Between 1979 and 1985, the City's average daily foreign exchange ('for-ex') turnover increased from $25 billion to $90 billion.[21]

The Conservative government had still not completed its first six months in office when it presented the City with an extraordinary opportunity. Without warning, on 23 October 1979, the Chancellor of the Exchequer,

Sir Geoffrey Howe, announced the scrapping of all remaining exchange controls. These restrictions on foreign investment had been imposed as an emergency measure at the outbreak of the Second World War and, in one form or another, had remained in place for the thirty-four years since Hitler's demise because of the Treasury's fear that if Britons were allowed to take significant sums of money out of the country they would surely do so, triggering sterling's collapse. What this meant for the British tourist and small investor is described above,* as is the role of North Sea oil revenue in negating the risk of a flight from sterling. For the City, the removal of the restrictions meant that decisions could finally be made to invest wherever in the world there was the hope of making the best return. This had profound consequences for the domestic economy. UK-based companies seeking City finance would henceforth find their competitiveness judged by global rather than purely national comparisons. Naturally, this removal of financial protectionism was condemned by the Labour front bench and by those who feared either that there would be a withdrawal of British investment from British companies, or else that continued investment would become conditional on the driving down of wage costs to the level of the cheapest competitor, which would have dire consequences for the British worker's standard of living. That, after all, was the logic of capital without borders seeking the best return. And the money appeared to follow the logic. While the City's net investment in UK securities increased from £1.9 billion in 1978 to £2.4 billion in 1982 (a rise of 26 per cent, which was negated by inflation), in overseas securities it soared from £459 million to £2.9 billion (up by 531 per cent). The foreign assets of British portfolio investors increased from £12.6 billion in 1979 to £215.2 billion in 1989.[22] Accordingly, these assets became one of the most important factors in the national wealth. By the end of 1988, the UK's net external assets represented one fifth of GDP, a higher proportion than for any other front-rank economy apart from Japan.[23]

Was this offshore prosperity garnered at the expense of those trying to run businesses and create jobs on the mainland? The extent to which a continuance of exchange controls during these years might have diverted investment from abroad to the UK cannot be easily assessed, partly because it is not a zero-sum equation. In so far as exchange controls would have damaged overseas opportunities, they might have curtailed the amount of new capital available to invest at home and thus proved wholly counterproductive. What was more, removing barriers fostered reciprocity. Much as British overseas investment soared during the eighties, so did investment by foreigners in Britain. Portfolio investments by foreign investors in the UK increased from

---

* See chapter three, p. 49.

£10.4 billion in 1979 to £110.7 billion in 1989.[24] By 1992, foreign companies (particularly American, but also European and Japanese) accounted for
one third of investment in British manufacturing and one fifth of its output.[25]
Nationalists and socialists were prominent among those who believed such
unrestrained free trade increasingly placed the country's economic base at
the mercy of decision-makers in distant lands. In 1988, widespread public
outrage greeted the news that the Swiss chocolatier Nestlé was to be permitted to buy Rowntree's of York. This astonished the trade secretary, Lord
Young, who mused that 'an outside observer would have formed the impression that chocolate was a strategic raw material'.[26] Then again, Kit Kat and
Quality Street were perhaps not the bow tie-wearing minister's principal
daily treat. When the government considered offers for Land Rover in
preparation for privatizing British Leyland, the possibility of the car and van
manufacturer passing into American ownership was met with vociferous
opposition from the Labour Party. Ultimately, it was Norman Tebbit who
offered the exasperated response to those who campaigned against foreign
ownership that 'surely it is better for the British people to buy Japanese cars
made by British workers than to buy German cars assembled by Turks?'[27] In
Tyne and Wear, where by 1989 over twenty Japanese companies had contributed a large share of the £825 million of foreign investment that was
finally rejuvenating the area, the chief executive of the region's local development company admitted that the national gulf in attitudes seemed greater
than the international one: 'Getting firms in from the South-East,' he said,
'had proved much, much harder than getting them from the Far East.'[28] This
foreign investment was not just a matter of attracting capital and securing
jobs. The ensuing change in the nature and ownership of British companies
opened them up to new approaches and different workplace cultures. As
with the money underwriting it, management was internationalized.

In helping to unshackle global capital markets, the abolition of exchange
controls further exposed the British economy to what at the time was often
pejoratively described as 'hot money' – the rapidly shifting flow of finance
between different markets and across national borders in search of the most
favourable return. A concomitant development was the birth of the London
International Financial Futures and Options Exchange (LIFFE) which was
established in the restored Royal Exchange building adjacent to the Bank of
England in September 1982. There, the dealing in options and futures
proved as vibrant as the multicoloured jackets worn by its famously uninhibited traders. Operating in a less restrictive manner, LIFFE was autonomous
from the Stock Exchange and the speed with which 'hot money' appeared
to be driving the integration of financial markets raised questions as to
whether the Stock Exchange's rules, regulations and traditional culture were
hopelessly out of touch with how global capital wished to do business.

In the early eighties, any person or institution wishing to buy or sell gilts (fixed-interest UK government securities) or shares in Stock Exchange-listed companies needed to do so through a stockbroker, who would act as their agent. The broker then approached a stock-jobber. Jobbers stood on the floor of the Stock Exchange close to their 'box' – a hexagonal pavilion providing telephone booths (mobile phones were not generally available until 1985 and not in wide circulation until 1987, and then primarily as car-phones), along with the latest market information – where they would offer brokers buying and selling prices for shares. Trading on their own account, jobbers made money through the 'spread' (the difference between the buying and selling price), while brokers made money by charging their clients commission for negotiating the deal. Under the Stock Exchange's rules, brokers could not be jobbers (or vice versa), nor could brokers compete with one another on the basic commission they charged their clients, the minimum rate for which was set by the Stock Exchange. Both regulations were widely presumed to be as old as the Stock Exchange itself, though in fact they dated from 1908 and 1910, respectively. With transactions in shares and gilts restricted to jobbers and with brokers accorded the privileges – including a stamp tax concession – conferred upon them by Stock Exchange membership, merchant banks and foreign competition were shut out from participating directly in the UK securities market.

In the City, there were about ten thousand stockbrokers and one thousand jobbers, the latter employed by just twelve remaining firms (down from 411 in 1920).[29] For the firms' partners, the benefit of retaining the existing structure was that it assured them a large cut of the profits (albeit with unlimited liability for the losses). The problem was that partnerships organized on this model had access to far less capital than was at the disposal of the vast US investment banks which dominated the securities market on Wall Street. If the rules were changed to let such investment banks trade on equal terms on the London Stock Exchange, they would speedily reduce the traditional partnerships to the status of impotent spectators. It was a reality that emphasized how the self-interest of the existing market-makers no longer served the wider interests of Britain's financial sector. It explained why, of the approximately $200 billion raised on global securities markets in the course of 1985, only $8 billion was raised through the London Stock Exchange.[30] Not only had London slipped behind its rivals on Wall Street and in Tokyo, it had even been surpassed by a second New York exchange, NASDAQ, which had been founded as recently as 1971.

Left to its own devices, the Stock Exchange seemed content to carry on regardless. Time, however, was running out for such insouciance. The warning shot had been fired as early as 1973 when the passage of the Fair Trade Act had widened the Office of Fair Trading's powers of investigation into restrictive practices to include the service sector. The subsequent Labour government duly initiated the OFT's inquiry into the Stock Exchange. Yet, even allowing for the complexity of the issues and the OFT's other distractions, the stay of execution had proved remarkably long and it was not until January 1984 that the case was scheduled to be heard in the Restrictive Practices Court. In the meantime, the status quo's defenders drew hope from the arrival in power of the Conservative Party. In 1980, the Stock Exchange's chairman, Sir Nicholas Goodison, tested the waters by calling upon John Nott, the trade secretary, and asking him to call off the OFT's inquiry. Nott refused. Frustratingly, it seemed the Conservatives meant what they said and actually intended to attack anti-competitive practices wherever they might be found. As Nott summed it up: 'I did not see how we could apply one law to capital and another to labour, given that we were about to launch an attack on the restrictive practices of the trade unions.'[31] Understandably, the defenders of the Square Mile's closed shop grew more alarmed as the date for the denouement in the Restrictive Practices Court drew nearer without any sign of ministerial intervention. The last prospect of salvation appeared lost when, in June 1983, Thatcher installed Cecil Parkinson as trade and industry secretary. The grammar school-educated son of a Lancashire railway worker, Parkinson had little instinctive sympathy, as he later put it, for an institution 'which had more in common with a gentleman's club than a central securities market', and which 'would become as redundant as the Manchester Stock Exchange unless we really opened it up to the big players'.[32]

Parkinson, however, wanted to see the reform properly embedded rather than imposed with the sudden force of a tornado. The latter was more likely if the Stock Exchange fought its corner in court and lost. Thus when Goodison went to see Parkinson he found him receptive to a compromise solution. The government would call off the OFT's inquiry on the condition the Stock Exchange fundamentally reformed itself. The central plank was the abolition of fixed minimum commission on share trading, but after that first step all the other major restrictions fell away. The division between brokers and jobbers would end. Stock Exchange membership rules would be relaxed. Where previously only individuals were entitled to membership, now corporate entities could belong. In particular, British merchant banks and foreign investment banks would be free to engage fully in the securities market – an invitation likely to ensure the annihilation of the traditional, and woefully under-capitalized, brokerages and jobbing firms.

Some of Goodison's colleagues were incredulous, believing that he had effectively surrendered without a fight and had agreed to implement everything that the OFT could have insisted on only if it had won outright. At the same time, Parkinson's critics thought he had been hoodwinked by a City cabal making hollow promises to reform itself. Having been happy to let the

Stock Exchange face the consequences in court, Thatcher was among those who needed persuading that her trade and industry secretary had not gone soft.[33] In fact, the Goodison–Parkinson deal made perfect sense. Its terms would change the City as much as if the OFT had won its case against the Stock Exchange, but instead of only having the mandatory nine months to implement the revolutionary change, three years had been secured to provide the necessary period of adjustment. That time would run out on 27 October 1986, a day whose gravity earned it the soubriquet 'Big Bang'.

In the three years between the Goodison–Parkinson accord and Big Bang, the City underwent the most fundamental transformation since the First World War disabled global capitalism and, with it, London's role at its heart. The loosening of the Stock Exchange's restrictions heralded the creation of integrated firms in which merchant banks were able to combine their traditional capital-raising, underwriting and asset management functions with the 'market-making' securities trading which had previously been the preserve of brokers and jobbers. For the British merchant banks, this meant having to learn how to become huge, multi-disciplinary and highly capitalized investment banks on the American model. Motivation was provided by the realization that American giants like Salomon Brothers, Morgan Stanley and Goldman Sachs already enjoyed the benefit of decades of experience of this sort of investment banking and could potentially run their *ingénue* British competitors out of the City if the latter failed quickly to master the art.

The process inspired mixed emotions for the partners of the old brokerages and jobbing firms. On the debit side, the venerable businesses to which they had, typically, devoted their adult careers, were about to cease trading as independent entities, swallowed up by the new generation of investment banks. Extinguished were such once familiar and evocative names as the brokers Kitcat & Aitken and the stock-jobbers Bisgood Bishop and Pinchin Denny. Mergers erased other finance houses, too, including the splendidly Dickensian-sounding bank of Charterhouse Japhet. On the credit side, premium prices were offered by purchasers seeking to outbid their rivals in the rush to acquire the pick of the partnerships. The best traders were paid salaries vastly exceeding their previous remuneration. The agreeable succour for the partners – of which there were roughly five hundred – was that they were able to depart as millionaires. In purchasing Akroyd & Smithers and Rowe & Pitman, the merchant bank Warburg's was generally assumed to be restructuring itself into an investment bank capable of taking on the big guns of Wall Street. And unlike in the United States, where between 1933 and 1999 the Glass-Steagall Act prevented 'high-street' commercial banks from being also investment banks, Britain's clearing banks were free to join the fray. Of the 'big four', only Lloyds resisted the temptation to develop a significant investment banking division. Barclays created its own investment arm, BZW, by buying the brokerage of De Zoete & Bevan and the jobbers Wedd Durlacher Mordaunt for a sum reportedly in the region of £150 million. This was a generous valuation considering that only three years earlier the combined capitalization of all the City's brokerages was estimated at £150–200 million.[34] Gripped by a mood that resembled panic buying, banks made almost $0.5 billion of such acquisitions in the lead-up to Big Bang.

Integration and adaptation on this scale were never likely to be a seamless process, especially given the unabashed self-confidence of some of the personalities involved. The clash of cultures was strongest where traditional City firms were bought by predatory American investment banks. When, in 1985, the American bond seller Michael Lewis was transferred from Salomon Brothers' New York office to its London outpost, he was astonished by the socially exclusive but professionally relaxed atmosphere permeating the British old guard. Emblematic of this fading establishment was one senior partner in a brokerage wearing 'an ill-fitted suit, scuffed black shoes and the sort of sagging thin black socks I came to recognize as a symbol of Britain's long economic decline', who assured Lewis over a two-hour lunch that working more than eight hours per day was counterproductive. The American was surprised that the boss of an operation employing several hundred people could look 'as if he had just awakened from a long nap', and amazed when the gent not only interrupted their discussion about the bond market to place a bet on a horse but proudly boasted that the two activities were closely aligned. Even more bewildering was the partner's effortless sense of superiority, particularly his insistence 'about how his small firm was going to cope with giants like Salomon invading the City of London'. The sober, hard-working, meritocratic values of the American investment banking community, in which the size of their salaries secured the loyalty of otherwise disparate individuals, could scarcely have differed more from the collegiate spirit that had helped keep generations of stockbrokers wedded to the same firm throughout their adult lives, and which helped ensure that an ever expanding salary was not the only test of corporate loyalty. The strong ex-public school predominance, cronyism, nepotism and admiration for those who could drink heavily at lunchtime and still conduct business sensibly in the afternoon were among the obvious manifestations of a native culture suddenly threatened by New World attitudes. What followed underlined the failings of the former way of doing business as well as its too easily concealed strengths: for all the conscious exclusiveness and periodic absurdity of the old City, its relative social homogeneity made it difficult for potential miscreants to break the 'my word is my bond' code without being shunned socially (and thus professionally as well). In that sense at least, the world that Big Bang destroyed possibly operated self-regulation more successfully than did the cut-throat culture that followed. Yet – unlike for so many whose socio-economic roles were undermined by the deregulations of the eighties – the change from the old world to the new was not without its consolations. Even the old-timer who had taken Michael Lewis to lunch recognized opportunity when he saw it. 'His firm, like so many small English financial firms,' noted Lewis with bemused incomprehension, 'was bought by an American bank for an enviable sum of money. He bailed out at just the right time, and floated the short distance to earth in a golden parachute.'[35]

The Predators' Ball

When dawn broke on 27 October 1986, the mergers and acquisitions necessary to create the integrated investment banks were all in place. In that sense, Big Bang was achieved before the moment assigned to it in the calendar. The Big Bang that was ignited on the allotted day was rather the computerized system that transformed how the securities markets operated thereafter. SEAQ (Stock Exchange Automated Quotations) provided an electronic share monitoring service based on the technology used in New York by the NASDAQ exchange, which was now linked up to London by satellite. Where previously brokers wanting to acquire or offload shares had to approach a jobber on the Stock Exchange floor, henceforth dealing could be done without leaving the office by market-makers watching price movements on a computer screen and making a telephone call (internet-based communications being not yet available). At the time, some bankers still believed that the new technology would operate alongside rather than instead of 'open outcry' (face-to-face) dealing on the Stock Exchange floor. Others suspected that it spelt the end of the old ways and that the floor would soon be gone for good. They were right; a tradition that, in one form or another, stretched back three hundred years was about to fall silent. As the market closed on the afternoon of Friday, 24 October, the contrasting moods of partying and pathos certainly suggested an era was coming to an end: a pantomime horse meandered erratically between the exchange's hexagonal kiosks while the remaining traders bade each other farewell, linked arms and struck up 'Auld Lang Syne'.

Only the Great Fire of London and the Blitz had brought swifter and more comprehensive change to the City's appearance than Big Bang. If the banks' market-makers were going to trade from behind batteries of computer screens and telephone extensions then each firm needed its own dealing floor. This required not only a large open-plan area but also sufficient space between walls and ceilings to run miles of telephone and computer cabling. Many of the old Victorian and Edwardian counting-houses could not be easily adapted, though Citibank did (admittedly unsuccessfully) attempt to create Europe's largest dealing room (28,000 square feet) within the ornate Victoriana of the disused Billingsgate fish market building; Richard Rogers provided the structural solution, though not how to combat the lingering aroma of haddock. In particular, the need for expansive dealing floors hastened the demolition of the City's collection of dismal post-war office blocks. Every bit as speculative as any activity that went on inside them, the 1950s and 1960s blocks proved to be mostly unfit for the technological requirements of the eighties. They were either demolished or transformed out of recognition. The new trading-floor requirements also helped drive forward the vast new developments at Broadgate and Canary Wharf, which got underway in 1985 and 1988, respectively.[*] Arriving on the new dealing floors could be an unnerving experience: 'It was the size of a football pitch with no natural daylight in my bit,' complained one veteran, who was used to sitting next to a window in a room sufficiently small that he could talk with ease to anyone in it. 'We had to use microphones to make ourselves heard. There were security guards on the front desk and machines, not tea ladies. It was like moving to another age.'[36]

That modern age formally began at 9 a.m., Monday, 27 October 1986, not with a big bang but a computer crash. In their curiosity to test out the new technology's capabilities, the traders overloaded the system, rendering it inoperable for an hour. It was not the best start, but the hiccup was soon forgotten in the ensuing months as the FTSE 100 index continued its seemingly irreversible rise. In 1986 alone, the turnover in equities rose by 72 per cent, to £181 billion. It surged again during the first three quarters of 1987, taking the total to £283 billion. Such was the competition that more than forty firms traded in a market that prior to Big Bang had been dominated by just five of the twelve jobbing firms. Such expansion made the fears of those long resistant to change appear fanciful. Despite the halving of the commission rate on share deals because of the abolition of the fixed minimum, the loss of income was more than compensated for by the increase in turnover, and revenue from state privatizations was proving particularly lucrative. The same was true for institutions advising on and organizing another City money-spinner, 'merger mania'.

By the twentieth century's end, aggressive corporate takeovers were routinely identified as among the central and distinguishing components of the 'Anglo-Saxon model'. Such tussles for control had become frequent in the seventies, but it was the feverish deal-making of the eighties that made them a principal characteristic of the British way of doing business. But the historic

[*] See pp. 273 and 274.

roots of this development were extraordinarily shallow – the first hostile takeover had only taken place in 1958, when stealthy share purchases by Warburg's secured Tube Investments' acquisition of British Aluminium. At the time, Warburg's tactics were widely condemned as ungentlemanly within the Square Mile. By the mid-eighties, such behaviour was not only deemed acceptable but defended as one of the beneficial roles that City institutions performed. The accelerating trend could be monitored by the value of UK companies involved in takeover bids of all kinds, which rose from £1.1 billion in 1981, to £2.3 billion in 1983, £15.4 billion in 1986 and £27.3 billion in 1989.[37] Prior to Big Bang, the Burton Group's £579 million hostile takeover of Debenhams in 1985 had set a record price tag. Thereafter, stakes were raised dramatically with, in particular, the food, drink and tobacco industries an open prairie enticing predatory salivations. Fear prompted an eat-or-be-eaten attitude which posited attack as the best form of defence. The drinks firm Allied Lyons saw off a £1.7 billion takeover attempt by the Australian conglomerate Elders IXL. Argyll Group bid for Distillers, only for Distillers to be bought – in questionable circumstances, as it later emerged – by Guinness. Imperial Group bid for United Biscuits, only for United Biscuits to launch a counter-bid for Imperial Group. This last battle in particular was fought in an especially uninhibited fashion – with the rival suitors taking out full-page newspaper advertisements setting out their claims, while investors were invited to ring premium-rate telephone numbers where they could hear minute-by-minute updates from City analysts on the latest odds. The contest ended with neither Imperial nor United Biscuits taking control of the other because Imperial, having exposed its flank, was instead taken over by Hanson Trust. Among Imperial's assets was the brewing firm Courage, which Hanson then sold to Elders IXL, whose original bid for Allied Lyons had kick-started the season of acquisitions.

Hanson was the most easily identifiable of the period's 'corporate raiders'. The term was used pejoratively by detractors not only on the political left but among industrialists who despaired at the manner in which business empires carefully built up over generations could suddenly be bought, decapitated and sold on by financiers who had never worked in the business sectors they intruded into nor seemed interested in learning from the experience of the management teams they could not wait to sack. The sight of James Hanson turning up at his new office and personally, dismissively, removing from its walls the historic portraits of the Courage family, who had created the brewing firm he had fleetingly bought as a means to securing a greater prize, symbolized a rapacious and unsentimental approach.[38] It suggested that corporate raiders were indifferent to custodianship and were merely asset-strippers, pocketing for themselves and their shareholders whatever sums could be extracted from companies they were content to reduce to a carcass or to sell on, without regard for the workforce. In providing the means through which the raiders' ambitions could be realized, the City stood accused of aiding and abetting a short-term vision which enriched the financial sector at the cost of wrecking the longer-term strategic objectives of British industry. 'If you create a company from scratch,' complained one of the decade's most publicly recognizable entrepreneurs, the boss of Virgin Group, Richard Branson, 'you get very little credit for it in the City. Whereas if you buy and sell companies and lay off people, the City thinks that is exciting.'[39] That James Hanson and his business partner, Gordon White, contributed large sums to the Conservative Party and were unabashed admirers of the prime minister – who responded by bestowing peerages upon them both – suggested that for all Thatcherism's exaltation of the entrepreneur, its greatest admiration was for the 'City slickers'.

Such was the caricature. Yet if Lord Hanson was a wheeler-dealer, he was also *The Times*'s 'Capitalist of the Year' for 1986 and acclaimed as the country's most impressive industrialist four years running, between 1988 and 1992, by company directors polled by MORI. It was hardly surprising that Margaret Thatcher and he admired one another. A grammar school-educated Yorkshireman, dapper, 6 ft 4 in, with a passable resemblance to a 1940s matinee idol, Hanson would have inherited the family haulage business if it had not been nationalized by the Attlee government. Instead, he teamed up with White, who had been a wartime Special Operations Executive agent behind enemy lines in the Far East, for a succession of buccaneering raids into hostile territory. Prior to his marriage this was supplemented by acquiring film-star girlfriends (Hanson was engaged to Audrey Hepburn, though he failed to close the deal), as well as bidding for more diverse if seemingly lower-yielding corporate entities whose true potential Hanson and White saw a means of unlocking. Profits were found by identifying where costs could be cut, often by divesting companies of their marginal operations and forcing them to concentrate on the core activities that had propelled them to prominence in the first place. The impressive returns for shareholders that this fat-trimming approach brought ensured money was readily forthcoming to fund ever larger acquisitions. Not content with paying £2.5 billion for Imperial in 1986, two years later Hanson stumped up £3.5 billion for Consolidated Gold Fields. By then, the company had become Hanson plc, a British success story on both sides of the Atlantic whose corporate logo drew together the Union Jack and the Stars and Stripes alongside the *nearly* self-effacing boast, 'a company from over here that's doing rather well over there'.

Hanson plc's commitment to shareholder value went so far as ensuring that it was structured in a way that minimized the taxes it paid over here and over there. Yet for all this, the company was far from being the best example for the critics of corporate raiding to attack. Neither Hanson nor White demonstrated – or even pretended to demonstrate – the long-term strategic direction and feel for product development that traditional captains of industry professed to possess, but their ability to take flabby companies and make them lean was not necessarily a bad place to start. The rationale of the takeover, after all, was to secure the most efficient allocation of capital. By returning Imperial Group's focus to its core tobacco business, Hanson increased the company's operating profits from £74 million in 1987 to £328 million in 1994.[40] By the time of Lord Hanson's death in 2004, Imperial Tobacco was worth £9.43 billion.[41] If this was short-termism, then there was much to be said for it. What took place in the meantime was also instructive. Enough of a realist to practise what he preached, Lord Hanson bowed to the power of his own logic by concluding that the conglomerate White and he had created was ultimately becoming too big for its own good. In 1997, he chose to break it up into its component parts before a hostile raider did it for him. Having acquired everything from Eveready batteries to precision golf clubs, Hanson plc was purposefully reduced to its bare essentials as a specialist in building materials. In 2007, its reward was to be bought by a German cement maker. Thus it shared the fate that the 'Anglo-Saxon model' had determined for so many other British firms – becoming a company that continued to do well over here by being owned over there.

Despite the recent history of the Stock Exchange's rearguard fight to protect its members from corporate and foreign competition, after Big Bang the City acted without nostalgia or patriotism when determining who owned which companies. The removal of the ancestral oil paintings only illustrated the truth that if the family that founded Courage had wanted to keep control of their brewing business, then they should never have merged with rivals and sold equity. Being bought by a publicly listed conglomerate like Imperial, in which shares could be traded, meant they could, in turn, be bought by Hanson and sold on to the Australian conglomerate Elders (which, in turn, sold Courage back to the British brewer Scottish & Newcastle). Companies that did not wish to be treated like courtesans had the option of not putting themselves on the market. Having listed his airline and record business on the Stock Exchange in 1986, only to see its share price slide, Richard Branson made his Virgin Group private again two years later by buying out the shareholders for £90 million – a deal from which he did particularly well. The downside of remaining, or becoming, privately owned was the higher cost of bank lending. The banking sector, nevertheless, was becoming increasingly indiscriminate in its lending criteria in order to compete with the sums that could be raised through share issues on the stock market. Vastly expanded bank lending also financed a succession of highly leveraged buy-outs of listed companies or their subsidiaries, often by their own management. The highest leveraged buy-outs took place in the United States where, in November 1988, the leading private equity firm of Kohlberg Kravis Roberts astonished even those jaded by large numbers with its record $31.1 billion buy-out of the tobacco and biscuit concern RJR Nabisco. The following year, the City of London was gripped by a similar contest when the corporate raider Sir James Goldsmith used a £13.4 billion war chest of borrowed money in an assault on BAT Industries. Backed by Jacob Rothschild and supplemented by a high-yield ('junk bond') issue by the controversial Wall Street bank of Drexel Burnham Lambert, Goldsmith's strategy – like that of Hanson with Imperial – was to strip BAT of its peripheral and extraordinarily diverse holdings and return it to its core cigarette business, where the true asset base of the company resided. The buy-out, however, would be funded wholly by debt. It fell through in 1990, leaving Goldsmith brooding upon the minor consolation that although BAT had escaped his grasp it proceeded to implement his strategy.

The sums that banks were making available were now without precedent. While British merchant banks dreamt of taking on Wall Street at its own investment banking game, the clearing banks also grew more ambitious, increasing their range of services and the scale of their lending. The smallest of the 'big four' was the Midland Bank, which less than forty years earlier had been the largest bank in the world. Its campaign to regain its former glory began in 1981 with the purchase of a major Californian bank. Unfortunately, the Crocker National Bank was a disastrous choice which proceeded to lose Midland's shareholders $1 billion. The sniff of blood brought the sharks circling: both Lord Hanson and the *Daily Mirror*'s owner, Robert Maxwell, started buying shares in the bank. The formal approach that signalled normal attitudes to banking were really in suspension was made in September 1987, when Charles and Maurice Saatchi asked for a meeting with the Midland. The ad men wanted to buy the bank. Midland acted promptly to quash talk of a deal which, it announced, lacked 'commercial or strategic logic';[42] but the fact that the world's largest advertising firm imagined it had a realistic chance of taking over a bank with $77 billion of assets, despite a total lack of banking experience, ought to have indicated that irrational exuberance was replacing the sensible assessment of risk and suitability. Unabashed by the rebuff, Saatchi & Saatchi looked into buying a merchant bank instead and decided to make a pitch for Hill Samuel. The signs were there for those looking out for them.

Sir James Goldsmith anticipated the coming crash, but few other investors benefited from his sense of foreboding. Far from concluding the prolonged bull market could be hurtling towards the precipice, the mood in the City was buoyant in the autumn of 1987, with especially high expectations for the government's latest sale of state assets – the £7.2 billion share offer in BP, which was due in October. The news that prime (short-term) interest rates were to rise by 1 per cent in the United States caused a tremor on Wall Street, but there was little activity going on in the City on the morning of Friday, 16 October. The Stock Exchange was shut and computer screens remained either blank or blinking ineffectually at almost entirely deserted dealing rooms because so few employees had made it to their desks – an unexpected hurricane having ravaged southern England during the night, disrupting commuter lines and destroying trees, roofs and much else besides. For metaphorical purposes, the destructive act of God was timed almost to perfection. The house of Mammon began trembling on the morning of Monday, 19 October – soon to be christened 'Black Monday' – as panic selling engulfed securities trading, wiping a record 249.6 points off the FTSE 100 index. Within forty-eight hours, almost 25 per cent had been wiped off the value of the stock market. On Wall Street, the Dow Jones took a comparable hit. The next day, shares began to fall on the Far Eastern stock exchanges as it became clear that global capitalism was succumbing to a convulsion. In London, the BP offer went ahead with none of the expected instant gains for the new generation of 'Sids'. Although the plunges of the first forty-eight hours were not repeated, the FTSE's slide, occasionally interrupted by ephemeral rallies, continued until mid-November, by which time it was clear that the City had taken a pasting.

Instant explanations were offered, not least by those seemingly not gifted with foresight. One theory latched on to the new computer technology because of the ease with which risk-highlighting software enabled traders to dump stock. This could never have been more than a minor contributory factor. After all, yelling 'Sell!' into a telephone receiver was not so very different from shouting it straight into someone's face, and as the crash of 1929 had demonstrated, cutting-edge gadgetry was not needed to offload investments in minutes. Human nature provided a better explanation of why a crash was long due. The FTSE index had been climbing year after year since 1974. Thus, only those with a City career dating back more than thirteen years had personal experience of how quickly what seemed like a one-way bet could prove to be an imprudent purchase at the top of the market. As one bond trader summed it up: 'You tend to get optimists working in the City and they can't cope in a crash because it's outside their normal psychological boundaries.'[43] The exact timing of the bubble's bursting might not have been predictable, but it strained credulity to imagine that some sort of significant correction to ever higher valuations could not be on the way. Yet if the prolonged good times numbed sensitivity to risk, then it was also true that the sharpness of the 1987 crash provoked equally exaggerated claims from the City's critics that its fundamental failings had been irrevocably exposed. On a longer view, the remarkable feature of the crash was less its severity than its shortness. Once the shock had passed, the sifting through the wreckage for newly undervalued stock began. Despite the turmoil of the previous autumn, equities turnover in 1988 was still twice as high as it had been before Big Bang, only two years previously. As the heatwaves of 1989's summer enveloped the country, recovery in the Square Mile was well under way. For all the City's prominent casualties, there were still more than 620,000 employed in financial services. And by then it was communism, not capitalism that was facing its endgame.

Relief and renewed optimism were understandable given that the widely assumed expectation – *pace* 1929 – that a stock market crash would be followed by a severe economic recession failed to materialize. Internationally, the lead was taken by Reagan's new appointment as chairman of the Federal Reserve, Alan Greenspan, who immediately indicated his readiness to pump liquidity into the US economy. Nigel Lawson announced the same intention. Judging the risk of inflation now secondary to that of a recession, he eased interest rates (albeit down to 8.38 per cent base rate in December 1987, which was high by later standards and represented a smaller cut than the opposition parties demanded at the time). Stimulating growth was still Lawson's objective the following spring, when his budget unleashed a slew of tax-slashing measures, including the cutting of higher rate income tax from 60 to 40 per cent and the basic rate to 25 per cent. As the Chancellor later put it: 'The actuality and *expectation* of cuts in tax rates were part of an important cultural change, which fuelled business confidence and economic growth' (italics added).[44] Delivering these promises was made easier by the Treasury's Gladstonian achievement at this time: a balanced budget and the paying back, rather than further accretion, of public sector debt. Thus the Lawson stimulus bore scant comparison to the debt-accumulating tax-slashing of 'Reaganomics', or the spending-driven budget deficits later run up by Gordon Brown.

One hangover that the boom years did bequeath the City was the revelation that the word of some of its most seemingly successful practitioners was clearly not their bond. The Financial Services Act 1986 retained the Bank of England's oversight of the banks while creating a new broking regulator, the Securities and Futures Authority (SFA). A step had thus been taken away from the gentleman's code of self-regulation which had left the Stock Exchange to police its own members, but had not given the SFA the powers enjoyed by the Securities and Exchange Commission (SEC) in the United States. In June 1987, it fell to the former joint head of securities at Morgan Grenfell to earn the dubious distinction of becoming the first person to be convicted of insider-dealing (he received a suspended one-year sentence and a £25,000 fine for using confidential information to net a £15,000 profit). Whether his and subsequent convictions revealed declining moral standards compared to the ethics of the 'old City' was a moot point. After all, prior to the Companies Act 1980, insider-dealing had not even been a criminal offence. Meanwhile, petitioning by Lloyd's of London successfully excluded it from the provisions of the Financial Services Act altogether. Evidence of malpractice in the insurance market was used both by those arguing for outside regulation and by those who maintained that the revelations showed that the existing procedures were capable of unmasking wrongdoing. In lobbying Parliament, it doubtless helped that one in eight Conservative MPs was a Lloyd's name,* many of whom were suspicious of outside interference. During the early nineties, losses incurred by Lloyd's syndicates exposed to natural disaster and asbestos claims, and legal action taken by financially ruined names, claiming mis-selling, suggested that a bit more outside interference would have been preferable.

Other scandals demonstrated that incompetence, naivety and a willingness to take individuals at their own estimation were capable of trumping due diligence whatever investigative structures were in place. The investment broker Peter Clowes, of Barlow Clowes, promised his fourteen thousand investors (many of them pensioners entrusting him with their life-savings) a guaranteed return from government-backed gilts, while actually spending their money on risky investments and personal embezzlement. His wheeze was undone by the 1987 crash, and when the Department of Trade and Industry belatedly looked into his dealings they discovered a £110 million shortfall. This sort of fraud seemed almost amateurish compared with that of Robert Maxwell, who left a £2 billion black hole in his transatlantic publishing and newspaper empire, representing 'the biggest plunder of public and private assets in Britain's history'.[45] In November 1988, with £3 million per day due in interest charges on the back of vast new borrowings, Maxwell had siphoned money from his public companies into his private companies, in the process robbing £400 million from the pension fund of his employees at the *Daily Mirror*. The deceit was only exposed after the media tycoon fatally tumbled over the side of his yacht in 1991. Auditing had not revealed his deceptions, nor had there been sufficient investigation of the suspicious complexity of his corporate structure or the fact that he alone retained the power to sign sizeable cheques. Particularly depressing was the willingness of the City to take on trust the word of someone who had been deemed 'unfit' to run a public company by the Department of Trade in 1971, and was

---

* A capital-committing, passive investor for whom membership of a Lloyd's syndicate provided a share of its profits and an effective tax shelter, alongside the risk of unlimited liability for losses.

popularly known, thanks to *Private Eye*'s double-entendre referring to his girth and his origins, as 'the bouncing Czech'. Determined and supposedly ruthless capitalists had allowed themselves to be hoodwinked by a man who was, in the posthumous verdict of *The Times*, 'a monstrously improbable socialist'.[46] The City's reputation was also besmirched by illegal share-support measures. The takeover by the recruitment agency Blue Arrow of an American competitor, Manpower, in 1987 was supported by an £837 million rights issue. Only after the deal's completion did it emerge that its success had been secured on the back of the misleading impression about the take-up of the subscription created by the County NatWest investment bank. A trial in 1992 secured convictions which the Court of Appeal later overturned. Similar share-support allegations were made following Guinness's £2.7 billion takeover of Distillers. The company's chief executive, Ernest Saunders, was one of the 'Guinness Four' arrested in 1987 and sent to jail three years later.[*]

The scandal damaged the reputation of Guinness's advisers, Morgan Grenfell, whose group chief executive resigned in January 1987 after pressure from the Bank of England. Alongside Warburg's, Morgan Grenfell was supposed to be the British merchant bank with the brightest prospect of becoming a world-ranking investment bank. During 1986, it advised on more mergers and acquisitions (111 of them, worth £15 billion) than any of its competitors and its flotation on the Stock Exchange was five times oversubscribed.[47] Thereafter, the losses run up by its securities trading division demonstrated how quickly the failings of its market-making arm could harm its traditional banking arm. In December 1988, the first time the company's 770 securities dealers learned that they were all going to be made redundant was when they read about it in the *Daily Telegraph*. As they arrived at their desks, they were brought to attention by the voice of the chief executive, Sir John Craven, abruptly crackling over the dealing-room loudspeaker: 'I'm sorry. You will have read in your newspapers that we're going out of the securities business . . . I want to thank you for everything you've done for us . . . We're bleeding at a rate of a million pounds a week. Please stop dealing now.'[48] Having been the great hope of British merchant banking, Morgan Grenfell was instead sold to Deutsche Bank the following year, taking whatever comfort it could from the £950 million price tag. Similar troubles beset County NatWest, the investment arm of NatWest. Among its Big Bang acquisitions had been the stockbrokers Fielding, Newson-Smith, one of whose senior partners, Dundas Hamilton, could not help but comment unfavourably on

---

[*] Saunders was released after ten months of his five-year sentence on the pretext of pre-senile dementia, from which he subsequently made a miraculous recovery; in 2000 the European Court of Human Rights pronounced that the manner of the Guinness Four's trial had breached their human rights.

the cavalier management style of his successors: 'A banker not a securities man ran it. It was a disaster,' he grumbled. 'Our firm was 130 years old and we had never, in my knowledge, had a loss in any year, not even the terrible slump year. We never had a redundancy. Every year we paid a bonus to our staff and made profits for our partnership but the new owners managed to lose money and staff after two years. It was a real tragedy.' Yet, like so many other partners, he had personally benefited from the change of ownership: 'The takeover suited me, personally, marvellously well. I was then 66. I should have retired from my firm at 65, which would have been in 1985, but they kindly kept me on for a year longer than I should have done in order that I should take my share of the sale proceeds without tax problems.'[49]

The investment divisions of the clearing banks NatWest and Barclays enjoyed a scale and capitalization that, with persistence and sound judgement, would have allowed them to take on the Wall Street giants. However, having made an uncertain start, the management of Barclays listened to more-immediate shareholder anxieties and sold BZW to CSFB (Credit Suisse-First Boston) in 1997, while at the same time NatWest began divesting itself of County NatWest to Bankers Trust, which was bought in turn by Deutsche Bank.* By then, the once august British merchant banks were also falling prey to foreign acquisition at a bewildering pace. During 1995, Warburg's was sold to Swiss Bank Corporation (SBC), Kleinwort Benson was bought by Dresdner Bank, Smith New Court was bought by the US investment bank Merrill Lynch, and, most sensationally of all, Baring's, having been brought down by its Singapore-based 'rogue trader' Nick Leeson, was sold to the Dutch bank ING for the derisive sum of £1. The other ex-merchant banks were snapped up in 2000 when Schroder's and Fleming's were sold, respectively, to the American banks Citigroup and Chase Manhattan. By that time, every one of the leading British merchant banks that had taken advantage of Big Bang in order to become investment banks was in foreign hands.

Did this foreign takeover of the City mean Big Bang's legacy was disastrous? Without the breaking of the old Stock Exchange restrictions and exclusions, the merchant banks could not so easily have embarked upon the path that led to their sale. Making a virtue out of necessity, one argument ran that, far from being a sign of their failure, their acquisition showed instead how much the Americans, Swiss and Germans were prepared to invest in the long-term future of the City. The material manifestation of this overseas

---

* These retreats did not end the participation of either clearing bank in investment banking. In 1997, Barclays Capital was established, and although NatWest's investment banking failures proved a major factor in its sale to the Royal Bank of Scotland in 2000, the RBS Group included its global banking and markets division.

faith was of such a scale that by the time of the financial downturn in 2007 it was becoming commonplace to suggest that the UK's banking sector had become *too* strong and was distorting the national economy. Even in 1989, before most of the famous names had changed hands, the City was home to 521 foreign banks, more than double the number hosted by any rival financial centre. The analogy of the Wimbledon tennis championships was widely trumpeted, whereby London thrived not because of the quality of its home-grown players but because it attracted the world's greatest talent, whose participation added lustre and considerably greater receipts. Indeed, so the argument went, far from betraying its heritage, the City's internationalization was in keeping with its most invigorating traditions. After all, such venerable British institutions as the banks of Warburg, Schroder, Kleinwort and Rothschild had been founded by immigrants. Far from wrecking the country's financial services sector, Big Bang had prevented it from sinking into a provincial backwater. In turn, global credentials bolstered the national interest. Such was London's continuing strength that even the UK's decision not to ditch sterling for the euro in 1999 did not damage the City, which proceeded to carry out more euro-denominated transactions than any of its rivals in the eurozone.

Yet for all its superficial appeal, the Wimbledon analogy was misleading. The international tennis championships were at least owned by the All England Club, whereas the investment institutions that came to dominate the City retained their headquarters in New York, Geneva and Frankfurt. Similarly, the reference to the émigré origins of the likes of Warburg, Schroder, Kleinwort and Rothschild missed the more substantive point that they were British citizens and their banks were British because, regardless of where and with whom they did business, they were headquartered in London. It was difficult to imagine that Deutsche Bank or Dresdner Bank would shift their headquarters from German soil, or even that they were structured in a way that would permit them to do so. In that sense, the keys to the City had been surrendered to those whose commitment to it was practical and self-interested, and which the advent of a less business-friendly environment in the UK might conceivably test to destruction.[50] This was, according to one's view, either a dangerous hostage to fortune or a welcome constraint on the country's political decision-makers, schooling them to understand that the City could not be taken for granted but rather needed to be appeased, otherwise its institutions and personnel would prove as mobile as the money that passed through it.

From a historical perspective, the admiring talk of 'Wimbledonization' represented wisdom after the event. The foreign takeovers may have been one of Big Bang's consequences, but they were far from having been the deregulation's intention. Alex Fletcher, who as minister for corporate and consumer affairs between 1983 and 1985 was charged with seeing through Big Bang, stated as his opinion in 1983: 'If we want to maintain London as a prominent market, I think it is very important that the Stock Exchange and the majority of the institutions here should remain very firmly in British hands.'[51] In March 1984, the Governor of the Bank of England, Robin Leigh-Pemberton, was clear that 'we would not contemplate with equanimity a Stock Exchange in which British-owned member firms played a subordinate role'.[52] By the twenty-first century there appeared to be no principled objection even to the Stock Exchange itself passing into foreign hands, as LIFFE did in 2002.

The original hope was that by becoming highly capitalized, integrated investment organizations, British merchant banks would take on the foreign competition, rather than be taken over by it. The reality was that too many of them when presented with the opportunity to think big went for broke. As one American financier put it: 'If you've never gone to the casino, you don't know how to manage risk.'[53] Part of the problem was that the integrated operations placed new managerial demands upon people who were used to running firms a quarter of the size, or less. Since they had gained their experience in a culture that separated broking from jobbing, and both from merchant banking, the City had a dearth of native Britons able to span these tasks, to manage much larger departments and to assess risk, all at the same time. Nick Durlacher was one of the experienced City businessmen who questioned the new framework, with its instant high rewards and focus on youth, followed by burn-out and pay-out. 'There was an innate discipline in the old hierarchical structure,' Durlacher suggested, 'an awful lot of businesses were partnerships where the senior people had their own money on the line – that gave a certain urgency to management supervision.'[54]

Instead, long-term loyalty to one firm – let alone personal liability – became wholly exceptional. In fairness, it was difficult to be loyal to a single firm when, after 1986, they were merging, acquiring and disappearing with a regularity comparable to that which their own mergers and acquisitions departments facilitated across the wider economy. The breaching of the introverted, rather self-satisfied, gentleman's club brought clear benefits in terms of drawing on a wider pool of talent, though the vastly greater remuneration necessary to stop its defection introduced potential risks that Kit McMahon, the Bank of England's Deputy Governor, had foreseen in September 1985 when he warned that:

> If key staff – and even on occasion whole teams – can be offered inducements
> to move suddenly from one institution to another, it becomes very difficult for
> any bank to rely on the commitment individuals will give to implementing its

plans and adds a further dimension of risk to any bank which is building its strategy largely around a few individuals' skills.[55]

Or, as a chronicler of 'the death of gentlemanly capitalism', Philip Augar, put it in a defence of the pre–Big Bang City: 'It was very hard to cheat on someone you saw every day.'[56]

Big Bang allowed the traditional merchant banks to go into securities trading. Notwithstanding periods of success, those that did so found it more difficult than the optimistic talk of 1986 had encouraged them to assume. The result was that they were subsumed into foreign-owned investment banks. But being permitted to enter a market is not the same as being forced to do so. Instructively, the firms that opted to stick to their historic niches continued to perform well. Cazenove was the only major brokerage to resist the blandishments of the banks, preferring to upscale its operations through borrowing from insurance companies. Retaining its socially distinguished clientele, it prospered and only dissolved its family-led partnership in 2001, being entirely taken over by JP Morgan in 2009. With John Nott as its chairman, Lazard's showed a viable way forward for merchant banking, and it remained in British ownership until 2000. Rothschild's was the one other major merchant bank that opted to focus on its strengths as an adviser on restructuring and mergers and acquisitions, rather than opt for the full multi-disciplinary investment banking approach. A quarter of a century after Big Bang, it alone of the City's historic merchant banks remained family-owned and free from foreign acquisition.

Could the pre–Big Bang regulatory structure have delivered better results if it had been left in place after 1986? That the performance as market-makers of so many of the much-vaunted banks fell far short of expectations was not, of itself, an argument for forbidding them from entering that market, or for encouraging others to buy them in the expectation that they would do a better job. If the City had continued to restrict its securities trading operations to the partner-structured, under-capitalized, smallish-scale firms with which it had entered the eighties, it is hard to see how London could have avoided becoming a near-irrelevance in international securities investment over the ensuing quarter-century. Moreover, marginalization as the price for retaining the old ways would hardly have been in the domestic economy's wider interests. For, as the Stock Exchange's chairman, Sir Nicholas Goodison, put it on the eve of Big Bang, its aim was 'to create in London one of the three major capital markets in the world'. Far from throwing over a sound national institution, the attracting in of foreign banks would create the great capital market that would finally give British firms 'a sound economic base'.[57] The liberalization certainly created the capital market.

Greed Is Good

In 1979, a director at Morgan Grenfell might have expected a basic income in the region of £40,000 per annum. Salaries, supplemented by bonuses, increased rapidly thereafter, but even the leading foreign exchange dealers did not take home more than £50,000 by 1982. By then, the Governor of the Bank of England earned a salary of £85,000 and directors at Rothschild's bank received around £100,000.[58] As late as 1983, Jacob Rothschild maintained that the City's highest earner was on £126,000 per annum.[59] Actually he was mistaken in this belief,* though it was revealing that someone of his considerable experience and social connections should be under such an impression.

Within three years, sums on this scale were unexceptional. As Big Bang approached, unprecedented inducements were offered by investment banks as they fought each other to secure the talents of the most highly regarded market-makers. A new lingo was coined during this bidding war. A 'golden hello' was a sizeable offer to entice those who were in demand. In an attempt to lock them in, 'golden handcuffs' guaranteed longer-term rewards (typically over five or six years) on condition that the wearer did not defect to a rival in the meantime. With so many partners selling out, particularly valued was the group just below the icing who became known as the 'marzipan set'. The money that the US investment banks offered was such that British institutions either had to raise the stakes or accept that they would be staffed by people deemed to be in the second or third XI. It was a sellers' market, in which the journalist Nicholas Coleridge estimated that by March 1986 there might be a couple of thousand investment bankers, stockbrokers and commodity brokers earning £100,000 per annum or more. 'Most are aged between 26 and 34,' he noted, 'and two years ago they were being paid £25,000, in some cases even less.'[60] That year, the directors at Morgan Grenfell made £225,000 each.[61]

These salaries, and the symbols of excess that went with them, were naturally contentious at a time when unemployment was still rising (it finally peaked during the summer of 1986) and leaving one in ten of the workforce unable to earn a living. However, those who assumed such striking wealth inequality was the conscious design – as distinct from the by-product – of Thatcherism might have been surprised by the reaction of the woman herself. Despite the company she kept, the prime minister had never entirely rid herself of her small-business, Methodist roots and the influence of a domineering father who regarded the Stock Exchange contemptuously as a form of gambling. In this, her *Poujadiste*† instincts stood in unreconciled

---

* In 1982, Ian Posgate, a Lloyd's underwriter, made over £320,000.

† A pro-small business, anti-elite, conservative movement that flourished in France in the 1950s.

conflict with her intellectual commitment to removing restrictions to free trade and facilitating entry to markets at whatever cost to equality of income. 'Top salaries in the City fair make one gasp, they are so large,' she exhaled in 1985, adding the following year: 'On salaries in the City, I am the first to say this does cause me great concern. I understand the resentment.'[62] But unless she was prepared to countenance higher-rate tax at a level that would act as an incomes cap, all she could offer were ineffectual words of restraint. Far harsher language was hurled at her Chancellor when, in the course of his 1988 budget speech, he announced a further series of tax-cutting measures. Lawson's statement that he was reducing the basic income tax rate from 27 to 25 per cent was shouted down by the Scottish Nationalist leader, Alex Salmond, who yelled: 'The Budget is an obscenity! The Chancellor cannot do this!'[63] Refusing to shut up, Salmond was expelled from the chamber for five days. Moments later, Lawson's announcement that the upper rate of income tax was to be cut from 60 per cent to 40 per cent attracted such a barrage of sustained abuse from Labour MPs that the chamber had to be cleared for ten minutes while tempers cooled.[64] Thereafter, the attacks continued in the newspapers, with the *Guardian*'s celebrated columnist Hugo Young declaring that such tax reductions represented 'the final disappearance of the last vestiges of the post-war consensus . . . Fairness and social justice, as registered through the tax system, have ceased even to be the pretended aspiration of the Conservative Party.'[65] If this was the criterion by which the Tories were to be judged, then Thatcher was on the social justice wing of her party – according to her Chancellor, she thought a 50 per cent top income tax rate a more practical proposition.[66]

Lawson, of course, did not accept his opponents' definition of fairness. As far as he was concerned, lowering high and potentially punitive levels of taxation was an economic stimulant which rewarded success as part of a virtuous circle that generated more wealth and jobs and thereby increased rather than diminished total tax receipts to the Treasury. Among those it most affected, at the upper end of the market, it certainly facilitated labour mobility. As Jack Spall, who worked in the City from 1947 to 1986, put it: 'Because of the high taxation rate [before 1979] it wasn't really worthwhile anybody moving from one company to another – if you got £10,000 per year more, you got £1,700 out of it and there wasn't much point in destroying your life for £1,700.' But as the top income tax rate fell first from 83 per cent to 60 per cent and then to 40 per cent, the marginal advantage of shifting jobs or even careers became more compelling, albeit 'employers became less loyal to their employees because they were paying vast sums of money and if they didn't perform they were out'.[67]

Accompanying and facilitating this mobility were the 'executive search' or 'headhunting' companies, a previously niche industry that was now coming to be regarded as a critical ancillary to corporate performance. As high-end City incomes soared, so other professional and management salaries rose too, in recognition that more would have to be offered to retain or attract talent that would otherwise be lured to the Square Mile. The rewards of this approach fell overwhelmingly at the very top and became an enduring feature of the next three decades, regardless of which political party was in power. In 1980, directors of FTSE-listed companies were typically paid ten times more than their average employee. By the end of the eighties, they were receiving seventeen times more. By 2008, the difference had risen to seventy-five times. The improving remuneration of those running the previously nationalized utilities attracted particular attention. For instance, the salary of British Gas's chief executive, which had been £50,000 when the company was privatized in 1986, stood at £370,000 five years later – an increase that could not be explained by the company's basting of its competitors in the intervening period, since it remained a monopoly provider. By 1994, the chief executive was earning £475,000, as much in a year as Sir Denis Rooke had done in almost fourteen years in the post between 1976 and 1989, during which time he had overseen British Gas's growth and steered it through privatization.[68] Sir Denis had to make do with the consolation of the Order of Merit.

Increasingly competitive levels of top-rate tax ensured that individuals who were in demand could use their tradability to maximum personal gain. Deindustrialization facilitated the process, because while physical plant usually comprised a major part of a traditional industrial company's asset base, the worth of many of the fast-developing service sector companies was primarily measured by its human capital. Of no eighties success story was this more true than Saatchi & Saatchi, whose share price halved in 1995 not because of a recent run of indifferent advertising campaigns but because Maurice Saatchi and several directors left the company, taking with them their personal input and contacts. Drawing its revenue entirely from the power of its ideas, advertising necessarily provided an extreme example, but it was nevertheless illustrative of one of the eighties' most marked economic developments. This was the widening of the UK's terms of trade, whereby mass low-value products were made more cheaply abroad and imported rather than manufactured in Britain, while national marginal advantage was sought instead by providing and exporting premium-value goods and services, which tended to be dependent on individual flair, insight and ability. Only through hyperactive redistributive intervention by the state could this process result in anything other than widening income inequality between those with the requisite skills to prosper in this market and those who lacked them.

The paradox of Conservative fiscal policy towards the rich was that by taking a smaller share of their income, a larger proportion of the total tax take was raised from them. In 1979, 11 per cent of total income tax receipts came from the richest 1 per cent of the population. Yet as the top rate of income tax came down from 83 per cent to 60 per cent and then to 40 per cent, where it remained until 2010, the proportion of total income tax receipts paid by the richest 1 per cent steadily grew, not just during the eighties but over the two successive decades. By 1999, the policy of remov-ing disincentives for the rich to get richer ensured that the top 1 per cent of them were paying 21 per cent of total income tax receipts, and by 2009 that 1 per cent was contributing almost one quarter of total receipts (and the top 10 per cent were contributing 54 per cent).[69] The paradox was easily explained: punitive rates of tax acted as income caps, making it scarcely worthwhile to be paid salaries within that bracket, with the consequence that relatively insignificant tax receipts were harvested. Concomitantly, the 83 per cent tax rate created a perverse incentive for those who did earn within that bracket either to use inventive accountancy methods to shift their income offshore where it was beyond the Inland Revenue's grasp, or to emigrate – a self-imposed exile familiarly referred to in the seventies as the 'brain drain'. Significantly, by the end of the eighties that term ceased to be much cited in public debate, not least because falling top-rate tax made the UK a more desirable place for the rich – and those with aspirations to become rich – to remain. It was less easy to measure the knock-on eco-nomic worth of attracting or retaining them (and their spare investment capital) than to compute the growing proportion of income tax receipts they contributed. Neither factor, however, impressed critics opposed on princi-ple to a philosophy that maintained 'we are intensely relaxed about people getting filthy rich so long as they pay their taxes'.[70] That that statement was made by neither of the two Tory architects of this approach, Sir Geoffrey Howe and Nigel Lawson, but in 1998 by Peter Mandelson, demonstrated the extent to which the Blair and Brown governments calculated that vast inequality of wealth was not the negation of the welfare state but rather the only means by which it could still be paid for without a vast tax hike for a far wider section of the electorate. To that extent it was social democracy that ended up pinning its survival upon the mantra of Gordon Gekko, the anti-hero of the 1987 film *Wall Street*, that 'greed, for lack of a better word, is good.'

Loaded, Landed, Leveraged

The equivalent of a *Debrett's* for the new plutocracy was launched as the *Sunday Times Rich List* in 1989. The surprise was perhaps that nothing com-parable had been published until that point, the fate of the one previous serious attempt having proved instructive. In 1982, the *Sunday Telegraph* began the task of producing a ranking of the country's wealthiest individuals, in response to a suggestion from Tiny Rowland, the chairman of the Lonrho conglomerate, that Britain lacked anything comparable to *Forbes*'s wealth rankings in the United States. Days into the research, the project was abandoned when the *Telegraph*'s proprietor, Lord Hartwell, was told bluntly by the Duke of Atholl that an offer to go grouse-shooting on his estate would be rescinded if an estimate of the Duke's wealth appeared in the list. Nor was outrage at the vulgarity of a social ranking determined by money rather than by class of peerage the only concern. The Sainsbury family was so perturbed by the *Telegraph*'s investigative insolence that it contacted Scotland Yard.[71]

Even by 1989, not everyone regarded it as a mark of distinction to appear in the first *Sunday Times Rich List*. The steel magnate Jack Walker condemned it as 'a beggars' and burglars' charter'.[72] But the *Sunday Times* was edited by Andrew Neil, a self-proclaimed meritocrat who had little regard for traditional deference and was not to be deflected by the threat of social *froideur*. Necessarily based upon estimates, the survey it produced was far from definitive, but contained much that was revelatory, particularly when subsequent editions permitted comparisons to be made concerning the changing nature of wealth and those who possessed it. In 1989, inherited wealth still predominated, accounting for 57 per cent of the top two hundred entries. Landowners accounted for one quarter, with eleven dukes, six marquesses and fourteen earls among them. A decade later, the *nouveau riche* had broken through, with self-made millionaires accounting for more than three quarters of entries. Even allowing for some intervening inflation, the scale of the fortunes also underwent a transformation. In 1989, the estimated £80 million owned by ex-Beatle Paul McCartney made him the country's eighty-third richest person. By 2008, those with £80 million were on the cusp of being excluded from the top one thousand. Another change was the internationalization of British-domiciled wealth. In 1989, only 11 per cent of those listed were born abroad. Twenty years later the proportion was nearing half of them.[73]

Vast wealth usually takes time to fructify, so it was understandable that those who began amassing personal fortunes in the eighties were not recognized among the echelons of established multi-millionaires until the following decade. What was striking during the eighties was how clearly demarcated the lines remained – at least in the popular perception – between those who had inherited money and those who were self-made. Indeed, the eighties brought into common parlance two terms that appeared perfectly to describe two identifiable, and rival, lifestyles associated with affluence and aspiration. These were the 'Sloane Ranger' and the 'yuppie'. The etymology of both terms was revelatory.

A wordplay on the Lone Ranger, the term 'Sloane Ranger' was actually coined by *Harpers & Queen* back in 1975, when the upmarket magazine's features editor, Ann Barr, commissioned Peter York to write about ex-public schoolgirls inhabiting flats in Chelsea close to Sloane Square who conformed to the type (it was only later that the term was applied to men as well). By 1976, the first classified advertisements were appearing in *The Times* seeking a Sloane Ranger to cook for private dinner parties on the Fulham Road.[74] The wider public remained oblivious to the meaning of this in-joke until 1982, when Barr and York edited *The Official Sloane Ranger Handbook*. In it they described a social group – 'movement' was the sort of sociological term they would have despised – that was self-consciously disconnected from modern egalitarian or even meritocratic assumptions, preferring to see worth in the supposed values of 'old money' and class distinction (supposedly tempered by *noblesse oblige*), and whose modes of speech and manners had not obviously moved on from the 'U and non-U' usages popularized by Nancy Mitford in the 1950s. That snobbery – or at any rate poshness – of this kind still existed was not of itself news. *The Official Sloane Ranger Handbook*'s achievement was to market the age-old notion as somehow trendsetting.

In this, Barr and York were assisted by the sudden public interest in the woman whose picture adorned the handbook's cover. Before her marriage, Lady Diana Spencer had seemed a stereotype Sloane, and while the perceived attractiveness of her personality may have owed much to her combination of shyness and good intentions, the admiration it generated also generated interest in her background, look and lifestyle. Combining an aristocratic lineage and ambivalence towards intellectualism – she was, as she famously put it, 'thick as a plank' – the future princess had left school without any O-level qualifications to pursue a cookery course, followed by nannying and assisting at the Young England Kindergarten in Pimlico. Alongside secretarial courses, degrees in fine art and internships with auction houses, such was the standard *curriculum vitae* of the classic young female Sloane. Her wedding to Prince Charles in July 1981 provided a reassuring distraction from the mounting unemployment and urban riots of that summer and was accompanied by nationwide celebrations. This was hardly surprising. At a time when the present day seemed beset with fear and uncertainty, the manifestation of tradition in the marriage of the heir to the throne to an engaging English aristocrat appeared to offer something comforting, rooted and stable. Three months later, nostalgia for the British aristocracy received a second fillip when ITV's eleven-episode adaption of Evelyn Waugh's *Brideshead Revisited* attracted eleven million viewers. Simultaneously, the content of newspaper and magazine fashion pages, the success of the country look promoted by the clothing chain Laura Ashley and the waxed-jacket maker Barbour, the shifting aesthetics of interior design, where chintz and heavy curtains were back in vogue, and the return – at least superficially – of classical detailing to the exterior of new architecture all suggested that 'reactionary chic' was undergoing a cultural renaissance.

This was the context that ensured the *Sloane Ranger Handbook* would be far more than a novelty guide to upper-class manners. In its first two years of publication, it went through fourteen impressions, selling more than a million copies and becoming the best-selling trade book of the decade.[75] Filled with advice about 'what really matters', where to shop and how to dress and behave like a Sloane, its sales extended far beyond the social group it depicted and suggested the presence of a considerable audience motivated by – or at least attracted to – social aspiration. By 1985, theatregoers were streaming into the West End for *The Sloane Ranger Review*, co-written by Ned Sherrin. The show, like the people it lovingly parodied, divided the critics, an acerbic *Times* reviewer insisting: 'How much more rewarding this show would be if it consisted of a march past of real Sloanes being pelted with real bread rolls.'[76] With their distinctive patterns of speech and sensibly traditional dress sense, the Sloanes were a stereotype easily sent up in mass advertising campaigns – most memorably and incongruously for Heineken lager in 1985 – and the presumption that they typically ended their sentences with the searching acknowledgement 'OK, yah?' bequeathed them the additional epithets 'yahs' or 'rahs', while their more boisterous, dinner-partying male counterparts came to be dubbed 'Hooray Henrys'. The Sloane, it seemed, was becoming as readily identifiable a feature of the first half of the eighties as were punks in the mid-seventies or Teddy Boys during the 1950s.

For all their reverence for 'old money', few could depend upon it to the extent of remaining wholly idle. During the early eighties, Sloane-ish figures were readily identifiable in the City. 'There's something about the way the City works,' the *Sloane Ranger Handbook* explained, 'the old-ness, the public-schoolness, the merchant bank "word-is-my-bond" code of honour – that makes it all seem like an ancient profession, not business at all. Even the dodgy side is a bit dashing and roguish, like eighteenth-century gambling. And the City is the last Empire, still controlling things everywhere, linked up with marvellous places like Hong Kong.'[77] This, however, was the clubbish, conservative and nepotistic City that Big Bang helped blow open to wider competition. After 1986, demand for the gentleman amateur – perhaps third or fourth in a line of close relations to have worked in the same venerable partnership, and proffering nothing higher than a 2:2 degree – slackened considerably. Those who came from Sloane-ish backgrounds who proved able to compete in the new environment tended to do so by dropping the act – at any rate, until the weekend's escape to the countryside. This changing mood in the City was in evidence elsewhere, too. Indeed, the woman who had helped propel the Sloane Ranger to prominence at the beginning of the decade came ultimately to exemplify the rejection of its values and prejudices. By the decade's end, Diana, Princess of Wales was mixing with an international jet-set that recognized no obvious distinction between an earl and a rock star or fashion designer. That thereafter she dated the Muslim son of the Egyptian businessman who – to Sloane-ish horror back in 1985 – had bought the Harrods department store underlined how much in the ascendant was the new admiration for wealth regardless of the social baggage with which it came.

This less class-bound attitude was embodied in the other aspirational social group to which the lingo of the eighties gave definition. 'Yuppie' was a term coined in the United States in 1984 as a part-acronym of 'young urban professional', though by the time it had achieved something approaching household recognition in the UK, round about 1986–7, it was widely interpreted as standing for 'young upwardly mobile professional'.[78] Thus in Britain the yuppie was assumed not to have inherited wealth or status but to be self-made. Those brought under the umbrella term – willingly or otherwise – included almost anyone perceived to be youthful and brazenly making large sums of money, be they City traders, estate agents, advertising executives (the definition of 'executive' was undergoing grade inflation), public relations consultants or those lucratively engaged in any of the other fast-growing service sectors. The breadth of this sweep inevitably scooped up many who, far from starting from scratch, had actually enjoyed a middle-class upbringing, perhaps with an expensive education included – for it was really an unapologetic attitude towards personal success, rather than social origin, that was the yuppie's hallmark. The sight of City traders, many of whom had recently grown up on council estates, volubly enjoying their good fortune over chilled champagne buckets in the bars around Leadenhall Market was unsettling to those – whether snobs or socialists – who regarded such behaviour as the product of social disorder. Nor was there any shortage of those happy to play up to the Harry Enfield-created stereotype of the newly prosperous plasterer boasting about his 'loadsamoney'.* Such behaviour also appeared on university campuses. At Exeter University, Professor Ted Wragg complained that 'these coves become leading lights in the Federation of Conservative Students. Some time ago they hired a white Rolls-Royce and drove it ostentatiously around the campus to demonstrate that some students have lots of money.'[79] The professor assumed that they were the product of his university's high public-school intake. Their behaviour, though, more closely resembled the nascent yuppie rather than the thoroughbred Sloane approach to irritating others. After all, for all their Tory sentiments, Sloanes were rarely political activists and were not likely to

---

* See p. 247.

admit to having to hire a Rolls-Royce – or to imagine that one painted white was a symbol of patrician taste.

The yuppie attitude displayed none of the old British coyness about making money or concealing success behind a mask of amiable self-efface-ment, and in this respect it was a distinctively transatlantic outlook. It was especially identified with the boom years of the eighties, and was propelled by the sort of individualistic energies supposedly unleashed by Thatcherite policies (which might explain why the term fell out of use after Thatcher's fall, even though there were plenty of young people who continued to make money and to act obnoxiously in the twenty years thereafter). The tradition-ally minded, 'High Tory' editor of the *Sunday Telegraph*, Peregrine Worsthorne, condemned such displays of affluence as 'bourgeois triumphal-ism' and urged Thatcher publicly to dissociate herself from them.[80] Naturally reluctant to condemn those being rewarded for their enterprise (who were, after all, her natural constituency), the prime minister did not take up Worsthorne's suggestion. But such was her sensitivity to Labour charges of growing inequality that when she selected 11 June 1987 as the date for the general election, the journalist Robin Oakley noted that she 'was deter-mined to rob Labour of the chance of exploiting the conspicuous consumption at the Ascot race meeting in the week of June 18'.[81]

Given their association with the mood music of Thatcherism, yuppies were predictably hate figures for those who regarded the 'Lawson boom' either as a mirage or as an insult to those who remained poor. By 1987, the expression 'yuppie scum' was easily tripping off tongues, for while Sloane Rangers were usually the subject of parody, yuppies were widely treated with loathing by the left. The basis of this contempt appeared to rest upon the notion that they were not the successes of a genuine meritocracy but merely latter-day spivs, making profits without creating the physical prod-ucts they bought and sold. Problematically, this definition could easily embrace a large section of the workforce in an increasingly post-industrial economy. The more stereotypical yuppies, however, tended to make them-selves readily identifiable not just by a cocky manner but also by adopting a dress code designed to amplify their unapologetic self-confidence: men wearing bold chalk-stripe suits with the trousers held up by pillar box-red braces, while women opted for power-dressing, often involving shoulder pads, primary colours and tailoring that appeared to have been inspired either by the military uniforms of the Napoleonic Wars or by the cut of the smarter sort of air stewardess. The yuppie accessory of a Filofax* became so ubiquitous as to be a source of comic ribaldry. There was even bemusement at how their sense of self-importance was revealed by their belief that they

---

* The favoured brand of leather-bound 'personal organizer' (a loose-leaf diary with add-ons).

needed the newfangled mobile phone to stay in touch while on the move
– literally and metaphorically.

It was as estate agents and property developers that Sloanes and yuppies
intermingled professionally. Yet, whatever the social timbre of those organizing property sales, they were engaged in the market that during the period
– even more than the expansion of share ownership – did most to broaden
and deepen the asset base of the greatest number of Britons. The average
house price rose from around £20,000 in 1979 to £34,000 in 1985, before
peaking at £62,000 in 1989.[82] Indeed, the increase between 1985 and 1989
represented a 70 per cent gain above inflation, and at their most feverish (and
unsustainable) in the first half of 1988 house prices rose by 30 per cent. In
1987, there was widespread incredulity in the press, and even in Parliament,
that a converted broom-cupboard in Knightsbridge, with dimensions smaller
than a snooker table, could be sold to a secretary for £36,500.* This proved
to be a sign not that the market was at its peak but rather that there was still
money to be made from even the most unpromising investments (at least if
they were in desirable areas). Furthermore, the increasing valuations were
crucially important to an ever larger number of individuals. The proportion
owning their own homes went up from 55 to 67 per cent between 1979 and
1989. The scale of this widening of home ownership was clear when put
into historical perspective: only one tenth of homes were privately owned in
1910, and renters still made up half the market as recently as 1970, when one
third of the population lived in council accommodation. 'Buying their own
home is the first step most people take towards building up capital to hand
down to their children and grandchildren,' declared the Conservatives' 1987
manifesto, neatly aligning the aspiration with Tory philosophy. 'It gives
people a stake in society – something to conserve. It is the foundation stone
of a capital-owning democracy.'[83] The rapid increase in home ownership in
the eighties was made possible by three clear strands of Conservative policy:
the sale of council houses, the extension of mortgage interest relief, and the
encouragement given to banks and building societies to relax their lending
criteria.

During the 1970s, it had not been impossible for tenants to buy their own
council houses in areas where Conservative-controlled town halls actively
facilitated the process, but the opportunities were patchy or non-existent
where Labour held sway. It was only with the passage of the Housing Act
1980 that the 'right to buy' became a statutory right regardless of the political
outlook of local councillors. The strength of demand immediately became
apparent and of the more than 5 million council homes occupied at the start
of the decade, 1.2 million had been sold to their (now) owner–occupiers ten

---

* It proved a shrewd long-term investment: in 2007 it was bought for £140,000.

years later. The scheme the former tenants took advantage of offered them a reduction on the market price proportionate to the number of years they had paid rent on the property (a reduction of between 33 and 50 per cent, depending on the length of tenancy beyond three years), though that deduction would have to be largely repaid if the home was then sold within five years. Such discounts cost the Treasury an estimated £2 billion, but the sales raised £18 billion, representing 43 per cent of the total receipts made from privatizations during the decade.[84]

The policy's by-product was to reduce the available housing stock for those on low pay, since the sale proceeds were directed towards reducing the debt burden and the proportion local councils could spend on reinvestment was steadily reduced over the decade. The funding of new or renovated council estates duly fell (thirteen thousand new council homes were being built per year at the end of the eighties, compared with twenty thousand annually during the seventies).[85] The problem for the Labour Party, which fought the 1983 general election promising to abolish the 'right to buy', was that the policy was especially popular among a wide section of what was – although it was ceasing to be – Labour's core support, who were on modest earnings and who saw home ownership as creating a valuable nest egg which would otherwise be beyond their reach. Reluctantly acknowledging this reality, Labour began to retreat from outright opposition and in 1987 opted for a more pragmatic stance, merely promising to redirect the proceeds towards reinvestment in council housing stock. This ran counter to one of the intentions of the legislation, which was to bring private investment into neighbourhoods that were otherwise dependent upon the budgets of central and local government, rather than merely to provide a new source of revenue with which to build more council estates. On those estates where significant numbers opted to buy their homes (often where the houses had gardens), the regenerative signs of 'gentrification' were widely discernible. Especially stark, therefore, became the contrast with those estates (often flats in tower blocks) where home ownership did not take off, a factor that also accentuated the 'north–south divide'. Such estates faced a spiral of decline, being dependent for refurbishment upon the council and, with the more prosperous or determined residents moving out, becoming home disproportionately to those dependent upon welfare benefits. In particular, housing benefit replaced rent control as the means through which accommodation was kept affordable for those without a regular income. In large part, this was a consequence of central government's reduction of the subsidies that had kept council house rents artificially low. Local authorities sought to make good the shortfall by charging market rents, which produced a surge in applications for housing benefit. The Treasury ended up paying out almost as much to individual applicants as it had previously done in providing councils with block subsidies.

The 'right to buy' policy accelerated rather than initiated changes in the social structure of council estates, since the process was already under way before the 1980 act; in fact, it could be traced to a private member's bill introduced by a Liberal MP, Stephen Ross, which the Labour government had brought on to the statute book as the Housing (Homeless Persons) Act 1977. This placed a legal obligation on local housing authorities to provide accommodation for the homeless. As the rough-sleepers making do in cardboard boxes in city centres attested, the need remained intense throughout the eighties, and the legislation's intent could scarcely be faulted – merely its failure to reach all those who remained in need. The unintended consequence, however, was fundamentally to change the social composition of many estates. In particular, the prioritizing of the most needy, regardless of where they came from, made sense on compassionate grounds but cut across the means by which traditional working-class estates retained their historic sense of community. Suddenly deemed discriminatory were the strict vetting procedures that had prioritized for tenancies local families and their relations and those in steady jobs. The result was the 'sink estate'.

The scale of the homelessness problem remained such that it was beyond the 1977 legislation's ability to end it. Indeed, it got worse as the eighties progressed, although there was disagreement as to how many it involved, with the National Audit Office suggesting that the numbers had risen from 53,000 in 1978 to 126,000 in 1989. Defining the homeless as those with no permanent address, local authorities estimated that, nationwide, almost 73,000 people fell into this category in the first six months of 1990. Most were being put up in temporary accommodation, whether in hostels or bed and breakfast residences.[86] It was the three to five thousand rough-sleepers who naturally attracted the most concern and popular outrage. The sight of (often young) people bedding down for the night in the shop doorways and on the pavements of The Strand provided a stark contrast between consumer plenty and abject poverty in London's West End. A similar scene of a cardboard shanty-town, inhabited mainly by older 'down and outs', in the concrete underpass outside Waterloo Station was the first sight of Thatcher's London that greeted commuters and tourists leaving the terminus. In an effort to stem the flow of the destitute into the capital, and other inner cities, the environment secretary, Nick Ridley, proposed in 1988 ending the benefit rights of homeless claimants who refused to stay in their 'home' local authority area. The plan was leaked, and was dropped after it was attacked as an attempt to hurt the vulnerable and shield them from metropolitan view, rather than to address their deep-seated problems.

The causes of homelessness included not just the absence of cheap housing but also the lack of jobs, the breakdown of the traditional family unit and the social atomization that resulted, the prevalence of recreational drug dependency, particularly among the young, and the effects of the 'care in the community' programme whereby those with mental health problems were treated with palliative medication rather than being restrained in asylums. While perceived to be driven by government spending restraints, 'care in the community' was nonetheless the continuation of a thirty-year liberal approach which decried asylums as the dehumanizing relics of Victorian institutionalization. As a result, the number of beds in mental hospitals had already been cut from 150,000 in the mid-1950s to 80,000 in the mid-1970s. The intention was for sufferers to take their medicine at home in an environment that fostered their re-engagement with society – though where patients failed to take their medication or did not respond to it, the danger was that they would enter into a downward spiral of personal problems, incapacity, homelessness and crime. Those – and the numbers were never adequately quantified – who fell between the cracks of community care had limited options. Only four thousand places in local authority hostels were created to accommodate the hundred thousand patients discharged from mental health institutions between 1955 and 1990.[87] Analysis by the St Mungo Association in the capital suggested that among younger homeless people one third had been in care immediately prior to sleeping on the streets. Two thirds had been in institutions at some stage during their lives.[88] The issue, however, was not just one of building new cheap accommodation. The Salvation Army reported that thousands slept rough within walking distance of their hostels, which had empty beds. For all the complaint that the 'right to buy' had destroyed the social housing market, the fact remained that by 1990 there were 100,000 empty council houses in England alone. The government set up a £300-million, two-year programme to renovate them. Furthermore, there were more than 600,000 privately owned properties standing empty, which became central to efforts to increase the available housing stock.[89]

The government's Housing Act 1988 proffered two solutions to the shortage of low-rent properties. The first was to encourage the growth of not-for-profit housing associations, which – where the residents voted for it – were allowed to take over the running of estates from local authorities. The grants that central government made to these charitable organizations increased from £50 million in 1979 to £1 billion in 1990, ensuring that they became responsible for building three times as many properties for rent as local government.[90] The second solution was to try to stimulate the private rental market. Until the 1960s, the country's private landlords had provided more rented accommodation than local authorities. Indeed, the sale of council houses in the eighties actually represented the second great wave of property sell-offs of the post-war period, given that in the 1950s and 1960s, private rental landlords had disposed of 2.3 million homes (one third of their total stock), mostly to private buyers. These properties tended to be terraced homes, which landlords concluded could no longer produce adequate rental returns in consequence of tight rent controls and the spreading availability of council housing. For most of the eighties, the private rental market showed no signs of recovery, remaining below 8 per cent of the housing stock until 1988, when the government freed landlords offering the newly created assured short-hold tenancies from rent controls, creating the potential for a greater return on their investment. In time, this provided the motivation for the 'buy to rent' market to take off, and by the late nineties the sector was staging a remarkable recovery – to the extent that by 2011 there were as many Britons renting from private landlords as from local authorities and housing associations.

That it took until 1988 for the government to address seriously the interests of those for whom renting remained the preferred or only option perfectly illustrated the priority given to creating the 'property-owning democracy'. The resources of the state were actively tilted to help those who wanted to buy. The main incentive was the income tax break offered by mortgage interest relief at source (MIRAS). The sweetener had actually been introduced by Roy Jenkins when he was Labour's Chancellor of the Exchequer in 1969, and represented a rare case of a state subsidy Thatcher was zealously keen to increase: between 1980 and 1990 its cost to the Treasury rose by 200 per cent, to £7 billion. It allowed applicants to claim for the first £30,000 of a mortgage. What was more, two cohabiting persons (so long as they were not married to one another) could each claim the relief, securing a £60,000 tax break on the same property. Lawson did away with this matrimonial disincentive in his 1988 budget, though the restriction was not implemented until more than four months later, during which time there was a surge in unmarried couples buying houses, forcing up prices at the very moment when the market was already overheating.

Prior to the eighties property boom, less than 5 per cent of mortgages were issued by banks, the primary lenders being building societies organized along mutual lines, without shareholders. It was a model that the intensifying desire for home ownership placed under considerable pressure, since building societies lent from the deposits they received from existing customers rather than from borrowed money, and this limited their ability to offer a sufficient supply of mortgages to meet the multiplying demand. The first relaxation in how these mutuals operated came in 1983 when Abbey National led the break-up of the cartel, organized since 1939 by the Building Societies Association, which fixed their lending and savings rates so that there was no competition between them. While the cartel had reduced the incentive for reckless lending, it also ensured a poor return for savers, resulting in insufficient funds and mortgage rationing. Its break-up was brought about not only by a newly cut-throat attitude on the part of some building societies, but because of the sensible apprehension that a relaxation of bank-lending criteria in 1980 would bring the major clearing banks into the mortgage market. The threat was real since banks' ability to offer credit by borrowing from the wholesale capital markets gave them the potential to reach a broader market – a particular advantage given that property prices were rising far more quickly than savings, making it impossible to fund the necessary mortgage lending from retail savings. Where previously home buyers might have hoped to secure a mortgage of two and a half times their annual salary, loans were soon being made of up to four times annual salary. In this way, Britain experienced a vast expansion of borrowing despite the fact that interest rates spent most of the eighties in double digits, far above the retail price index. The increasing value of loans offered for non-housing purposes, from £4 billion to £28 billion between 1978 and 1988, seemed positively miserly compared with the rise in mortgages from £6 billion to £63 billion over the same period.[91] By then, Lawson's policies were simultaneously taking the economy in two contrasting directions: while central government exercised mid-Victorian retrenchment by managing to spend less money than it raised, the private sector's credit-to-capital ratio expanded dramatically.

During the course of this expansion of credit, the services that both banks and building societies offered were transformed. In 1980, clearing banks still did not pay any interest on their customers' current accounts, and more than one quarter of Britons of working age did not even have a bank account (that proportion had stood at one half as recently as 1976).[92] Though larger payments might be made by writing cheques, most shopping was done with cash and until ATMs began to proliferate, from 1982 onwards, this necessitated standing in line for a bank teller to count out and hand over the notes. Building societies went through an even more fundamental change. Removing many of the restrictions on what they could and could not do, the Building Societies Act 1986 permitted them to borrow money like banks, to operate like banks and – if their members voted for it – to demutualize and effectively to become banks. The first fully to take advantage was Abbey National, which floated on the stock exchange in 1989 after its members had voted overwhelmingly in favour of demutualization – a decision sweetened by the offer of one hundred free shares for each of them if the flotation went ahead. Over the succeeding two decades, Abbey's major competitors all followed the same path, which mostly ended in their merging with or being taken over by the traditional banks.

The breaching of the rules and traditions that had long constrained and demarcated financial institutions provided an enormous stimulus to the property market. Yet, contrary to popular myth, the eighties was not a period of continuous house price rises. Only if sale prices are taken at face value, without regard to intervening inflation, does this misconception appear to be true. In reality, property values, like so much else, were depressed by the early eighties recession and (once inflation is factored in) the average price of a house was still lower in 1984 than it had been in 1979.[*] It was only with economic recovery and the accompanying relaxation of lending terms that property prices returned to their long-term trend. Only in the last three years of the decade did they sharply exceed that trend, ensuring that when the bubble burst at the end of 1989 those who were most over-leveraged suddenly found themselves holders of 'negative equity', because their outstanding mortgages were greater than the worth of their homes. Thus, the decade ended with the revelation that bricks and mortar, like stocks and shares, were not the one-way bet they had for so long seemed. House prices fell by 18 per cent between 1989 and 1995, which, when adjusted for inflation, represented a real decline of more than one third.[93] By 2007, twelve years of growth had made home-owning seem once again almost a prerequisite for personal financial security, the proportion of Britons pursuing the dream having at last caught up with that of the United States. And it was across the Atlantic that the same desire to widen property ownership beyond the middle class brought about the debt crisis that in 2008 threatened to bring down the major financial institutions of the Western world. The over-exposure of lenders to 'sub-prime' borrowers, whose means were not equal to the costs, left in its wake an unprecedented level of indebtedness. In Britain, vast liabilities would accompany what Nigel Lawson had outlined to the Conservative Party conference in October 1987 as the legacy of a property-owning democracy – the creation of 'a nation of inheritors'.[94]

---

[*] See Appendix: Nationwide Index of House Prices, 1979–90, p. 478.

15 AN END TO OLD CERTAINTIES

Ten More Years! Ten More Years!

'After a decade of achievement let us herald the decade of hope,' announced Thatcher in her New Year message on the eve of 1990. 'And let us do so in the knowledge that never since the Second World War have hopes – indeed expectations – for peace and progress in the world stood so high. Why? . . . The short answer lies in the 1980s – in the resolution of the West to defend our freedom and justice and the dawning realization in the communist bloc that their system simply could not compete with ours.'[1]

The dramatic fall on 9 November 1989 of the Berlin Wall and the Christmas overthrow of the Ceauşescu regime in Bucharest neatly aligned the end of the eighties with a great historic turning point – the collapse of Marxism–Leninism in Europe. Having formed her outlook through the prism of forty-three years of Cold War, and apparently lived to see her standpoint vindicated, what looked like the West's triumph in Berlin and the other capitals of Eastern Europe might have provided the fitting moment for the 'Iron Lady' to announce that there were no more crusades to go on and that she was hanging up her breastplate. But while the American neo-conservative thinker Francis Fukuyama gained immediate traction for his essay positing that the global triumph of liberal–democratic ideals represented 'the end of history', the British prime minister continued to see countless campaigns to mount. The task for the nineties, she continued in her New Year epistle, would necessitate 'assistance' to those turning towards freedom and, concomitantly, ensuring that the European Community was led 'towards the free trading, open, flexible and diverse group of nations' (and not, by implication, towards a tight, centralized union). Trumpeting what she saw as the economic achievements of the eighties at home, which had ended with unemployment falling rapidly and even manufacturing output 12 per cent higher than it had been in 1979, Thatcher sketched out a domestic agenda for the new decade that would be dominated by improving the quality of schools and hospitals, and the 'huge task' of 'protecting the global climate' (she surprised many by joining those expressing the new concern about global warming). Yet 'our prime task now' remained disappointingly similar to what it had been ten years earlier – 'damping down the fires of inflation . . . the only basis for improving the whole quality of life in British society in the 1990s'.[2] The next day, Thatcher won the Radio 4 *Today* programme listeners' vote for international 'Woman of the Year', an accolade she picked up eight times in nine years.

Was there any stopping her? When she strode on to the platform at the Conservative Party conference in Blackpool in October 1989, delegates broke into an ecstatic roar of 'Ten more years! Ten more years!' Everyone in the hall was standing, chanting, clapping, foot-stomping the bouffant blonde, 64-year-old sovereign of the Empress Ballroom. It had clearly occurred to her that she might dominate the coming decade as totally as the one that was drawing to its close. To *The Times* she expressed her intention to fight for a fourth term and then, less cautiously, assured a radio interviewer that if she stood and won that fourth term: 'I am quite prepared to go on to the fifth election.'[3] Displaying hubris on this scale was not clever politics, for the surest way to lose support was to take it for granted, and also because the signal it sent out to her Cabinet colleagues was that their ambitions to succeed her would be blocked for years to come unless they could engineer a way of securing her downfall in the meantime. At the end of 1988, by which time she was already the longest-serving prime minister of the twentieth century, it was her husband, Denis, who gently put it to her that she should stand down and thereby leave on her own terms. Fleetingly, she appeared to see the wisdom of his advice, only for Willie Whitelaw to confirm her suspicion that to stand down at that moment would divide her party.[4] Given the likelihood that the uncompromisingly pro-European Michael Heseltine might fill the vacancy, there seemed to be some wisdom in Whitelaw's advice. At any rate, convincing her to stay on proved a far easier task than persuading her to step down. The loyal and personally disinterested Whitelaw aside, the advice of political colleagues could easily be dismissed as self-serving. More useful might have been the counsel of long-serving personal – rather than political – colleagues, such as her media advisers Tim Bell and Gordon Reece. They shared her husband's view, but could not bring themselves to challenge her instinct for survival. When Bell beseeched Reece, 'You must tell her,' Reece replied, 'I can't. I love her.' At which point Denis interjected, 'Steady on. She's my wife.'[5]

One problem was that those who most wanted to succeed her seemed least committed to carrying on her legacy. And whatever her obvious unpopularity with a large section of the electorate, the inescapable fact remained of her record in garnering the votes where and when it mattered. On 11 June

1987, she had become the first prime minister in democratic times to be returned to office in three successive general elections, and the only one to have won two landslides in the twentieth century. With three quarters of the electorate voting in the 1987 poll, Labour's share of the vote increased to 30.8 per cent, from 27.6 per cent in 1983, while the SDP–Liberal Alliance slid by almost the same amount, from 25.4 to 22.6 per cent, leaving the Conservative vote shaved by a mere 0.2 per cent down to 42.3 per cent. The new Parliament duly assembled with 229 Labour MPs, 22 Alliance members and 376 Conservatives (down by just 21), leaving a government majority of 102.[6] The landslide was a blow to Neil Kinnock, three and a half years into his leadership of the Labour Party, whose presidential-style campaign had sought to contrast him favourably with the haphazard demeanour of his predecessor. As *The Times* pointed out: 'Eight years of the most vilified prime minister of modern times; three million unemployed and a country apparently enraged by the condition of its health service . . . In the end [Kinnock] still won only about a score or so extra seats than the hopeless Mr Michael Foot.' The problem, summarized the editorial, was as much the Labour Party's failings as the Conservatives' successes: in having become a refuge for single-issue activists claiming to speak for their chosen minority-interest group, Labour was simply unappealing to the bulk of 'ordinary' voters.[7]

In inner-city areas, Labour at least retained the foundations upon which to build. Beyond its age-old Liberal-held seats in Scotland and the West Country, the Alliance struggled to sustain such a boast. No nearer to 'breaking the mould' of British politics, the Liberals and SDP duly began the process of a formal merger, resulting – after understandable acrimony and horse-trading – in the creation of the Social & Liberal Democrats in March 1988. While managing to avoid adopting the hallucinogenic connotations of LSD, the SLD developed little brand awareness and the party was renamed the Liberal Democrats in October 1989. Three of the Gang of Four joined it – but not David Owen, who led his own 'continuing' SDP group into the wilderness: after its candidate polled fewer votes than Screaming Lord Sutch of the Official Monster Raving Loony Party at the Bootle by-election in May 1990, the party finally bowed to reality and was disbanded by its national executive. So ended with a whimper a remarkable experiment. As the authors of the SDP's definitive history concluded: 'Someone who returned to Britain in the mid-1990s after having lived abroad (and been out of touch) throughout the 1980s would find very little difference in the British party system – and almost no trace of the SDP.'[8] Having launched their appeal with such high hopes in 1981, the most discernible long-term consequence of the SDP's brief life was that it brought about the demise of the Liberal Party after 129 years of independent existence. Not that the Liberal Democrats proceeded to do better as a new unitary force, spending most of 1989 and 1990 ranging between 4 and 10 per cent in the opinion polls. It was small comfort that among extremist parties the performance was even more risible: out of over 32 million votes cast in the 1987 general election, the National Front and the British National Party between them received less than one thousand votes nationwide (settled immigration had by 1987 sunk to its lowest levels since the introduction of controls in 1961), while the Communist Party, the 'Red Front' and the Workers' Revolutionary Party could not quite collectively muster eleven thousand votes. For all the talk of divisive politics and a divided decade, the electorate showed scant inclination to endorse alternatives to the constitutional mainstream.

Yet divided the country clearly was between the two main parties, with the 1987 election confirming the geographically polarized nature of party support. Dominant in Scotland, Wales, the northern cities and the deprived boroughs of London, Labour struggled to claim a presence elsewhere. Outside the capital, the party only won three seats south of an imaginary line between the Severn and the Wash. With sixty-three seats in northern England, the Conservatives could make a better claim to being still a national party, but their failure in inner-city areas was laid bare. In Scotland, they lost ten seats from their 1983 total, though they retained eleven and were still the second-largest party, claiming the allegiance of almost one quarter of Scots voters. Much as Scottish Tories would subsequently blame the legacy of Thatcherism for their annihilation in 1997, they still did far better with the honourable member for Finchley as their leader than any of her five successors in the twenty years after 1990. Despite the simmering resentment at Thatcher's blanket refusal to discuss devolution, it did not translate into a swing towards the parties of Celtic independence. In terms of MPs returned and share of the vote, Plaid Cymru and the Scottish Nationalists were only the fourth-largest parties in their respective nations, in 1987 winning just three seats each and 7.3 and 14 per cent of ballots cast, respectively.[9]

Apart from a fleeting by-election triumph by 'Big Jim' Sillars in Glasgow Govan in 1988, the eighties were barren years for the Scottish Nationalists. Failure to secure even the modest devolution proposed in the 1979 referendum had checked the SNP's momentum, and the party was further debilitated by an internal split which ensured the temporary expulsion of (the future leader) Alex Salmond and fellow members of his 79 Group, who argued for a campaign of civil disobedience to create a 'Scottish socialist republic'.[10] The party encountered other problems, too. The economic case for Scotland's viability as an independent state was predicated upon gaining control of the revenue from North Sea oil. This was an argument that the oil price crash of 1986 went some way towards undermining. The Scottish economy, indeed, was going through as rapid a transformation as that of any region of the UK. In 1976, almost 30 per cent of Scotland's labour force worked in manufacturing. By 1990, only just over 20 per cent did so. Clydeside was once the world's greatest shipyard, yet during the eighties income from salmon fishing came to outstrip that from Scotland's shipbuilding industry. Amid this deindustrialization, the survival of the vast Ravenscraig steelworks at Motherwell assumed totemic status, and though it outlived the decade it was ultimately to close in 1992. Elsewhere, there were encouraging signs of adaptation and new growth. Nearly half of all UK computers for export were being made in the so-called Silicon Glen belt of central Scotland.[11] Over 45,000 Scots were employed in the sector. Scotland made one in eight of the world's semi-conductors and nearly a third of Europe's personal computers. Computerization also facilitated Edinburgh's rise as a centre for fund management, for Big Bang's introduction of the SEAQ electronic share-monitoring technology* made it easier for securities trading to be carried out outside the City of London. Scottish-based firms managed £50 billion of funds in 1986 and £211 billion by 1994 – by which time they represented the majority of Scotland's top twenty companies.[12] Thatcher did her best to trumpet such achievements, but what should have alarmed her philosophically was the manner in which her secretaries of state in both Wales and Scotland defended the party's record (and the case for maintaining the United Kingdom) by attributing the success stories to the role of subsidies and development agencies. To counter this, Michael Forsyth, the Scottish Conservative chairman between 1989 and 1990, endeavoured to win over the nation of Adam Smith to the benefits of market economics. His endeavours were not rewarded with conspicuous success.

Thatcher was unable to avoid giving the impression that she imagined Britishness to be an extension of Englishness, an assumption unlikely to appeal to Celtic sensitivities. Few could have been surprised that she demonstrated little empathy for the Irish nationalist outlook; and when the Cabinet secretary, Sir Robert Armstrong, mused in her hearing that in the long term a united Ireland was probably inevitable, she shot back: 'Never! Never!'[13] Yet she showed little understanding of unionist attitudes either, or rapport with their spokesmen (and men they all were). This was made manifest when, on 15 November 1985, she signed the Anglo-Irish Agreement, which affirmed that the Irish Republic was entitled to be consulted on policy within Northern Ireland, through the establishment of a joint committee with a permanent secretariat based on the outskirts of Belfast, and through regular meetings of an Anglo-Irish Intergovernmental Conference attended by British and Irish ministers. Counter-terrorism and 'the development of economic, social and cultural cooperation' were to be included in the discussions, though the nature and extent of the consultation remained vague.

---

* See p. 395.

While the government in Dublin kept the nationalist SDLP briefed on the negotiations leading up to the Anglo-Irish Agreement, London refused to involve the unionist politicians, whose opposition could be taken for granted and who duly reacted with outrage at being excluded from discussions about the administration of their own land. All fifteen unionist MPs resigned their seats in order to force by-elections to demonstrate that what they termed the 'diktat' was being imposed against the democratic will. Ian Paisley thundered indignantly before a 100,000-strong crowd outside Belfast City Hall: 'Where do the terrorists return to for sanctuary? To the Irish Republic! And yet Mrs Thatcher tells us that that Republic must have some say in our province. We say never! Never! Never! *Never!*'

In fact it was partly the Anglo-Irish Agreement's intention to improve cross-border security and to remove the virtual impunity with which those suspected of terrorist activity remained at liberty in the Irish Republic. In this respect, it proved a failure, especially after the more assertively nationalist Charles Haughey returned to power in Dublin in March 1987. There was no diminution in the ferocity of the Provisional IRA's activities, with republicans killing forty-two people in 1985, sixty-nine in 1987 and sixty-two in 1988.[14] It was not cooperation with Dublin but the vigilance of French customs officials that uncovered a major supply route to the IRA when, in October 1987, officers inspected a rusty cargo ship and stumbled upon a consignment that included one thousand AK-47 assault rifles, one million rounds of ammunition, fifty surface-to-air missiles and two tonnes of Semtex plastic explosive, sent from Libya. Under interrogation, the skipper revealed that he had already steered four previous shipments into the hands of the republican terrorists. Additionally, Colonel Gaddafi had sent them $10 million in cash. Clearly, far from being appeased by the establishment of cross-border committees, the IRA was planning to escalate hostilities and was stockpiling an arsenal on a scale sufficient for prosecuting a long war. Ten days later, their operatives detonated a bomb during the Remembrance Sunday service in the County Fermanagh town of Enniskillen, killing eleven civilians* and wounding more than sixty. By chance, an even larger bomb timed for the same moment failed to explode in the village of Tullyhommon, where its victims would have included the wreath-laying children of the local Boy's Brigade and Girls' Brigade. There was widespread condemnation from both sides of the divide, but no end to the terror. In March 1988, a lone loyalist gunman retaliated by firing at mourners at the funeral of IRA operatives who had been shot in Gibraltar by the SAS. Three days later, as one of his three victims was being given an IRA funeral, the mourners

---

* A twelfth victim, the former headmaster of Enniskillen High School, never regained consciousness and, after a thirteen-year coma, died in 2000.

spotted two British soldiers in a car, which they surrounded. In full view of television cameras, the mob dragged out the two corporals from their Volkswagen Passat and lynched them. Stripped, struck and battered beyond recognition, they were taken off and executed. The horrific scene produced one of the defining images of the Troubles: the Catholic priest Fr Alec Reid on his knees trying to administer the last rites to one of the broken and bloodied soldiers. Reid later played a role in the peace process – one that seemed a distant prospect amid the darkness of such late eighties atrocities.

Whitehall versus Town Hall

Four main factors conspired to sweep Margaret Thatcher out of Downing Street. The implementation of the poll tax and the signs of a weakening economy (in particular the housing market) badly hit the Conservatives' popularity, scaring Tory MPs into believing that unless the prime minister changed course they would all go down to a crushing defeat at the next general election, which was due by the summer of 1992. The other two factors principally concerned her deteriorating relations with her Cabinet colleagues, many of whom were tiring of her brusqueness and rudeness, and some of whom disagreed fundamentally on a major policy issue – her growing Euroscepticism. In the end, it was her falling out – personally and politically – with key members of the Cabinet that directly triggered the process by which she was toppled, but it was the poll tax that began the work of weakening her base in the country and at Westminster.

In its conceptual boldness, the poll tax appealed to Thatcher, for she was naturally attracted to radical solutions that upended conventional thinking. Her error was that, having been persuaded of the philosophical case for this new means of paying for local government, she proved unwilling to digest the mounting evidence that it could only become practical politics if so much Treasury money was thrown at it that it ceased to fulfil its original objective of holding town hall budgets to closer account. Earlier in her premiership, Thatcher's ability to marry idealism with the caution of a practised tactician had helped make her a formidable political operator. By contrast, the stridency with which she threw her weight behind the poll tax blinded her to its contradictions and shortcomings. It was as if experience was making her careless.

It might be supposed that, as the daughter of an alderman, admiration for local government would have been inbred in her. But because she believed her primary task was to restore order to the state's finances, she instead grew incandescent at what she took to be the refusal of local authorities (who were responsible for one quarter of all public sector spending) to show the same determination to bring their budgets into balance. As part of Whitehall's austerity measures, central government's grant to local government was slashed during the early eighties, falling from 61 per cent of local government income in 1979/80 to 53 per cent in 1982/3.[15] Councils were expected to make corresponding budget cuts rather than to carry on spending regardless, making up the revenue shortfall by taxing their residents more punitively. The second course, however, was the one generally adopted, increasing the tax burden on local ratepayers by 36 per cent above inflation between 1979 and 1983. The failure of many – especially Labour-controlled – councils to do as they were told forced the Department of the Environment (into whose remit local government fell) to chose between tolerating what it took to be gross irresponsibility as the price of local democracy or centralizing power in Whitehall. In 1981, with Michael Heseltine as secretary of state, it chose the latter course. Local councils were provided with a new block-grant formula and subjected to financial penalties if they then proceeded to spend more than Whitehall deemed appropriate for their circumstances.

The natural response to this was to point out that if town and city halls opted to tax their residents more highly than the voters felt reasonable for the services that they received then the councillors would face the consequences at the ballot box. That, after all, was the process by which central government was democratically held to account. However, in this respect central and local government were not comparable. By paying direct taxes (like income tax) and indirect taxes (like VAT), almost all voters contributed to some extent to funding the Treasury. By contrast, local government was funded on an entirely different basis, with only a minority of the electorate expected to shoulder the burden. Beyond the Treasury's grant, local government raised revenue through a tax on local businesses and a tax on householders called 'the rates'. As a tax on owning a home, the rates (calculated by estimating the 'rateable value' of a property) promoted the interests of those who rented and penalized those who took out a mortgage – a disincentive to home ownership that ran counter to the Conservatives' ambitions for a 'property-owning democracy'. It meant that out of an electorate of 40 million, only 18 million were ratepayers (though, in addition, many felt the consequences indirectly by being married to or living with a ratepayer). Particularly in areas of low home-ownership, (usually Labour) councils could set large rate increases without seriously fearing the effects of the ratepayers' wrath at election time: Sheffield's Labour group, for instance, was able to remain in power despite raising the rates by 41 per cent in 1980 and 37 per cent in 1981.[16] While nationally about half of the rates revenue came from the local business rate, in inner-city areas the number of homeowners was below average, ensuring that businesses there were contributing as much as three quarters of the revenue raised by the council. The resulting burden risked driving shops and companies either out of business or out of the area, worsening unemployment in already deprived areas.[17]

Although no lover of the rates, Thatcher came to power reluctant to initiate a fundamental overhaul of the system. In 1981, a green paper from the Department of the Environment examined three alternatives – a sales tax, a local income tax and a poll tax – without endorsing any of them. There were clear arguments against replicating the same fiscal systems that existed at a national level. A locally levied sales tax no longer appeared such an attractive option given the doubling of VAT, and might ultimately prove a breach of European law. Instituting a local income tax on top of a national income tax was bureaucratically difficult, because Inland Revenue data was not aligned with the record of home addresses in the electoral register. It would have simplified matters if, instead of running the same tax twice over, the Treasury were merely to increase the national income tax rate and to pass on the additional revenue to local authorities. But to do so would separate totally town hall accountability from revenue-raising. In any case, the Conservatives were committed to reducing income tax, not augmenting it. This therefore left the untried option, the poll tax, which – because everyone would have to pay it – would surely ensure maximum accountability for the leviers of the tax. As an idea, though, the green paper struggled to take it seriously. In England's history, ungraded poll taxes had only been tried twice before, in 1377 and 1380. Then, they had sparked the Peasants' Revolt and had been hastily abandoned.* A flat-rate tax on every adult, taking no account of the financial means of the payer, ran against the philosophical grain of three hundred years of fiscal policy and, more to the point, seemed essentially unfair. The debate appeared settled when in 1983 the Department of the Environment issued a white paper defending the retention of the rates, because 'they are well understood, cheap to collect and very difficult to evade'.[18]

Because of the unattractiveness of the alternatives, the rates might have survived without more than superficial tampering, but for two factors that caused a rethink. The first was the provocation provided by those Labour-controlled councils that deliberately flouted Whitehall's mechanisms for keeping their spending in check. The second was the panic spread by the Scottish Conservative Party, whose determined advocacy of a replacement for the rates forced the matter back to the forefront of Cabinet discussions.

The penalties imposed on councils deemed to be overspending met with some success, but failed to rein in the most determined from continuing to

---

* Seventeenth-century poll taxes were of a different nature because their rate was steeply graded according to the social rank of the payer. Even with this modification, they proved deeply unpopular and were replaced by property taxes.

fund their budget deficits through ever higher rate rises. To counter this, the Rates Act 1984 empowered Whitehall to set a legal 'cap' on rate rises. This remarkable infringement upon the autonomy of local government took effect the following year with the capping of eighteen councils, sixteen of which were Labour-controlled. But they did not submit quietly. Emboldened by the example of Liverpool city council, where the Trotskyite Militant Tendency held sway on the ruling Labour group, the sixteen councils – which included the Greater London Council, led by Ken Livingstone; Islington, led by Margaret Hodge; Lambeth, led by Ted Knight; and Sheffield, led by David Blunkett – announced that if they were not to be free to determine the size of their own budgets then they would set no rate at all. By deliberately abdicating their legal responsibilities in this way they would leave central government with little option but to step in and run local services directly, or see the these inner cities descend into chaos.

Being illegal, the tactic was risky and pitched the councils against their party's leadership since Kinnock, greatly alarmed by the destabilizing influence of the Militant Tendency, which he described as 'a maggot in the body of the party', was as determined as Thatcher to see the hard left's challenge basted. The result was bitter internal feuding among rival Labour factions and the crumbling of resistance amid demonstrations, sit-ins and internecine denunciations. By the end of May 1985, only Camden, Lambeth and Liverpool were still refusing to set a rate. Eventually, they set budgets well above the cap. Unable legally to meet its liabilities, and regarding looming bankruptcy as a valuable political manoeuvre, Liverpool city council dispatched statutory ninety-day redundancy notices to its thirty-one thousand staff, hand-delivered by shop stewards conveyed in thirty hired taxis. The tactic was designed to raise the stakes and to mobilize Liverpool for all-out civil disobedience against the government. Instead, it stirred Kinnock into action.

The previous year, the Labour conference had mandated the party to support the illegal no-rate-fixing rebellion, but in front of the assembled delegates in October 1985 Kinnock used the deteriorating situation in Liverpool to turn on its council's antics, thundering out against:

> the grotesque chaos of a Labour council – a *Labour* council – hiring taxis to scuttle round the city handing out redundancy notices to its own workers. I am telling you, no matter how entertaining, how fulfilling to short-term egos – [heckling] I'm telling you and you'll listen – I'm telling you, you can't play politics with people's jobs and with people's services.

At this, Liverpool's deputy leader, Derek Hatton, who was in the hall, started shouting 'liar! liar!' at his party leader, and booing rang out from a section of the audience. But as Kinnock kept going, raising his voice above the jeers, others found the courage of his convictions and started clapping and then cheering. It was more than a moment of political theatre, it was a public declaration that a *putsch* was being launched, for Militant, also known as the Revolutionary Socialist League, was a tightly disciplined force which had infiltrated not just constituency parties and local councils but trade unions too, and employed more full-time organizers than did the Labour Party. For his part, Hatton – surrounded by his personal bodyguards – seemed unconcerned by the approaching Night of the Long Knives but, as he would soon discover, Militant's hold on power rested upon its ability to operate within the Labour Party. After a series of hearings, in 1986 Hatton was among a number of Militant operatives expelled from the party (though after 1987 four Militant-supporting Labour MPs were returned to Parliament).[*]

Meanwhile, to stave off the shutdown of all its services, Liverpool adopted the un-Trotskyite contingency of turning to Swiss banks for emergency credit. There, and in the other flashpoints of civic insurrection, the revolt was finally brought to heel after the councillors who had delayed setting a rate were adjudged by the district auditor to be engaging in professional misconduct, given a five-year disqualification from standing for office and deemed personally liable for the interest surcharge. They had given the government a fright all the same, the prime minister having chaired a special committee over the winter of 1985/6 to work out what to do if the councils went bankrupt. The conclusion was that a breakdown into violence was likely and that the commissioners the government would then appoint to run the cities would need the protection of the police and armed forces. 'As we considered the various candidates,' the minister responsible, Kenneth Baker, later admitted, 'the shortlist became shorter and shorter and actually narrowed down to just one person.'[19] If more than one council had kept up the insurrection, the government would have been in trouble.

The climbdown by the rebel authorities represented only a qualified victory for Downing Street. It might have been comforting to imagine that the offending councils were being successfully compelled to adopt fiscal and budgetary discipline, but evidence duly built up that they were, in fact, turning to increasingly complicated accounting devices to hide their real priorities. Far from being concluded, the power struggle between local and central government was poised to enter a more intensive phase. In April 1986, local government was reorganized, with the abolition of the six metropolitan counties[†] and the Greater London Council. With the GLC's

---

[*] Ronnie Campbell (Blyth Valley), Terry Fields (Liverpool Broadgreen), Dave Nellist (Coventry South East) and Pat Wall (Bradford North).

[†] Greater Manchester, Merseyside, South Yorkshire, Tyne and Wear, West Midlands and West Yorkshire.

former powers over transport, planning and the fire and police services transferred to non-elected boards representing the constituent borough councils, the capital thus found itself in the peculiar position of being one of the world's greatest cities but without an elected city administration. The removal of this overarching tier of metropolitan democracy fitted in with Whitehall's growing conviction that quasi-autonomous non-governmental organizations (quangos) could make a better job of strategic planning and encouraging investment than another layer of elected politicians. The experience of Heseltine's Development Corporations for Merseyside and London Docklands seemed even to suggest that urban regeneration was made easier without the active intrusion of local democracy. Certainly, the disbandment of the six metropolitan counties caused noticeably little stir. Created as recently as 1974, they lacked a historic sense of identity, straddling communities that often felt themselves distinct from one another, and those of their powers that did not transfer to quangos were handed back to the old town and city corporations which more naturally appealed to local loyalties. The dismemberment of the GLC was different, since it was London itself that lost its unified democratic assembly. Opinion polls suggested that the GLC's abolition was opposed by three quarters of Londoners and in the London borough elections of May 1986 the Conservatives were severely punished.

If the government imagined that removing Ken Livingstone's GLC power base would rid the capital of a leader who combined sneering at the royal family with providing a platform for Sinn Fein, then they were to be speedily disabused since there were plenty of other municipal socialists ready to carry on the struggle. Lambeth council ruled that none of its publications could include the 'discriminatory' word 'family', though it did place advertisements making it clear that some senior council jobs were only open to black applicants. It also caused considerable irritation by proposing to spend £5 million renaming twenty-eight parks and civic buildings after black activists (Streatham Pool was to be renamed the Mangaliso Sobukwe Pool and Brockwell Park rechristened Zephania Mothopeng Park). Haringey council launched courses in homosexuality for nursery school children. Brent council began recruiting 180 'race advisers' to sit at the back of classrooms monitoring the 'progress and attitudes' of teachers towards their ethnic minority pupils (there were considerably more anti-racism advisers in Brent's schools than there were schools) – all at a time when the borough's education budget was under pressure and senior teachers were resigning over what they claimed was a culture of politically motivated witch hunts.[20] *The Sun* fulminated against the agenda of the so-called 'loony left', colouring the litany by adding some provocations of its own. Yet the reality was that in these councils and elsewhere the Labour vote continued to hold up, the burden of funding the policies falling disproportionately on those least likely to benefit from them.

The government responded with a slew of legislative acts clipping and curtailing the areas over which local authorities enjoyed direct control. The introduction of compulsory competitive tendering forced town halls to award contracts through an auction in which private contractors were able to bid against 'in-house' council providers who had previously enjoyed a monopoly over service provision. The process extended from tendering for constructing and maintaining roads in 1980, to refuse collection, cleaning and catering eight years later. After 1980, council house tenants enjoyed the legal right to buy their own homes even where their local authority was ideologically opposed to selling them, while, after 1988, those who continued to rent were given the right to transfer the management of their estates from the council to a not-for-profit housing association, if they so chose.*
Until the passage of Kenneth Baker's Education Reform Act 1988, local authorities' control of the state schools in their area extended to staff appointments and the allocation of resources within schools. Baker's act gave heads and school governors the right to manage how their budget allocation was spent and to decide who to appoint. They even gained the right, if parents voted for it, to opt out of local authority control altogether, allowing them to run their own affairs, with funds provided directly and without interference from Whitehall, as 'grant-maintained' schools. There was no rush to embrace this freedom, with only fifty schools (out of twenty-four thousand) choosing to do so by the end of 1990.[21] Yet although grant-maintained status was abolished by Tony Blair's government in 1997, it was resurrected three years later in the guise of academy schools. Two other facets of Baker's act aimed directly to undermine left-wing and 'trendy' priorities in the classroom. One was the abolition of the Inner London Education Authority (ILEA) which, under Tony Benn's former adviser, Frances Morrell, had particularly prioritized race and gender equality issues and championed such notions as teaching the children of immigrants in their 'mother tongue' rather than English. Its competences were devolved to borough level. The other change was the institution of a national curriculum to be taught in all schools, prescriptive in nature and designed to ensure the basics of English, maths and science predominated in the classroom, with compulsory testing at the ages of seven, eleven and fourteen. A national curriculum along these lines would permit easier comparisons to be made between succeeding and failing schools, with visits by inspectors and the collation and publication of comparative statistics. With these 'league tables' parents could supposedly make a more informed choice about where to send their children – schools

---

* See p. 421.

now being obliged to enrol all applicants unless they were already full. Establishing a national curriculum and the mechanisms to go with it was a protracted process, however, and it was not until 1992 that the curriculum and the accompanying league tables were launched.

Meanwhile, the government pushed ahead with devising a mechanism it hoped would spread more widely the financial burden of Labour's remaining town hall priorities and, in the process, make the Labour spendthrifts unelectable. The lever would be gradually to replace the rates with a poll tax, paid by every adult regardless of circumstances (save for the disabled, who would be exempted). It was bizarre that a proposal comprehensively dismissed in the Department of the Environment's white paper as recently as 1983 should have been resurrected so swiftly, but the catalyst for the volte-face came from the Scottish Tories. Rates were calculated by valuing properties and assessing their rentable value. Home improvements and rising house prices therefore served to put up the rates, and for this reason no revaluation of English and Welsh properties had been carried out since 1973. In Scotland, however, it was a legal requirement for a revaluation to be held by 1985 (the last one having taken place in 1978), and there was widespread outrage among middle-class Scots as the new tax demands arrived; in Edinburgh the rates increased overnight by 40 per cent.[22] Such was the sulphuric mood against the rate rises at the Scottish Conservatives' conference in May 1985 that it convinced the Scottish secretary, George Younger, that the system should be replaced with a poll tax. Similarly shaken by the extent of anti-rates feeling was the deputy prime minister, Willie Whitelaw, when he attended a meeting in the affluent Glasgow suburb of Bearsden. He promptly went to see Thatcher and told her something must be done. That Whitelaw's opinions tended to be guided by a perceptive instinct for the popular mood, rather than ideological zeal, made his judgement of particular value to the prime minister. Days later, a Cabinet committee began considering the problem and in October came out in favour of the poll tax. What was more, if the new system was good enough for Scotland it was presumably good enough for England and Wales too (though not for Northern Ireland, which remained immune from the reform). After all, a revaluation could not be postponed forever south of Berwick-upon-Tweed, and the longer it was put off the worse the English and Welsh rates rise would eventually be. On 9 January 1986, the Cabinet approved in principle the poll tax. Officially it would be called the 'community charge', a term to which only its most dogged defenders stuck in the increasingly bitter debates that attended its introduction.

During the fateful Cabinet meeting of 9 January, spirited opposition to the new tax might have been mounted by the former environment secretary, Michael Heseltine. Unfortunately, the ownership of Westland helicopters preceded the poll tax discussion on that day's Cabinet agenda. Heseltine chose Westland's fate as the cause over which to storm out of 10 Downing Street and announce his resignation to startled BBC reporters on the pavement outside, thereby losing the opportunity to influence the debate over the poll tax. The other sceptic who might have taken a lead was Nigel Lawson. This was not surprising, given that its guiding principle that every able-bodied adult should make at least some contribution to the cost of local services ran counter to the Chancellor's efforts to remove the high marginal income tax rate on the low-paid by lifting the threshold so they would not pay any direct tax for the central government services they used. The one aspect of the new proposal that Lawson did support was the nationalization of the business rate, which would thenceforth be fixed centrally and not at the whim of local councillors. It was the change to how residents would be taxed that, he warned, 'would be completely unworkable and politically catastrophic'.[23] However, he assumed its impracticality would become apparent before it was implemented, ensuring a U-turn and a proper examination of his own counter-proposal (which resembled the council tax that was eventually introduced in 1993). His assumption was wrong because once the Cabinet's approval had been secured for the poll tax it gathered its own momentum.

What was not true was the notion that the new tax was the idea of a right-wing cabal. Although the free-market think tank the Adam Smith Institute produced a paper advocating a poll tax,* this ran alongside the proposal being drawn up by government ministers rather than directly inspiring it. The two ministers most responsible for devising the tax were Kenneth Baker and William Waldegrave, who came, respectively, from the centre and centre-left of the party, while the early enthusiast George Younger leaned towards the 'wet' wing of the Cabinet. Of the two environment secretaries responsible for the later stages of the policy, Nicholas Ridley was a 'dry' and Chris Patten – though never a great enthusiast – was a 'wet'. Blame for the poll tax thus crossed the Tories' ideological divide, and far from being bounced into agreeing a policy they scarcely understood, the rest of the Cabinet had ample time to register any doubts. It was, as Lawson pointed out, the product of 'no less than two and a half years of intensive ministerial discussion . . . Nor is it true that ministers were uninformed about how the tax would work in practice.'[24] They were given a full briefing at a conference held at Chequers on 31 March 1985, during which none of them raised substantive objections; nor did they do so in the months thereafter while the detail was picked over in Cabinet committee. A further three years elapsed before the poll tax was implemented in Scotland, and four years before it came in in England

---

* Douglas Mason, *Revising the Rating System* (Adam Smith Institute, 1985).

and Wales, during which time no Cabinet rebellion manifested itself beyond demands for greater 'transitional' relief grants from the Treasury to soften its impact. The responsibility was collective.

The original intention was to introduce the poll tax gradually, starting at around £50 per head, alongside the rates, with the new tax only incrementally supplanting the old one over a ten-year period, or more. The argument for this gradual introduction was that it would soften the blow of the poll tax's launch and ensure that while the rates were slowly run down those owning large houses would still make proportionately larger contributions. Given that there were now millions of voters who, having never been ratepayers, were being lumbered with a new tax for the first time in their lives, there was much to be said for placing the burden upon them gradually. But running a dual system was cumbersome and expensive to administer. Also, gradual introduction would undermine the philosophical principle underpinning the poll tax – that it would make immediately transparent to all local electors the full cost of their council's budget. It was these arguments that triumphed when the Scottish legislation was framed, thereby ensuring that the poll tax would be introduced in one big bang rather than in stages. Having determined this approach for the Scots, it followed that the same should apply to the English and the Welsh. In an effort to make it seem fairer, Heseltine's lieutenant, Michael Mates, introduced an amendment in April 1988 that would have created three payment bands for the poll tax, equating to higher and standard rate income tax payers and those below the income tax threshold. With thirty-eight Tory MPs supporting the amendment and a further thirteen abstaining, Mates secured the largest Conservative back-bench rebellion of the Thatcher years, though it was still twenty-five votes short of carrying the day. The government preferred not to address income inequality through tax banding (which would create high marginal rates of tax for those whose earnings only just took them into a higher band), but rather to insist that, although all adults would have to pay it, there would be an 80 per cent rebate for the unemployed and those on income support (whose benefits would be increased to take account of the cost). Additionally, Kenneth Baker wanted to exclude students altogether. However, he was overruled and they, too, were expected to stump up 20 per cent of the full charge. This was consistent with the guiding objective that every adult should have to pay at least something for council services, but it was an error nonetheless. Students transpired to be among the most vociferous opponents of the tax, and their often peripatetic lodging arrangements made it especially difficult to track them down when they defaulted on payment.

The poll tax was introduced in Scotland on April Fools' Day 1989, a year before England and Wales, at the particular insistence of Younger's successor at the Scottish Office, Malcolm Rifkind, who miscalculated that the promise to abolish the rates would be a vote-winner north of the border.[25] Much as the process was a case of the Scottish tail wagging the English dog, it quickly became apparent that the early introduction in Scotland was widely seen as evidence that the English were using the Scots as guinea-pigs to test the new tax before it was imposed down south. Certainly, the Scottish experience offered little cheer for the tax's Sassenach supporters. Not only did eight of Scotland's eleven regions set a poll tax above the Treasury's estimate, but the level of public opposition was especially worrying. Kinnock's opposition to law-breaking ceded the initiative for a mass non-payment campaign to the SNP and the Militant Tendency, marshalled by the charismatic firebrand Tommy Sheridan – with the SNP's initial call for one hundred thousand Scots to take a principled 'Can Pay, Won't Pay' stance seamlessly followed by an alternative 'Can't Pay, Won't Pay' campaign, alongside Militant's slogan 'It's better to break the law than break the poor'. Six months after its introduction, 15 per cent of Scots had not paid the tax, and far from seeing their fortunes reviving, the Scottish Conservatives' support was ebbing further.

The government was in a hole of its own making. It was not too late to take cognizance of the inherent problems exposed by the launch in Scotland and to scrap, or at least postpone, the poll tax's introduction in England and Wales. But doing so would have confirmed Scots' suspicions that they were indeed being used as a laboratory by a party whose support came disproportionately from southern England. The second problem was the attitude of the prime minister, who had boasted to her backbenchers in July 1987 that the poll tax was the 'flagship of the Thatcher fleet' and who, when it came to U-turns, was still not for turning.[26] It may not have been her idea, but she had adopted it as an article of faith and getting her to back down appeared beyond the courage or ability of anyone in her Cabinet. Yet even those government ministers like Alan Clark who remained loyal to her and saw no principled objection to the tax, recognized that it would fail in practice. Those who 'overload local authority expenditure', Clark lamented in his diary, the 'slobs, yobs, drifters, junkies, free-loaders, claimants, and criminals on day-release', would refuse to pay it, while 'as usual the burden will fall on the thrifty, the prudent, the responsible, those "of fixed address", who patiently support society and the follies of the chattering class'.[27] Heseltine's foreboding proved especially prescient when, during the debate on the legislation's second reading, in December 1987, he suggested that it would not hold local government to account because popular outrage would instead be focused on the iniquity of a tax that presumed equality between 'the slum dweller and the landed aristocrat', with the blame falling on those in central government responsible for its introduction. It would, he prophesied, become known as 'the Tory tax'.[28] And as its implementation in England drew nearer, the scale of the iniquity became evident. The *Guardian* pointed out that, having previously paid £10,255 per year in rates, the Duke of Westminster would now be asked for £417, the same as his housekeeper and chauffeur.

The environment secretary, Chris Patten, forecast that so long as councils kept their spending close to their Whitehall-set targets, the average poll tax in England would be £278. Among the Conservatives' 'flagship' boroughs, Wandsworth set it at £148 and Westminster at £195, but these were the exceptions. The average levy proved to be £360.[29] On 31 March 1990, the day before the poll tax's introduction in England and Wales, the All-Britain Anti-Poll Tax Federation organized protest rallies in Edinburgh and London. Nearly one hundred thousand marchers joined the London rally and though police blocked the entrance to Downing Street they moved on to Trafalgar Square, where Tony Benn addressed them. This main rally ended peacefully, but a hard core of about three thousand stayed on to trade provocations with the police, who, in the absence of Tories, became the surrogate target for abuse, with bottles, scaffolding poles and other projectiles hurled at them. Wielding batons, the police responded with mounted charges, with the aim of dispersing a mob whose fury had turned to looting shops, smashing cars, setting street furniture ablaze and assaulting the South African embassy. The disorder spread to Soho and Covent Garden, with plumes of smoke rising from the heart of the capital, and by the evening's end there were 339 arrests, 250 incidents of damage to property, 374 injuries to police, eighty-six injuries to protesters and the public, and twenty injuries to police horses.[30]

The behaviour of those bent on violence was easily condemned, but more concerning for the government was the scale of the opposition. Much as Militant Tendency was active in the All-Britain Anti-Poll Tax Federation, the strength of feeling went far beyond what could be stirred up by professional agitators. Opinion polls suggested that three quarters of the electorate opposed the tax, and Labour's lead over the Tories stretched towards 24 per cent.[31] While rural and suburban England overwhelmingly paid the tax, the shortfalls from inner-city areas were noticeable. In Scotland, the situation was worsening. There, by the autumn of 1991, 23 per cent of the previous financial year's poll tax had not been collected, and 13 per cent was still outstanding from 1989/90.[32] While the numbers sent to jail for non-payment were small (though they included the Militant-supporting Labour MP Terry Fields), it was clear that the implicit social contract between government and people was being undermined by this level of civil disobedience.

The response was to throw Treasury money at the problem in the guise of 'transitional relief', in an effort to keep down the size of poll tax demands. Between 1989 and 1993, £20 billion from national taxes was diverted (in addition to the annual central grant) to fund local government and thereby keep down poll tax bills. This money was not all net cost to the public, since much of it would otherwise have been raised directly from the rates, but it completely undermined the poll tax's rationale. Instead of encouraging voter pressure on local councils to cut their spending, the new tax induced central government to shoulder a larger share of the cost. These Treasury subsidies – equating to increasing the basic rate of income tax by 4 per cent – ensured that the poll tax turned out to be a remarkably non-transparent measure of town hall efficiency and value for money. The poll tax also created costs that could not be shifted between Whitehall and town hall fiscal systems and that had to be written off as losses. Setting up, implementing and then scrapping the tax cost at least £1.5 billion. By the time it was replaced by the council tax in 1993, up to £2.5 billion remained uncollected – in contrast to the near-total collection rate previously achieved for the rates. Some of this sum was never recouped and an unknown number of individuals, estimated at 700,000, absented themselves from the electoral register in the belief that losing the right to vote was a worthwhile price to pay for escaping the poll tax.[33]

In her memoirs, Thatcher convinced herself that 'given time, it would have been seen as one of the most far-reaching and beneficial reforms ever made in the working of local government'.[34] In 1993, at the moment of its demise, the minister who had introduced the poll tax in England and Wales concluded otherwise. 'It was,' Chris Patten admitted, 'fundamentally flawed and politically incredible. I guess it was the single most unpopular policy any government has introduced since the war.'[35]

The Diet of Brussels

The issue that directly triggered the fall of Thatcher was not the poll tax but the European Community.* The drama had two sub-plots. The first concerned whether the British economy could be better managed if sterling joined the Exchange Rate Mechanism (ERM) of the European Monetary System. This intrigue pitted Chancellor against prime minister and resulted first in Lawson's resignation and then in Thatcher's capitulation to John Major, his successor at the Treasury, when he insisted that ERM entry could be deferred no longer. Though it seemed like a victory for Major at the time, ultimately it was a decision that ended up damaging his credibility far more than it did that of Thatcher. Much as it was a sign of her weakening

---

*The European Community was not renamed the European Union until 1993.

dominance, her grudging submission to conventional wisdom on the subject could have bought her short-term political capital but for the interweaving of the second sub-plot. This concerned not just the technicalities of an acceptable level of exchange rate volatility but the destiny of the nation. When Thatcher made it clear that she did not believe – or no longer believed – that the Treaty of Rome's promise of 'ever-closer union' within the European Community remained the goal of Her Majesty's government, she caused the resignation of her deputy prime minister, Sir Geoffrey Howe, in circumstances that goaded Michael Heseltine into duelling with her for the leadership of the party and inflicting a wound that proved mortal.

To Thatcher, the two sub-plots had long been inseparable. The ERM was established in 1979 to stabilize its member currencies by fixing their value (within narrow bands of movement) against the continent's leading currency, the West German Deutschmark. Back then, the prospect that this mechanism would hasten the replacement of Western European currencies with a single currency remained a vague aspiration. Nevertheless, sterling did not join and, despite the pound's subsequent volatility, the possibility of it being constrained within the corset of the ERM remained a technical one which rarely pushed itself to the forefront of public debate before 1985. It was unsurprising that Thatcher was no enthusiast. The ERM was a mechanism designed to make sure that interest rate policy was orchestrated towards keeping the value of the currency close to the value politicians wished to hold it at, whereas, as Thatcher assured the House of Commons in March 1988, 'there is no way in which one can buck the market'.[36] It was therefore fundamentally in conflict with her economic principles. What was more, in June 1988 the European Community's heads of government met at Hanover and (reluctantly in Thatcher's case) agreed to let the president of the European Commission, Jacques Delors, chair a committee looking into how European economic and monetary union (EMU) might be achieved. This gave substance to Thatcher's fear that the ERM truly was a ramp leading to the abolition of sterling. Thinking she was fussing unnecessarily, Lawson refused to believe that the two were necessarily entwined. He did not wish to replace the pound with the ecu (as the accounting unit that would become the euro was then called), but did believe that ERM membership would give sterling much-needed stability. In the process, it would enhance the UK's bargaining power if decisions about moving towards a European currency were eventually to be made. The battle between Chancellor and prime minister was thus between two Eurosceptics, though Lawson was assisted in the fight by those, like Sir Geoffrey Howe, who would emerge as Euro-enthusiasts and who shared Thatcher's analysis that the ERM would probably lead to a single currency, while dismissing her fears that this was necessarily a bad thing.

Exactly when the prime minister became a Eurosceptic* is not easily pin-pointed, not least because the changing role and aspirations of the European Community during the seventies and eighties altered the terms in which the debate was framed. Without demonstrating Edward Heath's ideological zeal, Thatcher had unhesitatingly campaigned for the UK to remain in the EEC (as it then was) in the referendum of 1975, appearing to see the 'Common Market' firstly as an economic and political adhesive to keep NATO's Western European countries together in the face of the communist threat from the Warsaw Pact, and secondly as the creator of treaty obligations that would prevent a future Labour government from establishing a socialist siege economy through high tariff barriers against Britain's nearest trading neighbours. Beyond this, her enthusiasm was muted. During the 1979 elections to the European Parliament, she stated her opposition to a 'fully fledged federal union' and 'a new super-state' – remote though those possibilities then seemed. Preferring to focus on practicalities, her Brussels diplomacy during her first term was dominated by a bruising and tenaciously fought battle (the substance of which she won) to limit the scale of the UK's otherwise dispro-portionately large contribution to the Community's budget.

Most tellingly of all, unlike many of her Tory colleagues – or, indeed, a large swathe of those in public life generally – Thatcher never demonstrated personal 'European' credentials. Being no great lover of holidays, travel was not the means through which she broadened her mind. Her cultural interests and social life were directed towards the 'Anglosphere', and the Anglo-American relationship in particular, rather than to friendships with 'continentals'. Following Gorbachev's rise to power in 1985, she developed a better rapport with the general secretary of the Communist Party of the Soviet Union than with any leader from the European Community. With West Germany's Chancellor, Helmut Kohl, there was no warmth. Italy changed its prime minister ten times during Thatcher's tenure in Downing Street and, as far as London was concerned, whoever was in office in Rome was usually irrelevant anyway. And while she was thankful for François Mitterrand's support during the Falklands War and content to establish with him the physical bonding of the *entente cordiale* through the construction of the Channel Tunnel (arguably a more practical continental commitment than was achieved by any of her three immediate successors in Downing Street), she was never likely to regard the French president or the philo-sophical traditions he represented as being in step with her own attitudes.

---

* The term is used here anachronistically, since although the *Oxford English Dictionary* has found a reference from 1985, it did not come into general use until the 1990s. There was no exactly comparable name in the 1970s and 1980s; the term 'anti-marketeer' (i.e. anti–Common Market) was used to describe outright opponents of EEC membership, but was hardly an apt description for someone of Thatcher's free-trading beliefs.

Obliged to attend bicentenary of the fall of the Bastille in July 1989, she bridled at the suggestion that the French Revolution represented the birth of Western liberty. As she reminded readers of *Le Monde*, Britons had gained their Bill of Rights a hundred years earlier and without recourse to the guillotine.

It was not Mitterrand but his former finance minister who became Thatcher's European bête noir. On 6 July 1988, the president of the European Commission, Jacques Delors, delivered a speech to the European Parliament in which he boasted that within ten years '80 percent of laws affecting the economy and social policy would be passed at a European and not a national level'.[37] On 8 September, Delors addressed the TUC conference in Bournemouth, where he received a standing ovation for calling upon trade unionists to see Brussels as their salvation and the defender of workers' rights against the free market. It was a sign that British politics was going through a major realignment, for, like the union delegates, the Parliamentary Labour Party was reversing its prejudices. Having fought the 1983 general election promising to take the UK out of the European Community, and going to the 1987 polls with a manifesto that papered over the issue by only referring to the Community in passing, it now saw both short-term opportunity and long-term advantage in being less critical of Brussels. The more that the Conservative leader riled against European integration, the less critical of the process became the Labour leader (and future European commissioner), with only Bryan Gould among Kinnock's senior front-bench colleagues continuing to resist conversion.

On 20 September 1988, two weeks after Delors's mission to Bournemouth and while he was busy with his committee devising the route to economic and monetary union, Thatcher delivered her riposte. A speaking engagement at the College of Europe in Bruges was the sort of occasion for which platitudes were usually deemed appropriate and the early drafts suggested by the Foreign Office contained all the usual *communitaire* genuflections. The problem was that the prime minister was no longer in the mood for this sort of self-effacement and duly worked with her like-minded private secretary for foreign affairs, Charles Powell, to craft arguably the single most historically significant speech of her premiership. Among sections of the speech cut out was Howe's suggested line: 'A stronger Europe does not mean the creation of a new Euro super-state but does, has and will require the sacrifice of political independence and the rights of national parliaments.'[38] The Foreign Office's 'interference and provocation', noted the trade minister, Alan Clark, who saw the draft script, 'turned a relatively minor ceremonial chore into what could now well be a milestone in redefining our position towards the Community'.[39] 'Europe is not the creation of the Treaty of Rome. Nor is the European idea the property of any group or institution,' Thatcher duly pointed out to the dignitaries, with a hint of the unabashed effrontery that Martin Luther had brought to his audience with the Emperor Charles V. To Thatcher, it was essential to wrest from the Commission the legitimacy to speak for the peoples of a continent. Given that the Berlin Wall remained firmly in situ, she showed foresightedness in holding up the dream not of a deeper but a wider Europe, which looked out to the peoples artificially cut off from it by the Iron Curtain. This led on to her main complaint about 'power . . . centralized in Brussels' and decisions 'taken by an appointed bureaucracy', since:

> it is ironic that just when those countries such as the Soviet Union, which have tried to run everything from the centre, are learning that success depends on dispersing power and decisions away from the centre, there are some in the Community who seem to want to move in the opposite direction. We have not successfully rolled back the frontiers of the state in Britain, only to see them reimposed at a European level with a European super-state exercising a new dominance from Brussels.[40]

The speech galvanized both sides. Inspired by its clarion call, an Oxford undergraduate, Patrick Robertson, founded the Bruges Group in February 1989, proceeding to attract mostly right-leaning politicians and academics including the historian Norman Stone and the philosopher Roger Scruton to the first of a new generation of Eurosceptic think tanks. But those perturbed by the Bruges speech were not just members of the 'appointed bureaucracy' in Brussels. They included diplomats and leaders of other member states,[41] and some of the prime minister's colleagues. Howe was appalled at the speech's impact, since he regarded its depiction of the Community's ambitions as veering 'between caricature and misunderstanding', leaving him to conclude in his memoirs that 'for Margaret the Bruges speech represented, subconsciously at least, her escape from the collective responsibility of her days in the Heath Cabinet'.[42]

If Thatcher was nervous about the path that Delors was paving towards a federal Europe, it was only with difficulty that she could accept that she had, even if inadvertently, provided him with the materials to undertake his task. At the time of his appointment to Brussels in 1985 she had preferred him to the alternative candidate, another French – but less effectual – socialist. As much as any European leader, it was Thatcher who lent crucial support to Delors's vision of a Community enjoying within its borders the free movement of goods, services, capital and people. This was the creation of the 'single market', and it represented the aspect of European integration that appeared to be not just compatible with Thatcherism but its triumph *sans frontières*. Much of the drafting to eliminate the internal barriers was done by

Thatcher's former trade secretary, Lord Cockfield, whom she dispatched to Brussels as commissioner for competition policy in 1984. Having removed, or being in the course of removing, regulatory restrictions within the British economy, she naturally wished to see a level playing field for Britons, their money and their products in the European market. It was, after all, vexing for her to have to endure lectures on being a good European from Mitterrand, who continued to barricade the French economy behind exchange controls that restricted the free flow of capital across France's borders, when the UK had led the way in abolishing this form of financial protectionism in 1979. The Single European Act directed that a European market without any internal restrictions would be established by 1992. Thatcher comforted herself that this was a free trade measure in British commercial interests, which included only an ambiguous reference to economic and monetary union and no firm commitment to include harmonization of national policies in other areas, like border controls and taxation, which she continued to regard as coming under the rightful jurisdiction of nation states. At Westminster, the legislation was passed, with remarkably little discussion, on a three-line whip. Yet in order to disable national obstructionism, it scrapped member states' vetoes by introducing qualified majority voting across a swathe of regulatory matters, establishing the legal framework within which European integration could gather pace unchecked.

The route map for where this integration was leading was clearly laid out by the publication in April 1989 of the Delors report, which detailed the European Commission's three-step approach to economic and monetary union: stage one, the removal of the remaining capital controls between member states by 1 July 1990; stage two, the independence of central banks from their governments and greater monetary convergence by 1 January 1994; and stage three, the replacement of national currencies with a new single currency, managed by a European Central Bank, from 1 January 1999. For Thatcher, the problem was that she was the only significant voice among Community heads of government who had doubts about stage two and was openly hostile to stage three. The headline from each successive meeting of the European Council was that she – and therefore Britain – was isolated. Her refusal to compromise on principles made her reluctant to make concessions on the details that underlay them. Lawson later argued that this tone 'was foolish and threw away many opportunities to build alliances', with the result that 'by 1989 she had become the Community's great unifying force'.[43] Her negative tone also animated the Conservatives' campaign for the European Parliament elections in June 1989, in which party headquarters overruled the pro-*communitaire* beliefs of most of its MEPs by running adverts featuring a plate of sprouts and the contrived slogan 'Stay at home on 15 June and you'll live on a diet of Brussels'. Gaining thirteen seats at the

Merchant Ivory Productions turned repressed emotions into cinematic art. In *A Room With a View* Julian Sands and Helena Bonham Carter briefly forget themselves under the Tuscan sun.

The British film industry's depth of talent and dearth of money was exemplified in the almost axed cult classic, *Withnail & I.*

Thatcher and her Cabinet at their 1984 party conference hours after surviving the IRA's mass assassination attempt. Absent from the platform is the Trade and Industry Secretary, Norman Tebbit, who had to be pulled from the wreckage of Brighton's Grand Hotel.

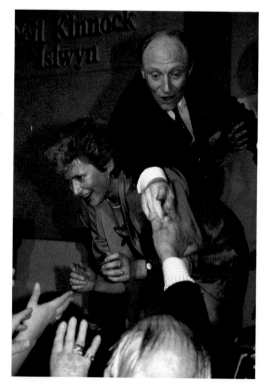

Leaning over his wife Glenys, Neil Kinnock tries to extend Labour's reach.

Liverpool city council's Derek Hatton and the Militant Tendency led the left's dual assault on Tory 'rate-capping' and Kinnock's leadership. At one stage, Militant employed more full-time organizers than the Labour Party.

The poll tax was met with rioting in Trafalgar Square. It ended up, in the verdict of the minister charged with its introduction, Chris Patten, as 'the single most unpopular policy any government has introduced since the war'.

Coates Wine Bar: Yuppies unwinding after a hard day's trading.

Heaven nightclub: A clubber unwinding during a hard night's raving.

expense of the Conservatives, Labour won the election. The Tories' performance (35 per cent of the vote against 37 per cent for Labour) was not especially poor for a mid-term government and the losses may have been primarily due to domestic politics, not least the looming poll tax, and the customary desire to record a protest in non-Westminster elections (the Green Party won 15 per cent of the vote). Regardless, Tory pro-European integrationists interpreted it as evidence of a popular yearning for a more positive attitude towards Brussels, even though only 36 per cent of the electorate troubled to vote.

None was more certain of this interpretation than the Foreign Secretary, Sir Geoffrey Howe. 'The party,' he suggested in his memoirs, 'was effectively being split by the defection of its own leader.'[44] On 20 June, Lawson and Howe jointly went to see Thatcher in her office to impress upon her the urgency of showing positive intent by letting sterling join the ERM. Once they had gone, she consulted her personal economics adviser, Sir Alan Walters, who drew up tough conditions as a prerequisite for joining, including the UK's inflation rate descending to the average inside the ERM. In the meantime, instead of consulting Lawson or Howe on the line to adopt in the coming Madrid summit of European leaders, where the Delors report was to be discussed, she turned to her personal entourage of Alan Walters, Charles Powell, Brian Griffiths and her press secretary, Bernard Ingham. A prime minister who no longer trusted the judgement of her Chancellor or Foreign Secretary was isolated indeed. On Sunday, 25 June, Howe and Lawson duly invited themselves to see her at Chequers just hours before she was due to fly to Madrid. They told her that unless she agreed to set a date for entry to the ERM, they would jointly resign. The threat was met with an awkward silence – one that continued on the flight out to Madrid, during which prime minister and Foreign Secretary addressed not a word to one another, the curtain across the gangway between them pointedly drawn throughout the journey. When the summit got under way the following morning, Howe was still in the dark as to what policy she would announce. In the event, she did just enough to keep her Foreign Secretary and Chancellor on board, by announcing her intention for sterling to join the ERM. But she did not set a date. A month later, on 24 July, she made a broad-ranging reshuffle of her Cabinet and removed Howe from the Foreign Office.

Howe was not expecting this reversal of fortune, even though his six years in the post had made him the longest-serving Foreign Secretary since Sir Edward Grey (1905–16). When the prime minister offered him the consolation of the office of either Home Secretary or Leader of the House, he went away to think about it and drafted a letter of resignation.[45] The subsequent history of the Conservative Party might have been very different if he had sent it. Instead, he put it aside and asked to be Leader of the House on condition he was also made deputy prime minister. This was an honorary position – as Thatcher's press secretary, Bernard Ingham, undiplomatically made clear – though Howe may have imagined it would give him the moderating influence that its last holder, Willie Whitelaw, had enjoyed. In this he was mistaken. Despite coming from different wings of the party, Thatcher liked and admired Whitelaw. For Howe, she could no longer conceal an irritation that bordered dangerously on contempt. In his place at the Foreign Office, she installed John Major, who was not known to be an ideologue for European integration – or, indeed, for much else, though he had impressed in his one year of Cabinet experience as Chief Secretary to the Treasury. Thatcher complacently assumed – as she put it to Nick Ridley – that the new man was 'one of us'.[46]

She had made the other appointment that really mattered in May when Sir Alan Walters had resumed his duties as her economic adviser (a role he had previously filled between 1981 and 1983, before taking up positions in American academia and the World Bank). Lean and fit, despite his greying demeanour (he was going on sixty-three), he cut a very different figure from the commodious frame of the Chancellor. His background was different, too, for Walters's path to professorial distinction was an unusual one, being the son of a grocer's clerk who had grown up in a slum in Leicester in the thirties and had left school at fifteen to become an errand boy. This made him no less sure of his abilities: his work table resembled a monument to disorganization with papers piled high and haphazardly, but there was room on it for his coffee mug, emblazoned with the boast 'Quiet – Genius at Work'.[47] No victim of low self-esteem himself, it was perfectly understandable that Lawson did not want Walters marking his homework. What was more, their personal rivalry was made far worse by their disagreement on fundamental issues. Walters opposed not just ERM entry but also the clandestine methods by which Lawson had been endeavouring to replicate the mechanism's stabilizing effects through a policy of shadowing the Deutschmark – initially without Thatcher's knowledge and thereafter without her support.

Since 1986, the Chancellor's efforts had been directed towards fine-tuning sterling's exchange rate value at between DM2.80 and DM3.00, raising interest rates when the pound slipped below that band and lowering them when it rose above. During 1987, this meant cutting interest rates, a policy accentuated by a further rate cut following the 'Black Monday' stock market crash in October. This was a credit stimulus in the midst of an economic boom and it created an inflationary bubble. The most unambiguous success of the government's record, bringing inflation under control, was now imperilled. Inflation doubled during 1988 from 3.3 per cent to 6.8 per cent, forcing Lawson to reverse his interest rate policy. By the autumn of 1989, the British economy stood on the brink of a downturn, the housing market already falling, yet still Lawson found himself hiking up interest rates, his determination to keep sterling at around DM3.00 leading him to respond to a rate rise by the Bundesbank in Frankfurt by following suit, taking interest rates to 15 per cent. It was a policy that highlighted the limitations of politicians prioritizing a preconceived notion of an appropriate exchange rate at a value the markets thought wrong. To Lawson and his supporters, however, it did not prove that Thatcher was right that it was ultimately impossible to 'buck the market'. Rather, they calculated that market pressure would surely ease – allowing interest rates to fall – if sterling was formally locked into the ERM.

On 18 October 1989, the *Financial Times* drew attention to an article Walters had written in June the previous year (before he was reinstalled as the prime minister's adviser) for the *American Economist*, describing the ERM as 'half-baked' and Lawson's policy of shadowing the Deutschmark as a 'tragedy'. Sensing opportunity, the shadow Chancellor, John Smith, baited Lawson in the Commons on 24 October, choosing the moment to complete the Labour Party's transformation from wanting to leave the European Community to now being desperate to join the ERM. While Lawson endured the pantomime, Thatcher was away at a meeting of Commonwealth leaders in Malaysia, and when she returned Lawson demanded to see her. The meeting was a difficult one, with Lawson making it abundantly clear that he was not going to have his authority undermined by Walters and presenting the prime minister with a choice: either sack her adviser or lose her Chancellor. Thatcher seemed genuinely surprised by this ultimatum and begged him not to resign, though her refusal to do as he commanded gave him no option. Thus, on 26 October, Lawson followed through with his threat.

When Thatcher asked John Major to come and see her at Downing Street, he found her still having trouble coming to terms with Lawson's dramatic gesture, claiming: 'It's unnecessary. He's being silly.' 'I thought she was close to tears at one moment,' Major later wrote, 'and briefly took her hand.'[48] He may also have been thinking that his own future would be unenviable if Walters were to continue at the prime minister's side – though fortunately Walters recognized that this would undermine Lawson's successor and almost immediately announced that he, too, was resigning, despite Thatcher's entreaties to him to stay. Thus, after only three months at the Foreign Office, the 46-year-old Major moved to the Treasury. In appointing him, Thatcher did not ask what he thought of the ERM.[49]

Scrapping the Iron Lady

Lawson was not the first member of the Thatcher Cabinet to conclude he could no longer work with her. She had survived what could have been a serious challenge to her Downing Street tenure in January 1986 when the defence secretary, Michael Heseltine, walked out of her Cabinet. The issue was the future ownership of the troubled Somerset-based helicopter manufacturer Westland, where the board and shareholders were seeking salvation from the American firm Sikorsky, but Heseltine was determined to prevent its sale other than to a European consortium. On the face of it, it was hardly an obvious cause for someone of Heseltine's evident personal ambition to sacrifice his Cabinet career over, and Westland's subsequent return to financial health with Sikorsky suggested that its management had a shrewder notion of what was good for their company than the defence secretary. Heseltine, however, made Thatcher's autocratic handling of the matter the reason for his departure. This sparring between strong personalities turned into a political crisis when the trade and industry secretary, Leon Brittan, took the blame for a civil servant in his department who had leaked a letter from the solicitor general disputing Heseltine's case. Those who believed the prime minister was directly, or implicitly, engaged in the leak hoped the questioning of her personal probity would bring about her downfall. But proof was never found and the storm soon blew over. Nevertheless, even from the back benches the imposing and charismatic Heseltine remained a potent threat to his leader. This was not just because his public profile continued to be higher than that of many Cabinet ministers but because he offered an alternative agenda – a more interventionist state which promoted strategically important businesses and drove forward urban renewal (much was made of his work to this effect in Liverpool).* Journalists were naturally attracted to this clash of Thatcher and Heseltine, the Tories' two bouffant blond(e)s. While courting his media contacts – Alastair Campbell at the *Mirror* was particularly helpful – Heseltine enjoyed the freedom from ministerial responsibility in other ways too, finding time to travel around the country speaking to the constituency associations of fellow Conservative MPs, who, it might be imagined, would return the favour by voting for him in a future leadership election. That he would be a candidate in such a contest was assumed, his oft-repeated formulation that he 'could not foresee the circumstances' in which he would challenge Thatcher leaving plenty of scope for the unforeseen. As early as January 1987, the Tory MP Michael Spicer was reflecting in his diary about a 'very agreeable' dinner with Heseltine at the Stafford Hotel. 'Clearly,' concluded Spicer, he 'thinks about nothing else but Thatcher's departure and how he is to replace her.'[50]

That moment, Heseltine calculated, was still not to hand when Nigel Lawson resigned. A month after the Chancellor's departure, a 'wet' MP, Sir Anthony Meyer, decided to challenge Thatcher for the party leadership

* See p. 97.

(under the party's rules, the leader faced reselection every year, though for Thatcher this had previously always been a formality). One of only two Tory MPs actively to oppose the Falklands War, Sir Anthony's dislike of the prime minister was well established: he had called for her resignation over Westland. Aged sixty-nine, a baronet and an Old Etonian, whose inheritance was sufficient to ensure he did not need to work for a living, he mixed a surprisingly complicated private life with a tendency to sneer snobbishly at the sort of people Thatcher admired. His belief in European integration was so fervent that he dismissively likened Britain's position as a sovereign nation to that of Albania.[51] It was not that he imagined he was prime ministerial material. His intention was rather to act as a 'stalking horse' who, having triggered a leadership contest, would then withdraw as soon as a credible alternative entered the race. It would have been astute of him to plot such an outcome before announcing his candidature. Instead, neither Heseltine nor anyone else rose to the bait, leaving Sir Anthony to rue that 'the wets were wet indeed'.[52] But having declared his candidature, he could hardly back down and, in the event, got thirty-three votes. Thatcher, who purposefully did not campaign, received 314. There were also twenty-four spoilt ballots and three abstentions which, combined, revealed that one sixth of the parliamentary party could not bring themselves to vote for their leader of fourteen years – a community that Kenneth Baker summarized as the 'dismissed, disappointed or disenchanted by Thatcher'.[53] Ominously, the abstentions included Heseltine, who ostentatiously hovered outside the door of the Commons committee room where the ballot was taking place without joining the queue. His time to strike was coming, but not in the company of the eccentric baronet.

During 1990, the Conservatives' popularity continued to slide. Losing by-elections was not necessarily a predictor of subsequent general election performance, but the size of the anti-Tory reaction suggested the party's difficulties were greater than could be waved off with the usual talk of 'mid-term blues'. In March, the previously safe Conservative seat of Mid-Staffordshire was lost on a swing of 22 per cent. On 30 July, Thatcher's former parliamentary private secretary, Ian Gow, was murdered by the IRA when they detonated a bomb under his car. His Eastbourne constituents might have been expected to respond to this outrage with a message of defiance to the terrorists, instead of which they chose the by-election as an opportunity to send a message to Downing Street, transforming Gow's 17,000 majority into one of 4,500 for the Liberal Democrats. By mid-October, MORI was suggesting that the Tories were trailing Labour nationally by 16 per cent.[54] The next general election was still potentially twenty months away, yet the proportion of Conservative MPs with grounds for feeling alarmed at their prospects was now extended significantly beyond those in marginal seats.

Simply ditching Thatcher was not necessarily the answer, since opinion polling suggested the party's support would drop further if she were replaced by such possible contenders as Kenneth Baker, Norman Tebbit or Sir Geoffrey Howe. By contrast, replacing her with Heseltine seemed to be the only option that would restore the party's fortunes, at least in the short term, with a December 1989 poll suggesting the prospect of a Heseltine premiership would stimulate a notional 13 per cent surge in Tory support.[55] During 1990, he continued to appear the only electorally viable alternative.

Whatever the apprehension on the back benches about the unpopularity of the poll tax, there was no sign of a decisive Cabinet rebellion on the matter. Rather, it was Thatcher's Euroscepticism that courted danger from her senior colleagues. At stake was not just her determination to keep Britain out of any rush towards economic and monetary union. Taken aback by the speed with which Eastern Europe's communist regimes had collapsed, she allowed her ingrained suspicion of latent German power to cloud her judgement about the threat a reunited Germany might present. At Brussels, on 3 December 1989, the West German Chancellor, Helmut Kohl, warned President Reagan's successor, George H. W. Bush, that Thatcher's 'ideas are pre-Churchillian. She thinks the post-war era isn't over yet.'[56] If anything, this was generous; some who heard her off-the-record comments during this period had grounds for wondering if she even thought the war era was over.[57] Particular embarrassment was caused when the *Independent on Sunday* published details of a colloquium of favoured historians she had convened on 24 March 1990 at Chequers to discuss the implications of a reunited Germany. Charles Powell's briefing paper summarizing German national characteristics as 'angst, aggressiveness, assertiveness, bullying, egotism, inferiority complex [and] sentimentality' was heavily criticized by the academics present,[58] but it was Powell's provocations rather than the scholarly modifications that made the headlines. There were plausible geopolitical reasons for Thatcher to be nervous about an over-hasty reunification of Germany, not least the potential destabilization of Gorbachev and the consequent possibility of his overthrow in Moscow by communist hardliners. She was also keen to clarify what pressures reunification would bring to the European Community, particularly with regard to who would pay for it and how it might stretch the Common Agricultural Policy.[59] The tone in which she articulated foreign policy, however, merely gave the impression that she was unable to adjust to changed circumstances and found herself on the wrong side of a great and historic upheaval. That her most supportive Cabinet colleague, the trade and industry secretary, Nicholas Ridley, was forced to resign in July 1990, after injudiciously drawing cheap parallels between European monetary union and the Third Reich in an interview for the *Spectator*, only strengthened the assumption that Euroscepticism — like

Germanophobia – was driven more by prejudice than reason. The reality was that Mitterrand also feared a reunified Germany but was able, by advocating a single European currency, to drive forward a policy he believed would keep Germans bound down within the European construct. Thatcher could articulate no alternative plan beyond unqualified opposition to a process over which she now exercised little control.

The first benefactor – or so it then seemed – of Thatcher's weakening grip was her new Chancellor, John Major, who transpired to be as keen as his predecessor on securing sterling's entry into the ERM. While the prime minister's conditions were that entry could only follow a decisive fall in inflation, Major argued that this was putting the cart before the horse, since it was the discipline exerted by ERM membership that would curb rising prices and ease pressure on the pound. Indeed, having publicly made it clear that entry was imminent, failure to follow through would risk undermining market confidence. Thus, despite the fact that inflation was running at 10.9 per cent, Major won the Treasury's long-running battle with Thatcher and, on 5 October, Chancellor and prime minister approached the press microphones outside 10 Downing Street. Putting on a brave face, Thatcher announced that sterling was joining the ERM. The BBC deemed the glad tidings worthy of interrupting its schedules with a news flash.

Overwhelmingly, 'informed' opinion rejoiced: the *Guardian* headline 'Shares Rocket In Market Euphoria' summing up the business response, while the *Financial Times* pronounced that 'both politically and economically, entry is shrewdly timed'.[60] Under the terms of entry, sterling's value was fixed within a 6 per cent band either side of DM2.95. This was roughly the rate at which the currency was trading at that moment – but proved sustainable thereafter only through a prolonged period of high interest rates, which certainly dampened down inflation, although at the cost of transforming what might have been a brief recession into a far more severe one. The dramatic denouement in September 1992, when sterling was pulled out of the ERM, left the policy's defenders hypothesizing that the problem had not been the principle of ERM membership but merely the rate to which sterling had been pegged – a more sustainable rate supposedly having been available during the years in which Thatcher had kept sterling out of the mechanism. Whether, in the long term, there was any such thing as a 'right' exchange rate remained the greater economic and philosophic question, but by then the Cassandra who had warned that the market could not be bucked could take little pleasure from the fulfilment of her prophecy, having herself been bucked by the enthusiasts for European currency-fixing.

It was two days in Rome that sealed her fate. There, at a summit of European heads of government on 27–8 October, Thatcher stood out as the lone voice opposing stage two of the Delors report's plan to move towards a single European currency. When she returned to Westminster to deliver her assessment to MPs, the mood in the Commons chamber was febrile. 'Her tantrum tactics,' taunted Kinnock, 'will not stop the process of change or change anything in the process of change.' The Liberal Democrat leader, Paddy Ashdown, was equally keen to be associated with the anticipated march of progress, announcing that 'as long as she hangs on to power, so long will Britain be held back from its future . . . she no longer speaks for Britain, she speaks for the past.' Rising to the challenge, Thatcher was not to be easily cowed, delivering her put-down of Kinnock as 'little Sir Echo' and insisting that, given the scale of the issues at stake, isolation was a price worth paying:

> Mr Delors said at a press conference the other day that he wanted the European Parliament to be the democratic body of the Community, he wanted the Commission to be the executive and he wanted the Council of Ministers to be the senate. No. No. No.[61]

Her remaining supporters cheered this defining articulation of opposition to submerging Britain into a federal Europe – the inevitable consequence, she maintained, of economic and monetary union. Rallying to her cry, the next day's headline in *The Sun* was 'Up Yours Delors'. It was memorable, but as far as Thatcher's survival was concerned, it was not helpful, for it was exactly the sort of shrill tone that convinced EMU's supporters that Euroscepticism was merely an expression of vulgar xenophobia. Most importantly of all, it offended the sensibilities of the deputy prime minister and Leader of the House, Sir Geoffrey Howe. He believed a parallel European currency (the 'hard ecu') could develop alongside national currencies and, if successful, replace them as a single European currency. Thatcher, however, had made it clear that would not happen on her watch, when she assured the Commons: 'This government has no intention of abolishing the pound sterling. If the hard ecu were to evolve and much greater use were to be made of it, that would be a decision for future parliaments . . . This government believe[s] in the pound sterling.'[62]

Having flunked resigning over his own demotion the previous summer, this time Howe decided he could tolerate Thatcher no more, handing her his letter of resignation on 1 November. It was a lengthy epistle built around the theme that Britain needed to be fully engaged in shaping EMU, which it could not do by asserting opposition to it from the outset. His resignation speech was delivered twelve days later. It proved to be a performance of breathtaking audacity, made all the more wounding by the quietness of Howe's delivery and the assumption that it represented a reserved man driven to breaking point by years of off-hand treatment from his boss.

Accusing the prime minister of creating unhelpful 'background noise' when her Chancellor and the Governor of the Bank of England were trying to promote the idea of a 'hard ecu', it was, he stated, 'like sending your opening batsmen to the crease only for them to find, the moment the first balls are bowled, that their bats have been broken before the game by the team captain'. This was an extraordinarily cutting comment from the man who had been successively her Chancellor, Foreign Secretary and deputy prime minister, but it was in his peroration that he openly threw down the gauntlet: 'The time has come for others to consider their own response to the tragic conflict of loyalties with which I have myself wrestled for perhaps too long.'[63]

As Conservative MPs filed out of the chamber, Alan Clark found those not too 'semi-traumatized' to speak weighing up whether Thatcher was finished. Norman Lamont seemed astonished at the thought that any government minister would be so 'quite monstrously disloyal' as to vote against the prime minister. To which Clark flashed back: 'I can see you weren't at Eton.'[64]

With Howe's departure there remained only one person in Thatcher's Cabinet who had been there since it was formed in May 1979 – and that was the prime minister herself. Her longevity gave her the dangerous distinction of being the prime minister who had sacked more ministers than any other in British history. More surprising was her failure to act as patron to those who were loyal to her. 'It was not just that she carelessly appointed her enemies (or those who were lukewarm about her) to key positions,' reflected the junior minister Michael Spicer, 'she actually fell out with, or sidelined, those who wished to serve her cause. As at the court of Queen Elizabeth I, and as a front-line politician, the closer you were to her the more brittle became the relationship.'[65] The passage of time had also removed from positions of influence loyal colleagues whose support she now needed: a stroke had forced Lord Whitelaw to retire as deputy prime minister back in January 1988; Lord Young had left the Department of Trade and Industry in July 1989 for the business world; while Norman Tebbit had retired as party chairman after the 1987 general election in order to care for his wife, who had been permanently crippled by the IRA – a commitment that made him unable to accede to Thatcher's blandishments when she asked him to return as education secretary following the Howe denunciation.

In preparing his attack, Howe had not plotted with Heseltine,[66] but the latter was inescapably the contender to whom the appeal was addressed. The following day, Heseltine duly announced his intention to challenge Thatcher for the party leadership. The date for the annual leadership election having been brought forward, the Howe and Heseltine statements were perfectly timed. Nominations were due to close the next day, 15 November, with the ballot held on 20 November, all Conservative MPs being entitled to vote. There would be two candidates, Heseltine and Thatcher, and the winner would be the one who secured a majority by a margin of at least fifty-six votes (this margin representing 15 per cent of those entitled to vote). A lead of less than fifty-six votes would necessitate the ballot going to a second round, which other candidates might enter.

To backbenchers primarily concerned by the issues most irritating voters, Heseltine was able to make the important promise that, if elected, he would review the poll tax. For those (usually) more senior politicians alarmed by Thatcher's Euroscepticism, he reaffirmed his pro-Brussels credentials: indeed, the previous year his book, *The Challenge of Europe*, had made unambiguously clear his belief that history was moving in one direction, towards unification, and it was necessary for Britain 'to commit all our national energies to the enterprise of Europe'.[67] With nearly five years outside of the Cabinet, Heseltine was free both to affirm his own beliefs and to offer a fresh start. By contrast, Thatcher felt that she 'could not now credibly tell an MP worried about the community charge' – as she still insisted upon calling the poll tax – 'that I had been convinced by what he said and intended to scrap the whole scheme'.[68] While Heseltine and his well-drilled lieutenants intensively canvassed MPs, Thatcher kept to her official schedule, which involved a trip to Northern Ireland and an event she was unlikely to want to miss, a summit in Paris where she was to join Bush, Mitterrand, Kohl, Gorbachev and other leaders in signing a major arms reduction treaty which would symbolize the end of the Cold War. While, in hindsight, Thatcher might have saved her skin by absenting herself from the summit and instead devoting the time to listening to the opinions and personal aspirations of her MPs, as she subsequently reflected: 'Tory MPs knew me, my record and my beliefs. If they were not already persuaded, there was not much left for me to persuade them with.'[69] A perhaps greater handicap was the ineffectualness of her campaign team. The former Scottish secretary, George Younger, was nominally in charge but appeared unable at this important juncture properly to tear himself away from his business commitments as chairman-elect of the Royal Bank of Scotland. Canvassing and confirming the support of MPs was run by a small team loosely under the direction of her parliamentary private secretary, Peter Morrison. Dangerously complacent – Alan Clark entered his office at a critical stage and found him enjoying a snooze – Morrison demonstrated an enviably optimistic view of human nature, assuring Thatcher that 'if you have not won then an awful lot of Conservative MPs are lying'.[70] According to his calculations, the verdict would go 220 to 110 in her favour.[71]

Thatcher was at the British ambassador's residence in Paris when the actual result was telephoned through to her: Thatcher 204, Heseltine 152, abstentions sixteen. She was four votes short of the 15 per cent rule. Put another way, if two Heseltine voters could have been persuaded to stick with her, she would have won outright. Striding outside to announce to the press her intention to stand in the second round, she then dressed and headed off to join her fellow world leaders for a banquet amid the gilded infinities of the Palace of Versailles' Hall of Mirrors. It was when she returned to Downing Street that she discovered the full extent of the disaffection and defection. Morrison suggested she see each of her ministers separately. While some were clearly angling for her to step down, even many who were loyal to her expressed the fear that if she stood, she would lose. The mood in Westminster seemed to be moving decisively in favour of Heseltine in the second ballot, the view being that Thatcher was now so badly wounded that it would be better to finish her off than let her limp on. For Heseltine's opponents, this meant moving the debate on from saving Margaret to denying Michael. The two obvious alternative candidates were the Foreign Secretary, Douglas Hurd, and the Chancellor, John Major, though because they had been Thatcher's proposer and seconder they could only enter the fray if she gave up the fight. Reluctantly, Thatcher bowed to this reality. During the morning of Thursday, 22 November, she announced her resignation at the meeting of the Cabinet and then attended an audience with the Queen. Not that she was quite relieved of her duties – in the afternoon she stood at the Commons dispatch box to defend herself in a no-confidence debate tabled by Labour. She delivered a performance of such assuredness and command – 'bravura' was the term bandied around in the press – that the cheering and waving of order papers by the MPs packed tightly on the benches behind her gave no indication of the fact that so many of them had just connived in her downfall.

Five days later, the Conservative Party had a new leader and the United Kingdom a new prime minister, when John Major came out top in the second ballot, gaining 185 votes to Heseltine's 131 and Hurd's fifty-six. The Thatcher age was over, its central figure standing briefly outside 10 Downing Street the following day to sum up her efforts: 'We're very happy that we leave the United Kingdom in a very, very much better state than when we came here eleven and a half years ago.'[72] Then the limousine drew up and, in a flicker of flashbulbs, she was gone.

What might have happened if she had been left to fight a fourth general election in 1992 can only be imagined. All that can be said is that her party won a fourth term with its new leader, a temperamentally different figure who attracted neither the widespread loathing nor the admiration that everywhere fixed upon the Iron Lady. Heseltine was put in charge of burying the poll tax, but Major never put to rest the debate over Britain and the European Union. That issue, and the manner in which some of Thatcher's most senior colleagues had brought down the Conservatives' most electorally successful leader, left a festering and debilitating wound. A presentiment of the internecine conflict to come was on display as early as 4 December 1990, when the party's MPs and peers gathered to acclaim Major as their new leader. Sir Geoffrey Howe, the Cassius to Thatcher's Caesar, found himself standing next to his former Cabinet colleague Keith Joseph, who had been her formative political and intellectual mentor and the man who by stepping aside had provided her with the chance to stand for the leadership back in 1975. Howe attempted to make conversation. 'I'm sorry, Geoffrey,' cut in Joseph as he prepared to turn his back, 'we're not friends anymore.'[73]

16 LEGACY

The recurring subjects that dominated the news in the early years of the seventies were still filling newspaper columns and television reports at the end of the decade: rapidly rising prices and soaring household bills; strikes and arbitration to halt their spread, along with great prominence given to pronouncements from trade union leaders; subsidies to the nationalized industries; concern at the perceived failures of management and general introspection about Britain's 'national decline'; the tax burden; serious violence in Northern Ireland; the forces of NATO and the Warsaw Pact facing each other across a dividing line separating two rival Germanys, with accompanying chilly rhetoric traded between the 'Free World' and the elderly men of the Kremlin. It was as if a decade of strife had unfolded without actually settling any of its persistent problems – except that increasing numbers of television viewers (but not newspaper readers) were able to see it all reported in colour. By contrast, a Briton gifted with the ability to switch seamlessly from the news of 1979 to that of 1990 would have been astonished to find that – despite the intervening prominence of unemployment and the continuation of the IRA's armed struggle – many of the daily staples of the seventies were either no longer major concerns by 1990 or else had been transformed out of all recognition, while those that remained were analysed and debated through the prism of almost completely different assumptions. Indeed, the transformation of the eighties, judged by this admittedly crude method, seems not only more profound than that which was wrought during the seventies, but also more primary in nature than the breaks in continuity that could be spotted by flicking between Britain in the respective summers of 1991 and 2001. Change over those years was startling in spheres influenced by the internet's spread and in some social attitudes, but far less fundamental in politics and economics. Compared with the decades that preceded and succeeded it, the eighties truly exploded with a decisive bang.

In 1979, democratic government was still the exception across most of the globe. Indeed, by then scarcely thirty-five democracies remained in the world. Thus the near worldwide collapse of communism as a viable alternative model to both capitalism and liberal democracy was patently the greatest turnaround of the eighties. That the consequences were felt most acutely in those countries that shed their Marxist–Leninist dogma ought not to detract from the enormous alteration to the parameters of thought and action in Britain that this epoch-defining change inspired. At its most basic level, the fear of imminent nuclear annihilation receded and with it one of the great alarms of the past forty years. But that was not all. At the start of the eighties, adherence to Marxist preconceptions was still not necessarily considered a mark of recondite eccentricity in academic circles; some self-confessed Marxists, like the Oxford economist Andrew Glyn, held senior lecturing positions and others from an older generation, like E. P. Thompson, Christopher Hill and Ralph Miliband, continued to be widely read and admired. Active membership of the Communist Party of Great Britain was no bar to being vice president of the NUM, a union so powerful that at least until 1985 it was credited with possessing the potential to bring the country and its government to their knees. At the decade's start, Labour Party membership remained open to Trotskyite 'entryists', many of whom proceeded, for a time, to wield considerable authority in local government. Gorbachev's *glasnost* and *perestroika* made Britain's far-left appear backward-looking in their ideas, while the fall of the Berlin Wall and the Soviet Union's subsequent collapse dealt them a grievous psychological blow. These events necessitated new thinking from the conventionally minded as well. After all, the Cold War's end transformed what the UK had, since the late 1940s, believed to be one of its primary responsibilities in the world, and, having adjusted to the loss of empire, the receding significance of the Royal Navy and the British Army of the Rhine after 1990 left Britain once again searching for its distinctive role. A major reassessment of government priorities followed. During the eighties, approximately as much of the state's total budget was spent on defence as on the NHS; by 2010, the NHS budget was three times greater than the defence budget.

The two issues that the Conservatives argued were the greatest concerns facing the UK at the outset of the eighties were inflation and trade union power. That neither remained front-rank worries in the nineties and noughties might be considered a testimony to Thatcher's ability to bring them to heel (though it was far from clear to observers in 1990 that inflation – which had temporarily swelled back to 10 per cent – was defeated). Certainly, the differences in the corporatist relationship between government, unions and inflation before, during and after the eighties could scarcely be clearer. The year of Thatcher's accession, 1979, began with trade union militancy exerting such a grip on the economy that the Labour Cabinet had considered calling a state of emergency and putting troops on the streets to keep essential supplies moving. It would not have been extraordinary if they had done so, since the similarly harassed Conservative government of Edward Heath had felt compelled to declare a state of emergency on five separate occasions between 1970 and 1974. Nor were the unions important merely because strikes caused disruptions and lost revenue. They were partners in government to the extent that they were accorded a critical role in economic policy, agreeing with government ministers' nationwide pay norms to prevent great numbers of employees – even in the private sector – from earning above a prescribed amount. In addition to this endeavour to restrain inflation through an incomes policy, there was a prices policy, with many medium- and large-sized companies statutorily obliged to send proposed price increases to the Price Commission, which would then decide whether to approve them according to the formula set by its Price Code. The principle of price regulation was to continue for major utilities where privatization did not create sufficient competition, but the notion that inflation might be controlled across swathes of the private sector by bureaucrats second-guessing whether thousands of companies had got their prices 'right', rather than leaving them to be determined by the market, conveys how differently those in authority looked at problems before Thatcher.

The incomes and prices policies were among the first restrictions her administration junked, along with exchange controls, whereby an entire department of civil servants had existed purely to prevent British companies, investors and holidaymakers from taking more money out of the country than they were allowed, to prohibit them from opening bank accounts in a different currency, and to stop them buying as many foreign shares or properties abroad as they liked. That the state should have the power to prevent its citizens from freely walking out of the country with their own money was, between 1939 and 1979, a generally accepted fact of life. Allowing Britons to invest their money wherever they liked was deemed 'reckless' and 'doctrinaire' by Denis Healey, the former Labour Chancellor of the Exchequer.[1] And he was firmly on the right of his party.

Indeed, in assessing the extent to which Thatcher's first and second administrations recast the political and economic climate, the telling contrast is not perhaps the obvious one between the Conservative manifesto of 1983 and Labour's counter-promises to erect tariff barriers around the UK in order to protect it from international competition, since even in the recession-hit Britain of that year the electorate overwhelmingly rejected this incarnation of 'socialism in one country'. Rather, the contrast is provided by the promises made in the 1983 election by the Liberal–SDP Alliance. Widely identified as straddling the moderate middle ground, the Alliance emphasized the absolute necessity of bringing back a permanent incomes policy, on a statutory basis if need be, restoring the Price Commission in a new guise and introducing a counter-inflation tax to be levied on those private sector companies that government officials adjudged were 'paying above the pay range'.[2] To this collectivist mindset, it was the state, rather than any compact between employer and employee, that was ultimately the arbiter of the fair rate for the job. Furthermore, the Alliance opposed privatizing any of the existing nationalized companies. The most remarkable characteristic of the SDP was that it was a new party with old ideas. Yet, by the end of the eighties such seventies solutions were off the agenda of all the main parties, and even Labour had given up on the prospect of renationalizing British Telecom, British Airways and the other major corporate entities whose ownership was now in the hands of millions of shareholders, unit trust investors and pension fund providers.

Thatcher 'forced the political debate in Britain on to the ground of who can best run a market economy', her admiring former Cabinet colleague Nicholas Ridley summarized, 'it is no longer about whether we have a market economy or a socialist one'.[3] It might be added that her name and her party were never on the ballot papers in countless other nations where this has also become the narrower choice. Nonetheless, it was decisions taken in the UK during her time that provided the critical impetus for a global revolution in economic thinking, which extended across the two succeeding decades. No country had previously attempted privatizations on the scale of those floated on the London Stock Exchange in the mid-eighties, and the British model was duly studied and followed around the world. Those most responsible for this export of an idea ought perhaps to have stood comparison with such once-revered mid-Victorian free-traders as Sir Robert Peel, Richard Cobden and John Bright, at least in terms of their worldwide influence. Eighties Britain was not just one more country caught up and pulled along in the trend of globalization. Alongside the expanding range of Wall Street, which Big Bang helped integrate with the City of London, Britain was the trendsetter of globalization.

The previous, mid-Victorian age of globalization had facilitated Britain's efforts to become the 'workshop of the world'. In contrast, late twentieth-century globalization saw Britain's share of international manufactured trade diminishing. By 1990, the number of Britons employed in wholesale and retail finally overtook the number engaged in manufacturing. It had taken the better part of two centuries, but Napoleon's claim that the country was '*une nation de boutiquiers*' was finally realized. Actually, it was not the French emperor who first coined the phrase. Fittingly, it was Adam Smith. His treatise on *The Wealth of Nations* was published in 1776, but might have been meant for the age of Thatcher:

> To found a great empire for the sole purpose of raising up a people of customers may at first sight appear a project fit only for a nation of shopkeepers. It is, however, a project altogether unfit for a nation of shopkeepers; but extremely fit for a nation whose government is influenced by shopkeepers.[4]

The outnumbering of makers by traders raises the question of whether this was a natural and benign development or, if it was preventable and malign, whether policy in the eighties should have been different. Could keeping exchange controls and other interventionist measures to shore up manufacturing companies have helped shield the country's industrial base, thereby providing jobs, income and self-respect to communities that were instead torn apart by the factory closures of the period? Making capital more mobile encouraged it to seek the best return for its investment wherever that might be found and to be indifferent to whether this benefited workers in Goa over those in Gateshead. Some consequences of this internationalization of capital and ownership are discussed in chapter fourteen.* But it should not be presumed that British industrial decline would have been reversible if capital movement had continued to be restricted and government had remained interventionist. In this respect, a cross–Channel comparison is instructive. When the UK's exchange controls were scrapped in 1979, the manufacturing sectors in the UK and France accounted for, at around 27 per cent, almost exactly the same share of their respective national GDPs. Instead of following the British Treasury's lead, the French continued to restrict the outflow of investment in an effort to keep capital tied up within France and to support French industry, only abolishing exchange controls eleven years after the British, in July 1990. By then, rather than diverging, the two countries' respective manufacturing sectors remained within a fraction of each other, at around 23 per cent of GDP. Nor did France's more interventionist tradition cast a discernible shadow over results thereafter. In 1999, the gap was still marginal, with the 19.3 per cent of French GDP generated by the manufacturing sector being scarcely different from the UK's 18.5 per cent.[5] By 2010, manufacturing was contributing 11 per cent to France's gross value added measurement to GDP and 12 per cent to that of the UK.[6] If it was specifically Thatcherism that destroyed British industry, how is France's comparable decline – much of it under the socialist Mitterrand – to be explained? What the UK's early abolition of exchange and other capital controls did ensure (and which France's delaying actions did not bequeath to Paris) was the renaissance of its financial sector, upon which the taxes to fund everything else became increasingly – and some believed overly – dependent.

In this environment, the competitiveness of what remained of British industry, as with other economic sectors, came to rely upon the effectualness of Thatcherite 'supply-side' reforms, which removed obstacles to productivity (for instance, disabling trade union militancy), delivered lower costs for purchasing the necessary equipment and raw materials (free trade),

---

* See, in particular, pp. 390, 394.

and lessened the risk and expense in taking on – and dispensing with – employees (fewer statutory employment rights, entitlements and restrictions). The subsequent replication, at least in part, of this approach throughout much of the world, alongside important technological advances like the internet, helped drive the twenty years of post-eighties low inflation. It may also be posited that had such 'supply-side' conditions existed to depress inflationary pressures at the beginning of the eighties – in place of the high prices that were the reality – then the tough interest rate squeeze of 1980–1, which finished off so many struggling industries, would never have become a requirement of monetary discipline and dole queues would have been kept much shorter. What might have been achieved in the eighties without the burden of three million unemployed remains the great 'what if?' of the decade.

The promotion of free trade and financial deregulation, which precipitated, accompanied and marked the near-worldwide collapse of Marxism–Leninism, allowed China and other low-cost economies to compete in the global marketplace. The cheaper goods that they exported reduced the cost of living for Western consumers and kept inflation down. One extraordinary consequence of this legacy came in a form that the eighties free-marketers failed adequately to foresee or warn against. The vast financial surpluses that emerging twenty-first century economic powers like China (aided by an undervalued currency) were able to generate by supplying the Western world with consumer durables needed to find an outlet, and were duly invested in the international bond markets. This massive financial injection allowed Western governments to borrow at such low rates of interest (sometimes at negative rates of interest in real terms) that they were encouraged to spend more than they raised in tax revenues, the cheapness of credit making a 'spend today, pay later' attitude appear both attractive and feasible. It also allowed Western governments, including that of the UK, to pursue what seemed like a vote-winning strategy of increasing public spending without ratcheting up taxes to pay for the public sector's expansion. Vast budget deficits resulted – the polar opposite of the firm control over public expenditure that Thatcherism (though not Reaganomics) believed to be essential. Nor were politicians the only ones caught up in this credit bubble. The same process was driving growth in the financial sector, especially in the United States and the UK, where banks and other institutions took advantage of cheap credit massively to increase their debt exposure far above the equity they held, leaving them heavily exposed in the event of a downturn. The Victorian values of thrift, of self-help, of building up savings – what might be termed the Grantham gospel of Thatcher's faith – were mocked to scorn in this age of leverage. By 2007, the UK's private sector debt was four times greater than the country's entire GDP.[7] This began to look unsustainable when the sub-prime debt crisis broke in the United States, sparking a trans-atlantic 'credit crunch', a near-calamitous run on the banks and the recession that began in 2008.

Commentators who marvelled, or despaired, at the way in which the governments of John Major, Tony Blair and Gordon Brown kept the dereg-ulatory supply-side reforms of the eighties in place, the powers of local authorities constrained, state ownership of public utilities off the agenda and income tax rates at, or below, the level established by Nigel Lawson natu-rally pronounced Thatcherism's enduring triumph.[8] By such yardsticks, any other conclusion would have been perverse. But the assessment was partial, for it ignored the post-2000 abandonment of Thatcher's Gladstonian attach-ment to balanced budgets, low debt ratios and public spending rising less quickly than private spending. In pursuit of these goals, much of the Treasury's effort during the eighties had been directed at bringing down the public sector borrowing requirement. A mixture of budget restraint, eco-nomic recovery, North Sea oil revenue and enhanced receipts from privatizations and council house sales brought borrowing down, and by 1987–8 the British government was a net *repayer* of debt. This achievement might have been expected to be repeated during the unprecedentedly pro-longed period of economic growth of the first decade of the twenty-first century. It was not, primarily because the Thatcherite belief in a smaller state was reversed through a return to borrowing. By 2010, with the long eco-nomic boom having turned to bust, the state accounted for half of the UK's entire GDP and the country was burdened with the greatest borrowing deficit in its post-war history.

One missed opportunity was that, despite lower unemployment rates in the nineties and noughties compared with the eighties, welfare dependency remained entrenched: the social security budget continued on its remorseless ascent and consumed one third of all public spending. Here was one dismal eighties legacy to which neither main political party had found a solution. 'I came to office with one deliberate intent,' claimed Thatcher in 1984, 'to change Britain from a dependent to a self-reliant society – from a give-it-to-me, to a do-it-yourself nation.'[9] Across large parts of the country there was little sign of this transformation taking place, and widespread evidence of greater, rather than less, reliance upon the benefactions of the state, particu-larly where demographic changes and the breakdown of the traditional family unit were most evident. How much these latter developments were caused by government policy in the eighties is as unquantifiable as the con-tribution made by changing social attitudes from the sixties onwards – attitudes that Thatcher showed no discernible ability to reverse. But welfare claimants were only part of a larger picture. The amount of goods and services pro-vided by the state is measured by government final consumption expenditure.

This fell from 22.4 per cent to 18.2 per cent of GDP between 1982 and 1998, only to be pushed back up during Gordon Brown's tenure as Chancellor. By the time Brown moved into his next-door neighbour's home, government final consumption expenditure was, at 22.3 per cent, again nudging its 1982 level.[10] Judged by this criterion, the eighties rolling back of the state was as temporary as it was selective. In its core objective, Thatcherism has not swept all before it after all.

The belief that the greatest victim of the eighties was the 'post-war consensus' also needs to be qualified. For the reality is that some of that consensus Thatcher attacked, some of it she kept in place with only modest reform, and parts of it she either left untouched or positively encouraged. Nationalized industries, Keynesian demand management to achieve 'full employment', and the corporatist partnership with the trade unions were dismantled. It should not have been surprising that a grocer's daughter had little truck with the attitude summed up by the old, if slightly misquoted, boast that 'the man in Whitehall knows best'.[11] In contrast, a cornerstone of the post-war settlement, the 1944 Butler Education Act, with its promotion of academic selection in grammar schools, specialist technical schools and generalized secondary moderns, was far closer to Thatcher's personal ideas on education than was the comprehensive system, yet her education secretaries did little to turn back the tide in favour of grammar schools, and only fifteen of the new-style technical schools, the City Technology Colleges created by the Education Act 1988, were ever opened. Much as the prime minister might not have wished it, schooling in the eighties represented the triumph not of the post-war consensus but of the sixties progressive, comprehensive ideal, albeit constrained at the decade's end by the imposition of a national curriculum. Meanwhile, on foreign policy, the Atlantic alliance and NATO, Thatcher was the devoted disciple of Clement Attlee and Ernest Bevin, leaving Labour under Michael Foot to turn its back on that aspect of its post-war heritage.

When Thatcher referred to the Beveridge Report it was usually in broadly favourable terms, reserving specific criticisms for the manner in which its insurance principles had been compromised and its support for additional private provision ignored.[12] Whatever anarcho-libertarian fantasies her detractors imagined she secretly entertained, judging by her words and deeds it was difficult to dismiss her protestation that 'our party has no more intention of dismantling the welfare state than we have of dismantling the Albert Hall'.[13] Despite increasing spending on the NHS by almost one third above the inflation rate, the government's funding of healthcare was a constant source of criticism during the eighties – though, in retrospect, what seems more significant is how limited were the reforms to the NHS, and the complete absence of plans to subject it to fundamental change. In these respects, it is possible to understand Thatcher's indignation at suggestions that she was taking her party away from the principles of the post-war generation. 'I don't think I have changed the direction of Conservatism' from that of the 1950s, she assured the journalist Hugo Young, before pointing out that as Chancellor and prime minister, Harold Macmillan's priorities had been to restrain inflation below 3 per cent and to hold public spending at a far lower level than it was at during the eighties. As she put it to another journalist, under her tenure, in 1984 the state consumed 42 per cent of GDP, whereas during 'the golden years of Harold Macmillan' it had accounted for only 33 per cent.[14] It was not the fifties from which she was trying to extract the country. Rather, she maintained, 'I think things started to go wrong in the late sixties', before degenerating completely in the seventies.[15] Instead of unpicking the handiwork of William Beveridge or Rab Butler, Thatcherism's quarrel was with the more immediate past, the 'management of decline' presided over by Harold Wilson, Edward Heath and James Callaghan. And it is in comparison with the seventies that the struggles of the eighties become comprehensible and the achievements more readily discernible.

However, the eighties look like a desperate disappointment if Thatcher's misattributed quotation of St Francis of Assisi is set as the measure of success. Where there was discord, nobody brought harmony. Some of the worst picket-line violence in British history was witnessed at Orgreave and Wapping, while the hooliganism afflicting football was the decade's ugliest youth fashion. The inner-city riots of 1981 and 1985 were of a ferocity not otherwise seen on the British mainland in the twentieth century. The disturbances in Trafalgar Square against the imposition of the poll tax were unsettling, but the massive nationwide campaign of civil disobedience by those who refused to pay it represented a greater threat to the social contract. Over in Northern Ireland, divisions remained unhealed: the Troubles claimed 853 lives during the decade. The only optimistic reflection on this tally was that it represented an improvement on the 2,092 fatalities claimed by the conflict during the seventies. Yet, for all the bloodshed, the IRA was neither closer to being defeated nor nearer to realizing its aims. In all parts of the United Kingdom, there were reasonable grounds for looking fearfully towards the future. Year after year, recorded crime reached unprecedented levels, while heroin and Aids wrecked lives and, if the wilder predictions were to be believed, threatened to increase exponentially. In this unsettling atmosphere, Thatcher's suggestion in 1987 that there was 'no such thing as society' was intended to emphasize the importance of personal responsibility and the requirement for individuals to support each other, rather than expecting some bureau of the state to do it for them. Nevertheless, that much of the public appeared to take the phrase, shorn of its context, at face value suggested the extent of unease about the direction in which the country was moving and distrust of the underlying philosophy guiding its leader. In the sort of expression that made traditional Tories wonder if their champion actually possessed something of the mind of a Marxist, Thatcher suggested in 1981: 'Economics are the method; the object is to change the heart and soul.'[16] She could no more make windows into men's souls than Queen Elizabeth I, but if opinion polls and social attitude surveys were any guide, she failed to shift basic attitudes on the value of the public sector over private endeavour.

In terms of greater sexual equality, educational experience and the opportunities and environment of the workplace, society was actually more cohesive in the eighties than it had been in any of the preceding decades since the war.* None of these gains, however, could be drawn on by the one in ten who, during the first half of the decade, found themselves out of work. Except in a few protected corners of the public sector, the expectation of a job for life with the same firm was gone. The loss of security this caused made for anxious times and for searing hardship, especially among those with few skills or with a specialism that was not easily transferable. For the well qualified or those with broad-ranging aptitudes, it offered greater opportunities, with so-called 'headhunters' and a profusion of recruitment agencies springing up to make labour market mobility as beneficial to employers seeking an injection of new blood and creative talent as to those who, in this more fluid system, were in demand and finally free to dictate their terms. 'The whole direction of politics in the last thirty years,' complained Thatcher in the same 1981 interview in which she spoke of economics and the soul, 'has always been towards the collectivist society. People have forgotten about the personal society. And they say: "Do I count, do I matter?"'[17] Critics of the trends of the eighties usually cited increased individualism as one of the decade's principal failings. It undoubtedly contributed towards greater income inequality. Yet it could represent a valuable freedom too – a liberty that in the labour market made it easier for talented adults to pursue their aspirations and, in doing so, to chip away at rigid hierarchies, outmoded stratifications and class-bound prejudices.

While liberal – even libertarian – conservatism was boosted by this dismantling of inflexible structures, social conservatism as well as socialist collectivism was undermined, a process that further makes the popular wisdom that the right won the eighties economic battle while the left won the cultural battle unhelpfully glib. The eighties began with, on average, 70 per cent of the nation's television sets switched to one channel (ITV) and ended with a far wider choice delivered through terrestrial, cable and satellite TV. Channel 4 was born with a remit that, besides high-quality and

---

* See pp. 339–40.

sometimes ground-breaking programming, also embraced minority tastes and lifestyles ignored by the BBC and ITV. Sky won the satellite 'Star Wars' with a promise to offer subscribers more of what they really wanted and to drive competition forward, while for the terrestrial channels government policy actively fostered the creation of an array of new and distinctive independent production companies. To sceptics and nay-sayers, this greater choice represented a consumer-led degradation of producer-determined taste, while increasing the range of options risked diminishing the sense of national cultural homogeneity created when a country of fifty-six million inhabitants could only watch one of three (or after 1982, four) programmes at any one time. In reality, such eighties creations as *EastEnders* and *Only Fools and Horses* proved just as capable of holding the attention of the masses and becoming collective cultural reference points as the evergreen *Coronation Street*. There was also much that was of low quality, though this was hardly a novel development. Anyone who thought the decade's tolerance of game shows was a new sign of the country's cultural Americanization or subservience to the zeitgeist of market-driven consumerism could not have watched much television in the sixties or seventies. The highlights of the eighties, meanwhile, stood reasonable comparison with the best of what came before and after, and the same was true in cinema, despite the financial constraints of the British film industry. More choice, in any case, did not necessarily mean a wider selection of undemanding commercialism, for, as the alternative comedy circuit and the indie music labels demonstrated, it could also provide a challenge to it.

In any *tour d'horizon* of a decade, there is a temptation to portray change as if it was inevitable and its advocates merely those best able to articulate the meaning of a revolution dictated by impersonal forces. Yet change, be it political, economic, social or cultural, is put in motion by specific decisions, no matter how well or badly those that take them are able to foresee the consequences. Labour's attitude to greater choice in broadcasting, for example, was far less permissive than that of the Conservatives, with results that could only have limited the spread of channels and production companies, regardless of the growing technical possibilities. There certainly was nothing inevitable about the right being in power in the eighties. If Callaghan had called a general election in the autumn of 1978 instead of waiting till the spring of 1979, Labour might have won a victory that could easily have spurred the Conservatives to ditch Thatcher, who many believed had performed indifferently as leader of the opposition. How different the Tories thereafter – led, perhaps, by Willie Whitelaw – might have been is mere conjecture, but different they surely would have been. That Britain was no longer a country gripped by a mindset of terminal retreat but was capable of overcoming difficult odds was demonstrated in the Falklands War. Whatever a Labour prime minister might have done, it is certainly not clear from the discussions that we know about that a Cabinet led by a senior Tory other than Thatcher would have possessed the martial resolve to call a halt to diplomatic obfuscations and instead retake the islands by force. Whether delivered by diplomacy or Exocet missile, what might humiliation at the hands of the Argentines have done for the nation's already battered morale? From a twenty-first-century perspective, where the country's mining industry has withered to a shadow of its former self, the defeat of the NUM in the strike of 1984–5 seems preordained. It was not. If Scargill had chosen his timing better, alienated fewer potential allies (and other miners) and known when to make a small compromise in order to gain the substance of his demands, then the miners would have won their strike. Who then would have considered trade union power a busted flush, and who would have been the leader subsequently to take the unions on? Who, indeed, could have predicted the next occupant of Downing Street if, at 2.54 a.m. on 12 October 1984, the IRA bomb at the Grand Hotel in Brighton had been placed slightly differently? The decade only unfolded in the manner that it did because a succession of potential turning points failed to turn.

The Labour leadership and its party, the Tory 'wets', the Argentine junta, Arthur Scargill, would-be IRA assassins – Thatcher, it is often suggested, was lucky in her choice of enemies. Partly, that may be true. If she had faced Denis Healey rather than Michael Foot, her fight would have been tougher. Or Labour might have imploded entirely, dashed to pieces between the two irreconcilable forces of Healey and the left. Certainly, the other popular notion that the Conservatives only remained in power because the creation of the SDP split the anti-Tory vote needs to be tested, resting as it does upon the false assumption that because the SDP's leadership were Labour defectors their voters must have been so as well. In fact, opinion poll data indicates that the SDP also attracted considerable support from those who would otherwise – if reluctantly – have voted Conservative. The detail of this psephological evidence suggests that, far from fatally dividing the left, it was only the intercession of the SDP that stopped the Conservatives beating Labour by even greater margins in the 1983 and 1987 general elections.[18]

The traits and peculiarities of Britain in the eighties become ever starker as the passage of time lengthens. The bitterness of the political divide and the extent to which the character and policies of the prime minister seeped into almost every aspect of national life were not repeated in the twenty years that followed. Having felt compelled to expose Thatcher's philosophical errors and corrosive social impact, few authors, dramatists and impresarios of the creative arts dedicated themselves to getting under the skin of John Major or Gordon Brown as a means of exploring broader truths about society. The state of the nation and the occupant of Downing Street no longer seemed so closely aligned. Tony Blair generated his share of anger and alarm, but mostly of a targeted and specific, rather than a general and all-encompassing, nature. Focused opposition formed against Blair's stance, for instance, on the war in Iraq, fox-hunting, civil liberties and the supposed triumph under his watch of 'spin-doctoring' and media manipulation, rather than coalescing in a relentless movement that stood against – or indeed for – everything he represented. In the eighties, politics assumed a more all-embracing tenor. It was far from uncommon for Britons to identify their own outlook in life primarily as either with or against the spirit of Thatcherism. By contrast, it was an unusual Briton who framed their personal identity first and foremost in terms of how it related to the supposed viewpoint of Major, Blair or Brown. The phrase 'Thatcher's children' enjoys a resonance as a description of those who grew to maturity during the eighties in a way that 'Blair's children' simply does not, even though both prime ministers enjoyed more than a decade in power.

This is why any history of the eighties becomes inextricably entwined with the politics of the period and, in particular, the politician who personified it – to an extent that might be thought more usual in a dictatorial regime than in a functioning and pluralistic democracy. During the eighties, there were three Britons whose level of recognition was truly international in scale: Margaret Thatcher; Diana, Princess of Wales; and (primarily as a consequence of her longevity and status) the Queen. All were women, but within their homeland only one of them was generally recognizable, without further explanation, as 'that woman'.

Placing Thatcher alongside Disraeli, Lloyd George and Ramsay MacDonald as one of only four authentic outsiders to have become prime minister over the previous one hundred and fifty years, the historian David Cannadine argued in 1989 that the full measure of her political dominance went far beyond her unprecedented three successive general election victories – 'She has brought her country military triumph unknown since the Second World War; she has survived a carefully plotted assassination attempt; she has been likened to Winston Churchill for her invincible courage; and she has given her name to a political style and a political philosophy, a distinction she shares with no other twentieth-century British politician.'[19] In doing so, she helped make the eighties a decade fixated on political issues and ideological debate to an extent that was simply not observable in the quarter-century thereafter. She is the reason that the 1980s began on 4 May 1979 and ended on 28 November 1990.

APPENDIX

UK ECONOMIC PERFORMANCE

ANNUAL INFLATION RATE (RPI) (%)

1979	13.4	1985	6.0
1980	18.0	1986	3.4
1981	11.9	1987	4.2
1982	8.6	1988	4.9
1983	4.6	1989	7.8
1984	5.0	1990	9.5

ANNUAL UNEMPLOYMENT RATE (%)
Percentage of estimated total workforce, seasonally adjusted

	UK	South-East	West Midlands	North	Scotland	Wales
1979	4.0	2.6	4.0	6.5	5.7	5.3
1980	5.1	3.1	5.5	8.0	7.0	6.9
1981	8.1	5.5	10.0	11.7	9.9	10.4
1982	9.5	6.7	11.9	13.3	11.3	12.1
1983	10.5	7.5	12.9	14.6	12.3	12.9
1984	10.7	7.8	12.7	15.2	12.6	13.2
1985	10.9	8.1	12.8	15.4	12.9	13.6
1986	11.1	8.3	12.9	15.3	13.3	13.5
1987	10.0	7.2	11.4	14.1	13.0	12.0
1988	8.1	5.4	8.9	11.9	11.3	9.8
1989	6.3	3.9	6.6	9.9	9.3	7.3
1990	5.8	4.0	6.0	8.7	8.1	6.6

Bang!

ECONOMIC GROWTH (GDP ANNUAL % INCREASE/ DECREASE)

Gross Domestic Product at factor cost, average estimate, 1985 prices

1979	2.8	**1985**	3.8
1980	−2.0	**1986**	3.6
1981	−1.2	**1987**	4.4
1982	1.7	**1988**	4.7
1983	3.8	**1989**	2.1
1984	1.8		

MANUFACTURING AS % OF GDP (INTERNATIONAL COMPARISON)

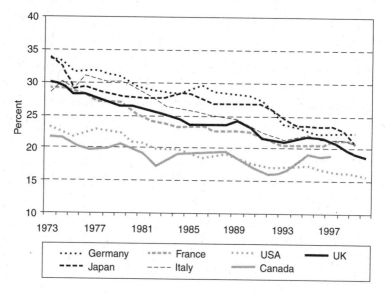

ECONOMIC GROWTH AND PUBLIC SPENDING
(% change in real terms 1979/80 to 1989/90)

Economic Growth (GDP)	+23.3
Total government spending	+12.9
of which:	
Law and Order	+53.3
Employment and Training	+33.3
NHS	+31.8
Social Security	+31.8
Education	+13.7
Defence	+9.2
Environment	+7.9
Transport	−5.8
Trade and Industry	−38.2
Housing	−67.0

SHARE OF PUBLIC SPENDING AS % OF TOTAL GOVERNMENT
BUDGET

Department	1979/80	1984/5	1989/90
Social Security	25.9	30.3	30.3
Education	14.1	12.9	14.2
NHS	12.1	12.7	14.1
Defence	12.0	13.0	11.6
Housing	7.1	3.4	2.1
Transport	4.8	4.3	3.9
Environment	4.3	3.4	4.1
Law and Order	4.1	4.7	5.6
Trade and Industry	3.7	4.0	2.1
Employment and Training	1.7	2.2	1.9
Other	10.2	9.1	10.1

TAX RATES (%)

	Income Tax (top rate)	Income Tax (standard)	VAT (main)	Corporation (top rate)	Inheritance
1978/9	83	33	8	52	75
1979	60	30	15	52	75
1980	60	30	15	52	75
1981	60	30	15	52	75
1982	60	30	15	52	75
1983	60	30	15	52	75
1984	60	30	15	45	60
1985	60	30	15	40	60
1986	60	29	15	35	60
1987	60	27	15	35	60
1988	40	25	15	35	40
1989	40	25	15	35	40
1990	40	25	15	35	40

NATIONWIDE INDEX OF AVERAGE HOUSE PRICES

Year	Price (average of Q1–Q4)	Real price (adjusted to 2010 prices)
1979	£19,829	£82,558
1980	£23,287	£82,363
1981	£23,953	£75,703
1982	£24,851	£72,255
1983	£27,622	£76,753
1984	£31,076	£82,258
1985	£34,377	£85,840
1986	£37,626	£90,816
1987	£43,164	£100,045
1988	£51,405	£113,429
1989	£61,513	£126,102
1990	£57,682	£108,169

POLITICS

OPINION POLLS: PARTY SUPPORT (%)

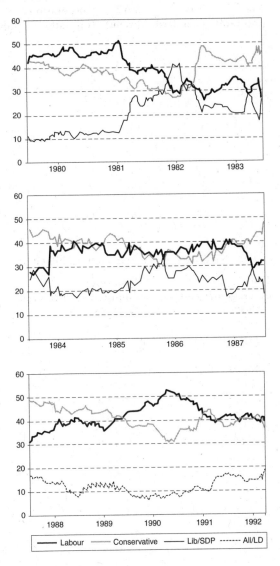

Labour — Conservative — Lib/SDP ------- All/LD

PRINCIPAL OFFICE HOLDERS OF STATE

PRIME MINISTER
Margaret Thatcher, May 1979–November 1990

LORD CHANCELLOR
Lord Hailsham, May 1979–June 1987
Lord Havers, June 1987–October 1987
Lord Mackay, October 1987–May 1997

CHANCELLOR OF THE EXCHEQUER
Sir Geoffrey Howe, May 1979–June 1983
Nigel Lawson, June 1983–October 1989
John Major, October 1989–November 1990

FOREIGN SECRETARY
Lord Carrington, May 1979–April 1982
Francis Pym, April 1982–June 1983
Sir Geoffrey Howe, June 1983–October 1989
Douglas Hurd, October 1989–July 1995

HOME SECRETARY
Sir William Whitelaw, May 1979–June 1983
Leon Brittan, June 1983–September 1985
Douglas Hurd, September 1985–October 1989
David Waddington, October 1989–November 1990

OPPOSITION LEADERS

LEADER OF THE LABOUR PARTY
James Callaghan, April 1976–November 1980
Michael Foot, November 1980–October 1983
Neil Kinnock, October 1983–July 1992

LEADER OF THE LIBERAL PARTY
David Steel, July 1976–March 1988

LEADER OF THE SOCIAL DEMOCRATIC PARTY
Roy Jenkins, July 1981–June 1983
David Owen, June 1983–June 1987
Robert Maclennan, June 1987–March 1988

LEADER OF THE LIBERAL DEMOCRATS
David Steel and Robert Maclennan, March 1988–July 1988
Paddy Ashdown, July 1988–August 1999

NATIONAL CONVENER OF THE SCOTTISH NATIONAL PARTY
Gordon Wilson, 1979–1990

PRESIDENT OF PLAID CYMRU
Gwynfor Evans, 1945–1981
Dafydd Wigley, 1981–1984
Dafydd Thomas, 1984–1991

LEADER OF THE ULSTER UNIONIST PARTY
James Molyneaux, 1979–1995

LEADER OF THE DEMOCRATIC UNIONIST PARTY
Iain Paisley, September 1971–May 2008

LEADER OF THE SOCIAL DEMOCRATIC AND LABOUR PARTY
John Hume, 1979–September 2001

PRESIDENT OF SINN FEIN
Ruairí Ó Brádaigh, October 1970–November 1983
Gerry Adams, November 1983 –

OTHER MAJOR OFFICES

ARCHBISHOP OF CANTERBURY
Donald Coggan, 1974–1980
Robert Runcie, 1980–1991

CABINET SECRETARY
Sir Robert Armstrong, 1979–1987
Sir Robin Butler, 1988–1998

CHIEF OF THE DEFENCE STAFF
Admiral of the Fleet Sir Terence Lewin, 1979–1982
Field Marshal Sir Edwin Bramall, 1982–1985
Admiral of the Fleet Sir John Fieldhouse, 1985–1988
Marshal of the Royal Air Force Sir David Craig, 1988–1991

DIRECTOR GENERAL OF THE BBC
Ian Trethowan, 1977–1982
Alasdair Milne, 1982–1987
Michael Checkland, 1987–1992

EDITOR OF *THE SUN*
Larry Lamb, 1975–1980
Kelvin MacKenzie, 1981–1994

GENERAL SECRETARY OF THE TRADES UNION COUNCIL
Len Murray, 1973–1984
Norman Willis, 1984–1993

ARTS AND SCIENCES

BOOKER PRIZE WINNERS

1980 William Golding (British) *Rites of Passage*
1981 Salman Rushdie (British) *Midnight's Children*
1982 Thomas Keneally (Australian) *Schindler's Ark*
1983 J. M. Coetzee (South African) *Life & Times of Michael K*
1984 Anita Brookner (British) *Hotel du Lac*
1985 Keri Hulme (New Zealander) *The Bone People*
1986 Kingsley Amis (British) *The Old Devils*
1987 Penelope Lively (British) *Moon Tiger*
1988 Peter Carey (Australian) *Oscar and Lucinda*
1989 Kazuo Ishiguro (British) *The Remains of the Day*

BRITISH NOBEL PRIZE WINNERS

Chemistry
1980 Frederick Sanger (shared with American, Walter Gilbert) 'for their contributions concerning the determination of base sequences in nucleic acids'
1982 Aaron Klug 'for his development of crystallographic electron microscopy and his structural elucidation of biologically important nucleic acid-protein complexes'

Economics
1984 Richard Stone 'for having made fundamental contributions to the development of systems of national accounts and hence greatly improved the basis for empirical economic analysis'

Literature
1983 William Golding 'for his novels which, with the perspicuity of realistic narrative art and the diversity and universality of myth, illuminate the human condition in the world of today'

Medicine
1982 John Vane (shared with Swedes Sune Bergstrom and Begt Sameulsson) 'for their discoveries concerning prostaglandins and related biologically active substances'

1988 Sir James Black (shared with Americans Gertrude Elion and George Hitchings) 'for their discoveries of important principles for drug treatment'

DECADE'S TEN BEST-SELLING ALBUMS

1 Dire Straits	*Brothers in Arms*	
2 Michael Jackson	*Bad*	
3 Michael Jackson	*Thriller*	
4 Queen	*Greatest Hits*	
5 Kylie Minogue	*Kylie*	
6 Whitney Houston	*Whitney*	
7 Fleetwood Mac	*Tango in the Night*	
8 Phil Collins	*No Jacket Required*	
9 Madonna	*True Blue*	
10 U2	*The Joshua Tree*	

CHART PERFORMANCE OF SINGLES RELEASED BY MADNESS

Release date	Title	Highest Chart Position
August 1979	'The Prince'	16
October 1979	'One Step Beyond'	7
December 1979	'My Girl'	3
March 1980	'Work Rest and Play' (EP)	6
September 1980	'Baggy Trousers'	3
November 1980	'Embarrassment'	4
January 1981	'The Return of the Los Palmas 7'	7
April 1981	'Grey Day'	4
September 1981	'Shut Up'	7
November 1981	'It Must Be Love'	4
February 1982	'Cardiac Arrest'	14
May 1982	'House of Fun'	1
July 1982	'Driving in My Car'	4
November 1982	'Our House'	5
February 1983	'Tomorrow's Just Another Day'	8
August 1983	'Wings of a Dove'	2
October 1983	'The Sun and the Rain'	5
February 1984	'Michael Caine'	11
May 1984	'One Better Day'	17
August 1985	'Yesterday's Men'	18
October 1985	'Uncle Sam'	21
January 1986	'Sweetest Girl'	35
November 1986	'(Waiting for) The Ghost Train'	18

MOST-WATCHED TELEVISION PROGRAMMES

	Programme	Channel	Date	Audience (millions)
1	*EastEnders*	BBC 1	25 December 1986	30.15
2	Royal wedding	BBC 1 & ITV	29 July 1981	28.40
3	*Coronation Street*	ITV	19 March 1989	26.93
4	*Dallas*	BBC 1	22 November 1980	21.60
5	*To the Manor Born*	BBC 1	9 November 1980	21.55
6	*Bread*	BBC 1	4 December 1988	20.97
7	*Neighbours*	BBC 1	4 March 1989	20.92
8	*Just Good Friends*	BBC 1	25 December 1986	20.75
9	News	BBC 1	25 December 1984	20.42
10	*Only Fools and Horses*	BBC 1	15 December 1989	20.12
11	*The Benny Hill Show*	ITV	7 January 1981	20.00
12	*This Is Your Life*	ITV	2 January 1980	19.75
13	*Porridge*	BBC 1	27 December 1984	19.36
14	*My Wife Next Door*	BBC 1	18 January 1980	19.30
15	*Jim'll Fix It*	BBC 1	1 March 1980	19.20
16	*Mastermind*	BBC 1	9 November 1980	19.15
17	*A Question of Sport*	BBC 1	5 February 1987	19.05
18	*Blankety Blank*	BBC 1	26 December 1980	19.05
19	*Open All Hours*	BBC 1	6 November 1985	18.96
20	*Wish You Were Here*	ITV	2 January 1985	18.95

SPORT

BBC SPORTS PERSONALITY OF THE YEAR

1980 Robin Cousins (figure skater)
1981 Ian Botham (cricketer)
1982 Daley Thompson (decathlete)
1983 Steve Cram (middle-distance runner)
1984 Jayne Torvill and Christopher Dean (figure skaters)
1985 Barry McGuigan (boxer)
1986 Nigel Mansell (Formula 1 racing driver)
1987 Fatima Whitbread (javelin thrower)
1988 Steve Davis (snooker player)
1989 Nick Faldo (golfer)

FOOTBALL: UK TEAMS IN THE WORLD CUP

1982 in Spain
England eliminated (on points difference) in the second round: W 3, D 2, L 0
Northern Ireland eliminated in the second round: W 1, D 3, L 1
Scotland eliminated in the first round (group stage): W 1, D 1, L 1
Wales did not qualify

1986 in Mexico
England eliminated in the quarter-finals (Argentina 2, England 1): W 2, D 1, L 2
Northern Ireland eliminated in the first round (group stage): W 0, D 1, L 2
Scotland eliminated in the first round (group stage): W 0, D 1, L 2
Wales did not qualify

FOOTBALL: FIRST DIVISION CHAMPIONS

1979/80	Liverpool	**1985/6**	Liverpool
1980/1	Aston Villa	**1986/7**	Everton
1981/2	Liverpool	**1987/8**	Liverpool
1982/3	Liverpool	**1988/9**	Arsenal
1983/4	Liverpool	**1989/90**	Liverpool
1984/5	Everton		

FOOTBALL: SCOTTISH PREMIER LEAGUE CHAMPIONS

1979/80	Aberdeen	**1985/6**	Celtic
1980/1	Celtic	**1986/7**	Rangers
1981/2	Celtic	**1987/8**	Celtic
1982/3	Dundee United	**1988/9**	Rangers
1983/4	Aberdeen	**1989/90**	Rangers
1984/5	Aberdeen		

CRICKET: THE ASHES

1981	England retained the Ashes, winning 3–1 (2 drawn), held in England
1982/3	Australia won back the Ashes, winning 2–1 (2 drawn), held in Australia
1985	England won back the Ashes, winning 3–1 (2 drawn), held in England
1986/7	England retained the Ashes, winning 2–1 (2 drawn), held in Australia
1989	Australia won back the Ashes, winning 4–0 (2 drawn), held in England

RUGBY: 5 NATIONS WINNERS

1980 England (Grand Slam)
1981 France (Grand Slam)
1982 Ireland (Triple Crown)
1983 France and Ireland
1984 Scotland (Grand Slam)
1985 Ireland (Triple Crown)
1986 France and Scotland
1987 France (Grand Slam)
1988 France and Wales (Triple Crown)
1989 France

TENNIS: FURTHEST PROGRESS OF BRITISH PLAYERS AT THE WIMBLEDON CHAMPIONSHIPS

Men's Singles

1980 Second Round (Mark Cox, Andrew Jarrett, Buster Mottram)
1981 Second Round (John Feaver, John Lloyd, Buster Mottram)
1982 Fourth Round (Buster Mottram)
1983 Second Round (Stuart Bale, Andrew Jarrett)
1984 Third Round (John Lloyd)
1985 Third Round (John Lloyd)
1986 Second Round (Stephen Botfield, Andrew Castle, Colin Dowdeswell, Nick Fulwood)
1987 Third Round (Jeremy Bates)
1988 Second Round (Jeremy Bates, Stephen Botfield)
1989 Third Round (Nick Fulwood)

Ladies' Singles

1980 Fourth Round (Virginia Wade)
1981 Fourth Round (Anne Hobbs, Jo Durie)
1982 Second Round (Anne Hobbs, Virginia Wade)
1983 Quarter-Finals (Virginia Wade)
1984 Quarter-Finals (Jo Durie)
1985 Fourth Round (Jo Durie)
1986 Third Round (Jo Durie, Anne Hobbs)
1987 Third Round (Jo Durie)
1988 Third Round (Julie Salmon)
1989 Third Round (Anne Hobbs)

OLYMPIC GAMES: BRITISH GOLD MEDAL WINNERS

1980 Moscow (5 gold medals)
Sebastian Coe (1,500 metres)
Duncan Goodhew (100 metres breaststroke)
Steve Ovett (800 metres)
Daley Thompson (decathlon)
Alan Wells (100 metres)

1984 Los Angeles (5 gold medals)
Sebastian Coe (1,500 metres)
Malcolm Cooper (shooting: rifle)
Andrew Holmes, Steven Redgrave, Martin Cross, Richard Budgett, Adrian Ellison (rowing: coxed fours)
Daley Thompson (decathlon)
Tessa Sanderson (javelin)

1988 Seoul (5 gold medals)
Malcolm Cooper (shooting: rifle)
GB team (men's hockey)
Andrew Holmes and Steven Redgrave (rowing: coxless pairs)
Michael McIntyre and Bryn Vaile (sailing: star class keelboat)
Adrian Moorhouse (100 metres breaststroke)

NOTES

Introduction
1 Charles Moore, *Sunday Telegraph*, 8 March 2008.

Chapter 1
1 In September 1978, Peter Jenkins went so far as to write in the *Guardian* that Britain could prove to be the first country to make 'the journey from developed to under-developed'.

2 'The Medium Term Assessment', memorandum by Gavyn Davies, 17 June 1977, in Kenneth O. Morgan, *Callaghan, A Life* (1997), p. 576.

3 While at Upper Clayhill, Callaghan kept to a strict early morning routine of patrolling around his farm. Morgan, *Callaghan*, p. 375.

4 MORI's private polling on 4 September 1978 suggested the Tories were on 47 per cent and Labour on 45 per cent (Morgan, *Callaghan*, p. 638). The following month, Gallup had Labour on 47.5 per cent and the Conservatives on 42 per cent, and in November, Labour on 48 per cent and the Conservatives on 43 per cent.

5 Morgan, *Callaghan*, pp. 639–40.

6 Lady Callaghan obituary, *Daily Telegraph*, 17 March 2005.

7 Morgan, *Callaghan*, p. 641.

8 Callaghan to Cledwyn Hughes, 5 April 1976, in Morgan, *Callaghan*, p. 474.

9 Quoted in Morgan, *Callaghan*, p. 320; see also Morgan, *Callaghan*, pp. 760–1.

10 Morgan, *Callaghan*, pp. 318–22.

11 BBC news footage of Callaghan's speech to the TUC conference, 5 September 1978.

12 *The Times*, 6 September 1978.

13 Cabinet Papers, 7 September 1978 (*The Times*, 1 January 2009).

14 David Steel, interviewed for *The Night the Government Fell: A Parliamentary Coup*, broadcast on BBC Parliament channel, 28 March 2009.

15 Edmund Dell, *The Chancellors* (1996), p. 390.

16 National Archives; quoted in 'Despot Planned Save Britain Fund', BBC News website, 1 January 2005.

17 John Campbell, *Edward Heath, A Biography* (1993), p. 589.

18 'Goodbye Great Britain', *Wall Street Journal*, 29 April 1975; quoted in Kathleen Burk and Alec Cairncross, *Goodbye, Great Britain: The 1976 IMF Crisis* (1992), p. xiv.

19 Transcript of conversation between Henry Kissinger and Gerald Ford, 8 January 1975, Ford Library, copy in Margaret Thatcher Foundation.

20 To the fore was David Stirling, the war hero and founder of the SAS, who established GB75, which he called 'an organisation of apprehensive patriots' aiming to prevent the constitution's subversion by the far left.

21 Nicholas Faith, *A Very Different Country: A Typically English Revolution* (2002), p. 195.

22 Susan Crosland, *Tony Crosland* (1982), p. 378.

23 Callaghan's speech to the Labour Party conference, 28 September 1976; quoted in Dell, *The Chancellors*, p. 427.

24 The M3 measure of the money supply averaged 12 per cent growth between 1976 and 1979. It was 10 per cent in 1975–6. Peter Clarke, *Hope and Glory* (1996), p. 351.

25 Dell, *The Chancellors*, p. 437.

26 *The Times*, 31 December 1976.

27 Paul Ormerod, 'Incomes Policy', in M. J. Artis and David Cobham, *Labour's Economic Policies 1974–79* (1991), p. 56.

28 Gallup tracked support of the two main parties as follows:

		Lab	Cons
1978	Oct	47.5	42
	Nov	48	43
	Dec	42.5	48
1979	Jan	41.5	49
	Feb	33	53
	Mar	37	51.5

29 Lipsey to Callaghan, Cabinet Papers, 5 October 1978 (*The Times*, 1 January 2009).

30 Jack Jones obituary, *The Times*, 23 April 2009.

31 The claim was made by Oleg Gordievsky, the KGB's bureau chief in London between 1982 and 1985, who stated he had paid Jones for information and 'had the pleasure of reading volumes of his files which were kept at the British department of the KGB until 1985 when they were transferred to the archives'. Gordievsky (who defected in 1985) claimed that Jones, given the codename 'Dream', was a 'very disciplined, useful agent' and that Jones's wife had been a Comintern agent since the mid-1930s. Jack Jones obituary, *Daily Telegraph*, 22 April 2009; Oleg Gordievsky, letter to the editor, *Daily Telegraph*, 28 April 2009.

32 *The Guardian*, 30 December 2008; *The Times*, 1 January 2009.

33 Philip Whitehead, *The Writing on the Wall* (1985); quoted in Faith, *A Very Different Country*, p. 218.

34 Lord Lever (Chancellor of the Duchy of Lancaster) to Lord Elwyn-Jones (Lord Chancellor) in Tony Benn, *Conflicts of Interest: Diaries 1977–80* (1990), p. 448.

35 Morgan, *Callaghan*, p. 679.

36 Michael Heseltine, *Life in the Jungle: My Autobiography* (2000), p. 172.

37 Recollection of Joe Ashton (Government Whip 1976–7), *The Night the Government Fell: A Parliamentary Coup*, broadcast on BBC Parliament channel, 28 March 2009.

38 Morgan, *Callaghan*, p. 679.

Chapter 2

1 Chris Horrie, '"Epoch-making" poster was clever fake', BBC News website, 16 March 2001.

2 Horrie, '"Epoch-making" poster was clever fake'; John Campbell, *Margaret Thatcher, Vol. 1: The Grocer's Daughter* (2000), p. 413.

3 MORI had the Conservatives on 51 per cent and Labour on 38 per cent on 1–2 April 1979, while Gallup had them on 50 and 40 per cent, respectively, between 6–9 April. With some fluctuations, this had slid to 45 and 37 per cent according to MORI on 2 May, and a knife-edge 43 to 41 per cent on 1–2 May according to Gallup. The actual result on polling day was Conservatives 43.9 per cent, Labour 37.7 per cent. David Butler and Dennis Kavanagh, *The British General Election of 1979* (1980), p. 264.

4 Butler and Kavanagh, *The British General Election of 1979*, p. 274.

5 When Thatcher pressed Callaghan in the Commons on the details of the IMF bail-out, he went so far as to offer the put-down: 'one day the Right Honourable Lady will understand these things a little better'. 8 June 1976, 912 HC Deb. cols 1192–3.

6 Thatcher to Michael Cockerell, interview for BBC *Campaign '79*, 27 April 1979, quoted in Dominic Sandbrook, *Seasons in the Sun: The Battle for Britain, 1974–1979* (2012), p. 783.

7 Campbell, *Margaret Thatcher, Vol. 1*, p. 436.

8 Butler and Kavanagh, *The British General Election of 1979*, p. 265.

9 Stephen Coleman, 'The Televised Leaders' Debate in Britain: From Talking Heads to Headless Chickens', *Parliamentary Affairs*, 51 (1998), pp. 183–4; Graham Stewart, 'Past Notes', *The Times*, 5 September 2009.

10 Butler and Kavanagh, *The British General Election of 1979*, p. 168; Campbell, *Margaret Thatcher, Vol. 1*, p. 427.

11 Campbell, *Margaret Thatcher, Vol. 1*, pp. 439–40.

12 *Times* diary, 11 September 1974. *The Times* concluded that 'her accent is unremarkable enough, and I think it is probably the pitch of her voice which irritates Mr Powell. It is a decibel or so too high for comfort. She speaks with undue deliberation and too little expression, having a rather mesmeric effect.'

13 Campbell, *Margaret Thatcher, Vol. 1*, p. 441.

14 Ronald Millar, *A View from the Wings* (1993), pp. 228, 227.

15 Michael Cockerell, *Live from Number 10: The Inside Story of Prime Ministers and Television* (1988), p. 234.

16 Thatcher's speech to Conservative rally in Cardiff, 16 April 1979, Margaret Thatcher Foundation.

17 Cockerell, *Live from Number 10*, pp. 251–2.

18 David Butler and Dennis Kavanagh, *The British General Election of 1983* (1984), p. 5.

19 Butler and Kavanagh, *The British General Election of 1979*, pp. 148–9.

20 Quoted in Butler and Kavanagh, *The British General Election of 1979*, p. 150.

21 Nigel Lawson, *The View From No. 11: Memoirs of a Tory Radical* (1992), p. 199.

22 Quoted in Butler and Kavanagh, *The British General Election of 1979*, p. 183.

23 Conservative Party 1979 general election manifesto.

24 Thatcher's speech to the Conservative local government conference, 2 March 1979, Margaret Thatcher Foundation.

25 Butler and Kavanagh, *The British General Election of 1979*, pp. 273–4.

26 BBC Gallup surveys 21–26 March and 3 March 1979, in Butler and Kavanagh, *The British General Election of 1979*, p. 342.

27 Quoted in Butler and Kavanagh, *The British General Election of 1979*, p. 188.

28 Quoted in Butler and Kavanagh, *The British General Election of 1979*, p. 195.

29 Graham Stewart, *The History of The Times*, vol. 7: *The Murdoch Years* (2005), p. 43

30 James Callaghan, election broadcast, 1 May 1979, in Butler and Kavanagh, *The British General Election of 1979*, p. 196.

31 Thatcher's speech to Conservative rally at Bolton, 1 May 1979, Margaret Thatcher Foundation.

32 Bernard Donoughue, *Prime Minister: The Conduct of Policy under Harold Wilson and James Callaghan* (1987), p. 191; quoted in Campbell, *Margaret Thatcher, Vol. 1*, p. 443.

33 MORI, in Butler and Kavanagh, *The British General Election of 1979*, p. 343.

34 *Guardian*, 5 May 1979.

35 There had, of course, been female prime ministers elsewhere in the world, like Golda

Meir in Israel and Indira Gandhi in India. Two months after Thatcher became prime minister in 1979, Maria da Lourdes Pintasilgo served as prime minister of Portugal for five months, but she was appointed rather than serving as the result of an election. As distinct from head of government, Vigdís Finnbogadóttir was elected Iceland's head of state (with minimal political power) in 1980. Isabel Perón had been appointed, rather than elected, Argentina's head of state in 1974–5.

36 Quoted in Campbell, *Margaret Thatcher, Vol. 1*, p. 446.

37 Campbell, *Margaret Thatcher, Vol. 1*, p. 446.

38 Campbell, *Margaret Thatcher, Vol. 1*, p. 1.

39 Campbell, *Margaret Thatcher, Vol. 1*, p. 29.

40 Campbell, *Margaret Thatcher, Vol. 1*, p. 19.

41 Margaret Thatcher, *The Path to Power* (1995), p. 28.

42 Campbell, *Margaret Thatcher, Vol. 1*, pp. 79, 84.

43 Dennis Walters, *Not Always with the Pack* (1989), p. 104.

44 Alfred Sherman, *Paradoxes of Power: Reflections on the Thatcher Interlude*, ed. Mark Garnett (2005), pp. 20–1.

45 Margaret Thatcher, interviewed by Margaret Howard on *The World this Weekend*, Radio 4, 16 May 1971.

46 Geraldine Bridgewater, *Ring of Truth* (2007), pp. 101–4.

47 Keith Joseph, speech to the Edgbaston Conservative Association, 19 October 1974; quoted in Andrew Denham and Mark Garnett, *Keith Joseph* (2001), pp. 267–8.

48 Thatcher, *The Path to Power*, p. 266.

49 *The Economist*, 30 November 1974; quoted in Alan Clark, *The Tories: Conservatives and the Nation State* (1998), p. 383.

50 Thatcher, *The Path to Power*, p. 269.

51 Richard Vinen, *Thatcher's Britain: The Politics and Social Upheaval of the Thatcher Era* (2009), p. 74.

52 Margaret Thatcher, interview for Scottish Television, 21 February 1975, Margaret Thatcher Foundation. Those who worked with her in opposition, such as George Gardiner, also noted her enduring admiration for Macmillan. George Gardiner, *Margaret Thatcher: From Childhood to Leadership* (1975), pp. 67–8.

53 Transcript of Thatcher interview with Hugo Young, 22 February 1983, Margaret Thatcher Foundation.

Chapter 3

1 Nigel Lawson, *The View from No. 11: Memoirs of a Tory Radical* (1992), p. 64. The credit for inventing the term 'Thatcherism' is generally given to the journal *Marxism Today*.

2 Christopher Johnson, *The Economy Under Mrs Thatcher, 1979–90* (1991), p. 38.

3 Jeff Rooker, Labour MP for Birmingham Perry Bar, Budget Debate, 12 June 1979, 968 HC Deb. col. 252.

4 Denis Healey in the House of Commons, 23 October 1979; quoted in the *Daily Telegraph*, 24 October 1979.

5 Edmund Dell, *The Chancellors* (1996), p. 464.

6 Eric Helleiner, *States and the Re-emergence of Global Finance, from Bretton Woods to the 1990s* (1994), p. 150.

7 Lawson, *The View from No. 11*, p. 32.

8 Minimum Band 1 Dealing Rate (the discount rate) <http://www.bankofengland.co.uk/statistics/rates/baserate.pdf> (August 2012).

9   Margaret Thatcher, *The Downing Street Years* (1993), p. 122.

10 *The Times*, 30 March 1981.

11 John Ranelagh, *Thatcher's People: An Insider's Account of the Politics, the Power and the Personalities* (1991), p. 227.

12 Lawson, *The View from No. 11*, p. 98.

13 Thatcher, *The Downing Street Years*, p. 138.

14 Patrick Minford, *The Times*, 7 April 1981.

15 Ian Gilmour, *Inside Right: A Study of Conservatism* (1977), p. 118.

16 Alan Sked and Chris Cook, *Post-War Britain: A Political History*, fourth edition (1993), p. 329.

17 Margaret Thatcher, *News of the World*, 20 September 1981.

18 Andrew Marr, *A History of Modern Britain* (2007), p. 386.

19 Thatcher, *The Downing Street Years*, p. 104.

20 Norman St John Stevas, *The Two Cities* (1984), p. 83.

21 Lord Ryder of Wensum to the author.

22 Michael Heseltine, *Life in the Jungle: My Autobiography* (2000), p. 232.

23 Lawson, *The View from No. 11*, p. 127. John Nott summarized her as 'aggressive' rather than 'dominant . . . On all sorts of issues there was a pretty good ding-dong discussion . . . Nobody kowtowed to Margaret Thatcher', while John Hoskyns believed she argued in order 'to satisfy herself that the thinking she was being given was good'. Nott and Hoskyns, interviews for *The Thatcher Factor*. The strengths and weaknesses of her arguing style are discussed by Cecil Parkinson, *Right at the Centre: An Autobiography* (1992), p. 21; George Walden, *Lucky George: Memoirs of an Anti-Politician* (1999), p. 191; and Alan Clark, *Diaries* (2000), p. 215 (14 June 1988).

24 Ronald Millar, *A View from the Wings* (1993), p. 327.

25 Paul Hirst, 'Miracle or Mirage? The Thatcher Years, 1979–1997', in *From Blitz to Blair: A New History of Britain since 1939*, ed. Nick Tiratsoo (1997), p. 193.

26 Ranelagh, *Thatcher's People*, p. ix.

27 Margaret Thatcher to Friedrich von Hayek, 18 May 1979, Thatcher MSS, THCR 2/4/1/8.

28 Peter York and Charles Jennings, *Peter York's Eighties* (1995), p. 11.

29 Recollection of Bruce Anderson, *The Times*, 31 August 2006.

30 Denis Healey, *The Time of My Life* (1989), p. 488.

31 Maurice Cowling, *The Times*, 4 February 1984.

32 Thatcher, *The Downing Street Years*, p. 109.

33 Thatcher on *Weekend World*, London Weekend Television, 1 February 1981, Margaret Thatcher Foundation.

34 David Parker, *The Official History of Privatisation*, vol. 1 (2009), p. 70.

35 Parker, *The Official History of Privatisation*, vol. 1, p. 70.

36 Jim Prior, *A Balance of Power* (1986), p. 122.

37 Thatcher, *The Downing Street Years*, p. 132.

38 Thatcher, *The Downing Street Years*, p. 52.

39 Thatcher, *The Downing Street Years*, pp. 129–30.

40 Thatcher to the *Guardian* Young Businessman of the Year lunch, 11 March 1981, Margaret Thatcher Foundation.

41 Thatcher, *The Downing Street Years*, pp. 151, 28–9.

42 John Junor, *Listening for a Midnight Tram* (1990), p. 263.

43 Thatcher, *The Downing Street Years*, p. 149.

Chapter 4

1   Andrew Glyn obituary, *The Times*, 8 January 2008.
2   Nigel Lawson, *The View from No. 11: Memoirs of a Tory Radical* (1992), p. 195.
3   R. E. Rowthorn and J. R. Wells, *Deindustrialization and Foreign Trade* (1987), pp. 180.
4   Christopher Johnson, *The Economy under Mrs Thatcher, 1979–90* (1991), p. 18 – at current price terms; the figures at 1985 constant prices painted only a slightly rosier picture of a fall from 27.1 per cent to 24.4 per cent from 1979 to 1989.
5   Christopher Langdon and David Manners, *Digerati Glitterati: High-Tech Heroes* (2001), p. 70.
6   Sidney Pollard, *The Wasting of the British Economy* (1982), pp. 2–3.
7   Sir Geoffrey Howe, budget speech, 12 June 1979, HC Deb. 5s., vol. 968, col. 237.
8   *Daily Telegraph*, 2 June 1979; quoted in Mark Garnett, *From Anger to Apathy:The Story of Politics, Society and Popular Culture in Britain since 1975*, (2007), p. 1.
9   Nicholas Henderson, *Mandarin: The Diaries of an Ambassador, 1969–1982* (1994), p. 406 (diary entry 4 July 1981).
10 Beatrix Campbell, *Wigan Pier Revisited: Poverty and Politics in the 80s* (1984), p. 169.
11 Matthew Parris in *The Times*, 23 January 1984.
12 Campbell, *Wigan Pier Revisited*, pp. 9–10.
13 Campbell, *Wigan Pier Revisited*, p. 14.
14 Low Pay Unit figures, *The Times*, 12 April 1989.
15 *Employment Gazette*, cited in Stephen Fothergill and Jill Vincent, *The State of the Nation* (1985), p. 50.
16 Ian Jack, *Before the Oil Ran Out, Britain 1977–86* (1987), p. 133.
17 George Orwell, *The Road to Wigan Pier* (1937), chapter five.
18 Jack, *Before the Oil Ran Out*, pp. 135–8.
19 Jack, *Before the Oil Ran Out*, p. 131.
20 Alexis Petridis, 'Ska for the Madding Crowd', *Guardian*, 8 March 2002.
21 Opinion Research and Communications poll for *The Times* and the Committee for Research into Public Attitudes, *The Times*, 10 September 1980.
22 This was the finding of 'Race Relations and the "Sus" Law', Home Affairs Committee, 1979–80.
23 Recollection of former PC Peter Bleksley, *The Reunion*, BBC Radio 4, 20 March 2011.
24 Martin Kettle and Lucy Hodges, *Uprising! The Police, the People and the Riots in Britain's Cities* (1982), p. 102.
25 Kettle and Hodges, *Uprising!*, p. 95.
26 Kettle and Hodges, *Uprising!*, p. 93.
27 Kettle and Hodges, *Uprising!*, p. 112.
28 Martin Huckerby, *The Times*, 13 April 1981.
29 Enoch Powell to the Commons, 13 April 1981, HC Deb. 6s., vol. 3, col. 25.
30 Kettle and Hodges, *Uprising!*, p. 191.
31 Kettle and Hodges, *Uprising!*, p. 159.
32 The journalist was Sasthi Brata, *The Times*, 15 April 1981.
33 Roy Hattersley to the Commons, 16 July 1981, HC Deb. 6s., vol. 8, col. 1408.
34 Kettle and Hodges, *Uprising!*, pp. 199–200.
35 *Police* magazine, May 1981; quoted in Kettle and Hodges, *Uprising!*, p. 185.
36 Michael Heseltine, *Life in the Jungle: My Autobiography* (2000), p. 221.
37 Heseltine, *Life in the Jungle*, p. 231.
38 Margaret Thatcher, *The Downing Street Years* (1993), p. 145.

39   *The Times*, 22 October 1981.

40   Thatcher to the Commons, 5 May 1981, HC Deb. 6s., vol. 4, col. 17.

Chapter 5

1   Ivor Crewe and Anthony King, *SDP: The Birth, Life and Death of the Social Democratic Party* (1995), p. 15.

2   Crewe and King, *SDP*, pp. 39–41.

3   Annual Conference Report 1980, pp. 31–2; quoted in Crewe and King, *SDP*, p. 49.

4   *The Times*, 30 September 1980.

5   Tony Benn, *The End of an Era: Diaries 1980–90* (1992), p. 11 (21 June 1980).

6   Benn, *The End of an Era*, pp. 33–4 (2 October 1980).

7   Benn, *The End of an Era*, pp. 35–6 (12 October 1980).

8   Benn, *The End of an Era*, p. 39 (20 October 1980).

9   Crewe and King, *SDP*, p. 75.

10   Anatoly Chernyaev diary, 5 December 1974; quoted in *The Spectator*, 7 November 2009.

11   *Time*, 16 February 1981.

12   David Kogan and Maurice Kogan, *The Battle for the Labour Party* (1982), pp. 45, 42.

13   Benn, *The End of an Era*, p. 9 (15 June 1980).

14   Benn, *The End of an Era*, p. 69 (24 January 1981).

15   Benn, *The End of an Era*, pp. 70–2 (25 January 1981).

16   *Sunday Times*, 25 January 1981.

17   Quoted in Crewe and King, *SDP*, p. 102.

18   Roy Jenkins, *European Diary, 1977–1981* (1989), p. 650.

19   Quoted in Crewe and King, *SDP*, p. 83.

20   *The Times*, 26 March 1981.

21   David Marquand, *The Progressive Dilemma from Lloyd George to Blair*, second edition (1999), p. 191.

22   Quoted in Crewe and King, *SDP*, p. 44.

23   See Crewe and King, *SDP*, pp. 111–113.

24   Julian Critchley, *A Bag of Boiled Sweets: An Autobiography* (1994), p. 195.

25   *The Times*, 29 January 1981.

26   *Daily Telegraph*, 3 March 2010.

27   Michael Foot obituary, *Daily Telegraph*, 4 March 2010.

28   Quoted in the *Daily Mail*, 4 March 2010.

29   Kenneth O. Morgan, *Labour People, Leaders and Lieutenants: Hardie to Kinnock* (1987), p. 287.

30   Benn, *The End of an Era*, p. 76 (27 January 1981).

31   Benn, *The End of an Era*, p. 146 (9 September 1981).

32   John Golding, *Hammer of the Left: Defeating Tony Benn, Eric Heffer and Militant in the Battle for the Labour Party* (2003), p. 191.

33   Benn, *The End of an Era*, pp. 149, 152 (19, 23 September 1981).

34   Kogan and Kogan, *The Battle for the Labour Party*, p. 114.

35   Patrick Seyd, *The Rise and Fall of the Labour Left* (1987), p. 136.

36   Kinnock to Ian Mikardo, 13 April 1981; quoted in Martin Westlake, *Kinnock: The Biography* (2001), p. 176.

37   Quoted in Robert Harris, *The Making of Neil Kinnock* (1984), p. 165.

38   *Daily Telegraph*, 12 June 1981.

39   Crewe and King, *SDP*, p. 54.

40   Quoted in Crewe and King, *SDP*, p. 140.

41 Crewe and King, *SDP*, p. 142.

42 Quoted in Crewe and King, *SDP*, p. 144.

Chapter 6

1 John Witherow and Patrick Bishop, *Winter War: The Falklands Conflict* (1982), p. 17.

2 Although the documentation remains classified, the claim that the Soviet Union passed on satellite data to Argentina during the conflict has been made by the Russian journalist Sergei Brilev, following interviews he conducted with senior Soviet intelligence and military officers of the time. *The Times*, 2 April 2010.

3 Hugh Bicheno, *Razor's Edge: The Unofficial History of the Falklands War* (2006), p. 106.

4 Estphal was labour minister at the time and was publicly voicing the private view of the West German Chancellor, Helmut Schmidt. *The Times*, 5 May 1982.

5 A full and dispassionate analysis of the history of the disputed claims to the Falkland Islands and its dependencies is contained in Lawrence Freedman's *The Official History of the Falklands Campaign*, vol. 1: *The Origins of the Falklands War* (2005), pp. 1–16.

6 The exact figure is disputed, with estimates ranging up to 30,000. The 11,000 figure has been suggested by Grupo Fahrenheit, using evidence gathered by the National Commission on the Disappeared (CONADEP).

7 Bicheno, *Razor's Edge*, p. 27.

8 Freedman, *Official History*, vol. 1, p. 153.

9 Freedman, *Official History*, vol. 1, pp. 77–8.

10 Freedman, *Official History*, vol. 1, p. 85.

11 Freedman, *Official History*, vol. 1, p. 163.

12 *The Times*, 31 March 1982.

13 Freedman, *Official History*, vol. 1, pp. 206–7

14 Freedman, *Official History*, vol. 1, p. 209.

15 John Nott, *Here Today, Gone Tomorrow* (2002), p. 258.

16 Alan Sked and Chris Cook, *Post-War Britain: A Political History*, fourth edition, (1993), p. 406.

17 Sir Lawrence Freedman, *The Official History of the Falklands Campaign*, vol. 2: *War and Diplomacy* (2005), pp. 12–13.

18 NOP opinion poll, *Daily Mail*, 6 April 1982.

19 Enoch Powell to the Commons, 3 April 1982, HC Deb. 6s., vol. 21, col. 644.

20 Margaret Thatcher, *The Downing Street Years* (1993), p. 181.

21 Michael Foot to the Commons, 3 April 1982, HC Deb. 6s., vol. 21. col. 638.

22 Tony Benn, *The End of an Era: Diaries 1980–90* (1992), p. 216 (27 April 1982), p. 213 (23 April 1982).

23 Benn, *The End of an Era*, pp. 207–8 (6 April 1982), p. 205 (5 April 1982).

24 Thatcher, *The Downing Street Years*, p. 186.

25 Freedman, *Official History*, vol. 2, p. 47.

26 Nott, *Here Today, Gone Tomorrow*, p. 305.

27 *The Times*, 14 May 1982.

28 Weinberger memoirs; quoted in Nott, *Here Today, Gone Tomorrow*, p. 286.

29 Bicheno, *Razor's Edge*, p. 123.

30 Thatcher, *The Downing Street Years*, pp. 205–8, 211.

31 Freedman, *Official History*, vol. 2, p. 171.

32 Freedman, *Official History*, vol. 2, p. 176.

33 Freedman, *Official History*, vol. 2, pp. 279–80; Bicheno, *Razor's Edge*, p. 126.

34 Bicheno, *Razor's Edge*, pp. 107, 109.

35 Sir Anthony Parsons, interview for the British Diplomatic Oral History Project, Churchill College, Cambridge; quoted in John Campbell, *Margaret Thatcher, Vol. 2: The Iron Lady* (2003), p. 145.

36 *Independent on Sunday*, 28 December 2003.

37 Peter Chippindale and Chris Horrie, *Stick It Up Your Punter!: The Rise and Fall of The Sun* (1991), p. 137.

38 Professor Bernard Crick, letter, *The Times*, 6 May 1982.

39 Tam Dalyell to the House of Commons, 21 December 1982.

40 Freedman, *Official History*, vol. 2, p. 746.

41 *Independent on Sunday*, 28 December 2003.

42 Draft US/Peruvian settlement, 6 May 1982; reproduced in Freedman, *Official History*, vol. 2, pp. 755–6.

43 Freedman, *Official History*, vol. 2, p. 327.

44 Freedman, *Official History*, vol. 2, p. 330.

45 Benn, *The End of an Era*, 29 April 1982, pp. 217–18.

46 Thatcher to the Commons, 20 May 1982, HC Deb. 6s. vol. 24 col. 483.

47 David Kynaston, *The Financial Times: A Centenary History* (1988), pp. 463–6.

48 Geoffrey Taylor, *Changing Faces: A History of the Guardian, 1956–88* (1993), pp. 228–33.

49 *New Statesman*, front cover, 30 April 1982; *New Statesman*, 'Mad Margaret and the Voyage of Dishonour', 9 April 1982.

50 *The Times*, 5 April 1982.

51 Graham Stewart, *The History of The Times*, vol. 7: *The Murdoch Years* (2005), p. 128.

52 Stewart, *The History of The Times*, vol. 7, p. 130.

53 Robert Harris, *Gotcha! The Media, the Government and the Falklands Crisis* (1983), p. 56.

54 Major General Julian Thompson (ed.), *The Imperial War Museum Book of Modern Warfare* (2002), p. 358, note 5.

55 Bicheno, *Razor's Edge*, p. 156.

56 Freedman, *Official History*, vol. 2, p. 559; Bicheno, *Razor's Edge*, p. 158.

57 Bicheno, *Razor's Edge*, p. 177; Freedman, *Official History*, vol. 2, p. 570.

58 Bicheno, *Razor's Edge*, pp. 186–7.

59 Freedman, *Official History*, vol. 2, p. 617.

60 Freedman, *Official History*, vol. 2, p. 647.

61 Max Hastings and Simon Jenkins, *The Battle for the Falklands* (1997), p. 350.

62 Freedman, *Official History*, vol. 2, p. 652.

63 Freedman, *Official History*, vol. 2, p. 652.

64 Freedman, *Official History*, vol. 2, p. 672.

65 Benn, *The End of an Era*, p. 229 (16 June 1982).

66 Benn, *The End of an Era*, p. 228 (15 June 1982).

67 Campbell, *Margaret Thatcher, Vol. 2*, pp. 139–40.

68 Thatcher to the Conservative Party rally, 3 July 1982, Margaret Thatcher Foundation.

Chapter 7

1 *The Economist*, 14 May 1983; quoted in David Butler and Dennis Kavanagh, *The British General Election of 1983* (1984), p. 206.

2 Butler and Kavanagh, *The British General Election of 1983*, p. 16.

3 Thatcher used the phrase in her New Year message of 31 December 1982 and it became a catchphrase for the Tories' 1983 general election campaign.

4 Butler and Kavanagh, *The British General Election of 1983*, p. 11.

5 Butler and Kavanagh, *The British General Election of 1983*, p. 40.

6 *The Challenge of Our Times*, Conservative Party manifesto, 1983.

7 *The New Hope for Britain*, Labour Party manifesto, 1983.

8 Butler and Kavanagh, *The British General Election of 1983*, p. 143.

9 Butler and Kavanagh, *The British General Election of 1983*, pp. 112–13.

10 *The Times*, 1 December 1982.

11 Butler and Kavanagh, *The British General Election of 1983*, p. 133.

12 Butler and Kavanagh, *The British General Election of 1983*, p. 144.

13 Butler and Kavanagh, *The British General Election of 1983*, p. 124.

14 *The Times*, 21 April 1982.

15 Quoted in Ivor Crewe and Anthony King, *SDP: The Birth, Life and Death of the Social Democratic Party* (1995), p. 165.

16 After the success at Glasgow Hillhead, the SDP lost by-elections at Beaconsfield, Birmingham Northfield, Coatbridge and Airdrie, Glasgow Queen's Park, Gower, Mitcham and Morden, and Peckham.

17 *Working Together for Britain*, Liberal–SDP Alliance manifesto, 1983.

18 Crewe and King, *SDP*, p. 254.

19 Graham Stewart, *The History of The Times*, vol. 7: *The Murdoch Years* (2005), pp. 162–3; Crewe and King, *SDP*, p. 498; Butler and Kavanagh, *The British General Election of 1983*, pp. 194–5.

20 *Daily Mirror*, 9 June 1982; *The Sun*, 9 June 1982; *Daily Express*, 9 June 1982.

21 Butler and Kavanagh, *The British General Election of 1983*, pp. 231, 234.

22 Butler and Kavanagh, *The British General Election of 1983*, p. 291.

23 Lord Pym obituary, *Daily Telegraph*, 7 March 2008.

24 Total taxes including social security contributions and local rates but excluding North Sea taxes as a percentage of national GDP, in Nigel Lawson, *The View from No. 11: Memoirs of a Tory Radical* (1992), Annex. 7, p. 1081.

25 Lawson, *The View from No. 11*, p. 481.

26 Nicholas Ridley, *My Style of Government: The Thatcher Years* (1991), p. 189.

27 Lawson, *The View from No. 11*, p. 536.

28 Lawson, *The View from No. 11*, pp. 339–40.

29 Brian Harrison, *Finding a Role?: The United Kingdom, 1970–1990* (2010), p. 259.

30 Lawson, *The View from No. 11*, p. 301.

31 Lawson, *The View from No. 11*, p. 526.

32 'Introducing the PSDR', *The Economist*, 19 March 1988.

33 Lawson, *The View from No. 11*, p. 195.

34 Andrew Marr, *A History of Britain*, BBC TV series.

35 Christopher Johnson, *The Economy under Mrs Thatcher, 1979–90* (1991), p. 158.

36 Johnson, *The Economy under Mrs Thatcher*, p. 131.

37 Christopher Harvie, *Fool's Gold: The Story of North Sea Oil* (1994), p. 312.

38 Harvie, *Fool's Gold*, p. 314.

39 Harvie, *Fool's Gold*, p. 319.

40 Thatcher to the Conservative Central Council, 15 March 1986, Margaret Thatcher Foundation.

41 Ian Gilmour, *Dancing with Dogma* (1992), p. 46.

42 In 1985, the equivalent figures for oil production were 79 million tonnes at a value of $16.7 billion for the UK and 32 million tonnes at a value of $6 billion for Norway. By 1990, the figures were 53.8 million tonnes and $9.4 billion for the UK versus 68 million tonnes and $11 billion for Norway. Harvie, *Fool's Gold*, p. 363.

43 Harvie, *Fool's Gold*, pp. 325–8.

44 John Hawksworth, 'A £450 Billion Question – Dude, Where's My Oil Money?' PricewaterhouseCoopers, February 2008, pp. 2–3.

45 *Independent*, 2 June 2010.

46 Hawksworth, 'A £450 Billion Question', p. 2.

Chapter 8

1 Anatoly Dobrynin, *In Confidence: Moscow's Ambassador to America's Six Cold War Presidents (1962–1986)* (1995), p. 528; quoted in John Lewis Gaddis, *The Cold War* (2005), p. 227.

2 Nathan Bennett Jones, 'Operation RYAN, Able Archer 83 and Miscalculation: The War Scare of 1983', paper for the University of California Santa Barbara International Graduate Student Conference on the Cold War, April 2008.

3 Gaddis, *The Cold War*, p. 228.

4 Ronald E. Powaski, *Return to Armageddon: The United States and the Nuclear Arms Race 1981–1999* (2000), p. 42.

5 Bennett Jones, 'Operation RYAN', p. 5.

6 Quoted in Lawrence Freedman, *The Politics of British Defence, 1979–98* (1999), p. 136.

7 Michael Heseltine, *Life in the Jungle: My Autobiography* (2000), p. 248.

8 Security Service Archives; quoted in Christopher Andrew, *The Defence of the Realm: The Authorized History of MI5* (2009), pp. 675–6.

9 Though he did not coin the phrase, the investigative journalist Duncan Campbell helped popularize the term with regard to Britain and used it as the title of his 1985 study of the 'Implications of American Military Power in Britain'.

10 By not buying the missiles, Britain paid only £10 million towards the cost of their deployment, leaving the American taxpayer to fund nearer £2.5 billion of the cost.

11 Margaret Thatcher, *The Downing Street Years* (1993), p. 268.

12 United Nations General Assembly resolution 38/7.

13 Thatcher, *The Downing Street Years*, p. 331

14 NOP opinion poll published in the *Daily Mail*, 9 November 1983; cited in Freedman, *The Politics of British Defence*, p. 134.

15 David Fairhall, *Common Ground: The Story of Greenham* (2006), p. 30.

16 Fairhall, *Common Ground*, p. 187.

17 Fairhall, *Common Ground*, p. 196.

18 Fairhall, *Common Ground*, p. 36.

19 *Daily Express*, 13 December 1982; quoted in Fairhall, *Common Ground*, p. 41.

20 NOP opinion poll, 23 May 1983, in David Butler and Dennis Kavanagh, *The British General Election of 1983* (1984), p. 182.

21 Fairhall, *Common Ground*, p. 84.

22 Fairhall, *Common Ground*, pp. 102–3.

23 A comparison between the German and English lyrics of '*99 Luftballons*/99 Red Balloons' can be found at <http://www.inthe80s.com/redger3.shtml> (August 2012).

24 Reagan in a radio broadcast, 7 August 1978; quoted in Gaddis, *The Cold War*, p. 217.

25 *Time* magazine, 3 December 1984.

26 Memorandum of conversation at Camp David, 22 December 1984, European and Soviet Affairs Directorate, NSC: Records (File Folder: Thatcher Visit – 1984 [1] Box 90902), Reagan Archive, copy in Margaret Thatcher Foundation. Memorandum of conversation at Camp David, 22 December 1984 (NSC, Box 90902).

27 John Campbell, *Margaret Thatcher, Vol. 2: The Iron Lady* (2003), p. 292.

28 Thatcher, *The Downing Street Years*, p. 467.

29   Memorandum of conversation at Camp David, 22 December 1984, European and Soviet Affairs Directorate, NSC: Records (File Folder: Thatcher Visit – 1984 [1] Box 90902), Reagan Archive, copy in Margaret Thatcher Foundation. Memorandum of conversation at Camp David, 22 December 1984 (NSC, Box 90902).

30   Heseltine, *Life in the Jungle*, p. 257.

31   Thatcher's speech to Joint Houses of Congress, 20 February 1985, Margaret Thatcher Foundation.

32   Michael L. Dockrill and Michael F. Hopkins, *The Cold War, 1945–1991* (2006), p. 144.

33   Vladimir Lukin (Russian ambassador to the United States, 1992–4) to the Carnegie Endowment for International Peace, Washington, DC; quoted in Paul Johnson, *A History of the American People* (1997), p. 776.

34   Thatcher, *The Downing Street Years*, p. 463.

35   Thatcher to press conference after addressing the UN General Assembly, 24 October 1985, Margaret Thatcher Foundation.

36   Dmitri Volkogonov, *The Rise and Fall of the Soviet Empire* (1998), pp. 414–15.

37   Thatcher, *The Downing Street Years*, p. 458.

38   Thatcher, *The Downing Street Years*, pp. 459–63.

39   Robert C. McFarlane, *Special Trust*, p. 301.

40   Mikhail Gorbachev, *Memoirs* (1996), p. 548.

41   Campbell, *Margaret Thatcher, Vol. 2*, pp. 297–8.

42   Gaddis, *The Cold War*, p. 226.

43   Kenneth Adelman to Paul Lettow, quoted in Paul Lettow, *Ronald Reagan and his Quest to Abolish Nuclear Weapons* (2005), p. 132.

44   Quoted in Gaddis, *The Cold War*, p. 232.

45   Thatcher, *The Downing Street Years*, p. 471.

46   Ronald Reagan, 12 October 1986; quoted in *The Times*, 13 October 1986.

47   Text in Thatcher, *The Downing Street Years*, p. 473.

48   Fairhall, *Common Ground*, p. 193.

49   Fairhall, *Common Ground*, p. 199.

50   Thatcher, *The Downing Street Years*, p. 472.

Chapter 9

1   *The Times*, 21 October 1981.

2   *The Times*, 2 June 1983.

3   Stephen Fay, *Power Play: The Life and Times of Peter Hall* (1995), p. 274.

4   *The Times*, 26 October 1982.

5   Robert Skidelsky, *John Maynard Keynes*, vol. 3: *Fighting for Britain 1937–1946* (2001), pp. 288, 290; Christopher Gordon and Peter Stark, 'Funding of the Arts and Heritage' <http:// www.publications.parliament.uk/pa/cm201011/cmselect/cmcumeds/writev/464/034.htm> (August 2012).

6   *The Times*, 31 March 1984.

7   Roy Strong, *The Roy Strong Diaries 1967–1987* (1997), p. 331 (14 April 1983); Luke Rittner, interview with the author, 16 March 2011.

8   *The Times*, 21 October 1981, 2 June 1983, 29 December 1989.

9   Statement by Iain Sproat, MP, minister for sport, 11 July 1994, HC Deb. 6s., vol. 246, col. 655.

10   Richard Cork, *New Spirit, New Sculpture, New Money: Art in the 1980s* (2003), pp. 13–15.

11   Cork, *New Spirit, New Sculpture, New Money*, p. 468.

12   Strong, *The Roy Strong Diaries*, p. 338 (12 July 1983).

13   Hanif Kureishi at the council meeting of the Royal Court Theatre, 13 July 1987, and Caryl Churchill at the 'British Theatre in Crisis' conference, 1988; quoted in Philip Roberts, *About Churchill: The Playwright and the Work* (2008), pp. 109, 110.

14   Michael Billington, *State of the Nation: British Theatre since 1945* (2007), p. 307.

15   Quoted in Nicholas Faith, *A Very Different Country: A Typically English Revolution* (2002), p. 234.

16   *The Observer*, 18 March 2007.

17   This point was made by Thatcher's biographer, John Campbell, *Margaret Thatcher, Vol. 2: The Iron Lady* (2003), p. 412.

18   Rittner, interview with the author, 16 March 2011.

19   Howard Brenton in the *Guardian*, 29 November 1990; quoted in George W. Brandt (ed.), *British Television Drama in the 1980s* (1993), p. 9.

20   Leonard Quart, 'British Film in the Thatcher Era', in Stanislao Pugliese (ed.), *The Political Legacy of Margaret Thatcher* (2003), p. 224.

21   Roberts, *About Churchill*, p. 109.

22   Billington, *State of the Nation*, p. 284.

23   Graham Stewart, *The History of The Times*, vol. 7: *The Murdoch Years* (2005), p. 115.

24   *The Times*, 4 April 1984.

25   Fay, *Power Play*, p. 302.

26   Fay, *Power Play*, p. 304.

27   *The Times*, 31 March 1981.

28   Strong, *The Roy Strong Diaries*, p. 412 (1 April 1987).

29   Cork, *New Spirit, New Sculpture, New Money*, p. 15

30   Cork, *New Spirit, New Sculpture, New Money*, pp. 15–16.

31   'De Kooning Work Sells For Record $20.6 million', *Los Angeles Times*, 9 November 1989.

32   Sir Harold Wilson to the House of Commons, 5 December 1979, and *Daily Express*, 6 December 1979; quoted in Peter Chippindale and Suzanne Franks, *Dished!: The Rise and Fall of British Satellite Broadcasting* (1991), p. 3.

33   Labour Party, *Labour's Programme 1982* (1982), p. 214.

34   Quoted in Des Freedman, *Television Polices of the Labour Party, 1951–2001* (2003), p. 121.

35   *The Times*, 1 November 1984.

36   Quoted in Jeremy Isaacs, *Storm Over 4: A Personal Account* (1989), p. 59.

37   Quoted in Isaacs, *Storm Over 4*, p. 65.

38   Matthew Horsman, *Sky High: The Inside Story of BSkyB* (1997), p. 2.

39   Quoted in Horsman, *Sky High*, p. 52.

40   Lord Whitelaw, House of Lords, 9 October 1990; quoted in Chippindale and Franks, *Dished!*, p. 268.

41   Andrew Neil, *Full Disclosure* (1997), p. 308.

42   Quoted in Horsman, *Sky High*, p. 75.

43   Chippindale and Franks, *Dished!*, Appendix.

44   Quoted in Horsman, *Sky High*, p. 69.

45   Nigel Lawson, *The View from No. 11: Memoirs of a Tory Radical* (1992), p. 314.

46   Brandt, *British Television Drama in the 1980s*, p. 142.

47   Recollection of Rupert Murdoch; quoted in Horsman, *Sky High*, p. 72.

48   Labour's submission to the Peacock Commission; quoted in Freedman, *Television Policies of the Labour Party*, pp. 137–8.

49   Quoted in *The Times*, 4 July 1986.

50   Quoted in Freedman, *Television Polices of the Labour Party*, p. 139.

51   Letter from Thatcher to Bruce Gyngell; quoted in the *Guardian*, 18 October 1991.

52   Alwyn Turner, *Rejoice! Rejoice!: Britain in the 1980s* (2010), p. 293.

53   William Shawcross, *Murdoch* (1992), pp. 350–1.

54   Studies by Monica Simms and Equity, 1985; cited in Brandt, *British Television Drama in the 1980s*, p. 219.

55   'The New Alternatives', *The Spectator*, 7 August 2010.

56   John Lloyd, interview, *Best Ever Spitting Image*, ITV, 26 June 2006.

57   Lord Steel and Lord Owen, interviews, *Best Ever Spitting Image*.

58   Bernard Ingham, interview, *Best Ever Spitting Image*.

59   Thatcher at the 1984 National Viewers and Listeners Association award ceremony; quoted in Brandt, *British Television Drama in the 1980s*, p. 82.

60   Paul Eddington in January 1984; quoted in Brandt, *British Television Drama in the 1980s*, p. 63.

61   *Variety*, 21 May 1986, and Herbert Kretzmer in the *Daily Mail*, 10 January 1986; quoted in Brandt, *British Television Drama in the 1980s*, p. 64.

62   British Film and Television Producers' Association statistics; cited in *The Times*, 23 December 1989.

63   Sarah Street, *British National Cinema* (1997), p. 22.

64   *Variety* magazine <http://www.variety.com/review/VE1117789506?refcatid=31> (August 2012).

65   A panel of Britain's leading film-makers voted *Withnail & I* the second-best British film made between 1984 and 2009. *Trainspotting* (1996) came first. *Observer*, 30 August 2009.

66   *The Times*, 23 December 1989.

67   *Daily Mail*, 30 June 1983; quoted in Turner, *Rejoice! Rejoice!*, p. 208.

68   Street, *British National Cinema*, p. 20.

Chapter 10

1   Among some architects, the loathing was so deep that even twenty-five years later, when, in May 2009, Prince Charles was asked to address RIBA in its 175th anniversary year, Peter Ahrends, whose proposed National Gallery extension the prince had singled out for particular attack, was among prominent architects, who also included Will Alsop and Piers Gough, who organized a boycott of his speech.

2   China Wharf, 29 Mill Street, completed in 1989 by CZWG, was on the cover of *The Phone Book*, London residential L–Z, December 1990.

3   Quoted in David Kynaston, *The City of London*, vol. 4: *A Club No More 1945–2000* (2001), p. 700.

4   Quinlan Terry, 'Origin of the Orders', in *Architectural Review*, February 1983, reprinted in Quinlan Terry, *Selected Works* (1993), pp. 126–8.

5   Alan Clark, *Diaries* (2000), p. 350 (17 November 1990).

6   David Watkin, 'A New Order for Office Buildings', *City Journal*, Spring 1996.

7   Peter Murray and Stephen Trombley, *Modern Architecture Guide: Britain* (1990), p. 12.

8   See, for instance, Quinlan Terry, speech to the Cambridge Union Society, January 1990, in Terry, *Selected Works*, p. 133.

9   Prince Charles, speech delivered at Hampton Court Palace for the 150th anniversary of the Royal Institute of British Architects, 30 May 1984, Prince of Wales website: Articles and Speeches.

10   Prince Charles, speech delivered at the Mansion House to the Corporation of London's

Planning and Communication Committee Annual Dinner, 1 December 1987, Prince of Wales website: Articles and Speeches.

11 *New York Times*, 9 September 1989.

12 Thatcher to the Conservative Party conference, 9 October 1987, Margaret Thatcher Foundation.

13 Charles Jencks, *Post-Modern Triumphs in London* (1991), p. 10; Martin Pawley obituary, *Independent*, 12 April 2008.

14 *New York Times*, 9 September 1989.

15 Martin Pawley obituary, *Guardian*, 11 March 2008.

16 Jencks, *Post-Modern Triumphs in London*, p. 16.

Chapter 11

1 Patrick Humphries, *Melody Maker*, 12 September 1981.

2 Quoted in Simon Reynolds, *Rip It Up and Start Again: Postpunk 1978–1984* (2005), p. 503. Horn also said: 'It's my job to enhance their ideas. No one complained when George Martin did that to The Beatles, adding a cello or harpsichord. Technology is there to be used.' Quoted in *The Times*, 14 February 1985.

3 Paul Morley interview, *The Quietus*, 15 December 2008.

4 Steve Strange, *Blitzed!* (2002), pp. 42, 46–8; David Rimmer, *New Romantics: The Look* (2003), pp. 53, 35; Rusty Egan interview, *The Guardian*, 15 May 2010.

5 Quoted in Reynolds, *Rip It Up and Start Again*, p. 375.

6 Reynolds, *Rip It Up and Start Again*, p. 531.

7 Reynolds, *Rip It Up and Start Again*, p. 413.

8 *The Times*, 11 December 1990.

9 Reynolds, *Rip It Up and Start Again*, pp. 286, 281.

10 Suggs, interview with Paul Gambaccini for MTV, 1983.

11 John Reed, *House of Fun: The Story of Madness* (2010), p. 193.

12 Johnny Marr, interview for *The South Bank Show*, ITV, 18 October 1987.

13 Quoted in Johnny Rogan, *Morrissey & Marr: The Severed Alliance* (1993), p. 215.

14 Paul Lester, sleeve notes to *The Very Best of The Smiths*, 2001.

15 Quoted in Rogan, *Morrissey & Marr*, p. 255.

16 Quoted in Rogan, *Morrissey & Marr*, p. 207.

17 Quoted in Rogan, *Morrissey & Marr*, p. 209.

18 Johnny Marr to *Hot Press*; quoted in Rogan, *Morrissey & Marr*, p. 256.

19 Quoted in James Nice, *Shadowplayers: The Rise and Fall of Factory Records* (2010), p. 184.

20 Dave Haslam, *Manchester England: The Story of the Pop Cult City* (1999), p. 170.

21 Vernon Coleman in *The Sun*, 19 October 1988; quoted in Matthew Collin, *Altered State: The Story of Ecstasy Culture and Acid House* (1998), p. 77.

22 Quoted in Collin, *Altered State*, p. 101.

23 Quoted in Collin, *Altered State*, p. 111.

24 *Daily Mail*, leading article, 26 June 1989; quoted in Collin, *Altered State*, p. 97.

25 *Daily Telegraph*, 17 April 2009.

26 Collin, *Altered State*, pp. 293, 306, 267, 132.

27 Shaun Ryder in *Melody Maker*, 13 May 1995; quoted in Collin, *Altered State*, p. 168.

28 Haslam, *Manchester England*, p. 179.

29 Quoted in Nice, *Shadowplayers*, p. 469.

30 Quoted in Nice, *Shadowplayers*, p. 484.

31 *Guardian*, 31 January 1991.

Chapter 12

1   Matthew Parris, *The Spectator*, 21 November 2007.

2   Thatcher interview transcript, 23 September 1987, Margaret Thatcher Foundation.

3   Thatcher interview, 23 September 1987, ibid.

4   Margaret Thatcher, *The Downing Street Years* (1993), p. 626.

5   Report of the Archbishop of Canterbury's Commission on Urban Priority Areas, *Faith in the City: A Call for Action by Church and Nation* (1985), p. 352.

6   See, for instance, Thatcher's reply to David Steel at Prime Minister's Questions, 23 March 1989, Margaret Thatcher Foundation.

7   A. H. Halsey and Josephine Webb (eds), *Twentieth-Century British Social Trends* (2000), Table 2.17, p. 62.

8   Central Statistical Office, *Annual Abstract of Statistics*, no. 127 (1991), Table 2.13, p. 24.

9   Central Statistical Office, *Annual Abstract of Statistics* (1991), Table 2.17, p. 30. The 1979 and 1989 figures are for the UK, the 2005 figures for England and Wales, the latter calculated by the Office of National Statistics, reported in *Daily Telegraph*, 22 October 2010.

10   Halsey and Webb, *Twentieth-Century British Social Trends*, Table 2.1, p. 50.

11   Brian Harrison, *Finding a Role?: The United Kingdom, 1970–1990* (2010), p. 224.

12   Thatcher to the Finchley Inter-Church Luncheon Club, 17 November 1969, Margaret Thatcher Foundation.

13   Thatcher, *The Downing Street Years*, p. 630.

14   Alwyn Turner, *Rejoice! Rejoice!: Britain in the 1980s* (2010), p. 219.

15   Central Statistical Office, *Annual Abstract of Statistics* (1991), Table 4.1, p. 75; Table 4.12, p. 83; Table 4.19, p. 87.

16   Thatcher to the Conservative Central Council, 27 March 1982, Margaret Thatcher Foundation.

17   Thatcher to the Conservative Party conference, 9 October 1987, Margaret Thatcher Foundation.

18   Thatcher to the Conservative Party conference, 12 October 1990, Margaret Thatcher Foundation.

19   Turner, *Rejoice! Rejoice!*, p. 89.

20   *The New Hope for Britain*, Labour Party manifesto, 1983, 'Law, Order and Justice' section.

21   Quoted in Peter Gerard Pearse and Nigel Matheson, *Ken Livingstone or The End of Civilization As We Know It: A Selection of Quotes, Quips and Quirks* (1982), p. 34.

22   Victor Bailey, 'Crime in Twentieth Century Britain', *History Today*, 38, no. 5.

23   Central Statistical Office, *Annual Abstract of Statistics* (1991), Table 4.3, p. 77.

24   Halsey and Webb, *Twentieth-Century British Social Trends*, pp. 698–9.

25   Central Statistical Office, *Annual Abstract of Statistics* (1991), Table 4.9, p. 81.

26   *The Times*, 29 September 1985; *Guardian*, 30 September 1985; *The Crisis*, 92, no. 10, p. 58 (December 1985).

27   *The Times*, 8 October 1985.

28   *The Times*, 9 October 1985; *Guardian*, 9 October 1985.

29   *Daily Telegraph*, 8 October 1985.

30   Quoted in Andy McSmith, *No Such Thing as Society* (2010), p. 275.

31   The Hillsborough Stadium Disaster, 15 April 1989, Inquiry by the Rt Hon. Lord Justice Taylor (HMSO, 1990), p. 5.

32   Virginia Berridge, *AIDS in the UK, The Making of Policy 1981–1994* (1996), p. 232.

33 *The Times*, 21 November 1984.

34 *The Times*, 13 December 1986.

35 *Daily Express*, 11 November 1986; *The Sun*, 11 November 1986, quoted in Berridge, *AIDS in the UK*, p. 110.

36 Peter Chippindale and Chris Horrie, *Stick It Up Your Punter!: The Rise and Fall of The Sun* (1991), p. 325.

37 *The Times*, 10 January 1985.

38 Author's recollection.

39 Berridge, *AIDS in the UK*, p. 1.

40 Harrison, *Finding a Role?*, p. 218.

41 Berridge, *AIDS in the UK*, p. 2.

42 *The Times*, 13 December 1986.

43 *The Times*, 12 December 1986.

44 *The Times*, 13 December and 12 December 1986.

45 Quoted in McSmith, *No Such Thing as Society*, p. 229.

46 Turner, *Rejoice! Rejoice!*, p. 219.

47 Richard Ingrams, *Muggeridge: The Biography* (1996), p. 243.

48 *Don't Die of Ignorance*, Government information leaflet (HMSO, 1986).

49 Harrison, *Finding a Role?*, p. 215.

50 Turner, *Rejoice! Rejoice!*, p. 219.

51 *The Times*, 28 February 1981.

52 *Guardian*, 21 March 2001.

53 Matthew Parris, *Chance Witness: An Outsider's Life in Politics* (2002), pp. 261, 265, 260.

54 Tatchell later claimed that a Liberal activist had confessed to him that his party was behind the smear. *Independent*, 27 January 2006.

55 *The Times*, 17 March 1987.

56 Quoted in Turner, *Rejoice! Rejoice!*, p. 218.

57 *New York Times*, 2 August 1988.

58 Thatcher to David Frost, transcript of interview for TV-am, 30 December 1988, Margaret Thatcher Foundation.

59 Peter Walker to the Rev. David Jenkins, Bishop of Durham, 5 October 1984; quoted in Francis Beckett and David Hencke, *Marching to the Fault Line: The 1984 Miners' Strike and the Death of Industrial Britain* (2009), pp. 136–7.

60 *The Times*, 27 March 1989.

61 Thatcher to Brian Walden, transcript of interview, Weekend World, 6 January 1980, Margaret Thatcher Foundation.

62 *Faith in the City*, pp. 208, 209, 190, 187, 211–13.

63 Quoted in Andrew Chandler, *The Church of England in the Twentieth Century: The Church Commissioners and the Politics of Reform, 1948–1998* (2006), p. 433.

64 Figures for England and Wales only. Dominic Hobson, *The National Wealth: Who Gets What in Britain* (1999), p. 912.

65 Hobson, *The National Wealth*, p. 912.

66 Figures for England and Wales only. Halsey and Webb, *Twentieth-Century British Social Trends*, Table 17.1, p. 589; Table 17.2, p. 590.

67 Halsey and Webb, *Twentieth-Century British Social Trends*, Tables 17.2 and 17.3, pp. 601–2.

68 National Trust figures for England, Wales and Northern Ireland. Halsey and Webb, *Twentieth-Century British Social Trends*, Table 17.18, pp. 610–11.

69 Charities Aid Foundation, cited in Halsey and Webb, *Twentieth-Century British Social Trends*, p. 598.

70 *Daily Telegraph*, 3 May 2010; David Rieff, *Prospect* magazine, July 2005. Contrary arguments to Rieff's thesis are offered by Brian Barder, Nicholas Winer and Jonathan Power in *Prospect* magazine, August 2005.

71 As measured by the General Household Survey. C. Jarvis and R. Hancock, 'Trends in Volunteering and the Implications for the Future', in Cathy Pharoah (ed.), *Dimensions of the Voluntary Sector* (1997).

72 Halsey and Webb, *Twentieth-Century British Social Trends*, p. 616.

73 House of Commons Library, 'Oxbridge Elitism', SN/SG/616, 9 January 2009, p. 5.

74 *The Times*, 11 April 1989.

Chapter 13

1 Arthur Scargill, interviewed by Dave Priscott, *Marxism Today*, April 1981.

2 Scargill interview.

3 Margaret Thatcher, *The Downing Street Years* (1993), p. 339.

4 Scargill to the NUM annual conference, 4 July 1983; quoted in Hugo Young, *One of Us: A Biography of Margaret Thatcher* (1991), p. 367.

5 Christopher Andrew, *The Defence of the Realm: The Authorized History of MI5* (2009), pp. 676–7.

6 Andrew, *The Defence of the Realm*, pp. 676–7.

7 Nigel Lawson, *The View from No. 11: Memoirs of a Tory Radical* (1992), p. 166.

8 Scargill interview, *Marxism Today*, April 1981.

9 *Sunday Times*, 10 June 1984.

10 Francis Beckett and David Hencke, *Marching to the Fault Line: The 1984 Miners' Strike and the Death of Industrial Britain* (2009), pp. 66–7

11 Quoted in John Campbell, *Margaret Thatcher, Vol. 2: The Iron Lady* (2003), p. 357.

12 Beckett and Hencke, *Marching to the Fault Line*, pp. 83–6.

13 *The Times*, 19 June 1984.

14 Quoted in Beckett and Hencke, *Marching to the Fault Line*, p. 93.

15 Testimony of Bernard Jackson; quoted in Beckett and Hencke, *Marching to the Fault Line*, p. 97.

16 Testimony of Bernard Jackson; quoted in Beckett and Hencke, *Marching to the Fault Line*, p. 97.

17 *The Times*, 19 June 1984.

18 Quoted in Beckett and Hencke, *Marching to the Fault Line*, p. 110.

19 Quoted in Beckett and Hencke, *Marching to the Fault Line*, p. 114.

20 Thatcher, interview for *The Downing Street Years*, BBC (1993), quoted in Campbell, *Margaret Thatcher, Vol. 2*, p. 366.

21 *The Times*, 18 June 1984.

22 *The Times*, 18 June 1984.

23 *The Times*, 18 May 1985.

24 Thatcher to the Conservative Party conference, 12 October 1984, Margaret Thatcher Foundation.

25 Thatcher to the 1922 Committee; quoted in *The Times*, 20 July 1984; rough notes for Thatcher's speech reproduced on Margaret Thatcher Foundation website.

26 Andrew, *The Defence of the Realm*, pp. 677–8.

27 *The Times*, 20 July 1984.

28 Earl of Stockton to the House of Lords, 13 November 1984, Hansard, HL Deb. 5s., vol. CDLVII, cols 240–1.

29 Thatcher, *The Downing Street Years*, p. 353.

30 Mick McGahey to the Scottish NUM, Usher Hall, Edinburgh, November 1984; quoted in Beckett and Hencke, *Marching to the Fault Line*, p. 163.

31 Mr Justice Nicholls, 10 October 1984; quoted Hansard, House of Lords, 11 December 1984, HL Deb. vol. 458, col. 156.

32 Andrew, *The Defence of the Realm*, pp. 679–80; Beckett and Hencke, *Marching to the Fault Line*, pp. 175, 185.

33 Interview with Roger Windsor in Beckett and Hencke, *Marching to the Fault Line*, p. 153; Andrew Neil, *Full Disclosure* (1996), p. 338.

34 The public divided 40 per cent in favour of the NCB and 33 per cent for the NUM in July 1984, but 51 per cent to 26 per cent by December 1984. Anthony King and Robert J. Wybrow, *British Political Opinion 1937–2000: The Gallup Polls* (2001), p. 337.

35 Quoted in Beckett and Hencke, *Marching to the Fault Line*, p. 245.

36 Peter Walker to Ian MacGregor, 12 February 1985; quoted in Beckett and Hencke, *Marching to the Fault Line*, p. 191.

37 Quoted in Beckett and Hencke, *Marching to the Fault Line*, pp. 206–7.

38 Beckett and Hencke, *Marching to the Fault Line*, p. 211.

39 Norman Tebbit, *Upwardly Mobile* (1989), p. 302.

40 Thatcher, *The Downing Street Years*, pp. 377–8.

41 Tony Benn, quoted in Alan Sked and Chris Cook, *Post-War Britain: A Political History*, fourth edition (1993), p. 452.

42 Quoted in Graham Stewart, *The History of The Times*, vol. 7: *The Murdoch Years* (2005), p. 221.

43 Stewart, *The History of The Times*, p. 219.

44 S. J. Taylor, *An Unlikely Hero: Vere Rothermere and How the Daily Mail was Saved* (2002), p. 180; Stewart, *The History of The Times*, p. 20.

45 Quoted in Brian MacArthur, *Eddy Shah, Today, and the Newspaper Revolution* (1988), p. 205.

46 Stewart, *The History of The Times*, pp. 224, 226

47 Quoted in Stewart, *The History of The Times*, p. 237.

48 Diana Wright, quoted in Roy Gleenslade, *Press Gang: How Newspapers Make Profits from Propaganda* (2003), p. 476.

49 Quoted in Stewart, *The History of The Times*, p. 257.

50 Quoted in Stewart, *The History of The Times*, p. 277.

51 *The Times*, 7 April 1986; Stewart, *The History of The Times*, p. 278.

52 Neil Chenoweth, *Virtual Murdoch: Reality Wars on the Information Highway* (2001), p. 63.

53 *Guardian*, 2 September 1993.

54 *The Long Good Friday*, film script by Barrie Keefe (Handmade Films, 1980).

55 Lawson, *The View From Number 11*, pp. 444–6.

56 Office of National Statistics.

57 Richard Hyman, 'Strikes in the UK: Withering Away?', European Industrial Relations Observatory online, 28 July 1999.

58 *Labour Market Trends*, Office for National Statistics (June 1999).

59 Certification Office and Labour Force Survey.

60 Alastair J. Reid, *United We Stand: A History of Britain's Trade Unions* (2004), p. 407.

61 Reid, *United We Stand*, p. 407.

62 *Guardian*, 5 June 2000.

Chapter 14

1 Nigel Lawson, *The View from No. 11: Memoirs of a Tory Radical* (1992), p. 222.

2 Peter Shore to the House of Commons, 2 May 1984, Hansard, HC Deb. Vol. 59, col. 354.

3 Lawson, *The View From No. 11*, p. 222.

4 Pablo T. Spiller and Ingo Vogelsand, 'Regulation, Institutions and Commitment in the British Telecommunications Sector', World Bank Policy Research Working Paper 1241 (January 1994), p. 17.

5 Lawson, *The View From No. 11*, p. 224.

6 Thatcher to the Conservative Party conference, 10 October 1986, Margaret Thatcher Foundation.

7 Lawson, *The View From No. 11*, p. 199.

8 Lawson, *The View From No. 11*, p. 208.

9 Richard Vinen, *Thatcher's Britain: The Politics and Social Upheaval of the 1980s* (2009), p. 197

10 'Selling at a Discount', leading article, *The Times*, 28 October 1982.

11 Philip Augar, *The Death of Gentlemanly Capitalism: The Rise and Fall of London's Investment Banks* (2000), p. 9.

12 Lawson, *The View From No. 11*, p. 232.

13 The Earl of Stockton (Harold Macmillan) sought to clear up the confusion as to what he meant in a speech to the House of Lords on 14 November 1985, 468 HL Deb. cc. 390–1.

14 Niall Ferguson, *The Cash Nexus: Money and Power in the Modern World 1700–2000* (2001), pp. 59–60.

15 *Britain Will Win with Labour*, Labour Party general election manifesto, 1987.

16 Spiller and Vogelsand, 'Regulation, Institutions and Commitment in the British Telecommunications Sector', p. 18.

17 David Kynaston, *The City of London*, vol. 4: *A Club No More 1945–2000* (2001), p. 747.

18 *Nice-Matin*, 3 November 1982; quoted in Kynaston, *A Club No More*, p. 717.

19 Augar, *The Death of Gentlemanly Capitalism*, p. 8.

20 Kynaston, *A Club No More*, p. 631.

21 Kynaston, *A Club No More*, pp. 664–5.

22 Dominic Hobson, *The National Wealth: Who Gets What in Britain* (1999), Table 29.6, p. 1063.

23 Brian Harrison, *Finding a Role?: The United Kingdom, 1970–1990* (2010), p. 10; Dennis Kavanagh and Anthony Seldon, *The Thatcher Effect: A Decade of Change* (1989), p. 15.

24 Hobson, *The National Wealth*, Table 29.6, p. 1063.

25 Harrison, *Finding a Role?*, p. 11.

26 Lord Young, *The Enterprise Years: A Businessman in the Cabinet* (1990), pp. 270–1.

27 Attributed remark, quoted in the *Financial Times*, 29 November 1991.

28 Dr John Bridge, quoted in *The Times*, 10 April 1989.

29 Bernard Attard, 'The Jobbers of the London Stock Exchange, An Oral History', *Oral History*, 22, no. 1 (Spring 1994), p. 43.

30 *Spectator*, 18 October 1986.

31 John Nott, *Here Today, Gone Tomorrow* (2002), pp. 182–3.

32 Quoted in Kynaston, *A Club No More*, p. 625.

33 Lawson, *The View From No. 11*, pp. 399–400.

34 Dominic Hobson, *The Pride of Lucifer: The Unauthorized Biography of Morgan Grenfell* (1991), pp. 211, 200.

35 Michael Lewis, *Liar's Poker* (1989), pp. 201–2.

36 Quoted in Augar, *The Death of Gentlemanly Capitalism*, p. 91.

37 Hobson, *The National Wealth*, Table 31.3, p. 1137.

38 *Independent*, 3 November 2004.

39 *Sunday Times*, 11 February 1990.

40 *The Times*, 3 November 2004.

41 *Daily Telegraph*, 3 November 2004.

42 *New York Times*, 19 September 1987.

43 Quoted in Cathy Courtney and Paul Thompson, *City Lives: The Changing Voices of British Finance* (1996), p. 141.

44 Lawson, *The View From No. 11*, p. 818.

45 Tom Bower, *Maxwell: The Final Verdict* (1996), p. 439.

46 Quoted in Bower, *Maxwell: The Final Verdict*, p. 305.

47 Christopher Reeves obituary, *The Times*, 5 December 2007.

48 Quoted in Courtney and Thompson, *City Lives*, pp. 112–13.

49 Quoted in Courtney and Thompson, *City Lives*, p. 65.

50 Philip Augar has suggested that the analogy may be not with the Wimbledon tennis championships but rather with Wimbledon Football Club, whose owners simply severed the club's Wimbledon associations and moved to Milton Keynes when it suited them, despite the views and hostility of the club's supporters. Augar, *The Death of Gentlemanly Capitalism*, p. 321.

51 *Financial Times*, 13 December 1983.

52 *Financial Times*, 7 March 1984.

53 Jack Hennessy of CSFB, quoted in Kynaston, *A Club No More*, p. 690.

54 Quoted in Kynaston, *A Club No More*, pp. 754–5.

55 *Financial Times*, 18 September 1985.

56 Augar, *The Death of Gentlemanly Capitalism*, p. 308.

57 Quoted in *Sunday Today*, 26 October 1986.

58 Kynaston, *A Club No More*, p. 713.

59 Hobson, *The National Wealth*, p. 593.

60 *Spectator*, 15 March 1986.

61 Kynaston, *A Club No More*, p. 715.

62 Quoted in Kynaston, *A Club No More*, pp. 713, 714.

63 Quoted in Lawson, *The View From No. 11*, p. 816.

64 *The Times*, 16 March 1988.

65 Quoted in Lawson, *The View From No. 11*, p. 823.

66 Lawson, *The View From No. 11*, p. 824.

67 Courtney and Thompson, *City Lives*, pp. 96–7.

68 Andy McSmith, *No Such Thing as Society* (2010), p. 171; *Observer*, 2 January 1994; *Sunday Times*, 14 November 2010.

69 *The Times*, 4 February 2010; Her Majesty's Revenue & Customs, Table 2.4: 'Shares of Total Income (before and after tax) and Income Tax for Percentile Groups, 1990–00 and 2011–12' <http://www.hmrc.gov.uk/stats/income_tax/table2-4.pdf> (August 2012).

70 Peter Mandelson, letter to the *Guardian*, 12 January 2008.

71 Kevin Cahill, 'Rich Pickings', *Guardian*, 29 January 2001.

72 Cahill, 'Rich Pickings'.

73 *Sunday Times Rich List* (2008); Hobson, *The National Wealth*, pp. 531–2.

74 *The Times*, 8 January 1976.

75   *Sunday Times*, 7 October 2007.

76   *The Times*, 14 November 1985.

77   Ann Barr and Peter York, *The Official Sloane Ranger Handbook* (1982), p. 11.

78   *Oxford English Dictionary* (1989 edition).

79   *The Times*, 8 August 1983.

80   *The Times*, 12 June 1987.

81   Quoted in Graham Stewart, *The History of The Times*, vol. 7: *The Murdoch Years* (2005), p. 313.

82   Nationwide Building Society survey.

83   *The Next Moves Forward*, Conservative Party general election manifesto, 1987.

84   Simon Jenkins, *Thatcher and Sons: A Revolution in Three Acts* (2006), p. 126; Simon Jenkins, *Accountable to None: The Tory Nationalization of Britain* (1995), p. 179.

85   Jenkins, *Thatcher and Sons*, p. 127.

86   *The Times*, 11 December 1990.

87   Rob Baggott, *Health and Health Care in Britain* (1994), pp. 224–5.

88   *The Times*, 11 December 1990.

89   *The Times*, 11 December 1990.

90   Jenkins, *Thatcher and Sons*, p. 127.

91   *Financial Times*, 5 November 2010.

92   Harrison, *Finding a Role?*, p. 171.

93   Niall Ferguson, *The Ascent of Money: A Financial history of the World* (2008), p. 263.

94   Lawson, *The View From No. 11*, p. 745.

Chapter 15

1   *Daily Express*, 28 December 1989.

2   *Daily Express*, 28 December 1989.

3   Independent Radio News, 24 November 1989, quoted in John Campbell, *Margaret Thatcher, Vol. 2: The Iron Lady* (2003), p. 678.

4   Campbell, *Margaret Thatcher, Vol. 2*, p. 673.

5   Kenneth Baker, *The Turbulent Years: My Life in Politics* (1993), p. 274.

6   David Butler and Dennis Kavanagh, *The British General Election of 1987* (1988), Appendix 1, p. 283.

7   *The Times*, 13 June 1987.

8   Ivor Crewe and Anthony King, *SDP: The Birth, Life and Death of the Social Democratic Party* (1995), p. 470.

9   Butler and Kavanagh, *The British General Election of 1987*, Table A1.2, p. 284.

10   *79 Group News*, December 1981.

11   Christopher Harvie, *Fool's Gold: The Story of North Sea Oil* (1994), p. 345.

12   Harvie, *Fool's Gold*, p. 346.

13   Recollection of Robert Armstrong; quoted in Peter Taylor, *Brits: The War Against the IRA* (2001), p. 268.

14   Henry Patterson, *Ireland Since 1939* (2002), p. 312.

15   David Butler, Andrew Adonis and Tony Travers, *Failure in British Government: Politics of the Poll Tax* (1994), p. 28.

16   Andy McSmith, *No Such Thing as Society* (2010), p. 242.

17   Butler, Adonis and Travers, *Failure in British Government*, p. 52.

18   Rates, Department of Environment white paper; quoted in Butler, Adonis and Travers, *Failure in British Government*, p. 39.

19   Baker, *The Turbulent Years*, p. 109.

20 *The Times*, 20 October 1986, 30 January 1987, 27 August 1988; Alan Sked and Chris Cook, *Post-War Britain: A Political History*, fourth edition (1993), pp. 458–9.

21 Campbell, *Margaret Thatcher, Vol. 2*, p. 544.

22 Butler, Adonis and Travers, *Failure in British Government*, p. 62.

23 Memorandum of 16 May 1985; quoted in Nigel Lawson, *The View from No. 11: Memoirs of a Tory Radical* (1992), p. 574.

24 Lawson, *The View from No. 11*, pp. 561–2.

25 Nicholas Ridley, *My Style of Government: The Thatcher Years* (1991), p. 125; Butler, Adonis and Travers, *Failure in British Government*, pp. 101–3.

26 Thatcher to the 1922 Committee, July 1987; quoted in Butler, Adonis and Travers, *Failure in British Government*, p. 107.

27 Alan Clark, *Diaries* (2000), p. 287 (25 March 1990).

28 Michael Heseltine to the Commons, 16 December 1987, HC Deb. col. 1141.

29 Butler, Adonis and Travers, *Failure in British Government*, pp. 150–1.

30 Hansard, 2 April 1990 HC Deb. col. 893; quoted in Butler, Adonis and Travers, *Failure in British Government*, p. 153.

31 Butler, Adonis and Travers, *Failure in British Government*, p. 259.

32 Butler, Adonis and Travers, *Failure in British Government*, p. 179.

33 Butler, Adonis and Travers, *Failure in British Government*, pp. 2, 180–1.

34 Margaret Thatcher, *The Downing Street Years* (1993), p. 642.

35 Chris Patten to Butler, Adonis and Travers, November 1993; quoted in Butler, Adonis and Travers, *Failure in British Government*, p. 1.

36 Thatcher to the Commons, 10 March 1988, HC Deb. vol. 129, col. 517.

37 Hugo Young, *This Blessed Plot: Britain and Europe from Churchill to Blair* (1999), p. 548.

38 Geoffrey Howe, *Conflict of Loyalty* (1994), p. 536.

39 Clark, *Diaries*, p. 227 (16 September 1988).

40 Speech to the College of Europe, Bruges, 20 September 1988, Margaret Thatcher Foundation.

41 *The Times*, 21 September 1988.

42 Howe, *Conflict of Loyalty*, pp. 537–8.

43 Lawson, *The View from No. 11*, p. 899.

44 Howe, *Conflict of Loyalty*, p. 572.

45 Howe, *Conflict of Loyalty*, p. 588.

46 Ridley, *My Style of Government*, p. 40.

47 Sir Alan Walters obituary, *Daily Telegraph*, 5 January 2009; *The Times*, 6 January 2009.

48 John Major, *The Autobiography* (1999), p. 134.

49 Major, *The Autobiography*, p. 134.

50 Michael Spicer, *The Spicer Diaries* (2012), p. 118 (14 January 1987).

51 Sir Anthony Meyer, obituary, *Daily Telegraph*, 10 January 2005.

52 Sir Anthony Meyer, obituary, *Daily Telegraph*, 10 January 2005.

53 Baker, *The Turbulent Years*, pp. 320–1.

54 MORI opinion poll in *The Times*, 22 October 1990: Conservatives 33 per cent, Labour 49 per cent, Lib Dems 14 per cent; ICM had the Labour lead at 13 per cent and Gallup at 14.5 per cent: *Guardian*, 13 October 1990; *Daily Telegraph*, October 1990.

55 *Sunday Telegraph*, 10 December 1989.

56 Transcript in Bush Presidential Library; quoted in *The Times*, 2 November 2009.

57 See Campbell, *Margaret Thatcher, Vol. 2*, p. 633.

58 Adam Sisman, *Hugh Trevor-Roper: The Biography* (2010), pp. 531–2; Campbell, *Margaret Thatcher, Vol. 2*, pp. 634–5.

59 Cabinet committee meeting as described in Spicer, *The Spicer Diaries*, p. 153 (8 March 1990).

60 Quoted in Major, *The Autobiography*, p. 162.

61 Kinnock, Ashdown and Thatcher to the Commons, 30 October 1990, HC Deb. vol. 178, cols 872–5.

62 Thatcher to the Commons, 30 October 1990, HC Deb. vol. 178, col. 875.

63 Howe to the Commons, 13 November 1990, Hansard HC Deb. 6s., vol. 180, cols 461–5.

64 Clark, *Diaries*, p. 347 (13 November 1990).

65 Spicer, *The Spicer Diaries*, p. 167.

66 Michael Heseltine, *Life in the Jungle: My Autobiography* (2000), pp. 354, 362.

67 Heseltine, *Life in the Jungle*, pp. 362–3; Michael Heseltine, *The Challenge of Europe: Can Britain Win?* (1989), p. 216.

68 Thatcher, *The Downing Street Years*, p. 837.

69 Thatcher, *The Downing Street Years*, pp. 836–7.

70 Richard Vinen, *Thatcher's Britain: The Politics and Social Upheaval of the 1980s* (2009), p. 268.

71 Thatcher, *The Downing Street Years*, p. 841.

72 Thatcher's remarks on departing Downing Street, 28 November 1990, Margaret Thatcher Foundation.

73 Howe, *Conflict of Loyalty*, p. 676.

Chapter 16

1 Denis Healey in the House of Commons, 23 October 1979; quoted in the *Daily Telegraph*, 24 October 1979.

2 *Working Together for Britain*, 1983 general election manifesto of the Liberal–SDP Alliance.

3 Nicholas Ridley, *My Style of Government: The Thatcher Years* (1991), p. 255.

4 Adam Smith, *An Inquiry into the Nature and Causes of the Wealth of Nations* ([1776] 1904 edition), Book IV, Part 7, p. 149.

5 Department for Business Innovation and Skills, 'The Government's Manufacturing Strategy', Chart 3, p. 11 <http://www.bis.gov.uk/files/file25266.pdf> (August 2012).

6 US Census Bureau; quoted in the *Spectator*, 4 February 2012, p. 16.

7 David Smith, *The Age of Instability: The Global Financial Crisis and What Comes Next* (2010), p. 96.

8 This case is most eloquently elaborated by Simon Jenkins, *Thatcher and Sons: A Revolution in Three Acts* (2006).

9 Speech to the Small Business Bureau conference, 8 February 1984, Margaret Thatcher Foundation.

10 Niall Ferguson, 'Conservatism and the Crisis: a Transatlantic Trilemma', Ruttenberg Memorial Lecture 2009, Centre for Policy Studies.

11 The original version appeared in Douglas Jay's 1937 work *The Socialist Case*, in which he asserted: 'In the case of nutrition and health, just as in the case of education, the gentleman in Whitehall really does know better what is good for people than the people themselves.'

12 Speech to the Conservative Central Council, 26 March 1983; interview on LWT's *Weekend World*, 5 June 1983; speech at Lord Mayor's banquet, 14 November 1983; and interview in the *Sunday Telegraph*, 19 July 1986, Margaret Thatcher Foundation.

13 Thatcher to the Conservative Central Council, 26 March 1983, Margaret Thatcher Foundation.

14 *Suomen Kuvalehti* [Finnish newspaper], 7 November 1984, Margaret Thatcher Foundation.

15 *Sunday Times*, 22 February 1983.

16 *Sunday Times*, 1 May 1981.

17 *Sunday Times*, 1 May 1981.

18 Ivor Crewe and Anthony King, *SDP: The Birth, Life and Death of the Social Democratic Party* (1995), pp. 290–98, 467, 508–9.

19 David Cannadine, *History in Our Time* (1998), pp. 288–9.

BIBLIOGRAPHY

Unless otherwise stated the place of publication is London

Adonis, Andrew and Pollard, Stephen, *A Class Act: The Myth of Britain's Classless Society* (Hamish Hamilton, 1997)

Andrew, Christopher, *The Defence of the Realm: The Authorized History of MI5* (Allen Lane, 2009)

Annan, Noel, *Our Age: The Generation that made Post-War Britain* (Weidenfeld & Nicolson, 1990)

Artis, M.J. and Cobham, David, *Labour's Economic Policies 1974–79* (Manchester: Manchester University Press, 1991)

Ashdown, Paddy, *The Ashdown Diaries, Volume 1: 1988–1997* (Allen Lane, 2000)

Augar, Philip, *The Death of Gentlemanly Capitalism: The Rise and Fall of London's Investment Banks* (Penguin Books, 2000)

Baggott, Rob, *Health and Health Care in Britain* (Macmillan, 1994)

Baker, Kenneth, *The Turbulent Years: My Life in Politics* (Faber and Faber, 1993)

Barr, Ann and York, Peter, *The Official Sloane Ranger Handbook* (Ebury Press, 1982)

Barr, Ann and York, Peter, *The Official Sloane Ranger Diary* (Ebury Press, 1983)

Beckett, Francis and Hencke, David, *Marching to the Fault Line: The 1984 Miners' Strike and the Death of Industrial Britain* (Constable, 2009)

Benn, Tony, *Conflicts of Interest: Diaries 1977–80* (Hutchinson, 1990)

Benn, Tony, *The End of an Era: Diaries 1980–90* (Hutchinson, 1992)

Berlinski, Claire, *There is No Alternative: Why Margaret Thatcher Matters* (New York: Basic Books, 2008)

Berridge, Virginia, *AIDS in the UK: The Making of Policy 1981–1994* (Oxford: Oxford University Press, 1996)

Bicheno, Hugh, *Razor's Edge: The Unofficial History of the Falklands War* (Weidenfeld & Nicolson, 2006)

Billington, Michael, *State of the Nation: British Theatre since 1945* (Faber and Faber, 2007)

Blake, Robert, *The Conservative Party from Peel to Thatcher* (Methuen Publishing, 1985)

Blythe, Daniel, *The Encyclopaedia of Classic 80s Pop* (Allison & Busby, 2002)

Bower, Tom, *Maxwell: The Final Verdict* (HarperCollins, 1996)

Brandt, George W. (ed.), *British Television Drama in the 1980s* (Cambridge: Cambridge University Press, 1993)

Bridgewater, Geraldine, *Ring of Truth* (Brighton: Pen Press Publishers, 2007)

Burk, Kathleen and Cairncross, Alec, *Goodbye, Great Britain: The 1976 IMF Crisis* (Yale: Yale University Press, 1992)

Butler, David and Kavanagh, Dennis, *The British General Election of 1979* (Macmillan, 1980)

Butler, David and Kavanagh, Dennis, *The British General Election of 1983* (Macmillan, 1984)

Butler, David and Kavanagh, Dennis, *The British General Election of 1987* (Macmillan, 1988)

Butler, David, Adonis, Andrew and Travers, Tony, *Failure in British Government: Politics of the Poll Tax* (Oxford: Oxford University Press, 1994)

Campbell, Beatrix, *Wigan Pier Revisited: Poverty and Politics in the 80s* (Virago Press, 1984)

Campbell, John, *Edward Heath: A Biography* (Jonathan Cape, 1993)

Campbell, John, *Margaret Thatcher, Volume I: The Grocer's Daughter* (Jonathan Cape, 2000)

Campbell, John, *Margaret Thatcher, Volume II: The Iron Lady* (Jonathan Cape, 2003)

Cannadine, David, *History in Our Time* (Yale: Yale University Press, 1998)

Chandler, Andrew, *The Church of England in the Twentieth Century: The Church Commissioners and the Politics of Reform, 1948–1998* (Woodbridge: Boydell Press, 2006)

Chenoweth, Neil, *Virtual Murdoch: Reality Wars on the Information Highway* (Martin Secker & Warburg, 2001)

Chesshyre, Robert, *The Return of a Native Reporter* (Viking, 1987)

Chippindale, Peter and Horrie, Chris, *Stick It Up Your Punter!: The Rise and Fall of The Sun* (William Heinemann, 1991)

Chippindale, Peter and Franks, Suzanne, *Dished!: The Rise and Fall of British Satellite Broadcasting* (Simon & Schuster, 1991)

Clark, Alan, *The Tories: Conservatives and the Nation State* (Weidenfeld & Nicolson, 1998)

Clark, Alan, *Diaries* (Weidenfeld & Nicolson, 2000)

Clarke, Peter, *A Question of Leadership: Gladstone to Thatcher* (Hamish Hamilton, 1991)

Bibliography

Clarke, Peter, *Hope and Glory: Britain 1900–1990* (Allen Lane, 1996)

Cockerell, Michael, *Live from Number 10: The Inside Story of Prime Ministers and Television* (Faber and Faber, 1988)

Cockett, Richard, *Thinking the Unthinkable: Think-Tanks and the Economic Counter-Revolution, 1931–1983* (HarperCollins, 1994)

Cole, John, *As It Seemed to Me: Political Memoirs* (Weidenfeld & Nicolson, 1995)

Collin, Matthew, *Altered State: The Story of Ecstasy Culture and Acid House* (Serpent's Tail, 1998)

Cork, Richard, *New Spirit, New Sculpture, New Money: Art in the 1980s* (Yale: Yale University Press, 2003)

Courtney, Cathy and Thompson, Paul, *City Lives: The Changing Voices of British Finance* (Methuen Publishing, 1996)

Cradock, Percy, *In Pursuit of British Interests: Reflections on Foreign Policy under Margaret Thatcher and John Major* (John Murray Publishers, 1997)

Crafts, Nicholas, *The Conservative Government's Economic Record: An End of Term Report* (Institute of Economic Affairs, 1998)

Crewe, Ivor and King, Anthony, *SDP: The Birth, Life and Death of the Social Democratic Party* (Oxford: Oxford University Press, 1995)

Critchley, Julian, *A Bag of Boiled Sweets: An Autobiography* (Faber and Faber, 1994)

Crosland, Susan, *Tony Crosland* (Jonathan Cape, 1982)

Dell, Edmund, *The Chancellors: A History of the Chancellors of the Exchequer 1945–1990* (HarperCollins, 1996)

Denham, Andrew and Garnett, Mark, *Keith Joseph* (Durham: Acumen Publishing, 2001)

Devine, T.M., *The Scottish Nation 1700–2000* (Allen Lane, 1999)

Dobrynin, Anatoly, *In Confidence: Moscow's Ambassador to America's Six Cold War Presidents (1962–1986)* (New York: Times Books, 1995)

Dockrill, Michael L. and Hopkins, Michael F., *The Cold War, 1945–1991* (Macmillan, 2006)

Donoughue, Bernard, *Prime Minister: The Conduct of Policy under Harold Wilson and James Callaghan* (Jonathan Cape, 1987)

Donoughue, Bernard, *Downing Street Diary, Volume Two, With James Callaghan in No. 10* (Jonathan Cape, 2008)

Fairhall, David, *Common Ground: The Story of Greenham* (I.B. Tauris, 2006)

Faith, Nicholas, *A Very Different Country: A Typically English Revolution* (Sinclair Stevenson, 2002)

Fay, Stephen, *Power Play: The Life and Times of Peter Hall* (Hodder & Stoughton, 1995)

Ferguson, Niall, *The Cash Nexus: Money and Power in the Modern World 1700–2000* (Allen Lane, 2001)

Ferguson, Niall, *The Ascent of Money: A Financial History of the World* (Allen Lane, 2008)

Fothergill, Stephen and Vincent, Jill, *The State of the Nation* (Pan, 1985)

Freedman, Des, *Television Policies of the Labour Party, 1951–2001* (Oxford: Routledge, 2003)

Freedman, Lawrence, *The Politics of British Defence, 1979–98* (Macmillan, 1999)

Freedman, Lawrence, *The Official History of the Falklands Campaign, Volume 1: The Origins of the Falklands War* (Oxford: Routledge, 2005)

Freedman, Lawrence, *The Official History of the Falklands Campaign, Volume 2: War and Diplomacy* (Oxford: Routledge, 2005)

Gaddis, John Lewis, *The Cold War* (Allen Lane, 2005)

Gamble, Andrew, *Britain in Decline: Economic Policy, Political Strategy and the British State* (Macmillan, fourth edition, 1994)

Gamble, Andrew, *The Free Economy and the Strong State: The Politics of Thatcherism* (Macmillan, second edtion, 1994)

Gardiner, George, *Margaret Thatcher: From Childhood to Leadership* (William Kimber, 1975)

Garnett, Mark, *From Anger to Apathy: The Story of Politics, Society and Popular Culture in Britain since 1975* (Jonathan Cape, 2007)

Gilmour, Ian, *Inside Right: A Study of Conservatism* (Hutchinson, 1977)

Gilmour, Ian, *Dancing with Dogma: Britain under Thatcherism* (Simon & Schuster, 1992)

Glancey, Jonathan, *New British Architecture* (Thames & Hudson, 1989)

Glover, Stephen, *Paper Dreams: The Story of the Independent and the Independent on Sunday by One of the Founding Fathers* (Jonathan Cape, 1993)

Golding, John, *Hammer of the Left: Defeating Tony Benn, Eric Heffer and Militant in the Battle for the Labour Party* (Politico's Publishing, 2003)

Gorbachev, Mikhail, *Memoirs* (Doubleday, 1996)

Greenslade, Roy, *Press Gang: How Newspapers Make Profits from Propaganda* (Macmillan, 2003)

Hailsham, Lord, *A Sparrow's Flight: Memoirs* (Collins, 1990)

Halcrow, Morrison, *Keith Joseph: A Single Mind* (Macmillan, 1989)

Halsey, A. H. and Webb, Josephine (eds.), *Twentieth-Century British Social Trends* (Macmillan, 2000)

Harris, Robert, *Gotcha! The Media, the Government and the Falklands Crisis* (Faber and Faber, 1983)

Harris, Robert, *The Making of Neil Kinnock* (Faber and Faber, 1984)

Harrison, Brian, *Finding a Role?: The United Kingdom, 1970–1990* (Oxford: Oxford University Press, 2010)

Harvie, Christopher, *Fool's Gold: The Story of North Sea Oil* (Hamish Hamilton, 1994)

Bibliography

Haslam, David, *Manchester England: The Story of the Pop Cult City* (Fourth Estate, 1999)

Hastings, Max and Jenkins, Simon, *The Battle for the Falklands* (Pan, 1997)

Healey, Denis, *The Time of My Life* (Michael Joseph, 1989)

Heath, Edward, *The Course of My Life* (Hodder & Stoughton, 1998)

Heffer, Simon, *Like the Roman: The Life of Enoch Powell* (Pan Edition, 1997)

Helleiner, Eric, *States and the Re-emergence of Global Finance, from Bretton Woods to the 1990s* (Cornell: Cornell University Press, 1994)

Henderson, Nicholas, *Mandarin: The Diaries of an Ambassador 1969–82* (Weidenfeld & Nicolson, 1994)

Hennessy, Peter, *The Prime Minister: The Office and Its Holders Since 1945* (Allen Lane, 2000)

Heseltine, Michael, *Where There's a Will* (Hutchinson, 1987)

Heseltine, Michael, *The Challenge of Europe: Can Britain Win?* (Weidenfeld & Nicolson, 1989)

Heseltine, Michael, *Life in the Jungle: My Autobiography* (Hodder & Stoughton, 2000)

Hillier, Bevis, *The Style of the Century*, second edition (Herbert Press, 1998)

Hobson, Dominic, *The Pride of Lucifer: The Unauthorized Biography of Morgan Grenfell* (Mandarin, 1991)

Hobson, Dominic, *The National Wealth: Who Gets What in Britain* (HarperCollins, 1999)

Horsman, Matthew, *Sky High: The Inside Story of BSkyB* (Orion, 1997)

Hoskyns, John, *Just in Time: Inside the Thatcher Revolution* (Aurum Press, 2000)

Howe, Geoffrey, *Conflict of Loyalty* (Macmillan, 1994)

Hurd, Douglas, *Memoirs* (Little, Brown & Co., 2003)

Hussey, Marmaduke, *Chance Governs All* (Macmillan, 2001)

Hutchinson, Maxwell, *The Prince of Wales, Right or Wrong?: An Architect Replies* (Faber and Faber, 1989)

Ingham, Bernard, *Kill the Messenger* (HarperCollins, 1994)

Ingrams, Richard, *Muggeridge: The Biography* (HarperCollins, 1996)

Isaacs, Jeremy, *Storm Over 4: A Personal Account* (Weidenfeld & Nicolson, 1989)

Jack, Ian, *Before the Oil Ran Out: Britain 1977–86* (Martin Secker & Warburg, 1987)

Jencks, Charles, *Post-Modern Triumphs in London* (Academy Editions, 1991)

Jenkins, Roy, *European Diary, 1977–1981* (HarperCollins, 1989)

Jenkins, Roy, *A Life at the Centre* (Macmillan, 1991)

Jenkins, Simon, *Accountable to None: The Tory Nationalization of Britain* (Hamish Hamilton, 1995)

Jenkins, Simon, *Thatcher and Sons: A Revolution in Three Acts* (Allen Lane, 2006)

Johnson, Christopher, *The Economy Under Mrs Thatcher, 1979–90* (Penguin Books, 1991)

Johnson, Paul, *A History of the American People* (Weidenfeld & Nicolson, 1997)

Junor, John, *Listening for a Midnight Tram* (Chapmans Publishers, 1990)

Kavanagh, Dennis, *Thatcherism and British Politics: The End of Consensus* (Oxford: Oxford University Press, 1987)

Kavanagh, Dennis and Seldon, Anthony, *The Thatcher Effect: A Decade of Change* (Oxford: Clarendon Press, 1989)

Kettle, Martin and Hodges, Lucy, *Uprising! The Police, the People and the Riots in Britain's Cities* (Macmillan, 1982)

King, Anthony and Wybrow, Robert J., *British Political Opinion 1937–2000: The Gallup Polls* (Politico's Publishing, 2001)

Kogan, David and Kogan, Maurice, *The Battle for the Labour Party* (Kogan Page, 1982)

Kynaston, David, *The Financial Times: A Centenary History* (Viking, 1998)

Kynaston, David, *The City of London: Volume 4: A Club No More, 1945–2000* (Chatto & Windus, 2001)

Langdon, Christopher and Manners, David, *Digerati Glitterati: High-Tech Heroes* (Jon Wiley & Sons, 2001)

Lawson, Nigel, *The View From No. 11: Memoirs of a Tory Radical* (Bantam Press, 1992)

Lettow, Paul, *Ronald Reagan and his Quest to Abolish Nuclear Weapons* (New York: Random House, 2005)

Letwin, Shirley Robin, *The Anatomy of Thatcherism* (Flamingo, 1992)

Lewis, Michael, *Liar's Poker* (W.W. Norton & Co., 1989)

MacArthur, Brian, *Eddy Shah, Today, and the Newspaper Revolution* (Newton Abbot: David & Charles, 1988)

McFarlane, Robert C. and Smardz, Zofia, *Special Trust* (New York: Cadell & Davies, 1994)

McSmith, Andy, *No Such Thing as Society* (Constable, 2010)

Major, John, *The Autobiography* (HarperCollins, 1999)

Marquand, David, *The Progressive Dilemma: from Lloyd George to Blair*, second edition (Weidenfeld & Nicolson, 1999)

Marr, Andrew, *A History of Modern Britain* (Macmillan, 2007)

Marsden-Smedley, Philip (ed.), *Britain in the Eighties: The Spectator's View of the Thatcher Decade* (Grafton, 1989)

Mason, Douglas, *Revising the Rating System* (Adam Smith Institute, 1985)

Melvern, Linda, *The End of the Street* (Methuen Publishing, 1986)

Meyer, Anthony, *Stand Up and Be Counted* (William Heinemann, 1990)

Bibliography

Millar, Ronald, *A View from the Wings* (Weidenfeld & Nicolson, 1993)

Morgan, Kenneth O., *Labour People, Leaders and Lieutenants: Hardie to Kinnock* (Oxford: Oxford University Press, 1987)

Morgan, Kenneth O., *Callaghan: A Life* (Oxford: Oxford University Press, 1997)

Morgan, Kenneth O., *Michael Foot: A Life* (HarperPress, 2007)

Murray, Peter and Trombley, Stephen, *Modern Architecture Guide: Britain* (Architecture, Design & Technology Press, 1990)

Neil, Andrew, *Full Disclosure* (Macmillan, 1997)

Nice, James, *Shadowplayers: The Rise and Fall of Factory Records* (Aurum Press, 2010)

Nott, John, *Here Today, Gone Tomorrow* (Politico's Publishing, 2002)

Oakley, Robin, *Inside Track* (Bantam Press, 2001)

Owen, David, *Time to Declare* (Michael Joseph, 1991)

Parker, David, *The Official History of Privatisation, Volume 1, The Formative Years, 1979–1987* (Oxford: Routledge, 2009)

Parkinson, Cecil, *Right at the Centre: An Autobiography* (Weidenfeld & Nicolson, 1992)

Parris, Matthew, *Chance Witness: An Outsider's Life in Politics* (Viking, 2002)

Patterson, Henry, *Ireland Since 1939* (Oxford: Oxford University Press, 2002)

Pearse, Peter Gerard and Matheson, Nigel, *Ken Livingstone, or The End of Civilization As We Know It: A Selection of Quotes, Quips and Quirks* (Proteus, 1982)

Pharoah, Cathy (ed.), *Dimensions of the Voluntary Sector* (CAF, 1997)

Pimlott, Ben, *The Queen* (HarperCollins, 1996)

Pollard, Sidney, *The Wasting of the British Economy* (Kent: Croom Helm, 1982)

Powaski, Ronald E., *Return to Armageddon: The United States and the Nuclear Arms Race 1981–1999* (New York: Oxford University Press USA, 2000)

Prince of Wales, *A Vision of Britain: A Personal View of Architecture* (Doubleday, 1989)

Prior, Jim, *A Balance of Power* (Hamish Hamilton, 1986)

Pugliese, Stanislao (ed.), *The Political Legacy of Margaret Thatcher* (Politico's Publishing, 2003)

Pym, John, *Merchant Ivory's English Landscape: Rooms, Views, and Anglo-Saxon Attitudes* (Pavilion Books, 1995)

Ramsden, John, *An Appetite for Power: A History of the Conservative Party since 1830* (HarperCollins, 1998)

Ranelagh, John, *Thatcher's People: An Insider's Account of the Politics, the Power and the Personalities* (HarperCollins, 1991)

Reed, John, *House of Fun: The Story of Madness* (Omnibus Press, 2010)

Reid, Alastair J., *United We Stand: A History of Britain's Trade Unions* (Allen Lane, 2004)

Reynolds, Simon, *Rip It Up and Start Again: Postpunk 1978–1984* (Faber and Faber, 2005)

Ridley, Nicholas, *My Style of Government: The Thatcher Years* (Hutchinson, 1991)

Rimmer, David, *New Romantics: The Look* (Omnibus Press, 2003)

Roberts, Philip, *About Churchill: The Playwright and the Work* (Faber and Faber, 2008)

Rogan, Johnny, *Morrissey & Marr: The Severed Alliance* (Omnibus Press, 1993)

St John Stevas, Norman, *The Two Cities* (Faber and Faber, 1984)

Sandbrook, Dominic, *State of Emergency: The Way We Were: Britain 1970–1974* (Allen Lane, 2010)

Sandbrook, Dominic, *Seasons in the Sun: The Battle for Britain, 1974–1979* (Allen Lane, 2012)

Seldon, Anthony and Ball, Stuart (eds.), *Conservative Century: The Conservative Party since 1900* (Oxford: Oxford University Press, 1994)

Seyd, Patrick, *The Rise and Fall of the Labour Left* (Macmillan, 1987)

Shawcross, William, *Murdoch* (Simon & Schuster, 1992)

Sherman, Alfred, *Paradoxes of Power: Reflections on the Thatcher Interlude* (ed. Mark Garnett) (Exeter: Imprint Academic, 2005)

Sisman, Adam, *Hugh Trevor-Roper: The Biography* (Weidenfeld & Nicolson, 2010)

Sked, Alan and Cook, Chris, *Post-War Britain: A Political History*, fourth edition (Penguin Books, 1993)

Smith, David, *The Age of Instability: The Global Financial Crisis and What Comes Next* (Profile Books, 2010)

Smith, Geoffrey, *Reagan and Thatcher* (The Bodley Head, 1990)

Spicer, Michael, *The Spicer Diaries* (Biteback, 2012)

Steel, David, *Against Goliath: David Steel's Story* (Weidenfeld & Nicolson, 1989)

Stewart, Graham, *The History of 'The Times', Volume 7: The Murdoch Years* (HarperCollins, 2005)

Strange, Steve, *Blitzed!* (Orion, 2002)

Street, Sarah, *British National Cinema* (Oxford: Routledge, 1997)

Strong, Roy, *The Roy Strong Diaries 1967–1987* (Weidenfeld & Nicolson, 1997)

Taylor, Geoffrey, *Changing Faces: A History of the Guardian, 1956–88* (Fourth Estate, 1993)

Taylor, Peter, *Brits: The War Against the IRA* (Bloomsbury Publishing, 2001)

Taylor, S. J., *An Unlikely Hero: Vere Rothermere and How the Daily Mail was Saved* (Weidenfeld & Nicolson, 2002)

Bibliography

Tebbit, Norman, *Upwardly Mobile* (Weidenfeld & Nicolson, 1989)

Terry, Quinlan, *Selected Works* (John Wiley & Sons, 1993)

Thatcher, Margaret, *The Path to Power* (HarperCollins, 1995)

Thatcher, Margaret, *The Downing Street Years* (HarperCollins, 1993)

Thompson, Julian (ed.), *The Imperial War Museum Book of Modern Warfare* (Sidgwick & Jackson, 2002)

Timmins, Nicholas, *The Five Giants: A Biography of the Welfare State* (HarperCollins, 1995)

Tiratsoo, Nick (ed.), *From Blitz to Blair: A New History of Britain since 1939* (Weidenfeld & Nicolson, 1997)

Turner, Alwyn, *Rejoice! Rejoice!: Britain in the 1980s* (Aurum Press, 2010)

Urban, George, *Diplomacy and Disillusion at the Court of Margaret Thatcher: An Insider's View* (I.B. Tauris, 1996)

Vinen, Richard, *Thatcher's Britain: The Politics and Social Upheaval of the Thatcher Era* (Simon & Schuster, 2009)

Volkogonov, Dmitri, *The Rise and Fall of the Soviet Empire: Political Leaders from Lenin to Gorbachev* (HarperCollins, 1998)

Walden, George, *Lucky George: Memoirs of an Anti-Politician* (Allen Lane, 1999)

Walters, Dennis, *Not Always with the Pack* (Constable, 1989)

Wapshott, Nicholas and Brock, George, *Thatcher* (Macdonald, 1984)

Watkins, Alan, *A Conservative Coup: The Fall of Margaret Thatcher* (Gerald Duckworth & Co., 1991)

Westlake, Martin, *Kinnock: The Biography* (Little Brown & Co., 2001)

Whitehead, Philip, *The Writing on the Wall: Britain in the Seventies* (Michael Joseph, 1985)

Wiener, Martin J., *English Culture and the Decline of the Industrial Spirit, 1850–1980* (Cambridge: Cambridge University Press, 1981)

Witherow, John and Bishop, Patrick, *Winter War: The Falklands Conflict* (Quartet Books, 1982)

Wyatt, Woodrow, *The Journals of Woodrow Wyatt, Volume 1* (ed. Sarah Curtis) (Macmillan, 1998)

York, Peter and Jennings, Charles, *Peter York's Eighties* (BBC Books, 1995)

Young, Hugo, *One of Us: A Biography of Margaret Thatcher* (Macmillan, 1989)

Young, Hugo, *This Blessed Plot: Britain and Europe from Churchill to Blair* (Macmillan, 1999)

Young, Lord, *The Enterprise Years: A Businessman in the Cabinet* (Headline, 1990)

INDEX

Index

British National Oil Corporation (BNOC) 188, 191

British National Party 178–9, 428

British Nationality Act (1981) 135

British Petroleum (BP) 188–90

British Satellite Broadcasting (BSB) 238–42

British Social Attitudes survey 315, 326, 328, 338

British Steel Corporation 72, 384

British Telecom, privatization 380–2, 383, 384, 385, 386

Britoil 188, 189, 190, 383

Brittain, Vera 117

Brittan, Leon 452

Brittan, Samuel 70

Brixton riots 88–92, 94, 95, 318–19; Brixton Defence Committee 92, 96, 97

Broadcasting Act (1980) 235, 237

Broadcasting Act (1990) 245, 277

broadcasting deregulation 277, 470–1

Broadgate 273, 396

Broadsword, HMS 150

Brocklebank-Fowler, Christopher 119

Brookside (TV programme) 236

Broughton, Sir Alfred 'Doc' 27

Brown, George 119

Brown, Gordon 177, 185, 402, 467, 468, 472

Bruges Group 447

Bruinvels, Peter 330

BSkyB 242; *see also* Sky

Buchan, Norman 244

budget (1975) 14; (1979) 52–6; (1981) 58–60; (1984) 180; (1988) 402

budget deficit 15–16, 58

budget surpluses 184–5

Buerk, Michael 336

building societies 422–3

Bush, George H.W. 454

by-elections 127–9, 174–5, 329, 427, 453

Cabinet: and the Falklands War 139; leaks 74; and the poll tax 438–9; reshuffle, (1981) 74–6; Thatcher's (1983) 179; Thatcher's first 62–4; Thatcher's relationship with 65–6

Cable & Wireless 383

Callaghan, Audrey 8

Callaghan, James: announces resignation 109; background 7, 9–11; comparison with Thatcher 30–1; corporatist government 17–18; decision not to call election (1978) 6–9, 11–12; desire for national revival 5–6; desperation 24; economic policy 104; economic situation facing 12–18; education 10; and the Falkland Islands 135, 136; and the Falklands War 154; general election (1979) 31, 34, 37–8, 40–2; as Home Secretary 10–11; Labour Party conference (1976) 16; lack of parliamentary majority 24–5; as leader of Labour Party 5–6; lost chance 471; political career 9; popularity 7; and public spending 50; replaced as party leader 105–14; Second World War service 10; take over as PM 7; TUC conference speech (1978) 11; TUC links 8; vote of no confidence in 26–8; Winter of Discontent 18, 19–24; world leaders' summit, Guadeloupe 22

Cambridge University 340

Cameron, David 312

Campaign for Labour Party Democracy (CLPD) 112–13

Campaign for Nuclear Disarmament (CND) 123, 167, 199–201, 219, 334

Campaign for Quality Television 244–5

Campbell, Alastair 452

Campbell, Beatrix 81–2

Campbell, Duncan 243

Campbell, John 42

Canada 145

Canary Wharf 274, 372–3, 396

Canberra (liner) 140, 158

capital expenditure 59

capital punishment 317

car industry 72

care in the community 421

Carlisle, John 236

Carlisle, Mark 63, 75

Carrington, Lord 62, 63–4, 143

Casey, John 70

Cashman, Michael 329–30

Castle, Barbara 8

Cazenove 408

CBI 73

Central Electricity Generating Board 359

Central Policy Review Staff 70

Centre for Public Studies (CPS) 68–9

Challenge of Europe, The (Heseltine) 458

Chambers, Quentin 304, 305

Channel 4 235–7, 246, 249–50, 256, 277, 470–1

Channel Four Films 256–7

Channon, Paul 260

Chariots of Fire (film) 255, 257

charities 335–8, 338

Charity Commission 335

Index

Index

Index

Index

National Society for the Prevention of
    Cruelty to Children 312
National Theatre 223, 230–1
National Trust 336
National Union of Journalists 362, 366, 371
National Union of Mineworkers (NUM)
    72, 107, 212; strike (1984) 341–60
National Union of Railwaymen 38, 368
nationalized industries 72–3, 385
NATO 15, 35, 57, 115, 145, 198, 199, 202,
    203, 216, 445, 461
NatWest 404–5
Neave, Airey, murder of 35
Neighbours (TV programme) 246–7, 289
Neil, Andrew 240, 413
Nena 208–9, 282
Nestlé 390
New Order 299–300, 308, 310
New Statesman (magazine) 155
New Statesman, The (TV programme) 253
New Zealand 145
Newcastle 82, 98, 125
News Corporation 241–2
News International 366, 369, 370, 371; *see
    also* Rupert Murdoch
News of the World 362, 364, 366, 370
Newton, Tony 327
Nichols, Monsignor Vincent 326
Nield, Robert 60
'99 Red Balloons' (song) 208–9, 282
1922 Committee 47
No Job for a Lady (TV programme) 250
Nobel Prize winners 482–3
no-rate-fixing rebellion 434–5
Norman, Edward 70
North, Ian 163
North Sea oil: bounty 185–6; casualties
    191, 192; depletion policy 193;
    discovery 186; exploitation 186–8;
    government control 187–9; investment
    in 187; management 194; medium-
    term assessment (1977) 6; Norwegian
    production 194; Piper Alpha disaster
    191–2; price collapse 191, 192; prices 52;
    privatization 188–9; production 186,
    190, 191, 192; and the property market
    195; revenue use 192–6; revenues 6, 55,
    181, 189, 192, 389, 467; and Scotland
    190–1; and the Stock Market 195; tax
    revenue 189, 192, 193; workforce 187,
    190
Northern Ireland: the Anglo-Irish
    Agreement 429–30; civil unrest 16;
    crime rate 315; devolution 102–3;

and the election campaign (1979)
    35; emergence of Sinn Fein 102;
    homosexuality legalised 328; Northern
    Ireland Assembly 102–3; Sands' funeral
    101–2; Sands wins Fermanagh by-election
    101; the Troubles 99–103, 430–1;
    unemployment 83
north–south divide 419
Norway 193, 194
Not the Nine O'Clock News (TV
    programme) 96, 251–2, 285
Nott, John 57, 63, 135, 137, 137–8, 142,
    143–4, 145, 168, 392, 408
Notting Hill race riots 86
Nottingham 81
Now That's What I Call Music! (album series)
    288–9
nuclear power stations 343, 359
nuclear weapons 108, 200, 212; anti-nuclear
    protests 199–201, 202–9; arms limitation
    talks 211; Church of England and
    334; deterrence 212–13; independent
    nuclear deterrent 199, 203, 216, 220;
    Intermediate-Range Nuclear Forces
    (INF) Treaty 221–2; mutually assured
    destruction 198–9, 214; nuclear-free
    zones 209–10; ownership 204; pop
    protest 208–9; public concern about
    210–11; replacement for Polaris 22;
    Reykjavik summit 219–21; START
    (strategic arms reduction talks) 219–22;
    strategic arms limitation talks (SALT
    II) 201; threat of 197–9; Trident 220;
    withdrawal of American 221–2
Numan, Gary 278–9, 286
NUPE 22
Nyman, Michael 272

Oakenfold, Paul 300
Oakey, Phil 277, 283
Oakley, Robin 417
O'Brien, Denis 259
Observer 176, 364
Office of Fair Trading 391–2
officers of state 480
Official Sloane Ranger Handbook, The (Barr
    and York) 414–15
oil: consumption 186; prices 52, 186, 191,
    192; production 186; *see also* North Sea
    oil
Old Grey Whistle Test, The (TV programme)
    276
Old Vic theatre 230
Oldfield, Mike 278

Index

Index